Eckhardt

FOCUS ON AMERICAN HISTORY SERIES
Center for American History
University of Texas at Austin
Edited by Don Carleton

ECKHARDT

There Once Was a Congressman from Texas

GARY A. KEITH

FOREWORD BY AL GORE

University of Texas Press
Austin

The publication of this book was made possible by a University Cooperative
Society Subvention Grant awarded by the University of Texas at Austin and a
generous contribution from the Jess and Betty Jo Hay Endowment.

Library of Congress Cataloging-in-Publication Data

Keith, Gary.
    Eckhardt : there once was a congressman from Texas / Gary A. Keith ; foreword
by Al Gore. — 1st ed.
        p.   cm. — (Focus on American history series)
    Includes bibliographical references and index.
    ISBN: 978-0-292-71691-9 (cloth : alk. paper)
    1. Eckhardt, Bob.   2. Legislators—United States—Biography.   3. United
States. Congress. House—Biography.   4. Legislators—Texas—Biography.
5. Labor lawyers—Texas—Biography.   6. Political activists—Texas—Biography.
7. Texas—Politics and government—1865–1950.   8. Texas—Politics and government—1951–   9. Liberalism—Texas—History—20th century.   10. Political
parties—Texas—History—20th century.   I. Title.
    E840.8.E28K45   2007
    328.73092—dc22
    [B]
                                                                            2007001065

This book is dedicated to all those who seek to practice a deeper democracy—of deliberation, of passion, of equality, and of caring for the commons.

Contents

Contents

Foreword

by Al Gore

Bob Eckhardt was an intellectual giant who made an indelible mark on the work of the U.S. House of Representatives during the fourteen years he served in that great institution. He was a Shakespeare-quoting, Renaissance man of high principles who had a lust for life that included a love affair with the Constitution and a consuming passion to craft legislation in the public interest.

Bob was a unique liberal. Just as Ralph Yarborough, of his native Texas, and my father, Albert Gore Sr., brought populism to the floor of the U.S. Senate in the 1950s and 1960s, Bob brought populism to the House in the 1970s.

Bob Eckhardt had a wonderful sense of humor. He could be flat-out funny, but he could also use his sharp wit to make a point in debate. That wit was manifested in (sometimes unflattering) drawings or sketches that depicted special interest lobbyists, hearing witnesses, or even his fellow members of Congress. Bob was a talented cartoonist who used that gift with poignancy and humor.

But first and foremost, Bob was a legislator, and an unusual one, in that he most often was his own legislative craftsman. He loved to write laws, and when so doing, he made certain they carried out their intended purposes. He brought his brilliant lawyer's mind to this work after spending years in the courtroom where he used laws as his sword and shield. He knew that weak, poorly-written laws could either be gutted by the executive branch or lead to unintended consequences.

At the same time, Bob Eckhardt also understood the fundamental responsibility of Congress to conduct oversight to ensure the adequacy of existing laws and the administration of those laws as Congress intended. He approached oversight just as he did lawmaking: with little regard for personal political consequences. And it didn't matter that his party was in the White House or that the focus of an investigation was on a vested interest in his political backyard. He was interested in pursuing sound public policy for the common good.

My first four years in Congress coincided with Bob's last four years. It was in the final two years, 1979–1980, when Bob became the chairman of the House Interstate and Foreign Commerce Committee's Subcommittee on

Oversight and Investigations, that I came to know him best. He was a mentor, and since I was second in subcommittee seniority, he occasionally asked me to chair a hearing in his absence, an opportunity I don't recall ever turning down.

Oversight and Investigations was an active subcommittee with very broad jurisdiction, including energy, health, environmental issues, and many others. During the two-year period, the subcommittee held ninety-four days of hearings, about half of them on environmental concerns, and a number of which examined various problems associated with hazardous waste disposal.

It was in the latter area that Bob may have made his most lasting contribution. Under his leadership, and almost immediately after he became chairman, the subcommittee initiated the first national study of waste disposal sites in the United States. A survey was directed to the fifty-three largest U.S. chemical companies to determine how they disposed of potentially dangerous wastes. In a closed-door gathering of company executives, Eckhardt convinced them of the wisdom of voluntarily disclosing their hazardous waste sites. The survey results revealed that the fifty-three companies had operated 1,605 facilities that, since 1950, had dumped wastes at 3,383 sites. Approximately two thousand of these sites had heretofore been unknown to the EPA.

The survey results, which became known as the "Eckhardt Report," and the hazardous waste disposal hearings led directly to legislation requiring the creation of a comprehensive inventory of all hazardous waste sites in the country (the EPA's National Priority List) and to legislation which became known as Superfund. As you may have guessed, Eckhardt played a key role in drafting this legislation.

Bob Eckhardt also was a constitutional scholar who cherished the rights that document bestows upon all Americans. I can only imagine his outrage today over proposed constitutional amendments aimed at limiting those rights. And we all would benefit from his erudite commentary on so many crucial constitutional issues facing the country today, such as warrantless surveillance programs and limitations on the rights of U.S. citizens designated as enemy combatants.

Bob Eckhardt was a great Congressman. He also could have been a great Senator or a great Supreme Court Justice. However, in the prime of his congressional years, he was cut down by the very politics that he had fought against for so long—the politics of cynicism, of duplicity, of right-wing shilling for the powerful. Those who campaigned against him in 1980 as "representing all that is wrong with America" should hang their heads in shame as the intervening years have proven what we all knew at the time—that Bob

Eckhardt represented all that was right with our best American dreams and values. Had we followed his path, we would be in a far better place today.

This scholarly work depicts the Bob Eckhardt that I knew and respected: the witty, genial colleague; the indifferent politician; the keen student of law, policy, and the Constitution; the genuine and persuasive debater; the man with an off-white three-piece seersucker suit, colorful bow tie, and panama hat atop a flowing mane, pedaling about Washington on a bicycle seemingly older than he.

More than anything, this story of the life of Bob Eckhardt provides a model of public service. It shows us what politics was like before the poisoned era that we find ourselves in today. It shows us the passion and sense of social justice of a man who used his considerable skills and talents on behalf of workers, consumers, environmental protection, and constitutional rights. And, in his story, perhaps we will find the way back—the way back to politics of optimism and hope, of caring for the commons and for the common man.

Acknowledgments

I feel greatly privileged to have known Bob Eckhardt. We spent many hours reminiscing, driving the countryside, and talking with his friends. I learned from him the wonders of Texas politics and the intricacies of the state legislative and congressional dances. I would like to acknowledge the great assistance of Bob Eckhardt's families in researching and interviewing for this book, as well as Milton Lower and the late Ann Lower, Don Carleton and the staff of the Center for American History at the University of Texas at Austin, and the scores of people who agreed to talk with me about Bob Eckhardt over this past decade. I regret that I did not get to interview others—so many people have wonderful Eckhardt stories. I would especially like to thank Tom Whatley for introducing me to Bob Eckhardt, planting the seed for this book, and providing valuable criticism along the way. Friends and colleagues who read parts of the manuscript and provided helpful criticisms and suggestions include Jeremy Curtoys, Hugh Davis, Dave McNeely, Julie Leininger Pycior, Mark Raabe, Sean Thierault—thank you all. Many eyes have helped correct inaccuracies in the text. Any errors that remain, of course, are solely my responsibility. Thanks to John Higley at the University of Texas at Austin for his support. Thanks also to those at the University of Texas Press who helped steer the book to publication, including William Bishel, Mary LaMotte, and Sally Furgeson. Finally, thank you to my wife Jacqueline Kerr and our boys Gabe and David Keith for letting me use the computer at all hours over the past many years. Now we can go outside and play soccer together!

Austin, 2007

Eckhardt

Introduction

Of all the things that are politics, one of the more obvious is that it is a never-ending battle between competing centers of power. Politics is also biography, and these two approaches to understanding politics come together in the life of Bob Eckhardt. He was a fascinating, colorful individual who spent his career fighting to wrest power from the economic centers and likewise to use public office to empower labor unions, to strengthen citizens against corporate power, and to invigorate environmental and consumer interests. He stood proudly and strongly with those centers that competed throughout the twentieth century against the economic centers of power. As a lawyer, state legislator, and congressman, Eckhardt made a lasting mark on public policies, breathing life into progressive politics in Texas and the nation and leaving a legacy of lawmaking.

And, oh, what a personality. Bob Eckhardt was truly a memorable character. Maury Maverick Jr. described him as "a delightful combination of 98 percent genius and 2 percent village idiot."[1] To speak of Bob Eckhardt is to conjure images and memories of his ever-present bow tie, his horses, his bicycle, his drawing, his Texas twang, his wit. He wore a big hat, sometimes dirty with the wear. When asked why, he replied, tongue in cheek and with a twinkle in his eye, "A man with a hat like that and a drawl like this couldn't be a liberal."[2] Eckhardt was a keen observer of his world, and his pen sketched cartoons that will long endure as a window into twentieth century politics.

From the 1940s to the 1960s, he was a leading figure in Texas political and legislative battles, aligning himself with labor unions, civil rights and social welfare causes, the reemerging populist wing of the Texas Democratic Party, and Ralph Yarborough. More than forty years later, people still talk about Eckhardt's spellbinding oratory on the floor of the Texas House.

Then, what Yarborough was to the U.S. Senate in the 1960s, Eckhardt was to the U.S. House in the 1970s: a champion of progressivism. Yarborough's defeat in 1970 was a severe blow to progressive politics; in 1980, the New Right won a sweeping victory, taking out Eckhardt and hosts of others. Yarborough was distressed that Eckhardt had lost. He wanted others to know Eckhardt's story.

"Tell the world," Yarborough wrote to Eckhardt. "Tell us about it. Let Texas and the Nation know that there was once a Congressman from Texas."[3]

To fully appreciate the importance of Bob Eckhardt, one must reconstitute that rich political, artistic, and intellectual stew that he stirred, and this book attempts to do that. Could one understand Texas and U.S. politics of that era without knowing of or understanding Eckhardt's role? Surely many do; after all, Eckhardt never became governor, senator, or president. Yet those who came to know of him only when he was in Congress missed the crucial and colorful contributions that Bob Eckhardt made before he ever reached there. He was such a fixture in Texas political lore of the 1940s, '50s, and '60s that he would have warranted a book had he never made it to Congress. But he did make it there, and he left his mark of liberalism and constitutionalism on environmental, consumer, labor, and war powers policies.

For four decades, Eckhardt appeared to be everywhere, present for all kinds of amazing and significant historical events. This, then, is a biography, a history, and a work of political science: An analysis of the workings of power in the political economy and in policymaking. A history of German immigrants and the four Texas congressmen the Kleberg-Wurzbach-Eckhardt families produced. A history of twentieth-century Austin and Houston. A history of the nation's postwar "Good Neighbor" policy, of labor politics in Texas and the United States, of Texas Democratic Party factionalism, and of state legislative battles over taxing the oil and gas industry. It is a history of a society divided by race and war in the 1960s, of the birth of the environmental movement in Texas in the 1960s and 1970s, and of the beginnings of the consumer movement nationally. This is a history of the congressional creation of the Big Thicket National Preserve, of the mammoth battles over President Jimmy Carter's energy policy in the 1970s, and of the passage of the War Powers Act in 1973. It is a history of the changing political landscape in Texas, of the rise of the New Right and of a two-party state.

And it is the story of the life of Robert Christian Eckhardt, who was born in 1913 in Austin, Texas, and died there in 2001. Eckhardt was engaged in all those battles, and he was one of the most intelligent, articulate voices in the public discourses. An honest and thoughtful biography must be somewhere between hagiography and kiss-and-tell. This book attempts to describe not only the public life of a public man, but also the character, the flamboyance, of Bob Eckhardt—all the characteristics that triggered admiration, loyalty, friendship, and exasperation. It was both his personality and his intellect that fashioned his ideas, speech, and writings and that made people sit up and listen.

Eckhardt's story is tied to the explorations of the Texas frontier and to the populist groundswell of the 1890s; his is the story of the linkages from a

Texas past of Sam Houston and Jim Hogg through the resurgence of popular democracy with Jimmie Allred and Maury Maverick to the next generation of liberals that included Ralph Yarborough, Creekmore Fath, Minnie Fisher Cunningham, Frankie Randolph, and Bob Eckhardt. Eckhardt was from an oil and gas state, yet he was a national leader for democratic control of energy policy, rather than laissez-faire political economics. He weathered repeated campaigns against him, fueled by the oil and gas industry, at the same time that he was a national leader on energy policy. In 1980, columnist Jack Anderson listed Eckhardt among the "Most Effective Members of Congress" and he was featured in the *New York Times Magazine*.[4] Yet in that same year, oil and gas opposition combined with the emerging New Right and religious fundamentalism to bring about his narrow defeat.

In a 1962 interview with Willie Morris, Bob Eckhardt made a seminal statement describing what he saw as the three major ingredients in his brand of liberalism:

> First, altruism. Second, pragmatism—the kind of experimentation and modification that was implicit in the New Deal. Third, respect for individual freedom and dignity—a kind of broad tolerance for individuals. In that sense, I consider myself a liberal. I believe in respect for the individual as an individual.[5]

He told Morris that, first, there was a need for "panzer troops," like the 1940s *Texas Spectator* and 1950s *Texas Observer* crowd of which he was an integral part, "setting down a conscience." Second, Eckhardt contended, we need the political organizer, like Frankie Randolph, who "holds people's feet to the fire," and third, we need the politicians, who must stand for something but must also win. "It's honorable and necessary for the panzer troops to set a standard to shoot at, and for the political organizer to devise a platform worth winning on, but the man in the position of the practicing politician has got to have at least the practical possibility of winning his race. He misrepresents his role unless he thinks he can win."

Eckhardt was often optimistic. "The longer view," he said, "is always in favor of the liberal. The liberal candidate may not win, but the conservative candidate has got to become more liberal. The drift of humane society is in that direction. The liberal trend is inevitable."[6] But by the time of his defeat in the Reagan election of 1980, then by the time of his death shortly after the September 11, 2001, attacks and the ensuing militarization of America, the country was clearly going in the other direction. Eckhardt is gone; others must lead the way back to democracy, constitutionalism, and progressivism.

EK
♡

Bob Eckhardt's story is that of a man you would want to have a drink with, to ride a horse with, as you explore the fascinating world of democracy in America. His is a story of social and cultural turmoil as the nation went through wrenching changes from the 1940s into the 1980s. Whether Bob Eckhardt's belief that tolerance, social justice, and liberalism will prevail in "the longer view" is something we must all ponder late in our own lives, and hand down to the next generations of democrats.

PART I

The Eckhardts of Texas

ONE

The German Texas Pioneers

Bob Eckhardt was part of a storied German-Texas family of Eckhardts, Klebergs, Wurzbachs, von Roeders, Engelkings, and Schmelzers. Each of those families immigrated to Texas in the nineteenth century—"gone to Texas and rooted there," in Eckhardt's words. His great-grandparents were German settlers Caesar and Louise Eckhardt and Robert and Rosa Kleberg. Bob was named after his grandfather, Robert Christian Eckhardt (1836–1887), who moved from Germany to Texas with his parents and married Caroline Kleberg, daughter of Robert and Rosa Kleberg. More than just an interesting family tree, though, Eckhardt's family history was a source of pride, values, and grounding for him. Those family lines produced a host of doctors, lawyers, ranchers, soldiers, and politicians—including state legislators and four congressmen.

Germans and Texas in the Nineteenth Century

The 1830s and 1840s brought hardship and violence to the German states. In this *Vormärz* period, peasant uprisings against the monarchs and Prussian troops led to backlashes, and in the ensuing persecution, thousands fled Germany. Then, in the Revolution of 1848, even more emigrated to numerous ports in the United States. Many who fled were of the intellectual and artistic elite—a highly educated class that based their readings and studies in ancient Greek and Roman cultures and in the Latin language. They came to be known as the *"Lateiners"* ("Latin ones"), and some of them formed freethinking *Lateiner* communities in the heartland of Texas.

One of the early German émigrés was Frederich Ernst. In 1831, he landed at Harrisburg (which would be a part of Bob Eckhardt's Houston congressional district in the 1960s). His party headed inland to Stephen F. Austin's colony at San Felipe, then founded the community of Industry. Ernst's letter back home, when published, spurred a steady stream of immigrants to Texas.

Soon, settlers decided to create a German state in Texas. The *Adelsverein,* or Society for the Protection of German Immigrants in Texas, sponsored voyages and planned the settlements that started at Matagorda Bay's Indian

EK
♡

Bob Eckhardt's Family Tree

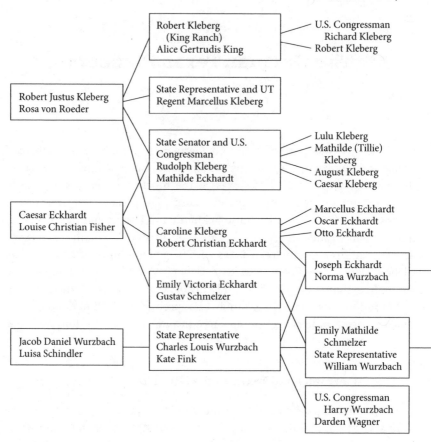

Point (Indianola), spread across the coastal plains into Hill Country settlements and included Fredericksburg and New Braunfels.

In 1842 and 1843, the princes and counts who began the *Adelsverein* purchased land near Industry, naming it Nassau Farm. Then in 1844, the new leader of *Adelsverein,* Prince Karl Solms von Braunfels, came to the wilderness wearing white gloves, high boots, and feathers in his cap, determined to be the nobleman who planted a New Germany.[1] The baron chose Indian Point as a permanent landing place. He hoped to colonize the area around Industry (in Austin County) that Ernst had founded. Indeed, he laid the groundwork for the Eckhardts' and Klebergs' immigration.

John Christian Justus Robert Kleberg was born in 1803 in Westphalia, Prussia. Schooled in Greek, Latin, German, and English, he read ancient and modern literature. As a law student, he became acquainted with fellow student Louis Ludwig von Roeder and, through him, his sister Philippine

ROBERT CHRISTIAN (BOB) ECKHARDT
   Orissa Stevenson
   Nadine Cannon Brammer
   Celia Buchan Morris

Orissa Eckhardt Arend
Rosalind Eckhardt Sanford
Sarah Eckhardt
Sidney, Shelby, Willie Brammer/Eckhardt
David Morris

Emily Wurzbach Mickler

Sophie Caroline Luise Rosalia (Rosa) von Roeder. The von Roeders were nobility. When their brother Sigismund killed a Prussian prince in a duel, the von Roeders, influenced by the Ernst letter, quickly decided to emigrate to Texas.

A small contingent of von Roeders went first, landing in coastal Texas in the summer of 1834 and heading inland toward San Felipe de Austin to file a claim. The first night, after settling near some springs, one of the men killed a wildcat, so they named their new home Katzenquelle (Cat Spring). Most of the remaining von Roeder family soon left Germany to join the scouting expedition. Rosa hastened her wedding with Robert Kleberg, and they went with Robert's brother Louis and the second von Roeder contingent, carrying Rosa's beloved piano. Robert Kleberg later wrote, "I wished to live under a republican form of government, with unbounded personal, religious and political liberty, free from the petty tyrannies, the many disadvantages and

9

evils of old countries. Prussia, my former home, smarted at the time under a military despotism. I was (and have ever remained) an enthusiastic lover of republican institutions, and I expected to find in Texas, above all other countries, the blessed land of my most fervent hopes."[2]

Theirs was a dangerous and challenging life. They sailed for two months, taking the *Congress* steamer to New Orleans, where they boarded a new ship. Just before Christmas 1834, they shipwrecked off Galveston Island. They salvaged some goods, including guns, wine, and Rosa's piano, survived on the bountiful deer on the island, and encountered no other humans. After several weeks, Kleberg and Rudolph von Roeder hailed a passing schooner that took them to the mainland. They found Stephen F. Austin's colony, then nearby Cat Spring. There, they learned that malaria had killed numerous settlers, including two of the von Roeders.

Kleberg retrieved the Galveston contingent in three trips on a hired steamer and a sloop and transported everyone to Harrisburg, the last of the group arriving by the fall of 1835. They then traveled by oxcart to Cat Spring, leaving in Harrisburg the piano, paintings, books, and other belongings. The new settlers built half-timbered houses of heavy timbers, filled between with red clay, using the ancient German tradition of cutting Roman numerals into the wood to show where to fit the joists, beams, and braces together.

Kickapoo Indians helped the newcomers. The two peoples were wary of each other, but soon learned that each side was friendly. Rosa was baking bread in the new cabin one day when a shadow fell across the floor. She looked up to see a tall Indian in paint standing in the doorway. He strode across the room, threw down a venison ham, snatched the hot loaves of bread on the table, muttered something about a "swap," and was gone before Rosa could say anything.[3]

The Germans' desire for a peaceful new life, far from the wars of Europe, was not to be. The Texas Revolution broke out in 1835, and Robert Kleberg, Albrecht von Roeder, and Louis von Roeder left their families and joined the fight. One day, Rosa saw a man running past their place, but going *away* from where the armies were amassing. Rosa asked him what was happening, and he claimed that the fight was all over. She yelled as he fled, "Run! Run! Santa Anna is behind you!"[4]

Louis fought at the siege of San Antonio in late 1835. He was with Sam Houston in Gonzales when Houston learned of the Alamo massacre in early March 1836. Houston decided on a strategy of retreating across the Colorado River, back to the Sabine River, collecting volunteers as he went. He also sent couriers across the countryside, urging the settlers to flee in what came to be known as the Runaway Scrape. Rosa could hear the cannons roaring as the armies engaged. She fled on horseback, with a baby under one arm and a rifle under the other, as the Kleberg and von Roeder families returned to Galveston Island.[5] While they were gone, Mexican soldiers burned their Harrisburg possessions, leaving only a pig and a lame ox. Louis, Albrecht, and Robert went on to fight in the decisive battle of San Jacinto on April 21, 1836, helping Houston and the Texans win.

It took some families a year or more to get back to their homes after the Runaway Scrape. Brother Ernst Kleberg, back in Germany, wrote to Sam Houston with letters for Robert and Louis, saying, "It is now near two years that we had no news of my two brothers" and asking Houston for news of them.[6] Mosquito season brought yellow fever, and more of the family died. The rest returned to Cat Spring. Robert received nearly 1,000 acres for his military service in the war. He grew tobacco, built the first store, and became chief justice of the county. In 1837, President Sam Houston appointed him associate commissioner of the Board of Land Commissioners, and he soon became president of the board. In 1845, he and the others in Cat Spring voted in favor of the annexation of Texas to the United States.[7]

New German settlements sprang up throughout Austin County and beyond to Fayette, Washington, and DeWitt counties. Otto von Roeder bought the *Adelsverein's* Nassau Farm in Fayette County. Von Roeder daughter Caroline married a German settler in nearby Millheim named Ferdinand Friederich Engelking. The Engelkings were the driving force in founding literary clubs, music clubs, and theaters in the German settlements (setting the genetic and cultural stage for twentieth-century cousins Bob Eckhardt and Bob Engelking and their artistic endeavors).[8] Bob Eckhardt, surrounded by his Kleberg, von Roeder, and Engelking cousins in twentieth-century Texas, studied this history of his family and of Sam Houston and the revolution. He was fascinated with the history of early Texas and the transitions from one political system to another. In a 1956 review of a book about the Texas Republic, he wrote:

> The intriguing thing about these facts and occurrences is not the end, annexation, but the means. It is interesting to note that the demagogic causes never ultimately succeeded in the Republic. Santa Anna was not shot, though the public clamor supported that course. The extremist war party never got the Republic into a war of conquest below the Rio Grande, though this was the vote-getting demagogy of the time. Indian land rights ultimately were legislatively recognized, though the rabble-rousing position was in the direction of persecution and nullification. It is only just to note that "Old Sam," willing as he was to "demagog" in small matters, was more than any other man responsible for this course of repudiating demagogy in great matters.[9]

Indians would stop by the Kleberg house on their way to and from their meetings with Sam Houston to discuss peace and the establishment of a reservation. Prince Karl also stopped by the Kleberg house.[10] He knew the von Roeders from Germany, as so many nobles knew each other. Rosa disdained the life of nobility. When they visited, Prince Karl and his entourage would not eat with their troops and servants, but Rosa would not stand for it and insisted that they all eat together.

A wave of immigration after the Texas Revolution brought the Eckhardt and Wurzbach families to Texas. Caesar Eckhardt (Bob's great-grandfather), born in 1806 in Laasphe, Germany, was a Prussian army officer.[11] His brother, Charles, decided to leave Prussia, landing in Texas in 1843, just eight years after the Klebergs. Soon, Charles enticed Caesar to emigrate. The Eckhardts brought with them the family coat of arms, with its declaration *"Helft der selbst, ser helft der Gott"* (he who helps himself helps God). Caesar brought his wife Louise Christian Fisher and their children, thirteen-year-old Robert Christian (Bob's grandfather and namesake), William, and Emily Victoria; Mathilde was born in Texas.

Charles settled near Indian Point, where he became a trader with the Germans who moved inland toward San Antonio and the area that became New Braunfels. However, the roads were long and out of the way, so he partnered with Captain John York to build a road through York's large ranch in DeWitt County. Charles oversaw the surveying and building of the road from Victoria, through York's ranch, and on to New Braunfels. He and York then founded Yorktown along the road. With the new road and the end of the Mexican War, business boomed in Indian Point, and town leaders wanted a more proper name for their town, settling on Indianola.[12]

Charles built the first log cabin in Yorktown in 1848 and laid out the town, which quickly became the largest German settlement in the region. In 1850, brother Caesar opened a store in Yorktown, known as C. Eckhardt & Sons. Built of stone, the store had a big water reservoir in the front room, as the threat of Indian attacks made frequent outside trips risky. Caesar also established a ranch four miles outside of town. (Today the building is a museum, and the Eckhardt Ranch is still in operation.)

The Eckhardts and Yorks soon had new neighbors. In 1847, hoping to maintain their German culture, with its emphasis on science, classical music, literature, and the Latin language, the Klebergs and Albrecht and Caroline Ernst von Roeder (Frederich Ernst's daughter) moved to a *"Lateiner"* community in DeWitt County just a quarter mile from the Eckhardt ranch. Robert and Rosa Kleberg had eight children (including Bob's grandmother Caroline, born in 1840). Sporadic but bloody battles with Indians continued for some time. In 1848, Kleberg, Captain York, Albrecht von Roeder, and others battled Comanches gathered around the new settlement of Yorktown, and York was killed.[13]

The Germans brought a sense of community, culture, and civic responsibility to the wilderness. The Eckhardts were Lutherans, Masons, and stalwart Democrats. Kleberg, too, was a Democrat. After their move, he served as DeWitt County commissioner and county chief justice.[14] As the cultures meshed, many immigrants continued to speak proper German, others brought their local dialects, and some became fluent in English and Spanish. They gathered for singing, dancing, poetry reading, neighborhood picnics, wine and beer. New Braunfels started the first singing society (*Gesangsvereine*) in 1850, and these *Saengerfests* spread throughout the communities. Rosa wrote back to relatives that her piano had survived, and would they please send to Texas "all the sheet music you can collect" as well as "the complete works of Goethe."[15] The Cat Spring Agricultural Society was founded in the 1850s to educate farmers. Robert Kleberg and Albrecht von Roeder built the first schoolhouse in DeWitt County. As early as 1856, Yorktown organized a theatrical group and singing society. Travelers between Indianola and San Antonio would stop in Yorktown to see the shows.[16]

The original settlers had spread out on the coastal plain—Cat Spring, Indianola, Cuero, Yorktown. Indianola was later wiped out by hurricanes, waves, and fires, first in 1875, then completely in 1886. Prince Karl and the *Adelsverein,* with Charles Eckhardt's help, had pushed inland and founded numerous German communities.[17] Not all German immigrants moved to rural Texas. A sizeable contingent settled in and around San Antonio, forming a close-knit society. They established breweries and a casino to which only Germans (and soldiers) could belong. They sponsored elaborate dinners and formally introduced their daughters at age sixteen.

These new San Antonians included Bob Eckhardt's Wurzbach and Schmelzer ancestors. Gustav Schmelzer was born in Prussia. He drove a stagecoach around Texas and was wounded in the shoulder by Indians. The Schmelzer house still stands in San Antonio. Jacob Daniel Wurzbach was a native of Mannheim, Germany. He emigrated to San Antonio as a civil engineer, working for the *Adelsverein* in 1844. Wurzbach brought his family with him, including young Charles Louis (later elected to the Texas legislature).[18]

The "Home Guard": Marriage, War, and Business

Within a few years of the German settlement of Texas, the Eckhardt, von Roeder, Kleberg, Schmelzer, and Wurzbach children bound the families together forever. At age twenty-four, Robert Christian Eckhardt married neighbor Caroline Kleberg, then his sister Mathilde married Caroline's brother

Rudolph. Emily Victoria Eckhardt married Gustav Schmelzer, who later owned the Alamo, and their daughter, Emily Mathilde Schmelzer, married William Wurzbach (Bob Eckhardt's uncle). As the families grew, Grandmother Rosa (called by the German name "Oma") would teach the children.

The Eckhardts farmed and ranched, in addition to running the Yorktown store. Caesar used a simple heart as his cattle brand, registering it in 1857 as the first Eckhardt brand. As the ranch grew, they employed Mexican cowboys and searched for horses. Three hundred years earlier, Cabeza de Vaca was running out of water on his ships, so he dumped Arab and Barbary horses overboard near Texas. The horses swam ashore, where they propagated so much that the area became known as the Wild Horse Desert.

Thus, horses were abundant—if they could be caught. Between Yorktown and Cuero, a large grove of old live oak trees intertwined, making a dense fence-like enclosure. Robert Eckhardt, the other young men, and the Mexican cowboys fashioned it into a kind of corral, with boughs between the trees. Mustangs that could not be lured or driven into an obvious corral could be caught in what came to be known as "Mustang Mott." The cowboys would swoop upon the wild herd, roping as many mustangs as they could before the horses jumped over or through the corral or ran out the end of the trap.[19]

When the Civil War broke out, Robert Kleberg gathered the families under a spreading oak. Though German Texans opposed slavery, and Kleberg respected Sam Houston and his stand against secession, Kleberg thought that *Texas* was now his country and his place, and thus he persuaded the men to become Confederates. Kleberg, at age 60, served as commissioner of war taxes. Caesar Eckhardt, 56, was commissioned as a lieutenant in the *Heim Wer* (home guard), and his sons Robert and William joined the Confederate Army, as did Otto and Rudolph Kleberg. (They survived, though some were grievously wounded.) The *Heim Wer* rounded up some aged horses and old military uniforms, decorated with their insignia from various duchies and principalities of Germany, and charged down the drill field, brandishing their Prussian or Masonic sabers. The women thought it silly and dangerous.[20]

Robert Eckhardt served in Texas, Louisiana, and Mississippi. A month went by after the surrender at Appomattox, and he had not returned. Then, a riderless mustang arrived at the ranch, his saddle scratched and torn. It was one of the Mustang Mott horses, and it belonged to Robert. A distraught Caroline, still holding out hope, often walked to the distant gate, looking, searching for any speck of movement over the broad pastureland. One day, in the cool of the evening, Robert came walking home, whistling a German tune. The mustang had broken his tether in deep East Texas and trotted on home, leaving Robert to make the long journey afoot.[21]

Caesar Eckhardt died three years after the war's end. Robert assumed management of the ranch, expanding it to 8,000 acres and building a new house in 1879. He imported shorthorn and Hereford bulls and used Eckhardt stock in developing the Texas longhorn cattle. He retooled the brand, placing "EK" above the heart, and registering it in 1873:

$$\begin{array}{c} \text{E K} \\ \heartsuit \end{array}$$

He and Caroline had eleven children, including the youngest, Joseph (Joe, who was Bob's father), born October 29, 1883.

Robert and his brothers ran the C. Eckhardt & Sons store with their mother. As Robert would ride home to the ranch from the store, he would whistle shrilly to let Caroline and the children know he was coming home. The store sponsored a Yorktown baseball team, using the $\overset{\text{E K}}{\heartsuit}$ symbol on their uniforms. During Governor Edmund J. Davis's Republican Reconstruction government, Robert served as the first mayor of Yorktown, though he was a Democrat. He also served as a school trustee.[22]

Expansion of the Eckhardt and Kleberg Families

Robert Kleberg's three most famous sons were Robert Justus Jr., Marcellus, and Rudolph. Marcellus served in the Texas House of Representatives in 1873, then moved to Galveston and became a local official. Robert Justus Jr. began a law practice in Cuero (near Yorktown), then moved to Corpus Christi. There, he had a longtime client named Richard King, founder of the famed King Ranch. When King died, his widow Henriette asked Kleberg to manage the ranch. He married a King daughter, beginning a multigenerational Kleberg leadership of the King Ranch. After fighting in the Civil War as a teenager, Rudolph studied law and married Mathilde Eckhardt. Moving to Cuero, he practiced law and edited the first newspaper in DeWitt County. In the 1870s, the long-running and bloody Sutton-Taylor feud produced daily murders, and Rudolph's articles about the feud helped restore a sense of peace. He was elected county attorney, then won election as a Democrat to the state Senate, where he served in 1883 and 1885. He served as U.S. Attorney for four years, then returned to practicing law while his sons August and Caesar attended St. Edward's College in Austin. Rudolph won election to Congress, serving from 1896 to 1903. After his congressional career, he moved to Austin, where he became official reporter for the Texas Court of Criminal Appeals.[23]

After graduating from college, Caesar Kleberg, Rudolph's son, helped his Uncle Robert run the million-acre King Ranch. Caesar traveled between

Kingsville, Alice, Corpus Christi, Cuero, and even Washington, helping with the ranch and with his dad's reelection campaigns in the district.[24] The Kleberg and Eckhardt families were letter writers, and even into the twentieth century, their letters would slip into German.

In San Antonio, Jacob Wurzbach's brother Emil became a Texas Ranger, and his son Charles (Bob's grandfather) became city attorney, county judge, and state representative (1876–1883, 1891). Charles and his wife Kate had eleven children, including the youngest, Norma (Bob's mother), born in 1889. Her brothers included William (who, like his father, became county judge and state representative) and Harry, who became a congressman.[25]

Back in Yorktown, Robert Justus Kleberg suffered a stroke in his last years, and he and Rosa moved in with daughter Caroline and her husband Robert Eckhardt. But the ranch saw great sorrow, as Robert Eckhardt died in 1887 and Robert Kleberg in 1888. When Robert Eckhardt died, youngest son Joe was only five. The eldest son Otto managed the huge ranch with his mother Caroline. Otto was wild and hot tempered. He would drive horses from south Texas, a pistol on one hip and a whiskey bottle on the other, sometimes dipping a tin cup in the river and mixing a bit of whiskey in it "to keep the typhoid germs away." He herded cattle to market at the railheads in Texas and to Louisiana. Otto made a lot of money, but also squandered a lot. He would return from a cattle drive, stuff his pockets, boots, and hatband with money and head to the German Casino at the Menger Hotel in San Antonio. After one particularly lucrative cattle trade, he reportedly spent $30,000 one night in the Menger.[26]

Otto's flamboyance must have caused tension in the family because "La Madama" Caroline eventually installed Marcellus as the ranch manager. Otto moved to Goliad and bought his own ranch. He had changed the ranch's brand, but Marcellus reverted to his father's brand.[27] All this time, young Joseph worked alongside his brothers on the ranch. Under a full moon, he and the other boys would go coon hunting on a donkey, pulling loose pickets off a picket fence for weapons.

The ranch always employed cowboys who worked alongside the family members. One ranch cowboy was William Wright, who later became captain of the Texas Rangers. After the Texas Revolution, many Mexicans were driven off their lands, harassed, and persecuted; after the Civil War, much the same happened to blacks. In South Texas, many became vaqueros or farmhands. King Ranch and Eckhardt Ranch vaqueros often worked on both places, even exchanging saddlery and equipment with each other.[28]

Thus, Joe grew up with Anglos, Latinos, and blacks. He worked with Gas Lewis, a black man who drove cattle up the trail. Joe rode on the knee of another black cowboy, Tom Smith, who ran the Eckhardts' cattle operations.

(Smith's nephew Lonnie, who became a political ally of Bob Eckhardt, gal-vanized black voting participation in the middle of the twentieth century through the *Smith v. Allwright* case). Joe's best friend was Decederio, a cow-boy who would get fired by Marcellus Eckhardt for roping cattle too hard, throwing them to the ground. The ranch owned the horse, so Decederio would take off his saddle and turn to leave the ranch, followed by young Joe. Marcellus would soon forgive them and take them back.

Like his brother Victor, Joe attended the new University of Texas (where Marcellus Kleberg was a regent). Being a bona fide cowboy, he took his horses with him. Joe would attend the UT football games at Clark Field and, after the games, race down the field in his two-horse carriage. He was a serious student and decided that he wanted to be a doctor. Joe continued to write Decederio letters in Spanish while he was in medical school.[29]

During a visit to her sister in La Grange, Norma Wurzbach from San Antonio admired a handsome young man riding a horse through town and asked who he was. Joe Eckhardt was on his way to ranch work. Norma's rela-tives knew him and introduced them, and they started dating. Joe graduated from the new University of Texas School of Medicine at Galveston in 1908, at the age of twenty-five.[30] He and Norma Wurzbach married and soon moved to Austin.

Life on the original settlers' ranch was over for Joe and, soon, for his mother Caroline. The Eckhardt Ranch would go on—it has now been in operation for more than 150 years. Years later, one of the Yorktown cousins, Carol Hoff, wrote award-winning children's books based on the story of the Kleberg-Eckhardt settling of Texas. In the novel, Cousin Ernst sends a letter from Texas to Germany and persuades Robert and Clara Friedricks to emigrate with their boy Johan, who is quickly redubbed "Johnny Texas" when they land in Harrisburg. The men fight with Sam Houston at San Jacinto, and the family learns how to survive in the rugged Texas landscape, building up their ranch.[31] The real Eckhardts moved into the urban and professional world of twentieth-century Texas, taking with them as much of their German heritage as they could. The original émigré Rosa lived on the ranch until her death in 1907. Caroline Kleberg Eckhardt left the ranch in 1911 to move in with Joe in Austin until her death in 1913. Robert and Rosa Kleberg and Robert and Caroline Eckhardt are all buried on the Eckhardt ranch. Granite tombstones shaped like soldiers' tents mark the graves and are inscribed, "Remember the Alamo! Remember Goliad!"[32]

TWO

Bobby Eckhardt in Austin

Life was hard and lonely for Caroline after Robert Eckhardt and Robert Kleberg died. She and her sons continued to manage the Yorktown ranch and store. By the time Rosa Kleberg died in 1907, Caroline's youngest son Joe was off in medical school in Galveston. Her brother Rudolph Kleberg retired from Congress in 1903, and he and Mathilde moved to Austin, as did her son Oscar and his young family in 1909. When Joe finished medical school in 1908 and married Norma, he practiced briefly in Yoakum, and then they too headed to Austin.[1] Caroline decided to leave the ranch and join the other Eckhardts and Klebergs in Austin.

In 1911, Caroline, Joe, and Norma bought a house at 2300 Rio Grande Street in Austin, near Seton Infirmary where Dr. Joe would see patients. Caroline was the dowager, and Joe played the role of youngest son, letting her run the house and tending to her needs. Norma gave birth to a boy on July 16, 1913. Dr. Joe brought home sterile equipment for the birth, but he forgot the calf gut for stitches, so he had to use hamstring. Caroline asked that they name the baby after her late husband. So it was that one of the earliest Texas Klebergs named Bob after one of the original Eckhardt settlers, his grandfather Robert Christian Eckhardt. The dark-haired boy, known during his childhood as Bobby, grew up to look like his dad, with the distinctive Eckhardt nose. Eight weeks after his birth, Caroline died. The family returned to the Yorktown ranch to bury her, next to her husband Robert Christian Eckhardt and her parents, Robert and Rosa Kleberg.[2]

The City of the Violet Crown

In the late nineteenth century, many Germans began living in and around Austin. A few *Saengerrunde* (singer round) provided recreation and entertainment. After landing at Indianola, Augustus Scholz made his way to Austin. He bought a house, café, zoo, and bowling alley that would become the famed Scholz's Beer Garden and Saengerrunde Hall, where he hosted German singing festivals.[3] Decades later, Scholz's would become Bob Eckhardt's favorite haunt.

At the turn of the century, the state capital was a city of about 30,000. The German Hill Country begins just to the west of Austin. When viewed from the city, the distant hills have a purplish hue. One of Austin's residents of note, William Sidney Porter (O. Henry), called his home "the city of the violet crown." The nickname stuck.

Austin was laid out as a square on the north bank of the Colorado River. Congress Avenue went right up the middle to the state capitol. After it burned, the new capitol was built there in the 1880s and '90s. Legislators and lobbyists would sit on iron benches on the capitol grounds under the corridor of trees lining the broad walk. In 1881, the legislature designated Austin as the site for the new University of Texas (UT), which opened two years later, nine blocks north of the capitol. Across the river to the south, Barton Springs was the city's gathering place. Young girls arrived on ponies, tethering them to nearby trees. Businessmen met at the springs over picnics of chicken and melon.[4] The cold spring-fed water provided respite in the era before air conditioning.

In 1902, the Daughters of Charity built Seton Infirmary at Twenty-sixth and Rio Grande Street. It expanded over the years and was renamed Seton Hospital in 1940. Joe Eckhardt practiced medicine there for more than four decades. Three banks dominated finances in town: Austin National Bank and American National Bank, soon joined by Capital National Bank. The new bank quickly became associated with the economic and political powers of the state, known as "the Johnson group" for their service to Lyndon Baines Johnson.

The Colorado River was both a key element of Central Texas development and a constant bane due to its flooding. A dam was built in Austin in 1893, but it leaked and eroded away with floods, causing constant rebuilding efforts. The state created the Lower Colorado River Authority (LCRA), and local Congressman James Buchanan secured the funding to dam the flood-prone river upstream. He soon died, his congressional seat filled by Johnson. LBJ helped push the project along, and Brown & Root Construction Company and others made fortunes building the Buchanan Dam. Still another dam was built in Austin, again with Brown & Root, costly overruns, and federal money.[5]

Drinking water was plentiful since Austin was on the river and over an aquifer. In the 1890s, an artesian well was dug to supply the new capitol. Public outdoor drinking fountains with eight spigots were fed by the well and ornamental fountains were added to the landscape. A grotto and pools were built on the east side. By the time the Eckhardts arrived, Austinites were taking morning rides and walks to the capitol to enjoy the grounds. When the city's water supply failed in 1921, the Eckhardts joined the lines that formed to get free water from the well. The scene was repeated in later water failures and after Colorado River floods, before the dams were completed.[6]

The Scarbrough Building, the Littlefield Building (catty-cornered on Sixth and Congress Avenue), and the Driskill Hotel (next to the Littlefield) were the center of commercial, professional, and entertaining life in Austin. Mid-century, they would become central to Bob's legal and political career. Emerson H. Scarbrough built his eight-story building in 1908; the street-level floor included his department store and Oscar Eckhardt's pharmacy. Joe Eckhardt soon opened his medical practice upstairs. After a stint as an army dentist in World War I, August Kleberg came back to Austin and opened his dental office in the Scarbrough Building. In his first year in practice, Joe hired sixteen-year-old Bessie Olle to work for him. When Norma needed to shop, she would cushion the infant Bobby on a pillow, place him in the carriage with her, drive the horse and carriage to the Scarbrough Building through the bustling downtown with its mixture of horses, carriages, and newfangled automobiles, and leave him with Bessie at the clinic.[7]

George Littlefield was a cattle baron, a banker, a UT regent, and the largest contributor to the university. Littlefield owned the Driskill Hotel where he established his American National Bank. After selling the Driskill, he built the Littlefield Building next door in 1910, moving his bank into its ground floor. The bank's solid bronze doors with bas-relief of cattle drives, his LFD brand showing on the cattle, were so unique that they were later acquired by UT. He included atop his lavish building a beautiful roof garden, which opened with an orchestral evening in 1912 and was the scene of numerous evening soirees. But Littlefield's ego got the best of him. Irate that Scarbrough's building was a bit taller, he enclosed the roof garden in 1917 and added a ninth floor, making it the tallest building between New Orleans and San Francisco.

Race relations in early Austin mirrored those of most Southern cities—segregation and control through terrorism. As the National Association for the Advancement of Colored People (NAACP) began its campaign for racial justice, Texas officials bristled. In 1919, John Shillady, the white executive secretary of the NAACP, came to Austin to talk with Governor William Hobby. He was detained and interrogated, then the county judge and a constable confronted him downtown and attacked him. "He was here apparently advocating social equality of the Negros and Whites," the judge wrote. "We gave him a pretty sound thrashing, using no weapons, and directed him to leave town." Governor Hobby's response was to tell the NAACP to keep their propaganda out of Texas. Shillady never fully recovered and later died from the wounds.[8]

African Americans and Mexican Americans worked as cotton pickers, servants, bootblacks, blacksmiths, and barbers' assistants. Blacks lived in East Austin and in neighborhoods such as Clarksville, Wheatsville, and (west of town) Masontown. The Eckhardts lived on the edge that divided white Austin from Wheatsville, which began at Twenty-fourth Street, a block north of the Eckhardt house. Clarksville was about fifteen blocks south. Bobby grew up with daily interactions with blacks and the understood deference that blacks had to show to whites. Even black adults addressed him as "Mr. Bobby." By the 1930s, expansion of the UT community, hardened segregation attitudes, and a city plan to concentrate blacks in one area led to the relocation of many blacks to East Austin.

Life at 2300 Rio Grande Street

The Eckhardt home was a warm and inviting, spacious two-story yellow brick house with large dining, living, and music rooms, two bathrooms, four upstairs bedrooms, and wraparound porches. The top porches were screened in and served as summer sleeping rooms. The house was surrounded by pecan trees that Joe planted. A building out back doubled as garage and barn, and the backyard held chickens, cows, and a grape arbor (for making wine). A streetcar ran down the middle of Rio Grande Street to take them downtown. Joe and Norma hired a hand who lived in quarters in the garage-barn.[9] They usually also employed a maid. Luisa came from Germany; a later longtime maid, Alla Mae, was African American.

Bobby was four years old when his brother Joseph Jr. was born, followed by Norman five years later. Joe Jr., like his namesake, attended the Galveston medical school, while Norman followed Bob into labor law. The whole family liked to swim and picnic at Barton Springs. Once when young Norman fell asleep, relaxing in his inner tube in the quiet waters, Bobby and Joe Jr. could not resist dumping their little brother over. The three were inseparable sidekicks through boyhood, and Norma and Joe referred to them as "the wild bunch." Joe Jr. and Norman looked up to older brother Bobby as a hero and model.[10]

Norma filled the house with the warm aroma of baking bread and the melodious sounds of her piano playing. Unlike her Wurzbach sisters, she did not buy into the prim and proper dress code of the day. A cute, seemingly carefree young woman, she wore flowery dresses, sometimes appearing gypsy-like. She was gregarious, exuding fun and love, and well liked throughout the community. Norma was very religious. Bob would later say that she was "an absolute literal Christian—I mean she really believed in it." She would dress to the hilt and take the boys with her to University Presbyterian Church, where she sang in the choir. When Norman became proficient as a musician, he would accompany her solos on his flute.[11] Norma became one of the most powerful influences in the boys' lives. She read Dickens to Bobby before he could read. He later remembered her as being "radical" about abuses in the English industrial society, adding that it helped influence him.[12]

Joe was a strict father. He often exhibited an ungovernable temper and hysterical outbursts of indignation, willing to do battle with injustices of the world. As Bobby grew up and learned about world affairs, he and the maid Luisa would argue about the World War. Luisa insisted that her Germany had not lost. But Joe would stop the arguments—he was the herr of the haus and did not want fights. Joe also underwent a change after leaving the ranch, perhaps due to his medical education or to the 1917 smallpox outbreak and 1918 influenza epidemic. When he was a cowboy, he was used to being out in the elements—amid dirt, flies, and insects—and eating on the ground around a campfire. As a physician and father, he was compulsive about germs and cleanliness. If a fly lit on some tomatoes, he threw out the whole bunch. At mealtime, he required the boys to wash their hands and walk from the washroom to the table with their hands up, so they didn't touch anything. Joe openly talked about the jackasses and damn fools he ran across. He was not a prudish man, but he did have stern lessons on sex and alcohol. He described syphilis to Bobby as "a night with Venus and two years with Mercury." He also cautioned against drinking, using as an example his older brother Otto and his wild flings at San Antonio's Menger Hotel.[13]

Dr. Eckhardt was a general practitioner, delivering babies, performing surgeries three blocks away at the Seton Infirmary, and making house calls in addition to his clinic practice downtown. He drove around town in his horse and buggy, charging three dollars for a house call (two dollars for an office visit). Later, he bought a fancy open-air Franklin automobile, with oak and aluminum trim. Bobby occasionally accompanied him on house calls. Dr. Eckhardt had a strong sense of justice and respected the dignity and individuality of his patients. Sometimes he brought home chickens received from patients who had no money. Bobby was sure that his dad was the best doctor in the world. And Joe and Norma thought their sons were the best.[14]

Bob's liberal race attitudes and politics were influenced deeply by his father. Joe would tell his son wonderful stories about Gas Lewis, Tom Smith, and Decederio from his ranching days. Joe spoke Spanish fluently, had a bilingual office staff, and attracted a large Hispanic clientele. Dr. Eckhardt was revered in the community, so he could get away with social practices that others could not. When fellow physicians pressured him to segregate his waiting room, he nearly threw them out of his office.[15]

The most visible political figure in Texas at that time was Governor Jim Ferguson, and Joe would take young Bobby to hear Ferguson and others downtown in Wooldridge Park. Joe did not identify himself as liberal politically, but he became a strong supporter of Franklin Roosevelt, voting for him and defending him. When Roosevelt ran for a third term, though, Dr. Eckhardt decided that FDR was becoming too powerful and supported Republican Wendell Willkie instead.[16]

Joe was now far removed from his cowboy days, but he always kept horses and passed on that love of horses to his boys. They rented a pasture three blocks away in the Wheatsville neighborhood, staking their horses there or down the hill on Shoal Creek then bringing them back to the barn at night. Joe and the boys would ride along Shoal Creek or go on longer rides over to Bull Creek. When Bobby was ten, he visited the Eckhardt Ranch and was thrilled when he got to put his horse riding skills to work helping run cattle. Joe thought that bicycles were too dangerous, so Bobby grew up without a bike (although it would become his favored mode of transportation as an adult). Horses were dangerous, but Joe was not as concerned about that danger; he was used to it. Young Bobby took some falls, including once when a horse reared up and fell over backward. One mare, YoYo, had a filly named Dixie (born on Jefferson Davis's birthday). Once as he was riding YoYo with Dixie following, Bobby neared a passing train. Dixie spooked and ran, and Bobby had to hold on tight to YoYo to keep from falling off as they chased the frightened filly.[17]

The Eckhardts, Klebergs, and Wurzbachs visited each other frequently. The house at 2300 Rio Grande was often full of Yorktown and San Antonio relatives. Grandfather Wurzbach would visit, as would Norma's brother William (a legislator) and his family. As one by one the young adults came to Austin to study at the university, they were included in the Eckhardt family affairs and outings. In 1918, William's daughter Emily came to live with the Eckhardts while she studied at UT. Emily was crazy about her Aunt Norma. She went on the outings to Barton Springs and taught Norma how to drive a car. Bobby liked to have Emily read to him and walk him the three blocks to school. She found Bobby to be an interesting and eccentric boy.[18]

Bobby grew up admiring politicians. "I thought it grand to be a congressman," he said of those days. He visited the long-bearded Great Uncle Rudolph in his office at the state capitol and at his home a few blocks away and heard stories of his days in Congress. Then Bobby would play with Great Aunt Mathilde and their girls Lulu and Tillie, who still lived at home. Son Caesar was a foreman on the King Ranch at that time, and August returned to Austin in 1918. There was some tension between the families in these years, as Rudolph and Mathilde sued the Yorktown Eckhardts (including her brothers), the von Roeders, and the Schmelzers over the bankruptcy of C. Eckhardt & Sons.[19]

Bobby frequently saw Uncle Oscar Eckhardt and his older cousins at Oscar's drugstore downstairs from Joe's office. Oscar's son James went to medical school in Galveston and returned to practice in Austin. Another son, Oscar Jr., known as "Ox," was one of the all-time great athletes at the University of Texas. He was a big fullback/halfback on the undefeated UT football team in 1923. "There goes Ox—through the line with a stiff-arm," the announcer would call again and again. Ox went on to play baseball and led Joe DiMaggio in batting average in the minor leagues in the 1930s.[20]

Bobby Makes Friends and Goes to School

Bobby was an active and imaginative boy who built birdhouses, set up a play office in the barn loft, and made friends with many of the neighborhood kids.[21] His best friend was Charles Black, who lived a block and a half down the street. Though Charles was nearly two years younger than Bobby, they were great playmates and became lifelong friends and colleagues (even co-authoring *The Tides of Power,* a book on constitutionalism and Congress). Their characters, their differences, and their competition came out even in these early days of play. When they built boats from boxes to sail down the Colorado River, Charles wanted to make a giant structure, but Bobby wanted to construct a much more practical boat.[22] They were Southern boys, so they played Civil War, complete with stars and bars on their uniforms. Theirs was the Great Southern Army. They shared the generalship, making Joe Jr. be a private and play the part of the entire enlisted service under their command. Charles was precocious. When his mother admitted to him that there was no Santa Claus, he told her "I suppose you'll soon be telling me the same thing about Jesus Christ."[23]

Bob Eckhardt's career as a cartoonist and caricaturist started early, and he continued to draw for the rest of his life, though he only took an art class once. By age five, he was filling the sidewalks around the house with his drawings. The UT students who lived next door in a fraternity house complained to Emily Wurzbach, saying, "Emily, for heaven's sake, make your cousin stop doing what he does. He gets that chalk out there and makes all those pictures on the sidewalks and won't let us walk on them. He makes us walk out on the road so we won't ruin his pictures."[24] Bobby also drew cartoons on the side of the house, and Norma cherished them and left them there. At Wooldridge Elementary School, Bobby would grab a chunk of limestone and draw on the sidewalks, all around the building, up the steps, right to the door of the school. Then, he would scoot across the drawings in his corduroy pants to rub them out to make room for more. The other kids would eye him to see if he was stealing school chalk—but he used the plentiful chalk rock, liking it better.

Charles Black had started early at a private school, then transferred to Wooldridge in second grade. So, though not the same age, they were in the same grade, from elementary school on through UT.[25] Norma would visit Bobby's and Charles's classes. Teacher Katherine Cook remembered them as "two of my finest and smartest boys." Sixty years later, they sent her a copy of their book on the Constitution.[26]

Bobby's play nurtured his creativity. In his retirement, he wrote that, like Robert Louis Stevenson in his writings, he did not want to give up this kind of boyishness. "I, like Stevenson, felt it was twelve when I could no longer, without embarrassment, make the sand pile my great imaginary universe—a place of fortresses and deep caves and pleasant beaches. When I first visited Corpus Christi, it was a disappointment in contrast with my imagined romantic beaches. . . . Imagination, and its companion, curiosity, are stronger usually in the boy . . . ."[27]

From Wooldridge, Bobby next went to John T. Allan Junior High School downtown. Almost all the white children of Travis County were merged together for junior high. And there, Bobby entered the world of adolescent prankster boys. Harold Preece would stand on a garbage can expounding his doctrines, one day Marxian, the next religious. Stinky Bowen would entertain everyone on the schoolyard with licentious expression. Once Stinky discovered the word "urinate," he used it whenever it suited him, as well as other words such as "poontang," secret code for nasty talk.[28]

The important relationship that Bobby made in junior high was with new friend John Henry "Johnny" Faulk. From the time he was able to speak, Faulk was funnier than anybody else and thus was the social king. He was also a troublemaker, but he got people—even the teachers—to laugh.[29] Johnny was just five weeks younger than Bobby, but he lived south of the Colorado River and had gone to Fulmore Elementary School, so they had not met earlier. The Faulks lived on a small farmstead on a dirt road named Live Oak Street. (After World War II, Johnny's sister would turn their house into Green Pastures Restaurant, a fashionable Austin eatery and gathering place.)

Bobby often visited the Faulk place, with its cows and chickens, guineas, dogs, and peacocks. He, Johnny, and friend Jack Kellam would head out into the curious world of South Austin, finding a dingy house where they would sit on the floor, eat rolled roast, and tell stories. Johnny learned to mimic sounds around him and could inhabit his stories with real characters, black and white, from South Austin. Bobby would laugh so hard that he would beat the walls, loosening the nails. The boys played along the banks of the Colorado, scooping up clay to sculpt into whatever shape suited their fancy, including forms to express their juvenile prurience.[30]

Bob Eckhardt, John Henry Faulk, Jack Kellam, Anne C. McAfee. From boyhood
through adulthood, Bob Eckhardt was friends and art comrades with John Henry
Faulk and Jack Kellam. Here, standing at the entrance to the Faulk farm in Austin
(1936), the three are joined by Faulk's niece Anne (later a printer of the *Texas
Observer*). Courtesy of Anne C. McAfee.

Johnny's father Henry was a lawyer (and Bob would later inherit his law
practice), but everyone called him "Judge Faulk." Henry was elected county
attorney in 1900. When he lost his reelection bid, he became disenchanted
with the establishment Democratic Party and became a Socialist, allied with
Eugene V. Debs, then Norman Thomas, the Socialist Party presidential candidates. Judge Faulk ran for Texas attorney general on the Socialist ticket.

In the 1920s, Judge Faulk had an office downtown, where he took on
the cases of poor blacks in their battles against loan sharks, land grabbers,
and funeral operators. Consequently, much of his legal service was, by de-
fault, free of charge. The Faulk household, like the Eckhardt home, served a
broad extended family. Eugene V. Debs stayed there when he visited Austin.
Mr. Faulk would leave his downtown office door open for those who needed
a place to sleep on the couch, putting up a visiting Wobbly or Communist.
When Bobby would go with Johnny into East Austin to collect rent checks
for Judge Faulk, he witnessed the poverty of black Austin. Henry Faulk and
his sense of social justice was a significant influence on Eckhardt. "I used to

kind of wonder," he later said. "Socialism is pretty radical, and I don't know that I want to go as far as old man Faulk, but it raised questions."[31]

Austin High School Years

In 1928, Austin High School opened at its new location at Twelfth and Rio Grande, just in time for Bobby's high school years. From his dad, he had learned about the family branding iron designed by his grandfather, and he adopted it as his own, signing his schoolwork $\underset{\circlearrowright}{EK}$.[32] It was later to become his trademark artistic and political signature as well. His classes included Shakespeare and physics. He studied Spanish with Lillian (Mrs. Roy) Bedichek. He loved Goethe and other German poetry. He served as president of the German Club in his junior year, sponsoring such projects as a picnic in New Braunfels. In his senior year, Bobby was one of four winners of the yearly declamation contest.[33]

Bobby's ever-expanding circle of friends and acquaintances at Austin High would interweave with his artistic, legal, and political life for decades. They included Charles Black and Johnny Faulk, Jack Kellam, Walter Richter, and Henry Holman. He got to know the Sutherland family; Alice Sutherland edited the school newspaper, *The Maroon*. Johnny continued to be a great influence on Bobby, and they frequently discussed politics. Eckhardt wrote of Faulk: "He influenced me toward a more socialistic view point and, more than that, he influenced me toward humanity. We used to read passages in *Pickwick Papers* aloud and others of Dickens' works: 'The law is a ass, a idiot,' said Mr. Bumble.'"[34]

When Bobby was a junior, a skinny boy named Creekmore (Creek) Fath moved to Austin. Creek and Johnny Faulk became debate partners. After Bobby, Charles, and Johnny graduated, they came back and egged Creek into running for student president, and the exes ran his losing campaign. It whetted Fath's appetite for politics. Eckhardt and Fath would become law partners and political allies.[35]

Bobby's interests in humor and art also found outlets in his high school years. He designed a full-color set of playing cards, a few of which have survived. The "seven" card was a man with a pipe in his mouth and a long knife in his hand; the "five" card was a blond woman with glasses sitting precariously on her nose, wearing pearls, a bracelet, and a purple dress.[36] In his senior year, he was the humor editor of the yearbook, the *Comet*. His cartoon sketches reflected a western and cowboy culture, one of the genres that he turned to throughout his cartooning years. Jack Kellam also drew for the *Comet* and would later draw with Eckhardt at UT.

Bobby and Charles Black started a renegade publication, the *Meatloaf Gazette,* so named because it was distributed in the lunchroom, where meatloaf was served every day, the only difference being that it was served with brown gravy on Mondays, Wednesdays, and Fridays and red gravy on Tuesdays and Thursdays. The *Gazette* caught the attention of the *Austin Statesman,* which mentioned it as a humorous paper at Austin High.[37] Bobby and Charles served as coeditors, just as they had been co-generals of the Great Southern Army a few years earlier. Their fierce competition extended to romantic advances with girls, and the rivalry spurred each of them to greater writing and intellectual heights. They both wrote for the *Gazette,* and Bobby drew cartoons and sketches, signed ᴇᴋ. When Charles ran for president of student council (losing to Zachary Scott, who became a 1940s and 50s stage, movie, and TV star), Bobby promoted his campaign in the *Gazette.*[38]

In one issue, Black wrote an editorial and Bobby drew the cartoon illustrating it. When Charles insisted on titling Bobby's cartoon, Bobby resisted, insisting that he would write his own caption. The dispute escalated to such a point that they dissolved the *Meatloaf Gazette* and refused to speak to each other for nearly three years.[39]

San Antonio: Eckhardts, Wurzbachs, and Mavericks

Throughout Bobby's school years, the Eckhardts not only entertained relatives at their home, but also often visited Grandfather Wurzbach, Great Aunt Emily Victoria Eckhardt and her husband Gustav Schmelzer, and aunts, uncles, and cousins in San Antonio. Their visits furthered Bob's political education and contacts. In 1914, Norma's brother William built a sturdy stone house near San Antonio, on what came to be named Wurzbach Road, and the Eckhardts would drive down for visits. Cousin Emily would take care of Bobby.

William Wurzbach was a rising star in Bexar County politics. He was active in the Democratic Party and in the 1930s he was elected county judge, as his father had been. Brother Harry practiced law in San Antonio, but after service in the Spanish-American War, he moved his practice to Seguin in Guadalupe County, where he also won election as county judge, serving from 1904 to 1912. Harry and his wife Darden visited William frequently and saw the Eckhardts there.

Like the rest of his family, Harry was a Democrat, and he wanted the nomination for Congress. But the Wurzbachs often lined up with reformers in their fierce battles with the San Antonio political machine of Bryan V. Callaghan Jr. and Harry could not get the Democratic nod. So, he took the Republican nomination and won the seat. From 1921 to 1931, he was the only Republican congressman from Texas. His Fourteenth Congressional

District—the same district that Rudolph Kleberg had represented—ran from the King Ranch up to Fredericksburg and contained many German-Texans. Harry was a delegate to the Republican National Convention in Cleveland in 1924, the same year that he spoke to an NAACP convention. Congressman Wurzbach voted anti-lynching and for that his enemies called him a black man. As his niece Emily Wurzbach Mickler said, "Uncle Harry and Poppa were very tolerant people. You see, that's one thing they had against Uncle Harry; they said he was a 'nigger lover.'" [40]

Eugene Nolte was the chairman of the Texas Republican Party and an ally of R. B. Creager, who ran the party. They hated Wurzbach. As the only Republican official, he controlled a lot of patronage, which Creager and other Republicans wanted to control. In 1926, in the first Republican primary ever held in Texas, Nolte and Creager recruited an opponent for Congressman Wurzbach, claiming that he was really a Democrat at heart. He won anyway. One time Wurzbach took young Bobby with him to Fredericksburg for a campaign speech. The local editor was anti-Wurzbach and pulled a dirty trick by printing an item saying that Wurzbach would not be there. Bobby watched as Uncle Harry used a megaphone to attract a crowd. [41]

In 1928, Creager and Nolte, desperate to defeat Wurzbach, supported the Democratic candidate in November. The election was so close that the vote tally went back and forth for weeks. Wurzbach eventually lost, but he appealed the election to the House, which delayed the issue for nearly a year before voting to seat him. The Democratic candidate and others involved in the effort were later indicted and acquitted for election tampering. [42]

Through his San Antonio kin, Bob entered the political orbit of the Maverick family, who were good friends of the Wurzbachs. In the nineteenth century, Samuel Maverick was not very interested in his ranching. He would not brand his cows and calves, and when they strayed around the countryside, neighbors knew that the unmarked livestock belonged to Maverick. Thus the term "maverick" came to mean one who is unbranded, difficult to keep fenced. In the early twentieth century, Samuel's son and his family lived on Sunshine Ranch northwest of San Antonio. Grandson Maury dated one of the older Wurzbach girls, Emma, and would call on her at the new stone home on Wurzbach Road, not too far from Sunshine Ranch. On one such visit, Maury, thinking that Mr. Wurzbach was out for the day, breezed through the door, saying to Emma and Emily, "Where's the old man tonight?" But Poppa walked in and said, "Here's the old man—what do you want?" Maverick was highly embarrassed. [43]

But neither that incident nor the end of the young romance (Emma believed that they were engaged to be married; Maury ran off to Ireland [44]) ruined the budding political partnership. In the 1920s, William Wurzbach teamed up with Maury Maverick in the Citizens League to clean up San Antonio from the corrupt governing Callaghan machine. Party affiliation was irrelevant in these local power battles. In 1930, Republican Congressman Harry Wurzbach endorsed the Democratic reform slate for Bexar County, which included Maverick as the successful candidate for tax collector![45]

Transition to College

Bobby graduated from Austin High in the spring of 1931. That summer he went to Houston to work at his Uncle Henry (Norma's brother-in-law) Schumacher's grocery supply store. It was hard work, and he learned respect for those who do physical work for little pay. He also saw a side of life that he did not like. He found his uncle (and others in the grocery business) to be conservative and anti-Semitic.[46]

Eighteen-year-old Bobby was ready to plunge into the college student life. Just as he did, though, Uncle Harry died unexpectedly. Congressman Wurzbach was loved by many, and Eckhardt long remembered his uncle's funeral, which attracted a large crowd, including Latinos, blacks, and members of Congress. He lay in state for a long time as people came by to pay their respects. For Bobby, it was a sad ending for an uncle he respected. Yet, unknown to him at the time, it was also a bridge into a new world of politics for Bob Eckhardt, Maury Maverick, and the nation.

THREE

Student Eckhardt on the Forty Acres

The Texas Constitution of 1876 affirmed a mandate for a public university "of the first class." Yet since its opening in 1883, the University of Texas (UT) has had to battle governors, legislatures, and boards of regents over efforts to restrict the education available—battles that Bob Eckhardt would be drawn into. In the 1930s, a few regents stood out as being committed to a university of the first class, complete with the resources and the freedoms necessary to that undertaking. Populist Democratic Governor James V. "Jimmie" Allred's regents were more progressive than most—notably oilman J. R. Parten, appointed by Allred in 1935. Parten loved UT and wanted to fashion it into a great university.

After the death of Harry "Bennie" Benedict, the distinguished-looking, white-haired president of the university from 1927 to 1937, Parten led a nationwide search that ended in the selection of 43-year-old Homer P. Rainey as president. Rainey, born and educated in Texas, was an ordained Baptist minister, who had already served as president of three colleges and universities. Parten was chair of the Board of Regents when Rainey took office in 1939, just as Eckhardt graduated from law school.[1] Both Rainey and Parten would become significant figures in Eckhardt's political life.

The UT faculty had giants in several fields. The triumvirate of Walter Prescott Webb, J. Frank Dobie, and Roy Bedichek provided the nation with a plethora of reading material on Texas, the West, natural life, and social life. The three intertwined with Eckhardt for decades. Webb taught history, published *The Great Plains* the year that Eckhardt entered UT, and became the premier theorist of the Great Frontier. His Friday Mountain Ranch, with its 1850s cabin, was a getaway and a great resource for natural research. "Pancho" Dobie taught English and directed the Texas Folklore Society. His Paisano Ranch was also a haven. Bedichek, or "Bedi," founded and served as the longtime director of the University Interscholastic League (UIL) based on the UT campus, running the Texas high school debate, speech, drama, and sports competitions. A self-taught naturalist, he spent a year at Friday Mountain Ranch writing *Adventures of a Texas Naturalist*. Both Bedichek and Dobie were mentors to John Henry Faulk. Webb, Dobie, and Bedichek were great friends, going on outings together, swapping dirty jokes and stories, and swimming regularly at Barton Springs, where they discussed politics, literature, history, and nature on their usual perch, "Conversation Rock."[2]

The UT economics department sometimes strayed from the mainstream of the era. Edward Hale Jr. taught Marxism. Clarence Ayres, intellectual leader of the department, was a former editor of the *New Republic*. Bushy-haired, with long sideburns, Robert H. Montgomery (known as "Dr. Bob") specialized in public utilities, was populist in his economics, and greatly influenced students. "He didn't have students; he had disciples," one of them would comment.[3] Montgomery would tell his students, "Texas is the richest colony of Wall Street."[4] Eckhardt would get caught up in the drama surrounding regents' attempts to fire Ayres, Montgomery, and others.

Forty Acres

When Austin was chosen as the seat for the university, the state set aside forty acres for the campus, just blocks north of the capitol—and the campus is still known as the "Forty Acres." Early regents and financial benefactors of the university included George Littlefield and George W. Brackenridge. But many of the campus facilities they helped fund were substandard throughout the early decades. As UT students in early 1900s, Maury Maverick and J. R. Parten railed against the inadequate "shacks" used for student housing.[5] These shacks grew even more inadequate in the 1920s as UT expanded beyond the tree-covered Forty Acres. The regents bought some abandoned buildings six blocks to the southeast of campus that came to be known as "Little Campus." Built in 1859 and the 1880s, the buildings had first been the state school for the blind, then in World War I, the Texas Aeronautics Academy. Those plain, rectangular buildings became men's dormitories and also housed Bedichek's UIL offices. They provided very basic accommodations and were referred to as "poor boys' dorms."[6]

President Benedict oversaw an extensive building program on the Forty Acres, finally replacing the firetraps that the oldest buildings had become. In Eckhardt's student days, the campus was a construction zone, as nine new buildings were dedicated. Benedict built new dormitories to replace the shacks, as well as beautiful limestone academic buildings with Spanish tile roofs. The old Main Building was still standing (precariously) when Eckhardt matriculated, but a new one was started and finished while he was a law student. The 307-foot Main Building tower stands nearly as tall as the state capitol dome. Its clock first tolled in 1937.

If you looked out from the tower in the years when Eckhardt was a student, you would see the peaceful campus and much of Austin. To the south, the pink granite state capitol dominated the skyline. Immediately surrounding Main, below your perch in the tower, were the Women's Building on the west side, then all the academic buildings, including on the southwest corner the library (now Battle Hall), Sutton Hall, and the Architecture Building. To the southeast was Garrison Hall, decorated with cattle brands and portraits of Texas statesmen, and to the northeast of Main stood the Journalism Building (now Gebauer Hall, the oldest building still standing). To the west and northwest, the new Union Building was under construction.

If you looked down the hill to the east, you could see George W. Brackenridge's storied yellow brick B Hall and, on the southeast corner of the Forty Acres, the Law School. Look beyond B Hall, across Speedway, and you could see the new Gregory Gym. Taylor Hall was under construction then on the former site of Clark Field (where Joe Eckhardt had raced his two-horse carriage across the field after football games). The new Clark Field could be seen to the east on the grassy area beyond the edge of the campus. Next to the field loomed the famed Billy Goat Hill, a limestone cliff that Longhorn outfielders scaled to chase down long fly balls.[7] South of Clark Field was Memorial Stadium, built after World War I, and beyond it, Little Campus. Looking to the north, a block from Main, you could not miss George Littlefield's red brick and red stone mansion across Twenty-fourth Street just off the Forty Acres (today it is inside the campus) and the new Littlefield women's dormitory. A block away from Main to the west was Guadalupe Street, which became known as the "Drag." University-oriented businesses lined Guadalupe, and streetcars took students, faculty, and townspeople to and from the Forty Acres for a nickel.[8]

And if you looked to the west beyond the Drag, before your eyes met the violet crown of hills outside the city, you would find, nestled in the trees, the residential area that housed the Eckhardts. When Joe Eckhardt returned to Austin in 1911, he chose to be near his beloved alma mater, locating his family just three blocks to the west of Guadalupe Street. The university was Bob's second home.

Bobby Becomes Bob, University Student

At the university, Bobby came to be called Bob. He enrolled in 1931 and graduated in 1935 with a BA degree. Eckhardt continued his study of German and further developed his interest in Shakespeare, Dickens, Burns, and Keats. But he majored in zoology as a pre-med student, trying to follow in his father's footsteps. Bob jumped into the world of science, putting his drawing skills to work on pen-and-ink sketches of the structure of a fertilized cell and drawing diagrams of primordial germ cells.[9] But he was a dilettante, more attentive to

33

the exciting campus life than to his studies. He struggled and often earned low grades. As he neared the end of his undergraduate years, Eckhardt simply could not go forward with his plan to become a doctor. He so enjoyed his verbal exchanges with students and professors that he decided he needed a profession where he could use his speaking skills. As he put it, "there's not much of a premium on bullshit in medicine," so he decided to become a lawyer. He entered the UT School of Law, graduating in 1939 with his LLB.

Few students owned cars, most lived on the Forty Acres or Little Campus, and it was easy to know a lot of students. Everyone knew Eckhardt because of his engaging personality, but also because he was an Austin boy, because his father was a well-known physician, and because some students saw his mother at church every week. Eckhardt stood out on campus. He tested his limits—drinking and carrying on. He was different. He kept and rode horses—common in his dad's day at UT, but not so much by the 1930s. Nobody wore sandals to school, but he did. While at law school, he started wearing white linen suits with red bow ties. Bob was admired by his fellow students as ethereal, as a Renaissance man with exciting ideas and great humor, and as an entertainer who played the concertina and sang German and Spanish songs, though he was not very fluent in either language.[10] Like other men in his family, he joined Sigma Chi fraternity, but he was not active in it.

Students loved Eckhardt's storytelling. He regaled them with stories about his German Texas family history. Once, Bob rode a dirty brown gelding named Bootlegger to visit a fellow student and told her the horse's story. Bootlegger was a small, twelve-hand, fine three-gaited horse, very fast, sporting a beautiful parade saddle with gold longhorn heads mounted on silver with ruby eyes that glinted in the sun. As Bob told it, Bootlegger belonged to Texas Ranger Captain Bill Sterling. Sterling had worked with the Klebergs of the King Ranch and had married Bob's cousin Zora Eckhardt, daughter of the wild Otto. Smugglers would take horses from Texas, swim them across the Rio Grande into Mexico, strap liquor or other contraband to their bellies, and swim them home. The Rangers captured Bootlegger during a raid of tequila smugglers. Captain Sterling bought the horse and gave him to his daughter, Inez, who rode Bootlegger in the 1931 UT Annual Roundup. Sterling let Joe and Bob ride Bootlegger, on the beautiful saddle that Will Rogers had given him.[11]

Student Eckhardt and His Cohort: A Generation of Politicians

Eckhardt's favorite pastime was sitting on the grass with fellow students, talking politics and Shakespeare—"For God's sake, let us sit upon the ground and tell sad stories of the death of kings."[12] They would argue under the streetlights long after midnight. Bob and his friends organized the Young Gentlemen's Coffee Colloquium and Yacht Club, meeting daily at 3:00 p.m. at the P-K Grille on the Drag, when coffee was free, to argue the campus and national issues of the day.[13] When Prohibition ended in 1933, Scholz's, the Tavern, and the Top Hat (just out of town, south of Johnny Faulk's home) became favorite meeting places for drinking and discussion.

There was an amazing group of students at UT in those years. Several Austin High friends joined Bob at UT, including Charles Black, Creek Fath, John Henry Faulk, and Jack Kellam. Early in their university careers, Bob and Charles were still not speaking to each other, fallout from the *Meatloaf Gazette* clashes. The only exception was when they were thrown into a tennis match: as the worst players, they competed with each other for the last place on the team and had to say "ready" and "serve" to each other.[14] But they reconciled and again became best of friends. Charles studied Greek classics. Johnny Faulk, with his penchant for mimicry and theater, explored the world of folklore with the best teachers and role models, Dobie, Webb, and Bedichek. Kellam pursued his artwork more at UT, and Creek became bitten deeply by the political bug.

Other key figures with whom Bob shared campus life included James Jarrell "Jake" Pickle, John Connally, Allan Shivers, Bernard Rapoport, Fred Schmidt, Thomas "Tommy" Sutherland IV, Clay Cochran, Hector Garcia, Gus Garcia, Henry B. Gonzalez, D. B. Hardeman, Walter Cronkite, and Stuart Long. Eckhardt would later reflect on the most successful of this assemblage, writing that "had the good Lord placed the most promising genetic qualities in one person, that man would have been a person of commanding presence, shrewd calculation and genial character. Such a man could be President. But the Lord, in His omnipotence, did not arrange it that way. As Bobbie Burns was wont to say: 'The Lord be thank it.'"[15]

Bob became friends with Tommy Sutherland, brother of Alice (editor of the Austin High newspaper, *Maroon*) and Liz (who became the famed Liz Carpenter). He was just the kind of person who would attract Eckhardt, as Sutherland quoted soliloquies from Shakespeare. He and his wife Lois lived near campus, and Bob would visit and engage Tommy in great discourses on British common law, Shakespeare, the virtues of Franklin Roosevelt, and the evils of Republicans.[16]

In Bob's sophomore year, the student body president was Allan Shivers, who would galvanize Eckhardt's political opposition twenty years later. Shivers was a six-foot-two, 195-pound man with a sharp mind, who was elected to the state senate at age twenty-six. He married Marialice Shary and became a part of that wealthy family. Shivers's life and his politics turned virulently racist. As lieutenant governor and governor, he turned against his labor allies and became their number one enemy. By the end of his electoral career, a voter said of him, "He's just the little brother of the big rich." [17]

Shivers made friends with fellow student Jake Pickle, who grew up in Big Spring in West Texas. Jake lived with about 130 other men in the "poor boys' dorms," in Little Campus, paying $25 a semester for a room. He got the milk route and walked bottled milk around to the rooms at 6:00 a.m. Later, he picked up and delivered laundry, then worked as a janitor, before finally landing a job at the capitol. Through all his jobs at the dorms, Jake came to know many students, which gave him a base for his political operations. [18]

Bernard Rapoport enrolled at UT in 1936. [19] His father David, being both a Marxist revolutionary and a Jew, had been banished from tsarist Russia after the 1905 revolt. David ended up in San Antonio, where he was a door-to-door salesman and Socialist organizer, and where he got to know Maury Maverick. His son Bernard, known as Barney or simply as "B", was also a door-to-door salesman. Barney became friends with Fred Schmidt, a boy from a poor German-Texan family (originally from Cuero, near Yorktown). Fred hung out at the Rapoport home playing chess, and the boys were high school debate partners. [20] They became like brothers. True to his father's roots, Rapoport was a Marxist when he arrived on campus. An aunt once told him how she had met rabbis from Biblical times, to which young B exclaimed, "how could you possibly know them?" He then marveled when, as he plunged into his studies at UT, he "met" Thorstein Veblen, and his philosophy started changing. He also got to know fellow student Clay Cochran and, under his and Dr. Bob's influence, learned about and embraced populism.

B and Fred would go to Bob and Gladys Montgomery's house on Friday nights for cookouts and discussions of politics and economics with a dozen or two of the other progressive students, and sometimes Dobie, Webb, and Bedichek. [21] Fred described himself in those early days as radical. In the 1950s, he became a labor leader, with Eckhardt as one of his lobbyists. After UT, Rapoport moved with his wife to her hometown of Waco and became a highly successful insurance company owner, national Democratic financier, one of the funders of Eckhardt's campaigns, and chairman of UT's Board of Regents under Governor Ann Richards.

The college men, of course, spent much of their time in dating endeavors. Bob loved the company of women, and he often dated more than one at a time. Bob's cousin and fellow artist Bob Engelking introduced him to Julya Thomson, a literature and art student who lived in a sorority house three houses down from the Eckhardts. [22] She would visit the Eckhardts and loved spending time with Bob, getting to know this eccentric and intriguing young man. They would frequently drink at the Tavern or Scholz's. She asked him once what made him stray from the path of goodness and light. He flippantly told her he decided to give up Christianity for alcohol. Julya returned to the Dallas area after leaving UT, studying and teaching art. Bob would take "La Belle Julya" to campus dances and football games, and then out to drink scotch. They fell in love, and Julya would be an important part of his life up to the day he died.

Tommy and Lois Sutherland introduced Bob to Orissa Stevenson, who had arrived from Houston as a freshman in 1936. She was a pretty, round-faced girl, with brown hair, sometimes kept long, sometimes cut short. She plunged into the social life, joining Kappa Kappa Gamma sorority as well as the prestigious Orange Jackets, the Ashbel Literary Society, and the Mortar Board. Julya Thomson was a year ahead of Orissa. They were good friends and roomed together at the sorority house near the Eckhardts. Named after a great aunt, who was named after a province in India, Orissa seemed mysterious to Bob, and he fell in love with her, too. He found her to be brilliant, and he admired her as a wonderful watercolor artist, coming from three generations of artists in her family. Orissa was not only one of the few women on campus who majored in architecture, she also won the American Institute of Architects award for having the highest scholastic average of architect students at UT for five years.[23] Bob and Orissa married immediately upon her graduation in 1942.

Student Eckhardt and the Politics of the 1930s

During his eight years on campus, Eckhardt became deeply attentive to the exciting world of politics involving President Franklin Roosevelt, Governor Jimmie Allred, and Congressman Maury Maverick. Whenever Roosevelt gave a fireside chat, every radio was tuned in, and his voice wafted over the campus. The Great Depression provided the fuel for a new political movement. In Texas, the movement was a regrowth of the populism of the 1880s and 1890s. Young Wichita Falls District Attorney James V. "Jimmie" Allred won the race for Texas attorney general in 1930, running against monopolies. In 1932, Roosevelt won the presidency, with Robert "Dr. Bob" Montgomery and suffragette leader Minnie Fisher Cunningham stumping across Texas for him, and the New Deal era began. Allred won the governorship in 1934, bringing a populist-laced New Deal to Texas.

When Uncle Harry Wurzbach died unexpectedly in 1931, Eckhardt's first cousin (once removed) Richard (Dick) Kleberg from the King Ranch ran for the congressional seat. Bexar County's new reform tax collector Maury Maverick supported Kleberg, and Kleberg won. Then, redistricting carved a new Bexar County (San Antonio) congressional district out of Kleberg's district. Kleberg supported Maverick in his bid for that seat, and Maverick won it in 1934.[24]

Kleberg was a southern "boll weevil" Democrat, never a strong New Dealer. Moreover, he was not a particularly hard worker and gained a reputation as a playboy congressman who enjoyed cockfighting. He hired young, hard-working Lyndon Johnson as his aide. Roosevelt did not support Kleberg, and with growing opposition at home, he was defeated in 1944. In his goodbye speech to the House, he fumed against "the almost complete Fascist state" of the New Deal and its "Marxist laws."[25] Maury Maverick, on the other hand, was one of the most aggressive New Dealers in Congress, sponsoring and pushing much of Roosevelt's program—and often pushing Roosevelt himself farther than the president was willing to go. But the battles between the Establishment and reformers back in San Antonio still raged, and Maverick won only two terms before losing in 1938. He fought back against the machine and won the mayor's office in 1939.

Eckhardt jumped enthusiastically into the potpourri of people, politics, and talk on campus. As John Connally wrote of the 1930s at UT, "Politics was the air we breathed. It was an easy time to find a cause, to choose sides and to go off in all directions."[26] The New Deal, the Spanish Civil War, the movements sweeping Europe—all were fodder for the university community. Maury Maverick and Dr. Bob hosted talks at the YMCA. Peace rallies drew large crowds. UT students were fervently engaged with the electoral campaigns. *Daily Texan* editor D. B. Hardeman boosted the New Deal campaigners in editorials and went to Washington and met Roosevelt.[27] D. B. went on to law school with Eckhardt, fought alongside him in the 1940s party wars, and became a Texas legislator before working for U.S. House Speaker Sam Rayburn. In this milieu, Student Eckhardt came to defend the New Deal, against left and right.[28]

Eckhardt was also active, with Rapoport and others, in the "Oxford Movement," a peace group. His hero Maury Maverick promoted isolationism in Washington,[29] and Eckhardt and his friends cheered him on. When Hitler marched into the Sudetenland in 1939, Law Student Eckhardt led a major rally at the Physics Building. He and other leaders declared the building off-limits and sought to prevent faculty and students from entering it. The demonstrators decried war and the growing appetite of the Nazis.[30] But with Hitler's continued military strikes, Eckhardt and many of the others abandoned pacifism and decided that it was, indeed, necessary to confront Hitler militarily.

Barbarians and Progressive Democrats

For three years, Creek Fath was president of the "Associated Independents," an anti-fraternity group. Creek and Clay Cochran organized the campus to the point of having ward heelers, with Creek as the campaign manager. Creek armed block walkers with maps of who lived where and sent them door-to-door. The fraternities (the "Greeks") gave them the derisive nickname the "Barbarians" (or simply the "Barbs"). The Barbs would be the troops for two Eckhardt campaigns on campus.

Intertwined with many of the Barbs was the campus Young Democrats (YD) chapter, including Fath, Cochran, Rapoport, Otto Mullinax, Herman Wright, Mark Adams, *Daily Texan* editor Joe Storm, and Chris Dixie. In student politics, they were Barbs, active against the fraternity candidates; in partisan politics, they were Young Democrats, active for the New Deal and against conservatives. They organized to take over leadership of YD chapters across the state. Vice President John Nance Garner wrote them a letter chastising them for their progressive activism and opposition to establishment policies. So they resigned their YD chapter and, with Dr. Montgomery's assistance, reorganized as the "Progressive Democrats," or PDs, and lived together in a cooperative house. In 1936, law students Dixie, Mullinax, and Wright all ran losing campaigns for the legislature from their home districts, with Fath managing Dixie's campaign.

The PDs pressed for progressive policies, including increased sulfur taxes and regulation of utilities, backing up State Senator Joe Hill's efforts at the capitol. The group found creative ways to put out their message. Every Saturday night, students could pay one dollar to attend a campus dance called a "German." Once, Creek held a PD German at Gregory Gym, where he used the microphone to take on the tax issue while standing under a banner across the stage, "For a higher tax on sulfur." Industry leaders railed against the students and complained to the state and university leaders about them.

Clay Cochran was the energetic, outgoing, intellectual leader of the PDs, and Creek was the activist leader. Both became law partners with Eckhardt. Cochran and Herman Wright had come from Amarillo. Wright became a labor lawyer and ran for governor in 1948 on the Progressive Party ticket, which was headed by the presidential candidate Henry Wallace. Cochran would go on to write against economic concentration and work for the Congress of Industrial Organizations (CIO). He eventually focused on rural power and housing issues and became the nation's leading rural advocate in Washington. Eckhardt entered one of Cochran's rural housing speeches into the *Congressional Record* in 1970.[31]

Otto Mullinax came to UT from East Texas. He joined Houston's premier labor law firm, along with Herman Wright and Chris Dixie, before moving to Dallas and founding his own labor law firm. Eckhardt partnered with Chris Dixie in law practice in Houston, after Dixie's clerkship for U.S. Supreme Court Justice Hugo Black. For two decades, Mullinax served on the board of directors of the independent liberal political organization, Americans for Democratic Action, bringing Eckhardt on board with him.

Mark Adams was a writer; indeed, he would later write about the PD trials and tribulations. After UT, Adams went into the printing and publishing business, providing writing and printing services to his favorite Texas campaigns. The PDs were, in Adams's view, "within the orbit of R. H. Montgomery." He was the greatest teacher they knew—the model of what a teacher should be—and never aspired to be department chairman or New Deal executive, though he had offers. Dr. Montgomery took students with him to Washington, providing valuable links between the young politicos and the New Deal.[32] He also took students to the governor's mansion for dinner and conversation with Allred and anyone else there that evening, such as Allred's former aide Ralph Yarborough and his UT regent J. R. Parten.[33] There, Eckhardt and Fath were introduced to the aromatic world of cigars and politics. On a typical evening at the governor's mansion, Jimmie and Jo Betsy Allred would host the group for dinner, then Mrs. Allred would leave the dining room and close the door behind her. Jimmie would open a cabinet, take out Roytan Senator cigars, pass them around, then open the windows. They would sit and smoke and talk politics and policy late into the night. Bob and Creek both became cigar smokers for much of their lives. Bob learned to use cigars as a prop in the courtroom and in political gatherings, to steal the focus and to stall for time to think.[34]

Two key and fascinating people Montgomery introduced Eckhardt and his fellow students to were New Dealers Minnie Fisher Cunningham and Walton "Hammy" Hamilton. Montgomery, like Clarence Ayres, had studied under Hamilton, a UT graduate who later became a leading economic theorist, worked with Thorstein Veblen, helped found the Brookings Institution, served on Roosevelt's National Recovery Administration Board, and directed FDR's cabinet committee on price policy. Hamilton went on to teach law at Yale and to serve as the lead Supreme Court litigator for Abe Fortas's law firm in Washington.[35]

Montgomery was a vocal advocate of regulation, speaking out in particular against practices of the sulfur industry. Business leaders, including Texas Gulf Sulfur lobbyist Roy Miller, concocted a legislative investigation in 1936 to discredit Montgomery, expose the PDs as Communists, and identify those who taught "communism, atheism, and other un-American and subversive theories and doctrines."[36] Otto Mullinax and Herman Wright were subpoenaed to testify, and they wore Roosevelt buttons to the hearing.[37] Governor Allred and Congressman Maverick sympathized with Montgomery and the students, and both were present at the hearings. Eckhardt, too, went down to the capitol to watch the show, which lasted days. The galleries were packed as more than fifteen hundred people showed up, many wearing red, white, and blue Roosevelt buttons.

Legislators grilled Mullinax and Wright for hours. "Three of us ran for the legislature on a program to tax sulfur, and were defeated on the charge of being Communists. Our issue was sulfur, not communism," testified Mullinax.[38] They were asked where they got the principles for the PD platform. "Part of them came from the writing of Thomas Jefferson, part of them were taken from President Roosevelt's campaign speeches, a few were selected from Gov. James V. Allred's platform, and three came from Dr. Robert Montgomery," Mullinax replied.[39] "Dr. Montgomery, do you believe in the profit system?" the legislators asked when he took the stand. "I most certainly do," he replied. "I would like to see it extended to 120 million people."[40] The chagrined legislators couldn't make the term "Communist" stick. Montgomery counterattacked, charging that utility interests and Republican leaders had offered to finance a Red Scare in Texas, starting with the legislative hearings.[41]

The whole ordeal served as a baptism by fire for the PDs. Mark Adams wrote that "they emerged from it as a cadre of blooded troops for armies of the democratic cause."[42] Eckhardt was energized and incensed by the red baiting. He wrote a letter to the *Daily Texan*—though it was censored and rejected—castigating the "red-baiting" legislature. He wrote, "In observing the manner in which this committee proceeded toward its end, one is reminded of the methods used in the Inquisition. . . . In attempting to stifle freedom of thought and of opinion, these legislative investigators, these red-baiters, have forsaken the tenets of that democracy which they profess to be championing."[43]

Cartooning

Even more than politics, the world of humor had its grip on Student Eckhardt. He would visit friends in their frat house and draw cartoons on the walls, much as he had drawn cartoons on the sidewalks and his house as a child.[44] He found his niche, though, in the student humor magazine, the *Texas Ranger.* He drew sketches that looked like those of cartoonist Don Herold, who drew for *Life* in the 1920s, and his brush technique was influenced by Peter Arno's *New Yorker* cartoons that began in the 1920s. Eckhardt met Arno when he came to an Austin art museum and he asked the cartoonist about his style and brushes.[45] At this time, Eckhardt was also developing his technique with wood block prints.

Eckhardt drew for the monthly *Texas Ranger* in his senior year and first year of law school, 1934–1936. The *Ranger*'s office was a large room in the basement of the journalism building next to Main. The long windows came down to the ground and, in those pre–air-conditioning days, were often open; Bob just climbed in through the open window. The *Ranger* showcased the talents of some remarkable students. John Henry Faulk sharpened his wit in its pages as "Canebrakes Correspondent" and "Backwoodsman." Jack Kellam and Jack Guinn practiced the cartooning that later became their professional calling. Charles Black wrote some brilliant poetry. Alyce Hamilton and Eckhardt's cousin Bob Engelking, descended from the original literary and artistic Engelking German immigrants, were regular contributors. Eckhardt drew cover sketches plus numerous cartoons scattered throughout the issues.

The staff leadership was apparently in chaos. As Bob started law school, he was editor at large, then acting associate editor, then associate editor. When the editor was booted out of school in the spring of 1936, Eckhardt was in line to become editor. Eckhardt thought his apparent ascendancy to the editorship a great occasion. The *Ranger* room had an enormous drawing table and two desks about twelve feet apart. As Guinn and Eckhardt celebrated Eckhardt's expected promotion, they stood on the desks throwing a gallon jug of wine from one man to the other in alternate gulps. They had been at it some time, finishing about two-thirds of the jug, when Paul J. Thompson, the straight-laced chairman of the journalism department who was in charge of the *Ranger,* phoned Eckhardt and asked him to come upstairs. Bob straightened his clothes, combed his hair, and went upstairs, deliberately walking very straight and not talking much. Thompson apparently did not notice Bob's altered state, or perhaps the chairman was not used to the smell of liquor. He told Bob that he was appointed editor. Bob thanked him, trying not to slur his words, and walked out, being careful not to bump the sides of the door.[46]

Editor Eckhardt decided to brighten the dingy office. He planned a mural of life-sized drawings depicting the decline and fall of Pancho Villa. He asked for permission to cover the walls with scenes of Villa, mountains, burning buildings, wrecked locomotives, and peasants. The answer came back—an emphatic "no."[47]

The position of editor was an elective one, so Bob had to run for the post for the following academic year. He designed his own campaign material (with the ♣ branding iron signature),[48] won the election, and settled in for a year of drawing and editing in 1936–1937. The job took a lot of time—so much so that he had to take an extra year to complete his law courses and pull his grades up.

In the *Ranger,* Eckhardt created his "Hobbs Boys" characters—country, hillbilly bumpkins. The pair would comment wryly, or foolishly, on matters of the day. One cartoon was a sketch of the two young men arriving at a party and talking with the butler at the door. "We understood this to be er—a—

semi-formal," says one of the young men. The butler is dressed in a tuxedo. The two young men are also dressed in tuxes—top hats, formal shirts and ties, coats, and carrying canes. The only trouble was that they had no pants or shoes, so they were only "semi" formal. In 1940—though Eckhardt was out practicing law by the time—the College Magazine Editorial Group polled seventy-five college editors around the nation, and Eckhardt's 1936 cartoon won first place.[49]

Censorship was the great issue of the day. Both the *Texas Ranger* and the *Daily Texan* challenged political and sexual mores. The *Ranger* staff pushed the limits, and their work (primarily sexual material) was frequently censored, as were the *Texan's* editorials. The administration was known to haul in wayward students for questioning, disciplining, and perhaps expulsion. Maury Maverick came to the students' defense, blasting the regents for "nazifying the University."[50]

Eckhardt deliberately provoked the administration, hoping to be censored. His photographer would take suggestive photos, but even mildly bawdy pictures would be censored, prompting Eckhardt to have to do some quick work, writing poems and sketching to fill the holes. The manager (and censor) for student publications was a man named William McGill. Bob skewered McGill by writing a poem with "Bill McGill" spelled out in the first letters of each of the first ten lines. Engelking once drew a sketch of a hill with a stream, a boy, and a girl. But the sketch contained a hidden picture, with a penis and with the hills doubling as a woman's breasts. McGill did not catch it, but the printer did and told Eckhardt that he had to reject it or Engelking would be kicked out of UT.[51]

Eckhardt's *Ranger* blended prose, poetry, and pictures. One issue included a takeoff on Chaucer, illustrated by Eckhardt. He also illustrated (with elaborate block prints on the cover and throughout the poem) a Charles Black epic poem in *terza rima,* the great Italian rhyme scheme.[52] He brought his knowledge of Shakespeare to bear on campus and national issues of the day, sketching Shakespeare characters in the style of *New Yorker* humorist James Thurber. McGill censored his bawdy Shakespeare sketches, so Bob substituted other versions. McGill even censored Shakespeare's lines that accompanied an Eckhardt sketch on King Lear: "Why brand they us with base? with baseness? Bastardy base? Base? Who, in the lusty stealth of nature, take more composition and fierce quality than doth, within a dull, stale, tired bed, go to th' creating a whole tribe of fops got 'tween asleep and wake?" Ingeniously, Eckhardt just ran the citation to the lines.

When the PDs and Dr. Bob were being investigated, Editor Eckhardt leapt into the fray. He was eager to be investigated, too, but the legislators never called him to testify. Eckhardt would describe himself as not being favorable to Communism, but he also was contemptuous of the smear tactics used by anti-Communists.[53] He designed a spoof of the whole affair in his "Communist edition," which featured a cover in red and white, with a giant hammer and sickle drawn by Engelking. Eckhardt peppered his sketches throughout the issue (it is also the issue that contained his prize-winning cartoon). And, long after their joint effort on the *Meatball Gazette* had gone awry, Eckhardt and Black collaborated on a joint cartoon depicting a student talking with his dad in his den. The caption read: "But Daddy, how do you think I feel when I have to tell my friends you're not a Communist?"[54]

After his editorship and all the way through law school, Bob occasionally contributed to the *Ranger,* but with the magazine no longer his canvas, he tried his hand at murals. In 1938, W. Lee O'Daniel was elected governor as Allred exited. O'Daniel's "Hillbilly Flour" campaign gimmick made biscuits a "special" on every menu. One of Eckhardt's friends opened the Hillbilly Café on the Drag. After convincing his friend that he needed big murals on his walls, Eckhardt painted for weeks as he was finishing law school. Reviving the Hobbs Boys, he drew twelve-foot-high pictures of hillbillies riding mules, hogs, and goats; hillbillies sleeping in mud holes; hillbillies eating biscuits. He got free meals out of the work.[55] Also in 1938, Creek and others started a newspaper called *The Drag: Forty Wise Acres.* In one issue, they featured a picture of Eckhardt painting the mural (see page 231). Both *The Drag* and the *Texas Ranger* ran Eckhardt-drawn Hillbilly Café ads, with the Hobbs brothers as characters.

Eckhardt drew more murals at a fraternity house and a private school, painting elaborate scenes of Mexican peons sleeping under shade trees. Another painting evoked images of Mayan civilization—it hung in the Eckhardt kitchen at 2300 Rio Grande for years. Unfortunately, none of the Eckhardt murals survive. But his legacy as a cartoonist, caricaturist, and muralist lived on. Five years after Eckhardt left campus, new student Eddie Ball kept hearing stories about the incredible Bob Eckhardt and his drawings, then got to meet him at a political gathering in Austin; they would become law, labor, and political allies. The *Ranger* office showcased an Eckhardt cartoon for ten years after he graduated. Forty years later, he was getting letters at his congressional office, reminding him of the "semi-formal" cartoon.[56]

Connally, Pickle, and Eckhardt

Texas Governor Allan Shivers (1949–1956), Governor John Connally (1963–1968), Congressman Jake Pickle (1963–1995), and Congressman Bob Eckhardt (1967–1980), like many politicians, started their political careers as student politicians. Running successfully for *Texas Ranger* editor and being loosely involved with the PDs and with state political affairs had whetted Eckhardt's appetite for politics. So, he decided to jump into the world of student politics. The only problem was that others had been at it a long time. Eckhardt would later say that since he had won election as the *Ranger* editor, "I thought I was a big shot. I liked to ride horses, drink whiskey, and draw cartoons. I didn't work hard."[57] He got steamrolled right out of student politics.

Barb leaders associated with the PDs were swept up in the New Deal politics; other Barbs, led by Jake Pickle and John Connally, were traditional in their politics. Connally ("Big John") already seemed destined for leadership. He was president of a debate club called the Athenaeum Literary Society and used that as a base for his political operations. Pickle moved out of Little Campus and into the law fraternity house, where he and Connally cemented a lifelong political alliance.[58] In 1936, they helped an independent beat the Greeks for student president. The next year, Jake decided to run for president, and Big John managed his campaign.

Lo and behold, Eckhardt jumped into the race. Pickle knew that Eckhardt was popular, and he feared that with two independents in the race, the Greek candidate would win. Pickle already had a lot of the independent organizations lined up, and he had run successful races before for the student assembly. He and Connally tried to talk Eckhardt out of running. Bob just laughed and said, "Oh, I think I'll run." He went to file, sat down and leaned back in his chair as he was chatting with the elections administrator, and promptly fell backward, gashing his head, which required stitching.[59]

Eckhardt considered Pickle to be friendly, a great organizer, who remembered names. Connally, on the other hand, he considered arrogant.[60] Pickle and Connally kept telling Eckhardt that he would split the independent vote and that he could not win. "Oh, well, we'll see," he would reply, with a grin. Jake and Big John spread rumors that Eckhardt was going to withdraw, hoping to win over some of his voters. All of the parties knew that it was likely that no one would get a majority, but that the fraternity candidate would win the most votes because of the split independent vote. Eckhardt took a proposal to the student council to require a runoff election instead of election by plurality.[61]

Connally and Pickle decided to push the runoff, too. They mounted a public relations campaign, arguing that democracy and fairness required a majority vote in an election, and cranked up a petition drive for a referendum to require a runoff election. That became the cause of the campaign, and it worked. They inflamed the campus, drew a lot of attention, and did, indeed, get a referendum, simultaneously with the election. The Pickle-Connally campaign was so successful that the runoff provision passed big, *and* Pickle came in first in the presidential voting, with Eckhardt a distant third. But now Pickle had to go into a runoff, which he won.[62] Eckhardt produced his last *Ranger* issue, complete with a sketch of his entire staff. He drew himself with a broken neck, trussed up on a board, from his fall off the chair, with the note, "You may have seen his picture on handbills in connection with some-thing or other. P.S.—He has retired from politics."[63]

Pickle served as president in 1937–1938. The next year, Connally ran for president, with Pickle managing the campaign. Connally came in second, then won the runoff. Pickle's majoritarianism paid off, but Eckhardt and Fath would soon trump them. Big John took office for the 1938–1939 school year, while Pickle graduated and went to work for Lyndon Johnson at the National Youth Administration in the Littlefield Building.

Connally's presidential year was Eckhardt's last year in law school. When the fall semester grades were posted, Fath and Eckhardt examined them. Eckhardt chortled, "Look! John is only passing nine semester hours—he's not passing these other courses." To serve in student government, one was required to be passing ten semester hours. They went to Eckhardt's old *Ranger* office and drafted a petition for the removal of Connally as president. They asked Tom Law, head of the Judicial Council, to call a meeting for the next morning. "On what grounds?" Law asked. They told him. "Oh, shit," Law whispered. The next morning, before the Council convened, Eckhardt read the *Daily Texan* with a front-page story reporting that Connally had resigned.

Eckhardt and the Study of Law

Dr. Eckhardt often interfered with things in Bob's life that were minor or that dealt with safety. But he stayed out of his sons' major decisions about profes-sions, romance, and marriage. Thus, he may have been disappointed that his oldest son was not following him into a career in medicine, but he did not try to dissuade him. He was more interested in seeing that Bob stuck with his studies rather than being pulled off into politics and cartooning. One day, Tommy Sutherland and Bob rolled out a long piece of butcher paper at the Eckhardt house and were painting a sign for an upcoming Democratic rally. Dr. Eckhardt saw them at work, paused, and remarked sadly, "Tommy, I wish you would just let him finish his degree."

Ira Polk Hildebrand was dean of the Law School and a source of irrita-tion for students. At one point, Connally bowed to Hildebrand's pressure to move the Athenaeum society debates out of the law building,[64] prompt-ing Athenaeum members (many of whom were PDs) to be disgusted with him—and to distrust him when he later ran for president. The incident also reinforced their contempt for Hildebrand. Eckhardt wrote a poem about Dean Hildebrand and the general feeling that he was a horse's ass:

> *The gods in council met and planned*
> *To fashion them a Hildebrand;*
> *No fitter pattern could they find*
> *To house so marvelous a mind*
> *Than Cherion's form, which is of course*
> *To Centaur's shape, half man, half horse;*
> *So be't, but e'en a spirit nods;*
> *In making him the mighty gods,*
> *Through some celestial imperfections,*
> *Forgot the first and middle sections.*

He readied the poem for the *Ranger,* but the censor deleted the reference to Hildebrand, and Eckhardt had to change "Hildebrand" to "candidate."[65]

As was the case in undergraduate school, Eckhardt met law students who would become important colleagues and friends. Gus Garcia was one of Eckhardt's classmates, and one of the few Latinos at UT. Garcia was born in Laredo in 1915 and graduated valedictorian in his high school class. He graduated from law school in 1938, a year before Eckhardt did. They would soon be in court together.

For the first time since second grade, Eckhardt did not have the company of Charles Black. Charles had studied the classics as an undergraduate and had no desire to follow his dad into law. Black wrote a poem expressing his feelings about law:

> *Give me a halter or a knife*
> *But do not make me spend my life*
> *Proving with reasons stout and strong*
> *That wrong is right and right is wrong.*

After UT, Charles roamed the country and Europe and kept in touch with Bob. When he returned, he studied Old and Middle English literature at Yale. With a master's in hand, Black decided, after all, to go to Yale Law School. He was, of course, an excellent law student. Eckhardt reminded him of his poem decrying the life of a lawyer. "Oh," he told Bob. "I don't care much about being a lawyer, but it's the only respectable way to be a miscellanist." Curious, Bob asked him what a miscellanist was. "An expert in miscellany," Charles replied.[66]

Even as a law student, Eckhardt, like Black, was skeptical of the role of lawyers, of the pecking order that they helped society continue, and of the status of clients. As he was engrossed in his studies, Eckhardt wrote a ballad about the law system. "Chancellors" was a play on words: it referred both to a traditional use of the term as a lawyer or judge and to an elite law student organization of that name:

> When I was leaving the public house
> I saw three Chancellors,
> And each had a note for the Law Review,
> And all I had was a bottle of brew—
> Heigh ho for the Chancellors.
>
> When I was passing the justice court,
> I saw three Chancellors,
> And each had a client of ill repute,
> A pimp and a bawd and a prostitute—
> Heigh ho for the Chancellors.
>
> When I was passing the county court,
> I saw three Chancellors,
> And each had a client of high esteem,
> A loan shark fat and a card sharp lean—
> Heigh ho for the Chancellors.
>
> When I was passing the district court,
> I saw three Chancellors,
> With suits so brown and shoes so tan,
> With a banker, a broker, a confidence man—
> Heigh ho for the Chancellors.
>
> As I returned to the public house,
> I thought of the Chancellors;
> Thought I, your clients of best repute
> Were the pimp and the bawd and the prostitute—
> Heigh ho for the Chancellors.

An incident back in the home neighborhood reaffirmed for Eckhardt the critical, and uneven, role that law played in people's lives. One day, he was out currying a colt in their horse pasture that bordered Wheatsville. Three Wheatsville boys—Luther and Lewis McQuirter and Bob Booty—were discussing Bob, not realizing that he could hear them as he groomed the colt. Lewis asked, "Is Mr. Roba a law?" His brother Luther replied, "No—he ain't a law! He don' wear no blue suit." But Lewis protested, "He go to d' law school." Still, Luther was having none of it. "He ain't no big hat law like raid Uncle Cornelius." Finally, Bob Booty settled it: "Aw, boy, you don' know. They's two kind of laws: one that puts you in an' one that gets you out." [67] As Eckhardt's sense of social justice deepened throughout his law and political career, he would use this story to illustrate two kinds of law: one applied against the poor and one for the rich.

PART II

Lawyer Eckhardt

Eckhardt's Shingle and Pen

Shortly after getting his law degree in 1939 and passing the bar exam, Bob Eckhardt hung his shingle, opening his law practice in Austin. He was an attractive bachelor and dated Orissa Stevenson, Julya Thomson, and other young women. Bob continued living at home—drawing cartoons, grooming and riding the horses, sharing his legal escapades with his family. The transition from town boy to professional lawyer in the same community can be awkward. Bertha Bennett Franklin, an African American woman who lived in Wheatsville, a few blocks from the Eckhardts, had known the family for years. Now that Bob was a twenty-six-year-old lawyer, he would occasionally run into her at the bank and, as she put it to him apologetically, "I always forget and call you Mr. Bobby instead of Lawyer Eckhardt."

Lawyer Eckhardt

As law students, Bob and Creek handled cases before the student judiciary council and found that they liked working together. When they graduated, they went to Houston for job interviews. The heavy coastal humidity persuaded them to stay in Austin. So, out of their joint UT work and their shared aversion to Houston, they decided to become partners. In 1939, they opened the Eckhardt and Fath Law Offices on the sixth floor of the Littlefield Building, across the street from Dr. Eckhardt's office in the Scarbrough Building. A floor above them was Uncle Oscar Eckhardt's new medical supply business. Next door was the county Democratic chairman, John Patterson, who had practiced law with Henry Faulk. Bob took up wood carving (learned from his woodblock print artwork) and crafted a sign that he put above his desk, quoting Shakespeare's *Measure for Measure*:[1]

> *We must not make a scarecrow of the law,*
> *Setting it up to fear the birds of prey,*
> *And let it take one shape, till custom make it*
> *Their perch, and not their terror.*

Eckhardt shared the Littlefield Building with the State Bar of Texas and with other lawyers, including Ralph Yarborough. He and Yarborough had met during Eckhardt's visits to Governor Jimmie Allred's mansion. In 1936, Allred appointed Yarborough district judge. Yarborough lost a race for attorney general in 1938, then resumed being a judge, also serving as president of the Travis County Bar Association and on the board of the Texas State Bar, before going off to war.[2] Early on, Yarborough was a reluctant politician. "It took a very long time before many of us who thought he ought to run for attorney general could get him to do it," Eckhardt would say. Then, they couldn't get him to stop! Eckhardt considered Yarborough to be "a hell of a good lawyer."[3]

Eckhardt had also come to know two other Allred aides, Everett Looney and Ed Clark. Looney was a determined legal strategist. Clark would gradually slide over to the Establishment side in Texas politics, allied with Lyndon Johnson. The two new graduates borrowed $100 from law partners Looney and Clark for their first month's operation, with which they bought furniture. A month later, they borrowed $200, paid back the first $100, and operated on the second loan. Bob and Creek paid off the loans within a year, but they survived on a shoestring basis for a while. "Our fervent hope," Eckhardt wrote, "is that the building manager and the furniture company decide to repossess at the same time so that we are not forced either to take up our desks and walk or to sit in the silent solitude of a bare and rugless office."[4]

John Henry Faulk's father died just as they opened their office, and the Faulks asked Bob and Creek to take his practice. Henry Faulk's library was great for historical research, but was not up to date. To remedy that problem, the two new lawyers managed to get advance copies of the *Southwestern Reporter,* put the pages together with brown paper covers, and hand-label the volumes. They also had a key to Charles Black's father's law library a couple of blocks away in the Norwood Building. They sometimes found Mr. Black there working. He would ask them what cases they were pursuing and was a great help in advising them.

Their shingle hung and their library open, they began to practice law, all kinds of law. Bob learned a lot about human character and, as he had done since he was a boy, he translated his understanding in visual, humorous art, drawing pictures of his opposing counsel in courtrooms.[5] Everett Looney persuaded Ralph Yarborough to appoint the new lawyers to the Anti-Usury Committee of the Travis County Bar, telling them that they might get some cases out of that. They served as counsel in five divorce cases in their first year of practice and so detested it that they vowed to never do divorces again. The clients from Faulk's practice were primarily poor, black, and Hispanic.

Lawyer Eckhardt in his law office. In 1939, Bob Eckhardt graduated from law school and opened a law office with Creekmore Fath. Here, Eckhardt stands in their new office in the Littlefield Building in downtown Austin. On the bottom bookshelf are law books that they bound and labeled by hand. Courtesy of Creekmore Fath.

They also provided legal services to students and faculty members, including J. Frank Dobie.

Their very first case was a usury case carried over from their law school work. They represented a carpenter in a suit against a lender, and, while the jury was out, the loan shark offered to settle, to avoid the possibility of triple damages. Creek called Looney and asked his advice; Looney yelled that they had won and had better not cave in now. Indeed, they did win. The *Austin Times* wrote them up in the front-page column, noting that these two brand-new lawyers had won a usury argument that other lawyers had tried for years to make. The novices had proved "to all the victims of high rate lenders that the courts will protect them. Their work in this suit is a fine beginning for two fine young men. The city and State needs more men like Eckhardt and Fath."[6] Bob developed usury as a specialty and soon became chairman of the Travis County Bar's Anti-Usury Committee.

Early on, Eckhardt brought suit against his alma mater, the University of Texas. A student protested against UT's requirement that he pay a $1 union building fee. Although it meant $30,000 a year for UT, his client would only win $1. But Eckhardt argued that the fee was unconstitutional. The judge was none other than Ralph Yarborough. UT fought hard. The university and Eckhardt battled back and forth with injunctions and fought over original mandamus in the Texas Supreme Court. Yarborough ruled for Eckhardt and the student. The ruling was eventually overruled, but UT, not wanting a battle at the legislature, dropped the fee. Meanwhile, the student had filed the case on a pauper's oath, leaving Eckhardt dunned for the court costs.

Travis County was growing, but the Depression was not yet over, and it was not easy to make a living. Clients with big interests, who could pay, went to established law firms, leaving the crumbs to the rest. Eckhardt brought numerous usury cases on small loans of $25 to $2,000, often recovering double the usurious interest. His fee was a one-third contingency, so he did not make much on this work. Once when the partners could not pay their office rent, the Littlefield manager changed the locks on their door. Eckhardt bitterly complained that her actions were harsh and peremptory. She replied, "But your partner, Mr. Fath, had told me how much you are making, and I read of your important cases all the time." She took the newspaper publicity about his UT case as evidence of a thriving law practice, but, in fact, Eckhardt was desperately trying to hang on. He had to persuade her of the truth of their meager practice before she would give him the key to the new locks.[7]

Eckhardt could not even pay his secretary, Nannie Lou Perry. Edmunds Travis, a friend of the Eckhardts, decided to pay her in order to help Bob. Travis was an oil lobbyist, city editor of the *Austin Daily Tribune,* and a conservative who hated President Roosevelt. But he liked Bob and would come

by Littlefield to argue politics. Eckhardt was not shy about discussing his political views. One day, a friend of Nannie Lou mentioned that she had heard
Eckhardt was a Communist. Nannie Lou, outraged and offended, replied,
"My boss is not a communist! He certainly is not. You might call him a sot
and a shyster, but he is *not* a communist!"[8]

One of Eckhardt's early clients was the longtime family acquaintance Bertha Bennett Franklin, who called him "Lawyer Eckhardt." As the UT student body became larger and wealthier, students started moving into Bertha's
neighborhood, Wheatsville. A fraternity wanted to buy the Bennett family's shanty, where Bertha lived with her aging mother. One family member
worked as a houseman for the fraternity and sold his one-twelfth interest in
the shanty to the fraternity. The fraternity then sued for possession of the
residence. Lawyer Eckhardt hunted down all the heirs and convinced them
to quitclaim their deeds to Bertha. She was then able to get a loan to buy out
the interest of the houseman and keep the house.[9]

Another early client was a liquor store, the Blue Moon Nite Club. Eckhardt
and Fath succeeded in collecting on a bill for the Blue Moon, but the store
owner still could not pay them. So they settled on a trade: Bob and Creek
were to come down to the South Austin club on Saturday and take the stock
that moved the slowest. For a while, they imbibed crème de menthe, rock and
rye, and sweet vermouth; after this period, though, Bob went back to scotch
whiskey, wine, and beer.

Some of the legal crumbs left to Eckhardt and Fath included allegations of
a treasure being whisked away by spirits to San Antonio. So they were introduced to the world of fraud and deceit. One of those dubious cases involved
the Red River Mining and Milling Company, which operated just off Red
River Street downtown. The company was quite an assembly of characters,
including an elderly, stately black man, Rayford Benton, who wore a big cowboy hat, and an itinerant Presbyterian preacher, Milton McGill, who would
try to convert Jews on Sixth Street. One day an old man named Deece, using
a witching stick, told McGill and Benton that silver was buried under Lewis
Silberstein's property on Red River Street. The witching finding confirmed
for Preacher McGill a story he had been told by a man named Juan Lopez,
who had heard from *his* grandfather that thirty Mexicans, with thirty burros laden with silver, had buried the treasure there long ago. The Red River
Mining and Milling Company had a lease for mining "minerals, metals, and
substance of any kind." So, using slant hole drilling, they started to work, trying to find buried silver under Silberstein's lot and buildings.

Unfortunately, their drilling and dynamiting bothered Silberstein's ten-
ants, making them especially nervous as they sat on the privy. Silberstein
wanted them to stop, so he sued them. Benton and McGill hired Eckhardt

to defend their lease and right to drill. Of course, they had found no buried treasure, only a rusty old .44 and some four-bit pieces. McGill wanted Eckhardt to use the story of the witching, as well as Juan Lopez's grandfather's recollection of the buried treasure, to persuade the judge that the mining company was operating with good intent. Eckhardt did not consider the story credible. He did not think it could be introduced, so he refused to use it. As they opened the case, Preacher McGill rose and, in a quavering voice, said to Judge Samuel Rogers, "Your honor, please, may we open the session with a word of prayer?" So, they did. But the case did not go well. Eckhardt tried to convince the judge that the discovery of the six-shooter and coins was evidence that they were legitimately mining for minerals as their lease permitted. At the end of the testimony and arguments, McGill again rose and asked, "Your honor, may we close this session with a word of prayer?" The judge agreed to let McGill pray, so he did: "Oh Lord! In thy infinite wisdom, inform this judge that in 1847, Juan Lopez's grandfather, at the time of this lease, brought thirty Mexicans with thirty burros upon this property and brought sacks of silver and buried them in that very hole. Now Lord, bless this court and give it wisdom. Amen." They lost.[10]

Some of the judges and legal procedures Eckhardt encountered were less than proficient. One client shot a bird on another man's property without the owner's permission. The owner filed a case with the local justice of the peace (JP). Eckhardt went to trial before Justice of the Peace J. C. Burch in Del Valle, just outside of Austin. It had been so long since a trial had been held there that the key to the door had been lost. Then, the window was stuck, so they had to pry it open with a crow bar and everyone crawled in. Judge Burch seated the jury on a long wicker bench and rolled back the top of his desk, dust flying over everyone. No one made a case for the plaintiff, so Judge Burch said, "Mr. Eckhardt, proceed to defend your client." Eckhardt replied, "Your honor, if this is all the case to be made against him, I would ask you to instruct the jury that they should acquit him." The judge was silent for a while, then replied, "Mr. Eckhardt, I understand a man is guilty until he proves hisself innocent." This reply surprised Eckhardt, of course, but he knew the power that judges wielded and the deference they expected. He said, "Your honor, there's a long line of precedent against that, from King Alfred, I think, but at least Magna Carta through the Constitution. All the judges in the courts of the Anglo-Saxon world have held that a man is innocent until he is proven guilty. I hadn't thought that question would come up, but I'll brief it for you." There was a long silence as Judge Burch thought and the jurors creaked back and forth on their wicker bench. Finally, the judge said, "What do I do now?"[11]

As a law student and now as a new lawyer, Eckhardt retained many friends from his high school and UT days, and along with his new professional acquaintances, they had great parties. Elmo and Jenny Hegman were good friends, and remained so for life. Elmo was older, a well-educated and well-read man from UT. He kept a wonderful library, collecting the finest writing in shelves filled to the ceiling with books. Elmo's dad had run a movie house, and Elmo took up the business, showing mostly westerns at the Ritz Movie House on Sixth Street. Sometimes after midnight, after the theater closed, the Hegmans, Bob, Creek, John Henry, Jack and Sally Guinn, and others would watch Charlie Chaplin films and other old movies. At other times, they would retire to the Hegmans' kitchen for dinner, Brahms, drinks, and rowdiness. Eckhardt wrote a poem about those heady encounters in Hegman's kitchen:

SOULS OF POETS DEAD AND GONE

What Elysium have you known
Better than the cheese and hams
Savored by the strains of Brahms

The tentacled and flitting Myers
Pricked by amorous desires,
Flicking flecks from Elmo's coat
And quoting clever quips by rote.

The bawdy ballads Brownie sings
'Bout whores and sores and English kings
And Faulk expounding many theses
Devoted, in the main, to feces.

The lures of corn patch, fig and alley
The lecher Guinn, the luscious Sally.
And amber beer in glass or stein
Make Romberg think of Madelein.

And Charley Ramsdell's muttered bitchin'.
Oh, what Elysium, Hegman's Kitchen! [12]

Young law partners Bob and Creek also kept their fingers in politics and kept up with the old PD gang. They decided to rejoin the Young Democrats and influence its direction, especially to oppose John Nance Garner in his bid to succeed Roosevelt. They conspired with Otto Mullinax and others to use a National Youth Administration conference in Austin as an organizing vehicle for their YD work. [13]

In 1940, just a year after opening their practice, an Austin legislative seat came open. Though only twenty-seven years old, Bob decided to follow the lead of his PD friends who had run in 1936. He plunged into the race, with Creek as his campaign manager. He ran in Place 2 of District 82, against four other candidates. By June, the *State Observer* reported, "Candidate for the Legislature Bob Eckhardt too shy to introduce himself to people and ask for their votes," and noted that although his friends said he would win the election, Eckhardt was noncommittal. Creek was determined to drum up publicity for Eckhardt, triggering this tongue-in-cheek response from the *Observer*: "For no reason at all we promised our friend Bob Eckhardt's law partner—a Mister Creekmore Fath—that we would mention Eckhardt's name in our paper. Bob Eckhardt." [14]

But Eckhardt and Fath did indeed campaign, attending rallies and meeting voters. In Manchaca, Bob bought cakes from a cake sale and handed them out, endearing himself to the recipients. (He saw the fickleness of politics when he learned that his opponent had handed out chickens.) In the Swedish farming area out of Austin, he shook the big rough hands of the farmers, watching their wary faces, unsure whether they liked him or not. [15] Bob embellished his campaign literature—mimeographed sheets of information—with sketches that symbolized the issues. He declared his opposition to a sales tax—an issue that he would work on for more than twenty years—and pledged that as a legislator, he would continue his anti-usury advocacy. Days before the election, the *State Observer* ran a front-page column with an Eckhardt poem in it, observing that the candidate had plenty of time to write poetry and skewering his work as being obscure. [16] It was full of allusions to the national and world events of the day and was prompted by what he had heard about one of his old law professors:

LINES TO BE INSCRIBED ON THE WALLS OF ALCATRAZ WITH A
KNITTING NEEDLE EXTRACTED FROM A BUNDLE FOR BRITAIN

I must confess I can't discern the reason
Why now opposing Roosevelt is treason
When former grubs like Knudsen and Stetinius
Are metamorphosed into aerial genius
And headstrong Frankie Knox is hotsy-totsy
And modest Lindbergh is now a bloody Nazi,
The latter once recipient of glories,
The former three denounced as blasted Tories,
Before the proud ascent of Martin Dies
Who found the F.B.I. a nest of spies.

The time is out of joint, O cursed spite
When cotton's cheap and clothing's out of sight
And rats grow fat while people die of scurvy.
O god, the whole damned world is topsy turvy.
But this is commonplace, routine and reasonable.
Hereafter, I'll swear that snow in summer's seasonable;
And April flowers follow rains in May—
Who ever thought I'd ever see the day
When I should find the man for blood most thirsty
Expounding Shakespeare at the University.

Eckhardt lost the Place 2 election, though he did well. He simply chose the wrong race: he actually got more votes than anyone running in Place 1. His conservative bankroller and debating partner Edmunds Travis scolded him, "Bob, what you do is you attack all the venal interests *except one,* and that's where you git your money. You attacked them *all.*"[17] After the loss, he refocused on the law practice.

Clay Cochran finished law school and decided that he should be associated with a law firm, though he did not really want to practice. Bob and Creek invited him into their firm, renaming it Eckhardt, Fath, and Cochran. When business did not pick up, Fath wrote a friend and got a six-week job as counsel to a House committee in Washington.[18] He left after the primary election, and Cochran never practiced, so Eckhardt was going solo. The corner office on the ninth floor of the Littlefield opened up, and Bob just had to have it, though it cost more. He moved upstairs and had the grandest view of Austin: he could look across the street to his dad's clinic in the Scarbrough, down Congress across the Colorado River to Johnny Faulk's old stomping grounds, and up Congress to the capitol.

Creek left with intentions of being back soon. Instead, his adventure took him into Franklin and Eleanor Roosevelt's White House and to the heights of politics, and he did not return permanently to Austin until Truman was president. When he told his law partner that he had a great job offer, Bob said, "Well, you've wanted to be a part of the New Deal, and this is your chance." Creek became chief counsel to the Select Committee on Interstate Migration of Destitute Citizens, the "Okie" Committee, where he plunged into the heady work for social relief programs and public works before going to work in the White House. After Pearl Harbor, Dr. Montgomery's friend and colleague Walton Hamilton borrowed Fath and Mark Adams for work on the Senate Committee on Patents to research German cartels and their relationship with American companies. Fath hired young UT grad Liz Sutherland (soon to be Carpenter) to help him. After Roosevelt's death, Fath worked in

Truman's White House and later for the Democratic National Committee, where his contacts would become invaluable for his later Texas political work with Eckhardt.

Eckhardt practiced general law from 1939 through 1941. Four things changed his career at this point. One was Creek going off to Washington. The second was that Bob was finding this type of work to be the most boring thing in the world. He did not like how slow the law moved. He thought of the disdain in Charles Black's poem: "But do not make me spend my life/Proving with reasons stout and strong/That wrong is right and right is wrong." Applying its sentiment to his practice, he thought, "What is the right and wrong side of a divorce case? The boundary dispute?" The third thing that ended his general practice was the war. Eckhardt, Fath, and Cochran all ended up in the armed forces. The fourth is that he and Orissa married, and his financial needs changed.

Coleman Flying School and Marriage

With Pearl Harbor, everything changed. Nearly all young men got pulled into the war effort. As the United States began a massive mobilization, one of the urgent needs was for pilots. So the army quickly went to work training soldiers to fly in the Army Air Corps. In order to fly safely and effectively, the trainees needed to know some basic science and math, theory of flight, and meteorology. The army contracted with private schools to provide the primary (ground) training for their aspiring pilots, so scores of contract primary training schools sprung up throughout the nation.

James Dibrell was a student at UT with Eckhardt, and they became great friends and campus political allies. Immediately after Pearl Harbor, Dibrell was hired to be the director of a ground school and opened it in his hometown of Coleman, a small town of about 7,000 in the heart of Texas. He set to work hiring old buddies from UT as his instructors. Bob decided that being a ground instructor was much safer than going into the war, so, in January 1942, he headed to Coleman. He had never flown and was, in fact, scared of flying. Ever the horseman, he told friends that he had never been higher than fifteen hands, and he had no intention of going higher than that.[19] And his teaching did not require him to do so. After a year and a half, he and the other instructors were officially inducted into the Air Corps Enlisted Reserves. He continued teaching and received an honorable discharge on October 24, 1944.

For the first time in his life, at nearly twenty-nine years old, Bob moved out of 2300 Rio Grande. During his service, he lived with the Dibrells in Coleman. James's father was a lawyer and had a large sixteen-room house where Bob roomed on the second floor.[20] He didn't have a car, so he took a bicycle with him, and, as he had never been without a horse, he also brought the old black mare Dixie. He continued courting Orissa and would ride the bus or get a ride back to Austin to see her.

Orissa was winding up a wonderful UT career, and they announced their engagement in April 1942. In May, she served as the toastmaster at the Annual Architects' Wind-Up Ball at the Stephen F. Austin Hotel, then a week later, just before graduation, received the American Institute of Architects' award for the highest five-year scholastic average.[21]

Family and friends then traveled to Houston for Bob's and Orissa's June 6th wedding at Palmer Memorial Chapel. Orissa wore a long-sleeved ivory satin dress embroidered with rose point lace. Bob wore his trademark bow tie and white coat. The whole chapel was decorated with magnolia blossoms. Charles Black came down from Yale Law School to be Bob's best man, and his brothers were his groomsmen. Orissa's entourage included her sister and friends from Houston. Uncle Oscar and Aunt Lila Eckhardt, as well as cousins Tillie and Lulu Kleberg came down from Austin. Norma Eckhardt sang the French musician Charles Gounod's "Entreat Me Not to Leave Thee" and German Carl Bohm's "Calm as the Night." After the ceremony, the Stevensons hosted the reception at their home, lavishly decorated with lilies, gladioli, and candles. The couple cut a large circular wedding cake, adorned with flowers. Everyone retired to the garden to toast the newlyweds with champagne. After the reception, Orissa changed into a dark dress and put on a hat. Bob kept his white suit, grabbed a suitcase, and they headed to Coleman to begin their new life.[22]

Bob moved out of the Dibrells' house and the newlyweds rented a house. Orissa taught math to public school students in Coleman. She loved interior decorating, and their house looked beautiful—even if some of the features were peculiar. The flooring was grass matting. Bob set up a woodshop and made the furniture.[23] But an ominous sign soon appeared in the life of the young couple. During his courtship with Orissa, Bob had seen some signs of mental problems with the brilliant architecture student and artist. Then, in Coleman, he would find Orissa wandering the streets lost at night. Orissa confided to him that she was having "spells" and that those spells were a living hell for her. When she was feeling well, their lives together were happy. But sometimes Orissa was seriously depressed and her behavior was erratic.

Bob would dress in his suit and tie, grab his pipe, and mount Dixie for the three-mile trip from home to the ground school. She didn't have much of a gait, but a good walk and trot. Once a train came by and scared her, as she had been spooked when she was a foal, and she ran away with him, full speed, down the main street of Coleman. Bob would stake her up close to the

Bob and Orissa Eckhardt. Orissa Stevenson started school at the University of Texas while Bob Eckhardt was a law student there. Upon her graduation, they married, while Bob was in the army. They had two daughters, Orissa and Rosalind. Courtesy of Orissa Eckhardt Arend.

school. She got loose one day and headed out to the runway. Bob found her chewing the leading cloth edge of a plane.

Eckhardt usually taught navigation, and occasionally meteorology, theory of flight, math, and physics. He would read the night before to know what he would be teaching the cadets the next day.[24] The students were eager to fly, though not so eager to spend time in the classroom. Still, they developed a camaraderie with the instructors, depicting Bob in their newsletter photos, writing, "Here we portray a few of the GODS of KNOWLEDGE who have seen some of the greatest minds in the country go down in shameful defeat. (There are a few of us who still support subversive sentiment among the compilers of those exams.)"[25] Bob would put formulas and diagrams on the board. Chalk in his left hand, he also entertained them by sketching caricatures and cartoons.

The students took ground instruction from the private school and flying lessons from army instructors. They flew the PT, a small teaching plane with one seat up and another back. They also had a larger trainer. Sometimes cadets would fly it to Mexico and pick up whiskey to bring back to the dry Coleman County. On one occasion, a Lieutenant Fox invited Bob to fly with him. Fox must have been persuasive. Or perhaps Instructor Eckhardt did not want to be accused of being too scared to see if his students had learned from him. Reluctantly, he agreed to go up. He checked to make sure that his parachute was under his seat, got in, and was so tall that he hit the shield. "I was scared shitless," he would later say. Fox told him that if he was worried about anything to just shake the joystick. But Eckhardt was scared to touch it. Lieutenant Fox kept turning his head back and talking, but Eckhardt couldn't hear a word. As his fear mounted, he kept trying to get the lieutenant to go back; instead, Fox took his captive up and turned over, looping. He threw it into reverse, throwing both of them against the sides of the plane. Then he put the PT into spins. Eckhardt felt absolutely lost, terrified, and by the time they landed, completely adrenalin-filled. Despite pleas to go up again, Eckhardt never did (and wouldn't fly for years).

One of Bob's students had to bail out and parachute as his plane crashed, and he was injured in his landing. Eckhardt visited him in the hospital, heard about the whole ordeal, and wrote friends about it. Rather than write on stationery, though, Eckhardt wrote the letters on bits of the tail fabric of the crashed airplane. "This is probably the most expensive stationery in the world," he wrote, "having cost about $25,000."[26]

They were sometimes reminded of the seriousness of their mission. Students came and went, and the instructors would hear news of their missions overseas. One student, Arthur Hartman, from Seguin, had been at UT and, like Eckhardt, had been antiwar at one time. Hartman was a German-American and had been pro-German while at UT. The intelligence lieutenant on base called Eckhardt in and asked him about Hartman. Eckhardt told him that Hartman was a tremendous and courageous man. "Hartman is the most honest man you could imagine; you don't have to worry about him a bit." Hartman went on through the school and became a B-17 pilot. Eckhardt and the other instructors soon got word that Hartman had been shot down in the Adriatic; he kept his plane intact, got everyone out, then went down with it into the sea. They heard a similar story about another student who went down with his plane in Alaska.

By 1944, though the war was still raging, the need for training schools lessened and the school closed. Eckhardt was transferred to Randolph Field in San Antonio, where he trained in meteorology and navigation (though he had been teaching these subjects for two years). He was discharged as a private on October 24, 1944.[27]

Eckhardt believed that the teaching was a good experience. He learned science beyond the base he had established as an undergraduate. Years later, his first committee assignment in Congress was on the Science and Astronautics Committee, and he believed that his Coleman and Randolph experiences were helpful even that much later.[28]

Starting Over in Austin

After the war, Otto Mullinax and Clay Cochran tried to get the old UT gang back together in Austin. Many of them did return, though *Daily Texan* editor Joe Storm was killed in the war. Others scattered around the state. New Dealers Minnie Fisher Cunningham and photographer Russell Lee and the students from Eckhardt's cohort—Mark Adams, Creek Fath, Chris Dixie, Clay Cochran, John Henry Faulk, Otto Mullinax—eventually came home to Texas (though Faulk soon moved to New York and national radio and TV fame). Bob and Orissa came back from Coleman in late 1944. The young couple moved into a house at Ninth and Baylor Streets, then bought an old stone house near the capitol, as Bob went to work for the Office of Inter-American Affairs.

Orissa flourished in those post-war Austin years. Her periods of depression became less frequent and less intense, and she plunged into a new furniture design business. On April 15, 1946, she gave birth to a baby girl at Seton Hospital, naming her the Stevenson family name, Orissa. They would be known as "Big Orissa" and "Little Orissa." A year later, she gave birth to another girl, named Rosalind. At thirty-two, Bob was now a dad, and he and his girls developed close, loving relationships, despite the harried nature of his legal and political life.

The young family would gather round a huge tree for Christmas at Joe and Norma's. In these years, Bob began a tradition that he kept up for years, printing a Christmas card from his original artwork. He carved a woodblock of a rooster crowing, designing it into a Christmas card with the Shakespeare quotation "Some Say that ever 'gainst that season comes, Wherein our Savior's Birth is Celebrated, The Bird of Dawning Singeth All Night Long," and "Greetings from Robert and Orissa Eckhardt."[29]

Bob reestablished relationships he had left behind for Coleman and renewed his acquaintanceships with UT professors, such as Dobie and Webb. Bob also plunged into new political activity. As the new president of the Travis County Young Democrats, he spoke at a labor rally at Wooldridge Park to a crowd of 1,500.[30]

The Political Presses

When Mark Adams returned to Austin, Eckhardt and Stuart Long came by for a visit, and the three UT friends shared a great evening of gab. Adams told them he hoped to begin a printing shop that would print material for their political causes. Long, too, had plans for a press, and had a commitment of $10,000 for his enterprise, so he and Adams pitched in together and started Long Publications. They did not, as they had hoped, get the contract to print the new liberal newspaper, the *Texas Spectator*, and their enterprise went bankrupt.[31] Still, Eckhardt, Adams, and Long would weave in and out of the world of political presses in Texas over the coming decades.

Texas has a long tradition of newspapers devoted to state politics, many evolving from earlier efforts that had died out. The *Austin Forum* started in 1901 as a pro-labor paper, then reemerged in the 1920s as the *Austin Forum-Advocate*. In the 1930s, Vann Kennedy, a close advisor to Jimmie Allred, took the paper over. Kennedy, who also served as secretary of the State Democratic Executive Committee, renamed it the *State Week and Austin Forum-Advocate,* then renamed it again the *State Observer.*

Kennedy's *State Observer* provided a professional starting point for UT writers and artists. D. B. Hardeman served as the managing editor in the late 1930s and early 1940s. Jack Guinn contributed poems, sketches, and block prints, then became art editor. Stuart Long was named associate editor in 1936. And Hardeman, Long, and Guinn used their ink to cover their friend Eckhardt in his artistic and political endeavors.

World War II disrupted everything, and the ownership of the paper changed hands. The new owner Paul Holcomb had always dreamed of a statewide Democratic newspaper, and he strived to make the *State Observer* that (though he also offered his religious prognostications).[32] After her 1944 gubernatorial campaign galvanized liberals, Minnie Fisher Cunningham became an *Observer* contributor. LBJ even got a regular column. For eleven years, Holcomb's *State Observer* was the liberal voice in Texas and the communication center for Democratic battles. In 1944 and 1945, following his discharge from the Army Reserves, Eckhardt took up his pen, contributing two cartoons: one depicting UT President Homer Rainey and his battles with the regents, the other lampooning the Texas Regulars, anti-Roosevelt

Democrats. Though for political and legal reasons they were unsigned, both cartoons were unmistakable, classic Eckhardts.[33]

For a short period, the *State Observer* had competition from a maverick publication patterned after Joseph Addison's eighteenth-century British *Spectator* and called the *Texas Spectator*. Eckhardt became a significant part of the new endeavor. Immediately after the war, Margaret Reading invited a host of would-be newspaper writers to her farm in Waller County. Eckhardt hopped in a car with Stuart Long, Joe Storm's widow Marion, and others and headed for the Reading farm, stopping at German beer joints along the way. At the farm, they met with C. Badger Reed and newspapermen Hubert Mewhinney (known audaciously as "The Mewhinney") and Harold "Kewpie" Young. Eckhardt bunked with Mewhinney and Young in an old log cabin. Inspired by the musings of that weekend, Reed, a wealthy man, established the *Texas Spectator*. Shakespeare adorned the masthead: "Fear no more the frown o' the great; Thou art past the tyrant's stroke." Young and Mewhinney quit their positions at the *Houston Post* to take on the *Spectator*. The Mewhinney, who wrote a column called "Meeting All Comers," was a complete character and a learned naturalist. He had a fondness for bourbon and branch water, dipping his first two fingers into the jigger and flinging the drippings on his breast. Eckhardt would later illustrate Mewhinney's *Manual for Neanderthals*.[34]

Eckhardt became the group's cover artist, and his political cartoons graced the cover of all but one of the 137 issues of the *Texas Spectator* from 1945 to 1948.[35] He reprised the *Ranger*-era sketches, depicting shysters and undertakers, but dressing them as statesmen and lobbyists, in the real world of Texas and national politics. The front-page index often provided brief commentary and captions to the cartoons. The small staff, with offices next to the capitol, developed camaraderie, often working (and partying) late into the night, and the *Spectator* experience became a formative one for Eckhardt.

His cartoons were usually post-midnight works of art. He would work in his house near the capitol right up to the Sunday night publication deadline, with Mewhinney, Young, or Reed breathing over his shoulder. Already at this stage in his political development, Eckhardt was concerned about the undue influence that powerful corporations—especially oil companies—had over Texas politics. At the time, Magnolia Petroleum Co. had leases on Governor Coke Stevenson's land and paid him handsomely in lease royalties for what seemed to be pretty worthless land. Eckhardt wanted to draw a magnolia blossom to use as a spoof of this relationship, but he could not remember exactly what one looked like. About 1:00 a.m., Eckhardt, Reed, and Mewhinney decided to do some research for the drawing. That it was after midnight—and that they weren't totally sober—did not stop them. They headed to the Old Zilker Place off East First Street where there was a great magnolia tree.

Eckhardt hoisted Mewhinney on his shoulders and they staggered around until Mewhinney could pluck a blossom. They raced back to the office with the blossom just in time for Eckhardt to draw the cartoon and meet the printing deadline.[36] The cartoon showed the governor picking the petals off a magnolia blossom ("she loves me, she loves me not . . . .").

Yet even his friends did not know that the artwork and caption commentary were Eckhardt's. Because of his work as a federal employee with the Office of Inter-American Affairs, Eckhardt had to be careful about his political advocacy. He decided to use a pseudonym rather than draw under his signature. A popular blues song from Bob's high school and college days was Blind Lemon Jefferson's 1926 "Jack o' Diamonds," with the line "Jack o' Diamonds is a hard card to play." Eckhardt chose that playing card character for his *Spectator* signature, incorporating a tiny jack-of-diamonds somewhere in each artwork, often with a political message implied in Jack's actions. Thus, he could skewer Governor Stevenson in a cartoon and then have him over to his house for a working dinner—without the governor knowing Eckhardt's alter ego. He sketched a cartoon of Stevenson yelling to Thomas Jefferson, "Agitator!" with Jefferson looking back, saying, "Well, Coke, I guess I was, at that," and Jack covering his eyes in embarrassment. When the ever-precarious magazine was in especially serious financial trouble, Eckhardt sketched the cover for a special issue appealing for money. It showed a blind Jack o' Diamonds with a cup, begging for money, asking simply, "You liberal?" People would laugh about the cartoons and describe them to Eckhardt, not knowing that he was the cartoonist. Bob would grin and say, "Yeah, that was pretty clever, wasn't it?"[37]

The barely thirty-year-old Eckhardt waded into a worldwide array of social and political issues with his *Spectator* cartoons. With the start-up of the cold war, a new Red Scare era dawned, accompanied by Eckhardt cartoons decrying the dangers of the movement. Just months after Hiroshima and Nagasaki, Eckhardt drew a prescient cartoon about atomic power and the already developing blindness about its consequences. The *Dallas News* mentioned it in a 1969 article: "One of Eckhardt's most memorable cartoons for *The Spectator* depicted the atom bomb as Gulliver, fenced in and surrounded by tiny generals as the Lilliputians. It was reprinted in Hong Kong and a friend sent him a copy of it with the lengthy Chinese description accompanying it. 'I never did figure out what it said,' Eckhardt said."[38]

When the legislature rewarded returning war veterans with a land loan program, Jack o' Diamonds smelled a rat. He drew a cartoon showing land speculators and the Texas Land Commissioner buddying up to a veteran. It foretold the scandal that would not break until late 1954. In his cartoons in later issues, Eckhardt decried what he saw as anti-Mexican changes that were underway at the Good Neighbor Commission, where he was a consultant. Though he was now several years out of UT, Eckhardt was still interested in affairs on campus, too. It was an era when academic freedom issues were hotly fought. His cartoons reflect the public battles over censorship by the Board of Regents and the Board's firing of President Homer Rainey, J. Frank Dobie, and other professors. The university was also fighting to remain a segregated institution, and Eckhardt took up the cause of Heman Sweatt in his successful court battle to integrate the law school.

In one issue, a reader complained that the artwork was bad. The editors replied, "Jack o' Diamonds has a screwy style of drawing; but all entreaties that he turn orthodox have been unavailing. And most of the customers seem to like his stuff. Frank Dobie, for instance, is a particular fan."[39] And he was. Dobie wrote that the paper "features the most devastating cartoonist who has ever made civilized Texans snicker. . . . I am guessing that the incognito cartoonist is one of our brave veterans; his only signature drawn with impudent variations, is the Jack of Diamonds."[40] Ironically, the issue with the critical letter to the editor included Eckhardt's cover cartoon of the unfolding veterans' land scandal, which he caught before most realized its depths. Soon, Jack o' Diamonds's cover was blown, as some readers came to know that Eckhardt was the artist.[41] As the paper planned its last few months of publication, Jack took off his disguise. His old *Texas Ranger* ran an article, with photo, on their former editor and his career of cartooning for the *Spectator.*[42]

The *Spectator* was more than a whimsical endeavor for Eckhardt, even if it was an after-hours labor. He threw his heart and soul into the effort. His cover for the final issue shows Jack o' Diamonds walking off over the horizon, disappearing from view. A few years later, Eckhardt wrote for the new *Texas Observer* about his experiences with the *Spectator,* complete with a new sketch of Jack o' Diamonds weeping over the grave of the *Spectator.* His article was signed simply "Jack."[43]

FIVE

Civil Rights and Labor

When Bob Eckhardt returned to Austin, drawing his political cartoons was but one way he found to engage his emerging passion for social justice and civil rights. He went to work for Nelson Rockefeller's Office of Inter-American Affairs (OIAA). In that capacity, he worked closely with the Texas Good Neighbor Commission (GNC) and was pulled into the battles over farmworker and education issues that pitted Establishment leaders against Hispanics and the young white professionals who sided with them.

With the demise of the OIAA and the capturing of the Good Neighbor Commission in 1946 and 1947 by anti–civil rights governors and their appointees, Eckhardt reopened his law office. He continued his involvement with Latino civil rights issues with his litigation of *Delgado v. Bastrop School District,* a key 1948 school desegregation case (paving the way for *Brown v. Board of Education*). At the same time, crucial changes were happening with labor unions, and he joined their legal and political battles. The short-lived Republican Congress passed the Taft-Hartley Act in 1947, severely restricting union activities. This legacy left unions desperately in need of legal help. The Texas legislature leapt at the opportunity to fight back against the New Deal and passed a series of anti-labor laws. Labor causes energized Texas politics throughout the 1940s and 1950s. Arguably, it was the AFL and CIO that brought pluralism back to Texas politics, and labor became a key component in the political party and electoral battles of that era.

Bob Eckhardt practiced labor law from 1946 into the early 1970s and was a crucial lobbyist for unions until his own election to office. Labor law revived his enthusiasm for legal practice. He found that labor law moved fast. When a picket line went up, there were quick legal moves back and forth. He was able to pursue the social and political objectives in which he was keenly interested. He believed that he had made the right decision in his choice of practice, even if it still was not lucrative. Years later, he wrote of his labor law practice, "I sometimes felt as if I were running a lobby of the hotel and someone else was renting the rooms. But I would not have traded my practice for any other, and only legislative service seems to me superior to it from the standpoint of my personal satisfaction."[1] He felt that he was on the right side, representing people passed over for promotions in favor of "brown-nosing" junior employees; organizers who were knocked down, kicked, and jailed; blacks fired allegedly because their varicose veins affected their work, though the firing coincidentally happened right after they joined a union. Eckhardt once told a friend who was counsel against him on a case, "I wish I were on your side. When you win you can enjoy the flush of victory and when you lose you know that justice has been done."[2]

Roosevelt, Rockefeller, and Latin Americans

President Roosevelt announced in his first inaugural address in 1933 his "Good Neighbor policy" to improve relations in the western hemisphere. It soon became apparent that the effort had to address the issue of discrimination against Latinos in the United States. For many Latinos in Texas, life was miserable and dangerous. The bracero guest worker program (1942–1964) assured farmers a pool of Mexican labor. These farmworkers were both a key component of cotton farming and the flashpoint for Anglo hostility. The contempt with which Anglos considered them was palpable. A placard in Texas restaurants of the day proclaimed, "No dogs or Mexicans." Sometimes growers would not pay wages, and working conditions were horrible. Farmers would bring in thousands of workers from Mexico, and local communities depended on their labor for a vibrant cotton industry, yet would refuse to let the workers use their restrooms or restaurants.[3] More ominously, newspapers carried stories of Anglos killing Latinos who crossed them.

News of violent and abusive treatment reached Mexico and strained U.S.-Mexican relations. The war effort became the turning point for Latino-Anglo relations. The U.S. military called up men of all races and national origins, and they went, some with great pride, to fight for their country. And that sense of pride, sacrifice, and accomplishment pushed Mexican Americans to reject the second-class treatment that they received from many Anglo Texans.

In 1940, Roosevelt created the Office of the Coordinator of Commercial and Cultural Relations between the American Republics—later renamed the Office of the Coordinator of Inter-American Affairs and then again renamed the Office of Inter-American Affairs (OIAA). Its task was to carry out Roosevelt's Good Neighbor policy to improve relations with Latin America and to counter Nazi propaganda that exploited U.S. discrimination against Latinos. Roosevelt appointed Nelson Rockefeller as its coordinator.[4]

Rockefeller decided that he needed staff in Texas and California, the storm centers for relations between Latinos and Anglos. He hired Eckhardt's UT friend Tom Sutherland, recently moved from Mexico to Washington, for the new position of field representative serving Texas, New Mexico, and Arizona.[5] Tom and Lois moved back to Austin in early 1943. They settled into his parents' house with their five girls, then moved into a larger two-story stone house at 901 Baylor. Tom opened his OIAA office in the Scarbrough Building.

The OIAA believed that education changes were essential to the improvement of Anglo-Latino relations. UT School of Education Professor George I. Sanchez, whose Spanish heritage was deeply rooted in New Mexico and who had just finished a term as president of the League of United Latin American Citizens (LULAC), was keenly interested in the OIAA initiative. The OIAA gave grants to UT and to the Texas Education Agency (TEA) to pursue an educational component of the initiative. University involvement was coordinated by a committee of professors chaired by Dr. Robert L. Sutherland (no relation to Tom) and including Dr. Sanchez. The UT committee used its OIAA grant money to hire the Spanish-speaking Pauline Kibbe, who had written a regular column for the *San Antonio Light* and radio programs in San Antonio concerning Latin America. In her UT/OIAA capacity, she worked closely with Tom Sutherland.

Texas Good Neighbor Commission

Farmworker issues were the most explosive ones for Tom Sutherland. The McAllen Chamber of Commerce complained to the State Department that examples of discrimination were "isolated" and reported that they were "getting burned up over the attitude of some Mexican officials regarding real or alleged discrimination. . . . If they get so much better treatment in Mexico, why don't they stay in Mexico or return to Mexico?"[6] In 1943, continued gross discrimination finally prompted Mexico to suspend the bracero program.

The Farm Bureau reacted with anger and political activity. They convinced the U.S. Consul General in Juarez to talk with Sutherland, who set up a meeting with Governor Coke Stevenson. In that meeting, Sutherland and Kibbe persuaded Governor Stevenson to create, as a part of his office, the Texas Good Neighbor Commission (GNC), funded initially by OIAA. Stevenson appointed as chair of the Commission wealthy Houston oilman Robert E. "Bob" Smith, a political independent, with Kibbe as GNC executive secretary.[7]

One of Kibbe's first acts in late 1943 was to visit the lower Rio Grande Valley, where she spoke to community groups, met with local officials, and went to farmworker gatherings with the new Texas Congress of Industrial Organizations (CIO) secretary-treasurer, Morris Akin. She then wrote a report on her findings and on the CIO's efforts to help Latino workers. Her efforts did not go unnoticed. UT Regent D. F. Strickland blasted UT President Homer Rainey for letting Kibbe travel to the Valley and lecture residents on how to get along with Mexicans. When Bob Smith got his copy of her report, he called her and demanded that she destroy it.[8]

Eckhardt Joins OIAA

In the summer of 1944, with the war still raging, Tom Sutherland decided to join the navy. He recommended that "the best Texan I know as a successor is Bob Eckhardt."[9] With Sutherland's recommendation, Eckhardt got the job as field representative, just as he was returning from the Army Air Corps Reserves. He went to work in the Scarbrough Building, seeing his dad frequently in his clinic downstairs.

The Sutherlands left 901 Baylor, and Bob and Orissa moved into the house, overlooking downtown and the capitol. They stayed there for a year before buying an old stone house on Trinity and Fourteenth, two blocks from the capitol. As the coordinator for the OIAA office, Eckhardt had to deal not just with the substantive issues, but also with the bureaucratic red tape that was a part of wartime operations. He rose to the defense of his office and employees. "I am entitled to an explanation as to why my office employees have not received regular reimbursement for their services," he wrote to Washington. "They are harassed by financial problems arising from spasmodic payment of their salary checks."[10]

Much of the OIAA work was policy development, but they also responded to requests for information and assistance from around the state. Sally Guinn, from Eckhardt's UT days and from the Hegman kitchen gatherings, was teaching at "the Mexican school" in Lockhart, while her husband Jack was at war. Sally wrote Bob about the "deplorable situation down here." Eckhardt assured her that he would keep confidential the source of the information she was providing, and that Pauline Kibbe, "a hell of a good gal," would also be discreet. Eckhardt tried to get Spanish-speaking attorneys in local communities to set up legal assistance clinics, but he also got pulled into legal advocacy himself. In 1945, he received a request for assistance from the United Latin-American Club in Taylor, just outside Austin, in an assault case. Eckhardt visited the victim in the hospital several times and informed the group when an arrest was finally made.[11]

Eckhardt began a news service with material in English and Spanish. In what could be considered a precursor to the Head Start program, he also helped start a preschool training program for Latino children. Shortly after he joined OIAA in October 1944, he worked with Pauline Kibbe on the Inter-American Relations Education Conference at the Driskill Hotel that she and Sutherland had planned. Eckhardt and Kibbe conducted similar conferences in colleges across the state throughout 1944 and 1945.[12]

Eckhardt was deeply involved with OIAA grant recipient TEA and its head, State School Superintendent Dr. L. A. Woods, but he was sometimes at odds with the agency. Eckhardt and TEA produced a series of "Spanish Speaking Americans in the War" pamphlets, which were very popular and in constant demand. He also worked on the TEA radio program "Americas United." When its content did not, in his opinion, reflect a good knowledge base of Latin American affairs, he urged TEA to use scripts that Kibbe had produced regarding democratic movements in Latin America. But TEA proceeded with its own version, at which point Kibbe withdrew. Eckhardt advised his Washington office that he and Kibbe had gotten the "brush-off" from TEA and that the TEA program and officials would be "either unclear or unreliable." [13]

As a part of his education project, Eckhardt wrote *State Aid and School Attendance in Texas, Report to the Office of Inter-American Affairs.* He documented that the South Texas region had low school revenue per student and was ranked lowest in per capita wealth and school attendance. He then articulated arguments that could still be heard in courtrooms in the Texas school finance battles a half century later—maintaining that any change in the constitutional method of school finance must provide an incentive for counties to promote school attendance and assure an equitable division of state expenditures without regard to racial, national, or economic background. To be effective, he wrote, such changes must take into account the real wealth or poverty of the counties and address the reality that "the education of the children of migrants, who may live in LaSalle County [in South Texas] and pick cotton in Lubbock County [in Northwest Texas], is the responsibility of the State as a whole." [14] In December 1945, he served as a delegate to the first regional conference on the education of Spanish-speaking people in the Southwest, organized by George Sanchez and held at UT's student union building. [15]

Within months of his arrival back in Austin, Eckhardt was making public presentations on issues of discrimination against Latinos. He spoke to UT's Pan American Student Forum, as well as to the new Austin chapter of the American Veterans Committee (AVC). The AVC, created in 1942, became an important organizing vehicle in the post-war period; more than one hundred chapters formed in Texas alone. Bernard Rapoport's friend Fred Schmidt returned from the war in the Philippines and went to work as the Southwestern chairman of the AVC, in which capacity he finally met Eckhardt. [16] When Eckhardt spoke to the Austin chapter of AVC, it was an unusual audience in that it was integrated. The group discussed racial discrimination in the university area by "housemothers" and landlords. Eckhardt maintained that the denial of civil liberties was widespread and decried prejudice and intolerance. "The myth of racial differences is a blight on the people of Texas," he said. Eckhardt argued that segregated schools were deplorable, noting that for Latin Americans, segregation was often based on lingual differences. "There is no pedagogical excuse whatsoever for segregation on the basis of language," he argued, presaging an argument he would make in *Delgado v. Bastrop School District,* a landmark desegregation case in 1948.[17]

Bob's new work took him on trips around Texas, the United States, and Mexico. Caesar Kleberg died in 1946, and Bob inherited his seersucker suit ("the cloak of Caesar," he would call it), one that stayed with him for his business and evening attire for years to come. Robert Sutherland smoothed the way for Eckhardt, inviting him to meetings at UT and with officials from other states. Eckhardt hosted Labor Department officials on a tour of Texas migrant camps in 1945, but the tour had to be cut short as a hurricane blew in.[18] He also went to Washington a few times (taking Orissa with him when he could) and met with Nelson Rockefeller.

Eckhardt and the Good Neighbor Commission

The 1945 legislature passed legislation transforming Governor Stevenson's Good Neighbor Commission into an official state agency. One of Stevenson's new appointees was Valley businessman Lloyd Bentsen Sr. Eckhardt found him to be extremely conservative, but friendly and open. At the first meeting, the reconstituted Commission reelected Bob Smith of Houston as chair, reappointed Pauline Kibbe as executive secretary, and named Eckhardt, who was still field representative of the OIAA, as general consultant. After the GNC meeting, Bob and Orissa hosted all of the appointees and Governor Stevenson at their Baylor Street house for dinner. As they ate and talked politics and policy, they looked out from the balcony of the hillside home to the capitol and the governor's mansion.[19]

Eckhardt did both policy and legal work for the Commission. Eckhardt took a particular interest in cotton and farmworker issues. He visited the area south of Corpus Christi, with its thousands of acres of rich black cotton land that was worked by migratory laborers. The crusty old owner of the Taft Ranch there seared into his mind the disdain, bitterness, and hostility that the economic elite had toward the New Deal and its attempts to alter management-labor practices. "I never was so happy as I was on the day that Roosevelt died," he told Eckhardt.[20]

By mid 1946, Eckhardt had worked for the OIAA for nearly two years. President Truman abolished the agency in May 1946 and transferred its functions to the State Department. Eckhardt closed down the OIAA Scarbrough office and reopened his law office there, continuing as consultant to GNC.

In addition to courtroom work, his new law practice included lobbying for Morris Akin (who had moved his CIO office to Austin), other labor union clients, and the GNC. He was also cartooning (anonymously) for the *Texas Spectator,* serving as chair of the Travis County Young Democrats, and coordinating gubernatorial candidate Homer Rainey's Travis County campaign.

In his work with the OIAA and the GNC, Eckhardt struck up a regular correspondence with Good Neighbor Commission Chairman Smith. In November 1946, Eckhardt traveled to Smith's city of Houston for a meeting of the Commission at the Rice Hotel. Eckhardt urged a focus on education and farmworker issues. He proposed the group study "changes in the state school fund allocations program . . . to protect . . . Latin-attended schools in the Valley, where attendance is affected by seasonal crop work."[21] But he also served as a legal-lobbying handyman for the GNC. The two-year legislative authorization for the agency was set to expire. Eckhardt, working with Chairman Smith, drafted a bill to establish the GNC as a permanent agency, and they presented it to the 1947 legislature.

In the meantime, Kibbe visited the Valley again and wrote a report about the conditions she witnessed. During the legislative process, growers and legislators reacted negatively to her report and were determined to neutralize the agency. Eckhardt's reauthorization bill was blocked in the Senate and, with Lieutenant Governor Allan Shivers's blessing, the senators' price for passing the bill was a behind-the-scenes agreement (reported later by one of the Commission members) to fire Kibbe. Shivers lied, denying the report of a backroom deal, but tellingly added that it wasn't Kibbe's business "to meddle in the affairs of the federal and Mexican governments."[22] Though the agency reauthorization bill passed, a separate anti-discrimination bill failed.

With those developments, and new Governor Beauford Jester's appointment of a slate of commissioners viewed as hostile to Latinos, Kibbe resigned rather than wait for the ax to fall. Smith wrote the lieutenant governor: "For your confidential information, this has all turned out as planned. . . . She resigned and that was exactly what I wanted her to do."[23] Shivers responded that Kibbe was like the "pinks and fellow travelers" in Washington—a contemptible red-baiting spin that would be a hallmark of his later gubernatorial politics.

Eckhardt Emerges as a Public Persona

Eckhardt would have none of it. He resigned as consultant and went public, with his action making front-page news. He wrote that the Senate trade-out for Kibbe's head had been made because of political pressure from large fruit growers in the Valley and that "under the influence of the Jester administration," the Commission was abandoning its most serious duty of protecting the rights and opportunities of Latinos. He said that he would have opposed his own bill recreating the agency "if the commission is to become a glorified tourist bureau for dignitaries traveling in Mexico."[24] He charged Jester and the Commission with being insensitive to civil rights violations, listing as shocking examples of charges that the Commission did not pursue: a recent killing for using a whites-only restroom at a filling station; the scalding deaths of two men who had demanded equal schools for their children; and the submachine gunning deaths of three by a sheriff.[25] But the deed was done, and an angry Jack o' Diamonds heaped contempt on Jester and the new Commission in his next *Spectator* cartoon, harking back to the old café signs, "No Mexicans Allowed"—only this time, the sign was on the door of the Commission.[26]

Eckhardt was emerging as a public persona at a time when discrimination was an issue throughout the country. Pennsylvania Republican Congressman John McDowell on the House Un-American Activities Committee was quoted as saying that there were "Fascist tendencies among people of Spanish descent in Texas." Eckhardt blasted back with a news release, picked up by papers:

> If Mr. McDowell would confine himself to observation of the other members of his committee and of the extremists in the Republican party, it is likely that he would find no less fertile a field for discovery of Fascism, than he will find among Latin-Americans of Texas. All during the time I worked with the coordinator's office, with access to FBI information, I never ran into any Fascist tendencies among our good people of Mexican descent; however, I did run into some fascistic tendencies on the part of a minority of our school boards who refuse our citizens of Mexican descent equal educational facilities.[27]

He suggested that McDowell's statement was "a gratuitous insult" to the American ethnic group that produced Texas Congressional Medal of Honor winners.

Latinos, of course, were not the only minority group experiencing the violence of racial hostilities. In 1946, a series of lynchings of blacks in South Carolina and Georgia ignited protests and demonstrations in Washington. President Truman, angered, set up a committee to report to him on civil rights issues.[28] Its October 1947 report would become a lightning rod in the 1948 presidential elections. The committee gathered information broadly on the issue of discrimination, and Eckhardt leapt at the opportunity to take the issue of Latino civil rights to the national stage. He submitted to Truman's committee a nineteen-page report on violations of civil rights and liberties in Texas, including examples of killings. He also submitted the report to the Good Neighbor Commission—which rejected it.

Lawyer Eckhardt Battles School Segregation

Now done with both the Office of Inter-American Affairs and the Good Neighbor Commission, Eckhardt returned to the full-time practice of law. This time, though, rather than a general practice, he sought out cases with social significance, particularly civil rights and labor cases. He immediately jumped into a Latino civil rights case that would have far-reaching ramifications.

In southern California, the League of United Latin American Citizens (LULAC) filed a lawsuit, resulting in a startling 1947 appellate decision that segregation of Latino students violated the Fourteenth Amendment. The case set the stage for Texas action. In April 1947, Texas Attorney General Price Daniel, responding to a request from the Cuero school district, issued an attorney general's opinion prohibiting segregation of Latinos, but allowing different treatment for language reasons.[29]

UT's George Sanchez wanted to press a similar lawsuit in Texas and turned to Eckhardt's UT Law classmate Gus Garcia. Garcia's San Antonio law practice included representation of the Mexican Consulate General's office. Garcia had gained a reputation as a great lawyer, an eloquent advocate for the impoverished, uneducated victims of discrimination. Other lawyers described him as the best lawyer they had ever known. In 1948, Latinos and blacks in San Antonio formed a coalition and, in an energized atmosphere, elected black businessman G. J. Sutton to the San Antonio Junior College board of trustees and Gus Garcia to the school board.[30]

Garcia and Eckhardt had kept up with each other, particularly through Eckhardt's OIAA and GNC work and through George Sanchez. Eckhardt had worked with Sanchez on OIAA and Good Neighbor Commission initiatives and offered his legal help for the case. Sanchez urged Garcia to file suit, using the California decision to attack segregation. Sanchez also tried unsuccessfully to get Jimmie Allred and Everett Looney to join Garcia's legal team.[31]

Garcia requested a clarification of the attorney general's opinion, and Daniel replied, "The law prohibits discrimination against or segregation of Latin Americans on account of race or descent." But, the opinion had little effect. Eckhardt and Garcia discussed the opinion and the California case. They brought in Al Wirin, a superb lawyer with the Los Angeles Civil Liberties Union, and Carlos Cadeña, who had been at UT law school with them. LULAC sponsored and helped raise funds for the suit, and Corpus Christi member Dr. Hector Garcia, who had gone to UT with Eckhardt and Gus Garcia, joined in the LULAC fundraising effort. Soon, Dr. Garcia launched the American G.I. Forum and raised money through his new organization for the lawsuit.[32]

UT students, through their American Veterans Committee, Laredo Club, and Alba Club, took up the cry for equal educational opportunity.[33] The four lawyers sent the students to Bastrop, Elgin, and points east and south of Austin to document discrimination. Eckhardt would say years later, "I suppose that we might have been engaged in a bit of barratry, though for me there was no money in it." (He got paid a total of $300 after the suit.[34]) He and Garcia drove out into the rural and small town areas to talk to prospective plaintiffs, most of them laborers who worked for companies such as the brick manufacturers in Elgin. Eckhardt's Spanish was limited, so when they encountered people who did not speak English, it was left to Garcia to explain that they would like the family to enter the law case for their children's sake. But he would warn them that the community and opposing interests could make it hard on them. An elderly gentleman replied that "it couldn't be worse" for them than it already was. One day, they saw ten families consecutively, and none turned them down. To Eckhardt, their spirit and willingness to join the lawsuit exemplified courage.

Garcia and Eckhardt filed suit in federal court for six-year-old Minerva Delgado and twenty others in January 1948, against the Bastrop, Caldwell, and Travis County school districts they had surveyed. *Minerva Delgado et al. v. Bastrop ISD et al.*, known as *Delgado v. Bastrop School District,* was heard in Austin by U.S. District Judge Ben H. Rice in June 1948.[35] Opposing counsel included Ireland Graves, who had practiced with Charles Black's father and who still shared offices with Mr. Black. During the negotiations, Eckhardt went to their Norwood Building offices, where, as a novice lawyer, he had gone to use their library. As he entered, Mr. Black, who was drinking heavily at the time, asked, "Well, Bob, what are you up here for?" Eckhardt told him he was there to see Mr. Graves about the school case. "Oh, Mr. Graves doesn't have a leg to stand on," the drunken Black opined.[36]

The Texas Constitution required segregation for Negroes. The lawyers could have argued that because Latinos were not Negroes (i.e., following LULAC's argument of Latinos being white), discrimination against them violated the Texas Constitution. But they deliberately decided to try the case on broader grounds, making arguments similar to those that would shortly be used by Thurgood Marshall, Charles Black, and others in the *Brown v. Board of Education* case.[37] An underlying and troubling issue was whether Mexican Americans were a cognizable class. But that issue had primarily been litigated in the context of jury service, so they argued that it was not relevant here. (Garcia and Maury Maverick Jr. would successfully argue that issue six years later.) They argued that segregation per se violated the Fourteenth

Amendment—that there were no constitutional grounds for discriminating at all.[38] From California, Wirin wrote to Garcia, "Both Bob and you should use . . . the very persuasive memo gotten up by Bob."[39]

State School Superintendent Dr. L. A. Woods, with whom Eckhardt had worked during the OIAA years, was sympathetic to the issue of equal educational opportunity. He, school district officials, and their attorneys decided to negotiate a consent decree. Eckhardt, Garcia, Wirin, and Cadeña insisted in establishing in court the evidence of discrimination so that they would have a binding decree. Judge Rice then accepted the consent decree and enjoined both the local districts and state officials from segregating Latinos in schools.[40]

Just as the later *Brown* decision would trigger resistance, the *Delgado* decision was greeted with hostility and contempt. Many local districts tried to establish "freedom of choice" policies to get around the ruling, allowing Anglos to opt into other schools. Second-class treatment for Latinos was so deeply embedded in the Anglo culture that court orders and administrative edicts could not defeat it, and Dr. Woods eventually paid the price. His job was elective; opponents of *Delgado* went to the legislature and got the elective position abolished. Woods lost his job, and a new superintendent was appointed who refused to require compliance with the court ruling.[41]

Thurgood Marshall, meanwhile, called Wirin and wrote Sanchez, congratulating them on the case and asking for copies of the case material and the benefit of their experience as he pursued school segregation cases.[42] *Brown* soon followed, as Eckhardt refocused his career on labor law.

Texas Labor Strife, 1900–1940s

While he was pursuing the *Delgado* case, Eckhardt was also busy at work for the local telephone workers' union and for the state CIO. Thus, he got pulled, inexorably, into the world of Texas labor. Their battles became his battles; their history became a part of his cloth.

Texas was a rural state, and out of the populist movement's collapse at the turn of the century grew the National Farmers Union (NFU), begun in Texas in 1902. The NFU favored taxes on natural resources, opposed sales taxes, and advocated alliances with the newly forming industrial labor groups. Texas had begun experiencing labor-management battles even before the turn of the century, with the old Knights of Labor railroad strikes. Nationally, the CIO broke away from the American Federation of Labor (AFL) in 1938. In the 1940s, the NFU worked with both the CIO and the AFL in Texas, and leaders were often invited to attend and speak at each other's meetings.[43]

There was virtually no unionization in Texas manufacturing when the New Deal started (union strength was in other sectors). But with increasing industrialization, Texas saw a phenomenal increase in production workers in the 1940s. Roosevelt also swung the New Deal behind labor organizing efforts.[44] Both the AFL and the CIO organized in this rich environment, and both jumped into the political and policy battles in Austin. It was a volatile, sometimes violent time, as labor developed its organizing skills. Labor strife in the field was accompanied by shrill battles in the political halls and party meetings.

Bob Eckhardt joined the more aggressive and progressive CIO branch of the movement—a homegrown, upstart organization, with strong, militant workers. It drew together a lot of people and clashed with the older AFL, which was inclined to stay out of politics. Their competition pushed both to greater organizing efforts. The labor movement was a threat to the traditional power held by Texas businesses, though the threat was often overblown. Militant unions such as that of the mineworkers frightened business and many politicians.[45]

With Jimmie Allred retiring from the governor's mansion in January 1939, the New Deal in Texas now faced a formidable opponent. During Pappy O'Daniel's governorship (1939–1941), there were major legal, political, and legislative battles over labor. In 1937, unions opposed sales taxes and advocated increased taxes on natural resources, pipelines, and utilities; in 1939, Governor O'Daniel proposed a sales tax plan, and the battle was on. He called a special session of the legislature in 1941 and demanded an "anti-violence" bill aimed at "communistic labor leader racketeers." O'Daniel warned the legislature about labor "racketeering and fifth-column activities."[46] After the legislature passed the bill, O'Daniel mailed a copy to every governor and touted it across the nation.[47] Labor was permanently set against him through the rest of his career.

Soon, a union official was convicted of violating O'Daniel's statute, even though there was no violence on the picket line in question. The legislature pressed ahead with new attacks. The 1943 Manford Act required unions to file financial statements and register before organizing. Over the course of several years, the U.S. Supreme Court and other courts held numerous provisions of the acts unconstitutional.[48] The 1945 legislature and Lieutenant Governor John Lee Smith pressed vigorously for Representative Marshall Bell's right-to-work bill, claiming that the war effort was being impeded by strikes. Though their effort was not successful, Roosevelt's death and the rise of a Republican Congress soon changed labor dynamics.

Republicans won control of Congress in 1946. President Truman removed price controls in a quick manner that, Eckhardt thought, destabilized labor-management relations, triggering new strikes. Eckhardt believed that had the president managed the transition more carefully, the nation could have moved into an era of labor organization that would have ratified labor advances.[49] Instead, Congress managed to do great damage to the New Deal, passing the 1947 Taft-Hartley Act to undo labor gains. Truman vetoed it, but Republicans and southerners—including Lyndon Johnson—overrode the veto. Taft-Hartley was one of the most significant policy changes of the twentieth century, beginning the long and slow erosion of American labor. In 1947, quickly following Taft-Hartley, the Texas legislature passed a right-to-work statute. Thus, the unraveling of the New Deal was coming to fruition at the time that Bob Eckhardt joined the battles as a labor lawyer and lobbyist.

Finessing the CIO and AFL Competition

In Texas, AFL unions coalesced into the Texas State Federation of Labor. Many in the AFL deeply hated the CIO and repeatedly blocked efforts for cooperation or consolidation as the CIO grew and challenged it. In 1937, numerous CIO locals met in Beaumont to form a statewide CIO council to compete with the Federation. The CIO's stronghold was in coastal areas with petroleum refineries. The locals that affiliated into the statewide organization included a wide variety of unions, from steelworkers to oil workers, shipbuilders, and garment workers. In addition, local area industrial union councils affiliated, including the CIO Councils of Harris, Tarrant, and Dallas Counties with which Eckhardt would work.[50]

In the war and postwar years, money flowed freely in the oil and steel industries, and union growth in those sectors was rapid. The oil workers' union became the CIO's strongest union in Texas, and Eckhardt went to work for them. In the 1940s, officials from the steelworker and oil worker unions dominated the CIO offices of president and executive secretary. Oil worker Morris Akin was secretary-treasurer of the Texas CIO State Council from 1944 to 1947. Akin was its chief lobbyist, and he moved the office from Houston to Austin's Littlefield Building, across from Eckhardt in the Scarbrough Building, so they got to know each other. Eckhardt saw the CIO as a dedicated bunch of people with great intelligence and ability, tremendous drive, ideological fervor, and commitment to democracy. He believed that the articulate Akin had a powerful intellect and could have been a great lawyer, as he grasped what the laws meant. Akin, in turn, came to value the advice that Eckhardt gave him on legislative and civil rights issues.[51]

The 1930s and 1940s were decades of struggle for control of the CIO among state, regional, and national leaders. But it was the struggle between Communists and anti-Communists for the soul of the organization that was even more intense. The anti-Communist faction, led by Akin, had won by 1944 and 1945, and the Council passed a resolution denouncing Communism.

Still, the internal battle fueled the red-baiting movement and damaged the union. The red-baiting led some in the National Farmers Union, for instance, to pull back from the CIO.

The AFL and the CIO intermittently decided that they needed each other or that they could live without each other. In 1943, after being defeated on the Manford Act, the CIO State Council called a meeting of all unions in Houston to work out a joint program. AFL, CIO, railroad, and other independent unions formed a United Labor Committee to support Roosevelt, work to abolish the poll tax, and oppose efforts to block New Deal programs. But centrifugal forces still pulled the unions apart. The Texas AFL devoted its 1946 convention to attacks on the CIO. The 1947 anti-labor bills jarred the unions and brought them back, again, to (minimal) cooperation. The National Farmers Union joined the fight against the 1947 anti-labor bills, and the CIO Council set up the Committee on Farmer-Labor Cooperation to continue and encourage that support.[52]

Labor's 1947 losses spurred on the CIO's efforts to build partnerships, and its race policies had to be changed to promote the needed alliances. Blacks and Latinos made up only about 10 percent of the CIO membership, and they were either segregated in Jim Crow locals or discriminated against in mixed locals. George Sanchez, directing the American Council of Spanish-Speaking People, and Ed Idar of the Texas G.I. Forum, criticized both the CIO and the AFL for not doing much to promote anti-discrimination. The CIO was caught between the national organization's anti-discrimination policies and the racist sentiments of many of its rank-and-file Texas members. When the CIO Council stood against racism, it faced the anger of those members.[53]

The 1947 Texas Legislative Labor Battles

During the 1947 legislative session, Eckhardt was a busy man. In April, the Eckhardts celebrated baby Orissa's first birthday, and a week later, Big Orissa gave birth to their second daughter, Rosalind. Bob surreptitiously drew his *Spectator* cartoons about the state's political escapades. In his role as private lawyer, he represented the Southwestern Telephone Workers' Union and other clients. But his heart, and much of his time, was at the capitol, where he represented the Good Neighbor Commission, Communication Workers of America (CWA), and the CIO Council. Minnie Fisher Cunningham drew him into her People's Legislative Committee and soon into the labor-affiliated Texas Social and Legislative Conference. And, by his own initiative, he jumped into the state's battles over tax policy, staking out a territory in oil and gas taxation that he would tend for decades. He quickly came to believe that one piece of the labor puzzle was that government tilted heavily in favor of business and the wealthy, while extracting taxes from the workers. So, beginning with his 1947 graduated oil tax bill, he spent a career attempting to make the tax system more equitable.

Shortly after restarting his law practice, Bob and his old UT friend Mark Adams were sitting in his Scarbrough office discussing the power concentration that they saw undermining the public good. They speculated about the possibilities of antitrust suits. Eckhardt thought that state antitrust action would not be successful. Adams thought that big oil companies could be vulnerable to state government action, since they could not leave the state. So the two men concocted a graduated tax on oil production, setting the gradations of the rate such that only eleven major companies would have their severance tax increased, while hundreds of other producers got reductions. The bill was projected to raise $38 million annually, with the money going for teachers' pay and farm-to-market roads. They took the bill to their friend who had reinvigorated the Young Democrats, twenty-four-year-old Jim Wright, just elected state representative from Weatherford. Eckhardt thought him the most liberal member of the House. Wright and Representative Jim Sewell decided to sponsor their bill. The bill drew immediate attention because it benefited so many, even in the oil industry, and it created quite a stir.[54]

Wright fought hard for it in a committee hearing on March 18. A comptroller's researcher told Wright, Eckhardt, and Adams just before the hearing that it would produce $120 million—far more than they had projected. But they feared they would be scoffed at, so they claimed in the hearing that it would raise $38 million. And no one else said anything about the revenue estimate. "Not a word," Eckhardt later said. "I'm sure they knew it, but they didn't want anybody to know how easy it was to raise $120 million."[55] They lost the committee vote 2–12, and the bill died. Wright had taken on the economic powers of the state and when he went back home to run for reelection in 1948, he was defeated. He learned from that lesson that economic populism can be detrimental to an ambitious politician.

The legislature considered a host of anti-labor bills and passed nine of them, including the right-to-work bill, the bill regulating picketing, the bill making unions liable for picketing, and the bill making secondary strikes and boycotts illegal. Eckhardt's old benefactor Ed Clark (who got his start with Allred, but now was a friend of LBJ and George and Herman Brown, of Brown & Root Construction Company) helped lobby through the crown jewel, the right-to-work law. Eckhardt did what he could to slow the march of the bills, advising Morris Akin and preparing information and arguments for testimony. The 1947 session was a devastating blow to labor. Akin resigned as secretary-treasurer of the CIO Council after the session and was succeeded by Jeff Hickman of the oil worker union.[56]

Eckhardt Moves to Fort Worth and Dallas

With the passage of the nine bills, labor leaders realized that they were in for a very rough period and that they had better step up their legal and political efforts. By then, Eckhardt was becoming well known in labor circles. The CIO's Akin, Hickman, and their regional political action committee head, Don Ellinger, all befriended and liked Eckhardt. Those CIO leaders introduced Bob to O. A. "Jack" Knight, head of Oil Workers International Union (OWIU), headquartered in Fort Worth. The city was a dynamic place for labor in the 1940s. The National Labor Relations Board had its regional office there, and the federal judiciary's Fifth Circuit held sessions in Fort Worth. With Taft-Hartley's passage and the new state laws, Knight decided that he needed help, and he offered Eckhardt a position with his legal team. The steady work that the job would provide, plus the chance to devote his efforts solely to labor law, was enough to entice him away from Austin.

Bob started to work in Fort Worth in late 1947 and he, Orissa, and the girls moved to Dallas in February 1948. They had just bought the old stone house in Austin a year earlier for $8,500 and were able to sell it for $15,000, a big boost for their financial condition. (The historic house was later moved to Symphony Square and restored; it remains there today.) Orissa soon got a job as a math teacher. Eckhardt plunged into the new environment, getting to know Dallas and Fort Worth people such as labor organizer and old socialist Harvey O'Connor, who wrote about the oil industry and its workers. Bob had lunch with him nearly every day and talked politics and labor.

Though he was no longer able to run down to the *Texas Spectator* office and produce last-minute cartoons, Eckhardt still managed to produce his artwork for each issue of the newspaper. It was during this period that his pseudonym as Jack o' Diamonds was finally blown, but he no longer needed the cover as he was not working for a government agency. In 1948, former Vice President Henry Wallace decided to run as a third party candidate against President Harry Truman. Union people stayed loyal to Truman. Eckhardt believed that Wallace was a man of high quality and ability, and he was concerned about cheap attacks on Wallace. He drew a *Spectator* cover defending Wallace. A little man wearing a button "Liberals against Wallace" was outdoors on a bright, shining day. He had an umbrella, wore galoshes, carried a raincoat, and was looking at a small cloud off in the sky. The caption to the cartoon was "The timid liberals." One of the Oil Workers' International Union officials saw the cartoon, went to Jack Knight, and said, "You have a Wallaceite working for you." Knight replied, "Well, when Bob's doing law, he's working for me; when he's drawing cartoons for the *Spectator,* he's working for Kewpie Young." [57] Eckhardt admired Knight for standing up for him.

Eckhardt's main job was to research and write about the legislative debates on the Taft-Hartley provisions.[58] Thus, in developing the legislative history of the act, he became well versed in it, became a valued asset to labor's legal team, and drew on that knowledge when he litigated. The job with OWIU, however, did not last long. Within a year of Bob's move, Knight decided to relocate the OWIU offices to Denver.

Eckhardt did not want to leave Texas, so in 1948 he left OWIU and returned to the Communication Workers of America. He became CWA general counsel, working out of Dallas. Eckhardt's work took him to states throughout the west, as well as to East Texas, where he met lawyer Franklin Jones. He practiced litigation and arbitration and traveled to Austin to continue his lobbying. In Dallas, Bob and Orissa became reacquainted with Julya, their old UT friend. Julya was now married to Guy Kirkpatrick. She had gotten degrees in literature, education, and fine arts, and pursued a career in art. The reacquaintance also rekindled the love between Julya and Bob, setting them all on a collision course. Julya and Guy had joined the First Unitarian Church of Dallas, and Orissa, too, decided that she liked the church. She and Bob and the girls attended. There at the church, Bob came to know labor organizers Carl and Laura Brannin. Carl had run for governor in 1936 as a Socialist.[59]

Bob also reconnected with Otto Mullinax. Just as Bob was moving to Dallas-Fort Worth, Otto opened a new practice in Dallas, teaming up with three other lawyers, including Nat Wells, a Columbia Law graduate who had worked for the National Labor Relations Board (NLRB). The two served as legal counsel for the Texas State Federation of Labor. The firm was to become a premier labor law firm.[60] Eckhardt worked with Wells on cases. There was plenty of work to go around, as companies all across the nation struck back at unions.

In 1947 and again in 1949, Eckhardt became a fixture in the lobbies outside the Texas House and Senate chambers. He got to know many of the leaders with whom he would later serve. The 1949 legislature included future Governor Dolph Briscoe and Eckhardt's future congressional colleague Jack Brooks. Eckhardt's sense of humor helped him engage legislators, lobbyists, and reporters. In 1949, the Speaker ordered the doors to the House chamber and inner lobby closed and guarded, thus forcing lobbyists out into the hall and rotunda area. Eckhardt remarked to reporters that they should stop using the word lobbyist. "They're not lobbyists anymore. They're rotundistas."[61]

In these post-war years, it was his labor and civil rights law that brought Eckhardt to politics. With his 1947 and 1949 lobbying, Eckhardt began a decade's work of writing and lobbying labor and tax legislation, simultaneously jumping into the vicious Texas Democratic Party battles from 1948 through 1958, until he emerged on his own as a legislator.

Eckhardt in 1940s Texas Politics

As Bob Eckhardt immersed himself in labor law, riding the wave of post Taft-Hartley labor-management clashes, he inevitably got drawn deeper into the world of Texas electoral politics. His blend of labor and civil rights concerns brought him full circle to his old UT crowd and to the raging battles between New Deal Democrats and anti-New Deal Democrats. During the ensuing twenty-five years of intense conflicts, Eckhardt was often engaged fully with the faction known by several names: Loyalists, national Democrats, or liberals. He emerged as a key player and often assumed leadership roles—in the pivotal Homer Rainey gubernatorial campaign of 1946, the 1948 party convention battles involving Lyndon Johnson and Harry Truman, and the merging of labor and liberal groups into the Texas Social and Legislative Conference. The internecine struggles of the Texas Democratic Party became his war; the titular heads of the liberal movement (Maury Maverick, Jimmie Allred, J. R. Parten, Homer Rainey) became his mentors; and the guerrilla leaders such as Minnie Fisher Cunningham and Creekmore Fath were his compadres. While Cunningham, Fath, and others did the trench work, Eckhardt served as lawyer, lobbyist, writer, cartoonist, and orator for the movement, before fully blossoming into a leader in his own right in the 1950s.

The 1930s New Deal spawned angry efforts to oppose it, and in Texas those efforts were made inside the Democratic Party. The party conventions and the State Democratic Executive Committee (SDEC) became battlegrounds between the two major factions of the party—those like Eckhardt who supported Franklin Roosevelt and Jimmie Allred and those who supported laissez faire government and thus despised Roosevelt and Allred. The assaults against the New Deal were led by factional groups (American Liberty League, Jeffersonian Democrats, Constitutional Democrats) and by leaders such as J. Evetts Haley (ranch manager for Houston·millionaire J. M. West).[1]

Key Texas congressmen who were early New Deal supporters included Sam Rayburn and Maury Maverick. About the time Maverick was defeated (1938), Lyndon Johnson took up the mantle of supporting Roosevelt. Maverick returned to Texas, won election as mayor of San Antonio, and continued as a strong New Dealer. One of Mayor Maverick's prized projects, the redevelopment of San Antonio's downtown river area and La Villita complex, would become a touchstone for Eckhardt and the Loyalists.

The LBJ–Brown & Root Machine

Lyndon Johnson and John Connally built a political machine that dominated Texas politics for forty years. Bob Eckhardt's political career ran on a track alongside their careers, from the 1940s through Johnson's presidency and Connally's presidential run. Their tracks sometimes merged, and sometimes wrenched apart. A key financier of the Johnson-Connally machine was the Brown & Root Construction Company. Johnson's relationship with Herman and George Brown and their empire became legendary and shaped public policy outcomes in Texas and the nation for decades.

In 1931, State Senator Alvin J. Wirtz persuaded his new congressman, Richard Kleberg, to appoint 23-year-old Lyndon Johnson as his secretary, having seen Johnson's political savvy during the primary campaign. Johnson tended to every little detail for Kleberg, writing, for instance, to Caesar Kleberg back on the King Ranch to get information for the congressman on their ranch dog, known as "Muscle Shoals Dick."[2] Later, Wirtz was chair of the Texas advisory board for the National Youth Administration when he and Sam Rayburn convinced President Roosevelt to appoint LBJ as the Texas NYA director. Wirtz also introduced Johnson to Herman and George Brown.

In 1937, Austin's congressman, James Buchanan, died. Minnie Fisher Cunningham, along with UT law students Clay Cochran and Creekmore Fath, rounded up money and New Deal support for Dr. Bob Montgomery to run for Congress. The strong-willed Mrs. Montgomery, raised as a tough army brat, said absolutely not, and that was the end of the "Draft Dr. Bob" movement.[3] Lyndon Johnson jumped into the race, supported by Wirtz. His campaign manager was Jimmie Allred protégé Ed Clark, who would soon help Eckhardt and Fath get started with their law practice. When Johnson won, he hired one of his campaign staffers, Eckhardt's UT nemesis John Connally, as his congressional aide. LBJ arrived in Washington just a few months after Houston elected a new congressman, Albert Thomas. (Eckhardt would succeed Thomas three decades later.) When Thomas was up for a Texas seat on the Appropriations Committee, Johnson challenged him, but the delegation voted to honor the seniority tradition (a system that would also affect Eckhardt's congressional advancement years later). Thomas won the appointment, and the two had a frosty relationship.[4]

Wirtz left the state senate and joined an Austin law and lobbying firm. The firm represented employers and thus was often at odds with the labor unions that employed Eckhardt. By far Wirtz's most virulent anti-labor client was Brown & Root. Herman Brown of Belton started building roads in the early 1900s. He formed a partnership with Dan Root, then brought in brother George, and they moved their headquarters to Houston. As the motor vehicle era set in, Brown & Root became road-building powers. Once they had established their ability to win contracts through their lobbying presence, they ventured out beyond road construction. Wirtz also worked as the general counsel to the new Lower Colorado River Authority. With the 1930s came a growing interest in taming the floods of the Colorado River, and the Brown brothers received contracts to build the dams. World War II brought military contracts to Brown & Root, greased by the brothers' relationship with Johnson and, through him, Roosevelt. These included ship building on the Houston ship channel in Congressman Albert Thomas's district. By the 1940s, Herman Brown had a reputation of being able to get any bill through the Texas legislature that he wanted and to block any that he did not want. And what he wanted were anti-labor laws, such as the 1947 right-to-work bill that he, Wirtz, and Clark helped lobby through the legislature, steamrolling Eckhardt and his allies.[5]

When Senator Morris Sheppard died in 1941, Governor O'Daniel called a special election and declared himself a candidate. Jimmie Allred decided to run, but backed out when his wife vetoed it. Lyndon Johnson had served little more than one term in the House, but decided to plunge into the Senate race, with Connally running his campaign. He opened his campaign office in Herman Brown's building close to the capitol.[6] O'Daniel won a bitterly fought runoff with Johnson, though his victory was tainted with charges of electoral fraud, and Connally never forgave himself for letting O'Daniel's people blindside them. It was a rare defeat for the Johnson-Connally machine, and they would later call on Eckhardt and his allies to avoid another loss.

The White Primary and the Poll Tax Battles

A defining reason for the strength of the Texas Establishment was its embrace of and institutionalization of racism in elections. In 1923, the legislature passed a law declaring primary elections to be for whites only. Moreover, in 1902, the legislature had required payment of a tax as a prerequisite for voting. The initiative was aimed at killing Populist electoral support; as side effects, it disenfranchised the lower classes and kept blacks out of the general elections.[7] Political and legal battles over the white primary and the poll tax raged for decades.

In 1924, Dr. Lawrence Nixon won a case overturning the white primary, but the state danced around it with new laws, and he and others lost a second round in 1935. The NAACP decided to open the fight again, this time in

Houston, with Dr. Lonnie Smith and Sidney Hasgett as the plaintiffs. They lost the lawsuit in 1942, then appealed the case. NAACP attorney Thurgood Marshall argued for Smith. In the middle of the 1944 elections, the U.S. Supreme Court ruled, striking down Texas's white primary in *Smith v. Allwright* (1944).[8] In so doing, the court changed southern politics forever, but in the short term, the decision energized the forces of racism.

Last Gasp Efforts against Roosevelt

As Roosevelt neared the end of his second term, the traditional end of a presidency, Vice President John Nance Garner from Texas received the support of those who hoped for an end to the New Deal. In 1939, Garner geared up a presidential campaign with Roy Miller, lobbyist for Texas Gulf Sulfur Association and the Progressive Democrats' old nemesis, as his head organizer. Steel executive and SDEC chair Eugene B. Germany pledged his support. But Roosevelt announced for a third term, and incoming House Speaker Sam Rayburn and Congressman Lyndon Johnson led the Texas national convention delegation for Roosevelt, who was still wildly popular among Texans. Roosevelt won the nomination and a landslide victory in November against Republican Wendell Willkie.[9]

Southern conservatives prepared again to stop Roosevelt in 1944. Governor Coke Stevenson's chair of the SDEC condemned the New Deal and urged precinct organizers to pass resolutions supporting an uninstructed national delegation. The 1944 state convention was held in Austin, in the Senate chamber, while Eckhardt was still in the army; its fallout affected his career for years.

In the overcrowded chamber, Alvin Wirtz moved to instruct the presidential electors to pledge to the party's nominee and lost. The New Dealers then bolted across the rotunda to the House chamber, holding a rump convention. The Senate chamber convention instructed Texas electors *not* to vote for Roosevelt and resolved against *Smith v. Allwright* and labor strikes. LBJ blasted the Senate convention as a bunch of "corporation lawyers, oil operators, [and] heads of big business . . . allied with the Republican old guard."[10]

Allred filed a pro-Roosevelt slate of electors, then organized an effort to win the second round of party conventions.[11] Meanwhile, SDEC leader Eugene B. Germany and other southern electors stated that they would not vote for Roosevelt. Germany wrote a letter to southern state electors, urging them to withhold their electoral votes so as to "control the electoral college" and win patronage. His letter ignited the factional fires. As Austin New Dealer Herman Jones put it: "There would be no appeasement of Germany—either Berlin or Eugene."[12]

After the national convention, the second round of county conventions produced fights throughout the state. Allred's organizational efforts paid off, and conservatives then walked out of the state convention. Allred and the delegates set to work purging electors (including Germany) who refused to support the president, installing a new chair, and replacing most of the SDEC members. When the secretary of state refused to certify the new electoral slate, the Texas Supreme Court overruled him and ordered Allred's Roosevelt electors on the ballot.[13]

Those losses propelled conservatives to form a third party, called the "Texas Regulars." Senator Pappy O'Daniel fired up his hillbilly band and toured the state for the Regulars. They stated eight party principles, including opposition to the "communist-controlled New Deal" and support of "supremacy of the white race."[14] They won support from the *Dallas News* and *Houston Post.* Regulars and Republicans negotiated to coordinate their efforts, hoping to deny Texas electoral votes to Roosevelt, but the cooperation effort eventually collapsed.[15]

The Roosevelt forces blitzed the state to assure a victory, with Allred, Rayburn, Johnson, and others regularly blasting the Texas Regulars. Their efforts prevailed, as Roosevelt amassed 71 percent of the state's votes. The Texas Regulars disbanded, but the conservative faction had won all the statewide offices in the primary, so the Regulars maintained a powerful presence inside the party and state government.

Even the Young Democrats got drawn into the ideological alignments in the party. In late 1944, when Eckhardt returned to Austin from the army, he joined the Young Democrats. Through them, he widened his circle of political friends, including the president of the Houston chapter, J. Edwin Smith, who would later serve as a key Eckhardt ally. Liberals took control of the state YD convention in 1945 in Fort Worth. They continued to control the organization in 1946, electing UT exes Stuart Long and Bernard Rapoport to the YD executive committee and Jim Wright, known as a "young, red-haired, good-looking war veteran, and a crack public speaker," as convention chair. Wright also chaired the credentials committee, with Eckhardt on his committee. Conservative delegates showed their contempt for the two by "inviting the committee chairman to keep quiet, or by inviting Bob Eckhardt of Austin, a committee member, to keep his hair out of his eyes."[16]

Minnie Fish and the Three Musketeers

The YDs were not the only ones that Eckhardt joined upon his return to Austin. Minnie Fisher Cunningham was also back in Austin. Cunningham was a longtime feminist driven to battle on issues of social and economic justice. A graduate of UT's pharmacy school in 1901 and relatively well off, she was one of the key influences on post-Allred liberalism and its practitioners, including Eckhardt. She had fought for women's suffrage as president of the Texas Equal Suffrage Association, establishing its headquarters in the new Littlefield Building.[17] In 1923, Cunningham moved to Washington and helped organize the League of Women Voters. She returned and ran for the U.S. Senate in 1928, unheard of for a Texas woman. During the New Deal, she moved back to Washington, worked for the Agricultural Adjustment Administration, and became close to Eleanor Roosevelt. The president nicknamed her "Minnie Fish," and that's what her close friends started calling her.

Upon her return to Texas, she worked out of the Littlefield Building with the Texas Committee to Abolish the Poll Tax. In 1944, Minnie Fish, John Henry Faulk, Margaret Reading, and others created a "Draft Dobie Campaign," hoping to convince J. Frank Dobie to run for governor against Coke Stevenson. He declined, so Cunningham ran (with Liz Sutherland as her press secretary).

After she lost the 1944 gubernatorial primary and just as Bob and Orissa returned to Austin in late 1944 from their Coleman sojourn, Minnie Fish persuaded Eckhardt to join her and "farmers and their wives" in a short-lived international peace effort.[18] He also worked with her during the 1946 Rainey campaign and for years to come. He considered her to be a highly intelligent, "very fine woman," who touched the consciences of the young men with whom she worked, preventing them from selling out.[19]

Minnie Fish had numerous disciples among women activists. One of those disciples was the short, feisty Lillian (Mrs. Jud) Collier. Another was Margaret Reading, at whose ranch the *Texas Spectator* was born. Minnie Fish, Collier, and Reading came to be known as "the three musketeers." Another younger, more independent disciple was Marion Storm, whose husband Joe (editor of the *Daily Texan* while Eckhardt was at UT) had been killed in the war.

The Rainey Affair and Campaign

Just about election time in 1944, the UT Regents fired President Homer Rainey, exacerbating the division between liberals and conservatives in Texas politics for years to come and setting the stage for Rainey's 1946 gubernatorial run that drew in Eckhardt. It all started with the 1938 election of Pappy O'Daniel as governor and O'Daniel winning control of the board of regents. O'Daniel wanted regents who would fire teachers who were critical of the Establishment. Thus began a nearly four-year war. After O'Daniel went to the U.S. Senate, Coke Stevenson appointed similarly-minded regents. Several O'Daniel-Stevenson regents were lobbyists for business interests, and in the pivotal political battles of 1944, many of them were anti-Roosevelt Texas Regulars.

J. Frank Dobie would say later that the UT regents "tried to build a Maginot line around this institution to keep ideas out." [20] Academic freedom, tenure, and research were not comprehensible to the reactionary regents. Allred's Regent Chair J. R. Parten received dozens of complaints from other regents about Dr. Bob Montgomery. Regents would read aloud some of Montgomery's writings. In an attempt to get rid of him, one regent moved to simply eliminate his salary. Parten overruled the motion as a violation of tenure. Lutcher Stark moved to eliminate Roy Bedichek's UIL budget, and Parten outmaneuvered him, too. [21] O'Daniel refused to reappoint Parten to the board when his term expired in early 1941.

At the first board meeting in 1942 after new Governor Stevenson had filled vacancies on the board, Regent D. F. Strickland, the motion picture industry's lobbyist, took from his pocket a small card and passed it across the table to President Rainey. Rainey looked at the card and saw the names Bob Montgomery, Clarence Ayres, E. E. Hale, and Clarence Wiley. Strickland told him, "We want you to fire these men." When Rainey asked why, he said, "We don't like what they are teaching." [22] Rainey resisted. Lesser-known professors were not so lucky, as the regents soon fired three economics instructors who criticized a Dallas rally held to oppose the Fair Labor Standards Act. Regents complained that the economics department was "swinging away from true economics and routing our children into the camp of state socialism." [23]

The regents' assaults were unrelenting. In 1943, a faculty member included on an optional reading list part of the award-winning *USA Trilogy*, by John Dos Passos. When the regents were informed about it (and about racy passages in the book), they whipped up a campaign to ban the book and to hang the incident around Rainey's neck, accusing him of hiring unqualified, immoral faculty members. In late 1944, after these repeated fights with the board, Rainey went public with sixteen charges against the regents. They fired him immediately.

The faculty and the Ex-Students Association protested. Five thousand students paraded down Congress Avenue to the capitol, carrying a casket representing academic freedom, and a general student strike ensued. The six regents who voted to fire Rainey offered their resignations, though the governor quickly rejected three of the resignations. J. R. Parten concluded that they had resigned "because they had done something they were ashamed of—like stealing eggs." [24] In the uproar that followed, Parten convinced the Texas Senate to hold hearings, with a full cast of luminaries testifying, including Webb, Dobie, and Bedichek. Dobie heaped contempt upon the regents, calling them "native fascists." [25] (They found a reason to fire him a couple of years later.) Newspapers and magazines around the nation excoriated the regents. *Harper's* wrote that "a group of unscrupulous, but very clear minded men, then, have destroyed the University of Texas as an educational institution."[26] As a result of the board's actions, the university was placed on probation by its accrediting body, and the American Association of University Professors censured UT.

In the charged atmosphere that the firing and the legislative hearings produced, Rainey became a household name, and the New Dealers rallied to his support. Barely a year after the firing, in early 1946, Rainey decided to run for governor. Not all progressives, however, were enamored of him—Bedichek, for instance, did not find Rainey to have the popular appeal necessary for political success. But for many, the Rainey campaign sparked a level of passion that even surpassed that of the New Deal fights. Rainey's platform included abolishing the poll tax, encouraging development of a two-party system, and purging the Texas Regulars.

Eckhardt and his friends and colleagues jumped wholeheartedly into the campaign. J. R. Parten recruited D. B. Hardeman to be the campaign manager. Jimmie Allred advised the campaign. Minnie Fish, fresh from her own loss in the 1944 gubernatorial primary, campaigned across the state for Rainey, supervised part of the campaign office, and put her financial resources behind him, working with Marion Storm and Lillian Collier. J. Frank Dobie was also active for Rainey. In Waco, Bernard and Audre Rapoport were Rainey's Central Texas campaign managers. College had been so important to Rapoport that already by 1946 he had saved $2,500 for a college education for his future children. But he was so passionate about Rainey and his promise for Texas politics that he gave it all to the campaign. In Austin, the Office of Inter-American Affairs was just dissolving. Eckhardt was reopening his law office and continuing as a consultant to the Good Neighbor Commission when he signed on as Rainey's Travis County campaign coordinator.

Parten rented his usual suite at the Stephen F. Austin Hotel, hosting Rainey. One day he invited Eckhardt to walk over from his Scarbrough office to talk campaign strategy with Rainey, Allred, and himself. The three asked Eckhardt, who was still cartooning for the *Texas Spectator,* to include the gubernatorial campaign in one of his cartoons, and he did. The cartoon featured Rainey's opponents, Attorney General Grover Sellers and Lieutenant Governor John Lee Smith, coupling them with corporate power and UT censorship issues, all in one cartoon. It depicted sulfur and oil carrying off the state of Texas, next to a stack of Dos Passos's *USA Trilogy* books, with a voter (and Jack o' Diamonds) behind the stack reading the book. "If he'll only just keep reading that book till we can take the whole dern state to Wall Street," said sulfur. "Well, we got this screen to hide behind . . . thanks to Grover and John Lee, rest their souls," said oil.[27]

E K

Rainey was leading in the polls in July, with Railroad Commissioner Beauford Jester coming up into second place. Eckhardt helped organize a major July 5 rally for Rainey in Wooldridge Park. Dobie introduced Rainey, who read a fiery populist speech (written by Parten and Allred), demanding an end to the monopoly of Texas resources by northeastern interests and blasting the Texas Regulars and their smear campaign against him on race, religion, and communism.[28] But Rainey's campaign had peaked too early. As he surged into the lead, the other candidates turned their fire on him, and the Establishment began rallying behind one candidate to stop Rainey. On election day, Jester came in first with 38 percent and Rainey second with 25 percent.

The runoff was on. Jimmie Allred campaigned around the state for Rainey. Eckhardt and the Austin and state campaign pulled together another Austin rally in August, drawing 8,000 people. Rainey delivered a great fighting speech, reminiscent of Governor Jim Hogg—enough, in Lillian Bedichek's opinion, "to make the people of Texas conscious of their real masters, and the sleeping giant may turn, even wake up."[29]

The runoff campaign was despicable by any standards. Jester charged that Rainey was supported by Communists. Rainey was accused of being a "nigger lover." Parten sent Eckhardt to Corsicana to check out a rumor that Jester had once joined the Ku Klux Klan (KKK). Eckhardt found a hotel run by a liberal woman in the area and stayed there a couple of days, poking around. He found an elderly man who had known Jester and had kept records of the area's families and happenings, including KKK affairs. The records weren't in good shape—he and Eckhardt dug them out of an old henhouse, covered with chicken droppings. He told Eckhardt that Jester had tried to join the Klan, but that he couldn't get in because of rumors that he was partly Jewish![30] Eckhardt reported back to Parten, and they decided there was not enough information to be useful.

Jester won the runoff, with Rainey carrying only Travis and six other counties. The governor's state convention was then held in San Antonio. Eckhardt, a Travis County delegate, was pictured in a front-page *American-Statesman* photo, behind Everett Looney. The Austin crowd had lost the election, and now they were to lose again. Jester purged the SDEC, installing Jester loyalists and Texas Regular members.[31]

Rainey's loss was a devastating blow to the hopes, dreams, and egos of the young New Dealers. Rapoport was crushed. Chris Dixie was putting down his roots in Houston, readying to go into politics. But after the primaries he wrote to Walton Hamilton, saying that he was "licking the wounds of a disastrous political defeat, going down with Homer Rainey," and considering his options.[32] They had all seen Rainey as the savior of Texas and the campaign as a critical effort to change the world, especially around education issues, and they all grew closer as a result of the campaign. The Rainey campaign became a defining event in all their lives.[33]

The Texas Social and Legislative Conference

After the gubernatorial runoff, Rainey supporters and "independent liberals" gathered in Fort Worth to discuss where to go next. Eckhardt represented the Southwestern Telephone Workers' Union. He joined Jim Wright, Otto Mullinax, Minnie Fish, Marion Storm, Margaret and Jack Carter, and others at the Fort Worth meeting. The Carters had been active in YDs with Eckhardt and would be key players in later party battles and in the founding of the *Texas Observer*. Further meetings were held at the Driskill in Austin and in Waco.[34] They decided to create the "People's Legislative Committee," with the goal of recreating a populist movement. Eckhardt was elected secretary-treasurer and co-chaired a twenty-one-member committee to research and draft bills. The group endorsed an income tax, higher natural resource taxes, approval of Agriculture Secretary Charles Brannan's farm plan for parity, a state labor relations law, and increased unemployment compensation and workers' compensation. They opened an office in the Littlefield Building, with Marion Storm as the staffer, and immediately gained press attention. The *Nation* even reported on their activities.[35]

The People's Legislative Committee soon found that it made sense to join efforts with a new labor-sponsored group that Minnie Fish had also helped to get started. After the Texas Farmers Union convention in early 1944, officials of the CIO and the Farmers Union had met with Minnie Fish (just back from her New Deal agricultural work) to discuss a liberal-labor-farm coalition. A week later, representatives of labor, old age pension groups, the Farmers Union, and others met to create a statewide committee. Out of the discussion came the formation of the Texas State Joint Social and Legislative Conference. In the labor tug-of-war, the AFL promptly withdrew, but was later coaxed back in.

Soon, the group shortened its name to Texas Social and Legislative Conference (TS&LC). After Rainey's defeat, the state CIO Council determined that the TS&LC needed to expand to be effective. It urged inclusion of the NAACP, Latino organizations, and all CIO unions. The Council wrote to its locals that this was "an opportunity for us to do the thing which we have never done before, that is, to have all of the labor organizations and friendly liberal organizations working in the same direction with the same program, with unified leadership, to attain our common objectives in the social, legislative, and political education field."[36] By the Conference's third convention in January 1947, it had picked up several new members, including the People's

Legislative Committee, the American G.I. Forum, and the black Progressive Voters' League.[37]

The Conference proved to be a key, short-term bridge for labor, leading up to the 1957 AFL-CIO merger. In the 1940s, the AFL's Harry Acreman would hardly speak to the CIO's Morris Akin. But they all knew that they had to have a common front to fend off the fierce post-New Deal assaults on labor. The Conference's fourth convention was held in Waco, January 1948. By this time, Eckhardt was working with the Oil Workers in Fort Worth and was close to Akin. He was also acceptable to Acreman and to railway labor, and he was deeply involved with the independent (non-labor) liberals, so they agreed on him to head the Conference, and the AFL rejoined.[38]

In his new role as TS&LC chair, Eckhardt helped plan the fifth convention, held in October 1948, with a focus on precinct organizing and candidate recruitment. New CIO leader Jeff Hickman came to believe that the Conference was "primarily responsible for the winning of the State Democratic Convention in 1948."[39] Eckhardt chaired the Conference and its annual conventions for five years.

The Conference constantly had funding woes, with the unions battling over who was paying their fair share. Eckhardt even threw in some money of his own. They hired Marion Storm as full-time executive secretary and research director. Her magnetism and ability helped keep the organization together. She worked out of the Littlefield office that the small group of liberals had managed to keep open with one activity or another ever since their failed attempt to draft Dobie to run against Stevenson in 1944.

Chairman Eckhardt and the Conference immediately got caught up in the fratricidal labor wars. At the 1949 CIO convention, a Maritime leader moved to not fund the Conference. Oil Worker and Auto Worker officials leapt to the support of the Conference, and a Packinghouse Worker official said that a vote against the Conference would mean they might leave the CIO. With that support, the CIO Council approved the budget item for the Conference. But disgruntlement over funding equity continued. Eckhardt was also serving as chairman of the legislative committee of the Communication Workers of America. He defended his and the Conference's activities to the CWA's legislative director, writing that it was through the Conference that the first caucus organizing the opposition to the Dixiecrats was called and that the TS&LC was more responsible than any other entity in carrying the Fort Worth convention for Truman. He argued that there may not be a pro rata share of expenses being paid by non-CIO unions, but contributions from unaffiliated liberals and some AFL unions showed development in the right direction. Also, he maintained, labor had advanced more from 1947 to 1949 than in any decade and that the Conference had energized those activities. "To say that because we have not gained our final liberal objective we should junk the machinery we have set up in the last two years and turn to the lack-a-daisical methods that have achieved little progress over long periods of time is to fly in the face of all reason and experience," he wrote.[40]

The Executive Committee held monthly meetings all across the state. Occasionally Orissa would travel with Bob to the meetings. The Conference encouraged creation of local conferences, and the Executive Committee meetings were sometimes held in conjunction with local organizing efforts. After chairing an Executive Committee meeting in Waco in 1949, for instance, Eckhardt spoke to Waco's local Conference.[41] In Austin, the local chapter included many of Eckhardt's longtime associates. The Austin group was integrated, which forced it to vacate its meeting place at the segregationist public library.[42]

The TS&LC was an invigorating, fun movement for its adherents, who saw it as a vehicle that was pure on the issues of the day, such as abolishing the poll tax, promoting labor initiatives, and opposing lynching. It worked mainly with volunteers and amassed a contact list of 6,000 people who would spring into action when called.[43] Eckhardt was a spiritual leader of the group. Marion Storm, Minnie Fish, and Margaret Carter showed the importance of women leaders. The work that they did in the late 1940s and on into the early 1950s helped to make possible the 1950s Ralph Yarborough campaigns.[44]

The 1948 Texas Campaigns

The 1948 campaigns saved the sitting president's and a future president's political lives and, even though he was no longer in the familiar political territory of Austin, Eckhardt was in the thick of it all, as a party activist and as the TS&LC chair.

In the presidential race, Truman was pressed by third party candidates Henry Wallace on the left and Strom Thurmond on the right. In Eckhardt's parting shot as consultant to the Good Neighbor Commission in 1947, he reported to Truman's civil rights committee on abuses against Texan Latinos. The committee issued its report in 1947. Truman then integrated the military by executive order and, in February 1948, sent Congress his "Ten Point Charter of Human Rights," all of which reignited Southern anger.[45] Many Texas liberals were torn between supporting Truman to assure a defeat for Dewey or voting for the man they wanted to win, Henry Wallace. J. Frank Dobie and Johnny Faulk sided with Wallace, and Faulk hosted a campaign meeting at his family's new Green Pastures restaurant in their old home. Despite Eckhardt's *Spectator* cartoon deriding timid liberals, he, Fath, and others stayed with Truman.[46]

When Eckhardt was elected chairman of the TS&LC in early 1948 and Beauford Jester announced for reelection, Eckhardt lashed out at the man who had beaten Homer Rainey and destroyed the Good Neighbor Commission. In a news release that was picked up by newspapers and that garnered a chilly response from the Democratic Party's spokesman, Eckhardt blasted Governor Jester's alignment with the oil industry and the anti-civil rights Democrats (and presaged the critical 1950s issue of tidelands oil):

> Is Jester speaking for the Democrats, or for the Texas Regulars? The tall talk about civil rights is just a smokescreen to cover up the effort of the major oil companies to get the tidelands oil cheap. If the oil put by nature under Texas coastal waters is controlled by state officials, the oil companies will get it for one-eighth royalties. If it is controlled by the federal government, then the oil companies will have to pay up to one-fourth royalties, with most of the money coming back to the states. . . .
>
> If Jester and his fellow Regulars were successful in defeating Pres. Truman's re-election, who would be elected? A Republican, from a party historically pledged to a civil rights program which contains all the allegedly objectionable features of President Truman's civil rights report.
>
> Texas should not allow the oil crowd to distract the attention of true Democrats from the real issue: Who will run Texas, Texans or the Northern oil companies? [47]

By 1948, Senator O'Daniel had become an embarrassment even to the Texas Establishment. He sensed that he had lost his base. With O'Daniel's announced retirement, the hot 1948 campaign was the famous U.S. Senate race between Congressman Lyndon Johnson and former Governor Coke Stevenson that produced the twice-told tale of Box 13. Johnson decided to make a second run for the Senate (with Connally again managing his campaign). Thus, his central Texas congressional seat would be open. Creek Fath had just left his job with the Democratic National Committee and moved back to Austin, reopening his law office in the Littlefield Building. He ran for LBJ's congressional seat, but lost in the primary to Homer Thornberry.

Conservatives won many of the precinct conventions in 1948, triggering the usual credentials battles at the county and state conventions. Though a brand-new Dallas resident, Eckhardt plunged right into its politics. He was selected as a delegate to the state convention, where, with Governor Jester leading the anti–New Deal forces, Eckhardt's group was ultimately unseated.[48]

After the May convention, it was back to the primary campaigns. Angry with LBJ for voting for Taft-Hartley in 1947, the AFL supported Coke Stevenson; some CIO unions supported LBJ.[49] Stevenson led with 40 percent to LBJ's 34 percent, setting up an August runoff. LBJ whipped around the state in his famous helicopter tour, pulling off an upset in the runoff by 87 votes. John Connally would later acknowledge that they deliberately held back votes from South Texas so that they would not be the victims of similar tactics by Stevenson, as they had been by O'Daniel in the 1941 race. The LBJ campaign then reported their results, including the disputed votes in Box 13 of Jim Wells County, where, interestingly, many of the votes were cast in alphabetical order. Had LBJ lost, he was prepared to challenge the East Texas county totals that favored Stevenson.[50] Instead, it was Stevenson who challenged the results. He got a federal restraining order to stop certification of the LBJ victory. But LBJ's lawyers Alvin Wirtz, Ed Clark, and, in Washington, Abe Fortas, got the order overturned.

Meanwhile, at the Philadelphia national convention, former Texas Governor Dan Moody led a losing battle against Minneapolis Mayor Hubert Humphrey's civil rights plank. Though Texans did not bolt, other southern delegates did, forming the States' Rights Party and nominating South Carolina Governor Strom Thurmond for president.[51]

Liberals regained control of the September governor's state convention by winning the precinct and county conventions, just as they had in 1944. Eckhardt was again elected a delegate. The convention and a State Democratic Executive Committee meeting were held in Fort Worth and became the final battlegrounds in the LBJ-Stevenson election. The SDEC met to certify to the convention the primary results. Governor Jester's supporters on the SDEC were split between Stevenson and Johnson. The committee voted 29 to 28 to certify LBJ as the winner of the Senate primary.[52]

At the convention, a whole day was spent on credentials. The issue of which delegations would be seated was important both to the Truman campaign and to Johnson, who feared that Stevenson delegates could work to undo his SDEC victory, reopen Box 13, and give the nomination to Stevenson. Connally huddled with Eckhardt, Akin, and other labor leaders. Eckhardt was not particularly interested in protecting the Taft-Hartley supporter LBJ, but he was interested in protecting Truman by getting loyal electors. So Eckhardt, Connally, and the others worked out a deal to protect LBJ, in exchange for Johnson helping Truman by not seating the disputed (conservative) Harris County delegation.[53]

The first order of business was five hours of wrangling over Harris County. J. Edwin Smith chaired the Houston Truman delegation against the Houston Dixiecrats. Smith was born in San Marcos in 1911. He attended Southwest Texas State there (as had LBJ), then UT Law School with Eckhardt, editing the *Law Review*. Known as J. Ed or Smitty, he would come to serve as Eckhardt's attorney and campaign treasurer. They made an unusual pair—the six-foot-two Eckhardt towered over the five-foot-five Smith—but they shared an intellectualism and a passion for constitutionalism and the law. Smith framed the Bill of Rights for his office and quoted Sir Edward Coke and Justices Oliver Wendell Holmes Jr. and Louis Brandeis.[54]

The convention voted to unseat the Harris County anti-Truman delegation, many of whom were also Stevenson supporters, and to seat Smith and his delegation. When the Loyalists (and LBJ) won the delegate battles, the Stevenson/Texas Regular/Dixiecrat delegates bolted, their leader shouting, "You can't put me in bed with Truman and his Commiecrats." Since the conservatives had been in charge of organizing the convention, they retaliated by taking with them all their furniture and equipment! They took Sam Rayburn's table. He stood up and protested; they took his chair.[55] Maury Maverick talked for two hours while the Loyalists reorganized the convention. Jimmie Allred got the delegates to raise enough money to keep the hall open. In a replay of the 1944 scenario, delegates then ousted the May presidential electors who would not pledge to Truman. They required party officials to make a written pledge to support the party's nominees.[56] With no such pledge forthcoming, they then chose new Truman-supporting SDEC members.

Sam Rayburn, with D. B. Hardeman at his side, stumped for Truman across Texas and the South. Eckhardt campaigned around the state for Truman, and Fath helped organize the campaign's whistle-stop tour through Texas. In November, Truman won 66 percent of the vote in Texas to Dewey's 25 percent and the Dixiecrats' 9 percent. Most of the States' Rights votes came from East Texas Black Belt counties, as the Dixiecrat campaign had focused more on race-conscious whites than had the Texas Regulars' economic conservative campaign of 1944.[57]

In 1949, Eckhardt battled at the legislature against the new onslaught of anti-labor legislation, representing the TS&LC and the CWA. After the session, newly reelected Governor Jester died. Lieutenant Governor Allan Shivers, who had been UT student president when Eckhardt was at UT, assumed the office. The 1940s ended with Eckhardt as a rising star in the Texas labor movement and in the resurgent Loyalist Democratic faction; with the legislature dominated by anti-labor forces; and with the governor's mansion occupied by anti-labor Allan Shivers. The Eckhardts moved to Houston on January 1, 1950, and Eckhardt took his legal and political careers into the heart of the state's labor strength, which would propel him into the Texas legislature and ultimately into Congress.

SEVEN

Brother Eckhardt Goes to Houston

On January 1, 1950, at age thirty-six, Bob Eckhardt moved to Houston (Harris County) to work with Chris Dixie in labor law, and there he made his electoral career. His *Texas Ranger* cartooning friend Jack Guinn immediately profiled him in the *Houston Post* and included a sketch he drew of Eckhardt with the caption, "Jack O'Diamonds Rests His Brush." Guinn described Eckhardt as "a medium-large man with lots of black hair, eyes full of humor and a nose which wanders around a little before it becomes a nose."[1] Bob brought his family, his horse, his art tools, and his passion for progressive politics. Fifty years later, he would be named one of the top ten Houston political figures of the twentieth century.[2]

Becoming a Houstonian

Orissa got a job with an architectural firm, and they soon decided to build a house. They found a lot on a dirt road in a West Houston wooded area just being developed. Bob and Orissa would visit the lot and lie on the ground, talking about their plans. Looking up through the canopy of oak trees, Bob said, "there ought to be a skylight," so she designed one. For months, Bob, Orissa, and the girls would picnic at the lot, watching their new home go up.

It was a beautiful house, and they came to love living at 4527 W. Alabama Avenue. The L-shaped red brick house was set back on the lot, built around three large oak trees. The Eckhardts did not fit in well with what developed as a manicured suburban neighborhood. They planted trees, bamboo, and other plants to grow a barrier. With a lot of glass in the front, a large, open living room/dining room with a giant fireplace, and the skylight, the house was very bright. Orissa did not like a lot of people in the kitchen while she was cooking, so she designed a small kitchen. They built a roof deck and spent time there or on the brick patio, where Bob grilled steaks, an outdoor activity he loved and continued throughout his life.

Orissa didn't share Bob's passion for horses, but he was determined to have one in Houston. Robert Smith, the former chair of the Good Neighbor Commission, was a baseball aficionado who had funded the nearby Bob

Smith Ball Park. Smith agreed to let Eckhardt keep a horse there. Brother Norman gave him June, a descendant of Dixie and YoYo, the horses from their boyhood days at 2300 Rio Grande. So Bob tethered, watered, and fed her in the park, eventually building a little shed and getting a second horse. When he needed rope for the horse, he would leave from work, buy it downtown, sling it over his shoulder, and head back to his office. In the elevator, he encountered jokes—"Who you gonna lynch?"—that reminded him he was definitely in the South.[3]

Eckhardt soon bred his horses, proud that they had descended from YoYo. They were quarter horse–American saddle horse breeds, well gaited with a very smooth ride. Just as the first Robert Christian Eckhardt had a distinctive whistle that he used when he approached the Eckhardt Ranch, Bob also had a unique whistle, and his horses would come running at the sound of it.

Bob and the girls would ride at a fast trot through Memorial Park and in the neighborhoods. Horses and Bob went together, and though she was afraid of horses, Little Orissa learned that if she wanted to spend time with Poppa, she would do so on horseback. Riding allowed them quiet time together. One horse, Buck, often reared up, and Bob would use his big weight against his neck to bring the horse down. Once when Rosalind was riding Buck, he reared up and she threw her tiny weight against his neck. The horse fought back, expecting Bob's weight, and toppled over backward with Rosalind. She was terrified, but Bob insisted that she get back on him. Rosalind inherited his love of horses; forty years later, he would be riding *her* horses in Colorado.

Bob had gone with Orissa to the Unitarian church in Dallas. In Houston, Orissa joined the First Unitarian Church on Main Street. She went to church on Sundays, but Bob preferred to take the girls horseback riding. Still, he would go occasionally. He even got invited to preach, and did so once, delivering a sermon about Huck Finn rafting down the Mississippi River, agonizing over whether to turn in Jim.

The Eckhardts socialized in and outside of Houston. Hubert Mewhinney was back at the *Houston Post,* and the Eckhardts and Mewhinneys often dined together. Mewhinney learned how to flake flint and in 1957 published *A Manual for Neanderthals* on Stone Age flint tools and weapons, with Eckhardt drawing its sketches of Neanderthal men.[4] The Texas-based members of the UT and Austin gang, led by Fred Schmidt, decided to regularize get-togethers as family campouts. They named their group the Maverick Society, in honor of one of their mentors, Maury Maverick Sr. The Maverick campers—Schmidts, Eckhardts, Wellses, Mullinaxes, Carters, soon the Duggers, and others—would gather at Walter Webb's ranch and other places around Texas to enjoy a weekend picnicking, kids playing together, swimming, and talking. Eckhardt would sit around the fire and *think* and talk with the others, bringing philosophy to the woods.

Bob's labor and political work often took him to Austin, so he frequently saw Norma and Joe. Then, in 1953, Joe Eckhardt died. Bob wept at the news of his father's death. As he and little Orissa were filling June's water trough, he was deep in thought about his dad. As his eyes began tearing, he said, "He was the best man I knew."[5] Dr. Eckhardt had been a powerful influence on Bob's life. He was also a direct link for Bob back to the original German Eckhardts and Klebergs who had landed nearby in Harrisburg.

The Magnolia City

Galveston had been the nineteenth-century center of life in Texas, while Houston was a humid, mosquito-infested inland city in Harris County. The county is on the coastal plain, the San Jacinto River running through it, the Trinity River just to the east. In 1915, completion of a deepwater seaport and a ship channel from the Gulf of Mexico inland to Houston, by then nicknamed the Magnolia City, triggered booming growth and the resulting decline of Galveston (already devastated by the 1900 hurricane). By 1950, Harris County's population had burgeoned to 800,000.

In the early 1900s, the ship channel and deepwater seaport provided an advantageous location for oil refineries, near the booming oil fields of East Texas. By 1950, natural gas—no longer a nuisance—had become strong in the Texas economy, and Houston the most important gas center in the nation. Paper, steel, and other industries saw the advantage of being close to an energy supply and transportation system. By the 1970s, more than one hundred companies were crowding the channel.[6] Shipping, too, became critical to the local economy. As industry grew, so did industrial problems in the whole coastal area. In 1947, Texas City, between Houston and Galveston, became the site of the largest man-made disaster in Texas history when ships and refineries exploded, killing 600 people and forever etching the catastrophe into the history of the area.

HOUSTON'S ESTABLISHMENT

The hugely important captains of Houston industry intertwine with Eckhardt's political careers in Austin and Washington. Jesse Jones and other wealthy businessmen built a downtown Houston to showcase to the world—including the Shamrock, Lamar, and Rice Hotels. Jones, a master financier, served Woodrow Wilson and Herbert Hoover before cementing his stature as a superpower by working with Franklin Roosevelt. Jones owned the *Houston Post,* then bought the *Houston Chronicle* and sold the *Post* to William P. Hobby.[7]

Other magnates included Gus Wortham, Walter Mischer, James Elkins, Joe Foy, Hugh Roy Cullen, and James Abercrombie. The Liedtke brothers— J. Hugh and William C.—partnered with George H. W. Bush to found Zapata Petroleum and Zapata Offshore Company.[8] J. R. Parten had moved his company's headquarters to Houston in the 1930s. Good Neighbor Commission Chairman Robert Smith was a Houston-based oilman who allied with State Representative Roy Hofheinz, helping elect him mayor in 1952 over the Establishment's powerful 1920s–1950s mayor, Oscar Holcombe.

At the center of the Houston Establishment was another pair of businessmen, long a part of Eckhardt's legal and political affairs. During World War II, George and Herman Brown established Brown Shipbuilding, constructing ships for the Navy. After the war, they bought Texas Eastern Transmission Co. and thus became players in the oil and gas industry. As George Brown recalled, "we just formed one corporation after another" in ships, oil and gas, and construction.[9] Later, when President Kennedy started pushing for a manned spacecraft center, the focus turned from Cape Canaveral to Houston, partly as a lure for Albert Thomas to support appropriations for the project. George Brown lobbied his friend Thomas for the Houston location, on Humble Oil & Refining Co. land, and Brown & Root Construction Company became a prime contractor on the new facility.[10]

The legal, financial, and communications arms of the Houston Establishment were extensive and so intertwined as to make it impossible to separate them. Houston's lawyers were, like characters in George Orwell's *Animal Farm,* indistinguishable from their clients, leading the boards of directors of banks, corporations, Rice University, and the University of Houston, and taking their law clients to their banks. Socially, the families intermarried.[11] This Establishment was not just a happenstance, but also a coordinated political enterprise. Wortham, Elkins, Jones, Hobby, and the Brown brothers would meet in the Browns' Suite 8-F at Jesse Jones's Lamar Hotel. They became known as the "8-F Crowd" and continued to meet and coordinate their political recruitments, endorsements, and finances for decades. Searcy Bracewell, an Eisenhower Democrat, senior partner in Bracewell and Patterson, and confidant of the 8-F Crowd, became their legislator in the Texas House and Senate, then a lobbyist for them.

THE COLOR LINE

The city that Eckhardt moved to was highly segregated, with a sad history in race relations. When black troops were stationed in Houston after the Civil War, white citizens rioted. In 1917, black troops and white policemen clashed, sparking riots that left sixteen dead. Lynchings scarred early twentieth-century Houston. The Democratic Party chose to hold its national convention in Houston in 1928, though the city was firmly and deeply ensconced in the segregation culture. Black delegates were forced to sit separately, behind chicken wire.[12]

Houston's labor unions were also segregated. Many in the surging labor movement were racist, while others in the movement fought for inclusion. In the year that Eckhardt began his Houston labor law practice, premier Houston labor lawyer Arthur Combs was bitterly criticized in union meetings for denying blacks the right to attend the Democrats' Jefferson-Jackson Dinner.[13]

Local leadership emerged from within the black community to fight the racism. Carter Wesley published the *Houston Informer* and became a leader of the community. The Houston NAACP was a proud and active chapter, taking on the white primary and sponsoring Heman Sweatt's integration case against the UT Law School. The Houston NAACP so antagonized the Establishment that Governor Shivers and Attorney General John Ben Shepperd filed barratry charges against it![14]

Black voter registration in the South was nearly nonexistent as late as 1940, and the white primary made registration worthless anyway. The 1944 *Smith v. Allwright* decision and the postwar organizing by black leaders stirred political activism in the community. Houston blacks showed their increasing political clout in 1958 by electing the first black to office in Harris County since Reconstruction: Mrs. Charles E. White won election to the school board.[15] The 1965 Voting Rights Act further energized black voter registration and participation.[16]

Alongside the residential and political segregation of blacks in Houston was the segregation of Latinos. Though their early numbers were small, Latinos grew as a percentage of Houston's population throughout the twentieth century. They resided predominantly in south Houston, including the barrio known as Magnolia, or "Little Mexico."[17] By the 1950s, Houston Latinos were becoming more politically active. John Herrera, who had served as the LULAC counsel in the *Delgado* case with Eckhardt and Gus Garcia, served as national LULAC president, as did fellow Houstonian Felix Tijerina. Tijerina launched the "Little Schools of the 400" project to teach 400 English words to preschoolers.

LABOR

As industry boomed in Houston in the 1930s and 1940s, the need for a sizeable labor pool increased. The employment growth created an environment ripe for union organizing. By the late 1950s, there were nearly 100,000 union members in Harris County, making up about 20 percent of the labor force, and by the time Eckhardt went to Congress in the late 1960s, 56 percent of Houston companies recognized union representation.[18]

Houston's labor growth occurred as unionization at the state level was maturing. In 1953 young, liberal Jerry Holleman became executive secretary of the Texas State Federation of Labor. Two years later, Eckhardt's friend Fred Schmidt with the Oil, Chemical and Atomic Workers was elected executive secretary of the State Council of the CIO. National talks for merging the AFL and the CIO produced agreement in 1955, and Holleman and Schmidt completed the Texas merger in the summer of 1957. The new Texas union decided on a dual leadership structure. Holleman was elected president of the new Texas AFL-CIO and Schmidt was elected secretary-treasurer.

Eckhardt's Houston Labor Law Practice

The Houston law firm of Mandell and Combs did most of the coastal area labor law practice in the 1930s and 1940s. Eckhardt's UT friends Chris Dixie, Herman Wright, and Otto Mullinax joined that firm before Mullinax moved on to Dallas. Soon, the big four labor lawyers in the state were Dixie and Wright in Houston and Mullinax and Nat Wells in Dallas.

News of Eckhardt's move to Houston rippled through the law community. From the Abe Fortas law firm in Washington, Walton Hamilton congratulated Eckhardt. "You will soon be the established and yet the pioneer firm in the Southwest," Hammy wrote. "You can no more stay out of politics than can Chris, but I hope that the two of you hit upon exactly the right mixture."[19] Eckhardt's work won him respect in the legal community. In 1952 he was elected vice-chair, and in 1953 chair, of the Labor Law Section of the State Bar.[20]

With offices in the Scanlan Building (built on the site where Sam Houston had lived when he was president of Texas), the law firm soon included Chris Dixie, Thomas Ryan, Meyer Jacobson, Al Schulman, Bob Eckhardt, and Ed Ball.[21] Their legal secretary was a stickler for doing everything by the book. Eckhardt would tell Schulman, "I'd have to jump in the out box to get out of here." Eckhardt became a prolific and brilliant brief writer. But, true to form, he turned in his work at 11:59 p.m. on the day it was due, and considered that quite good.[22]

Eckhardt and Ryan later separated from the firm, forming Ryan, Eckhardt and Adams (James N. Adams), but continued to work and share offices with Dixie.[23] Later, Eckhardt moved to the Sterling Building. His office was a mess—stacks of books and papers everywhere. He built his own cabinets and somehow found time to start carving a frieze for his wall, planning to go all around the office.[24] Adams eventually left, and the firm of Ryan and Eckhardt continued into the 1970s.

Lawyer Eckhardt in his Houston office. Throughout the 1950s, Eckhardt practiced
labor law in Houston. Here, he puzzles over a brief. He built the bookshelves on
which he placed his carving of the same Shakespeare quotation he had in his first
law office in Austin's Littlefield Building. Courtesy of the Center for American
History, University of Texas at Austin, DI 02933.

Eckhardt represented steelworkers, teamsters, reporters, and other unions,
but his primary client was the Communication Workers of America.[25]
Eckhardt would serve as counsel for CWA local unions in disputes before the
American Arbitration Association's Voluntary Labor Arbitration Tribunal.
He hated driving and loved the train, so Orissa and the girls were always
taking him down to the train station. He was invariably late, often forgetting
important papers. Sometimes they would rush with him to the track with
goodbye kisses and hugs, watching him jump on the train as it was pulling
out. Once as he jumped on the Pullman, disheveled and grabbing his legal
papers, tied together with strings, a porter commented to another porter,
"There's an upper berth passenger if ever I saw one!"[26]

He traveled to Little Rock, New Orleans, St. Louis, and other locations. He
won cases where telephone workers brought charges against Bell, and he won
reversal of company decisions to suspend workers.[27] The clients he helped
remembered him. Years later, he received a letter from a woman fired from
her job with General Telephone Co. in Port Lavaca in 1958. Eckhardt won re-
instatement for her with all her seniority rights. "I have never forgotten you,"

she wrote, "and have followed you in the newspapers regarding your efforts in the political game in Washington. . . . I want you to know I appreciate all you did in regaining my job for me."[28]

Representing individual workers was the bread-and-butter work of his practice, but he was also deeply involved in the major battles that erupted between businesses and unions, each trying to defend their interests and test the boundaries of the new labor laws. In the late 1940s and early 1950s, Southwestern Bell was enjoining strikes, often through a state judge in Midland. Bell argued that the strikes were illegal under both state and federal law; therefore, they could bring action in the favorable state courts (where they would plead only the state issues). But once during the legal battles over a Pecos CWA strike, Bell made the mistake of joining the state and federal issues together before the state judge, and Dixie and Eckhardt decided to counterattack. Dixie went to Midland, while Eckhardt went to a federal judge and filed a petition for removal of the case to the federal court. He argued that because the case was both federal and state, regardless of where it was pleaded, once federal questions were raised the case could be removed to the federal level. The judge granted the petition for removal.

Persuading a federal judge bought time and forced negotiations. Eckhardt used this tactic all across the trans-Pecos area and beyond. With such tactics and victories, the firm gained a reputation of having some of the best labor lawyers in the country. There were so many labor actions in Texas that Eckhardt and his colleagues knew more about how to counter business tactics than just about anyone.[29]

In 1950, Brown & Root sought an injunction against the AFL and ninety affiliates. Nat Wells defended the unions, but Eckhardt and other CIO lawyers jumped in, too. Brown & Root won a series of ten-day restraining orders lasting 180 days, stopping ninety-two unions from any activity against the company, then won a temporary injunction.[30] Eckhardt later regretted that they did not have the case removed to federal court, at least to stop the injunction for a week while the motion was debated, but they had not yet come up with that tactic.[31]

Labor actions could sometimes get rough, even for the lawyers. Eckhardt once had to get a union member out of jail. The part-time sheriff was powerful in the community, working simultaneously for oilman Hugh Roy Cullen. Twice, Eckhardt brought him surety bonds and the sheriff, surrounded by his mastiffs, refused to accept them. The second time, he took off his pistols and threw Eckhardt out of the building physically. So Eckhardt engineered a call from a politically powerful person who knew the sheriff. When Eckhardt came rapping on the door a third time, now with a writ of habeas corpus, the sheriff finally was pressured into giving up the union member on bond.[32]

Eckhardt's Emerging Political Leadership

Walton Hamilton was right. Eckhardt could not stay out of politics. Upon his arrival in Houston, he jumped into the Houston political scene. In the 1950s, an ultra-right organization named the "Minute Women" stirred up a Houston Red Scare to go along with that of Joe McCarthy in Washington.[33] Eckhardt, Dixie, and their allies were involved in the fierce school board election battles of 1952 and 1954 between the Minute Women and the progressive faction. The *Houston Post* took heat for running articles that exposed the Minute Women and their dubious tactics. Unions sponsored a testimonial dinner for the reporter who wrote the nationally acclaimed stories. Eckhardt bought his tickets to the event from a young reporter named Keith Ozmore. This was the first time that the two met; Ozmore would later become a key Eckhardt staffer.[34]

Labor politics were exclusively Democratic, and Eckhardt's state party initiatives were immediately recognized in the kitchen of Gulf Coast labor politics. In the fall of 1950, a CWA delegate to the Houston Area Industrial Union Council reported that "Brother Eckhardt" had given a "good solid Democratic address" during the state Democratic convention. Eckhardt would speak to the Council in his role as CWA attorney, explaining the right-to-work law and legislation for the 1951 session.[35] He also went to Washington for the CWA. Young Congressman Lloyd Bentsen Jr., son of the Good Neighbor Commission appointee Lloyd Bentsen with whom Eckhardt had worked, was one of the few congressmen that Eckhardt found he could really talk to. Bentsen was quite conservative and wouldn't necessarily support labor's position, but Eckhardt was impressed that Bentsen would listen and talk.

As Texas Social and Legislative Conference chair, Eckhardt continued to travel the state, meeting with its board each month and reporting to them on the legislative agenda. He brought in and introduced guests such as his old hero Maury Maverick, his old Oil Worker boss Jack Knight, the NAACP's Donald Jones, and the G.I. Forum's Dr. Hector Garcia.[36] Bob was assisted by Marion Storm and Margaret Reading. Marion developed as a respected organizer in the liberal community. She had helped organize both the People's Legislative Committee, bringing it into the Conference, and local Conference organizations around Texas, and she was elected as a member of the State Democratic Executive Committee. On July 2, 1950, Storm headed north from Austin to Fort Worth, but she never made it. Near Temple, a two-car collision spun one of those cars head-on into her car, and she died. She was only thirty-five years old. The Conference, the People's Legislative Committee, and allies on the SDEC were devastated by her death. Eckhardt and others put together a Marion Storm Memorial Fund.[37]

EK
♡

1950 Elections

Newly minted Governor Allan Shivers, wearing his bright blue tie with a Lone Star flag, ran for the office for the first time in 1950, just a year after Governor Jester's death. Shivers was unquestionably a dynamic, strong leader. A key leader of his troops was Jake Pickle, just as Connally had become LBJ's key leader. Pickle organized every county for Shivers in 1950, and Shivers won an overwhelming victory.

Liberals planned a strong push at the governor's convention in Mineral Wells, but so did Shivers. Walter G. Hall, a banker from Dickinson in the Houston-Galveston area, was one of the liberal organizers for the convention and would become a close Eckhardt ally and financier over the next thirty years. But all the planning and organizing was to no avail. Shivers and Pickle used an array of dirty tricks—denying liberals hotel rooms, having police run them out of a park, disabling their microphones, and impounding their cars.[38] They blocked the seating of liberal delegates and put Shivers's supporters on the SDEC, leaving but a few of the 1948 Fort Worth Democrats in place.

Meanwhile, in San Antonio, Maury Maverick's son Maury Jr. was running for the Texas House of Representatives. Henry B. Gonzalez, who had briefly been at UT during Eckhardt's years there, was also running for another San Antonio seat in the legislature. Both Maverick and Gonzalez made the runoffs, and they teamed up in the runoff campaign; Maverick won his seat, but Gonzalez lost his. But Henry B., as he was known, was to become a fixture in Texas and national politics for decades, while Maverick would serve in elected office only briefly before becoming a famed civil liberties lawyer. In 1953, Gonzalez won a San Antonio city council seat and pushed through an ordinance desegregating city facilities.[39] He would energize the Latino community in 1956 when he ran against an incumbent state senator. He won and entered the orbit of statewide progressive politics with Eckhardt.

Lobbyist Eckhardt, 1951

During the 1951 legislative session, labor lobbyist Eckhardt plied the road between Houston and Austin. He began his habit of meandering the back roads, looking for ripe field corn, antique shops, and old Eckhardt/Kleberg settlements, such as Cat Spring. The old *Daily Texan* editor and Homer Rainey campaign manager, now State Representative D. B. Hardeman led the liberal forces in 1951, teaching them how to count votes. Liberals would gather at D. B.'s apartment, where he would get a few drinks down and make an inspiring address, imploring his colleagues to keep fighting. Sometimes he got such a hangover that he wouldn't show up at the capitol the next day.[40] As a result of the hard-fought tax battles, Hardeman was defeated in 1952 but won again in 1954, then went on to work for U.S. House Speaker Sam Rayburn.

Eckhardt would join his legislative allies as they drank and plotted, helping them strategize and feeding them information. Once, he sat in the gallery writing a speech for Representative Edgar Berlin; ever the procrastinator, Eckhardt had not finished writing the speech, and Berlin was already speaking. So Eckhardt dropped down a page at a time as he wrote it, with Berlin then reading it, not knowing what words he would find next![41] Eckhardt was such a likable character that he made friends with capitol politicos from many camps. One such friend was young Bill Hobby Jr., son of *Houston Post* owners William and Oveta Culp Hobby. Bill Jr. was in and out of the capitol, covering the legislature for the *Post*. He and Eckhardt got to know and like each other. The senior Hobby had been governor, and Mrs. Hobby had served as parliamentarian for the Texas House and later as the first woman cabinet member, in Eisenhower's administration. In 1959, Bill Jr. became parliamentarian for the Texas Senate during Eckhardt's first session as a House member.[42]

Eckhardt's CWA and TS&LC lobbying blended together. Eckhardt and other labor lawyers drafted a package of bills sponsored by the Conference. On the other side, anti-labor Senator George Parkhouse sponsored a resolution to investigate unions for violations of the 1947 labor laws. He also introduced SB 267, making union preference agreements antitrust violations. Eckhardt wrote that the prime objectives of the Conference in the session should be fighting the anti-labor and sales tax bills, and he sent the Conference's program to each legislator, with a note from him. Parkhouse wrote back that he was pleased to have it "to guide me in my voting because whatever you are 'fer' I'm 'again' and vice versa."[43]

When the TS&LC board met in March 1951, they got a kick out of reading aloud Parkhouse's letter, but Eckhardt also warned that SB 267 was as bad as the nine 1947 laws. With wounds from the 1950 legal battles with Brown & Root still smarting, Walter Hall wrote that the bill "relieves Brown & Root of the cost of prosecuting those whom they feel have done them harm." Indeed, they fought it hard, but lost.[44]

The labor-liberal coalition was keenly interested in election legislation, fearing that changes could tilt the system even more to the Establishment. Eckhardt appointed a TS&LC committee to watch congressional redistricting, already foreseeing it as a crucial issue, years before it became his ticket to Congress. Governor Shivers supported "cross-filing" of candidates in more than one party's primary. He argued that it "will not damage the Democratic Party in any way," while Walter Hall expressed the view of labor and liberals that the bill (which passed) "is a plan suggested by [Harry] Byrd of Virginia, who advises that all Southern States nominate Republican candidates." Margaret Carter wrote to Eckhardt that the bill would "put the electoral vote of Texas in the Governor's pocket."[45] The issue would influence the next year's presidential politics.

THE RED SCARE

As Joseph McCarthy, Richard Nixon, and Martin Dies were whipping up the Red Scare that would come to mark the years known as the McCarthy Era, and as Houston was experiencing its own version with local tyrants (the Minute Women), the anti-Red virus spread across the state. Political leaders infected by it saw the scare as a powerful weapon that could be used against their ideological opponents. Maury Maverick Jr. wrote that if you believed in unions, academic freedom, dignity for African-Americans, and a living wage for Mexican-Americans, you were tarred as a Communist.[46]

Leaders of the scare movement charged that Reds were sweeping all over Texas. The 1951 legislature featured a revival of hearings on Communism at UT. This time, they aimed at Economics Professor Clarence Ayres, with a resolution urging his firing for advocating an income tax and opposing loyalty tests. Eckhardt and his Conference worked into the night producing letters that went all over the state to whip up opposition. The anti-Ayres effort fizzled out in the Senate.

The social, psychological, and political pressure to join the witch hunt was intense and pervasive. The few brave souls willing to fight it met nightly at Hardeman's apartment. Twenty-nine-year-old Maverick Jr. was among them. Eckhardt was one of the few people who would try to pep up the holdouts, encouraging them to keep going and keep proposing amendments. He would sit in the gallery and draft amendments, floating them down to allies on the floor.[47]

Even Maury Jr. got scared. When the Ayres resolution came to the floor, he lost his courage. He so feared what might happen to him if he voted "nay" that he decided to duck the vote. Only Johnny Barnhart, a friend of Eckhardt's from his UT days, voted nay. The next day, Maverick Sr. called his son and said he had noticed that the name Maverick was not listed as voting on the resolution. "Where were you?" he demanded. Maury Jr. replied, "Papa, I was hiding in the toilet." Senior said, "You little shithouse liberal," and slammed the phone down. Maury Jr. was humiliated.[48]

THE GAS HOUSE GANG

To shore up the state budget, Governor Shivers, businesses, and Establishment Democrats supported an omnibus tax bill that included a sales tax.

Senator George Nokes and Representative Jim Sewell introduced a competing bill proposing a "gas-gathering" tax on natural gas pipelines, similar to
Eckhardt's 1947 graduated oil tax bill that Sewell and Jim Wright had carried.
Sewell, a Corsicana lawyer who had been blinded by an explosion on his ship
in World War II, was a war hero others would eagerly follow. He fashioned
a rural-urban coalition and packaged the tax bill with funding for Representative (and future Governor) Dolph Briscoe's rural roads program, thus
broadening their coalition.[49] Amazingly, Sewell pushed it through the House.
But the Senate would not go along and Shivers called a special session for the
summer.

The House coalition hunkered down. To beat the economic crunch of a
special session (they were paid only $5 per day), they pooled resources and
rented a big house at 1700 Rio Grande Street, announcing that they would
stay as long as it took to defeat the sales tax bill. Up to twenty-two people
lived there at one time or another. Eckhardt cheered them on, along with
many other allies. Liquor lobbyists sent bourbon. Supporters sent crates of
fruit, rounds of cheese, sides of bacon, and homemade jam, furniture, linens,
and ashtrays. Even the county judges' organization sent grand luncheons and
gallons of milk. The stalwart legislators—primarily rural, poorer members—
quickly gained the name "the Gas House Gang" and draped across the front
porch of the house banners that read "The People's Legislative Headquarters"
and "Let Texas Gas Pave the Way—the Free Ride's Over." D. B. would walk
back and forth across the living room with a dry Beefeater gin martini in his
hand imploring everyone to fight.[50]

With all the attention that the Gas House Gang won and the coalition they
built, Sewell and Hardeman won a compromise version of the tax. When
Shivers realized that they had beaten him, he sat down with them. "OK, boys,
you win this one; maybe I'll win the next one."[51] It was the first major change
in the Texas tax structure since Allred's administration. But perhaps Shivers
knew something they didn't. Seven pipeline companies filed suit in January
1952 and won a decision declaring the tax unconstitutional.[52] Eckhardt made
mental notes for the next round on taxes.

Organizing Democrats

Eckhardt's Texas Social and Legislative Conference was soon joined by other
arms of the liberal effort to gain control of the Texas Democratic Party—
particularly two new organizations, the Loyal Democrats of Texas and the
Harris County Democrats (HCDs). After the 1951 summer legislative session, the TS&LC board met at Margaret Reading's farm in Waller County.
They discussed contacting D. B. Hardeman and seeing how the Conference

could help him and the other members of the Gas House Gang. Then Eckhardt adjourned the meeting to a barbecue at the county fairgrounds. Maury
Maverick Sr. joined them for the afternoon meeting and offered his Sunshine
Ranch for the next meeting. That meeting at Maverick's ranch featured beer,
barbecue, and a speech by Sewell on the tax bill. The group selected a committee, including Eckhardt and Walter Hall, to help organize local Democratic clubs.[53] At the same time, CIO leaders huddled with others to plan a
statewide Democratic organization. They worked with Eckhardt and Hall on
plans for a kickoff fund-raising breakfast for the new "Loyal Democrats of
Texas" that would include the local clubs.

For the October annual TS&LC convention, the board invited Truman's
Agriculture Secretary Charles F. Brannan to speak, with plans to then use him
at the fund-raiser for the Loyal Democrats of Texas. The day the Conference
opened its convention, the Loyal Democrats held their "Brannan Breakfast"
in Austin's Commodore Perry Hotel. More than three hundred of the liberal
community from around the state attended, including Eckhardt. Brannan
spoke, then Walter Hall was chosen to chair the new group.[54] After the breakfast, Eckhardt and many of the others walked over to the Driskill, where he
called the TS&LC convention together. Eckhardt told the delegates of the big
victory on the Sewell-Nokes bill and a victory on an old age pension bill, then
lamented the passage of the Parkhouse bill. "Next year," he said, "our most
important work will be in organizing our precinct, county and state conventions to insure that the Texas delegation to the National Democratic Convention will carry out the wishes of the majority of the people of Texas."[55] Fagan
Dickson and Creekmore Fath would soon prevail upon Hall to form a key
Volunteer Legal Aid Committee, to be chaired by John Cofer and to include
Eckhardt, Fath, Maverick Jr., Dixie, and Nat Wells.[56] Dickson and Cofer led
legal battles against the poll tax and for party loyalty oaths. Cofer would go
on to become a judge, and Dickson ran unsuccessfully against Jake Pickle for
Congress.

Meanwhile, the CIO crowed to their members that "our representatives
working through the Texas Social and Legislative Conference initiated the
plan for the Brannan breakfast."[57] It is particularly perplexing, then, that labor turned against the TS&LC. Bob and Orissa hosted the December board
meeting at their new Houston home, where a labor representative complained, "We've been a miserable failure." That got Minnie Fish's blood boiling. She recounted the founding of the Conference and added, "This has been
no miserable failure. It has been a glorious success and has a glorious future.
Our failure has been in not asking for the finances to run the conference."
Farm and liberal bloc members defeated labor's motion to cut staffing. Orissa

brought out lunch from her small kitchen, then they discussed the upcoming poll tax drive in the afternoon.[58]

About the same time, a Harris County labor-liberal-minority coalition effort was born—a coalition that Eckhardt would later chair. Eddie Ball, who had been introduced to the cartoonist Eckhardt in Austin, headed the Houston Truman campaign in 1948. He saw a need to form a local organization separate from the party, but it would take several years before the Harris County Democrats formally organized. After Dixie successfully pushed him to get his law degree, Ball acted as the key political organizer for the group, joining Dixie and Eckhardt in their law firm before going to work for the steelworkers union.[59]

One day during the 1952 presidential campaign, a woman walked into the Houston campaign office and asked how she could help. Mrs. R. D. (Frankie) Randolph had arrived and would orchestrate liberal Democratic organizing in Texas for years. Her family was from East Texas and had gained wealth from the lumber industry. Ball told her that he could use help organizing all the files. She paid for filing cabinets, phones, typewriters, and furniture, then started organizing precinct chairs. Frankie had a hearty laugh and a deep, husky voice. She liked conversation and good Scotch and became revered as a hard-working leader and organizer. She attracted others, including twenty-four-year-old Billie Carr. Billie worked side-by-side with Frankie and took over once Frankie retired in the 1960s.[60]

Immediately after the 1952 election, about a dozen people met and decided to create a permanent organization. They planned a kickoff meeting for March 2. That integrated gathering of the new Harris County Democrats drew 110 people, including Eckhardt, Eddie and Eleanor Ball, Chris Dixie, African American dentist Lonnie Smith (of *Smith v. Allwright* fame), and Christia Adair, a leader of the NAACP. J. Edwin Smith was elected chair. Smith would serve four years (1953–1957), to be followed by Eckhardt (1957–1961).

The Harris County Democrats was a three-legged stool—minorities, white liberals, and labor. They met in union halls because other facilities were segregated. Once, they could not find a banquet site that would accept black guests. The Rice Hotel finally agreed, but only for a buffet where no one sat down together. Some elderly African American women sat in the few chairs that were left in the room, prompting the management to come in and remove those chairs. HCD referred to their standing-only gathering as "vertical integration." (Only later, when Conrad Hilton bought the Shamrock Hotel, was a truly integrated banquet held.)[61] Still, many of the minority members of HCD resented labor's influence in the group because many unions were racially segregated and because labor precincts could not be counted on to support black candidates. It was not until 1968 that the first black chair of HCD was elected. Many minorities believed that the group was controlled by a small clique of whites connected with labor or with Dixie's law firm and that the HCD did not deal with their issues.[62]

Yarborough v. The Establishment, Round 1

Ralph Yarborough had lost his 1938 race for attorney general, then got pulled into the war and his law practice. As the 1952 political season began, Attorney General Price Daniel was running for the Senate, so Yarborough began generating support for another race for attorney general. In a colorful exchange that was to have repercussions for decades, Yarborough reported that he ran into Governor Shivers in the capitol rotunda. Shivers told him that John Ben Shepperd had already been slated as the candidate for attorney general. Yarborough headed to the Littlefield Building, huddled with Fagan Dickson and Creekmore Fath, continued his tour of the state, and returned to Austin to announce that "if I'm going to fight an organized machine, a conspiracy against democracy . . . then I might as well buck the lead dog," and he went down to party headquarters and filed to run against Shivers.[63] Eckhardt began what would become two decades of campaigning for Yarborough. Though Yarborough lost, his 37 percent of the vote against the incumbent governor was higher than most had expected.

Phenomenally large crowds gathered at the May 3, 1952, precinct conventions. The Loyalists tried to repeat 1944, asking their followers to walk out of any convention that refused to pledge loyalty. But Shivercrats defeated the Loyalists, except in Maverick's Bexar County, Hall's Galveston County, and San Angelo. County conventions then became battlegrounds, and rump county conventions erupted. In Houston, the Loyalists lost at the county convention, and Eckhardt led their bolt down Rusk Avenue.[64]

The state convention convened in San Antonio, and Maury Maverick Sr. rented his beloved La Villita Assembly Hall for the eventuality of a rump convention. Numerous rump delegations, including Eckhardt and the Harris County Loyalists, were refused recognition, and Loyalists lost a vote to require a loyalty oath. Shivers also decided he was not going to let the liberals on his State Democratic Executive Committee—he was the governor, and he was the head of the party. Pickle was in charge of the nominations committee and orchestrated Shivers's selections onto the SDEC.[65]

Maury Maverick spoke after the Loyalists lost the votes, and yelled, "Who'll go with me to La Villita?" At that point, Eckhardt joined seven hundred delegates and supporters, marching in the rain, a mile down the street, to reconvene at La Villita, where Maverick and J. R. Parten led the convention.[66]

Eckhardt chaired the Credentials Committee, meeting in a corner. His general rule was that anyone who would take the loyalty pledge could be a delegate, including those from counties where no bolt had occurred.[67]

Eckhardt did not go to Chicago, but helped organize for the national convention.[68] Shivers chaired his national delegation, which included 1948 States' Rights and 1944 Texas Regulars leaders. Shivers assured Rayburn that the Democratic nominees would be on the ballot in Texas and convinced Rayburn that he would be loyal, so Rayburn decided to seat the Shivers delegation.[69]

After the convention, Shivers reneged on his party loyalty pledge, turning Sam Rayburn into his powerful enemy. Shivers had served with Dwight Eisenhower in the war. He got the governor's convention to endorse the Republican ticket. Then he moved to create a new party called the "Texas Democratic Party," with Eisenhower and Richard Nixon as its nominees, and to list Adlai Stevenson as the "National Democratic Party" candidate, hoping (wrongly) that his action would be taken as an honest attempt to comply with his pledge. Fath and Dickson filed suit and won a court decision blocking Shivers's action. True to Walter Hall's warnings about the cross-filing law, Shivers, Daniel, and the entire Democratic ticket (except for Agriculture Commissioner John White) then allowed the Republican Party to file them as Republican candidates, too, in an effort to boost Eisenhower's chances of getting Texas votes. Eisenhower won Texas, becoming only the second Republican (after Hoover) to ever carry Texas in a presidential election.

Throughout the 1952 campaigns, the TS&LC board continued to meet, and their financial problems deepened. At the August meeting in the Littlefield offices, Eckhardt defended the successes of the Conference. "In 1947 this group actually drew up the natural resource tax bill that culminated in the successful . . . Sewell-Nokes bill," he said, and he trumpeted the group's initiation of the Brannan Breakfast, "which ended in Governor Shivers taking the pledge at Chicago."[70] Just before the October annual convention, Minnie Fish wrote that "constitutionally Bob cannot succeed himself as Chairman even if he wanted to, which he does not."[71] Eckhardt opened the annual convention at the Driskill and Stephen F. Austin Hotels, in his last act as chair. There was talk of abolishing the Conference. While that did not happen, the battles took their toll, and the Conference soon faded away. Its legacy, though, was already being played out, as the new political groups dug into the elections.

Lobbyist Eckhardt, 1953

Labor held legislative workshops every Wednesday during the 1953 session, and Mondays and Wednesdays in the 1954 special session. Dozens of delegates from locals would start with breakfast at an Austin hotel, with Eck-hardt and other guest speakers briefing them. They would get an orientation to the legislature and study voting records before heading to the capitol.[72]

The 1953 House membership included freshman Representative Don Ken-nard, twenty-two years old, who would spend years in Austin and Washing-ton with Eckhardt. Kennard served through 1962, when he was elected to the state Senate. The liberal delegation tried to replace the voided Sewell-Nokes natural gas pipeline tax, but failed. Maverick and others pushed a bill to re-peal cross-filing, but it, too, stalled out. (The legislature would abolish cross-filing in 1955.)[73]

Shivers was determined, again, to win a sales tax. To counter the move-ment, Eckhardt wrote a twelve-page piece entitled "Texas and Taxes—It's Up to You," under the auspices of the TS&LC and published by the CIO Council. Its format looked amazingly like *Bob Eckhardt's Quarterly Reports* that he would produce years later as a congressman. The booklet featured a front-page Eckhardt sketch of an emaciated cow, being sucked dry by bloated ticks. The caption said, "One of the Bad Things About Sales Taxes is that we rarely realize how much they hurt." Eckhardt explained taxes and state spending in the context of a "big family budget," arguing that sales taxes were inequitable for working families and illustrating his points with sketches and self-drawn graphs. To show that Texas was awash in money, rather than impoverished, he depicted a man sweeping up cash off the street, but looking warily over his shoulder. The rich were represented by a martini-sipping man with a gold chain, smoking a cigarette in a long holder. A citizen was shown burdened under a big bag of sales taxes, while a fat man in a three-piece suit, labeled oil, gas, and sulfur, bears a lighter load of severance taxes.[74]

Yet again, no CIO legislation passed in 1953, but labor did defeat many bills, including the sales tax bill. It was the first session since 1947 in which anti-labor legislation did not pass. The big labor fight was over Senator Parkhouse's Ford Motor Company Bill. It sought to deny unemployment compensation to locked-out Dallas Ford employees. Eckhardt worked vigorously against the bill and managed to delay action enough that time ran out, forcing Park-house to get two-thirds support to suspend the rules; he got a majority, but not two-thirds.[75]

The Red Scare reared its venomous head in the 1953 session, as it did throughout the 1950s. Maury Maverick got back the courage that he had lost in the '51 session on the Ayres bill. The leadership backed a resolution to set up the "Un-American Activities Committee," with power to subpoena and browbeat anyone the leaders considered suspicious. Edgar Berlin, Johnny Barnhart, Doug Crouch, and Maverick stalled the resolution, then when it made it to the floor in the last few hours of the session, they attacked it with amendment after amendment, thwarting the attempt to whisk the bill through. As the clock ticked down to the last few minutes of the session, Maverick held the floor, speaking against it, hearing legislators threaten to pull him away from the microphone and knock him to the floor. With Crouch standing by, fists ready to defend him, Maverick kept speaking until the session ended—winning a rare victory over the forces of the Red Scare.[76]

By this time, the Loyal Democrats of Texas had dissolved, as the organization was created primarily for the 1952 election. Fath called for a meeting to set up a permanent organization. Eckhardt joined nearly three hundred people at Lake Buchanan on Sunday, May 17, 1953, for what came to be a watershed meeting in Texas politics. They created the Texas Democratic Organizing Committee. Fath brought back former Agriculture Secretary Charles Brannan as their keynote speaker.

From the Lake Buchanan meeting, the Committee spread across the state and began organizing for the 1954 elections. Sam Rayburn, fearing the battles that would ensue with the new organization, twisted arms and got it changed to a Rayburn-sponsored Democratic Advisory Council.[77] This cooptation of the group soon soured liberals on Rayburn, even if he was assisted by one of their own, D. B. Hardeman.

Eckhardt loved the intensity of Texas and Houston politics in the early 1950s. He and Orissa hosted organizing meetings at their house, with Mrs. Randolph and the other activists in the movement. Orissa was quiet and not very active in these political endeavors. She tried to make ethical sense of political events, but was appalled at the social injustice she saw.[78] The Eckhardts enjoyed a creative mix of artistic and political friends, and Orissa related well with them. She sometimes offered her name to help with the new friends she made through the political gatherings. In 1953 and 1954, she joined Minnie Fish's Texas Democratic Women's State Committee, and in 1956, she was one of fourteen women forming the Committee for Minnie Fisher Cunningham, urging her selection as chair of the Texas delegation to the national convention.[79] But over the years, as Bob became ever more deeply involved with politics, Orissa came to resent the time that he spent away from the family. She did not like the publicity, the campaigning, and the time lost with Bob, and she would often cry about it.[80] But politics was Bob's calling, and Houston and Austin were his extended family.

EIGHT

Eckhardt, the *Texas Observer*, and Yarborough Come of Age

Bob Eckhardt's political life in the mid-to-late 1950s was bound up with Ralph Yarborough's permanent campaigns, the stirrings of racial integration, the continued evolution of liberal organizing, the founding of the *Texas Observer*, and his own election to the Texas House of Representatives. The *Texas Observer* was a compass point in the dark ages of McCarthyism, and Eckhardt was associated with it for the rest of his life as a cartoonist and artist, a writer, and a subject of its coverage. Throughout the 1950s, he was involved with the panoply of liberal organizing efforts. He often spoke at these gatherings, telling stories in his southern preacher cadence. His ability to speak at any time, often without notes, served him well in energizing and educating people and in elevating his own position in the constellation of Texas politics.

Yarborough v. the Establishment, Round 2

Ralph Yarborough never stopped campaigning after his 1952 race, and Eckhardt stayed with him in the political trenches. Yarborough became such a dynamic and magnetic leader that Frankie Randolph dubbed him "our head alligator." In 1954, he again challenged Allan Shivers in the primary, and as Yarborough's campaign for governor gained steam, Shivers realized that he was in serious trouble. He decided that the best way of putting Yarborough on the defensive was to use the controversy created by the *Brown v. Board of Education* decision to ramp up the segregation issue. "While I'm governor," he said, integration "is not going to happen." After the election, a confidant said that Shivers "didn't like to demagogue, but he was about to lose the race. He had to have a white charger to ride in order to win."[1] Integration alone, though, was not enough. Shivers linked integration, Communism, and labor—all in one tidy demagogic package that tainted (and offended) Eckhardt and anyone associated with liberal/labor politics. Shivers charged that Yarborough was controlled by "the C.I.O. and the National Association for the Advancement of Colored People."[2]

In Shivers's hometown of Port Arthur, retail and office workers went on strike. After Shivers's Industrial Commission accused the local union of being

Communist, the national CIO sidelined the union and took over the bargaining.[3] Shivers then called a special legislative session in which he asked for a "Texas Communist Control" bill, outlawing the Communist Party and executing its members. He even proposed an administrative board to conduct the inquiries, rather than a jury trial! Once again, Eckhardt encouraged and supported the brave few legislators standing against the Red Scare initiatives, just as he had in 1951. A week before Joe McCarthy began his nationally televised army Communism hearings, the Texas House Criminal Jurisprudence Committee convened its hearing. The committee chair, Price Daniel's brother Bill, took names of everyone who dared to show up to watch the show. Representing the CIO, Eckhardt was one of the few bold enough to testify against the unconstitutional proposal. "A man could be tried and his reputation ruined on hearsay testimony" before the administrative board, he argued.[4]

The tireless Yarborough lit a fire across the state. Even with his red-baiting and race-baiting tactics, Shivers could not hold a majority on the first ballot against Frankie's head alligator. Yarborough shocked Shivers by coming within 23,000 votes of him out of 1.35 million votes cast.[5] Now forced into a runoff, Shivers was running scared. So, Jake Pickle's public relations firm concocted a propaganda film to turn the tide. They produced the "Port Arthur Story," a film supposedly showing how the ruinous, Communist-instigated strike had paralyzed business in Port Arthur, turning it into a near-ghost town with deserted streets. In reality, they shot the film at 5:00 in the morning, though they did not disclose this bit of trickery. They also cut in some frames showing integrated picket lines, race baiting as well as red baiting. Years later, Pickle would call it a "negative, misleading campaign ad" that "left a bad taste in my mouth."[6]

Businesses showed the film across the state and the *Dallas Morning News* picked up the theme: "In Port Arthur you can't earn your living without the permission of a labor union conceived in communism and dedicated to dictatorship."[7] The film and its spin-off campaign did the trick. In the second election, Shivers won 53 percent to 47 percent. The CIO lost several legislative runoffs, too. But there were some victories. Labor helped Jim Wright defeat Congressman Wingate Lucas, the sponsor of several Taft-Hartley provisions. Eckhardt's Young Democrats ally was on his way to Washington, arriving there twelve years before Eckhardt.[8]

Liberals redoubled their efforts for the September governor's convention. Eckhardt was concerned that Shivers would handpick the State Democratic Executive Committee, so he wrote a *State Observer* piece arguing that liberals must go to the Fort Worth convention "to keep Allan Shivers from illegally imposing his will on the Democrats in the convention as he did in 1950 and 1952." He advised that if Loyalist state delegates chose loyal Democrats as their nominees for the SDEC, Shivers would be obligated to accept those nominees and not insist on his own people.[9] But conservatives controlled the convention, where they called for continued segregation and commended the anti-Communist movement.[10] Shivers reaffirmed that he was not going to let liberals on his SDEC. Jake Pickle was again in charge of the nominations committee. If a senatorial caucus nominated a liberal, as Eckhardt counseled, Pickle would knock the nominee off and nominate a Shivers person. Years later, Pickle would recount those times, chuckling, "I was working for Shivers, and I said, 'well, you're the boss.'"[11]

Launching the *Texas Observer*

In 1948, Paul Holcomb, publisher of the *State Observer,* proposed to sell his newspaper to the CIO for $5,000, but the CIO turned it down. By 1953, Holcomb had decided to retire. Mark Adams and Yarborough aide Lyman Jones negotiated with Holcomb, but were not able to consummate a deal. Minnie Fisher Cunningham and Lillian Collier were interested, but Holcomb would not sell to women. Holcomb then wrote an editorial suggesting that Democrats organize a corporation to buy the paper.[12]

After the narrow Yarborough loss in the summer 1954 runoff, Holcomb wrote that he was going to quit and asked what Democrats wanted to do about not having a statewide newspaper and about the defeat of Loyalist Democrats in the primary.[13] In 1953, Eckhardt's lawyer friend Franklin Jones had bought the *Democratic Bulletin* and changed it to *The East Texas Democrat.*[14] Within a year, Jones was ready to sell and talked with Minnie Fish and Lillian Collier. Jones met with the two women and Paul Holcomb at Hill's Café on a hilltop in South Austin, and Minnie Fish broached the subject of combining the two papers.[15]

About thirty members of the liberal and labor communities then huddled at the Driskill in October 1954, with Eckhardt as one of the planners and legal advisers. Ever so lawyerly and drawing on his own experience, he explained that lack of funding had led to the demise of his beloved *Texas Spectator* and that funding for the risky *Observer* initiative could sap campaign contributions from liberal candidates. The group decided that it was worth the risk and named Frankie Randolph as the publisher. Eckhardt hurriedly set to work drafting legal documents for the venture, as the option to purchase the *State Observer* had already been extended once.[16]

Both Mark Adams and Minnie Fish wanted the editorship.[17] But the group, familiar with twenty-four-year-old Ronnie Dugger's editorship of the *Daily Texan* in 1950–51 and his graduate work at Oxford, offered him the job, sorely disappointing Minnie Fish. Dugger immediately wrote a five-legal-size-page letter to Jones, Randolph, Cunningham, and Eckhardt. "I am very honored by the invitation to edit the new *Observer*," he wrote. "I feel that the name of the newspaper should be *The Texas Observer* rather than the *State Observer*, because the former name seems to have more authority and scope." He argued for the paper being "pro-Democratic as an independent, not as a Democrat," stating that he would take the job only if he had exclusive editorial control. Frankie liked Dugger's spunk. She arranged a follow-up Houston luncheon meeting at which Eckhardt, as trustee for the group, received funds for the paper. They discussed with Dugger the terms of a contract and came to agreement.[18]

The masthead statement that Dugger penned troubled some of the planners: "We will serve no group or party but will hew hard to the truth as we find it and the right as we see it." Minnie Fish and others in the group wanted the paper to be a Democratic party organ.[19] Told to drop the statement or to change it, Dugger was ready to turn down the job, convinced that he would not have editorial freedom. But he was coming to know Eckhardt and to trust him, so he asked Eckhardt's advice about the issue. Eckhardt advised him to stand up to the pressure and run the masthead as he had written it. And he did.[20] Eckhardt wrote to Minnie Fish, outlining the tentative plan for organizing the paper. Demonstrating his approach that would serve him so well in legislative encounters, he broached the subject of the discontent that some felt with the independence that Dugger wanted:

> Ronnie, understandably, wants advance commitments granting him a maximum of freedom. I have heard expressions of concern in this area about ultimate control. . . . It has been my experience that conflicting views are much more likely to exist in the planning stage than in the working stage in any liberal activity. This is because we are more likely to agree when a problem is presented in such a way that there can be no question of what the problem is. When the facts define the problem rather than the surmises of the planners, we agree on its solution.[21]

Dugger set up his office on Twenty-fourth Street in Austin, near the old Eckhardt home, and soon opened a Houston branch office on Welch Street, where Eckhardt would join Frankie Randolph as she hosted well-attended "Wednesday Club" luncheons, with speakers or forum discussions.[22] The first issue of the *Texas Observer* was published December 13, 1954, "incorporating the State Observer, East Texas Democrat, State Week, and Austin Forum-Advocate." Dugger immediately turned to Eckhardt for artwork. Eckhardt drew a stump that served as the logo for the "Letters to the Editor" section—a symbolic stump for all to climb up on and orate from. He sketched an alert

hound dog to symbolize the *Observer's* investigative journalism. And he illustrated the paper's mail-out appeals for financial support. The first issue
included an Eckhardt political cartoon lampooning the anti-free speech sentiments sweeping the land in the McCarthy era: a man with a cane, top hat,
long braid, and top coat, saying, "I do not agree with anything you say, and
I will fight to the death your right to say it." Just as Eckhardt had embraced
the *Texas Spectator* in the 1940s, he now embraced the *Observer,* referring
to it as "this little star in the murky night of Texas journalism."[23] In an early
issue, Eckhardt wrote an article lamenting the passing of the *Spectator* and
reminiscing about his experiences with it. He drew a new sketch of Jack o'
Diamonds weeping over the grave of the *Spectator.*[24]

From 1954 to 1990, Eckhardt drew nearly one hundred cartoons and
sketches for the *Observer.* His visual editorials fit in nicely with the *Observer*
stance. Sometimes he would simply submit a piece. "Haven't drawn any cartoons lately," he wrote Dugger in 1955, "but state officials' actions have been
so grotesque recently that the cartooning medium may be the only way to
treat them. I will try to get you some drawings."[25] Once he drew two cartoons
about Senator Jimmy Phillips and Lieutenant Governor Ben Ramsey and
thought they were his best work. He gave them to Dugger, who put them in
his coat pocket and headed to Scholz's Beer Garden. When Dugger got ready
to leave, someone had stolen his jacket; he and Eckhardt were both distressed
at the loss of the new coat and the never-to-be-seen cartoons.[26]

Other times, Dugger would tell him what story he was working on and
ask him to draw something for it. Eckhardt's cartoons captured the person-
alities, societal changes, and issues of the day: Eisenhower, Shivers, and the
turmoil that the Democratic Party went through over presidential politics;
the deep ideological split within the party; the reigns of Texans Sam Rayburn
as Speaker of the U.S. House and Lyndon Johnson as majority leader of the
U.S. Senate; the violence that accompanied school desegregation mandates;
and the continued fading of the old cowboy traditions and their replacement
with faux cowboys.

Eckhardt took pride in his work, paying attention to style, technique, and
materials in his cartooning. He bought a French designer's red sable brush, of
the type that Peter Arno had told him he used, and found it to be a wonderful
tool, allowing beautiful bold strokes. He would write that the trouble with his
drawing "is that I don't get sleepy when I am doing it and can easily stay up
all night. Then I'm pretty bushed in the morning."[27]

Dugger admired both Eckhardt and his cartoons. He liked an Eckhardt
thematic series of sketches and captions so much that he pitched them to
Harper's, writing that Eckhardt was "one of the most civilized persons I

know. . . . He is the intellectual leader of the Houston liberals—his keynote at the Harris County Democratic convention, for example, quite out of place at such a rowdy affair, was an attempt to draw the victors back to the deeper issue, who shall rule, the corporations or the people—and he is also a vintage character who seems to have been transplanted, whole and unflustered, from the Gladstone-Disraeli era of British politics." [28]

In 1955 Dugger hired an associate editor—twenty-six-year-old Bill Brammer. He and his wife Nadine had moved to Austin, where he became an award-winning writer with the *Austin American-Statesman*. Bill and Nadine had two girls, Sidney and Shelby, and Willie was born in 1957; all the Brammers would become a part of Eckhardt's life. Billy Lee, as he was sometimes known, became a character of the Austin scene, drifting in and out of it for twenty years, and he wrote colorfully of that scene. Brammer and Eckhardt became friends and observed the social scene that swirled around the legislative and lobbying dynamics of Austin, including Scholz's. They would talk about the whorehouses frequented by legislators and lobbyists—Hattie's on South Congress and one tucked away across from Scarbrough's. (One legislator told Eckhardt that the Austin brothels were better than the famed Chicken Ranch at La Grange, but Eckhardt would swear that he never frequented them.)

Brammer left the *American-Statesman* and went to work for the *Observer*, but within months, Lyndon Johnson offered him a job, so Bill and Nadine moved to Washington, joining other Texans in the LBJ world, such as Liz Sutherland Carpenter, Walter Jenkins, and Jack and Mary Margaret Valenti. Brammer's observations of legislative life in Austin, followed by his work for LBJ, served to channel his energies into fiction writing. His forte was satire through dialogue, which he used both in his *Observer* pieces and then in his fiction.

In the mid-to-late 1950s, he worked on what came to be an award-winning novel of 1961, *The Gay Place*. His fictional characters in an Austin political setting were amalgams of the real characters he encountered, including Eckhardt and his frequent forays into antique shops, and Nadine and her wild lifestyle in Austin. His Governor Fenstemaker was an unmistakable knockoff of LBJ. Brammer blended into the novel local haunts such as Scholz's (known in the book as The Dearly Beloved). His parachutist was based on Galveston's wealthy, eccentric State Representative Maco Stewart Jr. Representative Roy Sherwood was based on Eckhardt's friend Bob Hughes. Willie Morris and Ronnie Dugger also became part of the cast; Dugger would later show his irritation by writing that Brammer's writing showed contempt for Texas liberals and admiration for the cunning of their adversary, LBJ.[29]

Lobbyist, Cartoonist, and Party Organizer, 1955

The 1955 legislative session opened with flourishes of Eckhardt's pen in the new *Texas Observer.* The first-of-the-session issue also featured an article by Willie Morris, editor of the *Daily Texan,* who would become a fixture in Eckhardt's life.[30] Eckhardt pointed the *Observer's* wary eye with sketches of "The Pillar of Society" and "The Corporation Lawyer," followed in the next issue by a front-page sketch of Allan Shivers. Land Commissioner Bascom Giles resigned at the end of 1954 in the unfolding veterans' land scandal, and Eckhardt used the *Observer* to update his old *Spectator* cartoon that had foretold the scandal. Giles was convicted for taking bribes to accept land speculators' inflated appraisals. Shivers, serving on the land board with Giles, came under fire, the legislature reprimanded him, and Shivers's popularity plummeted.[31]

The session began in the charged anti-labor atmosphere just months after the "Port Arthur Story." Senator Parkhouse again targeted the Ford strike with Senate Bill 44. His SB 45 outlawed recognition and organizational strikes; it was more restrictive than even Taft-Hartley. In the battles over these bills, labor—and Eckhardt—lost. Eckhardt fought SB 45 and wrote a piece on it for the *Observer,* arguing that the bill, "providing no alternative to a strike as a means of gaining recognition, thus 'mousetraps' the union into striking and affords a means of permanently enjoining any further union activity after an election is held." Eckhardt wrote that SB 45:

> Could be used to take away every means available to intrastate workers to assert their rights to be recognized as a majority representative of the employees of an employer. Thus, every avenue of organization of Texas workers whose work does not affect interstate commerce is completely shut off if the employer refuses recognition. . . . Little people with low wages, such as bell-hops, laundry employees, waitresses, and store clerks, would become the forgotten people in our industrial society, and their wages would remain at a level far below the other half of the Texas working community, whose work affects interstate commerce.

Eckhardt worried that if passed, SB 45 would be "worse than all the other Texas anti-labor legislation put together."[32]

As sine die—the last day of the session—approached, Eckhardt's friends, Representative Alonzo Jamison and his wife Liz, wrote a song called "Sine Die," to the tune of "This Ole House," depicting the despair of liberals. "Ain't a-gonna need this House no longer/Let's go home and face the facts!" the song ended.[33] Eckhardt took it up and memorialized the end of the session with a front-page *Observer* cartoon, "This Ol' House." The cartoon showed a legislator leaving the capitol, whistling, with an open umbrella, while the tax structure crumbles, the lobby thumbs its nose, labor is sick, and state colleges are falling apart.[34]

After the session, the battles shifted to the filling of a vacancy on the Democratic National Committee, with Eckhardt brokering the deal. Loyalists wanted the seat, but LBJ and Rayburn wanted to placate Shivers by giving it to Lieutenant Governor Ben Ramsey. The Democratic Advisory Council met in Waco on November 5, 1955, with Rayburn in attendance. In a move intended as a slap at Rayburn, Creek Fath moved that the DNC position be left vacant until the May convention. But his old friend Eckhardt offered a substitute motion that, *in the future*, committeemen would have to be active Democrats. The Eckhardt amendment won, though Rayburn and others considered even it too stringent.[35]

Yarborough v. the Establishment, Round 3

The big question going into the 1956 elections was whether Governor Shivers would run for reelection. Shivers's public approval collapsed as a result of the land fraud scandal and a series of scandals involving insurance companies and Shivers-appointed regulators.[36] When Shivers ultimately decided to retire, Senator Price Daniel came home from Washington to run for governor. With Shivers out of the way, Yarborough was tasting victory. Then, a ghost from the past emerged, as Pappy O'Daniel tried another statewide race. In the first primary, Daniel led by 162,000 votes over Yarborough, with O'Daniel third.

Presidential politics intervened in the 1956 gubernatorial dances. In an effort to deny Shivers the leadership of the Texas delegation to the national convention, Rayburn cleverly pushed LBJ (now U.S. Senate majority leader) as a favorite son presidential candidate. It quickly got ugly: Shivers attacked LBJ as a radical, while LBJ called Shivers a "Democratic party traitor" and urged him to become a Republican.[37] At the May conventions, Loyalists and LBJ mobilized their troops and won a smashing victory. LBJ was apparently willing to use the liberal-Loyalists to help assure a Democratic victory, but he was not about to become one of them. Once he beat Shivers, he announced, "The next fight will be to knock down the extreme left wing."[38]

J. Edwin Smith chaired the Harris County convention, where liberals won a rousing victory, and Eckhardt gave the keynote address. As liberals booed the conservatives, Chris Dixie and Smith waved the crowd for silence, knowing that they would win if they did not overplay their hand. One young conservative spoke passionately for a states' rights resolution, but was heckled. When he left the stage, he told Eckhardt, "You guys could hold that crowd against God."[39]

In his keynote address, Eckhardt told the delegates that they faced a new era. Drawing a historical parallel, he said that the Shivers regime had been similar to the last Republican regime. Eckhardt quoted his 1890s hero, Governor Jim Hogg: "The question is: shall the corporations or the state control?" Eckhardt then offered his own analysis: "Today, the question is the same. . . . The major oil and gas companies . . . are now in the saddle in Texas, and for the first time in history the Governor openly confers with their lobbyists before making important decisions." Unafraid to broach the volatile race issue, Eckhardt blasted Shivers because he "does not believe in equality of opportunity for our Negro citizens." He ended with more unfavorable comparisons of Shivers with his hero Hogg: "The spirit that the Governor represents is a sort of political Bridey Murphy. It is the same spirit that animated Clark, who ran against James Stephen Hogg. It is the spirit that was reincarnated in W. Lee O'Daniel—though that vehicle is now fortunately collapsed like the wonderful one-horse shay." [40]

Shivers had just pressed for defiance of the *Brown v. Board of Education* decision by placing referenda on the ballots to reinforce public opposition to integration, a popular move among the white electorate. One referendum exempted compulsory attendance at integrated schools. Eckhardt drafted a mock amendment stating that if a school was shut down, persons "engaged in the violence provided for in this act shall also not be subject to the compulsory school attendance law." [41] But they could not defeat it in the legislature, and in November the referendum passed overwhelmingly, including in Eckhardt's Harris County. [42] In the charged atmosphere, Shivers then shamelessly sent troops to Mansfield (near Fort Worth) to enforce *segregation,* rather than to protect blacks from the violent whites. Eckhardt drew an *Observer* cartoon about the Mansfield incident, showing thugs buying "school supplies" of rope and kerosene. [43] He came to treasure this piece as his best cartoon ever.

The day before the state convention in Dallas, the Democratic Advisory Council caucused and planned its move to oust Shivers's SDEC. Pickle was again orchestrating the convention, this time for Daniel. His plan—not a new one—was to deny admission to liberal delegates. Back in Austin, Eckhardt's old Austin High schoolmate Henry Holman heard a rumor of such a plan, so he counterfeited and distributed hundreds of admission tickets, and liberal delegates used them to get into the convention. [44] Just before the convention, LBJ hosted Fred Schmidt and Jerry Holleman at his ranch, insisting that labor not support Frankie Randolph, who was a candidate for the Democratic National Committee. [45] The night before the convention, Rayburn and Johnson spoke to twelve hundred delegates. To both applause and booing, they urged caution. The Harris County delegates caucused, endorsing Randolph for the

DNC, and then Eckhardt moved a resolution to purge the SDEC of Shivers's supporters and replace them with supporters of the national nominees.

Ralph Yarborough's speech received a rousing reception; LBJ drew a more mixed reaction, presaging what was to come. LBJ and Rayburn were still furious with Shivers and would not even put him on the delegation to the national convention. Still, LBJ and Rayburn recommended keeping the SDEC as it was until the September convention.

LBJ's aide George Reedy met with Democratic Advisory Council secretary Kathleen Voight and others. Voight agreed to oppose Eckhardt's motion if LBJ would agree to dissolve the Democratic Advisory Council and instead support a switch to a liberal SDEC at the September convention. On the floor, J. Edwin Smith offered the Eckhardt motion from the Houston caucus. John Connally spoke against it, and with Voight's decision to go with LBJ, the motion lost. Eckhardt drew an *Observer* cartoon suggesting that LBJ would return party control to Daniel, against the liberal-Loyalist bloc. Indeed, in September LBJ reneged on what Voight had taken as a commitment to support SDEC changes, creating a rift between him and liberals that was never bridged.[46]

After defeating the Eckhardt-Smith motion, LBJ moved to seat Beryl Bentsen, wife of Congressman Lloyd Bentsen Jr., as a DNC member. Loyalists made a floor nomination of Frankie Randolph. LBJ refused to seat the liberal Dallas delegates before he won the Bentsen vote, but delegates were offended at LBJ's strong-arm tactics and roared their disapproval. LBJ had to allow the credentials report, and the conservative Dallas delegates were thrown out.

LBJ supporters urged Mrs. Randolph to withdraw, but she refused. Liberals printed handbills showing Lloyd Bentsen's 1952 statement that he would not support Adlai Stevenson and a picture of Beryl Bentsen with an Eisenhower sign. LBJ set up an office behind the stage, with Connally in charge of twisting arms. They called J. Edwin Smith to the back room. LBJ, knowing that Smith was interested in a federal judgeship, threatened him, "J. Ed, if you pursue this, you'll never be a U.S. judge" (and he was right).[47] But with his support crumbling, LBJ withdrew Bentsen's name, and Randolph was elected by acclamation, creating a huge institutional presence for the liberal-Loyalists and a burr under the saddle of LBJ, Rayburn, Daniel, and Connally.[48]

In Chicago, Adlai Stevenson won on the first ballot, with only Texas and Mississippi voting for LBJ.[49] Gus Garcia was a delegate on Senator John Kennedy's failed vice presidential bandwagon. Back in Houston after the convention, Eckhardt ran into Garcia outside the Scanlan Building. Garcia was very agitated. "Everything I touch turns to shit. I couldn't even sell John Kennedy to the Catholics," he said.[50]

The Daniel-Yarborough runoff featured the highest voter turnout of any Texas Democratic gubernatorial primary—31 percent.[51] Daniel escaped with a 3,000-vote victory, 698,000 votes to Yarborough's 695,000. Yarborough and his camp immediately made vote-stealing charges, but eventually Yarborough decided to not contest the election.

In the run-up to the September convention in Fort Worth, Rayburn first announced his support for the contested liberal delegations. But LBJ, chairing the Blanco County delegation, supported conservative delegations and brought Rayburn with him. When it came time to decide whether to seat the conservative Houston delegation or the liberal delegation, the convention voted to let the conservative Houston delegation vote on whether to seat itself or the liberal delegation! With that parliamentary gimmick, the conservative group was certified, with LBJ and Rayburn voting with the conservatives against Eckhardt and the rest of the liberal Harris delegation.

With Houston Loyalists losing the credentials vote, DNC member Frankie Randolph was not seated as a delegate and not even invited to attend as a party official. Jake Pickle was again in charge of the nominations committee. Pickle blocked liberal nominations to the SDEC, and the Johnson-Rayburn-Daniel rout was complete. Liberal-Loyalists were outraged and blamed Johnson for the intimidation tactics of armed guards threatening liberal delegates at the 1956 convention.[52] It is understandable that Johnson would want to assure his ally Daniel control of the Texas political machinery, now that Shivers was out of the way. It is baffling, though, why he chose to do so in a steamroller manner that locked in liberal hatred and suspicion of him for the rest of his career. J. R. Parten went backstage and chewed LBJ out, saying, "Mister, you're making the biggest mistake of your life here." Minnie Fish vowed, "I have a 'vocation' to be a thorn in Lyndon's side."[53] In 1958, gadfly newsman Archer Fullingim wrote in "Both Barrels," his column in the *Kountze News,* that Johnson "did it in 1956 at the state convention and now he did it again." Fullingim continued:

> Democrats might as well get used to the idea that Johnson has deserted us for the Eisenhower Democrats. We might as well quit eternally hoping that Johnson will see the light and get with us. . . . Let us see him henceforth as he is, The Enemy, because we would have won both in 1956 and again in 1958 if Lyndon had not turned his back on his friends. . . . How does it feel, Lyndon, to double cross your oldest friends, the ones who put you in office, and side in with those who voted against you . . . ?[54]

Eckhardt believed that the closer Lyndon Johnson was to Texas, the more conservative he was; the farther away from Texas, the more he became like a mainstream Democrat. He found LBJ to be "half please-ball and half states-man," but "a politician par excellence."[55] Eckhardt wrote "a little Doxology" about LBJ and his machinations through Alvin Wirtz, Everett Looney, and Ed Clark:

> *Praise him through whom all blessings come.*
> *Praise him who dwells in Washington.*
> *Praise him all of the common herds.*
> *Praise Everett, Ed, and Alvin Wirtz.*[56]

Yet, Eckhardt also worried about the dynamics of the liberal movement and the ability of the LBJs to take advantage of political blindness in the movement. Liberal leaders, he wrote, "take the extremest position possible on the liberal side to show that you are a simon-pure, blue ribbon liberal, uncompromising and therefore altogether trustworthy. But when this position is taken by enough of the leaders, the group then becomes to the public just a highly partisan elite guard of the left, and persons begin to drop off at the fringes, and finally the faction cannot muster enough votes to gain election."[57]

Yarborough v. the Establishment, Victory in Round 4

In many ways, the 1957 legislative session was a typical one. The Establishment proposed raiding the Permanent School Fund to avoid adopting a natural gas tax, and legislators continued their resistance to integration. But this time, the Senate was not all Anglo. New Senator Henry B. Gonzalez filibustered the leadership's anti-NAACP and pro-segregation bills and was named by the NAACP as their "man of the year."

Eckhardt was back (one last time) lobbying on labor and social welfare issues. He took Little Orissa with him to Austin, where she lived with Oma Eckhardt and went to fifth grade at his old Wooldridge Elementary. Early in the session, a legislator was tape-recorded taking a bribe. Eckhardt drew a front-page *Observer* cartoon on it.[58] Bill Brammer must have been taking notes from Washington, as a legislator bribe was at the center of the novel that he was working on at the time.

In the middle of the session came a special election for Daniel's U.S. Senate seat. Shivers and Daniel had managed to keep Yarborough out of the governor's mansion in 1952, 1954, and 1956. The price for the 1956 victory was Daniel's resignation of his Senate seat. Yarborough announced his candidacy for the Senate in January 1957, just as the legislature convened. Statewide, his vote counts had increased from 37 percent in 1952 to 47 percent in the 1954 runoff to 49.9 percent in the 1956 runoff. In Harris County, Yarborough won the 1956 runoff.[59] Clearly, he was a bigger threat than ever.

Outgoing Governor Shivers appointed conservative, millionaire business-man Bill Blakely as interim senator and new Governor Daniel then called a special election for April 2. Another ghost from the past emerged, as Communist-baiter Martin Dies announced his candidacy, as did up-and-coming Republican leader Thad Hutcheson. In a multi-candidate race, Democrats were nervous that a strong Republican campaign could produce a first-place finish for Hutcheson, giving the U.S. Senate to Republicans and stripping LBJ of his majority leadership. But Johnson was no fan of Yarborough and his strong labor entourage.

Unlike primary elections, there was no runoff in special elections. So, to head off a probable Yarborough plurality victory or a possible Hutcheson victory, LBJ ally State Representative Joe Pool sponsored an emergency measure to require a runoff. Arm twisting and calls from Washington garnered the necessary votes, and it passed in the House, but it then ran into trouble in the Senate. The bill passed as a regular measure (thus having consequences for 1961), but it didn't get the two-thirds vote needed for emergency bills, so it could not become effective for the Yarborough special election.

As before, Eckhardt campaigned for Yarborough. This time, the head alligator prevailed, with a 72,000-vote plurality. After six years of organizing and campaigning, Ralph Yarborough—and with him the whole of Texas populist Democrats—had won a jubilant victory. With machinations by Walton Hamilton and UT's Bob Montgomery, Majority Leader Johnson appointed Yarborough to the Senate Committee on Labor,[60] giving Eckhardt and the Texas CIO a strong voice in national labor policy.

Democrats of Texas

Incensed at their treatment by Johnson and Rayburn in the 1956 political battles, the liberal-Loyalists returned to their organizing. Eckhardt was elected the chair of Harris County Democrats in early 1957 to press ahead their victories in the local party. On the state level, Creek Fath decided to organize yet another effort to carry the banner of the Lake Buchanan group that had created the Texas Democratic Organizing Committee in 1953. In December 1956, fifty organizers met at the Stephen F. Austin Hotel, with Frankie Randolph as the temporary chair, before they elected Eckhardt to preside. They chose as their new name the "Democrats of Texas" (DOT) and gave Eckhardt the job of drafting a constitution. They called a statewide meeting for May 18, 1957, and named Eckhardt, Fath, and Kathleen Voight as the convention planning committee.[61] Randolph, attending a meeting of the DNC, told the press the group had the sanction of the national committee. The group's purpose was "to work for the platform and the candidates of the Democratic party," she said.[62] Ever the cynic, Eckhardt's friend The Mewhinney later reflected on Randolph's and Eckhardt's leadership, saying, "You'll be getting a little bit done when the bomb falls, but it won't make any difference."[63]

More than one thousand people from 106 counties attended the May 1957 meeting of the Democrats of Texas at the Stephen F. Austin Hotel, and they triumphantly marched through a wet downtown Austin. It was a time of exuberance, and the star of the show was new U.S. Senator Ralph Yarborough. "I'll never forget those who upheld our cause in the hours of our darkest adversity," Yarborough told the crowd. "You have been my friends in time of need. And I'm your friend in this time of triumph."[64] He urged them to remember the 1952 Maverick-led march to La Villita and the 1953 Buchanan Dam meeting. The convention approved Eckhardt's constitution and set to work electing

Eckhardt speaks to Democrats of Texas. The Democrats of Texas was one of a series of organizing ventures by national (liberal) Democrats. Here Eckhardt, identified by his name tag as a board member, speaks to the statewide DOT gathering in 1958. Photo by Russell Lee. Courtesy of the Center for American History, University of Texas at Austin, CN 12136.

Creekmore Fath speaks to Democrats of Texas meeting. The Eckhardt and Fath Law Offices lasted only a short while, but Fath became one of the lead organizers for the liberal faction of Democrats, and the two continued to work together politically. Photo by Russell Lee. Courtesy of the Center for American History, University of Texas at Austin, DI 02934.

Randolph chair and Fath vice chair of the group. A thirty-seven-member executive board was appointed, including Eckhardt as an at-large member. The new DOT office was Fath's law office in the Littlefield Building.[65]

Now the new regime of Governor Daniel, Speaker Rayburn, and Senate Majority Leader Johnson set to work, with Senator Yarborough, the DOT, and Randolph positioned against them. The founding of the DOT created a political firestorm. Shivercrats and moderates who had thrown in with Daniel were outraged. At SDEC meetings and elsewhere, Governor Daniel heatedly condemned Randolph and referred to the DOT as "the splinter Democratic group."[66] Rayburn said he would not join the DOT. Daniel's aide and SDEC secretary Jake Jacobsen said that the name "Democrats of Texas" was not legal. The DOT began a newsletter called the *Democratic Reporter*. Eckhardt drew a cartoon for it showing two politicians, with one saying, "Don't look now, but I think the people are trying to steal the party again."[67]

Eckhardt was the point man in the DOT's public relations campaign. He told the *Houston Chronicle* that it took a popular groundswell in 1944 and 1948 for the conventions to be won back from the anti-Roosevelt leaders, noting the 1952 usurpation of the party for Republicans and the 1956 rejection of duly selected committeemen. He charged that Jake Pickle is "now actively engaged in preparation for a 1958 convention of the same stamp." He said that "it is with ill grace that Pickle, who engineered the disenfranchisement of Harris, Bexar, El Paso and . . . others, is appealing to those areas to support the very forces that disenfranchised them."[68] Under his own artwork rendition of the *Observer's* "Letters to the Editor" stump, Eckhardt also defended the group in a long letter, signing it as chair of the Harris County Democrats. He wrote that duly elected Bexar officials had been "illegally removed from the [State Democratic Executive Committee] because they would not go along with the cynical stealing of the Harris and El Paso County votes which permitted Price Daniel and associates to control a convention that they had lost in the precincts and the counties of the state."[69]

Eckhardt also rallied his troops against a conservative, anti-Communist group, "Freedom in Action" (FIA), that had formed earlier in the 1950s and now tried to gain control of the conventions. Its president was Abner McCall (Baylor Law School dean and former Texas Supreme Court member), and its executive secretary was oilman and former Democratic State Representative Jack Cox (who would soon turn up as a Republican gubernatorial candidate). Randolph mocked the FIA as "Fascism in Action."[70] By 1961, the John Birch Society was endorsing FIA.[71] In a Harris County Democrats letter to "Loyal Democrats" in Houston, Eckhardt warned of what he called these "Dixiecrat" efforts to woo them. "This simply means that we are going to have to work harder than ever," he wrote. "Lyndon Johnson—who sold us out in Fort

Worth—has said he's going to stay out of precinct fights this year. But we know that some of his people are pushing the new Dixiecrat group."[72]

Liberal Steamroller, 1958

The liberal-Loyalist work of the 1940s and 1950s finally paid off. Bob Eckhardt was elected to the Texas legislature in 1958. This proved to be a watershed year for Democrats and liberals across the nation, a year that, as the Eisenhower administration faded, set the stage for the liberal politics of the 1960s. Frankie Randolph returned from a DNC meeting in Washington, endorsing Chair Paul Butler's pro-civil rights stand. "The whole thing [is] based on this feeling that the Democratic Party must become a liberal party," she wrote to the DOT, concluding that the majority of the DNC believes "the Democratic Party must move forward now with a liberal, progressive program on every front."[73]

By 1958, labor was strengthened in membership and in organizing in Texas, but nervous about their political potential. Labor organizer Don Ellinger reported to national officials on the state labor convention that although "Johnson had not been a friend to organized labor, he was still our elected senator for a couple of years, and it was best to try to get along with him." Some labor officials were becoming more and more uncomfortable backing Congressman Albert Thomas, though Eckhardt's ally Eddie Ball, now a steelworker official, was a strong Thomas backer. Ellinger noted, "We are not convinced that we can field a candidate against [Thomas] and our local people are very pessimistic about it. However, the state leadership is still pushing to see that something is done so that Albert is at least threatened with a liberal candidate from an overwhelmingly liberal district."[74] Labor began casting about, eyeing Eckhardt as their candidate.

The top focus for the 1958 Texas campaigns was twofold: the need to cement a six-year term for new Senator Yarborough and the race against Governor Daniel. Gubernatorial candidate possibilities included, among others, newly famous State Senator Henry B. Gonzalez and Corsicana Judge Jim Sewell, who, with an introduction by Eckhardt, spoke at a Harris County Democrats meeting early in the year. Then, lo and behold, Pappy O'Daniel tried yet again. Eckhardt loved the sentiment expressed by Gonzalez as he filed for the race—that he didn't want the people to just have a choice between "Tweedledee and O'Tweedledee."[75]

The liberal community was split, with labor wary of Gonzalez. Eckhardt's Harris County Democrats endorsed Yarborough, but not Gonzalez.[76] The *Observer* supported Gonzalez. Gonzalez told the *Observer* that he didn't believe in putting his friends on the spot. He wanted DOT votes, but would not ask for an endorsement. "I realize some think a Mexican-American might hurt a ticket." He wrote Randolph, offering to forego an endorsement that might create dissension within the group. He told the *Observer* that Randolph and Bob Eckhardt "were concerned that if DOT does not endorse him 25 percent will be angry, and if it does, another 25 percent will be angry."[77] Some in the DOT had qualms about Gonzalez being Mexican-American, Catholic, and pro-integration. Fath believed that supporting Gonzalez would hurt the group and urged DOT to soft-pedal the racial issue to placate East Texas members. The most important objective for the group, he said, was to keep Yarborough and to win control of the party. In the DOT steering committee, a motion was made to not endorse. When a substitute was offered to endorse both Yarborough and Gonzalez, Eckhardt moved to table the substitute, and he won. Though Fath did not even want Gonzalez to speak, they did invite him to speak, and he got a rousing reception.[78]

So, Eckhardt chose the path that seemed most pragmatic, countering his personal sympathies. He later said that the primary objection to an endorsement was that "he couldn't win," but Eckhardt believed that by running, Gonzalez "did a wise thing. He launched himself into a prominent position, gave Latin-Americans a feeling of pride," and was good "for educating a broad liberalism."[79]

In the primary, Yarborough won easily, 59 percent to Bill Blakely's 41 percent. Daniel, too, won going away, with 60 percent to Gonzalez's 18.6 percent and O'Daniel's 18.4 percent. Jake Pickle stayed in place as the acknowledged "hatchet man" for the crowd. At the September state convention in San Antonio, Daniel and Pickle stripped the remaining liberals off the SDEC, rammed their choices through, and quickly adjourned. They literally slipped out the back door, with armed officers at their sides.[80] The DOT delegates were furious and marched out for a rally. But it was all over, again.

Candidate Eckhardt

Yarborough's 1957 victory, the huge organizing effort of the DOT, and success with the Harris County Democrats persuaded Eckhardt that the time was ripe for him to make the leap from lobbyist/political activist to candidate. Reprising his 1940 role, he decided to run for state representative. In early 1958, he wrote a letter to labor leader Sherman Miles in Austin, adding: "P.S. I intend to announce for the House, Place 2, Sunday. Wish me luck—Bob."[81] He did not pull his punches—even as he filed, he wrote an *Observer* article criticizing Governor Daniel.[82]

Harris County had eight state representatives (all running countywide), and six of those seats were open. The July primary was a feast for liberal candidates. They ran against a general sales tax and for a dedicated natural gas tax. Eckhardt's platform supported education spending and a tax shift to chemical, natural gas, and other industries.[83] He made the runoff against Genevieve Turner, leading her 36,421 to 35,441, with 25,919 votes for two other candidates. With liberals making it into all the House runoffs, the campaigns intensified. Eckhardt campaigned hard, scared that the "sweet little female rattlesnake" would snatch victory away from him.[84] The Harris County Taxpayers Committee, financed by Texas Manufacturers Association (TMA) members, urged the defeat of Eckhardt and four others, warning against "a dangerous political machine, the labor boss-D.O.T. left-wing splinter-group." Eckhardt charged that the "taxpayer" group "has cynically plotted to foist a series of special sales taxes on the people."[85]

Genevieve Turner described Eckhardt as a hatchet man and lobbyist, bought and paid for by unions. She hoped to capitalize on racism among union members. She accused Eckhardt of spending his time in the Third and Fifth Wards, drinking beer to get the black vote. She then made an explicit appeal to segregationists:

> Are you men wholeheartedly in favor of integration in your union, in your public schools, in your social functions? Mr. Eckhardt's past and present affiliations with various race organizations proves he is in favor of integrating your entire organization. If you doubt this statement get him to publicly answer or deny his feelings. . . . Ask Mr. Eckhardt who wrote the civil rights bill of your union. I can tell you—a Negro lawyer.[86]

Her campaign backfired. Eckhardt received the highest number of votes of any of the House candidates, 41,076 (59 percent), and Turner, the lowest, 28,400. The vote in the black precincts was 7,383 for Eckhardt, 591 for Turner. She received her biggest support in the silk-stocking areas of River Oaks, Bellaire, and West University Place.[87] Woodrow Seals, the DOT candidate, won his race for county chair, and all the other Harris County liberal state legislative candidates also won rousing victories. Across the nation, Democrats and liberals won congressional seats that year in a landslide.

Eckhardt had begun his electoral career fashioning a coalition of white liberal, labor, black, and Latino voters. Frankie Randolph believed that the Harris County Democrats had come of age, with Eckhardt as chair. "This is the victory of the precinct workers," she wrote. "It is almost unbelievable that you could do what you did with all the money poured out and all the propaganda against you."[88]

Labor was ecstatic. Local and state labor officials were proud of the organizing work that their members had done; they also realized the power of coalition politics and urged labor leaders "to take a more active part in the Harris County Democrats."[89] Don Ellinger reported to national leaders introducing new state representative nominee Eckhardt to them as "attorney for the CWA and longtime attorney for the CIO unions in the state and the architect of much of our legislative programs in the past."[90]

After the thrill of the primary elections, the post-primary precinct conventions produced their usual splits and rumps, setting the stage for battles at the San Antonio governor's convention. Eckhardt served on the DOT's steering committee planning for the convention. The convention was chaotic, with each side winning some battles. Daniel's choice for temporary chair won over Yarborough's candidate, Jim Sewell. Freedom in Action had won several delegations; they moved to oust Randolph from DNC, and all hell broke loose. In the midst of the chaos, Pickle and Daniel called in Rayburn and Johnson, and they all decided to just adjourn the convention. The two groups took to the streets, with police escorts.[91] But with the election and the convention behind him, Bob Eckhardt turned his attention to his new role as political broker and state representative.

PART III

Pygmies, Giants, and Knights at the State Capitol

Lobbyists at the state capitol are "the knights of Congress Avenue who have done more to injure Texas than all the highwaymen combined."

—GOVERNOR JIM HOGG

The Texas Capitol was "built for giants and inhabited by pygmies."

—BOB ECKHARDT

NINE

Freshman Legislator of the Year, 1959

Bob Eckhardt had lost his quixotic 1940 bid to become a twenty-seven-year-old state legislator. Now at forty-five, on January 13, 1959, he was sworn into office, and he served continuously as an elected official until January 1981. State Representative Eckhardt had a powerful and uplifting impact on the Texas legislature. *Texas Observer* editor Willie Morris later wrote that Eckhardt would rise to speak about a bill, beginning with a sad lament, and transforming it into a passionate analysis of what had gone wrong with state government. This would stoke his allies in the legislature, such as Don Kennard, Malcolm McGregor, and Franklin Spears to join the fight.[1] At the end of his first session, even before he passed his first piece of legislation, the capitol press corps named Eckhardt the "most outstanding freshman legislator."[2]

Eckhardt would have many successes as a legislator, but many defeats as well. As a labor lobbyist, he had worked against what Governor Jim Hogg had called the "Knights of Congress Avenue"—the powerful business lobbyists who controlled state government. Now, he would battle against them on the inside. From his new vantage point on the House floor, he spoofed the lobbyists through caricatures in the *Observer*.[3] Eckhardt had learned through his own lobbying that there were a few brilliant and ethical legislators not controlled by the business lobbyists, but they were outnumbered. He would remark to Willie Morris that the Texas capitol was "built for giants and inhabited by pygmies."

Eckhardt built a reputation for being a legislative craftsman. Early in his tenure, he discovered that most who have a strong interest in legislation "are principally concerned with making things work . . . it's not particularly ideological; it's mechanical."[4] He told his constituents that "we are faced with legislative problems which we must solve just as an architect solves the problem of designing a house to fit a need. We should not hide behind labels. Most of the issues in Austin can't be defined as liberal or conservative."[5] Eckhardt believed that the lobby operated intelligently under this philosophy, but that too often his side did not. "Liberals are like quail hunting bird dogs," he would wryly note about his legislative colleagues.[6] He appreciated the interplay of politics, ideology, conscience, and activism. "To become a liberal legislator," he maintained, "you first have to get elected to the legislature."[7]

Eckhardt may have been a freshman in 1959, but he had fought so many legislative battles over his decade of lobbying that he knew how power worked. As he later wrote:

> The first important and practical lesson I learned in the Texas legislature is that you have to lobby with the lobby. The interest group proponents of a measure have a lot more time than a legislator does to devote to a single issue; and, with their specialty interest and their institutional format, they have frequently developed a greater access to leadership in a legislative body than even most of the members of that body. Also, though you as a member may know more about how the inside process works, they understand better the interplay between real power outside the official doors with the real powers within. There is not just the "military-industrial complex" that Eisenhower recognized but an industrial-governmental complex which exercises the real power more than ever before.[8]

He plunged into classes on parliamentary procedure, becoming knowledgeable about the technical tricks of this power game. Though he had worked around the legislature for twelve years, now that he was on the inside, Eckhardt was impressed with how little he knew about the "intricate human relations" in the legislature, and he came to admire even more D. B. Hardeman's and Jim Sewell's 1951 success with the Gas House Gang.[9] With the combination of his experience and this humility, Bob Eckhardt began his legislative career not as a quixotic knight tilting against windmills, but as an ideologically committed, skilled tactician—with a personality and a manner that could, sometimes, win converts.

Pre-Session Maneuvers

After Eckhardt's 1958 primary election victory, he quickly became immersed in a legislative-political issue and a policy issue. The House was in the midst of a campaign for the speakership. Most speakers served only one term, but Speaker Waggoner Carr decided to run for reelection. Eckhardt had known Carr ever since he had supported the Gas House Gang in his freshman year in 1951. Carr was not liberal, but his opponent, Joe Burkett, was anathema to labor and liberals. The liberals' sweep of the Harris County primary elections reenergized Carr's campaign. Eckhardt rounded up the new representatives and produced a package of pledges for Carr, which put him over the top.[10] He ultimately won a 79–71 vote.

The 1958 policy issue involved one of Eckhardt's passions, natural resources. He and Orissa and the girls had come to love the beach. They would pile in the car for day trips to Galveston, where they would drive down the beach until there were no more people and cars, then swim and enjoy the sun. Just as Bob was winning his election, the issue of access to the beaches blew wide open. In 1958, the Texas Supreme Court ruled in *Luttes v. Texas*[11] that landowners could drill and take oil in the foreshore. From that, some landowners concluded that they could bar traditional use of the beach to the public, so they began putting up fences. Beachgoers became outraged and went public with their demand for access to the beaches.

Eckhardt reacted to the dynamic with his lawyer's mind. He mulled over whether the court case did, indeed, wipe out the right of public use of the beaches and came up with the idea of an "open beaches" law. He believed that beaches had always been thought of as open to certain traditional uses. With that assumption, Eckhardt then used a law analogy of land title as a bundle of sticks. When title is attached to beaches, Eckhardt thought, that bundle does not necessarily contain a stick to drive off the public. Therefore, he concluded, why couldn't the legislature declare that, in the ordinary instance, traditional beach uses prevail? He grabbed this issue and, as the calendar turned to 1959, began preparing it for his debut as a legislator.[12]

Austin's Social and Legislative Setting

Eleven years after moving away from Austin, Bob was back home. He returned to 2300 Rio Grande and stayed with his mom, sleeping once again on the sleeping porch and reveling in getting away from "the foul humors of the Houston atmosphere."[13] John Henry Faulk, in the midst of his blacklisting battles, returned from New York City to Austin in 1959, so Bob got to see him again. He also could share Austin with his legislative compadres. Orissa and the girls occasionally came up from Houston. Bob and Orissa and Ronnie and Jean Dugger would spend evenings and weekends together; Orissa would cook a wonderful corn patty for breakfast, and they would talk *Observer* and state and national politics. Once when the Duggers and Eckhardts were camping, Bob forgot to bring the grill. He thought for awhile, then gathered bunches of green twigs, wove them into a grill, and cooked the steaks. He grabbed the finished meat off the grill just as it started to collapse into the fire.[14]

During his lobbying days, Eckhardt had come to know Malcolm McGregor, a young El Paso legislator. McGregor became a passionate leader for the liberals, and he and Eckhardt remained friends for life. When Bob traveled to El Paso, Malcolm would take him across the border to buy his favorite footwear, huaraches. Sometimes young Representative Don Kennard accompanied

Eckhardt, and the three visited the border hot springs. In Austin, Kennard and McGregor rented a house that became dubbed the "Russian Embassy," where they, Eckhardt, and other liberals plotted strategy, cussed their defeats, and shared good whiskey. Malcolm and his wife eventually moved about ten miles out of Austin. It was expensive for Bob to keep horses in Houston, so Malcolm invited him to keep his horses on his place. Bob brought them up, and he, the girls, and the Duggers would go out and ride and picnic.[15]

His political opponents begrudgingly respected Eckhardt, and his friends greatly admired him for his legislative skills, for the camaraderie they shared, and for his entertaining ploys, carried with him from his days as a UT gadfly. Once, his *Observer* friend from Marshall, Franklin Jones, visited him at the capitol. After seeing a letterhead for a dubious company in which a physician had invested unwisely and lost his money, Jones decided to adopt it, tongue-in-cheek, for his personal correspondence. His specious letterhead for "Stearns Patent Horse Detacher Co." had a sketch of a horse and carriage stuck on railroad tracks, with a train coming. He showed it to Eckhardt, who suggested that Jones should be the general counsel for the imaginary firm. So, Jones redesigned his letterhead. Thenceforth, he was general counsel and began sending a series of "Stearns letters" to Eckhardt and other political friends.[16]

Most politicians are circumspect about their public comments on unpopular issues. Not so Eckhardt—he kept his cartooning tools close by for wry commentary. Over a breakfast caucus one morning, he sketched a caustic cartoon about oil lobbyists, and McGregor copied and distributed it around the capitol.[17] Eckhardt found that mixing cartooning with a political career could be risky. In 1959, Houston civic leaders embarked on a silly campaign to get the Boy Scouts to help weed out pornography. Eckhardt thought it hilarious that the anti-smutters would engage boys to search for *Playboy*-type images—and expect them to turn them in, no less—so he drew a cartoon for the *Observer* showing scoutmasters and boys diligently looking at pictures of naked women. A constituent was not amused and wrote him a scathingly critical letter. Eckhardt, ever the gentleman, replied (in a letter published in the *Observer*) with a sympathetic take on the constituent's concerns, but also with a very revealing self-description. He wrote that during the daytime, he always worked hard, but that his alter ego—the cartoonist—came out at night, like a Mr. Hyde to his Dr. Jekyll. He agreed that his constituent had every right to object to his cartoon, but added that he had been associated with Mr. Hyde so long that "I do not wish to give him up, though he is infrequently in accord with majority public opinion. But as a lawyer and a legislator I absolutely refuse to take his case or to defend him publicly. He is incorrigible."[18]

Scholz's, of course, was a favorite watering hole for legislators. They would huddle at an inside table or retire to the outside garden, dragging a chair up to a table on the dusty caliche floor. Everyone could tell when legislators had been to Scholz's, as the bottom of their trousers would be brushed with the chalk dust. After session, they would lament the day's losses, celebrate their victories, and implore each other to stand up for virtue and justice in the next day's votes, much as earlier groups had done in D. B. Hardeman's living room. With the help of the brew, Eckhardt's Houston ally, Representative Bill Kilgarlin, would use wild gestures and rise to elocutionary heights as he made his fervent appeal to his fellow Scholz's legislative drinkers.[19]

Lobbyists, too, found a home at Scholz's, where they were close to their prey. One day Bob took his two girls to eat lunch there. When Bob asked for the check, the waitress said, "Oh, it's been taken care of." When Bob asked by whom, she said, "The gentleman over there," pointing to a lobbyist. As Bob waved his acknowledgement, young Rosalind asked, "Daddy, who paid for the lunch?" When Bob pointed out the man, she continued her inquiry. "Is he a friend of yours?" Bob replied, "Well, not exactly a friend, but he's interested in some of my legislation. I know him." Doing some quick analysis, Rosalind cried out, "Oh Daddy, he made a bribe!"[20]

Inside the Texas House

Eckhardt came to Austin as a new player of a very public role. He recognized that and hoped that his fellow legislators accepted the public nature of their roles, too. To begin the session, he penned a series of sketches for the *Observer,* strewn throughout the session-beginning edition in which Dugger asked, "Does the capitol belong to the people?" Eckhardt's text for his sketches was the UT school song:

> *The eyes of Texas are upon you,*
> *All the live long day.*
> *The eyes of Texas are upon you,*
> *You cannot get away.*
> *Do not think you can escape them,*
> *At night or early in the morn.*
> *The eyes of Texas are upon you,*
> *'Til Gabriel blows his horn.*

Eckhardt's sketches show a carefree young legislator, followed by a host of eyes, presumably those of the public, staring at him. He then tries to hide from the eyes—in his coat, in his bed, running away from them, pleading with them to leave him alone—before finally, when he cannot escape them, happily embracing Gabriel as the archangel blows his horn.[21]

Humor and patience are necessary for survival in the legislative setting. Members engaged in humorous interplays at the microphones. Legislators would rise to recognize Miss Watermelon Thump or the Buckaroos of Breckenridge High, to much applause, and often did not give much attention to serious legislative business. Eckhardt joined in the fun. Fellow Houstonian Criss Cole sponsored a resolution to name little Orissa and Rosalind as official "mascots" of the House, as many members' children were. Off the floor, cigarettes and liquor stoked the deliberations. Some would even bring their beverage of choice onto the floor of the chamber—sipping gin from a 7-Up bottle. Legislators did not have individual offices. They had to work from their desks on the floor, using a pool of secretaries in an antechamber behind the speaker. Eckhardt decided to handcraft file boxes and, in typical Eckhardt fashion, used what was handy and convenient—whiskey boxes. The wooden Cutty Sark or Berry's boxes were just the right size for his files, and he fashioned handles for convenient carrying to the floor. They also served as amusement, as an icon for his style, and as a source of irritation for some who objected to a legislator keeping whiskey boxes in plain view in the capitol. That liquor lubricated the legislative machinery was supposed to be hidden, hypocritically, from the public.

Eckhardt was at home on the House floor. He sat on the very back row, next to his anti-Communist, anti-labor nemesis Marshall Bell.[22] The speaker convened the House at 10:00 in the morning, and they adjourned about 1:00 for committee meetings. Eckhardt found the chamber to be an intensely personal legislative environment. Everyone was on the floor at the same time: 150 men (and, occasionally, one or two women members) milling around, talking, negotiating, then debating and voting. He would walk down the aisle, sit next to a member, and say, "Look, I've got this bill, and here's what it does. I think it's good for these reasons." He felt that he was successful in persuading some to vote with him.

Eckhardt fully immersed himself in the process of legislative sausage making. In debate, he would stroll to the back microphone, referred to as the "snorting pole," to parry with his opponents or support his allies. He was already known for his draftsmanship, as he would write amendments when he was a lobbyist. Now, he would mull over the bills, listen to the debate, then go sit on the carpeted steps going up to the speaker's desk, scribble out an amendment, plop it on the speaker's desk, and wait his turn at the mike.[23] Eckhardt had lobbied for the CIO, so he had more legislative experience than other newcomers, and he led the group of liberal legislators. He was not so

State Representative Eckhardt and his whiskey boxes. When Bob Eckhardt was
a freshman member of the Texas House of Representatives in 1959, members
did not have offices. Eckhardt fashioned whiskey crates into file boxes, attached
handles, put his EK signature on them, carried them to the House chamber, and
used them at his desk. Photo: AP/ Wide World Photos.

much the coordinator of their activities as he was their brain—and his intellectual leadership took them more to the left than they would have gone
without him.[24] But his role was not that of a legislative workhorse in the sense
of passing a great deal of legislation. In fact, he authored only six bills in his
first regular session—and none of them passed.

Labor, Human Services, and Criminal Law

Freshman Eckhardt was rewarded for helping clinch the speaker's reelection with a choice committee assignment—Labor. He was also appointed to the committees on Conservation and Reclamation (where Don Kennard was vice chair), Constitutional Amendments, Public Lands and Buildings, and Examination of Comptroller's and Treasurer's Accounts.

Eckhardt was now much more than a labor union advocate, but he certainly continued to play that role, working for pro-labor and health and human service legislation. The recent merger of the AFL-CIO was a catalyst for the liberal bloc. Jerry Holleman and Fred Schmidt provided support to their legislative troops from their new joint labor office two blocks from the capitol, and Eckhardt worked closely with Schmidt.[25] Though Speaker Carr had been supported by liberals, he gave conservatives majorities on committees, so labor and liberals were primarily in the opposition.[26] The Labor Committee battled over unemployment compensation eligibility, workers compensation, a fifty-cent minimum wage, and industrial safety. Eckhardt supported Charles Hughes's industrial safety bill, but it was watered down in committee and never brought up on the floor. Eckhardt and Clyde Miller sponsored a bill to advance collective bargaining in interstate commerce. The committee gutted the bill; undaunted, Eckhardt moved on the floor to report the ungutted bill on a minority report. He told the House that not once since World War II had a labor bill made it to the floor that would advance worker protection rather than restrict it. He came close, but lost 65–73.[27]

Mossback legislators pushed efforts to emaciate the state's already enfeebled social service system and to stigmatize the poor, as they always did, while the liberals tried to humanize the system. A liberal bill proposed to delete from birth certificates the baby's legitimacy status. During one debate, Eckhardt shocked his fellow legislators when he said, "I am not so much worried about the natural bastards of this state as the self-made ones." He also opposed (unsuccessfully) an amendment to reduce spending for needy children by barring payments if the household had more than one illegitimate child. He told reporters, who were frantically scribbling down his words, that he could not see why it took less to feed the second bastard than it did to feed the first one—but editors refused to use the quote. Infuriated at the proposal, Eckhardt took to the snorting pole in the late night debate in an impassioned speech. "Mr. Speaker, we're talking about the little chil'ren here!"[28] He insisted on printing in the *House Journal* the reasons for his opposition: "I will not be a party to taking food from the mouths of little dependent children either in the name of economy or in the name of virtue, for there is no economy in loosing upon the State underfed, unattended, and neglected children, and there is no virtue in punishing an innocent child because his mother has twice erred. This is a monstrous amendment," he cried.[29]

By the end of the session, the AFL-CIO rated Eckhardt as having cast twenty-four good votes and one bad (he voted to increase truck load limits). He continued his labor initiatives after the regular session. Eckhardt, Hughes, and others held hearings in Houston to build public attention and pressure for the industrial safety legislation that had died. An industrial accident that resulted in the escape of phosgene gas in La Porte served as a backdrop for their push, and they used it to remind people of the six hundred deaths in the 1947 Texas City tragedy.[30]

Criminal procedure is always a volatile subject for the legislature. In 1959, the House considered a bill requiring state courts to appoint attorneys for indigent defendants in all felony cases, instead of only in death penalty cases, but it was not until the 1965 U.S. Supreme Court case *Gideon v. Wainwright*, requiring state courts to provide lawyers for defendants, that Texas was pushed to constitutionality. To prevent police brutality, Eckhardt sponsored a measure requiring the police to tell suspects their legal rights under the Constitution and requiring any confession to be signed before a judge—an amazing initiative that predated by five years the Supreme Court's *Miranda v. Arizona* decision. He got the bill reported from the Criminal Jurisprudence Committee, but it died. He wasn't above spoofing himself. He sat at Scholz's and sketched caricatures for the *Observer* suggesting that about the only support he had for his proposal was from society's ne'er-do-wells.[31]

Election Politics on the Inside

Looming over the 1959 session was a non-member: Lyndon Johnson. In April, LBJ spoke to the House, unofficially kicking off his presidential campaign.[32] The only problem was that LBJ's Senate term was ending in 1960, and he did not wish to gamble on being out of public life by giving up his Senate seat and losing the presidential race. Rayburn, LBJ, Daniel, and their legislative team, led by Senator Dorsey Hardeman (no relation to D. B.) and Representative Marshall Bell, concocted a threefold strategy for helping LBJ—and winning the biennial intraparty battles. First, they pushed SB 458, which allowed candidates to run for president or vice president *and* one other office simultaneously. It came to be known as the LBJ Law and has had powerful consequences for state and national politics. Next, they pushed HB 158 to accomplish the other two parts of their strategy: to move the party primary elections up to May and June to help LBJ and to simply abolish the confrontational governor's conventions.

Eckhardt and Dean Johnston led the opposition to the Bell and Hardeman bills. Walter Hall advised Eckhardt about possible nefarious effects of HB 158 *and* its potential as a vehicle for helping them. He wrote Eckhardt that the bill needed to stipulate hours at which precinct conventions should be held. "I think the precinct conventions ought to be held one hour after the closing of the polls. . . . if the hour is stipulated by law, it would prevent such stuff as Jake Pickle promoted by having a few precinct conventions held around noon and then having the results put on newscasts throughout the state."[33] On the floor, Eckhardt moved to change the formula for convention voting strength to use the votes for the party's candidate for *president,* instead of *governor*—which would have yielded results based on higher turnout, and probably a more liberal electorate; it was tabled 83–50.[34]

The strategy was for LBJ to get an early 1960 primary renomination for the Senate, in advance of the national convention, so that he could concentrate on his presidential campaign. But that was an unseemly reason for the bills. Sam Rayburn called and pressured legislators to support the bills. Representative (and future Congressman) Eligio "Kika" de la Garza from South Texas spoke to Rayburn, and then took to the front microphone to suggest another explanation for his own support of the bill. "There's a reason many people have not voted," he argued. "We have a great number of cotton pickers in my district." He went on to explain that the pickers moved on to other cotton areas, such as Corpus Christi, so that "by June my people are not in my district" and cannot vote. Zeke Zbranek couldn't resist the moment and stepped to the back mike. With Eckhardt and others laughing, he said, "Kika, I would observe caution—you've been elected many times when your people were not in your district!"[35] In the Senate, Henry B. Gonzalez filibustered SB 458, but it finally passed.

Tax Equity, Again

Eckhardt now was in a place to continue the tax equity efforts he had pushed ever since the 1947 session. The comptroller forecasted deficits, so there were intense battles, not ultimately resolved until the special sessions called after the 1961 session. Texas was one of only two states with neither a sales nor an income tax. Governor Price Daniel proposed a sales tax on automobiles, a corporate franchise tax, and a flat-rate natural gas tax. Walter Hall complained to Eckhardt that the bill "is like everything else about Price—timid, inadequate, and a bit on the dumb side."[36] But Daniel was a peculiar character on taxation. He had successfully led the "Immortal 56," the legislators who fought against Pappy O'Daniel's 1939 sales tax, and he still vehemently opposed a general sales tax. He also blasted away at the oil and gas industry for tax avoidance.

Malcolm McGregor and Alonzo Jamison introduced an income tax bill. Eckhardt introduced a graduated oil tax bill and a natural gas contracts bill. He marveled that he could call Daniel's office for help garnering witnesses to testify on his gas tax bill.[37] Eckhardt was consumed with the issue of taxing oil and gas—he wanted taxes to fall heaviest on industries that extracted natural resources, rather than on manufacturing and processing. He particularly wanted to target resources that went out of state to assure that the extractor "who has a large spread between the price he pays for the gas and the price he sells it for pays more tax than the one who buys his gas at a reasonably high rate."[38] In his maiden speech to the House, he quoted the broadside in the Texas Declaration of Independence against the Mexican government for not funding public education out of its "boundless resources." He suggested that modern-day Texas had boundless resources in oil, gas, and sulfur, and it was incumbent upon legislators to use them to support education.[39] He was equally determined to address the regressivity of the tax system, separating the small and big oil companies to make the tax system progressive. Yet, he also realized that compromise was essential. As a result of the 1947, 1951, and 1957 battles, he had a profound knowledge of the constitutional limitations. McGregor concluded from working with Eckhardt that he was sincere and operated in total good faith.[40]

Eckhardt could not get his bill out of committee so, on the floor, he proposed his substitute to the governor's proposal, replacing Daniel's taxes with a graduated tax on oil and on dedicated gas contracts, producing the same amount of revenue as Daniel's bill. The tax would apply to the seventeen major oil companies, with the uppermost rate applying to companies that produced more than five million barrels a month—which meant Humble Oil, now a subsidiary of Standard of New Jersey. Eckhardt argued, "There is a need for a return to some of the old Texas conscience against monopolies. We even recognize the evil of monopoly in our Constitution—the only Constitution I know of in the world that does so. Texas has suffered from repeated monopolies, in railroads, lumber, and so on. I think the anti-monopoly approach is the tradition of Texas and in the tradition of Jim Hogg." He debated, armed with graphs, Federal Trade Commission reports, and the Texas Constitution. He and Kennard kibitzed at the mikes for votes, but they lost badly, 47–91.[41]

Neither bloc could prevail, though the moderates and liberals beat back the sales tax bloc, led by Joe Burkett. But Waggoner Carr sided with Burkett, alienating those who had voted for him over Burkett for speaker. Legislative leaders huddled with Herman Brown and other business leaders to salvage their sales tax.[42] Ultimately, the legislature was stalemated, so Governor Daniel called them back into special session.

Over the short break, Eckhardt took his usual sightseeing trip home to Houston, driving through Cat Spring, where he found a good supply of roasting ears. After the family feast, he still had enough of the corn for one of his favorite foods, a corn mush.[43] When he returned to Austin, he reintroduced his tax bills and again they went nowhere. The stalemate prevailed for the thirty-day special session, so Daniel called another, beginning the next day. Eckhardt lost his efforts in committee to get his bills out, so he had to vote on and work on others' proposals. He believed that one member's gas tax proposal would magnify inequities, but it was the only severance beneficiary tax that he thought was going to pass. He wrote a constituent after the session, "I thought it was at least a step in the right direction in levying the tax at the pipe-line level and voted for it though I have some disagreement with its operation."[44]

Eckhardt and the proponents of a gas pipeline tax finally prevailed in the House. Kennard then moved to instruct the House conferees to stand solidly behind their gas pipeline tax; his motion carried 76–72. Kika de la Garza moved to delete the tax, but was defeated 73–69.[45] That session, too, ended with no final deal. By the end of the shorter third special session, the legislature had not passed a comprehensive and far-reaching solution to the budget woes, but rather a collection of patchwork proposals: increased selective sales, corporate franchise, and utilities taxes, and new taxes on numerous products, including natural gas beneficiaries. By December 1960, a state appeals court would vote 2–1 to sustain a ruling that the natural gas pipeline tax was unconstitutional.[46]

Daniel's leadership on the tax issue had mixed results. His calling of the special sessions set the stage not only for bruising tax battles, but also for a prime Eckhardt issue that he was still developing—open beaches.

The Story of Open Beaches

In 1859, the Texas Supreme Court recognized partly public and partly private rights to the beaches, holding that Texas owned the foreshore to the demarcation of the "mean highest high tide line." In 1958, however, the court ruled in *Luttes* that the state owned to the line of mean *higher* high tide.[47] The difference in the two standards was up to 200 feet.

Throughout the regular session of 1959, Eckhardt was still researching and drafting his open beaches bill.[48] Meanwhile, along West Beach on Galveston Island, landowners and developers were driving posts into the sand and extending these barriers right into the sea in order to prevent swimmers, sunbathers, and picnickers from driving down the beach, the way the Eckhardts had for years. Bob and the family took new trips to the beach, measuring how far the tide came in and the fences extended. This expansion of fencing stirred what had been a quiet beehive of concern into a swarm of angry public protest. Not just working quietly in the capitol, Eckhardt was also developing public opinion to sustain the open beaches position by writing papers, doing radio and TV interviews, and soliciting editorials criticizing the fencings.[49] He walked around and talked to every member of the House about his idea during the session. He was able to draw on the public outrage and his power of quiet persuasion to entice more than half of the House members to appear as co-sponsors of his bill.

They may not have known it, but those legislators were signing on not just to a bill to overturn *Luttes,* but also to a historical understanding and a legal philosophy that Eckhardt had coaxed from his studies. He began with a historical-legal argument. The concept of public access, he argued, lay deep in the roots of Roman and Spanish civil law and English common law, which distinguished (1) the fee-title of an individual owner, (2) the rights of the sovereign, and (3) the people's rights to access to the beach. The sea, he argued, is the sovereign's to hold, control, and mine. The foreshore, or tidelands, had historically been held by the sovereign *in trust for the public.* The general and historical use of the beaches by the public is related to *access* to the sea. Seafarers and fishermen traditionally use the beach to land their boats and dry their nets, as a source of shellfish, as a mode of travel, and as a place to enjoy the sun and surf. Therefore, Eckhardt reasoned, "the line between private and public ownership generally may be placed at the landward border of the foreshore. . . . The normal common law rule puts this boundary at the mean high tide line. . . . Thus, it may be seen that the foreshore is generally conceded to be available for public use." [50]

He cited common law from an old English law tract: "yet the common people of England have regularly a liberty of fishing in the sea, or creeks or arms thereof as a public common . . . and may not without injury to their right be restrained of it" [51] and "the shores of the sea, incontestably belong to the nation . . . and they belong to the class of public things common to all mankind." He also found that the term "highest wave" had been used in commentaries on the civil or Spanish law. He came to believe that *all* of the Texas beaches exposed to the open sea are subject to the "immemorial customary right of the public" to access.[52]

Eckhardt then brought that historical-legal argument home to Texas and, in so doing, indulged his interest in Texas history. He explored J. Frank Dobie's writings on the "brush country" ranches, including those along the barrier islands. Long before the the nineteenth century, barren, unpopulated, or sparsely populated beaches were treated as a common. Ranchers began to establish rancheros along the sparsely populated coast and continued the common usage of beaches. Eckhardt cited an 1841 news article describing a stagecoach traveling along the beaches near Galveston: "As the coach traveled, the coach horses' feet were wetted with the spray of the sea along the hard, smooth beach, and the passengers heard 'the music of the ocean . . . as one travels.'"[53]

Thus, open beaches had been the rule under civil or Spanish law as well as the English common law; the Republic of Texas followed this concept; and it had been carried forward when the Republic became a state. After 1959, his reliance on this historical language in the drafting of the bill proved key in court rulings sustaining the law. As he later wrote: "the Open Beaches Act must tally with the common law, recognizing that long before the Act of 1959, the immemorial customary usage of the public beach has existed."[54] Eckhardt concluded that the people's right to the beaches as a public easement is a *vested* property right that cannot be divested by the sovereign without compensation and due process. It was just as important to protect that right, he believed, as those of the fee owner.

Eckhardt was, of course, keenly aware that constitutional challenges would be brought to his bill. As expected, resource development interests became alarmed. They got the attorney general to review the draft Eckhardt was circulating, as a tactic to kill it. The dean of the UT Law School, Page Keeton, spent one evening lobbying the attorney general's office for an interpretation that would hold, as Eckhardt believed, that the legislature could resolve the customary use issue in favor of the public.[55]

Three weeks into the First Called Session, with the clock ticking and the legislature deadlocked on taxes, Eckhardt had his open beaches bill ready and asked Governor Daniel to add it to the call for the session. Daniel could see the benefit of having a popular bill in the mix, supported by the anti-sales-taxers, as he was trying to keep together and expand the coalition to support his tax bill. So, he added the bill to his call.

Eckhardt was ready. His opponents were ready, too, led by his hometown freshman senator, Robert Baker. Eckhardt introduced three bills: one just to stop fencing along the beach, one to protect shores and surf, and then his comprehensive open beaches act. His Conservation and Reclamation Committee quickly reported the open beaches bill with six amendments, and it was brought to the floor. After adopting two minor committee amendments, the House then considered an amendment to exempt islands from the bill. Eckhardt offered a substitute (simply encouraging state, federal, and local cooperation on island recreation area issues) and won, 75–56. It was a good test vote for how large the pro- and anti- blocs were. He appeared to have the upper hand.

Eckhardt then offered an amendment on the definition of "line of vegetation," and the House did what it often does when battle lines are drawn and neither side is sure of victory—they fought over whether to adjourn so that the sides could regroup. They eventually broke for lunch, then came back and adopted a compromise to Eckhardt's definition, establishing a maximum of 200 feet for the line of vegetation. Opponents lost a couple of other thrusts before the House approved the bill. Eckhardt fretted that, across the rotunda, Senators Baker and Phillips were trying to emasculate the bill, and he concluded that their bill actually took away public rights to the beach. But after all that work, the session ended without Senate action.

Daniel called a second session to begin the next day—he was determined to get his tax bill through—and he added the open beaches bill to the call again. Eckhardt introduced it as HB 14. Senator Baker introduced his own bill, SB 9, which appeared to guarantee beach access, without changing the *Luttes* ruling. Whereas Eckhardt's bill would provide 100–200 feet of public beach, Baker's bill would have only declared a strip of land exposed during low tide as public land—providing no relief, or in some cases, up to fifteen feet. Eckhardt considered the Baker bill to be worthless, and he knew he would need to beat it back if he were to win the full-rounded open beaches concept in his bill. So, he dubbed Baker's bill "the Volkswagen Beach Bill," saying it would allow only a vehicle the size of a Volkswagen to drive down the beach at low tide, if it hurried back before the tide came in.[56]

Eckhardt let Baker and the Senate take the lead this time around. The Senate passed SB 9, with an amendment exempting Padre and Mustang Islands, and it was reported to the House Conservation and Reclamation Committee. Representative Sam Bass carried the Senate bill. The subcommittee chairman, Bill Shaw from the Valley, refused to call a meeting to work on the bill. Eckhardt finally cornered him in front of reporters and put a hand on his shoulder to stop him and talk to him. "Get your hands off me. I'm getting tired of all this," Shaw said. Eckhardt replied, "I'm getting tired of all the runaround. . . . When are you going to stop representing Dallas landowners of Padre Island and start representing your constituents?"[57] When he got the hearing, Eckhardt offered a redraft of Baker's bill back to the version the House had passed a few weeks earlier and convinced the committee to endorse his version.

House members who had voted against Eckhardt were inclined to go along with the Baker bill, knowing that they would curry favors with developers, while at the same time reassuring angry constituents that they had voted for open beaches. Eckhardt called on the public support for his bill to pressure wavering members. He had a 4,000-signature petition dropped, in fan style, from the balcony, to demonstrate support for his version, and he talked with reporters, blasting the Senate version as a "worthless bill."

Bass opened the floor debate on SB 9 by putting up a substitute, as is the legislative custom, as a vehicle to "perfect" the bill, but it was essentially the Baker bill all over again. During the debate on the Bass substitute, Representative Harold Parish successfully offered an amendment providing an exception that the bill would not apply to islands or peninsulas unless they may be connected to the mainland by public road or ferry facility. When the amendments to the Bass substitute had been considered, Eckhardt then offered as a substitute to the Bass substitute his version of the bill, as Committee Amendment No. 1.

The House debated open beaches all day on July 9, 1959, in Eckhardt's toughest legislative fight yet. Opponents derided his bill as "a fundamental change" in law.[58] Ben Glusing tried to delete the crucial subsection assuring public rights and failed on a tie vote, 68–68. Another amendment stipulated that the public must pay to use the beaches, and Eckhardt easily tabled it, 111–21. He then lost on two other minor amendments on close votes. Once those amendments were considered, then the decision for House members was whether to approve the Eckhardt substitute, as amended, or kill it. Approving it meant that the Bass substitute (Baker's weak Senate bill) was dead; defeating the Eckhardt substitute meant that the Bass substitute would still be alive. The motion to table the Eckhardt substitute lost, 60–78. His margin had held. Debate then continued on the Eckhardt substitute. After a few more amendments, Eckhardt's motion to strike out all that existed in SB 9 and replace it with his amended substitute was approved, 74–61.[59]

Senator Baker was apparently feeling the heat of public pressure from his Houston-area beach-loving constituents. When SB 9 arrived back in the Senate with Eckhardt's amendments, Baker moved to concur with the Eckhardt amendments. But developers were not willing to give up so easily, and in a highly unusual development, the author's motion was defeated. The vote to not concur triggered a House-Senate conference committee. Though Eckhardt had delivered the Houston delegation to Waggoner Carr, and thus assured his speakership, Carr refused to return the favor. He put open beaches opponents (Glusing and Bass) on the conference team with Eckhardt.

Then, an unexpected front in the battle opened up. Chief Clerk Dorothy Hallman had certified the Eckhardt substitute as passed by the House, with its Sections a, b, and c. But when the *House Journal* for July 9, 1959, was printed, a subsection "d" was printed with the Eckhardt House Amendment No. 1. When he looked at it, it was obvious that it was the Parish (island exemption) amendment, which had been in the defeated Bass substitute, but not in his amended substitute. Eckhardt considered Dorothy Hallman a person of impeccable veracity and competence. He knew that she would not have made such a mistake. But, because they were immediately going to conference with the Senate, with time running out, he was not able to ferret out who was behind this backroom deal to sneak the provision in. In conference, he did not feel that he could oppose "the House's position," so he hewed to the *House Journal* version.

Eckhardt had to hold a majority of the House conferees, keeping Max Smith and W. T. Oliver in his corner. Then he had to bring around three of the five senators. Brownsville's Senator Hubert Hudson often stood with the progressive factions; he had stood with Henry B. in his 1957 filibuster, helping him to defeat some of the pro-segregation bills. But businessmen wanting to develop the South Texas coast had persuaded him to vote for the Senate exemption of islands, and they were now pressuring him to vote against Eckhardt. He was wavering. Eckhardt was determined to press aggressively. He had public opinion going for him. So, in a heated private conversation with Hudson, he yelled out to the senator that if he supported the weaker version, "I'll burn your ass in your district." Baker, too, had seen the potential backlash to his career if he persisted with gutting Eckhardt's bill. Recently elevated from the House to the Senate, Baker saw the progressive tidal wave in the 1958 elections in Houston, and there were already rumors of Eckhardt running against him. Baker said to Hudson, "Let's give Eckhardt something— give him his little amendment."[60] Thus, the conference committee approved Eckhardt's "little amendment," which included virtually his whole bill, plus the Parish amendment. The conference bill went to the House and Senate chambers, where it was finally passed on July 16, 1959—quite a present for Eckhardt's forty-sixth birthday.

The Outstanding Freshman Legislator had prevailed. The press immediately reported that Eckhardt was a strong liberal contender to take on Baker in a future election.[61] Eckhardt's victory assured that both immemorial custom and the statutory rights of property in the open beaches became vested property that could not be removed without due process. Yet, just as had happened with his earlier victories in getting gas taxes passed, he knew that his legislative victory could be cut short. Indeed, in the half century since the adoption of the law, it has been repeatedly tested by litigation, by the legislature itself—and even by hurricanes.

Five years after Eckhardt's victory, the Houston Court of Civil Appeals established judicially that Galveston's beaches were statutorily and constitutionally public beaches, and the Texas Supreme Court declined the case, thus assuring the constitutionality of Eckhardt's Open Beaches Act. Oregon and California courts soon cited the Texas law and case in protecting beach access in those states.[62] The cases kept coming, and the courts continued upholding not just the law, but also the legal philosophy that Eckhardt had espoused.[63]

Years later, after twenty-two years of legislating in the Texas House and the U.S. Congress, Eckhardt described the 1959 Open Beaches Act as "my best bill." He tried to extend his idea nationally once he was in Congress, but was not successful there. Back in Texas, the legislature has repeatedly considered amendments sponsored by developers to create exceptions to the law. Even now, the legislative assaults continue, and the state's elected officials nervously look for ways to avoid enforcing the act.

Eckhardt's stellar research and draftsmanship has kept alive his open beaches victory, an improbable victory against the Knights of Congress Avenue. It was already clear in 1959 that, in the capitol's world of pygmies and giants, Robert Christian Eckhardt would become one of the legislative giants, revered through the years.

TEN

The Veteran Legislator

With the end of the 1959 sessions, Bob Eckhardt spent the next seven years as a veteran legislator, still involved as well in the wider political battles beyond his legislative seat. These early legislative years were intense, and he shined in the glare of the lights. He won his Open Beaches Act and he would lead the legislative forces for progressive taxation, environmental protection, and worker safety.

Eckhardt's era as a veteran legislator began with a poignant nod to the progressive past—in September 1959, Jimmie Allred died. The man who had defended Dr. Bob Montgomery and brought J. R. Parten to UT and Ralph Yarborough to Austin, the man responsible for the Texas version of the New Deal, the man who had shared cigars with Bob and Creek in the governor's mansion, was gone. Allred had carried the Jim Hogg wing of the Texas Democratic Party through and beyond the Depression—and Eckhardt, as exemplified in his leadership on behalf of Yarborough and in his 1956 county convention speech, sought to carry that anti-monopoly, populist message forward.

Jimmie Allred had tried to use the state's tax system to provide equity among Texans and to sustain his populist vision. Pappy O'Daniel had gone the other direction, with his sales tax proposal. For decades, progressives argued and voted for income and natural resource taxation, while the business community continued to fight virtually any tax. Eckhardt had jumped into that fray in 1947 and again in 1959 with his natural gas tax proposals. Eckhardt's 1961 sophomore legislative season would see the climactic battle in the tax wars, and the business community would come out victorious with a general sales tax. Eckhardt skillfully led the House to adoption of a natural gas tax, though the Knights of Congress Avenue once again seeded it with a poison pill.

To continue the populist traditions as a legislator meant that Eckhardt was constantly aligning himself in battles against the Knights. Eckhardt sketched an *Observer* cartoon, "Texas Chess," with the hands of two players on either side of a chessboard, which only had pawns on it. "Any number of lobbyists can play," read the caption. He wryly described his sketch, saying, "The game

EK
♡

may be played for money."[1] Eckhardt argued that the lobby "operates now like a kind of foreign service, with its ambassadors in Austin representing the business interests in Houston and Dallas and elsewhere. It's become less a purveyor of beef and bourbon than an ambassador for the local chambers of commerce."[2] Being a legislative technician, he was disgusted that lobbyists got their bills through committee with little or no change, then lobbied the floor for up or down votes, "without any concept of accommodation or amendment.... [it was] lobbying that called for an unreasoned, uncompromised result."[3] He and his allies would win a few battles and lose a lot. Despite the Knights' repeated efforts, it would be years before they checkmated Eckhardt out of politics.

Divorce, Dating, Remarrying

Lauded and admired for his wit and legislative acumen, Eckhardt still held a sense of reticence about politics becoming his whole life. He wanted to engage more deeply with his family and his friends on matters other than politics. When Little Orissa's horse died, he saw his daughters' anguish and avowed that "my little girls' emotion made my love for them gush forth." He knew that politics pulled him away from that love and from his friendships. I "want a very few people to love me a great deal rather than a great number of people to love me a little bit," he wrote, and offered his own list of "my warm friends: Charles Black, Tommie Sutherland, Ronnie Dugger, Maury Maverick Jr., and a few others." Then there was the campaigning and politicking that made him so uncomfortable. "Politics is an alligator pit," he wrote. "Nobody ever does anything except to get credit.... Though there are several things I like about politics—an opportunity for self expression, to put over a program or a reform that I think is desirable, etc.—I constantly find myself hating the aspect of politics related to this pushy type of activity that not only makes others obnoxious to me but *me* obnoxious to *me* for being sucked into it."[4]

By the end of the 1950s, the strain of his constant political activity—and an extramarital affair—pulled Bob and Orissa's marriage apart. Bob had maintained an on-and-off relationship with Julya (Thomson) Kirkpatrick ever since their UT days. When Orissa discovered that they were continuing an affair, she confronted them and insisted that he stop. Bob loved Orissa and felt close to her; he did not want a divorce, yet he also loved Julya and would not give up his relationship with her. Could he really have imagined that he could continue relationships with both? Orissa could not put up with it any longer. Immediately after his reelection in November 1960, they separated. They had to talk with Rosalind and Orissa, and Bob cried as he told them.[5] He moved out of the house that Orissa had designed and they had built together and into a small apartment two blocks away. Bob bought an old red Volkswagen and Orissa kept their Corvair.

Bob had never lived alone. He stocked his refrigerator with wine, but didn't get around to buying food for some time. At his folks' house, their maids had always cleaned up after him, and then Orissa had. In his bachelor apartment, he began a pattern that would repeat itself throughout his life (and cause huge problems): he would not take care of his home, and there was no one to pick up after him. The floor of his apartment was completely strewn with dirty clothes, books, and kitchen items. He would prop his type-writer on two empty whiskey cases close to the gas heater, typing away in the cold apartment. He knew how his lifestyle looked to others, describing it as a *kitchen midden*—a city where primitive people dwelled, moving on when their abode became so cluttered and befouled that they could not live there anymore.[6]

What would he do now? Reconcile with Orissa? Be a bachelor? Finally get together with Julya in a permanent relationship? Julya, too, was married, and though she considered it, she never divorced. But Bob and Orissa could not reconcile and divorced in early 1961.

Bob gave up the bachelor apartment and moved back home to 2300 Rio Grande during the 1961 session, pasturing his horses on Malcolm McGregor's rented ranchland. He had to find a permanent Houston home, so he soon sold some of his parents' land in Austin that he now owned, and he and Eddie Ball bought some wooded acreage on Cypress Creek in northeast Harris County. Ball soon sold his part of the land to Eckhardt.[7] Bachelor Eckhardt put up a tent and camped on the shores of the creek. He started planning to build his house among the Cypress Creek oaks, beeches, magnolias, and pines.

Bob believed that he and Orissa were still on good terms with each other. She continued her architecture career and her painting. Complicating their marriage, and now their post-marriage relationship, was the resurgence of Orissa's mental illness. She had improved in the years after the war, but as time went on, she experienced bouts of severe depression. After the divorce, Orissa would be found wandering Houston, incoherent, as she had in Coleman fifteen years earlier. She was hospitalized several times for depression and psychotic episodes. Bob came to regret that medications for manic-depressive illness were not readily available then, as they would later come to be.

Bob's divorce happened about the same time as a divorce of two of his friends. Bill Brammer had left Senator Lyndon Johnson's staff, then had a series of brief jobs in Washington, New York, and Austin. Bill and Nadine struggled financially, and Nadine moved back to Austin with Sidney, Shelby, and Willie. Nadine thought they would reconcile, but not until or unless Bill became more stable with jobs and money. Bill, in turn, despaired of Nadine's Austin lifestyle. Their financial situation did not improve, even with his novel now finished and on the market. Brammer published *The Gay Place* with Houghton Mifflin, receiving their Literary Fellowship Award. By May, the book was on bestseller lists and would soon be reviewed in *Time, New Republic,* and other publications. Bill came to Texas for a book tour, and he and Nadine had high hopes for a movie deal. The royalties helped, but did not solve their financial (or marital) woes. After being separated for three years, they filed for divorce in April 1961.[8]

After Nadine's return to Austin, she went back to the capitol, where she had worked briefly before Bill and she had left to work on LBJ's staff. Eckhardt offered Nadine a position as his legislative secretary, but she decided instead to work for his new desk mate and ally, Bob Mullen. Eckhardt was angry with her for not working for him, and she mollified him by bringing him coffee when she came to the floor. Gradually, their relationship turned in another direction. Bob would visit Nadine at her pink Austin house, where they would laugh, call friends such as Walter Jenkins in Washington, and write mocking lyrics about John Connally now being head of the queen's navy in his new position in the JFK Administration.[9] Bill still harbored hopes of reconciling, writing Nadine, "I adore you, so, have sent Bob Eckhardt a timebomb in the mail. Hope you don't mind."[10] Nadine went to work at UT after the session, and Bob and she continued dating and fell in love, exchanging passionate letters when they were separated. Bob broke off his relationship with Julya in 1962, not to see her again for twenty-five years.

Eckhardt's life was hectic, mixing law and politics with seeing Nadine in Austin as often as he could. He was an observant man, visually oriented, and would soak up the sights around him on his trips. In November 1961, he rode the train to St. Louis for CWA negotiations with Southwestern Bell. He returned to his room at the Hilton and took a streetcar to Gaslight Square, then after more negotiations the next day, he took a long stroll along the sycamore-lined streets on the south side, near the brewery, observing the people of St. Louis. Each one produced in his mind a caricature of features, some reminding him of people he had seen in other parts of the country. That night, when he wrote to Nadine, he didn't just describe the people, but also sketched cameos of three different duos: one, characters of "middle European stolidity," one of "homo sapiens Arkansana," and one describing the scene at Gaslight Square, "cats like these," a young black man and young white man.[11]

Over the Christmas break, while vacationing in Mexico, Bob and Nadine decided to marry. They married on March 8, 1962, and Eckhardt suddenly found himself with a huge family. They camped on his wooded acreage, cooking on an open fire, bathing in the creek, and riding the horses, as Bob built a shack. They soon tired of roughing it, so they also rented an apartment in Houston. Norma Eckhardt was still energetic and would come down and watch the kids while Bob and Nadine worked on the rustic shack that would last for years, nestled in and around the trees. Bob bought a pot-bellied iron stove at an antique shop. Soon they built a barn, where they stabled Giji, June, Misty, and Rebel. Willie learned to ride—Norma even rode the horses—and they enjoyed a new colt born on the land. The girls kept hens, and they all learned target shooting.[12] It was a crude existence, as they did not have electricity for some time. One winter morning, Bob got ready to take Rosalind to school and head on to Austin, but they could not get the old red Volkswagen to move. Bob discovered that the parking brake was frozen. He got a candle, crawled under the car, and heated the brake with the candle, then raced to the school and on to Austin.[13]

For her junior and senior years (1962–1964), 'Rissa transferred to St. Stephen's Episcopal boarding school in Austin. She loved the new school and its social setting and was eager to have her dad visit when he drove to Austin.[14] Bob and Nadine rented one of the apartments that Norma had built behind her house, so they would have a place big enough for the kids. They also rented a "hideaway" one-room apartment in the "cloakroom" building across a side street from the capitol. There, they entertained guests such as Ronnie Dugger and John Silber, chair of the Department of Philosophy at UT, and, during the session, provided a place for strategy gatherings.[15] The Brammer girls went to school in Austin, while Willie was a frequent companion to Bob and Nadine at the capitol. Rosalind stayed in Houston with Big Orissa and would come up some weekends to see them and sister Orissa. She would write (to "the sweetest daddy in the whole world"), filling Bob in on how her mom was doing, reporting that some days she didn't seem as blue as others.

Transitions for the *Texas Observer* and Labor

By 1960, Ronnie Dugger had edited the *Texas Observer* for five years, seeking Bob Eckhardt's counsel, drawing on Eckhardt's cartooning pen, and covering him in the Democratic political battles and now as a new political official. Ronnie and Jean Dugger vacationed with the Eckhardts in Mexico and in Maverick Society gatherings around Texas. Dugger not only admired and revered Eckhardt as an intellectual and a political leader, but also loved him as a brother and friend.

Dugger had to constantly raise money and soon convinced Bernard Rapoport to be the *Observer's* financial backstop. The editor also frequently had to recruit new staff members, who then became comrades of Eckhardt's.

Ronnie Dugger, Bernard Rapoport, and Bob Eckhardt. Bob Eckhardt and Bernard
Rapoport were both students at the University of Texas in the 1930s, then became
active in Democratic politics together. In 1954, Eckhardt was one of the founders
of the *Texas Observer*. Ronnie Dugger was the first editor, and later the publisher,
of the *Observer,* and the two became fast friends for life. Eckhardt drew cartoons
and wrote articles for Dugger, and Dugger covered Eckhardt upon his entry to
elected office. Rapoport became one of Eckhardt's largest campaign contributors
and a crucial financier for the *Observer*. In this photo, the three friends talk at
the 1976 Democratic National Convention. Courtesy of the Robert C. Eckhardt
Collection, Center for American History, University of Texas at Austin, CN 12137.

When Dugger decided to take a break, Willie Morris took over as editor in
March 1961, with Robert "Bob" Sherrill as his associate editor. Morris had
come from segregationist Mississippi to UT in 1952, and it changed him, as
he describes in *North Toward Home*.[16] As editor of the *Daily Texan* in 1955–56,
his criticism of oil and gas agitated the UT president and board of regents,
and his writing was censored. Like Dugger before him, Morris went off to
Oxford after his UT years. Then he and his wife Celia returned and Willie
went to work as Dugger's associate editor, then editor. Morris, too, would
come to deeply admire and respect Eckhardt. He saw Eckhardt as "a gentle
and learned man, undoubtedly one of the outstanding men in state politics
in America," a genius with anecdotes and stories.[17] In 1963, Morris left the
Observer and Dugger returned as editor.

Bob met Celia Morris during those years, but neither paid much attention to each other. Born in Houston as Celia Buchan, she attended UT, graduating Phi Beta Kappa in 1957. After London and the *Observer* with Willie, she went to graduate school, and they had a son, David. Celia received her PhD before she and Willie divorced in 1969. She taught at UT, City University of New York, and Pace College, then became senior editor of *Change* magazine. Her memories of Eckhardt in the early 1960s were somewhat less glowing than those of her then-husband. Celia remembered observing Eckhardt eating at Scholz's, cutting his bread with his pocketknife and plunging the bread into his gravy, swirling the bread around, then eating it with a look of immense satisfaction.[18] She was not impressed.

Like the *Observer*, labor was experiencing restlessness and change in its ranks. The 1960 JFK-LBJ victory may have been good for labor, but it also set off an internal Texas labor fight. Texas AFL-CIO President Jerry Holleman worked to keep labor support for LBJ in the party battles, and LBJ got Kennedy to name Holleman assistant secretary of Labor. Texas AFL-CIO Secretary-Treasurer Fred Schmidt was eager to step into the presidency, but Education and Research Director Hank Brown challenged him for the office. It was a quick but bitter race, stirring the industrial union-craft union-ideology wars.[19] Eckhardt supported Schmidt, but Eddie Ball and others were hostile to Schmidt's democratic socialism. Hank Brown won in a secret ballot. Dugger later wrote that Schmidt "was vulnerable in the union movement because he was an intellectual . . . ."[20] Eckhardt had lost his friend as a key labor ally.

Campaigner Eckhardt in the Early 1960s

Already well regarded, Eckhardt emerged from his freshman sessions with even greater stature. He was a battle-sharpened, respected forty-seven-year-old political and legislative veteran, and speculation was swirling about his future. Labor wanted him to be their man to win a Houston congressional seat, and pledged $25,000 for that purpose. Possible targets included conservative Bob Casey and sometimes labor ally, sometimes Brown and Root ally Albert Thomas. The state Senate was also a possibility, as was taking his leadership of the House liberal bloc into a speakership campaign. Early in 1960, the *Dallas Morning News* wrote that Eckhardt, "generally recognized as a mighty smart mind in the growing House liberal bloc, has his eyes on a race for Speaker in 1963. Reportedly he had that in mind when he rejected suggestions that he run against Congressman Bob Casey."[21]

But Eckhardt concluded that he could never win in a war against the Knights, who almost always controlled the speakership. As for the congressional seat, Mrs. Randolph and some others in Harris County Democrats did not think that Casey was beatable. Eckhardt learned that Congressman Thomas was ailing with a slow-developing cancer, and he thought that Thomas would soon retire. Moreover, he wasn't ready to leave the Texas legislature or his law practice. "I like being a lawyer; I like being a politician, and I like being a cartoonist," he wrote. "I'd have to choose to be a pretty full time politician to go to Congress. I find the job [as Texas Representative] fascinating, a sort of Dimaggio-of-the-Little-Leagues position, as [journalist] Bill Kittrell very flatteringly put it."[22] So, he bought a new seersucker suit and ran for reelection.

Yet Eckhardt never seemed to find the intense energy for campaigning that he found for his broader organizational work. "It's pretty grim to have to go to the San Jacinto Battleground on San Jacinto day," he wryly commented. "Isn't that what those men fought for: to keep us from having to do things like that?" After attending an opening of a chamber of commerce office, he wrote that supporters "demand that I demean myself. . . ." He continued:

> It removes supporters' inferiority complexes. They think, "yeah, he gets elected to that high and mighty office of Representative, Place 2, but look how silly he looks jumping up as high as he can with his shirttail hanging out, nailing a political placard out of reach; look at him with his pockets all bulging with stuff about himself, trudging through the supermarket parking area." It's sort of like a fraternity initiation. When you've done enough demeaning exercises to hate yourself and everybody around you, they think you're fit for their company—and I suppose you are.[23]

If he wasn't a keen, aggressive campaigner, he had admirers who were committed to him and pulled him through—Ed Ball, Frankie Randolph, Billie Carr. As Billie noted, "You couldn't even get Eckhardt to campaign. . . . the Harris County Democrats had to do all the work."[24] He wouldn't focus on his campaign responsibilities—even forgetting once to pick up Mrs. Randolph and take her with him, as he had promised her.[25]

Sometimes when campaigning at black churches, Bob would take his family along. At one church, the preacher introduced him, telling the congregation that Eckhardt may be white, "but he has a black heart." Eckhardt had to explain to his daughters that this was a high compliment.[26] Eckhardt had struck up an acquaintanceship with Lonnie Smith, the African-American dentist who had dealt the deathblow to the white primary in *Smith v. Allwright*. Knowing that Dr. Smith was from Yoakum, near Yorktown, Eckhardt told him about when his dad rode on a plow with Tom Smith, who ran the farming operation for the Eckhardt Ranch. Dr. Smith told him that Tom Smith was his uncle! Dr. Smith would take Eckhardt to bars and other places to introduce him to black Houstonians.

Bob's campaigns were a family affair. Norma Eckhardt would come to Houston, eagerly plunging into the work at the campaign office. The girls would be hauled into the campaign events. They all got drawn into the labor and race issues of the day that were embodied in his campaigns. Sometimes the girls would ask someone to vote for Daddy, only to hear, "Oh, I wouldn't vote for that pinko commie." One day when Norma was working the telephones, a voter let her know in no uncertain terms that he just could not go along with Bob's attitudes about integration. "Oh, that's my fault," Norma replied. "I taught him to be a Christian." [27]

As Eckhardt vied for reelection in 1960, candidates started jockeying for other positions. LBJ announced that he would run for the presidency—*and* for reelection to his Senate seat. Price Daniel decided to go for a third term as governor. The Democrats of Texas met at the Rice Hotel in Houston in February 1960, hearing William Wayne Justice, Creek Fath, and Walter Hall. Eckhardt spoke as chair of the Harris County Democrats, then introduced the main speaker, U.S. Senator Wayne Morse from Oregon, who praised Yarborough. [28]

The right was resurgent in 1960. In the state legislative multi-member countywide races, the *Houston Chronicle* endorsed the conservative slate— including attorney Tom Norman to defeat Eckhardt. Although Eckhardt easily won (84,745 to 57,229), most of the class of '58 lost. [29] Rice University sociologist Chandler Davidson found that Eckhardt won 87 percent of the black vote, but only 57 percent of the white vote. Precincts in the lowest income ranges gave him 64 percent; the highest income precincts, only 29 percent. His lowest support was in the white River Oaks precinct (perhaps the most affluent residential area in the South), where he received only 20 percent. [30]

Around the state, there were many bolts from county conventions. The anti-Communist Freedom in Action forces were victorious in Harris County, so Loyalists bolted. Eckhardt, Dixie, Randolph, Ball, and county party chair Woodrow Seals were not even seated as delegates. [31] The loss of the county convention prompted Eckhardt to draw an *Observer* cartoon, likely inspired by his sketch for Mewhinney's *Manual for Neanderthals*. The cartoon showed a delegate on his way to the fairgrounds for the convention, then stopping, pulling out a stone tomahawk from his briefcase, and heading into the convention, whooping. The caption: "Neo-Neanderthal." [32]

At the state convention in Austin, Randolph and the others were not seated, and she was stripped from the DNC. In Los Angeles, Rayburn pulled hard for LBJ, but Kennedy prevailed. The shocker of JFK adding LBJ to the ticket as the vice presidential nominee halted everyone in their tracks. Fath predicted, correctly, that the LBJ nomination meant the end of the Democrats of Texas, as everyone would be pulled into the energized national effort

1960, Eckhardt, JFK, and LBJ. In 1960, Democratic presidential nominee John F. Kennedy and his running mate Lyndon Johnson made a campaign stop in Houston. As chairman of the Harris County Democrats, Bob Eckhardt leapt into the campaign. Courtesy of the Eckhardt family.

for the ticket. Eckhardt immediately called a meeting of his Harris County Democrats' executive committee and got their unanimous support to send his telegram to the Kennedy-Johnson campaign offering their service "in carrying Harris County for you."[33]

Eckhardt plunged into the local Kennedy campaign, in which volunteers, including a young African-American lawyer named Barbara Jordan, went door to door. In September, the presidential campaign made a swing through Texas. When the plane touched down in Houston, Eckhardt met them at the airport. The crowd greeted JFK and Frankie Randolph with the largest rounds of applause.[34] Yarborough came to town in October to campaign for Kennedy, and Eckhardt introduced him to the crowd. Harris County Democrats sponsored a Kennedy Ladies Tea, attracting more than three thousand to gather with Lady Bird Johnson and others.

Eckhardt organized and drew artwork for a last-minute get-out-the-vote campaign called "Operation Shoe Leather." His logo for the letterhead and name tags depicted a collection of shoes and boots, women's and men's.

On the Saturday before the election, three hundred volunteers slapped on Eckhardt's Shoe Leather name tags at the East End YMCA and set out to work the streets for Kennedy. On election day, Eckhardt easily won, getting 162,271 votes to beat Republican Carlos G. Watson's 84,972 votes.[35] Kennedy and Johnson lost Harris County, barely carrying Texas and the nation.

UP OR OUT?

As the 1961 legislative session began, a nonpartisan special election was being held to fill Johnson's Senate seat. Henry B., Jim Wright, and Maury Maverick Jr. all ran. Eckhardt, Harris County Democrats, the Harris County AFL-CIO Council, and the state AFL-CIO campaigned hard and enthusiastically for Maverick.[36] But Republican John Tower, who had never stopped campaigning after losing to LBJ in the November Senate race, won a runoff, starting the crack in Texas's one-party Democratic system.

Labor leaders and the Loyal Democrats huddled in Austin to strategize. One issue that concerned everyone was patronage in the new Democratic administration. They appointed Eckhardt to head a committee to meet with Johnson, Yarborough, and Rayburn (who soon died). The strategizers also discussed the 1962 elections and pushed Eckhardt to run for governor, lieutenant governor, attorney general, or the state supreme court.[37] He discussed these political winds over lunch with Minnie Fish in Austin one October weekend, then they attended a meeting of the "Democratic Coalition," a newly emerging organization to replace the Democrats of Texas—an effort that some of the participants jokingly referred to as IDIOTS—Intractable Disorganized Independents of Texas, Syndicated.[38]

Though Eckhardt was clearly an influential force in the House, it was obvious that he and his allies were outnumbered, and the speakership was an unlikely grail. Before the next elections, he decided that it was time to move on. In October 1961, he announced his candidacy against Senator Robert Baker of the Volkswagen Beach Bill.[39]

The reaction was not what he expected. Some of Bob's labor allies were furious with him. Ed Ball took him aside and told him that they were determined to get him in Congress, and they didn't want a new part-time, low-paying state Senate job (or losing the race) to sidetrack him. Ball had spoken with Congressman Albert Thomas about what would happen with his seat when he retired, and Thomas told Ball, confidentially, that he thought Eckhardt was by far the best person to succeed him. Indeed, Albert Thomas and Lyndon Johnson both said the same thing about Eckhardt: that he was born and bred to be a congressman.[40] Ball told Eckhardt that labor wanted him in the race for Thomas's seat—if not in 1962, then in 1964, when Thomas was expected to retire. Reluctantly, but with a bit of hope for the future, Eckhardt retracted his announcement and ran for reelection to the House.

ECKHARDT, CONNALLY, AND JORDAN

As the 1962 political season approached, Governor Daniel was undecided about whether to run for a fourth term. Waiting in the wings, off in the Kennedy-Johnson administration, was John Connally. By the time Daniel decided to run, Connally would not back out. He ran with sizable contributions from Brown & Root, with whom he had long been associated.[41] Houstonian Don Yarborough (no relation to Ralph) decided to run and was backed intensely by liberals. Governor Daniel did not even make the primary runoff. Connally and Don Yarborough went into a runoff, which Connally won.

Eckhardt also had to campaign for his own renomination, against businessman Russell Cummings. He asked his Austin friend and revered New Deal photographer Russell Lee to shoot photos for his campaign material.[42] Eckhardt told his constituents that his Open Beaches Bill "has been upheld in court, and the fences across Galveston beach have come down" and highlighted his worker safety and environmental stance.[43] Nadine and the kids helped at the headquarters, rallies, and coffees, where the kids would filch cookies.

The Harris County Democrats proved again to be the backbone of Eckhardt's campaign. Liberals and labor had benefited from HCD organizing by getting Eckhardt and others elected. But HCD had not yet cracked the race barrier. Like many other U.S. cities in the 1960s, Houston was experiencing racial tension. Blacks protested school segregation and police killings of minorities. Students at Texas Southern University sponsored sit-ins. The Negro Baptist Ministers' Association and the Harris County Council of Organizations were influential, but there were few black candidates to support. African Americans simply could not win running countywide, with a large Anglo plurality in the county.[44] Then, Barbara Jordan joined Harris County Democrats, as a result of her work with the Kennedy campaign and her NAACP school integration efforts. When Eckhardt stepped down as chair, Chris Dixie was elected. Dixie, Eckhardt, Randolph, and Ball all admired Jordan, and she was elected vice chair. Dixie urged her to run for the legislature in 1962; she borrowed the filing money from him and ran.[45]

The heady days of the liberals' 1958 victories, though, could not be replicated. Don Yarborough lost in the governor's race. Bill Kilgarlin, who had lost his House seat in 1960, did win the county party chairmanship for the liberals. Eckhardt and Charles Whitfield were the only Harris County liberals to win without runoffs. Eckhardt won 66,965 to 49,537, though Cummings outspent him about $13,000 to $4,000.[46] Barbara Jordan did not even make the runoff. Blacks complained that labor had not contributed a substantial vote for Jordan, while some liberals complained that blacks had voted for her, but ignored other races in which white liberals opposed conservatives. Jordan felt that she had been used.[47]

In the fall 1962 campaign, Russell Pryor was the Republican nominee against Eckhardt. Also, Price Daniel's 1960 Democratic opponent, oilman and FIA leader Jack Cox, now mounted a campaign as the Republican nominee for governor. Both Connally and Eckhardt had intense campaigns on their hands. Eckhardt had never liked Connally, but Cox was even more of a danger: "a real pitch man," he described him, "a modern W. Lee O'Daniel for the white collar crowd."[48] So Eckhardt campaigned actively for Connally. Cox and Connally battled to a draw in Houston, while statewide Connally won the close election. The victorious Connally thanked Eckhardt profusely for all he had done for him in Houston.[49]

As the campaign unfolded, Pryor asked voters to "Help Pry Mr. Income-Tax Eckhardt Out of Office." Eckhardt argued that he had voted against the 1961 tax bill and that he was the only one of the conferees who refused to support "the biggest and worst tax in Texas history."[50] Eckhardt won in his closest race to date, 114,877 to 86,893, despite being outspent. Yet how much either side spent was more a mystery than an exact reporting. Eckhardt filed and found that he was spending more than Pryor. Then, lo and behold, late campaign finance reports came in after the election, showing that Eckhardt had, after all, been outspent considerably. He saw this time and time again in his legislative election campaigns: with no enforcement mechanism, candidates would hold back their reporting so that it would not be known until after the election.[51]

Rebuking Superciliousness and Tyranny

With his 1960 and 1962 decisions to stay in the House, Eckhardt leapt into the policy and political skirmishes in Austin. Returning to the capitol, he ordered his official state letterhead printed with the family brand, now his personal logo, $\overset{EK}{\heartsuit}$. His sophomore session in 1961 showcased his leadership abilities in an environment that appreciated his skills and positions. It was a brief moment. His junior session in 1963 demonstrated the power of a resurgent Establishment to marginalize those like Eckhardt.

As 1961 dawned, the comptroller forecasted budget deficits, and legislators faced another marathon of sessions. Eckhardt developed key relationships with newcomers Neil Caldwell and, from East Texas, future Congressman Charlie Wilson. Meanwhile, Eckhardt's county delegation convened in angry meetings with screaming and shouting as the ideological electoral battles carried forward into the halls of the capitol.

The first task of the House was to elect a speaker to succeed Waggoner Carr. Conservative Wade Spilman and East Texas populist Jimmy Turman ran. Eckhardt was an early supporter of Turman, who put together a coalition of liberals, East Texas neighbors, and others and won 83–66. Turman gave liberals good committee assignments, but he did not shut conservatives out.[52] Speaker Turman rewarded Eckhardt by making him chair of Criminal Jurisprudence. The new chair of House Administration tried to confiscate Eckhardt's whiskey boxes. Bob tried to protect them, but this time, his opponents found a way of forcing him to remove them. Speaker Turman decided that, for the first time, a few legislators would be allowed to have individual capitol offices. As a committee chairman, Eckhardt was one of the first to get an office—so that he would get his whiskey boxes off the floor! He could look out at the UT Tower from his new office "up on the third floor of this wonderful old capitol building—built for giants and occupied by midgets," he wrote.[53] He liked his quip. When he repeated it to Willie Morris, it was "built for giants and inhabited by pygmies."

Eckhardt also got a prize appointment to the Revenue and Taxation Committee. He stayed on Labor as well as Conservation and Reclamation, and he also served on Federal Relations, chaired by Don Kennard. The new Turman majority quickly passed its reform bill, the Legislative Reorganization Act of 1961. It allowed representatives to choose one committee in order of seniority, (thus limiting the speaker to selecting about three-fourths of the membership of committees).[54]

Eckhardt introduced twelve bills in the 1961 Regular Session, and none of them passed. His natural gas tax bill was postponed on a 64–61 floor vote, thus allowing its death by calendar. Yet, he was often effective in persuading members on the floor to vote with him, even on his populist proposals, such as a successful amendment to a Railroad Commission bill stipulating that the bill would not alter laws against monopolies.[55]

ECKHARDT, BUDDING ENVIRONMENTALIST

Here at the dawning of the environmental movement, just as Rachel Carson was finishing her seminal work *Silent Spring*, Bob Eckhardt was poised to follow up on his 1959 Open Beaches Act by becoming a key voice in environmental policymaking. He used his seat on the Conservation and Reclamation Committee and his chairmanship of Criminal Jurisprudence as his launching pads. Environmental policy would feature prominently in Eckhardt's career for the next two decades, and it began with Houston-based issues.

In 1953, Harris County hired Dr. Walter Quebedeaux to head its new pollution control unit.[56] He immediately alienated the City of Houston by charging it with dumping sewage into the bayous that flowed into the ship channel, and he filed numerous suits against polluting companies. Then in 1961, in his lawsuit against Stauffer Chemical Company, an appeals court ruled that local courts had no authority to exact fines.

Eckhardt supported Quebedeaux and admired his stamina. In response to the Stauffer pollution and the court cases, he introduced three bills: declaring corporations to be entities that can be sued, providing for criminal process on a corporation, and providing fines against corporations. He got the bills through his Criminal Jurisprudence Committee, but the conservative clique knocked all his bills off the calendar.[57] Eckhardt later wrote that "highpowered lobbyists, being threatened at the local level, had thwarted attempts to amend the laws so that local officials might haul their clients into court."[58]

TAX EQUITY, AGAIN

Governor Daniel continued his opposition to a general sales tax, but Speaker Turman was undecided. Business at first opposed such a tax, wanting selective taxes. Yet, the business community soon came around to supporting a general sales tax rather than face other taxes that would have hurt them directly, including Eckhardt's oil and gas taxes. The Knights, using the name "Citizens for a Sales Tax," went office to office, telling representatives they should vote for a sales tax and business would not oppose them in the next election.[59] Eckhardt publicly named the big-time lobbyists who led the group and described it as a front for oil, gas, and interstate corporate interests.

Daniel proposed a grab bag menu package for legislators to choose from. Eckhardt, with a seat at the table on the Revenue and Taxation Committee, suggested that anyone who opposed Daniel's program should be willing to offer alternatives, and he did just that. He proposed a corporate net profits tax to replace the franchise tax, a tax on stocks and bonds dividends, a graduated oil production tax, and a natural gas dedicated reserves tax, arguing that his package would make the Texas tax system more equitable.[60]

Eckhardt proved dangerous, especially to those unfamiliar with his style and mannerisms. Willie Morris wrote that lobbyists flying to Texas for corporate testimony were forewarned by their bosses to look out for a legislator named Eckhardt, with a dirt farmer drawl, who knew more than they did.[61] He challenged every major lobbyist for the pipeline companies at the tax hearings. When a paper company lobbyist warned the Committee against taxes and threatened to pull his company out of Texas, Eckhardt pressed him on why his company had located in Texas. "I wonder if it had anything to do with water and trees," he drawled (wahduh an' treees), and he attacked big corporations that "come down here and take our natural resources out of our earth, and take our water and our trees, and use our roads, and send their children to our schools, and don't begin to give us a proper social payment in return."[62]

Eckhardt finally got his gas tax bill to the floor; he lost by two votes, then on a second effort lost again by three votes.[63] The sales tax bill made it to the House floor over Eckhardt's opposition. Eckhardt offered a floor amendment to declare that a sales tax is regressive and to include a "regressivity compensation factor" based on income. It was a mild form of income tax intended to make the omnibus tax bill come out with a proportional tax result. He did not actually believe that it would pass, but offered it to demonstrate how the poor were paying a higher percentage of their earnings than the rich; on the outside chance that it would be adopted, he offered it as a "poison pill" to lessen the bill's chances of passing—a tactic often used against his bills, and a rationale that would become important in his reelection campaigns. His motion was tabled 125–17.[64] Eckhardt then offered as an amendment his graduated oil occupation tax. His allies came back to him, but it wasn't enough: he lost 52–89. The session ended with no tax bill.

A few weeks later, legislators were back for a special session. Eckhardt revisited his first cartoon as a legislator from 1959, in which he had depicted the eyes of Texas watching legislators; this time, he showed a hand sneaking up from behind a desk, where the legislator hid from the public's watchful eyes, to push a button for a sales tax.[65] Labor met in their annual convention, and Eckhardt spoke to them in a broad-ranging speech outlining a host of alternatives to the sales tax.[66] The Knights made it clear that they would block Eckhardt's efforts. He decided to use the route of humor, going public with the joust by taking his artist's pen in hand and printing: "Members of the lobby will please take note that the undersigned will request an immediate hearing on the Eckhardt-Hinson bill. . . . 25 copies thereof are deposited with the sergeant-at-arms for your use. This will constitute de-facto notice so that you may have an opportunity to prepare your presentations. Eckhardt." The *Austin American* then photographed him grinning as he tacked his note on the House bulletin board.[67]

Eckhardt introduced his Dedicated Reserve Gas Tax to replace the 1959 tax that was declared unconstitutional. But he could not even get a hearing in the Revenue and Taxation Committee that he sat on. The omnibus bill made it to the floor, where Eckhardt again offered his gas tax as an amendment. In fine form, Eckhardt's calm, logical, but pithy oratorical style began persuading wary legislators. One freshman conservative was asked why he voted for the amendment, and he said, "I listened to Eckhardt and he just simply convinced me." The alarm rang loudly as Eckhardt prevailed, 92–51.[68] His victory could not be sustained in the Senate, though, and the session ended in stalemate.

Governor Daniel immediately called another session, and the battle continued. The House readopted its package, including Eckhardt's tax, and the

Senate passed its version, with an altered version of Eckhardt's tax. Turman appointed Eckhardt to the conference committee, which held painstaking work sessions to produce a compromise version of the omnibus bill. Eckhardt eyed the work of the powerful lobbyists, led now by his former ally, Ed Clark, "the Jupiter of the lobbyists," who worked with "the gods of the Senate" to write the final tax bills. He worried presciently that Clark could "insert an unconstitutional provision in the dedicated reserves tax."[69] Eckhardt's usual demeanor was gentle, sweet, and humorous. But he also had a temper and was supremely confident. When he got riled, he would confront his opponent, poking a finger in his chest fearlessly. When Eckhardt looked at the final tax bill wording that was presented to the committee, he got angry. He was the only conferee to vote against the bill, and he stormed out to hunt down Judge "Twinkletoes" J. H. Foster, lobbyist for Phillips Petroleum. He shook his fist angrily and shouted, "You ruined my tax, Judge. You made it unconstitutional, and you *know* it."[70]

He pressed on against the Knights, angrily requesting permission for a personal privilege speech on the House floor. He charged that "for the third time a secret power, a kind of anti-attorney general's office, has written unconstitutionality into a gas bill. There is a secret force in this State, more devious and powerful even than the lobbyists we face here. This force, with the talents of the finest lawyers in the State at its disposal, devotes these talents to writing unconstitutionality into bills." He concluded:

> The powerful, secret, behind-the-scenes force that I have called the anti-attorney general's office has inserted exactly the same kind of language in the Dedicated Reserves Tax of 1961. . . . I went before the Senate State Affairs Committee when it was considering HB 20 and proposed an amendment which would . . . be workable and constitutional. . . . Instead of accepting the change . . . the Senate subcommittee added a non-severability clause . . . . The Senate then adopted HB 20 with this combination of fatal clauses. . . . I do not intend to let the same thing happen again in the 1961 Legislature that happened in the Legislature in 1959, and before that in 1951. . . . The $128.5 million relied upon by the Senate in this Dedicated Reserves Tax would then be simply a pot at the end of a rainbow, and the people of this State would be duped by the passage of a hollow sham of a gas tax.[71]

Eckhardt would not give up on his complaints about the backroom dealing that had fouled his tax. He took to the floor in a second personal privilege speech. Though he opposed the bill, he also saw the need to establish a record on its interpretation. He argued that the Conference Committee's language exempted taxation "after processing," but that other portions of the bill taxed gas upon severance.[72] But, of course, Eckhardt's first analysis was correct—two years later, the tax was declared unconstitutional.

When the speeches were finished, the omnibus bill won final approval, 83–62. The capitol had the atmosphere of a carnival and a wake. Citizens for a Sales Tax and other lobbyists celebrated, jubilant with their victory. One legislator declared, "The TMA [Texas Manufacturers' Association] flag is flying over the Capitol tonight."[73] Eckhardt wrote an eight-page pamphlet for his constituents, blasting the tax decision and continuing to make the argument against it. Titled "The Worst Tax in Texas History and Why I Voted Against It," the pamphlet was similar to his 1953 piece for the Texas Social and Legislative Conference, including analysis of revenues that would have been produced from better alternatives and equity figures showing how the sales tax gouged those with lower incomes. He wrote a separate piece, "The Sales Tax Hoax," and got twenty-one members to sign it. They told their voters that "we favored the Carriker-Eckhardt Amendment because it honestly met the problem of raising $360 million without a general retail sales tax."[74]

Real damage was done in these 1961 House floor showdowns. In the decades-long war between Establishment Democrats and populist Democrats, control of the tax system was the golden ring, and it could not be firmly grabbed by either of the two sides. Progressive income and natural resource taxation were possible, and closely fought over, in the 1940s and 1950s. Now, with the sales tax victory in 1961, the war was over. The Establishment had won by cementing into place a regressive tax system, making tax equity an impossible dream. The Knights' sales tax victory assured that the upper classes would continue to have unchallenged economic power in Texas, and it signaled the death knell of Texas populism.

Soon, there was another legislative session. The Third Called Session was tame by comparison with the earlier ones. It is notable only for Eckhardt's humor. What got Eckhardt's dander up was the continuing flood of "memorializing" resolutions. Members would offer resolutions to tell Congress all kinds of things, from opposing Jimmy Hoffa to supporting neighborhood schools. It was a tool that conservatives constantly used to get liberals on the record on the hot-button issue of the day. Eckhardt voted against a resolution opposing federal aid to education and told the House "I don't vote to memorialize Congress and I don't want Congress to memorialize me."[75]

That gave him an idea. He wrote a resolution asking Congress to memorialize the Texas legislature, then whipped out his artists' pen and embedded in the text of the resolution a sketch showing a Texas legislator running after a congressman, trying to tap him on the shoulder and show him a memorializing resolution, with the congressman paying absolutely no attention. Eckhardt stepped up to the front mike to ask that his resolution be introduced, and explained, "If there is anything I hate, it is the supercilious attitude of Washington" in refusing to memorialize the Texas House. "It ought to be a two-way street," he said, to Charlie Wilson's cheering. "But if there is anything I hate more than this supercilious attitude, it is controversy. I like tranquility and I've always tried to maintain that attitude with the Harris County delegation," he added, tongue-in-cheek, to Wilson's whooping and clapping. The sketch was a part of the resolution, and Eckhardt insisted that the cartoon be printed in the *House Journal* and preserved as a part of the official resolution.[76] It is the only known artwork ever to be a part of a legislative bill or resolution.

LEGISLATING IN BIG JOHN'S TEXAS

In 1963, John Connally rode into Austin as the new governor, just as the legislative session began—a session that would test the patrician-populist confines of Texas politics. Eckhardt disdained the new governor as an aloof, aristocratic leader. Despite having helped Connally win, Eckhardt could never get through to Connally when he tried to call him, unlike his experience with Price Daniel. For his part, Connally was dismissive of liberal politicians. He got his history wrong in trying to defend himself, arguing, "I could not please the liberals even when I championed issues that were dear to them. . . . I was the first Texas governor to call for the creation of a public utility commission."[77] Governor Jimmie Allred, of course, was a fierce champion of utility regulation, back when Connally and Eckhardt were still UT students. Dr. Bob Montgomery wrote Allred's utility regulation bill, which they got through the House in 1937, but could not move through the Senate. Connally admired the political power of the wealthy. He wrote that his oil mentor Sid Richardson, as well as the Rockefellers, DuPonts, Mellons, Carnegies, Hearsts, Gettys, and Hunts were "mandarins" with "a deep and, I think, healthy interest in the [political] system that made their wealth possible."[78] Eckhardt, on the other hand, believed that such "interest" corrupted democracy and did not like the Establishment dogma that Connally took into the legislative battles.

With Jimmy Turman's exit from the House in 1962, a speaker's race developed. Eckhardt's name had been bandied about for two years, but he knew that he was a lightning rod and would attract intense opposition. Byron Tunnell emerged as the leading candidate from the Establishment faction and won the race. Tunnell began preparations for taking power and let it be known that he intended to roll back the 1961 rules reforms. His young ally Ben Barnes said that they had the votes to get rid of the modified seniority system. Eckhardt wrote a public letter to Tunnell, suggesting that killing the reforms would be interpreted "in light of the widely held view that the lobby was pretty solidly behind your candidacy for speaker." He argued that a fresh, powerful Speaker could write rules with no opposition in a way that "will ul-timately be disastrous for the democratic proceedings of this House." Subtly paraphrasing Shakespeare, Eckhardt cautioned: "Byron, it has been said that 'it is good to have a giant in power, but it is tyranny to use it like a giant.' And when one enters the speakership position unopposed, as I feel quite sure you will, he has a giant power. At least until he uses it like a giant."[79] On Eckhardt's subsequent motion to keep the reformed 1961 rules, he and the liberals lost badly, 108–39. The die was cast for a miserable session. By its end, Tunnell and Barnes had sneaked through a resolution that stripped from members the right to vote on top officers of the House. Eckhardt denounced it as "a pick-pocket theft."[80] He did not like the tyranny that he thought Tunnell represented.

Eckhardt was banished to the sidelines. Tunnell would not even give him a seat on the Criminal Jurisprudence Committee that he had chaired. His legislative program was blocked. Eckhardt revived his three environmental criminal penalty bills, but he could not get them out of the committee. Ever since his freshman year, Eckhardt had pursued industrial and worker safety issues, designing a regulation scheme that was based on the belief that ad-equate regulation prevented tort suits. He would try again in 1963, unsuc-cessfully, and would have to wait until he joined LBJ and his allies later in pushing a similar scheme on the federal level that became the Occupational Safety and Health Administration (OSHA).[81]

In the 1963 hearings on his worker safety bill, witnesses argued that it was impossible to legislate safety, that workers were usually the ones at fault for accidents. Eckhardt replied, "Well, you know in the lumber mills, those big hooks that come down and grab a log and pull it into the saw, sometimes they grab a worker and pull *him* into the saw. But I guess you'd call that worker failure, because the machinery was workin' just right, and it sawed up that worker just like he was a log."[82] When he could not get a vote to report his bill, he made a floor motion to discharge the bill from committee, losing on a tie vote, 70–70. Representative David Finney brought to the floor a bill to create an industrial safety coordinator, saying that he had Connally's support. Eckhardt helped kill it, arguing that it was a sham designed to thwart his stronger bill.

It was the field of environmental policy where Eckhardt and Connally re-ally clashed. Eckhardt was emerging as a defender of coastal interests against business interests that dredged shells out of the bays to use for concrete and other industrial uses. He supported the oyster industry that depended on a clean, viable ecological setting for oyster growth and harvest. The state's long-time director of the Texas Game and Fish Commission also opposed the shell dredgers. The 1963 legislature merged the Commission with the state parks

Representative Eckhardt speaking from floor microphone. Famed photographer Russell Lee photographed Bob Eckhardt on several occasions. Here, he captured Eckhardt speaking to the Texas House in 1963. Courtesy of the Russell Lee Collection, Center for American History, University of Texas at Austin, DI 02931.

board. Connally got to appoint the new commissioners, who promptly fired the anti-dredging director. Eckhardt and sportsmen and oyster fishermen opposed the infringement on live oyster reefs, but the new commission approved a rule permitting dredging close to the shell reefs, which led to contamination of many of the oyster beds off the Gulf Coast.[83]

Connally's pet issue for the session was higher education, and the session ended in battles over his proposals. Tunnell and his anti-tax team were hostile and defeated the higher education funding. Connally told a jammed press conference that he was deeply disappointed, and negotiations began. But those who supported his program became disgusted, as they were kept in the dark about what Connally would agree to. Eckhardt returned from the news conference and took to the floor, blistering Connally for his leadership:

> The governor is right that the appropriations bill is inadequate in the field of higher education. But he is wrong in asking that the pie be cut in such a way as to take from the afflicted and unfortunate in order to give to the talented and the fortunate. There was no reason why Texas needed to make such a choice. The governor at an earlier date could have put his foot down on tax cuts and giveaways and preserved enough money in the treasury to take care of both needs. . . . Where was the governor when these slashes in our present tax structures were made?

Eckhardt argued that if the pie had shrunk, "it is not the responsibility of those who sliced the pie, but of those who baked it." Connally's "excellence in education" program, Eckhardt concluded, "is but a pitchman's cry, a fraud, and a mockery." [84]

National Tragedy

When the session ended and everyone headed home, the news came that President Kennedy had appointed LBJ's congressional successor, Homer Thornberry, to a federal judgeship. Jake Pickle leapt into the special election for the congressional seat. Pickle had extensive contacts from his campaigning for Johnson and Shivers for years, and he won the seat in December, beating Eckhardt to Washington by three years.

Eckhardt focused again on his labor law practice. Nadine and Willie would go to the office with him, where Willie would sleep on a mattress as they worked. The shack was still a favorite gathering place. Bob and Nadine held parties there, entertaining Malcolm McGregor and others when they were in town. They also started building a new house up the hill from the shack, moving into it in early November.

As President Kennedy planned his fateful trip to Texas, Eckhardt served on the Welcome Committee for the Austin dinner, planned for November 22. Albert Thomas did not retire, and instead planned a gala event in Houston for November 21 to kick off his 1964 congressional campaign and to demonstrate his drawing power, in case anyone dared challenge him. His Arrangements Committee included a full array of Houston's finest—but not Eckhardt. Bob and Nadine went to the dinner, where Jackie Kennedy spoke briefly, including a few words in Spanish. The highlight of the evening was President Kennedy, and everyone left the coliseum enthusiastic. Kennedy's opponents, of course, were also active. As Bob and Nadine left, they encountered a man on the corner handing out anti-Kennedy leaflets. "I hope nothing happens to the president while he's in Texas," Nadine commented to Bob. The next day, Bob, Nadine, and the girls gathered around a small black and white television in their new house, watching in shock the news of the assassination in Dallas.

ELEVEN

Readying for Congress

During 1964, Bob faced numerous changes in his home and political families, including memorable births and deaths. 'Rissa graduated from St. Stephen's. Eckhardt wanted his daughter to go to UT, but he also encouraged her to be independent. So, she took his independence advice. In the fall, 'Rissa headed off to Philadelphia, plunging eagerly into college life at the University of Pennsylvania, observing the differences between southern and northern life. She found Philly to be old and dirty "but not without a certain dignity and stableness."[1] On September 18, Nadine gave birth to a girl, whom they named Sarah. The big family now had an infant to fawn over. It was the era of TV ads for Sarah Lee Pies, so they nicknamed their baby "Pie."

In June, Gus Garcia died at age forty-nine, broke and hooked on the bottle. Sadly, the same day that the Eckhardts celebrated Sarah's birth in Houston, J. Frank Dobie died, just a year after Walter Webb's death. "And so now," wrote Mewhinney, "all three of them are gone from us: Roy Bedichek, Walter Webb, and Frank Dobie."[2] Then in December, Minnie Fisher Cunningham died, drawing together the liberal family at her memorial service. Eckhardt and Yarborough served as pallbearers.[3]

Politically, 1964 was a topsy-turvy electoral year. In the liberal community, the grief from Kennedy's horrible death was processed simultaneously with the reshuffled political deck. Their old jousting partner Lyndon Johnson was now president, running for election and needing their support. Ralph Yarborough was up for reelection, and he and Johnson were bitterly estranged. Yet, LBJ kept opponents out of Yarborough's primary race, not wanting to reopen those old wounds while he was trying to win a national campaign. The chief statewide race in November was Yarborough's, as Republicans, emboldened by John Tower's victory in 1961, ran Houston millionaire oilman George Bush against Yarborough. Bush campaigned aggressively, but Yarborough's popularity, his populism, and the Democratic loyalty of voters proved enough to secure his reelection. No one then knew that it would be the last big populist electoral victory in Texas for a generation.

With Albert Thomas's firm grip on the seat, Eckhardt could not yet run for Congress, so he geared up for another campaign for his Texas House seat.

In the 1964 primary season, liberals lost even more legislative races than in 1960 and 1962. Barbara Jordan ran and lost. Again, she was frustrated with Harris County Democrats, but it was becoming even clearer that an African American simply could not win in the at-large countywide races, with a predominantly white electorate and race-based voting.

Eckhardt was, as usual, a reluctant campaigner, and Nadine and others worked the ropes for him. He would drive Frankie Randolph crazy: "Bob, don't be so damned lazy! Now get out and do some ward heeling," she told him.[4] But he preferred spending time in the woods with his horses. His old Volkswagen finally died, and he bought a new open-air Jeep. When he came driving up to the campaign headquarters in the Jeep, Frankie gruffly chastised him: "Where have you been? This is a campaign."[5] As a campaign staffer recalled, "we said, 'Bob, get up off your fanny and go shake hands or something or you'll lose this election,' and he said, 'Well hell, we've got three whole days.' Well, he did get a move on. We didn't see him for 72 hours and when we finally found him he was sitting on a street corner, beard grown out, dirty as all get-out. He'd been out hammering up his posters and shaking hands on a non-stop basis."[6]

His 1964 opponents were Art Forbes and William Montgomery. Arming himself with *House Journals,* Forbes went on television, arguing that Eckhardt had supported an income tax. Eckhardt's response was one that he later admitted was "misleading but not literally false." He said that he had never offered a bill calculated to get a personal income tax into law because he knew that it would never pass, but that he had, rather, calculated to defeat or at least expose the regressive nature of the sales tax.[7]

Each race was more expensive. Forbes spent the then-incredible amount of $27,000, forcing Eckhardt to raise money aggressively.[8] His campaign staff organized the "Bob Eckhardt Open Beaches Appreciation Dinner," getting help from the state AFL-CIO in putting on the dinner.[9] Eckhardt ended up spending $6,000. Forbes's well-financed campaign nearly did the trick, but not quite. Eckhardt won with only 52.5 percent, just enough to avoid a runoff. He had 74,821 votes to Forbes's 50,421 and Montgomery's 17,626. As Forbes later lamented to Eckhardt, "We spent a lot of money to get your record researched way back and got all the evidence and the props and the expensive TV time and you just stood there and said you hadn't gone to pass an income tax, and they all believed you."[10] In November, Eckhardt's Republican opponent was Tom Overton. Eckhardt won big in his last countywide race, 229,234 to 126,954.

Eckhardt meandered to the capital in January 1965 in his Jeep for what would prove to be his last session. With all their other kids in school, Bob and Nadine brought Pie to the capitol with them. She was soon big enough to scoot around the House floor in her rolling walker, entertaining the mem-

Bob Eckhardt on his horse. Joe Eckhardt had brought his horses from the Eckhardt Ranch to Austin with him, and he taught his son Bob to love horses. Bob kept horses in Austin and Houston. Here, he sits astride June, in his Cypress Creek woods. Courtesy of the Eckhardt family.

bers.[11] Eckhardt's 1965 session again featured policy jousts with John Connally and the Knights of Congress Avenue. But most important for Eckhardt was the Gordian knot of redistricting. Would redrawing the congressional lines allow him to finally run for Congress, or would those lines prove the Grail to be a mirage? Looming over the redistricting battle was the question of Albert Thomas's intentions. By the end of the session, the outcome was becoming clear. Soon, Bob Eckhardt would be leaving the pygmies, knights, and a few giants behind in Austin to head off to Washington.

Congressman Albert Thomas

By the mid-1960s, Albert Thomas had served Houston (and Brown & Root) faithfully since his election in 1936. Thomas had scaled the heights of power in Washington, chairing the House Appropriations Subcommittee on Independent Offices and bringing home the bacon for projects such as the medical center and NASA (built by Brown & Root). His steadfast support of

Brown & Root had alienated some in labor. The AFL-CIO vote ratings for the 1940s and 1950s listed Thomas as being 50 percent for and 50 percent against them—yet he represented a strong labor district.[12] But Thomas was a natural politician and very diligent in his local politicking and constituent relations. So long as he wanted to continue, he could not be beaten.

When Eckhardt won reelection in 1962, he and others had already begun planning for a 1964 run for Thomas's seat. In April 1963, Thomas announced that he was battling cancer and would retire after that term. Bob began putting out feelers to his broad base of supporters. From Yale, Charles Black let Bob know that he was ready to help.[13] Bob and Nadine went to the Political Association of Spanish-Speaking Organizations (PASSO) convention in San Antonio in early June, where they made valuable political connections and raised money. Eckhardt talked with Ralph Yarborough, Maury Maverick Jr., and his former House colleague, now State Senator Franklin Spears about the congressional race, and Maverick urged him to talk directly to Thomas about the seat.[14]

The Houston business community and Thomas's ally Lyndon Johnson had other plans for the seat. County Commissioner V. V. Ramsey wanted the seat, but he would not run against Thomas. Eckhardt's good friend from Harris County Democrats, Woodrow Seals, told him that LBJ's confidante Jack Valenti was also interested in running. Nadine had worked on LBJ's staff with Mary Margaret Valenti, so she and Bob had dinner with Jack and Mary Margaret, then they all headed out to the country place for drinking and talking. Bob's political spadework must have disquieted Establishment leaders; LBJ and others pressured Thomas to run again, so late in 1963 he withdrew his retirement announcement, dashing Eckhardt's and Valenti's plans.[15] Valenti met Eckhardt at a downtown outdoor restaurant on Fannin Street to discuss the race. Eckhardt wanted the seat, but he knew that taking on Thomas was politically unwise. He told Valenti that he would not run against Thomas. After Thomas won, Eckhardt wrote him, deciding to be up front as Maverick had earlier suggested, letting Thomas know of his interest in running in 1966. But Thomas had his secretary respond, saying that he would run again in 1966. Thomas's earlier quiet statement to Eddie Ball that he thought Eckhardt should succeed him seemed to be a conviction of the past.

Connally and Eckhardt

Big John Connally had survived the hail of bullets in Dallas, was overwhelmingly reelected in 1964, and was at his strongest politically. As legislators readied to descend on Austin for the session's beginning, an unexpected change in leadership occurred. Connally was angry with Speaker Tunnell for failing to support his higher education initiative. Tough-minded, ideological, aloof, and independent, Tunnell required high maintenance, from Connally's point of view. Connally decided that he had to push Tunnell out of the speakership if he was to have more success in the 1965 session.

When Connally announced for the governorship and began his campaign rounds in 1962, twenty-three-year-old State Representative Ben Barnes introduced him in his district in Brownwood and signed up with the campaign. Barnes was also savvy in his inside politics at the capitol, eagerly siding with the Establishment bloc and supporting Tunnell's speakership campaign. Former State Representative Bob Bullock, an auto dealer lobbyist and a key adviser to Connally, suggested that Barnes garner "second" pledges for himself to line up support for a 1967 speaker's race. Connally wrote of Barnes that "he would be more visionary, more progressive, and more loyal than anyone else in the speaker's chair and I needed that help." Barnes was his man.[16]

Bullock called Barnes and alerted him to the plan. When a seat opened up on the Texas Railroad Commission, Connally appointed Tunnell to that higher paid statewide office. Sure enough, Tunnell accepted the appointment. Barnes flew to Austin, where Connally and Bullock met him at the Driskill. Barnes called in his legislative and lobbyist allies and began a blitzkrieg round of phone calls to legislators. Within thirty-six hours, Barnes had the speakership sewn up, just days before the session's start. Eckhardt did not like Tunnell, but he was worried and appalled at what had happened. He said that the manner in which Barnes was elected was "something unique and dangerous in Texas politics. It means perpetual control of the House by the lobby."[17]

Barnes led the House with much of Tunnell's old team. Connally liked working with Barnes, and they consistently defeated Eckhardt and his allies throughout the 1965 session. Connally proposed to extend statewide offices from two-year terms to four-year terms. Eckhardt was among the most outspoken opponents of the measure. Connally got the constitutional amendment through the legislature with broad-based support. But Eckhardt joined with Yarborough and labor to campaign against the proposal, and voters defeated it.[18]

With Tunnell out of the way, Connally returned to his 1963 theme of improving the quality of higher education. He proposed a statewide Coordinating Board to oversee institutions of higher education. Eckhardt, suspicious of the proposal, voiced his distrust of the governor and his frustration with the legislative process under Connally and Barnes. Mirroring his 1963 floor speech blasting Connally, Eckhardt again took to the floor, where he argued that "the house and the legislature have in large measure become the rubber stamp of the executive branch in this session. When HB No. 1, the Higher Education Coordinating Board bill, was acted on, we did not materially change it in its entire course through the house and the senate. Because of some strange fascination with the governor's power we acted as though we could not change it."[19]

Eckhardt in Redistricting Politics

For decades, urban growth stalled legislative and congressional redistricting in Texas. The rural-dominated legislature refused to redistrict.[20] A 1936 constitutional amendment even specifically limited urban representation. In 1950, Harris County elected eight representatives, when it should have had fifteen. Moreover, the legislature preferred multi-member at-large districts rather than single-member districts that could allow labor or racial and ethnic minorities to win.[21] With the 1950 census, the state gained one congressional seat; rather than redistrict, though, the legislature chose to keep the old lines and make that seat an at-large statewide seat. The legislature finally did draw new districts for the 1958 election, creating a second seat in Harris County (won by conservative Democrat County Judge Bob Casey) to go along with Albert Thomas's seat.

The 1960 census triggered the decennial round of redistricting for both the legislature and Congress. Texas gained yet another congressional seat; once again, the legislature could not agree on redistricting and made it an at-large seat for 1962 and 1964 (won by Joe Pool, of the infamous 1957 Pool Bill attempt to keep Ralph Yarborough out of the Senate).

The districts were still far from equal in size. Then, in 1962 and 1964, the U.S. Supreme Court ruled that redistricting was a justiciable constitutional issue, requiring a one man-one vote standard (even for the state senate). No longer would the legislature be allowed to keep the redistricting ball in its own private arena. State and federal courts would henceforth become major players, potentially shifting the balance of power.

Transplanted Connecticut Yankee, then West Texas oil businessman George Bush (whose father was Republican U.S. Senator Prescott Bush from Connecticut) had moved to Houston and was serving as Harris County Republican chair. Bush and other Republicans brought suit, challenging the congressional districts. Harris County had two seats, but was 410,142 over the ideal population for two seats. Clearly, Houston was due a third seat. In October 1963, a federal court declared Texas congressional districts unconstitutional, writing that over-representation and under-representation around the state were "spectacular"; the U.S. Supreme Court affirmed that decision in March 1964.[22] The district court then stayed its order until January 11, 1965. Connally ordered a study of redistricting issues, and his committee recommended three districts in Harris County.

State legislative redistricting fights were to become inextricably linked with the congressional redistricting fights. Bill Kilgarlin, Eckhardt, Franklin Spears, Don Kennard, and Jake Johnson filed suit challenging the state legislative districts, and they won.[23] In Connally's speech kicking off the 1965 session, he recommended that the legislature support a U.S. constitutional amendment to allow the state senate to be based on variables other than population. Coming out once again on the wrong side of history, Connally warned, "I feel very strongly that the very essence of representative government is damaged if this proposal fails."[24]

The redistricting dynamics were stirring just as Albert Thomas's health was in serious decline. Thomas was presumed unable to run for reelection in 1966. Eckhardt went to visit Gus Wortham and others in the Houston business establishment. He told them that with three districts, it was likely that one would be a Republican district, that conservative Congressman Casey would get the second district, and that the third should be a liberal-labor district. This would ensure that all three camps had a voice. Wortham was noncommittal about Eckhardt's proposal for a liberal-labor district, saying, "I'm not in that district." But Eckhardt knew that Wortham, a powerful friend of Albert Thomas, had his hand in all of Harris County and Galveston County politics.[25] Wortham eventually tried, behind the scenes, to defeat Eckhardt.

Eckhardt immediately jumped into the battles as the legislature convened, filing his congressional redistricting proposal and a proposal for single-member state legislative districts that could elect minority Democrats. Conservative Democrats got the Legislative Council to propose a system similar to Connally's interim study committee's plan: east-to-west horizontal Houston congressional districts. Their analysis was that "Conservative Democrats can nominate both Congressional and Legislative candidates in the Primaries, in the CENTRAL and SOUTH Districts," conceding that the north district might go liberal. As for race issues, their analysis made the disingenuous statement that "Negro population divided between three districts—no discrimination."[26] Eckhardt denounced the Council's plan as "schizophrenic." As he saw it, "the principle should be to keep people of the same viewpoint together in order to keep the maximum number of people satisfied with their congressman."[27]

Eckhardt proposed a pie-shaped configuration of three congressional districts, carving out an east Harris County congressional district from the labor-dominated communities (including his Cypress Creek land). The Republican Party mapped out a new west Houston district for George Bush, a southern county seat (Casey's District 22), and District 8 (Thomas's seat) as a northeastern Harris County district. Eckhardt's and the Republicans' aims were not very different: a Republican district, a Democratic district dominated by business-establishment conservatives, and, depending on exactly how the lines were drawn, a district that could be won by Harris County Democrats or by Establishment Democrats. The Council's plan came to be called "Plan A," and the alternative came to be called the "Eckhardt/Republican" Plan.

For the state legislative districts in Houston, the Legislative Council concluded: "conservative candidates can be nominated in the *primary* but must have the liberal/loyal Democrats to win in November." [28] Eckhardt could not convince redistricting chair Gus Mutscher and his committee to support the idea of single-member districts, but he stirred up a lot of support in Houston. Curtis Graves, a young up-and-coming African-American leader in Houston, went to Austin with others to witness the hearing on Eckhardt's proposal. Graves decided, as he watched the committee at work on the House floor, that he wanted a seat in the legislature. [29] Eckhardt struck a compromise for something in between countywide state legislative districts and single-member districts: three multimember state legislative districts, each within a congressional district, with six legislative seats inside each congressional district.

Graves believed that Eckhardt and the others worked to craft a strong legislative/constituent coalition of the black, Mexican-American, and labor-white communities. [30] That coalition building produced eager candidates for the legislature, ready to buy into the proposal. The state senate redistricting bill would give Harris County four single-member districts, finally allowing Barbara Jordan to run from a black-centered district. Thus, the Bush and Kilgarlin/Eckhardt lawsuits, coupled with Eckhardt's redistricting scheme and coalition building, helped bring to office in 1967 the first blacks elected to the Texas legislature since Reconstruction (Jordan, Graves, and Dallas's Joe Lockridge) as well as labor-liberal stalwarts such as Otto Mullinax's law partner Oscar Mauzy in Dallas.

With the state-level agreement with Mutscher, Eckhardt got a strong hand in drawing the lines for the congressional districts. Eckhardt wanted District 8 to include his Cypress Creek property, and his desk mate William Miller wanted to be in the redrawn District 7. Barnes's team agreed to the "Eckhardt-Miller line," putting both of them in their desired districts and cracking the county's Republican vote among the three districts. Houston's black community was split up. Their numbers were likely not large enough to have produced a black district in 1966, but blacks' vote power was not immediately strengthened by the plan. More of the black community was placed in District 8 than in the other two districts, but the district was only 26 percent black. [31] District 8 comprised very segregated communities. The Northeast and Acre Homes areas were overwhelmingly black, Denver Harbor was overwhelmingly Latino, and the remaining neighborhoods were white.

Overall, the House's congressional redistricting bill was consciously devised to protect conservative Democrats. After the deal was proposed, Eckhardt gingerly approached his allies to tell them about the plan. He needed their votes to get it passed, and sheepishly confessed to them, "I sold out." But his friends so admired and respected him that they responded, "Bob, if you get to Congress, it's worth it—we'll vote for it."[32] After rancorous debate, the legislature approved all three redistricting bills. Yet, on the last day of the session, after voting for the bill, Eckhardt filed a personal privilege statement *against* the congressional plan. He got twenty-five other members to sign his complaint charging that the plan violated the one man-one vote rule.[33] Bush and the Republicans, too, were dissatisfied, and filed suit. Still, on January 5, 1966, a Houston court upheld the plans.

Family Tragedy

In the midst of the 1965 political and legislative battles, the Eckhardts faced tragedy. Big Orissa had struggled more and more with her depression and her psychotic episodes—as had her sister, Anne. Orissa had long periods of coping well with her illness, but they were interspersed with dark depressions. She attempted unsuccessfully to take her life by overdosing on sleeping pills. Her sister Anne underwent a frontal lobotomy after the Stevenson family decided that her mental illness required severe measures. She was not mentally competent to care for herself afterward and lived in her mother's house, then in a nursing facility. When Orissa declined so severely, they decided to try electric shock therapy—a horrible, traumatic experience for her and the family. Soon, like Anne, she moved in with her mother. 'Rissa and Rosalind stayed with them for a while, before moving into the boarding school at St. Stephen's in Austin, a relief from the chaotic environment around their mother. Then, in the summer of 1965, Orissa took her life by slitting her wrists. Rosalind stayed with Grandmother Stevenson before heading off to college in Pennsylvania with 'Rissa.

Statewide and Houston Politics in 1966

With the 1965 session behind him, Eckhardt returned to juggling his law practice, his interim legislative work, his political leadership, and now, the delicate task of negotiating his way into Albert Thomas's congressional seat, with Thomas still in it. Then, after decades of liberals' failed attempts to repeal the poll tax, the Supreme Court killed it with one swift stroke.[34] Connally called a special legislative session to reestablish Texas's voting system. The legislature set up an annual voter registration period, with no poll tax.

In his last hurrah as state representative, Eckhardt tried, but failed, to win a more open and flexible registration system.[35]

By the 1960s, Bob Eckhardt was a magnet for political support in Houston because of his connection with labor, his pro-integration stance, his leadership in the emerging environmental movement, and his role in political organizing, particularly through Harris County Democrats. His engaging personality attracted people even in outlying conservative areas such as Humble, where committed volunteers would work intensely to win Eckhardt votes. He had a core group of campaign volunteers, such as pipe fitter Hartsell Gray. The Harris County AFL-CIO Central Council had developed into a political powerhouse with its endorsements and organizational help for candidates. Central Council leaders Ed Ball and Don Horn were key Eckhardt supporters. The shell dredging issue continued to stoke reaction, and people like Rex Braun, who later won a state legislative seat, joined Eckhardt in his support for the oystermen and shrimpers.[36] House candidates Curtis Graves and Lauro Cruz admired Eckhardt and his efforts to bolster minority political participation and leadership. The three of them campaigned together. In the midst of the 1966 campaigns, Graves gave Eckhardt a proclamation: "This is to certify that Robert C. Eckhardt is hereby proclaimed an honorary Negro and all the rights and privileges appertaining thereto. Namely: Chitlins, Ham Hocks, Hog Maws, Collard Greens, Red Beans, and one free pass to the Club Matinee."[37] He soon wrote to Eckhardt in Washington, "Hope to work the Churches with you soon."[38]

Barbara Jordan ran strong races for the House in 1962 and 1964. With the redistricting, she decided to aim her sights higher because the state Senate seats were now single-member districts. Her first hurdle was winning the endorsement of the Harris County Democrats. HCD had backed Charles Whitfield in his successful House campaigns, and he, too, was running for the Senate seat. But Jordan had developed strong support in the group. Eckhardt, Randolph, Dixie, and Ball decided to back her. The executive committee endorsed her, and they strongly supported her before the full membership. Eckhardt argued that the labor-liberal-black coalition could not continue to expect blacks to be a part of a coalition in which they had no leadership roles. "We couldn't say: 'You ought to support us but we won't support you,'" he concluded.[39] Whitfield was furious and campaigned aggressively against Jordan throughout the spring, but Jordan won with 64 percent.

Running for Congress

Albert Thomas's illness created dilemmas for everyone involved. It did not appear that he would live long. Still, Thomas filed for reelection in January

1966. As Thomas's health deteriorated, Gus Wortham decided that he had to act to preserve the seat, even if he seemed disloyal to Thomas. Wanting to block Eckhardt, Wortham quietly arranged for a name to be filed at the last minute.[40] Meanwhile, Bob, Nadine, Ed Ball and other labor leaders, and Harris County Democrats huddled to decide what to do. They did not want Thomas to die in the middle of the campaign and not have a candidate in place for the seat. But Eckhardt had promised Thomas that he would not run against him. As he was trying to decide what to do, his constant campaign aide Hartsell Gray came to the house and urged him to file, as the clock ticked down to midnight on February 7, the last filing day. Gray drafted a statement for Eckhardt, reiterating that he would not run against Thomas but would file in the event that the congressman could not run. So Bob, Nadine, and Hartsell jumped in the car and drove to the courthouse and filed, just before midnight. The next day, Eckhardt issued a news release saying that he was filing only as a second candidate and would vote for Thomas if he lived. But Eckhardt was not the only last-minute filer. Wortham's backup plans also kicked in. George Brown's ally and former aide to conservative Mayor Louie Welch, Larry McKaskle (McRascal, Bob would call him) had planned to run for the legislature, but instead filed for Thomas's seat.

Congressman Thomas died a few days later, on February 15. Now there would have to be both the Democratic nomination and a special election to fill the seat for the rest of the year. The day after Thomas's funeral his widow, Lera, announced that she would run in the special election. Beaumont Congressman Jack Brooks (who had known Eckhardt since his days in the Texas House in 1947 and 1949) called Eckhardt and asked him to withdraw. Brooks told him that Mrs. Thomas just wanted to finish out the term. Eckhardt decided to play coy for a few days, with the newspapers covering the suspense. He then issued a statement saying that he would "step aside" and not run in the special election, allowing Mrs. Thomas to finish out the term, but he would run for the nomination. Then, again at the last minute, McKaskle jumped into the special election. It seemed like an effort to block Eckhardt: if McKaskle won the seat, he could defend it, as the incumbent, against Eckhardt.

The Harris County AFL-CIO Central Council invited Eckhardt to address their regular meeting a few days later. Eckhardt pledged his full support to Mrs. Thomas in the March 26th special election and stated that he would push as hard as he knew how to be elected for the full term. The Council voted to recommend "unanimous and unqualified support" for Eckhardt, and "further we join with State Representative Eckhardt in support of Mrs. Thomas to fill out the remaining few months of her late husband's term." They knew that they had to keep Mrs. Thomas in the seat so that "McRascal" did not get a powerful advantage for the primary nomination. PASSO followed with its endorsement of Eckhardt.[41]

The special election split the Houston establishment. The *Chronicle* endorsed Mrs. Thomas, but the *Post* endorsed owner Oveta Culp Hobby's favorite, McKaskle. Mrs. Thomas won the race. Then, turning her attention to the primary, she supported a move to win the nomination for her deceased husband (whose name was still on the ballot), which would allow the Harris County Democratic Committee to name her or another candidate other than Eckhardt. She campaigned actively against Eckhardt.

Eckhardt knew that he would need a more intensive and better-fueled campaign than he had ever had for his legislative races. He borrowed money, then to consolidate his debt at the end of the campaign, he borrowed from his long-time ally, Dickinson banker Walter Hall.[42] Eckhardt, Harris County Democrats, and labor fanned out across the district and campaigned neighborhood by neighborhood, door to door. Eckhardt opened multiple headquarters across the large district, which stretched from Houston into the rural areas of northeast Harris County. Norma came down from Austin again to work at the headquarters. A car dealer loaned Eckhardt a black car, complete with a then-rare car phone, for the campaign. Hartsell Gray served as Eckhardt's driver. Nadine laughingly referred to them as Batman and Robin, riding around in their Batmobile.

The AFL-CIO endorsed a slate of six candidates for state representative, and they all campaigned together, with Eckhardt. After one event in Humble, Bob and Nadine invited Curtis Graves to their Cypress Creek home, and they became steadfast friends. Dr. Lonnie Smith and Graves would take Eckhardt to black churches. They would start with a Mexican breakfast, then hop in the Batmobile and head to the early Catholic masses. Later, Graves would use the car phone to call ahead to the Baptist ministers. At each service, Graves would go up with the minister, speak briefly, then introduce Eckhardt, who would wave from the pews. Then the three campaigners would all head to the next church.[43]

Eckhardt wrapped himself around the JFK and LBJ administrations, using a 1960 photo of himself with Kennedy and Johnson. "I am 99 percent for" LBJ, he declared. "I've been a New Dealer, a Fair Dealer and a member of the Great Society. And I hope to be in the mainstream of Democratic party activities in Washington." He even embraced LBJ's position on the war: "there are battles that must be fought at the barricades of democracy. The Vietnamese war is one of these, and I stand with our President in saying that we must stand firm but seek peace."[44]

In his campaign brochure, he wrote: "the Democratic Party's goal is to build a great society which will give the maximum scope for humanity to flower. I want to accomplish this goal in the Eighth Congressional District. We are the shops, the yards and the docks of Harris County, the sinew of its industry—not its country club or its front office." He addressed environmental and social justice issues, before those terms were coined: "The Fifth Ward should not be forced to breathe the smoke of burning hide and hair from rendering plants and incinerators nor Baytown, the smell of decaying fish killed by bayou pollution. I intend to see that the federal Water Quality Control Act's minimum standards are met."

The campaign against Eckhardt intensified. Despite Eckhardt's critical help in his 1959 speaker's race, Attorney General Waggoner Carr campaigned twice with McKaskle.[45] Brown & Root mobilized their troops to fight against Eckhardt in the Eighth District. More than three hundred of their employees served as paid handbill-pushers in nearly every precinct, and Brown personally intervened with Oveta Culp Hobby to win the endorsement of the *Houston Post* for his candidates.[46] When Bill Hobby learned this, he called Eckhardt to tell him that the paper was going to editorialize against him. Eckhardt told Hobby that he was going on a boat ride with the mayor of Baytown and others and asked if the *Post* would cover it. Bill sent a reporter, who took pictures of Eckhardt on the cruise down the Houston Ship Channel. The photo and story got great play in the *Post,* even as the paper editorialized for his opponent![47]

On election day, Nadine worked the Humble box, while Bob traveled from spot to spot. As the polls closed, Bob, Norma, and Nadine gathered at the Harrisburg headquarters (near the original nineteenth-century German landing place) to listen to the returns. They watched as the results came in, showing him beating Thomas and McKaskle without a runoff. The watch party became an exhilarating victory party with a crowd of screaming supporters and lots of drinking. At 2:00 a.m. Bob and Nadine went to Barbara Jordan's headquarters to celebrate her victory in the state Senate race. After partying there (and getting even drunker), they drove home.[48]

Eckhardt won 20,327 votes (53 percent), the deceased Albert Thomas won 10,261 (25 percent), and Larry McKaskle won 8,521 (22 percent).[49] McKaskle demanded a recount. "This is the first time I've ever heard of the third man in a race demanding a recount," Eckhardt said. The recount changed only a few votes. McKaskle then appealed to the Justice Department, claiming voting irregularities, but in a few days, the Justice Department reported they had found no basis for intervention.[50]

Bob had no Republican opponent in November. He was the presumptive congressman, even with Lera Thomas filling the official seat in Washington. For the rest of the year, he was in great demand as a speaker at labor and political gatherings, even traveling to Harvard to speak on southern politics.[51] He penned an irreverent verse about his soon-to-be Washington compadres:

> When the armored car is jerking
> And the Viet Cong is lurking
> And the Theoretician's working on a Tennet,
> Lyndon Johnson's Never Shirking
> And McNamarrer's Perking
> And Everett Dirkson's Ferking up the Senate.[52]

Eckhardt also now had two daughters to support at college, as Rosalind began her freshman year at the University of Pennsylvania in fall 1966, joining sister Orissa. 'Rissa and Rosalind were proud of their poppa being a new congressman. They wrote to Bob and Nadine, filling them in on their new boyfriends and expressing enthusiasm about their courses.[53] But ominously, Orissa was having difficulty with her eyesight and developed a spot on her eye. She visited an ophthalmologist, who removed the spot, then told Bob that her condition was pre-melanoma. Yet, Bob did not tell Orissa how serious it was. In November, the doctor wrote Bob that he was continuing to treat and monitor her and that he found no sign of the melanoma. He told Bob that he wanted to see her again in six months.[54] Bob continually asked Orissa if she was going in for her monitoring, but because he did not let her know how serious it was, sometimes long periods lapsed between visits.

With no Republican opponent, Eckhardt got 92 percent of the vote in November against a Constitution Party candidate. The key statewide campaign was Senator John Tower's reelection campaign against Attorney General Waggoner Carr. The November races focused on the Senate contest and, in Houston, the Seventh Congressional District. Republican George Bush, having lost in his statewide race against Yarborough in November 1964, lowered his sights in 1966 to the new Houston House seat that he had helped create with the Republican lawsuit. He beat Democrat Frank Briscoe. On election night, Eckhardt went to Bush's campaign office to congratulate him.

Before they headed to their new positions in Washington, both Eckhardt and Bush received an invitation from Texas A&M University to talk about the new politics.[55] On November 29, they drove to College Station together, getting to know each other. The next summer, they would both sit on a University of Houston panel, discussing the new Congress, and they would debate each other on Houston television in 1967 and 1968. Little could they know that only Eckhardt would be beginning a long congressional career, and that Bush would instead take many detours that would lead him (and his son) to the White House.

PART IV

Bob Eckhardt:
America's Second Congressman

TWELVE

Inside Congress, Inside Washington

Bob Eckhardt arrived in Washington during the heyday of the Great Society, amidst the blooming of a hundred flowers of the counterculture, with the swelling power of public interest groups, and as the time bomb of the Vietnam War was running out of fuse. He focused the rest of his career on national and international issues. Eckhardt told Studs Terkel, "I had a rather broad program, a lot of it to do with environmental protection, consumer protection, industrial safety. Real issues, I thought, rather than issues brought up by professional advisers, by ideological organizations that stamp you liberal or conservative." He added, "I always think of liberal and conservative as adjectives, not as nouns."[1] Eckhardt immediately stood out as an unusual congressman, both in his work and in his personal appearance. Speaker Tip O'Neill wrote that Eckhardt was a "maverick" congressman—a perhaps unintended high accolade for this longtime admirer and friend of the Maury Mavericks of San Antonio.[2]

Eckhardt would win awards and kudos during his fourteen-year congressional career, including being listed among the brightest, the best, and the most effective. Known as the "Philosopher Congressman" and the House's constitutional lawyer, he went to Congress the same year that Willie Morris's *North Toward Home* was published. In that memoir, Morris voiced his admiration for Eckhardt as a lawmaker and quoted Eckhardt's line about the Texas capitol being built for giants but inhabited by pygmies.

Eckhardt became an admired and award-winning congressman because of his prowess as a crafter of legislation and (sometimes) a skilled insider in getting his proposals adopted. "Legislation is my field," he would say, "and I should like to be thought of as a craftsman in it."[3] He became an anomaly—a congressman who actually listened to and participated in floor debates. Back in his office, the phone would ring and a reporter would request a copy of "the Eckhardt amendment" that just went on a bill, and the staff would have to ask, "What Eckhardt amendment?" The presumption in Washington was that legislation was carefully drawn in advance by staff and lobbyists, but Eckhardt would often write his own amendments. Jake Pickle said, "Some men like to gamble or drink whiskey or chase women," but Eckhardt "liked to legislate. He would sit there and listen to them, then he'd get that pencil in his left hand and he'd start writing an amendment. I don't care what the bill was, Eckhardt would have an amendment for it."[4]

Eckhardt believed that the Great Society legislation suffered from LBJ being a "legislative entrepreneur—result-oriented—not a craftsman. Too little of that legislation was governed by a firm view of what a bill is supposed to accomplish and how. . . . Congressional acts, like the common law, ought to move carefully from precedent to precedent."[5] His determined craftsmanship reflected his wariness over executive authority. "In our zeal to cover a wide range of administrative matters," he argued, "we have delegated too much authority calling for subjective judgment of the administration without protecting the process from permitting the exercise of this subjective judgment corruptly."[6] Eckhardt also valued the *legislative process* as key to good policy. Within weeks of being sworn in, he responded to constituents' queries: "As a member of Congress, I will take part in this process, and as I do, my thinking may change. . . . a creative legislator must do more than make up his mind and vote. He must try as best he can to shape politics and laws which respond to national needs."[7] Young congressional staffer Bill White (later mayor of Houston) concluded that "watching Bob Eckhardt in action gave you a glimpse of what it might have been like to watch Madison or Lincoln—politicians who knew their own mind and wrote their own speeches."[8]

Eckhardt brought to Washington the same speaking wit and style that he had honed in Texas courtrooms and legislative debates. He would cite the Constitution, Shakespeare, Voltaire, and his own experiences in his efforts to persuade his colleagues. He would remember a quotation and ask the Library of Congress staff to dig it out for him. In opposing a reorganization of Volunteers in Service to America (VISTA), Eckhardt sparred with a colleague: "I want to carry on the Shakespearean theme a little further by saying: do you not fear that the VISTA program might go 'we know not where, to lie in cold obstruction and to rot,' its 'sensible warm motion to become a kneaded clod' if this reorganization plan should go into effect?"[9] During the 1970s energy crises and bitterly cold winters in the northeast, he drew on a Thornton Wilder passage on a cold winter in *Skin of Our Teeth*: "There are some that are trying to go South and the roads are crowded; but you can't take old people and children very far in a cold like this."

Eckhardt loved the congressional process much more than the lobby-driven process in Austin. Still, he became exasperated when the process became too Wizard of Oz–like. "Whenever I go before the Rules Committee," he wrote, "I have that awful feeling that I am in the presence of the Delphian oracle. There is great prescience there because there is the power to influence the result—to tilt the marble machine so to speak, or to fix the one arm bandit so it pays off or doesn't pay off. But when one listens to the questions and hears the debate one sometimes feels that he is in the inner sanctum of an oracle gone mad."[10]

In Austin, Eckhardt had battled the Knights of Congress Avenue; in Washington, he was just as skeptical of the lobbyists. In a hearing on telecommunications, he said, "During some eighteen years of practicing labor law, many of them for the CWA, I had many dealings with Ma Bell, and was able to raise her voluminous petticoats just high enough to see her scarlet stockings!"[11] He told the press, "I served a good number of years in a legislative body which was very sympathetic with the gas pipeline companies and I have had the experience of their long arm reaching right into a conference committee of the Texas legislature to render a tax unconstitutional. I thought I had escaped this tampering when I came to Congress, but I underestimated their reach."[12] He carried his populism with him to Congress. "I sometimes fear," Eckhardt wrote, "that the power of the special interest lobby groups to defeat pro-people programs is limitless."[13] He was even indifferent to lobbyist campaign contributors on his own side, maintaining what he jokingly referred to as a "healthy ingratitude" toward them. Some became disgusted with his indifference to them, seeing it as arrogance. Bernard Rapoport, though, commented, "I couldn't get [Eckhardt] to move. And I like that—if I can't get him to move, he can't be bought."[14]

Settling In

In January 1967, the Eckhardts moved from Texas to Washington, D.C. Where were they to live in their new environment? Where, and how, would the new congressman set up his office? Would he need to dress more formally? How would he get around the capital? How would the family, now spread over different locations, keep together? It was a time of settling in.

THE ECKHARDT HOME

Nadine had lived in Washington in the 1950s when she and Bill Brammer worked for LBJ, so she knew she wanted to live close to downtown to avoid the hassles of commuting and to have a place that would be convenient for Bob's constituents, friends, and staff to visit. Transplanted Texans Chris Little and Robert and Mary Sherrill helped them search, and they soon found a house for rent in nearby Georgetown.

It was a wonderful high-ceilinged vintage 1815 house with four stories, bedrooms and baths for a family of six, kitchen and dining in the basement, fireplaces, a yard, and a patio. In the upstairs master bedroom, Bob set up his drafting board for when his cartooning muse, Mr. Hyde, would visit. They

Bob, Nadine, and Sarah Eckhardt. Bob Eckhardt and Nadine Cannon Brammer
married in 1962 and Sarah was born in 1964. Courtesy of Nadine Eckhardt.

liked their neighborhood and would walk over a couple of blocks to Martin's
Tavern, sharing drinks with Georgetown's political and literary elite.

BOB'S OFFICE

Bob was assigned two complete offices in the Longworth Building, covering
an entire inner hallway. It afforded privacy since it was off the main row of
offices, but the only view from the windows was the unattractive inner court-
yard. Across a side street was the Cannon House Office Building, where his
old sparring partner Jake Pickle had his offices. As Eckhardt gained seniority,
he had the opportunity to move to better, newer offices in the Rayburn Building, named for Speaker Sam Rayburn, but he never wanted to move. Thus,
for fourteen years, he would rush through the Longworth Building tunnel to
the Capitol for votes.

Along the back roads between Houston and Austin, Eckhardt had taken
many beloved detours into antique shops. Now, in Washington, instead of or-
dering standard pieces of furniture, the new congressman rummaged through
the basement for abandoned old pieces, gleefully claiming big stuffed leather

chairs, huge, heavy oak tables in pieces, and a piece of red carpet from the House Un-American Activities Committee room. He had the oval committee tables brought up and reassembled. The largest one became the desk for his inner office. Behind his table, Eckhardt hung portraits of Abraham Lincoln, Sam Houston, and Great Uncle (Congressman) Rudolph Kleberg. One of the maroon leather chairs that Eckhardt reclaimed had been from the "Board of Education" hideaway where Sam Rayburn and his cronies (including LBJ) met for drinks. One story has it that Harry Truman was sitting in that very chair when he heard that FDR had died and he was now the president.[15]

Eckhardt's table was the centerpiece of his office. Covered with books, stacks of bills and reports, yellow legal pads, and papers with his doodlings and calculations, it would be cleaned off on two occasions. One, when it was time to paste up *Bob Eckhardt's Quarterly Report,* he cleared the table. This was *his* newsletter, and he did it himself, spreading out the pages on the big oak table, taking great joy in cutting and pasting his hand-drawn graphics, charts, and cartoons. Two, when it was time for a party, the staff would clear his table and spread out food for "eat-ins," and Nadine would bring a big jug of white wine. Whoever happened to be in town—Willie Morris, new friend and *Texas Observer* editor Molly Ivins, and others—would join in the luncheons.

BOB'S EYE-RAISING ATTIRE AND MANNERISMS

For Bob Eckhardt, going to Congress meant a pay raise. The year he was elected, the annual pay increased to $30,000 (he had never before made more than $17,000).[16] His style and quality of dress, however, did not change with his income. In 1946, Bob had inherited a white seersucker suit from Caesar Kleberg. "I'm wearing the cloak of Caesar!" he would exclaim, and he wore it for years. He liked the airy coolness of seersucker and linen in the heat of the South. But linen wrinkles easily, and Eckhardt's appearance was more disheveled than debonair. As he was campaigning once, an aide overheard a small girl say, "Mama! We just *have* to help that man. He looks so poor." The aide was concerned about the impression that Eckhardt was making. "Look," he pleaded, "you really have to buy a decent-looking suit. You haven't had a new one in five years." Eckhardt thought, quietly, as was his wont, then replied, "Well, okay—but don't think you're gonna talk me into buying one of those expensive $80 or $90 numbers!"[17] When 'Rissa moved to New Orleans, he would visit her and buy seersucker or linen suits from Godchaux's and panama hats from Meyer the Hatter.[18] In his second term, he also listened to the hearings on the dangers of cigarette smoking and decided that cigars weren't so bad! He reconsidered his earlier decision to stop smoking the cigars that

Jimmie Allred had gotten him started with, and determined that one cigar a day would be okay.[19]

Thus, he became known for his dress—an old and wrinkled white linen or seersucker suit, gold watch chain, a broad panama hat over long flowing gray hair, a brightly colored bow tie, and an occasional cigar. Sometimes his eccentric dress worked against him. He made *Washingtonian* magazine's list of the Capital's Worst-Dressed Men and head of its "Bow Tie Gang." A constituent wrote about his clownish appearance.[20] Yet he commanded respect. Curtis Graves, who later moved to Washington, said of Eckhardt: "There are a lot of eccentricities among Congressmen. He was so bright it didn't hurt him."[21] Even an oil industry spokesman wrote that "perhaps the word that best describes Congressman Bob Eckhardt of Texas is 'gentleman.' Despite his ever-wrinkled, out-of-date suits and narrow bow ties, he has an air of dignity that commands respect."[22] Bob Sherrill wrote that Eckhardt "has about him a Spanish-moss quaintness and an elegant corniness that people tend to associate with Southern politicians."[23]

As if traversing the capital in a 1920s Southern plantation style of dress did not make him stand out enough, "Bow tie Bob's" *mannerisms* helped him garner a reputation as an eccentric southerner. He took the South with him to Washington. He would have cookouts for staff and friends, using a "corn scraper" on field corn and boiling it down into a mush. He loved red-dyed pistachios and would walk around popping them in his mouth with machine-like efficiency, his thumbnails stained red for days.

BOB'S SYMBOLIC BIKE

Then there was his bicycle. Eckhardt was never fond of driving, and he could not have his horses in the capital. So he bicycled, earning him the additional moniker "Bicycle Bob." Because he was miserly, he would buy an old bike, hook a horn to the handles, and attach his whiskey file box, with a lid and lock, to the back. Eckhardt's three-mile ride from his Georgetown home took twenty to thirty minutes as he pedaled alongside the Potomac River and the Lincoln Memorial, past the reflecting pool, in his white suit, bow tie, and panama hat, puffing a crooked cigar. Sometimes he arrived covered in ice and snow; sometimes he showered in the congressional gym to get rid of the sweat. "The terrain is ideal, but the traffic is terrible," he told Carl Bernstein for a *Washington Post* article, with a photo of him on the streets of Washington.[24] He became a known fixture in the Washington street scene, grinning and waving "hello, Evie" to labor lobbyist Evie Dubrow, greeting other friends, and worrying friends, family, and strangers with his near misses in the traffic. Once he got knocked off his bike by a bus, and he yelled and cursed out the driver.[25] Arriving at the Capitol, he would sometimes lock the bike to whatever was near. When he forgot where he had left his bike, staff members would search for it, or police would call the office and a staff member would retrieve the errant bike.

President Johnson took note of Eckhardt's bicycling. When Eckhardt bicycled to the White House for a meeting in 1968, photographers snapped

THE WHITE HOUSE
WASHINGTON

March 11, 1968

Dear Bob:

The Curator of the White House tells me that during the 168-year history of the White House, Congressmen have arrived on foot, on horseback, in automobiles, helicopter, bus and trailer -- but as far as we know you're the first to show up on a bicycle.

Here are some prints which can prove your strength to your constituents.

Sincerely,

Lyndon B. Johnson

Honorable Robert C. Eckhardt
House of Representatives
Washington, D. C.

Congressman Eckhardt riding his bicycle at the White House. Without his horses in Washington, Eckhardt took to the bicycle for transportation, even pedaling to the White House. White House Photo; courtesy of the Eckhardt family.

Eckhardt's bicycle card. One of Eckhardt's signature art pieces was a linoleum
block print of a self portrait made in the midst of the energy crises of the
1970s—Congressman Eckhardt riding his bicycle, with the Emergency Energy Act
tucked under his arm. Courtesy of the Robert C. Eckhardt Collection, Center for
American History, University of Texas at Austin, CN 12140.

a shot of him. LBJ signed it and sent Eckhardt a note: "The Curator of the
White House tells me that during the 168-year history of the White House,
Congressmen have arrived on foot, on horseback, by automobile, helicopter,
bus and trailer—but as far as we know you're the first to show up on a bicycle." The photo and note graced Eckhardt's wall for the rest of his life.

When the energy crisis erupted in the 1970s, people applauded his gas-
saving transport. Eckhardt delighted in the attention and incorporated it

into his persona. For his 1973 Christmas card, he got out his linoleum blocks and carved a caricature of himself riding his bicycle, decked out in bow tie and panama hat, with a copy of the emergency energy bill tucked under his arm—a self-portrait that newspapers eagerly reprinted.

The LBJ-signed photo was later supplemented with another photo of him at the White House, bicycling back from an energy policy meeting with President Carter—this one published across the nation and in Mexico. A Californian wrote, "Only a Texas gentleman with a German name as you are will have the determination in using his bicycle in your high duties in Washington D.C. This, your humble act, makes you a great man, a true leader." [26] Eckhardt pushed provisions to study bicycle riding impediments and incentives and bikes' energy conservation potential. *Bicycling* magazine put him and his bike on its cover in 1980 and wrote a story about him. [27]

BOB'S FAMILY

Bob mixed family affairs, congressional work, and travel. He returned to the district about every other week. Because he hated flying, he would drive or take the train whenever possible, though those days were numbered as he got busier. Sidney and Shelby were teenagers, Willie nine, and Sarah two. Orissa had moved to Ithaca. Rosalind was nineteen and not far away in Philadelphia. He would go to Philadelphia or New York, and sometimes the girls would come to Washington for visits with daddy, who would buy them clothes and send them money and prints from woodcuts he carved.

Orissa's eye doctor continued to monitor the condition that had been diagnosed in 1966. In June 1967, her doctor concluded that there was no recurrence, suggesting that Orissa be seen once or twice a year. She married Larry Arend, who had been a year ahead of her at St. Stephens, then went to Cornell. After Ithaca, they moved to New Orleans and Orissa finished her degree at Tulane. A year later, her New Orleans doctor discovered melanoma, and she lost her eye to the cancer, which, amazingly, did not spread. Bob felt a deep sense of remorse for not being involved enough with her to detect the condition before she lost her eye, and for trying unsuccessfully and tragically to protect her by not fully informing her of the doctor's concerns. Orissa recovered and, when she graduated, got a job teaching at an all-black New Orleans school. She made New Orleans her permanent home and became a counselor and writer.

From the Great Society to Nixon

For the first two years of Eckhardt's congressional career, he shared Washington with Lyndon Johnson, then with Richard Nixon and his team, including

John Connally. It was a tumultuous time across the nation, and the street tensions that welled up from the bitter divisions in society were reflected in Eckhardt's Congress as they fenced with Johnson, then Nixon.

THE CONGRESSIONAL FAMILY

Eckhardt reveled in the camaraderie of Congress. His friendliness and charm allowed him to communicate easily with members, even across ideological and party divides. He would meet quietly with Republicans and fashion compromises that would help him win votes. He also won friends, allies, and breakfast companions in informal groups of Democratic outsiders, such as "True Believers," the "Hard Core" and "The Group"—typically reform-minded, antiwar Democrats.

Eckhardt joined a Congress composed of 248 Democrats and 187 Republicans. He joined the twenty-three-member Texas House delegation. He was, of course, friends and allies with Ralph Yarborough in the Senate, and Yarborough hosted a welcoming reception for Eckhardt as soon as he got to Congress.[28] Upon Yarborough's defeat in 1970, Opal Yarborough wrote Nadine, saying how much the Eckhardts had meant to them in Washington.

Eckhardt loved dealing with what he saw as a real Democratic structure in Washington. He found some natural allies in the Texas delegation—his 1940s Young Democrat compatriot Jim Wright and his Texas legislative associate Henry B. Gonzalez, plus Jack Brooks and Wright Patman. Later, Barbara Jordan would join them, followed by Mickey Leland. Other members of the Texas delegation were often Boll Weevils (southern Democrats who voted with Republicans)—among them, Joe Pool (who died in 1968), who was serving on the Un-American Activities Committee, John Dowdy, Eligio "Kika" de la Garza, Omar Burleson, George Mahon, Bob Casey, and Chick Kazen. Jake Pickle moderated over the years as his Austin district became more liberal and shifted between the national Democrats and the Boll Weevils, though still successfully maneuvering to keep reformers out of power.[29] Pickle was soon joined in the middle by newcomers Charlie Wilson and Bob Krueger. Eckhardt concluded that some Texans would go along with the party's national positions when it was necessary to do so for Democrats to keep power, so Kazen and others moved away from Boll Weevilism over time.[30]

Eckhardt observed and made judgments about his new colleagues, gleefully repeating a comment made by Speaker John McCormack about a fellow congressman: "He is a gentleman who enjoys my minimum high regard."[31] At the end of his congressional career, Eckhardt reflected on the changes he had witnessed. The 1960s members of the House were just as reactionary as the ones in 1980, he remarked, "but they stood on a kind of principle. I wrote a poem about three of them one time." They were H. R. Gross (R-Iowa), Frank Bow (R-Ohio), and Durward Hall (R-Mo.).

> *It's good enough for Mr. Bow*
> *To just preserve the status quo.*
> *And Dr. Hall will gladly tell them*
> *His status quo is ante-bellum.*
> *"What bellum then?" cries Mr. Gross.*
> *"The Civil War is much too close.*
> *I'd fain retreat with right good speed*
> *to England prior to Runnymede."* [32]

Eckhardt would build a critical, but delicate, relationship with John Dingell (D-Mich.). Eckhardt thought Dingell brilliant, circumspect, and shrewd, but also arrogant, ruthless, and devious.[33] Their relationship on the Commerce Committee would become an important dynamic in the energy battles of the 1970s. While he was briefly on the Science and Astronautics Committee, Eckhardt built a relationship with committee member Tip O'Neill. He would later take Speaker O'Neill on a tour of the Houston medical complex. Eckhardt thought O'Neill was very provincial—O'Neill couldn't believe that all this medical research was happening in Texas instead of Boston! Eckhardt particularly admired Mo Udall (D-Ariz.) and considered the Arizona congressman the best person he worked with in his congressional years. Eckhardt supported Udall in a failed run against Speaker McCormack in 1969, and then again in a failed run for the presidency in 1976.

Once Barbara Jordan made it to Congress in 1973, he and Nadine hosted a reception for her. He admired Jordan and liked working with her. As her physical condition deteriorated as a result of multiple sclerosis, it become difficult for her to move from her Longworth office to the chamber in the Capitol, so she stayed on the floor of the House. This was Eckhardt's favorite hangout, too, so they would talk there.[34] Yet, he became disappointed in Jordan. Observing that she rarely led on women's or blacks' issues, he commented, "She has no sex and no race." [35]

On the other side of the aisle, Eckhardt and George Bush built a Houston-based amicable relationship, following up on their trip to Texas A&M after the 1966 election. In the summer of 1967, they anchored a University of Houston panel discussion, "The First Seven Months of the 90th Congress." Bush was conservative, yet he would sometimes come under attack from the right. Eckhardt was just as predictably liberal, yet sometimes his liberal supporters would be dismayed at a particular vote he cast. Bush and Eckhardt came to a jocular agreement to help each other with the extremes of their bases of support: if Bush was attacked from the right, Eckhardt would criticize him as a conservative Republican; likewise, if Eckhardt came under fire from the left, Bush would criticize him as a liberal Democrat. In this way, they rallied each other's troops to their defense. But, over time, Eckhardt came to see Bush as having "no conception of the constitution of government," someone who "only flitted amongst the flowers of popularity."[36]

ECKHARDT'S COMMITTEES

Democrats were assigned to their committees by the Democratic contingent on the Ways and Means Committee. Majority Whip Hale Boggs (D-La.) was in charge of Texas, so Eckhardt talked with him. Eckhardt's first choice was the Committee on Interstate and Foreign Commerce, a powerful committee with far-reaching jurisdiction into the world of business, labor issues, even environmental issues. His second choice was the prestigious Foreign Affairs Committee. He was also keen to focus on environmental and conservation issues, so his third and fourth choices were the Interior and Insular Affairs Committee (natural resources) and Merchant Marine and Fisheries (coastal issues). But he didn't get any of his choices. Eckhardt's original committee assignment was to the Science and Astronautics Committee. By 1967, the blossoming NASA presence in Houston made Science and Astronautics an attractive assignment. He served there with fellow Texans Earle Cabell and Tiger Teague; down the table was a young Republican from Illinois named Donald Rumsfeld. Eckhardt found little to do on the committee, which gave him plenty of time to be on the House floor, learning the ropes and beginning his engagement in floor debates.[37]

After winning reelection in 1968, Eckhardt again sought a seat on the Interstate and Foreign Commerce Committee. He went hat-in-hand to the Ways and Means Democrats, finally winning the assignment and dropping the Science Committee. With the congressional reforms of the early 1970s, members were assured two committee assignments, and in 1973, Eckhardt won appointment to the Merchant Marine and Fisheries Committee.

Proud of his assignment to Commerce, Eckhardt saw his role as continuing the work of Texans John Reagan and Sam Rayburn on that committee. He served on the committee for the rest of his career, joining none other than Jake Pickle. "We always got along" on the committee, Pickle said. "He would vote against me—I was a little bit closer to business than Eckhardt was."[38] Eckhardt was assigned to the Commerce and Finance Subcommittee, chaired by California's John Moss. Commerce was often involved in hot-button regulatory issues of the day. One of those issues was cigarette labeling, and the 1969–70 hearings confirmed Eckhardt's resolve to not smoke cigarettes.[39] He objected to the committee's bill, filing a minority report that the required warning on packages, absent stiffer regulations, "lulls us into the belief that the public is protected and preempts further investigation."[40] He would spend the rest of his career championing consumer protection.

In 1973, under pressure from the Democratic Study Group in the House, the Democratic Caucus reined in committee chairs by setting up a vote to affirm or reject the seniority-designated chairs. All chairs were confirmed that year, but the unraveling of the tight power structure was unstoppable. The Caucus stripped its Ways and Means members of their committee-selection powers and gave them to the Caucus's Steering and Policy Committee. Eckhardt won a rules change requiring a majority vote to close committee sessions. His basic idea was to shift the burden from those who want to open the doors to those who want to close them.[41] The 1973 "Subcommittee Bill of Rights" forced chairs to share authority, allowed Democratic members to select subcommittee chairs, and mandated a larger number of subcommittees. Changes in 1975 allowed subcommittee chairs to hire staff.

All these changes, plus the upheavals of the 1974 election in the midst of the Watergate scandal, stirred more changes in 1975. With the large turnover of House membership, there was an opening on the Ways and Means Committee that the Texas delegation was due, and Eckhardt decided to go for it, seeing an opportunity to revive his tax equity persona. But his old oil and gas enemies worked to block him. Back in 1936, when Albert Thomas beat out Lyndon Johnson for appointment to Appropriations, it caused such a rift that they did not speak to each other for years. The Texas delegation then enforced a system of strict seniority for its committee choices, and that norm was followed religiously.[42] Charlie Wilson had joined the delegation in 1973 and he too wanted the Ways and Means appointment. Most of the Texas delegation supported the centrist Wilson, but Eckhardt was due the assignment on seniority grounds.

Jake Pickle became the dealmaker. Pickle supported Wilson, knowing that he would work closer with business than would Eckhardt. Pickle tried to persuade Eckhardt to step aside, much as he had tried to ease him out of the student body presidential race in 1938. But Eckhardt knew that, by the delegation's system of seniority, the position was his. Pickle told Eckhardt that he thought it likely that the delegation would violate the norm and not vote for him, but Eckhardt refused to back down. So, Pickle and the others made an end run around Eckhardt. Pickle did not necessarily want to give up the seniority he had earned on the Commerce Committee, but others in the Texas delegation persuaded him to apply for Ways and Means, thus blocking Eckhardt out by seniority. It worked. Pickle went on to make his career as a Ways and Means specialist. Eckhardt moved up in seniority on Commerce and became a legislative craftsman and subcommittee chair on the committee that took center ring in the major consumer, environmental, and energy legislation of the 1970s.

As a consolation, Eckhardt got an appointment to the committee he had first requested back in 1967. He dropped Merchant Marine and Fisheries to join the Committee on Interior and Insular Affairs, where he worked with Mo Udall, who chaired his Energy and the Environment subcommittee.

STAFF

As a Texas legislator, Eckhardt had been able to hire one staff aide. Now, he had a budget and hired Washington and Houston staff. By the end of his tenure, his staff numbered twenty-one, with a salary budget of $300,000, and as he gained in committee responsibility he hired subcommittee staffers as well.[43]

When Eckhardt won office in 1966, he flew to Washington and was met at the airport by Robert Cochran. Bob Cochran and his wife Gloria had been friends of Bob and Nadine in Houston. When Cochran was fired as a *Houston Chronicle* editor (for supporting Eckhardt and his ilk), the Cochrans moved to Washington, where he worked with Jack Valenti writing speeches for LBJ. Eckhardt asked Cochran to help him set up his office, then made him his Administrative Assistant, or AA (the top congressional staff position). Cochran was a lawyer by training, but a writer by choice, publishing in numerous magazines and newspapers over the years. He was a history buff, his interests were eclectic, and he had a great sense of humor. He served as AA only until 1968, but he and Eckhardt continued their friendship for years.[44]

Cochran brought with him a talented secretary named Frances Gray. Gloria Cochran also came along, volunteering to help with the office. Soon, Eckhardt said to Gloria, "I think it's time we put you on the payroll," and she and Fran stayed with Eckhardt for the entirety of his congressional career.[45] Eckhardt would hire a young lawyer for his Legislative Assistant (LA), usually a woman, and tell her that he expected her to work only a couple of years to gain experience as she began her career.

A congressman's relationship with his staff can be a delicate matter. Eckhardt could be distant, self-absorbed, egotistical. His inner circle worked closely with him, but he did not interact much with the rest of the staff. He was not a demanding, barking boss as some members could be, but he rarely gave staff feedback and was usually so preoccupied that he talked with them about the issue in front of them, but not much else. When a floor vote came up, Frances would call the staff person who was working on that issue and he or she would explain it to Eckhardt in the five-minute walk to the Capitol.

Eckhardt often appeared as the absentminded professor. Staff members were always retrieving his hat or bicycle. He had trouble remembering names. Though Gloria worked for him for years, one day he appeared in the doorway of his office to ask her a question. He looked straight at her and said, "Umm, umm, umm—Gloria???"[46] Yet, despite his scattered interactions with his staff, they came to greatly adore and respect him, referring to him as "The Congressman," were extremely loyal, and cherished the years they spent with him. Other staffers were envious of them for getting to work with the legendary Eckhardt. Even thirty years later, Eckhardt staffers would gather with each other for social affairs, sometimes in his name or honor.

THE ADAM CLAYTON POWELL AFFAIR

From the beginning, Eckhardt loved the job, the excitement, and the controversy of being in Congress. Immediately upon being sworn in, he was pulled into the Adam Clayton Powell storm. The House voted to not seat Congressman Powell, who chaired the Education and Labor Committee. Powell, the pastor of Harlem's Abyssinian Baptist Church, was first elected in 1944, one of two African Americans in Congress. Powell had an engaging, charismatic personality. By the 1960s, he was attired in expensive dress, and his office was adorned with Persian rugs and antique furniture and stocked with French and Spanish wines and sherries. He had Playboy bunnies and models on staff and sipped martinis as he met with callers in his office. Powell was often gone to his second home in Puerto Rico or to other far-off places—he wasn't even present for the final vote on the Civil Rights Act of 1964. Members joked about Powell, though the joking was often mixed with admiration and a boyish sense of "I wish I could get away with that." Yet, members became increasingly disturbed over his practices, including his abuse of members' franking privilege and his placement of his wife on his payroll and apparent pocketing of her salary. Andrew Young later said, "It was left to Adam Clayton Powell to integrate corruption."[47]

Eckhardt called Houston to consult new State Representative Curtis Graves about the Powell affair, then voted against the successful motion to block Powell from taking the oath of office. A committee wrestled with whether to block Powell from the House, to fine him, or to seat him then expel him. The committee recommended to "exclude" Powell (there is no constitutional language on exclusion). In his maiden congressional speech, Eckhardt argued that the House had no constitutional authority to refuse to seat Powell. The Constitution, he said, only allows *voters* to determine whether members are qualified. He urged the House instead to approve Mo Udall's motion to seat Powell, then strip him of his committee chairmanship as punishment for his violation of House rules and ethics. But by majority vote the House "excluded" Powell from its membership; Eckhardt voted nay in what he called "my most difficult vote." With the House's action, Powell's seat was declared vacant and a special election called to fill it. Powell won the election, but was excluded again.[48] Eckhardt wrote a *Texas Law Review* article arguing that the House had violated the Constitution.[49] The Constitution alone, he wrote, spelled out the qualifications for members. He cited constitutional convention debates to sustain his position that Congress could not judge the qualifications of its members, as the House had done in its resolution. Only *after* a qualified (elected, meeting the constitutional requirements) member was seated could the House, *by the constitutionally mandated two-thirds vote*, expel the member. The House had not done so in the Powell case because it could not get two-thirds.

Powell sued the House and successfully won reelection in 1968 (he was seated, then fined for his unethical behavior). A district judge agreed with House lawyers that courts had no jurisdiction, as did Warren Burger's Court of Appeals. But in 1969, the Supreme Court overturned the House's action, vindicating Eckhardt's constitutional arguments. Indeed, Chief Justice Earl Warren quoted Eckhardt's law review article, noting, "The views of Congressman Eckhardt were echoed during the exclusion proceedings."[50] Thus, Eckhardt began gaining his reputation as a serious constitutional scholar and lawyer. Yet, the arrogant Powell, banished from his chairmanship and his luxurious Rayburn offices to small Longworth offices, was unrepentant and never even thanked Eckhardt for his efforts.[51]

LBJ, ECKHARDT, AND VIETNAM

Within weeks of being sworn in, Bob and Nadine were at the White House spending an evening with Lyndon, Lady Bird, and Hubert Humphrey. Eckhardt had campaigned as a supporter of LBJ, even of his Vietnam policy. In 1965 and 1966, President Johnson poured troops into the Vietnam conflict, transforming it into a major war. By early 1967, the war was not going well, casualty numbers were rising, and opposition was growing. As Eckhardt ascended to the national stage, the dynamics of Vietnam and the dissension across the nation were ever present in the Eckhardt-Johnson relationship. LBJ cultivated their longstanding relationship, extending presidential privileges such as having Eckhardt join him on a flight back to Texas on Air Force One. Yet, by April 1967 Eckhardt, as the keynote speaker at the Texas Young Democrats convention in Austin, urged unilateral de-escalation. He said that he was "neither a dove, for we cannot 'coo' ourselves out of the situation which we had so much to do with coming about, nor a hawk." He supposed, he said, that he was a *paisano*, a roadrunner with his feet on the ground, but a word that can also mean a countryman, sympathetic with those who are upholding their own nationalism.[52]

In June, Eckhardt was in Paris with his Science and Astronautics Committee. There, he literally and ominously saw the writing on the wall. He wrote to Nadine, "I saw three writings on walls near Quai Malaquiais: 'US=Nazis,' 'ala porte Humphrey,' and 'Victorie au Vietcong.' I don't think Mr. Johnson's image is holding out very well."[53] On Bob's fifty-fourth birthday, they were at Congressman Richard Bolling's house for a party when Lyndon and Lady Bird dropped by. The president played with Sarah Pie and gave Eckhardt the "Johnson Treatment," saying how much he appreciated him—without ever mentioning Eckhardt's new antiwar statements.[54] That fall, John Henry Faulk sent Bob and Nadine a postcard, showing an Indian in full headgear and ceremonial dress, beating a drum. With typical Faulk humor and social commentary, he wrote: "Alert Joe Pool! Just caught this character sending smoke signals. One glance and I saw he was un-American. Probably a premature Hippie Red! Admits grandpa didn't even speak English! Says he understands how North Vietnamese feel. Same thing happened to *his* folks. I'm off on a lecture tour. Have spoken in 26 states in 26 days! And the folks ain't happy in the land, Bob. Hope to see you in Wash. soon—Best John Faulk."[55]

Eckhardt's evolving position on Vietnam was influenced by critiques from constituents, his own observations about the damage the war was doing, and pressure from his daughters. Orissa became distressed that Johnson's actions in Vietnam were undermining his domestic leadership. Like many college students, Rosalind believed Johnson to be a warmonger. She went to New York in April for a march from Central Park to the United Nations, wearing beads and bell-bottoms and carrying a sign that said "Texans for Peace." Rosalind argued with her dad that he was wrong to insist that the war was not LBJ's fault. Eckhardt replied to a Baytown constituent's antiwar letter that we "should withdraw from Vietnam." In his reply, Eckhardt despaired that "the war poisons the wellsprings of the Great Society." He wrote that it is necessary for us "to accept in our own minds a lesser goal than the absolute insistence, under all conditions, on a sovereign, separate state of South Vietnam. Unless we envisage at least the possibility, ultimately, of a unified Vietnam free of western surveillance, I do not think there is any possibility of meaningful negotiation.... Our commitment is to humanity, not to any military junta."[56]

Just a few months into his inaugural year, Eckhardt began meeting with others in the House who were turning against the war. He went with a group of members to meet with Secretary of State Dean Rusk in April, where they expressed their dissatisfaction with the course of events in Vietnam. The next day, Eckhardt huddled with a dozen of the participants to discuss their strategy. Eight of them had formed "The Group" to work up antiwar support, and

EK
♡

they began going public with their opposition.[57] Eckhardt could not get into The Group in his first term—he believed that his southern accent caused suspicion among the northern antiwar contingent—but he was later welcomed and became good friends with members Don Edwards, Bob Kastenmeier, Phil Burton, Robert Drinan, Abner Mikva, Brock Adams, and others.[58] The Group grew and designated a rotating monthly chair, meeting sometimes in Eckhardt's Longworth office.

By late 1967, Eckhardt was becoming bolder with his opposition. In November, he went to the Bronx with Congressman James Scheuer to be on a panel with John Kenneth Galbraith and others. Eckhardt argued that "we were wrong even in the early fifties to envisage ourselves as the single force in the world powerful enough to stand against the Communist bloc and thus destined to do so. From this position we have developed the conceit that we had a commitment to save the Saigon government." He concluded that "the war poisons the wellsprings of the Great Society," and "I cannot see how even a clear-cut victory in Vietnam would justify the sacrifice."[59] In 1968, Eckhardt joined a new group, Members of Congress for Peace Through Law, and in the spring of 1969, he joined colleagues in a "Congressional Conference on the Military Budget and National Priorities"; they followed it with other hearings and published books to publicize the growing opposition to the war.[60]

THE END OF THE GREAT SOCIETY, AND NIXON COMING

By the time Eckhardt settled in as a congressman, he was running for re-election. Bob Cochran and Nadine planned fundraising within the first few weeks of being in office. He ran unopposed in the 1968 primary, then easily beat Republican Joe Stevens in the general election, 63 percent to 37 percent. It was apparent to the Houston establishment that Eckhardt was a formidable force, whether they liked him or not. John Connally joined Houston's powerful Vinson & Elkins law firm in 1969, and the partners invited Eckhardt over for a peace meeting with them and Connally.[61] Even George Brown began warming up to Eckhardt. They all accepted the inevitability of his congressional tenure. Harris County Democrats continued to do most of the legwork for Eckhardt's campaigns. He would come in from Washington and join the headquarters activities, grabbing scissors and cutting up the registered voters' lists to make walk lists, then head out for campaign speeches and meetings. But he never was much of a strategist or technician. Nadine or his staff aides steered him from appointment to appointment, as he would become engrossed in conversation and simply forget or ignore campaign obligations.[62]

Without strong opposition in his own campaign, Eckhardt's primary political engagement in 1968 was the presidential campaign. The antiwar fervor was reaching a fever pitch, and Senator Eugene McCarthy challenged President Johnson for the nomination. In March, LBJ shocked the nation by withdrawing from the race. Eckhardt reflected on his understanding of the dynamics in a statement to the press, carefully praising Johnson and urging continuation of a Democratic government. He argued that national unity was required to resolve the problems of Vietnam, and that "to get this unity the President must be above partisan politics or the suspicion of self-seeking. . . . The President obviously thinks—from what he said last night—that such a unified Party cannot be led by an incumbent who is a contender for the Presidential nomination. I think what he is doing is in the highest tradition of the great office of the Presidency."[63]

So the race was on, though Connally and Johnson quietly maneuvered to keep alive the possibility of a "Draft Johnson" effort. Eckhardt and his congressional allies endorsed McCarthy, believing that he "brought sense and reason into the Vietnam debate."[64] McCarthy greatly energized college campuses, but when Robert F. Kennedy jumped into the race, the left was split. Rosalind went to a Kennedy speech and reported to Bob that RFK got mad when a student asked, "How do your views differ from McCarthy's?" She found him to be an awkward campaigner, nervous in a crowd.[65]

Then, Martin Luther King, Jr. was assassinated. Eckhardt released a statement: "There has not been a time since the assassination of John F. Kennedy when so insignificant an assailant has done so much harm to the cause of humanity."[66] The nation was shocked, and riots erupted in city after city. In New York, on the night of the assassination, Celia Morris shoved Willie, screaming, "You southern boys have a lot to be guilty about!"[67] A few short weeks later, Bobby Kennedy, too, was assassinated.

Connally's efforts to use his control of the Texas delegation to keep the nomination process open failed. Humphrey prevailed at the raucous Chicago convention, and it was time for an intense fall campaign. Eckhardt campaigned for Humphrey, hosting a coffee for him at Houston's Rice Hotel in September. Johnson, Yarborough, and Connally coordinated the Texas campaign. Each was responsible for turning out his part of the Democratic coalition. And they did. Humphrey won a narrow victory in Texas. In Eckhardt's district, he drew 46 percent to George Wallace's 28 percent and Richard Nixon's 26 percent.[68] Nixon was impressed with Connally's and Johnson's ability to turn out the Texas vote and began sizing up the conservative Connally for inclusion in his administration.

Eckhardt's relations with President Nixon were minimal. When he and Nadine visited the White House, they found Pat to be friendly while Richard was cold.[69] His dealings with the Nixon administration often proved combative. Eckhardt and Bush appealed successfully to Secretary of Interior Walter

Hickel to appoint career conservationist Dr. Leslie Glasgow as assistant secretary, and Eckhardt was irate when Glasgow was later fired.[70] Eckhardt was
particularly alarmed at Nixon Attorney General John Mitchell. Mitchell's
anti-crime bill brought back memories of Eckhardt's 1940 trial before Justice
of the Peace Burch, who presumed the defendant guilty until proven innocent. Eckhardt was also irritated at Vice President Spiro Agnew's attacks on
the press. He used his wit to upbraid Nixon officials, even Mitchell's sharp-
tongued wife Martha. When Agnew stated that journalists and some members of Congress would like him to "simply shut up and disappear," Eckhardt,
believing that Agnew's caustic rhetoric was damaging to the administration,
couldn't resist a comeback. He addressed the House: "I simply want to disas-
sociate myself from any Members of the Congress who want the Vice President to simply shut up and disappear. I hope that he will not shut up, that he
will not disappear, and that goes also for the charming and ebullient wife of
the Attorney General."[71]

Nixon continued and widened the war, and Eckhardt increased his antiwar leadership. He began appearing on the weekend television news interview shows to discuss particularly sensitive issues before Congress, such as
the Pentagon Papers and the My Lai massacre. He told *Face the Nation:*

> Our choice of fighting a war of this nature, which has encompassed, for
> instance, the moving of whole villages out of their villages . . . and into
> detention camps, to in effect flush out the Viet Cong that may be in that
> area, is something that simply creates a situation in which the game is not
> worth the candle. What do you do for a people if you destroy its culture in
> attempting to bring it peace? What do you do for a people if you lay waste
> its forests and its fields, and leave hundreds of thousands of refugees and
> many dead?[72]

His appearances brought him congratulatory mail from all over the nation. He spoke at Rice University on Vietnam Moratorium Day in 1969, and
as the Cambodia invasion exploded into the news and the antiwar movement
peaked in 1970, he spoke at Rice, Cornell University, and Millsaps College. In
1971, Eckhardt joined Representatives Don Edwards and Bella Abzug, Senator Mike Gravel, and others in a national tour, speaking at antiwar rallies;
Eckhardt spoke in Ohio and Connecticut.[73]

National Democratic Leadership

Eckhardt was a seasoned legislator, a scholar of the Constitution, an experienced practitioner of the law, and a longtime speaker on national political

issues. He was not reticent about jumping into big issues. Seeing the disaster that fell upon the Democratic Party with the 1968 primary battles and divisive national convention, he introduced the "Presidential Nominee Selection Act of 1969," with a proportional representation scheme for conventions, federal funding of primary elections, abolition of the unit rule, a shortened campaign period, and televised debates. He decried the national political dialogue descending "into a pitchman's hullabaloo" and argued that his proposal would restore the public stump for genuine dialogue.[74] He did not, however, support changing the Constitution to get rid of the Electoral College. He lectured his fellow members that such a move "may have the most far-reaching effect of any matter upon which you and I will ever vote." He continued:

> Therefore, above all others, this issue deserves deep philosophic consideration of what the change could do in altering a fundamental balance in our government. . . . I believe the result of the change is not nearly so simple, nor so wholesome, as I know some of my very sincere friends believe. . . . I very deeply fear that the passage of this bill would do severe damage to a system that has worked well for 180 years."[75]

Eckhardt's voting record lined him up squarely and consistently with the national party and its constituent groups, and both members and lobby groups started turning to him for help with bills and amendments. He was becoming an icon in the liberal political community. Willie Morris's good friend Edwin Yoder profiled Eckhardt in a 1970 *Harper's* article, and Representative Robert Tiernan placed it in the *Congressional Record*, noting that it "catches the spirit, personality, and brilliance of my good friend from Texas."[76]

Over the course of his long career, his cumulative voting record from labor, environmental, consumer, civil rights, and public interest groups was in the range of 85–98 percent support.[77] His Democratic Party Unity Score in 1970 was 82 percent, bettered only by Henry B. Gonzalez among his fellow Texans; his LBJ Support Score was 87 percent.[78] Early in his career, Eckhardt was invited to Rules Committee Chair William Colmer's office for a huddle of Dixie Democrats who were plotting against the Speaker.[79] When it became apparent that he was not like other southern Democrats, he wasn't invited back. In 1968, the bellwether liberal group Americans for Democratic Action rated Eckhardt and Gonzalez 100 percent; they were the only southerners to score 100 percent. In contrast, Americans for Constitutional Action (the leading conservative group vote analyzer) scored him 0 percent. His old UT friend and longtime Americans for Democratic Action activist Otto Mullinax helped get Eckhardt elected as a vice chairman of ADA in 1971.

Eckhardt maintained close ties with labor, both Texas and national. His cumulative career score from AFL-CIO's Committee on Political Education was 94 percent, leading the Texas delegation in labor vote rankings. He followed up his Texas legislative push for workplace safety by cosponsoring LBJ's bill creating the Occupational Safety and Health Administration (OSHA). One of the puzzling aspects of Eckhardt's congressional career was that, although he continued his interest in and ironclad alliance with labor, he never focused on or specialized in labor affairs during his years in the House.

1970 Elections

In his second reelection effort, Eckhardt drew as a primary opponent Bobby Carley, a local school board member and former Marine. Carley was clearly out of his league in a congressional race, but his campaign foreshadowed some of the issues that, a decade later, would defeat Eckhardt. Running against gun control and trade with Communist countries, Carley supported a stronger war effort, criticizing Eckhardt's participation in antiwar rallies. He also denounced Eckhardt's vote to abolish the Un-American Activities Committee and his vote against a flag desecration bill.[80] Eckhardt touted his consumer class action legislation and his national Open Beaches legislation. In a dismal turnout, Eckhardt swamped Carley 77 percent to 23 percent, then had no Republican opponent.

In the Houston area campaign, Frankie Randolph had retired, and the coalition just didn't work together the way it had with her.[81] The liberal and labor camps became cross-wise, especially under Billie Carr's leadership. Eckhardt, close to both labor and liberals, felt caught in the middle. He had earlier proposed a reorganization of Harris County Democrats, but he did not win; now he pled with the group to work out its differences in quarterly caucuses. "Like the gospel says, 'Ye must be born again.' The Harris County Democrats have got to quit bickering and get together," their former chairman urged.[82] But his Houston staff was favorable with one group or the other and would tell tales. Eckhardt hated to get involved in such infighting, so he would ignore it as long as he could. When relations between the factions continued to deteriorate, with his staff in the thick of the battles, he fired a staff member and concluded he was partly to blame because he had not spent enough time in Houston.[83]

The big race in 1970 was Ralph Yarborough's reelection campaign, with multimillionaire Lloyd Bentsen Jr. running against him in the Democratic primary. Bentsen defeated Yarborough, and the old party rift was again wide open. With Republican George Bush running a strong campaign for the seat, some Democrats, angered by Bentsen's pro-war, anti-civil rights campaign, joined Bush. After the elections, Texas progressives could see the corrosive effects of having anti-progressive forces in control. They realized the need to fire up, again, their old organizing efforts. Eckhardt traveled to Austin to huddle with Hank Brown, State Senators Barbara Jordan and Joe Bernal, and other progressives. They followed up with a February meeting at which Yarborough and former U.S. Attorney General Ramsey Clark spoke.[84] Eckhardt chaired the meeting, with Bernal and Jordan as vice chairs, and Bernard Rapoport was elected treasurer. But the ensuing organization never achieved much clout. The next year, Frankie Randolph died and Yarborough lost his comeback effort, trying again to win the Democratic primary for the Senate seat held by John Tower. The movement had lost its passion and its iconic leaders. The 1970s weren't looking promising for Congressman Eckhardt's brand of politics and policy.

THIRTEEN

The Veteran Congressman

Members of Congress live in the world of government in Washington, the world of the local constituency, the world of their personal affairs, and the world of international affairs. The international world was a new one to Eckhardt. He became a world traveler—Lisbon, Munich, Paris, Stuttgart, Ottawa, the Middle East—engaging with parliamentarians from other countries on consumer, environmental, and energy issues. Most of his attention, of course, was focused on affairs in Washington and the nation. Eckhardt became a regular at the semiannual Brookings Institution policy conferences, and he was increasingly in demand as a speaker at university campuses.

Meanwhile, Back in Houston

Eckhardt also had to work at being a part of his Houston community. Young lawyer Lynn Coleman hosted Eckhardt at a Vinson & Elkins gathering, and several of the lawyers who were Democrats became Eckhardt supporters.[1] The congressman learned to be an ombudsman for constituents' concerns with the federal government. He joined the Steel Caucus and championed his Houston steelworkers' concerns, cementing their undying support for him. When he reluctantly started flying, Eckhardt took the three-hour flight from Washington to Houston on Friday morning, returning Monday about noon. He would spend the weekend in his Rusk Street office and around the city on constituent matters and political affairs. When he was on Cypress Creek, he wore patched and torn blue jeans, checkered shirts, and boots with cracked leather, even as he hosted guests. A reporter described Eckhardt's hair as "down to here and all uncombed and going every which way." He wrote, "If you met him on the road you might think he was about to ask you for half a buck to buy a bowl of chili. . . . But get in close and The Look is still there. They all have it, after they've been in public life a few years. There's a sort of shrewdness showing in the eyes, and a slick show-biz quality in the face. It's something they can't hide with old clothes."[2]

Congressman Eckhardt cultivated his relationship with Houston's black community. His black precincts were well organized by activists devoted to his campaigns, such as Reverend Floyd Williams. Eckhardt had built and maintained a relationship with Dr. Lonnie Smith who, along with Williams and Curtis Graves, shepherded Eckhardt around to events in the black community. When Smith was elderly, he took ill and asked for Eckhardt. But Eckhardt did not make time to go see him until Smith was hospitalized and called for him again. Smith was dying and asked for Eckhardt's help with a man he thought was wrongly arrested. Ashamed that he had not gone to see him earlier, Bob wept in the parking lot as he was leaving, saying that Smith was far better to represent the district, but that he, Eckhardt, had gotten the position because he was white.

In Houston as well as in Congress, the school busing issue was a hydra, one that kept rearing its heads even into his 1980 campaign. Eckhardt opposed anti-busing constitutional amendments, saying, "I can't vote for anything that would undermine the principle of *Brown*."[3] Hundreds of anti-busing letters from constituents poured into his office. In an obviously orchestrated campaign, scores of them asked for "freedom of choice"—the same phrase used in the late 1950s to resist integration. Eckhardt replied that he opposed forced busing, but would have to be convinced that "freedom of choice" was "not just a screen for unconstitutional segregation of the public schools." He wrote many long, often very direct, responses himself. He wrote back to one anti-busing leader that he could not support his position, out of a "deeply felt conviction that state-imposed segregation was, and is, unjust."[4] The most difficult case Eckhardt had to address was that of the Harlem School in an all-black community near Baytown. Eckhardt helped devise and get adopted a voluntary desegregation plan under the magnet school process, which he considered to be a model for solving the very difficult problem of integration.

1972: Jordan, Nixon, McGovern, and Connally

The dynamics of both the presidential election and the Texas congressional elections dominated 1972. In the 1970 reapportionment, Texas had gained one congressional seat, and much as Eckhardt worked to draw a seat for himself in 1965, now his State Senate allies Charlie Wilson, Don Kennard, Oscar Mauzy, Babe Schwartz, and Barbara Jordan wanted the new seat. Jordan was close to Lieutenant Governor Ben Barnes, and he supported her effort to get this new seat. Eckhardt went to Barnes's office to discuss the redistricting dynamics, and Barnes made sure that all the incumbents, including Eckhardt, had districts they could continue to win.[5] Eckhardt had supported Jordan and loved the idea of her coming to Congress. Yet, he had to be careful, as he had to give up black precincts in his district to the new district next to his.

Both he and Jordan were able to get what they needed: he kept his workshop district, and she got many, though not all, of the minority communities in her district.

At the same time, he got caught up in a rift among black allies. Barnes and most of the senators had come to like and trust Jordan. She worked well with them, and they considered her an insider. Curtis Graves, who was definitely not an insider, wanted Jordan's state senate seat. Barnes and senators were alarmed at that possibility and decided to block him. Jordan went to Lauro Cruz, who was on the redistricting conference committee, and asked where Graves's house was on the map. She took out a magic marker and drew a line around his house, into the district that extended into River Oaks, the wealthy, white area of town, and that map was passed. Graves was furious. Knowing that he could not win (indeed, the seat went white), he instead filed to run for Congress, and Jordan and Graves battled each other in the primary, with Jordan winning the nomination. Eckhardt had to stay neutral.

Eckhardt was opposed in the 1972 primary by mechanical engineer David Shall, who ran against busing and against the federal government. Eckhardt beat him handily, 77 percent to 23 percent. In November, he beat Republican Lewis Emerich, 65 percent to 34 percent. Congressman John Dowdy's resignation opened a seat in East Texas. Like Jordan, the other new representative to Congress came from the Texas Senate and had been a boisterous colleague of Eckhardt's in the Texas House—Charlie Wilson.

On the presidential campaign front, new Treasury Secretary John Connally headed the group, "Democrats for Nixon." Connally publicly stated that he was a Democrat and that prospects for his changing parties were "very remote." In an interview for CBS's *60 Minutes,* Eckhardt, Pickle, and Dugger all predicted that Connally would switch to the Republican Party. The two old UT rivals resumed their battle positions. Eckhardt compared Connally to a Roman military leader: "You know Coriolanus fought for Rome and when they didn't give him enough recognition, why he fought for the enemies of Rome." He described Connally unflatteringly as a "man who likes to exercise power. I don't know that John Connally has any particular political philosophy. He's a political pragmatist, I suppose." Pickle said that Connally was "born a leader." [6] When Connally did jump to the Republican Party, as Watergate was decimating the Republican Party, Eckhardt likened him to a man who had left his hat on an airplane and was going back in to get it, having to push against the crowd going the other way.

The antiwar fervor propelled the Senate's leading antiwar spokesman and national party reformer, George McGovern, to the Democratic nomination for president. In Houston, Curtis Graves organized a McGovern meeting, and Eckhardt spoke. He said that he had not thought McGovern to be the Democrats' strongest candidate earlier, but that the primaries had shown him to have the best chance to defeat Nixon.[7] As McGovern neared the nomination, he set to work to find a running mate. He wanted Senator Edward Kennedy to join him on the ticket, but Kennedy would not take the offer. So McGovern broadened his list, and the *New York Times* reported that Eckhardt was on it.[8] Tactical though the mention may have been, the mere reporting of his name by the *Times* set Eckhardt and his staff to work composing responses to potential media queries about a possible vice presidential nomination.[9]

Despite the early stench of scandal from the botched break-in at the Democratic headquarters in the Watergate building, Nixon won a landslide victory. Within weeks of the election, Lyndon Johnson died. Eckhardt attended LBJ's Washington memorial service in the Capitol rotunda, where he listened to Jake Pickle give a warm personal eulogy and John Connally deliver a cold campaign speech.[10] Connally went back to governing with Nixon, though the Watergate debacle soon sucked them all under. In 1974, Eckhardt was the first Texas congressman to state publicly his intent to vote to impeach Nixon, believing the White House recordings contained shocking revelations of "the callous view of the underlings who ran afoul of the law."[11]

Mr. Hyde Goes to Washington

Turned loose in a new national environment, Eckhardt soon found more material for his cartooning alter ego, "Mr. Hyde." He still drew editorial cartoons; when Humble Oil changed its name to Exxon in 1972, he skewered the change—the transformation of a meek and humble oil company—in a cartoon in the *Texas Observer*. But more often he would produce spur-of-the-moment sketches. How did the busy congressman find time for his art? Mr. Hyde may have continued to emerge at night, working on the drawing board in his bedroom, but it was the boring, tedious committee sessions that served as his new muse. Eckhardt would draw on whatever was available—committee or White House stationery, placemats, notebook paper. The most distinctive are those he sketched right over the printed text of the *Congressional Record*.

He drew sketches of witnesses, lobbyists, and members and sketches of the famous people who spoke before the committees or the House—John Kenneth Galbraith, Ralph Nader, Robert Novak, Lyndon Johnson, Richard Nixon, Gerald Ford. Eckhardt's rendering of Nixon was often the classic profile view highlighting the president's ski-jump nose. One was of Nixon as a snake-oil salesman. Eckhardt used his linoleum-block technique for a cartoon of Nixon as a train conductor trying to get the nation to go one direction, while a southern congressional chairman was trying to go the other direction. His drawing of a somber and stern-looking President Ford is especially eye-catching, appearing in a *Congressional Record*.[12]

Eckhardt whiled away the hours during boring parts of meetings with his pen and ink. One cartoon showed a witness saying, "let me be brief," as committee members rolled their eyes knowingly at the windbag. Another, sketched on White House stationery, showed a large man sitting on and hanging out beyond a tiny chair, with the caption "these are times that try men's asses." During committee work sessions, he would stop sketching to tally in the margin the votes for and against a measure. Sometimes the sketches would be passed around the table, breaking the monotony and drawing snickers and guffaws. Listening to hours of hearings and floor debates, hearing the same phrases over and over, would stir in him a desire to visually frame (or sometimes mock) a recurring statement or theme. The congressional clichés "that old dog won't hunt," "biting the bullet," "interface," "high profile," and "leveling the playing field" were just too tempting for Mr. Hyde to pass up. His thematic collections include sketches and caricatures of "types" of people, noses, chins, or countenances. He drew a "proud people" series in the *Record*. During the debate over rising tensions between Greece and Turkey, he kept hearing members say, "The Turks are a very proud people." Eckhardt thought, "Who is not?" So with that inspiration, he sketched different poses for different nationalities, to reflect "proud" Russians, Spaniards, Mexicans, Germans, and Turks.[13]

Eckhardt also continued his tradition of designing his own Christmas cards. Most contained a thematic production or a sketch, though one year he printed into the card a photograph showing him, other committee members, and staffers looking bored to death at a hearing. The 1968 card demonstrated his admiration for Franklin Roosevelt and the New Deal, with classic block carvings of several New Deal figures (including Roosevelt and his Scottish terrier, Fala), and the text from Alfred, Lord Tennyson's *Idylls of the King* description of the Knights of the Round Table: "A glorious company, The flower of men, to serve as model for the mighty world and be the fair beginning of a time." The 1976 bicentennial year card was a series of linoleum block carvings of the founding fathers: Washington, Franklin, Hamilton, Marshall, Jay, Madison, and Jefferson, all lined up on the card, talking to each other. For years, Eckhardt drew a scene each year from the "Twelve Days of Christmas." One depicted President Nixon and Attorney General Mitchell as pipers.

Bob Eckhardt clearly had fun with his cartoons, caricatures, and sketches. But throughout his life, he also incorporated serious commentary into his cartoons, and thus they served as a vehicle to get across his political message. Eckhardt appreciated and studied the art and history of political cartooning. He even wrote an article on political cartooning for his old *Observer* friend Bob Sherrill, published in *Lithopinion* magazine.[14]

Collage of Eckhardt's artwork. Bob Eckhardt was an accomplished and published cartoonist, caricaturist, and sketcher. This collection depicts some of his artwork, from his high school *Meatloaf Gazette,* to his Jack o' Diamonds for the *Texas Spectator,* to his state legislative resolution sketching and congressional sketching, to his 1960 campaign sketch for the Kennedy-Johnson campaign, to his congressional newsletter, *Bob Eckhardt's Quarterly Report*—and, of course, his family cattle brand, his political signature. Collage by author; materials courtesy of the Eckhardt family.

As staffers and reporters learned of Eckhardt's cartooning, his work was picked up and appeared in the *New York Times, Washington Star, Detroit Free Press, People, Texas Observer,* and Texas newspapers.[15] Additionally, as Eckhardt had become a political figure himself, the *Observer* ran sketches of him drawn by other artists.

Bob Eckhardt's Quarterly Report

Eckhardt's constituents also got to view his sketches, but in a different medium. Like most members of Congress, Eckhardt produced a newsletter. But *Bob Eckhardt's Quarterly Report* was unique. He drew the masthead and often included cartoons, sketches, and block drawings. He designed and laid out the newsletter on his cluttered office table. Bernard Rapoport loved the *Quarterly Report,* helped fund it, and sent it to his friends around the nation, telling them that Eckhardt had "one of the most creative minds in the Congress" and that he was "that rare kind of congressman that represents America."[16] Other allies, though, were frustrated with the highbrow publication, which they did not believe helped Eckhardt politically in the district.

Bob Eckhardt's Quarterly Report was a source of political and legislative *news*—on Vietnam, urban issues, industrial safety, tax reforms, consumer and energy legislation, and later, the battle against inflation. But primarily, the newsletter was a source of sophisticated *policy analysis*—often containing sober lessons on the nation's economics, foreign policy, and social dilemmas—written by Eckhardt himself and footnoted as if it were an academic paper or law journal article. He commented that the *Quarterly Report* filled "a kind of peculiar need. It's not just a casual letter to constituents. It helps me organize and formulate in my own mind what the whole picture is in Congress. It helps me catalog my special goals and desires."[17]

Just as his cartooning became a subject for news stories, so did his unique *Quarterly Report.* The *Dallas Morning News* described it as "unlike any other correspondence emerging from a Capitol Hill office."[18] The *Texas Observer* occasionally reprinted whole articles from the *Quarterly Report*—especially Eckhardt's detailed analyses of energy policy and his rationale for control of natural gas and oil prices. Sometimes Congressional colleagues would enter entire *Quarterly Report* articles into the *Congressional Record.*[19]

Constitutional Lawyer

As a congressman, Bob Eckhardt retained his intellectual fascination with the law and cultivated an interest in constitutionalism. He loved giving guest lectures to law forums around the nation. Instead of litigation and arbitration being his outlet, he now turned to writing law review articles and occasional briefs as his vehicle for legal thinking.[20] He wrote three amicus curiae briefs to the Supreme Court, including in the 1971 Pentagon Papers case. (Eckhardt made the oral arguments before Judge Gerhard Gesell and before the Court of Appeals.)

Eckhardt was geographically close to Charles Black again. Black had become one of the nation's preeminent constitutional scholars. He would come down from Yale to testify in Congress, bringing Bob and Nadine his latest poetry. They would eat and get rip-roaring drunk. Sometimes Eckhardt would drink so much that it showed the next day on the Hill, and sometimes Black, too, would show up inebriated in the Capitol. Black would write to Nadine, thanking her and "the Great Man" for their help.[21] Eckhardt and Black shared long, elaborate conversations about their understandings of the Constitution. As Black became engaged in the Nixon impeachment dynamics, they discussed the process, and Black consequently wrote a well-publicized book, *Impeachment: A Handbook.* Though Eckhardt did not serve on the Judiciary Committee, he jumped into the fray, writing an analysis of the role of the House and suggesting an ad hoc team of House investigators (Speaker O'Neill did not think Eckhardt's proposal wise, and kept the question of impeachment before the Judiciary Committee).[22] Eckhardt also reviewed Black's book in the *Washington Post* just a month before Nixon's resignation in August 1974.[23]

Eckhardt and Black's conversations gave them the idea to put together a book about the Constitution. They sat down with a tape recorder, and the result was hours of conversation, edited by Yale University Press and published in 1976 as *The Tides of Power: Conversations on the American Constitution.*[24] The unique book got attention. Former Hugo Black law clerk Frank Wozencraft reviewed it in the *Houston Post,* and Max Beloff lauded it in the *Times Literary Supplement.*[25]

One of the dynamics nurturing their conversations was the growing tension between Congress and President Nixon over the Vietnam War. Antiwar members of Congress believed that both Johnson and Nixon had violated the Constitution in exercising war powers. As early as 1969, Eckhardt was telling his colleagues that, essentially, Jim Wright had been duped with a resolution supporting the peace process and that the amended resolution was "improper insofar as it delegates to the President congressional authority." He cajoled the members, arguing that "ultimate policy decisions respecting war and peace must continue to be the function of Congress. . . . It is not appropriate nor is it consonant with the authority and dignity of Congress to give any general affirmation to an existing and continuing course of action of the Presidency so as to erode such role of Congress."[26] Throughout 1973, support gathered in Congress for a reassertion of its constitutional role in war powers.

A war powers bill was originally drafted by Yale Law Professor Alexander Bickel. Eckhardt played a significant role in the legislation, though he ultimately opposed the bill that emerged, believing that it was an unconstitutional *grant* of power to the president. Eckhardt grilled the House author, Clement Zablocki, on whether the bill would extend greater powers to the president. Numerous amendments were offered, but only Eckhardt's was approved. It had the effect of limiting presidential war authority to occasions when there was no time for Congress to act. However, the entire substitute that the House was debating was defeated.

Eckhardt then offered his own complete floor substitute to block a president from committing troops unless Congress specifically authorized the commitment or unless such an action was *within* the president's constitutional authority.[27] His proposal also established timetables for reporting to Congress. Eckhardt proposed "a clear warning to the President that overstepping these authorities, after Congress had expressed itself by concurrent resolution, would be considered most seriously as to whether the President had faithfully executed the law,"[28] raising the specter of an impeachable offense. The leadership opposed him, and Eckhardt lost 153–262.

After both chambers approved Zablocki's bill, Nixon vetoed it, and an intense override campaign was waged. Eckhardt opposed the bill and the override, even in the face of pressure from labor, Americans for Democratic Action, and other liberal groups to support it. But the veto override prevailed.[29] "I feel as I have said in the well before," Eckhardt told the House, "that by formalizing Presidential engagement of U.S. troops in hostilities for up to 90 days the Congress provides the color of authority to the President to exercise a warmaking power which I find the Constitution has exclusively assigned to the Congress. . . . This bill, it seems to me, would encourage adventurism in international affairs."[30] He continued to battle for his understanding of the constitutional limitations on presidential war-making powers. In 1975 congressional action on the Sinai Accord, Eckhardt won an amendment saying the joint resolution gives no new authority to the president that he did not already possess to introduce U.S. military forces into hostilities.

Nadine

Nadine had been a crucial part of Eckhardt's life all the way through the 1960s. Theirs was often a passionate and romantic relationship. Eckhardt considered himself to be, in some senses, an eighteenth-century man, with the interests and passions of that era, and Nadine a part of that passion, love, romance, and bawdiness. They shared a sense of skepticism about and freedom from many societal norms. They both were rebellious and independent. Thus, they were attracted to and loved each other; yet their independence also served to strain their relationship. Nadine was involved in the protest movements of the time, with the counterculture, and with the women's movement. She came to feel that Bob was too abstract and that he would not communicate with her. Indeed, Eckhardt was intellectually immersed in his policy persona. He acknowledged that his policy and legislative focus was akin to a mistress, keeping him distant in his relationship with Nadine and others. When he did disengage from his public persona, he could engage with Nadine, but she increasingly found that to be not enough. The life of a congressional wife was too Establishment for her. Feeling too much an attachment to Bob and not enough her own person, Nadine moved back to Houston in 1973. She and Bob would remain a marital and political team for the next three years, long distance. Nadine continued to help with the 1974 campaign and with political chores, proving an essential part of the 1974 campaign for the Democratic Study Group chairmanship.

The Houston separation worked for a while, but, perhaps inevitably, it served to cement the alienation in the relationship. In the end, it proved for Nadine to be a way station, much as her Austin separation from Washington-based Bill Brammer had been in 1960–1961. She developed her own life in Houston. As it became apparent that the separation was permanent, Bob began socializing with others. Always a fascinating character, he began meeting new people, men and women who would be friends for the rest of his life. He also developed a romantic relationship with Celia Morris in New York, who had divorced Willie in 1969.

By spring 1976, Nadine decided that she wanted a divorce. Bob had to retreat to the shack now when he was in Houston. She retained a lawyer and filed in September—in the middle of the fall campaign. Bob retained J. Edwin Smith as his lawyer.[31] Nadine alleged adulteries, and her charges reminded Eckhardt of the story of a man whose wife's lawyers brought him divorce papers alleging seven adulteries. He looked at the list, took out a pen, scratched through several of them—then added three others! Only two of Nadine's charges were true, Eckhardt would say, and one of those was Celia, during the separation with Nadine when they were already discussing divorce.[32]

In the divorce settlement, Nadine got six acres and the big house that they built together. Bob kept eighteen acres, but he now had no Houston domicile. He used the shack for a while and soon developed a fascination with nineteenth-century log cabins. He found an 1850s dogtrot log cabin in East Texas that was being used as a hay barn.[33] Eckhardt decided to buy it and restore it to its original condition. He and a crew of helpers took the cabin and its chimney apart, numbering its log, brick, and sandstone pieces, and moved it to his Cypress Creek land. It took a while to reassemble the structure. Its two sixteen-by-sixteen-foot rooms were divided by the eight-foot dog run. He built a long covered porch along the side. Over the years, the cabin served as a camping place and a campaign cookout site, but it never became the completed domicile that he had wanted. He would hold "chinking" parties, drawing in friends and supporters to help him mud in the spaces between the logs.[34]

After Nadine returned to Houston with the kids, Bob gave up the house in Georgetown for an apartment on Capitol Hill, within sight of his office building. With Nadine gone, he was forced to fend for himself. But he was never attentive to domestic chores, and his living environment became as disheveled as his personal appearance. Once he invited his staff to the apartment, but he asked them to wait a while before arriving. He rushed home and hurriedly cleaned enough to entertain. As they were eating and talking, the phone rang, and Bob disappeared into the closed bedroom to answer it. He emerged and sheepishly told Legislative Assistant Martha Patterson that the call was for her. She went into the closed room to take the phone call and discovered that his "cleaning" had consisted of shoving debris from the living room and kitchen into the bedroom![35] His propensity for a messy domicile would create big problems for his personal life. Molly Ivins later commented that, though Eckhardt was a wonderful man, no woman could live with him.

Campaigns and Elections

Once the Houston Establishment decided that they had to live with Eckhardt, he had little electoral competition, winning easily through 1974, and not having to spend much money to do it. He spent $15,000 in the general election in 1972; $13,000 in 1974.[36] He had the Democratic nomination locked up, though Republicans tried to defeat him from the 1972 election on. Yet, the seeds of his eventual loss were already planted. With Kennedy and Johnson gone and the turmoil of 1968 past, the swing to the right had begun. George Wallace won nearly a third of the vote in Eckhardt's district in 1968. Labor saw that it was losing its membership to the right and tried to stem the tide by establishing schools to teach its new members about politics, economics, and labor. Moreover, Curtis Graves sued to include in Barbara Jordan's congressional district a higher percentage of the Houston black population than Jordan had negotiated, and with Graves's victory, Eckhardt lost even more black constituents (and his house was even drawn outside the Eighth District).

In the 1974 primary, Eckhardt again faced David Shall, who had run against him in 1972. J. Edwin Smith managed Bob's campaign, and John Henry Faulk came down to emcee a fundraiser. He won as big as he had two years earlier,

77 percent to 23 percent, and the *Houston Chronicle* wrote that he "proved one of the top vote getters in the county."[37] In November, he increased his margin of victory over the 1972 general election, beating Donald Whitefield 72 percent to 28 percent. Eckhardt was at the pinnacle of his strength.

By this time, Ronnie Dugger and others were urging Eckhardt to run for the Senate; Dugger even boosted him for the presidency. But Eckhardt believed that a winning Senate race would cost far more than he would ever be able to raise. "I prefer the warm sugar teat of the 8th congressional district to the cold bosom of Texas in a statewide race," he remarked in Austin to the 1976 state Democratic convention, and he never ran for the Senate.[38] Dugger came to believe that Eckhardt knew he was an anomaly. "I've got to have a wide margin of safety," he told Dugger, and going statewide would, he feared, bring him down, whereas he could continue being in public life by holding on to his House seat.[39]

Like many politicians, Eckhardt found the money race to be quite distasteful. He saw a need for free air time for candidates, to create "a national Wooldridge Park" for an open political dialogue.[40] After his career, he drafted a speech in which he stated:

> Both sides in an election campaign drag their nets through Washington fund-raisers. And for four of my election cycles, I would not participate in this corrupting endeavor. Incumbents and opposing candidates, thought to be rising stars in the political firmament, announced that the lobbyist would appear as little less than a command-performance, shelling out the contribution and allotting the minimum price of attendance.[41]

He thought that too often, rather than doing the detailed work inside Congress necessary to producing good legislation, members focused on introducing bills, generating press coverage, sending franked letters to supporters already in agreement on the issue, and working the issue in the district or for honoraria outside the district. The need to raise money, he felt, exacerbated the situation. He found a "Postscript" in an old edition of the *Saturday Evening Post* to illustrate his point:

> *"Father, may I go out to stump?"*
> *"Yes, and the Lord be with you.*
> *Keep the partizans on the jump,*
> *But never go near the issue."*[42]

In 1976, Eckhardt won his primary in a breeze, beating Perry Roach 81 percent to 19 percent. In May, *Texas Monthly* named Eckhardt one of the best members of Congress, but reported that warning flags were flapping, noting "his slipshod treatment of the folks back home" and saying that he "doesn't try to keep his political fences mended." The Democratic Study Group Campaign Fund surveyed the Eighth District and found alarming dynamics: only 28 percent of the respondents knew his name, and those who did were ambivalent. "The fact is that many voters are simply unaware of the job that Congressman Eckhardt is doing in Washington, D.C. Thus, there is considerable distance between the Congressman and his constituents."[43] Republicans licked their chops.

In 1975–1976, Eckhardt led the successful House effort against oil and gas deregulation, angering Houston oilmen, who poured money into the fall campaign against him. *Petroleum Independent* magazine gave Eckhardt a rating of zero and urged industry leaders to circulate and remember the record.[44] As Democrats in Harris County prepared for November, Eckhardt was advised to bring a more intense effort to bear in his campaign. Even his staff recognized that "we have tended to ignore" connections to the district.[45] During the campaign, Eckhardt wrote letters to black ministers, thanking them for letting him speak to their congregations, and adding a handwritten note: "I will not be so remiss in the future in visiting you *between* elections."[46]

There was still a lot of progressive organizing in Houston, battling against the always-strong conservative/business community. Ann Lower had been active in the women's political caucus, Harris County Democrats, and the mayoral campaign of Fred Hofheinz. The Steelworkers' Ed Ball and Sam Dawson decided that she was just what Eckhardt needed: a campaign-seasoned, well-connected organizer. They took her out to the Cypress Creek woods, where Eckhardt was camped out in the shack. They sat outside around a fire, she and the congressman and the labor organizers. She thought it a strange setting for a discussion about running a campaign for a veteran congressman, but she decided to sign on, and they started jotting down names of key supporters. With Lower came closer Eckhardt ties with the new wave of Democrats in Houston.

Eckhardt's 1976 Republican opponent was a serious threat because he was well-known KHOU-TV news director and anchor Nick Gearhart. Oil and gas backed him heavily. John Connally may have buried the hatchet with Eckhardt in the late 1960s, but by now Connally was a Republican, and he keynoted a Gearhart fundraiser.[47] Gearhart tried to make inroads in the black community, but did not fare well. Georgia Congressman Andy Young came to Houston to counter the effort. It was the hardest campaign Eckhardt had yet faced, and he did so as he was going through his divorce with Nadine.

Gearhart was one of the highest spending candidates in the nation—and two-thirds of his $303,587 came from the oil and gas industry. Eckhardt held his first-ever Washington fundraiser. He spent more than he ever had—$125,587—and ended with a $10,000 debt. Gearhart ran a slick, professional campaign, pulling Eckhardt with him into the modern world of campaign consultants and big money, a world that Eckhardt detested. Eckhardt took out his pen, sketched some characters, and wrote a brief spoof about the libel and shakedowns of campaigns, creating a consultant firm with the wonderful name of Grimes, Fablemacher, & Smoot:

> I want to tell you about our public relations firm. I am Arnold Fablemacher, in the tweed suit. Morley Grimes, our senior partner, is at right. We don't let him come into the campaign until the last day. Though he is sometimes very effective, even now, his is an older technique, not so well fitted to the day of immediate media response. Our junior partner is Julius Haldeman Smoot. We bring him in earlier but not at the beginning of a campaign. He likes to personalize the candidates, particularly the opposition. As he always says, "Nobody's perfect." His technique got a big boost from the Supreme Court case of *New York Times v. Sullivan*. I come in at the very beginning. . . . We don't always win our campaigns, but we maintain a good average. We have a rule of thumb that a candidate who can pay us a hundred thousand dollar fee is what we call in the trade a "fat pigeon" who can, with our help, walk proudly in the flock.[48]

Eckhardt won big, 61 percent to Gearhart's 39 percent, but it was the best showing against him since his initial 1966 race. Jimmy Carter, too, won big in Eckhardt's district, 63 percent to Ford's 37 percent.[49] To the chagrin of those in the Eckhardt camp who had hoped that Ann Lower could become a district political manager, Eckhardt took her with him to Washington after the campaign. Over time, this decision would prove costly.

In 1978, Eckhardt's Democratic primary was an even more difficult race. He had angered many trial lawyers with his support for no-fault automobile insurance, and local attorney Joe Archer ran against him. The sons of James Elkins and Hugh Roy Cullen, of the old 8-F Crowd, fashioned Archer's organization and financing, and oilman Harry Lucas served as finance chair. Archer paid Lance Tarrance, the former research director of the Republican National Committee, to work with his campaign. Tarrance had cowritten *The Ticket Splitter*, with strategies to get Republicans to cross over to the Democratic primary elections.[50] Archer induced the community newspapers to run his news releases, copied word-for-word from the National Republican Campaign Committee, without attribution to the NRCC.[51] During the campaign, Eckhardt met with officials of the National Rifle Association, supported their bill of the session, and held a news conference with them. But the NRA endorsed and financed Archer, running ads for him and against Eckhardt. "They want you to be a devotee of their cause of anti-gun control," Eckhardt replied. "I'm not anybody's devotee." [52]

Archer campaigned aggressively, even coming to Washington to raise money from anti-Eckhardt forces there. He made a determined effort to split the black community. Barbara Jordan publicly endorsed Eckhardt because of his "demonstrated depth of sensitivity" on issues significant to blacks.[53] Eckhardt shored up his support in the Hispanic Denver Harbor area of Houston, campaigning with new leader Ben Reyes and touting his 1948 work on *Delgado v. Bastrop School District.*

Eckhardt started the year with no money in the bank. He raised $125,000 for the primary, while Archer spent about $175,000.[54] Speaker O'Neill headlined an Eckhardt fundraiser in Houston. But Eckhardt and Lower did not run a particularly good campaign. As the early returns came in on election night, he was losing, and everyone monitoring the campaign in Houston and Washington was scared. The later boxes, though, were his. He won, but with a smaller percentage of the vote (54 percent) this time and with a larger debt ($15,000) at the end of the campaign.

Nick Gearhart grabbed the Republican nomination again. Eckhardt anticipated a vigorous campaign from Gearhart. But Eckhardt had led on oil and gas compromises in 1978, and the industry did not fund Gearhart as aggressively as they had in 1976. Eckhardt raised money more intensively than ever from Washington and Houston fundraisers. Rosalyn Carter made a campaign swing through Houston. As he had in 1976, Andy Young, now UN Ambassador, flew in to help in the last days of the campaign, appearing at a breakfast at the Shamrock Hilton with Mickey Leland and others. Eckhardt was able to raise his largest amount yet, $285,000 and, for a change, spent more money than his opponent. This time around, Gearhart was able to raise only $139,000. Still, Eckhardt ended the campaign with an additional $10,000 debt, on top of the earlier deficits.

Three issues hurt Eckhardt in the 1978 campaign. First was the no-fault issue. Second was President Carter, who was extremely unpopular in the fall campaign. Members were shunning him in their reelection campaigns. Eckhardt told columnist David Broder, "I don't defend him or attack him. I just make a point of not bringing the subject up." [55] But the president's mother was popular, so in October, Eckhardt had Lillian Carter campaign with him in Houston, speaking to a seven-hundred-person luncheon.

Third was the issue of the proposed amendment to the Constitution known as the Equal Rights Amendment (ERA). Early in his congressional years, Eckhardt was skeptical of a constitutional amendment. By 1971, he had changed his position. He told his colleagues, "I enter the well, if not as a convert, at least as one who, like Saul on the road to Damascus, had seen the light. I must say my position was, before I saw the light, somewhat like that of the agnostic who attends church in order to get the business patronage of the other members of the congregation. But I have now seen what the basis of this women's rights amendment is."[56] He became a strong supporter of the amendment and voted for it. The New Right mobilized and stopped its ratification, so women's groups pressed Congress to extend the deadline for ratification, which they did. Eckhardt voted against the motion, arguing, "I'm for the ERA, but I'm not for extending it through what I consider an unconstitutional process."[57] He did not think it constitutional for Congress to extend, by majority vote, a measure that had required a two-thirds vote to pass. Women's groups, his staff, and Celia were dismayed. He had to go to his old First Unitarian Church and speak to the Harris County Women's Political Caucus, defending his position. It was an angry meeting, and though Celia disagreed with him, she leapt to his defense when women challenged his integrity. Still, the caucus did not care about his constitutional argument; they rescinded their endorsement of him.

In the much smaller turnout of the midterm election, Eckhardt won by a slightly larger margin than he had in 1976, 61.5 percent to Gearhart's 38.5 percent. Ominously, a Republican (Bill Clements) won the Texas governorship for the first time in more than one hundred years. The November 1978 election proved to be Eckhardt's last general election victory.

Celia, Norma

In 1975, estranged from Nadine and moving in different social worlds in Houston and Washington, Bob called Celia Morris in New York and soon went to visit her. Their romance flourished throughout 1976 in New York and Washington. They shared lunches and dinners, visited bookstores, went to plays. They stayed at each other's apartments, sipping wine and eating cheese, bicycling, and reading together. After the divorce with Nadine was finalized, Bob and Celia announced their engagement. Willie Morris sent Bob a warm note and wrote his son David a letter, saying he couldn't think of anything better than for David to be Bob's stepson.[58]

In the spring of 1977, Celia came to Washington for the weekend and they went house hunting. Bob found an ad for a house not far from his apartment, so they bicycled over to Third Street. He was immediately taken with the two-story, high-ceilinged house with two fireplaces and chandeliers. She was wary, especially of the small and old kitchen, but they decided to buy it. Celia's desire for a comfortable home immediately clashed with Bob's procrastinations. When she did not get the bookshelves that he had promised to build, she threw ice water in his face.[59]

In the midst of his divorce from Nadine and his engagement to Celia, Bob was also dealing with the deteriorating condition of his mother. When Bob moved to Washington in 1967, Norma was seventy-seven years old. None of her three sons lived in Austin anymore, so they decided it was impossible for her to continue living at the 2300 Rio Grande house. Because Bob was frequently in Houston, Norma moved there and they sold the Austin house. In 1970, the three sons decided to hire an in-home assistant for Norma, as she was still socially active and very alert. But when she fell and broke her hip, her alertness and physical condition deteriorated. There ensued tensions among the brothers over the finances as the estate became depleted and they tried to work out a fair distribution of the expenses. Norma Wurzbach Eckhardt died on August 9, 1977, and was buried in Austin next to her husband Joe.[60]

Celia was in Europe that summer. After Norma's funeral, Bob flew to France to meet her, and from there, they went to Switzerland. But it was not the happy-go-lucky outing that they wanted. Celia was irate when she heard the divorce terms, and they got into heated arguments as she tried to persuade him to sell some of the Cypress Creek acreage to pay his debts. When they returned, they were married on September 6, 1977, in Washington, by Judge Gerhard Gesell of Watergate fame, with Charles Black as the best man. But the storms in their young relationship would not abate. Celia continued pressing Bob to sell some land. He finally got angry and yelled at her, "I'm going to keep it all!"[61]

Chairman Eckhardt

In his last three terms in Congress, Eckhardt served one term each as chairman of the Democratic Study Group (1975–1976), the Commerce Committee's Consumer Protection and Finance Subcommittee (1977–1978), and the Commerce Committee's Oversight and Investigations Subcommittee (1979–1980). His advances to these positions resulted directly from the congressional reforms that began in the late 1960s and matured in 1974–1975, with Eckhardt's active leadership. Still, he had to accumulate seniority before he could seriously challenge for these positions. "Seniority is like a frigid, flirtatious shrew," he would say. "When I was courting her, she made me miserable. Now that I have her, she gives me no satisfaction."[62]

In 1957, young members of Congress had written a "Liberal Manifesto," which was followed by the wave of liberal freshmen elected in 1958. Those efforts coalesced in the 1959 creation of the Democratic Study Group and the ensuing pressure for rules reforms. In the years after Rayburn's death and the liberalism of the Kennedy and Johnson administrations, the DSG became a significant power center, pressing for empowerment of the Democratic Caucus, reform of the seniority system, and liberal public policies. Eckhardt had been accepted by liberal members with his antiwar stances, and he joined the DSG. By 1972, he was on the executive committee, serving as vice chairman. Early evenings, he would huddle with DSG Chair Phil Burton and others from the inner core. Over whiskey, they strategized House reforms, often turning to Eckhardt for his incisive legal analysis of the proposals.[63]

Eckhardt decided to run for the DSG chairmanship. No southerner had ever held that post, as most southern Democrats were outside the mainstream of the party. Eckhardt began running in late 1974, readying for the vote that would be taken in early 1975 between himself and William Ford of Michigan. Nadine and the staff plunged into the campaign, helping with phone calls and orchestrating contacts.

Eckhardt won a narrow victory and served two years as the DSG chair. The first year of his term was significant for the DSG. With the Watergate class of 1974, the DSG grew even larger—more than 225 members—and pressed for reforms in the Democratic Caucus. Moreover, the DSG Campaign Committee had provided professional polling and other services to one hundred candidates in 1974 and repeated the strategy in 1976 to protect the new freshmen and others. Anticipating a Democratic presidential victory in 1976, Eckhardt and the DSG hosted "An Evening with the Next President and First Lady Jimmy and Rosalynn Carter" at the Washington Hilton.

The end of Eckhardt's DSG chairmanship coincided with a shift in the Committee on Interstate and Foreign Commerce. Harley Staggers, longtime West Virginia congressman, chaired both Commerce and its powerful Investigations Subcommittee. Eckhardt usually got along with Staggers, but sometimes opposed him, especially his efforts to censure CBS for its controversial documentary, *The Selling of the Pentagon*. Staggers was seen as a consumer advocate, though not as much as John Moss (D-Calif.). Moss chaired the Commerce and Finance Subcommittee, on which Eckhardt served, and developed a reputation as a champion of consumer protection and the regulatory state.

In the mutinies stirred by the Watergate class of 1974, Staggers was stripped of his Investigations Subcommittee chairmanship and Commerce's subcommittees were reorganized. Moss won the chairmanship of the newly named and expanded Oversight and Investigations (O&I) Subcommittee. Eckhardt served on the newly reorganized Consumer Protection and Finance Subcommittee, headed by Lionel Van Deerlin (D-Calif.), and on the Energy and Power Subcommittee, chaired by John Dingell. In 1976, Van Deerlin decided to chair the Communications Subcommittee, which left Consumer Protection and Finance open.

Outgoing DSG Chair Eckhardt decided to campaign for the Consumer Protection and Finance chair position. He had now been in Congress ten years, though he was still not in the top seniority ranks. Indeed, to run, he had to take on David Satterfield (D-Va.), a more senior member. Such a move always made senior members nervous. John Dingell had climbed near the top in seniority and came to prize the power conferred by that system. Eckhardt thought that Dingell feared that Bob, if not stopped now, might eventually challenge him for the chairmanship of the full committee.[64]

Members returned to Washington in the heady first days of the Carter administration, and the Commerce Committee huddled to choose its leaders. The first vote was whether to confirm the senior members as subcommittee chairs or not. The committee rejected Satterfield 12 to 17. With that victory, Eckhardt could now be nominated for chair of the Consumer Protection and Finance Subcommittee. He won 22 to 5 with 1 abstention.[65] Under the reformed rules, subcommittee chairs could not be members of other subcommittees, so Eckhardt left his Energy and Power Subcommittee. His ranking Republican member on the Consumer Protection and Finance Subcommittee was James Broyhill of North Carolina, and they would establish a good working relationship that paid off over the years.

Moss's O&I subcommittee was a powerful vehicle for the consumer movement. With a growing staff and numerous hearings, O&I established a rich history of investigations. But just two years after assuming the chairmanship, Moss decided to retire from Congress. With Moss's departure, Eckhardt was now sixth in seniority among the committee Democrats. He knew that O&I was a stronger and more prestigious subcommittee. He decided to go for it and announced his candidacy for the chairmanship in late 1978. The *Houston Post* wrote, "The subcommittee is one of the most glamorous in the House."[66]

Eckhardt was involved in his intense reelection campaign in the fall of 1978. On November 1, he was speaking at a campaign breakfast before a black audience at Houston's Shamrock Hilton, Andy Young by his side at the head table. Suddenly, Eckhardt became gravely ill. When he collapsed, three doctors in the audience rushed to help him.[67] At the hospital, tests revealed that he had several blocked arteries. The doctors explained that his heart was failing, and he needed bypass surgery. But he returned to campaigning that afternoon and won reelection a few days later.

Should he go ahead with the campaign for the chairmanship and wait until the session convened before having the surgery, then miss congressional sessions? Or go ahead and have the surgery in the midst of his campaign for the subcommittee spot? He decided that he had to have the surgery. Dr. Denton Cooley performed triple coronary bypass surgery in Houston on December 16. In his hospital recovery and boredom, Bob asked for a copy of Chaucer to read. He was flooded with stacks of telegrams, dozens of bouquets, and endless telephone calls. He continued his chairmanship campaign over the telephone by his hospital bed. He left the hospital on Christmas Eve, and after Christmas, he returned to Washington so that he could campaign personally. But when he became feverish on New Year's Eve, Celia and a staff member rushed him to Naval Medical Center in Bethesda. They called Dr. Cooley, who decided that they did not have time to get Bob to Houston. He was wheeled into surgery to clean out the infection. Friends and colleagues were worried about whether he would pull through.

As Bob emerged from the second surgery, a powerful colleague, New York's John Murphy, announced that he was running for the O&I chairmanship. His Commerce committee seniority trumped Eckhardt's, so the vote would technically be on whether to accept or reject Murphy. Only if Murphy lost would there then be a chance for Eckhardt. Murphy's ideological image was mixed. He campaigned as a "moderate alternative," a not-too-subtle dig at Eckhardt. He was pro-union, yet also pro-business and conservative on foreign policy issues. Murphy was a staunch ally of Nicaraguan dictator Anastasio Somoza, the Shah of Iran, and the South Korea military, which turned some liberal members against him. Additionally, he was seen as being more captive of local interests, and the consumer and environmental community feared that a Murphy chairmanship would not be aggressive. The *New York Post* wryly noted: "We are usually elated to watch hometown boys make good. But this is the wrong job for the wrong man at the wrong time. Murphy's elevation would be a triumph for the backroom influence-peddlers and a major blow to a distinguished Congressional committee." [68] In the final days of the campaign, Murphy became the subject of a federal investigation for his relationship with Iranian and Nicaraguan agents.

Eckhardt emerged from the hospital and made it to the Capitol for the first day of the session, shocking members with his ghostly pallor. He wanted to be there to make clear that he was serious about winning. He returned to writing, calling, visiting with members, and campaigning at gatherings. The competition raised tensions, as some members and staff thought Murphy was taking advantage of Eckhardt's health woes, and as Ann Lower and the Eckhardt staff distributed news clippings about Murphy's ethical woes. With Barbara Jordan's retirement from Congress, State Representative Mickey Leland had just won her seat, and the ailing Eckhardt hosted a Rayburn Building reception for him. Leland had also joined the Commerce Committee, so Bob was able to engage even more members on his own turf.

On January 29, the *Wall Street Journal*, not liking their backyard congressman, opined that "the House leadership would be embarrassed if Congressman Murphy won," [69] and the *New York Times* that same day endorsed Eckhardt as "eminently qualified" and "a liberal Democrat noted for his intellect

Congressmen Bob Eckhardt chairing subcommittee. For four years, Bob Eckhardt
chaired two key subcommittees of the House Committee on Interstate and
Foreign Commerce. He held more than two hundred hearings in those four years.
Here, he chairs a hearing. Subcommittee member Al Gore sits to his far right.
Courtesy of the Robert C. Eckhardt Collection, Center for American History,
University of Texas at Austin, CN 12142.

and legislative skill." The *Times* blasted Murphy for "the close correlation between his committee assignments and his campaign contributions," adding
that giving him the O&I chairmanship "would be an unfortunate acting
out of the old saw about setting the fox to guard the chicken coop."[70] On
January 30, the Commerce Democrats caucused for the vote. In the secret
balloting, Murphy was rejected, 9 to 18, and Eckhardt won the chairmanship,
26 to 1.[71] The color returned to his cheeks, indicating the flush of victory and
better health.

Eckhardt's O&I subcommittee included an amazing collection of Democrats, many highly loyal to him as a result of his supporting the 1974–1975
congressional reforms and his work with them over the years. It included Al
Gore, Phil Sharp, Jim Santini, Toby Moffett, Andy Maguire, Mickey Leland,
and Tim Wirth. He became a mentor to them, and was so confident in his
position that he had no hesitation in sharing the power with them. Or perhaps he didn't realize what he was giving away. His staff would work to put

together a great public relations event for him, but he would turn to Gore and say, "Al, can you do that for me?"[72]

Eckhardt's O&I would produce a monumental amount of work over the next twenty-three months, and he immediately drew media attention.[73] He knew that he would need a strong staff to help him take on the private power centers that he wanted to examine. In mid-February, he asked a Commerce committee staffer, ex-FBI agent Mark Raabe, to be chief counsel and staff director. Eckhardt's O&I had the largest subcommittee budget ($850,000) and staff in the House (twenty-four Majority staffers and two Minority staffers).[74] He kept most of Moss's staff and brought over some from his Consumer Protection and Finance staff, including economist Milton Lower, Ann's husband.

In his two-year O&I chairmanship, Eckhardt used his bully pulpit to advance many issues, from those that he had worked on from his days as a labor lawyer, such as environmental health, to the critical issues that he had become a floor leader on, such as energy and consumer protection. It was the perfect pulpit for him. He saw two functions of oversight: "To Keep the Big Boys Honest," and "To Keep the Government Frugal and Responsive."[75] Throughout 1979 and 1980, he became a sharp thorn in the side of many businesses and many Carter administration regulators.

Jim Wright's Election as Majority Leader

Over the years Jim Wright had moved up in House seniority and leadership, both in committees (briefly chairing Public Works) and in the Democratic Caucus (becoming deputy majority whip). Speaker Carl Albert retired after the 1976 election and Majority Leader Tip O'Neill ascended to the speakership. Albert's announcement touched off a fierce battle for majority leader throughout 1976, with moderate Majority Whip John McFall and liberal leaders Phillip Burton and Richard Bolling all vying for the post. Then, later in the campaign, Wright jumped into the race.

Wright's appeal was that he was well liked and worked well with his fellow members. Eckhardt had long known and worked with Wright, and the natural tendency would have been for him to support his fellow Texan. Wright's former aide Larry L. King was a friend of Eckhardt's, and Bernard Rapoport and Eckhardt's Texas legislative colleague Don Kennard jumped in and helped Wright raise money for the campaign. But Wright had been telling members that he would not run. Eckhardt had worked with Phil Burton in the antiwar efforts, the congressional rules reform battles, and the DSG. He pledged his support to Burton, liking his liberalism and his forceful leadership. Texan Jack Brooks and Wright had never gotten along very well, and Brooks, too, had pledged to Burton. Eckhardt and Brooks both told Wright of their pledges to Burton, and Wright accepted their need to honor their pledges.[76]

At the time, Eckhardt was serving as chairman of the Democratic Study Group, and the candidates came to speak to DSG gatherings. When Wright spoke, he told the story of his 1947 oil tax bill that he had worked on with Eckhardt. Eckhardt thought that Wright embellished the story in an effort to reestablish his liberal credentials.[77] Even though they had long worked together, there was now quite an ideological gap between the Americans for Democratic Action 100-percent rated Eckhardt and Wright. Burton had averaged an ADA score of 93; Bolling 67; McFall 52; and Wright only 28.[78]

Burton was perceived by many members as abrasive and Bolling as arrogant. When Burton's brash personality and methods of operation became the story of the campaign, Eckhardt and thirteen other members signed a "Dear Colleague" letter, praising Burton's coalition building as essential to the legislative process.[79]

The balloting rule was that the lowest candidate in the vote tabulation would be dropped from the ballot, another vote taken, and so on, until one candidate got a majority. On the first vote, McFall fell far behind. Burton led, and Wright and Bolling tied. In the second ballot, with McFall out of the race, Wright beat Bolling by two votes to make the final ballot with Burton, who continued to lead. So where would the Bolling votes go? To the liberal, but abrasive, Burton, or to the moderate, likeable Wright? On the final vote, Wright beat Burton 148 to 147. Eckhardt stayed with Burton all the way, as he had pledged. Referring to LBJ's 1948 election victory, Wright told the press "We Texans are not new to landslides."[80]

FOURTEEN

Public v. Special Interest: Environmental and Consumer Policymaking

Bob Eckhardt became a leading congressional force for the maturing environmental and consumer movements in the 1970s. Ralph Nader praised him as "the number one consumer champion in the House," and the Consumer Federation of America gave him its Philip Hart Public Service Award. He led the Texas delegation in scoring by the League of Conservation Voters and was awarded the National Recreation and Park Association's Congressional Award. In the wake of his leadership came real and significant changes: the cleanup of Galveston Bay and the Houston Ship Channel, creation of the Big Thicket National Preserve, landmark regulation of toxic substances, improved automobile safety, and the institutionalization of product safety regulation—all before he served as a subcommittee chair and gained widespread attention with his hearings on Love Canal's hazardous waste, his Foreign Corrupt Practices Act, Ethics in Government Act, and others. Eckhardt's subcommittees had an incredible flurry of activity—holding nearly 200 hearings in the four years that he chaired them. His fingerprints were all over many other members' key consumer and environmental protection bills—including the Alaska Lands Bill, Superfund, Clean Air Act, Securities Act, and Federal Trade Commission Warranty Act.

To achieve this record, Eckhardt often battled corporate powers, whose lobbyists understandably fought efforts to regulate their relationship with consumers and the natural environment. Though Eckhardt had a hefty record of successes, he also absorbed numerous defeats. His actions created powerful enemies for him in the strengthening anti-regulation communities. Eckhardt had fortified the powers of regulators, and he was determined that they use those powers to protect public health and to enforce measures against recalcitrant corporations. Siding with the public interest against the special interest of corporate power was, of course, a familiar role for him. His regulatory persona developed from his labor law and state legislative background, jousting with the Knights of Congress Avenue in Austin. In Washington, he faced the dominating lobbyists of national trade associations and corporations.

As is often the case with national policy leaders, Eckhardt built his activism out of dynamics in his home district, and he had to wage local battles

EK
♡

while crafting nationwide policy on the broader policy issues. Houston-based aide Keith Ozmore became Eckhardt's go-between with the emerging environmentalist community in Texas, helping Eckhardt delve into one issue after another. Eckhardt had strong staff support in his consumer initiatives, too. When Ann Lower became his chief assistant in the Capitol, her husband, UT-trained economist Milton Lower, also moved to Washington, and Eck-hardt hired him for the Consumer Protection and Finance Subcommittee. The lawyers who ran the staff were highly wary of economists, but came to embrace Dr. Lower as they learned that not all economists were of the Mil-ton Friedman anti-regulation school of thought. In 1979, Eckhardt brought Dr. Lower over to his Oversight and Investigations Subcommittee. The Lower husband-wife team thus became a policy, legislative, and political team for Eckhardt in the pinnacle of his career.

Eckhardt's Houston labor allies became strong environmental support-ers over time—coupling issues such as air pollution and worker health—but sometimes, Eckhardt would take positions that they did not support. The Eighth District had three can plants and hundreds of steelworkers. When Eckhardt supported a bill requiring deposits on cans and bottles, Steelworker official Jim Ward called. "Eckhardt, have you lost your mind?!" he asked. Eckhardt reflected for a while, then replied, "Well, that's a fair question." [1]

In his consumer advocacy, Eckhardt was far from alone. Not since the 1930s had Congress managed to pass any significant consumer protection policies.[2] The 1960s and 1970s brought a new heyday of congressional ac-tion and a reinvigorated consumer movement. Much as they had financed Eckhardt's Texas Social and Legislative Conference in the 1940s and 1950s, now labor was a financier of the Consumer Federation of America (CFA), born out of a 1967 planning assembly of labor unions, the Consumers Union, rural electric cooperatives, and others. Added to this effort was a new en-trepreneurial leader, Ralph Nader. As a result of public reaction to Nader's landmark 1965 auto safety book and Senate testimony, Congress approved auto safety legislation in 1966.[3] Nader then institutionalized the new wave consumer movement with a potpourri of task forces and advocacy groups issuing investigatory reports and with "Nader's Raiders" disrupting the usual insiders' lobbying game.

When Jimmy Carter won the presidency for Democrats, everyone wanted to get their people into the administration. Eckhardt nominated Creekmore Fath for chair of the Federal Communications Commission, then later for membership on the Federal Trade Commission, but Fath did not get either appointment. Several consumer movement leaders—Carol Tucker Foreman, Michael Pertschuk, Joan Claybrook—did move into the administration. They had close ties to Eckhardt, though they had to learn to get comfortable with his style. Pertschuk was in Eckhardt's office lobbying him once and asked him a question. Silence. As the silence grew longer, Pertschuk became more uncomfortable, and silently angry. What was up? Finally, Eckhardt spoke, and Pertschuk realized that he was actually *thinking* before responding.[4]

The Story of the Big Thicket

When Bob Eckhardt bought his land on Cypress Creek, it was near-wilderness, thickly forested with at least eleven species of trees, muscadine grapes growing among them. Bob especially liked the magnolias that he had grown up with in Austin; here on the Cypress Creek, some of the native magnolias grew to about sixty feet. He would camp among the trees, and he once saw a wolf slink off into their protection. Bob loved riding his line-back dun gelding through the woods, imagining them as endless, imagining them as they were when the original Robert Christian Eckhardt rode through the motts not too far from Houston, rounding up mustangs.

He knew that his land was a postage stamp–sized leftover from a three-million-acre primitive ecological wonder known as the Big Thicket, stretching from the Sabine River in East Texas to the Trinity River and beyond, toward Eckhardt's land. The Big Thicket is a conjoining of ecosystems into arguably the most biologically diverse area on the planet. The rainy Thicket contains seven major ecological systems. More than 350 species of birds live in its dense trees and shrubs; more than one thousand varieties of plants thrive there, from cactus and ferns to carnivorous plants, orchids, and camellias. For centuries, that primitive ecosystem sustained three Indian tribes. Mexico deeded the area to Lorenzo de Zavala, but it was Anglo Americans from the South who moved into the area in the eighteenth century. Eckhardt described them as "land-seeking adventurers who had hidden in the no-man's land between Texas and Louisiana, escaping prison or debt. . . . There was as much misdirection in the woods as there was to be in Congress, later, when the Big Thicket became a political issue."[5]

Early in the twentieth century, the abundant woods attracted lumber companies and paper mills. The discovery of oil further endangered the Thicket. Salt water spills created wastelands. The Big Thicket was soon in danger of death by development, logging, and pollution. Local resident Lance Rosier founded the Big Thicket Association in 1964. Like Roy Bedichek in Central and West Texas, Rosier was a self-taught naturalist who came to know his East Texas woods intimately; Bedichek visited Rosier and they learned from each other.[6] Rosier devoted his life to his passion and become known as "Mr. Big Thicket." The Association held a meeting at the Alabama-Coushatta Indian Reservation in 1966, and congressional candidate Eckhardt was invited. As he drove to the reservation, he was appalled at the piles of hardwood stacked along the edges of the Thicket in preparation for building "corduroy" roads to oil well sites. Soon, Eckhardt would become a part of Rosier's political and public opinion support structure.

As a new congressman, Eckhardt had to be careful because East Texas Congressman John Dowdy was an enemy of Big Thicket protection. But Ralph Yarborough was not so constrained; he had a statewide constituency and a new leadership role in environmental measures. Yarborough began beating the congressional drum to designate the Big Thicket as a national preserve in the early 1960s. In 1969, John Dowdy and Dallas Congressman Earle Cabell also introduced a bill, seen as the timber industry's attempt to kill the idea or limit the acreage to a small park—hyped as a "string of pearls"—totaling less than 15,000 noncontiguous acres (over time, increased to just under 35,000 acres). Yarborough increased the acreage in his bill to 100,000, and public support swelled. In June 1970, Eckhardt testified in support of Yarborough's bill and proposed that the largest unit in the park be named the "Lance Rosier Unit." Eckhardt then introduced his own bill to create a 185,000-acre park. George Bush, too, introduced a bill, for 150,000 acres. Eckhardt and Bush did not work closely together on their bills, but as Eckhardt later wrote: "Knowledgeable individuals who formulate the initial ideas . . . (particularly the congressional staffers) exchange information, ideas and plans, freely between the congressmen, borrowing each other's drafts; and that is the way a bill is formulated. That is why it is not unusual that the Eckhardt and Bush proposals came together in the twin introduction."[7] None of the bills advanced in the House.

Two things thrust Eckhardt into the leading role in the creation of the park. One was Lloyd Bentsen's defeat of Yarborough in the 1970 primary. Suddenly, the biggest champion of the idea was gone from the scene, and new Democratic nominee Bentsen went on to defeat Bush in November. Second was John Dowdy's conviction on bribery charges and his replacement by Charlie Wilson from Eckhardt's Texas legislative days. Wilson was more moderate on the issue than Dowdy, though "Timber Charlie" still championed the industry's perspective.

Eckhardt had known Bentsen's father back in his days with the Good Neighbor Commission. And when young Lloyd was briefly a congressman in the 1950s, Eckhardt had lobbied him on behalf of the CIO. So he knew Bentsen casually. When Bentsen assumed the Senate seat, Eckhardt urged him to take up Yarborough's initiative. Bentsen did sponsor the bill, but Eckhardt concluded that the new senator did not seem very interested. Eckhardt was encouraged, though, that Bentsen did not put up roadblocks.[8]

Eckhardt reintroduced his bill, this time covering 191,000 acres. "Hell, Eckhardt, why don't you just go ahead and make it half a million," Wilson

Eckhardt with Senator Ralph Yarborough. Bob Eckhardt met Ralph Yarborough
in the 1930s and campaigned for him throughout the 1950s and 1960s. Here,
Representative Eckhardt has just finished speaking at a fund-raising dinner for
Senator Yarborough in Yarborough's 1970 campaign. Representative Barbara
Jordan looks on. Courtesy of the Ralph Yarborough Collection, Center for
American History, University of Texas at Austin.

chided him.[9] Eckhardt knew that in the end he would have to compromise
and that Wilson would need some wiggle room, too, if timber companies
were going to support a park. Eckhardt proposed tying together the "string
of pearls" with broad corridors along the East Texas streams, rather than just
preserving isolated pockets of wilderness that would not protect wildlife.

In the face of a fairly solid Texas delegation against his broader Thicket
proposal, Eckhardt joined with Jack Brooks on a new bill. They got the House
subcommittee to come to Beaumont for a hearing in June 1972 to see the
beauty of the Thicket—and its ongoing destruction. Congressmen, Park Service personnel, and Big Thicket advocates toured the Thicket and walked
among the big trees with Eckhardt. Still, the bills stalled out again.

Concern over the state of the Thicket was mounting rapidly. Lumber companies hurried to cut acreage, ultimately succumbing to pressure for an informal moratorium on logging in the immediate areas under consideration. The

idea of a park had grown a national constituency by this time, through the Ad Hoc Committee to Save the Big Thicket. Still, the coordinating committee for the effort reluctantly decided that the idea of a giant park would not fly. Keith Ozmore and the advocates reconfigured the bill to 100,000 acres.

In early 1973, Eckhardt took to the well of the House to tell his colleagues that the area was "succumbing to the hungry bit of lumbermen's saws and land developers' bulldozers." He said, "It is my hope that this Congress, unlike its predecessors which failed to create a national park as originally proposed by the distinguished former Senator from Texas, Ralph Yarborough, will act to preserve a portion of this uniquely beautiful and historic area." [10] Eckhardt introduced his 100,000-acre bill, and Wilson introduced a 75,000-acre bill. By this time, the industry's small "string of pearls" proposal was dead. The industry had damaged its own efforts by stalling the proposals so long and logging so intensively that support for the park solidified. Wilson came to Eckhardt's office and they huddled over the maps spread across Eckhardt's oak table. Eckhardt knew that Wilson could not agree to all the acreage; they compromised on a figure of 84,550, with the intent to add acreage over time. On December 3, 1973, they won the House floor vote, and the campaign shifted to the Senate.

Across the rotunda, senators bought assurances from timber companies that they would, in good faith, continue a voluntary moratorium on logging. [11] So, they deleted the "legislative taking" provision in favor of the normal acquisition policy. They also adjusted boundaries and acreages. The conference committee came to agreement, and both chambers adopted the report on October 11, 1974. Newly inaugurated President Gerald Ford signed into law the bill authorizing a Big Thicket National Preserve. [12]

"In my 22 years as a member of legislative bodies," Eckhardt wrote, "never can I recall an issue on which there were so many starts and stops, wins and losses as there were in this process." As a result of this success, the National Recreation and Park Association gave Eckhardt its 1974 National Congressional Award. Yet Eckhardt still referred to Yarborough as the father of the Big Thicket bill. Yarborough became president of the Big Thicket Association and lent his name to Eckhardt's 1976 reelection campaign, saying, "I know of no member of the Congress who has done more toward saving the Big Thicket than Bob Eckhardt. Without his efforts, I am certain that we would have wound up with a far smaller Preserve than we did." [13]

Lumber companies knew that they were about to lose a cheap source of lumber forever. In 1975 and 1976, some abandoned their pledge of a moratorium and put the bulldozers and chain saws into overdrive, ripping away at the areas designated for the Preserve. Eckhardt and Wilson jointly sponsored a measure to reinsert their legislative taking provision. "The people who fought so long for the creation of the Big Thicket National Preserve are heartsick as they see timber being cut in what may become the National Preserve," they said, and they got local editorial support for their proposal.[14] Its adoption in 1976 stopped the saws in a part of the Thicket. Later that same year, the lumber companies tore into another part of the proposed Preserve, and Eckhardt got the Park Service to use the new provision for a declaration of taking, thus silencing the saws.

With the first purchases, it was time to celebrate the historic victory. Bill Daniel, brother of Price Daniel, hosted the party on his ranch on the edges of the Thicket, with Eckhardt, Wilson, Yarborough, and scores of celebrants. Eckhardt knew Daniel, as he had testified before his state legislative committee in the 1950s, opposing Shivers's red-baiting bill. Eckhardt couldn't resist a chance to ride a horse, and he and Daniel ended up having a horse race.

After Eckhardt's congressional career ended, the Big Thicket lived on. Charlie Wilson and Lloyd Bentsen pushed legislation to increase its size, and by the 1990s, the Preserve acreage was up to the 100,000 that Eckhardt had pushed for.[15]

Clean Water

The industrial conglomeration on the Houston coast fed tons of foul pollutants into the air and water. In the 1967 Clean Air Act amendments, Eckhardt supported stricter pollution control standards and enforcement and worked on regulating industrial growth in nonattainment areas.[16] But it was the water issues to which he devoted intense energies.

Throughout his congressional career, Eckhardt had a keen interest in Galveston Bay, the Houston Ship Channel, and broader national coastal issues. Three dynamics drove Eckhardt's activism and policy posture. One was having constituents who relied on viable bays and estuaries for their livelihood. The second was the rapidly growing environmental movement and consciousness of the 1960s. And the third was the recreational dimension that underlay his 1959 Open Beaches Act.

Galveston Bay is the largest estuary on the Texas coast, with 245 miles of shoreline.[17] Pouring into it is the Houston Ship Channel. By the 1970s, Houston had more than one hundred industrial companies along the channel. Federal Water Control Administration Commissioner James Quigley acknowledged that the Houston Ship Channel "may be the most badly polluted body of water in the world."[18]

Under the 1965 Water Pollution Act, the commissioner could call pollution enforcement conferences. Eckhardt requested Quigley to call such a conference in 1967. Quigley came to Houston and he, Eckhardt, Keith Ozmore,

Don Kennard, and others cruised the ship channel, gliding past the industrial facilities. Yet, Quigley would not or could not get the political support necessary for enforcement. The federal act required the governor's blessing for an enforcement conference, and Governor Preston Smith would not approve the request. Pressure built for a new approach to water pollution control.

It was not until Nixon's creation of the Environmental Protection Agency (EPA) that the polluted ship channel received more serious federal attention. In 1971, EPA gave Houston grants to construct water and wastewater treatment facilities—contingent on meeting special water quality conditions.[19] The newly empowered EPA then insisted on enforcement measures. Governor Smith relented, and the first Galveston Bay Enforcement Conference was held in June 1971 at Houston's Rice Hotel.[20] Eckhardt spoke, breathing fire about the effects of pollution and shell dredging on oyster life, the health effects from polluted waters, and the four-year foot-dragging in calling the conference. "We environmentalists have been buoyed in recent months by the militant position taken by Administrator William D. Ruckelshaus. But now we are wondering, will the same thing happen to Mr. Ruckelshaus that happened to Interior Secretary Walter Hickel and his assistant secretary, Dr. Leslie Glasgow? Is this . . . a program of appeasement for big business? If this be true, then again we are up the polluted Houston Ship Channel without a paddle."[21]

The enforcement conference was followed by a second and a third enforcement conference, and the efforts began to pay off.[22] The conference established load limits, then a new Clean Water Act of 1973 required tougher permit requirements. As a result, water quality began improving and marine fish, crabs, and shrimp began migrating into areas of the channel where they had not been seen for years.[23]

In addition to chemical waste emissions from industrial facilities, Eckhardt was convinced that shell dredging and destruction of wetlands was killing Galveston Bay.[24] As a state legislator, Eckhardt had sponsored a series of hearings on dredging, but Connally's appointees had kept control of the issue in the hands of the dredgers. New Congressman Eckhardt immediately leapt at the chance to bring federal power to bear on the issue. He persuaded John Dingell to hold hearings on the shell dredging issue and to allow him to sit with the subcommittee. Members peppered Eckhardt with questions, and he responded with detailed knowledge of the dredging issues. He, in turn, grilled Corps of Engineers officials, repeatedly reading from federal law requirements for dredging permits in navigable waters. "Are you doing this?" he asked the Corps. The barely audible answer: "No sir, we are not." None of the dredging firms had permits, and most had never even applied for one. He next asked, "Do you plan on doing this?" The answer was a humiliated, "Yes sir, we do."[25] The Corps began holding public hearings on dredging permits.

In 1968, Eckhardt told a Baytown audience: "Texas conservationists have won a major victory—the last big commercial shell dredge has left Galveston Bay . . . we still have not been able to assess the full damage of shell dredging upon the oyster reefs in the Galveston Bay Estuary. We've been concerned about whether the entire oyster fishery was going to be destroyed. . . . [but] I think that we can say that the major reef structures have been saved."[26]

The attentive community took note of Eckhardt's doggedness on natural resource protections. *Outdoor Life* included him among "Our 10 Best Friends in Congress":

> Surf casters everywhere ought to offer up a silent prayer for Bob Eckhardt every time they wet a line, because if it weren't for him a lot of them would never have access to salt water. The right of access to marine beachfront is pretty well taken for granted now, but it was not always so. . . . [Also] a great deal of the credit for the slow—and bitterly contested—clean-up of the Houston ship channel is his. Another notable triumph was scored when he spearheaded attempts to stop the dredging of oyster shell in the Galveston Bay complex.[27]

On the recreational front, in 1969 Eckhardt introduced a national Open Beaches Act, modeled after his Texas act, reintroducing it each session throughout his congressional tenure.[28] The legislation proposed to give the public the right to use the nation's beaches, forbid anyone from limiting access to a beach, give the U.S. attorney general power to sue to protect the public's right to the beaches, and create a federal-state partnership with federal money to help state governments interested in establishing the public right to the beach. One front of opposition was that the federal government had no right to get involved with issues that the states controlled. So, in 1973, Eckhardt and Charles Black both wrote law review articles arguing that the bill was constitutional, and Black defended the bill's constitutionality in new hearings.[29] Eckhardt stoked interest in the issue across the nation.[30] Yet Eckhardt and Black were no match for the private property forces that opposed the bill, and one of the biggest failures of Eckhardt's congressional years was his inability to win approval of the open beaches legislation that was so important to him.

Toxic Substances

Because he represented a district on the Gulf Coast and had many constituents who were oil and chemical workers, Eckhardt was always concerned about environmental health issues. He described the consumer and environmental work of the 1960s–70s Congresses—OSHA, the Clean Water Act, the Clean Air Act, and the Consumer Product Safety Act—as pillars of environmental and health protections. In his broad understanding of the law and his long involvement in policy deliberations, he saw not just a single bill here and there, but a logically connected series of laws. Yet, he became convinced that crucial gaps remained: the testing of chemicals used in products and the disposal of those chemicals after their use. He argued that it would be more effective to address the issue at the point of origination, rather than having to address the hundreds or thousands of later points of use.[31] He believed that agencies needed new preventive tools. Thus, he became the chief craftsman of the Toxic Substances Control Act, designed, in his words, "(1) to close gaps, (2) to cut off the main valve through which danger flowed, and (3) to coordinate a safe treatment of a product throughout its whole life cycle from manufacture to disposal."[32] Yet, in speaking to the industry, he had to joke about his predicament of having a district heavily populated with chemical companies: "When I undertook to author the Toxic Substances Control Act I thought to myself: Eckhardt, you should have left this to a member from North Dakota."[33]

The idea of a toxic substances control measure germinated throughout the early 1970s.[34] The Manufacturing Chemists Association successfully blocked the bills for years. Then the industry became convinced that a bill was going to pass and that they had better negotiate in good faith (though smaller companies were determined to continue blocking any bill). Knowing that passage of such a major bill would require public pressure as well as negotiations with industry, Eckhardt spoke for the bill in many forums. In New York, he argued to a chemical industry investment seminar that testing of suspicious chemicals was essential if the industry was to avoid health disasters. In South Carolina, he told industry seminar participants that "economic and employment dislocation are minimized when regulatory action against hazardous chemicals occurs early in the lifetime of a chemical rather than after major commercial investment and associated labor force are committed to the production of the product."[35]

Eckhardt's 1975 bill landed in the Consumer Protection and Finance Subcommittee, with Eckhardt as a member. It authorized testing and review of chemical substances prior to their introduction into the stream of commerce, strengthened legal tools to deal with unreasonably dangerous chemicals by authorizing direct controls at the point of manufacture, and coordinated collection of data concerning hazardous substances. Negotiations were intense. In March 1976, Eckhardt called in Richard Heckert, DuPont's senior vice president and chair of the Manufacturing Chemists Association's committee on toxic substances, for a huddle around the table in his office with Janie Kinney and Martha Patterson of his staff and other industry representatives. Heckert's intransigence irritated Eckhardt so much that he walked out of the negotiations. "It was a terrible initial meeting," according to Kinney. "Heckert didn't realize the importance of getting down to basic issues." The Senate passed its version overwhelmingly, CBS's *60 Minutes* ran an exposé on chemical hazards, and action returned to the House. Industry representatives reentered negotiations. When Eckhardt next met with them, he said, "I guess you're ready to jump on the cart now." [36]

The hardest negotiations involved requirements for pre-market notification and authority for EPA to hold a new chemical off the market. They approached a compromise and Eckhardt met with labor and environmental groups to win their support. Back at home, the Texas Chemical Industry Council lobbied Eckhardt to weaken the bill's provisions. The industry turned to Republican Jim Broyhill, and he and Eckhardt delicately finalized the compromise. Eckhardt agreed to some of Broyhill's changes and he got Broyhill to agree to support the House version in conference. [37]

After dealing with him for months, the Manufacturing Chemists Association praised him, saying, "Eckhardt is a good man. We are in good shape with him as a supporter. Unlike most congressmen, he understands the bill without having to be propped by the staffers." [38] Yet, to win that kind of praise from industry, he had accepted compromises that some of his allies could not swallow. Steadfast ally and admirer Toby Moffett (D-Conn.) opposed the substitute as too weak. Eckhardt won quick passage through Commerce, then opponents in industry swarmed the Capitol during House debate, but Eckhardt ran over them, winning 319–45.

In conference committee, industry, labor, and Joan Claybrook of Nader's Congress Watch all jumped into the fray, and brinksmanship almost brought the bill down before more tweaking saved it. Eckhardt introduced the final compromise, it was approved, and both chambers voted for it. Reluctantly, President Ford signed the bill. To the list that included OSHA, the Clean Water Act, the Clean Air Act, and the Consumer Product Safety Act, Eckhardt now added the 1976 Toxic Substances Control Act as being one of the "five pillars" of environmental protection that Congress had passed. [39]

Eckhardt came to be seen as a policy expert on toxic substances. In 1979, he spoke in Paris to the International Conference on Toxic Substances; in 1980, he spoke at Harvard and gave the luncheon address at a Washington seminar on American and European toxic substance regulation. Yet, the battle was never over. His O&I Subcommittee soon criticized EPA for exempting PCBs from the Act's provisions.

Eckhardt, Gore, and Love Canal

In 1976, Eckhardt supported passage of the Resource Conservation and Recovery Act (RCRA), a crucial legal link in environmental protection addressing disposal of hazardous wastes. Shortly after passage of his Toxic Substances Control Act, Eckhardt's Consumer Protection Subcommittee issued an extensive report on hazardous waste disposal, setting the stage for his Oversight and Investigation work, including the Superfund initiative. Then, chairing O&I in 1979, he held hearings on RCRA implementation, as EPA dragged its feet in developing a strong regulatory program to identify disposal sites.

Eckhardt worked particularly well with O&I subcommittee member Al Gore. Eckhardt and Gore appeared on *Good Morning America* (ABC) and the *Today Show* (NBC) in 1979 to discuss their hazardous waste findings, and they encouraged the public to provide information. They got hundreds of responses and referred seventy-five of them to the EPA.[40] But RCRA did not address problems with respect to cleanup responsibility and liability for *inactive or abandoned* sites. In the spring of 1979, Eckhardt conducted thirteen days of hearings in Washington and other cities, publicizing Love Canal and other contaminated sites. His staff was able to ferret out information that had not been revealed before, such as Hooker Chemical and Plastics Corporation's internal files documenting groundwater contamination at their sites.[41]

With the storm caused by the Love Canal affair, Congress and the Carter administration worked intently on creating a "Superfund" for cleanup of hazardous waste sites. Eckhardt jumped in with his own bill, which would require inventories and surveys of disposal practices and locations, federal-state partnership for cleanup programs for emergency containment, site monitoring, and planning for future disposal. He was convinced that general revenues should pay for the cleanup, to avoid problems that a fee-based system would trigger.[42]

One investigatory vehicle developed by Eckhardt's O&I Subcommittee came to be known as the "Eckhardt Report," a 1979 Waste Disposal Site Survey. Gore discovered in a 1978 hearing, focusing in part on Love Canal, that the EPA did not have a database of hazardous waste disposal sites—did not even know where they were. So Eckhardt, Gore, and Mark Raabe developed their own survey, sent to the fifty-three largest domestic chemical companies. They then called in officials from those companies, in a locked-door meeting, so that they could talk freely. Industry knew that Raabe was an ex-FBI investigator, and they knew that O&I under John Moss had been aggressive in issuing subpoenas. During the lengthy meeting, Eckhardt and Gore adopted a good cop-bad cop routine: Gore was absolutely insistent that they turn over the requested material, then Eckhardt talked with them, reasoned with them, and eventually persuaded them that they should cooperate.

So the companies set to work producing the material. Astonishingly, the O&I study found 3,383 dumpsites, and follow-up investigations found additional ones. Eckhardt held a news conference with the president of the Chemical Manufacturers Association, releasing the subcommittee report. It was turned over to EPA, which compiled and released the results of its Eckhardt Report.[43] With this information, it was clear that Love Canal was not an isolated, aberrant event, but instead a waste disposal story that raised the specter of many Love Canals. It was time for a comprehensive hazardous waste disposal policy.

New Jersey Representative Jim Florio developed the "Superfund" bill to clean up abandoned hazardous waste sites. But Florio could not get enough agreements to get a bill marked up and through the subcommittee, which created room for Eckhardt to step in. There followed a dance between Florio and Eckhardt, with each contributing to the outcome. In the full Commerce hearing, the committee rejected Eckhardt's amendment to make companies liable for twenty years. On the floor, the House rejected Gore's amendment giving the EPA power to sue. Eckhardt won a voice vote approval to require owners to report the existence of sites. The House and Senate finally approved Superfund in December 1980.[44] Many years later, at Bob Eckhardt's Washington memorial service, Gore lauded Eckhardt's efforts, saying that the combination of the Eckhardt Report and his crafting of the Superfund bill represented Eckhardt's finest work in Congress.[45]

Caveat Emptor No More

As the Democratic Study Group was becoming the leading vehicle for liberal leadership in the 1960s House, Eckhardt joined a DSG Task Force on Consumer Affairs. It recommended a federal consumer protection agency, product safety and labeling requirements, provisions for class action lawsuits, and increased enforcement powers for the Federal Trade Commission.[46] This 1969 DSG wish list was to become Eckhardt's consumer agenda for the 1970s. He often played a key role in shaping others' bills, such as John Moss's Securities Acts amendments of 1975, but he also authored bills of his own, such as his Dispute Resolution Act, adopted in 1980.

AUTOMOBILES

Some of the most persistent issues pursued by the consumer movement were automobile design and highway safety.[47] Consumer advocates and their allies in Congress were concerned about safety design features in new automobiles and repair costs for car owners. Commerce held hearings on repair costs in 1971. John Moss then developed a catchall Motor Vehicle Information and Cost Savings Act, which passed in 1972 with Eckhardt as a cosponsor. Eckhardt had a separate bill with a provision to prohibit tampering with odometers and a requirement for stronger bumpers. His bumper standard was designed to increase protection from damage due to low-speed bumps, requiring bumpers to be able to absorb an impact up to 5 miles per hour with no damage to the car (thus reducing repair costs). He was not able to get his bumper requirement on Moss's bill in committee, so he took it to the floor. There, Eckhardt successfully opposed a California amendment to permit states to enforce more stringent bumper standards.[48] Eckhardt then prevailed with his bumper amendment, establishing a national requirement.

Ralph Nader and his Raiders worked closely with Eckhardt on the auto safety initiatives—and they all found themselves at odds with John Dingell, who came from Detroit and fiercely advocated the auto industry's position. During one floor vote on a measure pushed by Nader representative Joan Claybrook, both Dingell and Eckhardt were standing at the back of the chamber, working against each other to get members' commitments (as they came in to vote). Dingell goaded Eckhardt lightheartedly by asking, "When Joan Claybrook comes to your office, where does she park her broom?" Eckhardt replied, "John, if the implications of your question were correct, she'd have turned you into a toad long ago." Dingell shot right back, "Then I would have kissed her."[49]

Eckhardt became passionate about auto safety as a policy issue. In 1971, he flew to Stuttgart, Germany for the Second International Technical Conference on Experimental Safety Vehicles. In 1972, he was a featured speaker at the First International Congress on Automotive Safety in San Francisco. By the time that the Commerce Committee was holding oversight hearings on the implementation of Moss's act, Eckhardt had come to be extremely wary of the industry. After one witness's comments, Eckhardt took the mike to say, "What you said satisfies a question of curiosity I have had for a long time. That is, why the Plymouth Company should have named one of its automobiles after a mythological creature; Thysias, a woman's head and torso that makes men mad. And now I know."[50]

By 1975, auto manufacturers had co-opted President Ford's Department of Transportation, which sponsored the industry's proposal to weaken Eckhardt's bumper standard. Eckhardt argued in hearings against the change, and prevailed.[51] By 1977, Eckhardt chaired hearings on the auto warranties and repairs, charging that Ford's administration had treated the issue with "benign neglect" and pressing DOT to finally issue the standards that the act required.[52]

Eckhardt and Ann Lower developed the concept of "avoidable cost" to use on the automobile repair question. They used that concept on the auto bumper issue, then on numerous other issues as inflation became a crucial political and policy issue. Eckhardt also used his chairmanship to push for passive restraints in automobiles. In 1977, Brock Adams, Eckhardt's old House colleague and friend and now President Carter's new Secretary of Transportation, reversed the Ford administration and ordered Detroit to install air bags. But under the guise of legislative vetoes, Congress got a shot at the passive restraint regulations. Eckhardt's subcommittee reviewed DOT's auto safety standard requiring automatic crash protection. Eckhardt quoted Adams's estimate of air bags saving nine thousand lives a year. Eckhardt and Henry Waxman (D-Calif.) used parliamentary procedures to defeat the veto resolution, and President Carter thanked Eckhardt profusely for stopping the resolutions.[53] The next year, Eckhardt pushed funding for research and development into passive restraint systems, but he lost a close vote on the floor, 180–194.

Of all the auto-related issues that Eckhardt dealt with, none hurt him politically except for the issue of no-fault automobile liability insurance. In 1966, Harvard Law Professor Robert Keeton (brother of UT Law School Dean Page Keeton), partnered with then-state legislator Michael Dukakis, pushed for no-fault insurance in Massachusetts. They got it enacted in 1971, which helped propel Dukakis to the governorship. Eckhardt was originally skeptical, opposing his allies Philip Hart and John Moss. He wrote magazine articles for *Trial* and *Trial Lawyer Forum* expressing his skepticism, yet also offering possibilities for a combination system.[54] In 1971, Eckhardt testified to the Senate Commerce Committee, urging a federal insurance system to "eliminate fault or the negligence suit concept," to remove the incentive for aggressive adversary action, to create an incentive for prompt payment, and to "leave intact traditional measures of damages and finance medical and hospital elements of recovery through a tax-supported national health plan."[55] No bill emerged from the efforts. Senator Hart would run into Eckhardt and say, "Well, Bob, what are you doing over in the House to get no-fault moving?"[56]

Eckhardt committee staffer Peter Kinzler became a passionate advocate of no-fault and pushed Eckhardt to fully embrace it. Eckhardt took his subcommittee to Massachusetts, Florida, New York, New Jersey, and Michigan to observe the state systems. He expressed caution: "The Subcommittee has no preconceived notion as to the success or failure of state no-fault laws."[57] Allies in the legal profession began telling him that they did not want him to continue these hearings. Eckhardt shot back, "I am pro-lawyer, but do not expect me to arbitrarily kill anything that has potential consumer service. I will explore it fully."[58] His bill would provide medical and work loss benefits to compensate losses of accident victims regardless of fault. But it would permit victims to sue to recover overdue benefits, to recoup economic losses not compensated by the no-fault benefits, and to compensate for pain and suffering in serious injuries.

Eckhardt's Houston legal and political ally Jim Kronzer testified to his committee. He worried about "the unbridled attack upon the lawyers, juries and the entire judicial system," and urged that, unless the federal government was ready to directly regulate the casualty insurance industry, it had better leave this issue to the states.[59] In 1978, trial lawyers tried to get Commerce to recommit the bill to subcommittee (and thus kill it), but Eckhardt won 24–18. Then, after a massive lobbying push, trial lawyers picked up four votes and killed the bill 19–22.[60]

How much political damage was done by his advocacy of a policy that split his consumer and trial lawyer communities? He talked with Houston lawyer John Patterson at a reception in Baytown, and Patterson nosed around for him. He reported back that Eckhardt had problems, though perhaps not as serious as Eckhardt feared. Members of the Texas Trial Lawyers Association, he reported, "are opposed to 'No Fault' almost to a man without knowing exactly why." He went on to caution, "I did hear last week that you have become too much Potomac oriented," and he urged Eckhardt to get back to the district frequently to blunt the criticisms leveled against him by trial lawyer Joe Archer, who then ran against him for the 1978 Democratic nomination. Patterson noted, "This is going to be a campaign issue."[61] Indeed, opponents struck a blow so hard that Eckhardt was weakened financially and politically, allowing other opponents to strike harder in 1980.

CONSUMER PRODUCT SAFETY AND WARRANTIES

Eckhardt was particularly proud of his work on the Consumer Product Safety Act, which established the Consumer Product Safety Commission "to protect the public against unreasonable risks of injury associated with consumer products." It was the first independent regulatory commission established since the New Deal. Eckhardt was a key ally of John Moss in steering the Act through in 1972. Five years later, the agency was already becoming fenced in. Eckhardt pushed through the compromises necessary to extend the Commission. He became exasperated that Carter had not filled vacancies on the Commission in 1977 and 1978.[62]

Product warranties were also crucial to consumer protection, yet meaningful warranties were resisted intensely by business. The Senate passed a strong warranty bill repeatedly, only to have it die in the House. John Moss shepherded it through his subcommittee, with Eckhardt's support, but they were blocked in full committee. Finally, the Commerce Committee approved a weak version in 1974, and on the House floor Eckhardt offered an amendment to restore the Senate's stronger provisions. "Consumer fraud continues to be profitable and not subject to full redress unless the Federal Trade Commission has the authority, in a proceeding before a court and after proof of violation of the rule, to act," he argued. Moss backed him up, but they lost 180–209, as Republicans argued that it would cause a "radical change."[63]

But much of the Senate's bill passed intact, and the watershed 1974 Federal Trade Commission Warranty (Magnuson-Moss) Act gave the Federal Trade Commission new authority to bring action on behalf of defrauded consumers, go directly to court to enforce consumer rights against deceptive practices, and set trade regulation rules establishing fair conduct in businesses affecting commerce. It also mandated resolution of warranty disputes, required warranties and guaranties of consumer products to be fair in their terms and in their disclosures, and made it illegal to contract away an implied warranty. As a result, it became the target for business in the ensuing years.

CLASS ACTION

Another of Eckhardt's abiding concerns was the ability of consumers to join together to sue in order to protect their rights in the marketplace, a concept known as "consumer class action." He believed that people's rights are vulnerable unless they have recourse to a lawyer for bringing action, and that class action lawsuits were essential to make that a reality in cases where a person's claims were too small to warrant the services of a lawyer. Eckhardt argued that too often there was a "false protection" by the Federal Trade Commission. He would call forth the old Shakespeare quotation that he had carved into a wooden block for his original lawyer's desk: "We must not make a scarecrow of the law, Setting it up to fear the birds of prey, And let it keep one shape, till custom make it Their perch, and not their terror."[64]

Eckhardt introduced a class action bill early in 1969, as the idea of broader class action policies was winning wider support. President Nixon included it in his consumer message to Congress later that year.[65] Eckhardt was surprised to hear Nixon's proposal; he modified his bill and reintroduced it, arguing that his legislation could be used to implement Nixon's suggestions, but with more expansive rights. His bill defined unfair consumer practices that would allow individuals to bring class actions and provided damages, with court costs and attorney fees. Nixon's bill would require action by the Justice Department or the FTC *before* consumers could take action. Eckhardt sketched a cartoon of Nixon as a huckster, selling "Snake Oil Remedy for Consumers." He brought in Charles Black and Bess Myerson Grant, New York City's commissioner of consumer affairs, to testify.[66] He also held a news conference with Nader, who blasted business opposition to the bill. Eckhardt wrote law review articles and lectured on the issue at the Brookings Institution's Seminar for Business Executives, criticizing an American Bar Association committee for its opposition to consumer class action. Those lawyers, he said:

> are saying, "please throw us in the briar patch," the briar patch of the Federal Trade Commission. Indeed, this is exactly where they want to be thrown. As Ralph Nader has pointed out, administrative agencies have fallen down in their duty to protect the public interest. They have become the hospitable briar patch into which malefactors against consumers wish to be thrown, and the lawyers for these interests do not even have the subtlety of Br'er Rabbit but plead directly their preference for the briar patch of the Federal Trade Commission. What a comfortable and sound hedge against effective action this has become! It is a familiar ground of the Washington lawyer who can speak directly to the commissioners and other administrative personnel of the agencies. He cannot speak directly to the judge who is trying the case in which he is involved about the merits of that case. He has come to be more comfortable with those before whom he may plead over lunch than before those he must address at the bar.[67]

It soon became obvious that Nixon would not put the power of his presidency behind his rhetoric and instead recommended further study through a new institute, which Eckhardt labeled a "root-a-de-toot institute" for consumer protection.[68] Eckhardt wrote Staggers, "There is a wave of consumerism now which I feel must be taken at its peak or we may not have legislation for years. . . . Secondarily, if the Republicans desire to use all their strength to prevent the President's proposed consumer program from coming to the floor of the House, I am desirous of having them make that record, too."[69] But consumer class action legislation was dead. Eckhardt reintroduced the legislation over the next eight years. The Business Roundtable and chambers of commerce accused him of urging a "lawyers full employment act," and he was never able to get it passed.

CONSUMER PROTECTION AGENCY

When societal changes create new centers of power, Congress sometimes reacts by expanding the president's cabinet to include the new power center. In 1959, Senator Estes Kefauver (D-Tenn.) tried to create a cabinet-level department of consumer affairs. But the consumer movement was not powerful enough at that time. Representative Benjamin Rosenthal (D-N.Y.) pushed the idea in the 1960s. Eckhardt joined the fray at the height of the battle, cosponsoring Rosenthal's bill in 1968.

With Nader's leadership of the movement in the 1960s and 1970s, the idea evolved to an independent agency rather than a cabinet office. The role of a consumer advocacy agency was not to regulate, but to monitor activities of regulators and intervene on behalf of consumers. It had various names in its several incarnations: Consumer Protection Agency, Agency for Consumer Protection, Agency for Consumer Advocacy, and Office of Consumer Representation.

Throughout the 1970s, the bill would pass one chamber, but not both, or it would be killed in conference committee, with Eckhardt working intensely with Nader and the broader community to push it along. The U.S. Chamber of Commerce, National Association of Manufacturers, Business Roundtable, and National Federation of Independent Business coalesced repeatedly to defeat it. President Carter lobbied for it, yet it was defeated in 1978, 189–227.[70] Speaker O'Neill commented, "I have been around here for 25 years; I have never seen such extensive lobbying." Nader bitterly blamed "the corrupting influence of big business campaign contributors."[71]

Battling the Legislative Veto

Congress has always had the responsibility of oversight of agencies and programs and has long grappled with the best tools for such oversight. The Constitution speaks to the president's ability to negate—or veto—a bill. Yet by the 1930s, Congress devised its own tool known as the "legislative veto." It has numerous manifestations, but essentially allows Congress to step in after an executive agency has issued a rule or regulation and veto it. With the environmental and consumer statutes and regulations of the 1960s and 1970s, businesses lobbied for legislative vetoes of rules and regulations that they had not been able to kill in the administrative process. Eckhardt long opposed the legislative veto as a congressman, as a constitutional scholar, and, even after his congressional career, as a lawyer. He argued that the legislative veto politicized an independent regulatory agency and that it amounted to "standing the Constitution on its head."

In 1975, he argued against a broad legislative veto: "Once we get to delegating authority with the idea that we can pull back like a yo-yo, we will delegate authority with less procedural safeguards. The result is a far greater delegation of congressional power than has existed heretofore."[72] He continued to work tirelessly to block veto proposals in one bill after another,[73] and made speeches with his constitutional and policy arguments against the legislative veto, including at UT's Texas Law Review Association banquet.

In 1979, Eckhardt authored a crucial bill to reauthorize the Federal Trade Commission and expand its powers. He included class action lawsuit provisions in the FTC bill, with Carter's endorsement.[74] Eckhardt managed to get his bill through Commerce, but business lobbyists stalled it for five months, then he lost control of much of his own bill. Corporations were at their strongest in organizing against the consumer movement and managed to shred the bill with amendments, including a powerful legislative veto provision. Eckhardt told the House: "What we are doing in this legislation today is commencing a plucking of the powers of the only agency that we can call a consumer agency in the entire U.S. government."[75] He finally got a weakened bill passed.

In conference, Eckhardt won the battle to keep a legislative veto out of the bill. But when the bill emerged from conference in February 1978, the House rejected the whole bill, rather than give up on the idea of a strong legislative veto. They sent it back to conference. When Eckhardt got it out in August, he suggested a compromise on congressional cancellation of FTC rules, through a House and Senate *joint* resolution of disapproval (with deadlines, and with the possibility of a presidential veto of the resolution). He was forced to get a waiver from the Rules Committee for his proposal, but when he got the bill back up on the floor, it was, to his great disappointment, rejected again, killed finally this time, 175–214.[76]

Eckhardt was tilting at windmills, as an assertive Congress with powerful interest group ties saw the legislative veto as a great vehicle to protect business. He had allies in his constitutional battle. Immigrant Jagdish Rai Chadha got caught up in the clashes over the legislative veto when the House vetoed an administrative law judge's stay of his deportation. Chadha's lawyers then sued, arguing that the legislative veto was unconstitutional, and Eckhardt and his congressional allies saw an opportunity to strike a blow against the veto. Eckhardt penned a brief to the Supreme Court. In *Chadha v. INS,* the Supreme Court validated Eckhardt's position by striking down a one-house legislative veto, ruling that the Constitution only allows congressional action by final votes in both chambers. The legislative veto is not dead, but because of *Chadha,* it is harder for interest groups to block unwanted regulations by getting a few key congressional allies to do their work for them. They must work it through both chambers, as Eckhardt repeatedly argued.

Eckhardt's legislative veto battles demonstrated that, by the late 1970s, the consumer protection moment had passed. Consumer advocate and former FTC chair Michael Pertschuk wrote: "I knew, but hadn't learned, that the FTC served two masters—the public interest and the Congress. The public interest was a malleable absentee master, but the Congress held the whip."[77] By 1979, Eckhardt could no longer hold that whip, having lost it to the growing rabble fed by the business community rather than the public interest. One thing that great legislative craftsmanship like Eckhardt's cannot overcome is a sea change in the distribution of power. One business leader proclaimed, "This is war. The battle is not over our economic system. The battle is over our political system." In that environment, Eckhardt was in the middle of the bulls-eye.[78]

FIFTEEN

The Oil and Gas Wars

In 1973, in reaction to the Arab-Israeli war, OPEC turned off the oil spigot. In the ensuing energy wars, Bob Eckhardt led fierce battles against the oil and gas giants, whose Knights of Congress Avenue had earlier jousted with him in the Texas capitol. Regulation, taxation, inflation, alternative energy sources, energy conservation, and transportation issues all got dragged into the fights. Eckhardt wrote his version of the wars, a story "about how pricing by a cartel brought a ten fold increase in oil prices in the world spot market in six years; about how Congress tried to control the price of domestic oil with mixed success; and about how the removal of these controls . . . triggered the most frightful inflation in 30 years."[1] Those super profits and super inflation created a political implosion that brought down the Carter presidency—and ended Bob Eckhardt's career.

The essence of Eckhardt's position was that an extremely high price would not produce much more oil. The remaining hard-to-get resource was trapped in subterranean sand and rock, and the technology of capturing it was not yet adequate, so an unregulated price would serve only to recover little of the resource, while soaking customers and lining the pockets of the super-wealthy industry. The industry's basic theory, Eckhardt concluded, was that the high prices needed for *new* oil exploration and extraction should also apply to *all* the flowing oil explored for and produced in the past at much lower cost. He found such a position revealing of the brazen arrogance of monopolies, and he considered it government's job to stand in for consumers in quashing such greed. Bob Eckhardt's role was to fight big oil and gas, much as Jim Hogg and Jimmie Allred had fought the big powers of their days.

Oil and gas policy was a particularly delicate issue for Eckhardt because he represented Houston, where many of the companies were headquartered. Yet, he didn't often pull his punches. In a *Texas Observer* sketch, Eckhardt skewered the name change of Humble Oil to Exxon ("humble no more"), and he illustrated his *Quarterly Reports* with unfavorable cartoons about the industry. Joe Foy of Houston Natural Gas supported Eckhardt's compromises on pricing and deregulation, but most industry giants deemed him a dangerous opponent. Eckhardt sympathized with independent producers in their battles against the majors. Independent oilmen J. R. Parten, George Mitchell, and Jack Warren were Eckhardt supporters, but neither he nor the independents were faithful partners in their strained marriage. Parten and Mitchell abandoned him in the end, and Warren finally wrote Celia, "If you can't get Bob to vote with us, we're just going to have to beat him."[2]

Big Oil, Big Gas, Big Congressmen

In 1901, the Spindletop oil well erupted east of Houston, ushering in the twentieth-century addiction to oil. Energy policy matters then demanded the attention of federal and state lawmakers and regulators throughout the century. Because of overproduction and violence in East Texas oilfields in the 1930s, crude oil prices and production levels came under state controls. Then, once oil companies realized that they could make money from the natural gas that they had been burning off, they started developing their gas resources. In 1938, Congress passed the Natural Gas Act, regulating gas sales. In 1954, the Supreme Court validated regulation of the sale of gas going to the interstate market. The industry learned to manipulate intrastate/interstate legalities to their advantage, as Eckhardt learned in his battles at the Texas legislature.

Oil and gas had powerful protectors in Washington: Oklahoma's Bob Kerr and Carl Albert, Louisiana's Russell Long, Texas's Lyndon Johnson and Sam Rayburn, and others. Eckhardt believed that the industry was a multinational, multiparty force that permeated the policy determinations of every president and debilitated and subverted every executive agency charged by Congress with control of the industry. The 1938 and 1954 decisions spawned persistent efforts by the natural gas industry to overturn government's regulation of its prices. Yet, as powerful as the industry and their congressional allies were, they had not been able to get rid of regulation.

OPEC Saves Big Oil

With OPEC's embargo came the so-called energy crises of the 1970s. The gas industry controlled state legislative and regulatory politics and pushed up their prices in intrastate markets from 12 cents to more than $2 per thousand cubic feet. The Federal Power Commission raised the interstate prices to about half a dollar. So, companies had created the wedge that would prove their ultimate weapon. They then withheld gas from the interstate market, doubling the crisis. Eckhardt was convinced that industry played upon the fear of oil and gas running out as a means of making high prices acceptable to the public. Robert Sherrill wrote a *New York Times Magazine* exposé showing the enormous supplies that the companies had in 1973, while claiming shortages and shutting down facilities.[3] Indeed, a congressional report showed that the *1973 natural gas production was the highest ever.*[4] The companies were in a position to make their prognostications come true long enough, Eckhardt thought, to create a crisis mentality, so they set the stage for increased prices.

After President Nixon and Congress acted with quick emergency measures, Senator Henry "Scoop" Jackson (D-Wash.) pushed through a comprehensive National Energy Emergency Act, but Nixon vetoed it. Both chambers began anew. Jackson proposed rolling back the price of oil to $5.25 per barrel, then allowing it to go up to $7.06. In the House Commerce Committee, Eckhardt successfully offered a price rollback provision to the levels of November 1, 1973, the beginning of the embargo. "Old" oil would be priced at an average $4.25 per barrel; "new" oil would be $6.17. Eckhardt's proposal was amended to exempt small producers of new oil ("stripper" well producers) to provide incentives to small independent producers to continue exploring and developing.[5] The House first supported the rollback, then stripped it off. In a close vote, the House defeated the new bill altogether, and the bill was dead. New oil was by then up to $10 and, by late 1975, $14 per barrel. New President Gerald Ford vetoed another bill that Congress quickly sent him, then he tried to impose price decontrols, but the House voted disapproval of the plans.

Staggers, Dingell, Moss, and Eckhardt were solidly in favor of continued regulation. They were joined by Commerce's 1974 freshmen, the mop-headed Naderite Toby Moffett from Connecticut and New Jersey's Andy Maguire. The Subcommittee on Energy and Power decided on a lower price than President Ford's proposal. Eckhardt believed that a single price of $7–$8 per barrel would have prevented production of more costly new oil that was needed, so he offered a rollback provision to $6 per barrel, exempting some new oil from independent producers. Maguire pushed the amendment, huddling with Eckhardt on the technicalities. He won in Commerce, but could not get the two-thirds he needed for suspension of the rules on the floor.

Maguire considered Eckhardt a brilliant technical writer with a vast knowledge of the industry. But he noticed that when Eckhardt tried to explain proposals, members' eyes started glazing over. Also, neither Maguire nor Moffett believed that Eckhardt was sharp on building coalitions. But the three of them made a good team: Moffett and Maguire fanned out among the newer members and Eckhardt provided the intellectual and legalistic foundation for price controls.[6] They were almost done in by Speaker Carl Albert, who represented oil state Oklahoma. Albert tried to undermine the committee when the bill got to the floor. Eckhardt saw this as a flagrant violation of the norms and as evidence of the reach of the industry into the Speaker's office.[7]

Staggers, Dingell, and Eckhardt prevailed, and the House established seven price categories. Eckhardt thought Senator Jackson's rollback proposal overlooked critical technical issues as well as the dynamic of encouraging production.[8] But the House-Senate conferees felt it better to defer classifications to administrative determination. So, the Energy Policy and Conservation Act established a *composite* price of $7.66, created a Strategic Petroleum Reserve, and required the president to prepare a standby gasoline-rationing plan. Ford did not veto this bill. Eckhardt came to believe that Congress had boosted Ford politically, as prices at the rate he proposed would have exacerbated the recession and unemployment. Eckhardt was proud of the work that the subcommittee had done. He thought it remarkable that, over the opposition of Ford, Albert, and the industry, the House had prevailed to sustain regulation. Of course, Eckhardt paid for his leadership—the oil and gas industry sank $200,000 into the effort to defeat him the next year.

A Shakespearean Duel

Enter freshman Texas Congressman Bob Krueger. Longtime Hill Country and West Texas Congressman O. C. Fisher retired, and Krueger won the seat in 1974. Krueger grew up in New Braunfels, earned a doctorate from Oxford, and taught Shakespeare at Duke University. Once he arrived in Washington, though, he went to work for the oil and gas industry. Thus, the 1975–76 battle was on between Shakespeare Professor Krueger and Shakespeare-quoting Lawyer Eckhardt, chairman of the liberal Democratic Study Group. One observer listed both Krueger and Eckhardt among the congressmen with the highest IQs.[9] Paul Burka, writing for then-new magazine *Texas Monthly* noted that Eckhardt was on the opposing side from Krueger and "that spelled very bad news for supporters of deregulation. Eckhardt's casual air and slightly disheveled appearance belie a brilliant legislative mind; he is one of the few liberals in the House who understands how the petroleum industry works." Eckhardt, Burka wrote, was "the man who is reputed to be the best technical legislator in the entire Congress."[10]

The battle resembled a chess match, with intricate moves and breathtaking moments when the consequence of a particular move was uncertain. In the Energy and Power Subcommittee, Krueger proposed to decontrol *crude oil* prices immediately. Eckhardt lost, 12–10. The second match was before the full Commerce Committee, where Eckhardt and his allies eventually won, after three close votes.

Krueger wasn't finished. He found a parliamentary vehicle to ride his proposal to the House floor. The debate was long and bruising, as the industry cranked up its lobbying might. Eckhardt used his folksy approach to get members to think in his direction. "A person can pay me to jump 2½ feet [high] for $5, but he cannot get me to jump 6 feet for $15. I just cannot do it. Such is analogous to the theory that you can bring in new oil quickly by merely raising the price."[11] By this time in his career, Eckhardt's old ally of the 1947 battle to tax oil and gas, Jim Wright, had gone over to the side of oil, and he urged his colleagues to vote with Krueger.

The battle raged for days in the summer heat, with Eckhardt losing the price rollback provisions, then gaining them back. After Krueger had stripped out Eckhardt's language, Eckhardt teamed up with Committee on Interstate and Foreign Commerce chairman Harley Staggers to elevate the stature of the pro-regulation forces. The Staggers–Eckhardt amendment then prevailed, beating Krueger, 218–207, with a version even stronger than Eckhardt's first effort. The House–Senate conferees adopted a version retaining controls.[12] Eckhardt concluded from the battle that freshman Krueger, who had the whole industry with him, was smart, but not a particularly good politician.

The next battlefield for the Shakespeareans was *natural gas* deregulation. Lloyd Bentsen had moved a deregulation bill through the Senate in 1975. Dingell and Staggers had a bill to allow interstate gas pipeline companies to buy intrastate gas in emergencies. They crafted it narrowly to block Krueger from making a broad and long-term deregulation amendment like Bentsen's bill, and they defeated him in committee when he tried anyway. When Dingell and Staggers tried to get a rule to disallow floor amendments, the industry prevailed upon Speaker Albert to intervene, and Krueger got a rule that he could offer his amendment. The issue lay smoldering over the Christmas break, ready to reignite in early 1976.

Krueger had as an ally the wily Charlie Wilson. Wilson took over the politicking from the inexperienced Krueger and put together a coalition of independent producers and business consumers. Thus, the old Texas state legislative colleagues Eckhardt and Wilson, who had just gone toe-to-toe on the Big Thicket, would go toe-to-toe repeatedly over energy policy. Eckhardt thought he and Wilson got along "so-so," but they eventually made good partners for compromising. Wilson felt that Eckhardt would sometimes give him a vote on an issue favoring independents, but that Eckhardt would not work the issue.[13]

Dingell called a huddle in Albert's office with Krueger and Eckhardt. Krueger refused to budge. *Texas Monthly* described the Democratic Caucus meeting on the February morning of the vote, where an outraged Dingell blasted Krueger, the Rules Committee, and the Speaker for flouting the committee system by allowing a vote on Krueger's amendment. Staggers, too, defended the Commerce Committee. Finally, Eckhardt rose to speak. His remarks were classic Eckhardt—not, like Staggers and Dingell, angrily supportive of seniority and the System but casting the dispute in the mold of the lobby battle and the dynamics of legislative compromise.

The trouble with this process is that it's just like the Texas Legislature. There's virtually no committee action [there]. A bill springs full-blown from the lobby and makes it to the floor in the identical form. What's wrong with this is that it polarizes debate—you're either for the bill or against. There's no opportunity to compromise. Give us a chance to hammer out a solution between men of good faith. That's what the committee system is for.[14]

On the floor, Krueger won, as Republicans and enough Democrats voted to approve the rule for debate, 234–183. The battle was engaged.

Eckhardt led the charge for three days, in the finest moments in his congressional career. His skillful draftsmanship and questioning of the technical consequences of Krueger's proposal turned the tide, as members came to see that perhaps the committee polishing stage had indeed been skipped on this one. Meanwhile, as Eckhardt delayed a final vote with his amendments and debate, the Commerce staff worked furiously to draft a fallback proposal for Eckhardt, Dingell, and Staggers. Eckhardt was winning, but Pickle and others would ride to Krueger's rescue.

The floor battle was accompanied by a staff and lobby battle for public opinion. Moss warned that his O&I subcommittee had discovered that producers were holding back gas to pressure for deregulation. Labor unions publicly rallied to Eckhardt's side. Staff planted information with the *Washington Post* about Krueger's campaign debts and contributions from the oil and gas industry making it harder for the Shakespearean professor to argue dispassionately that his was simply the right way to address the crisis.

Dingell, Eckhardt, and Neal Smith of Iowa proposed a compromise to deregulate *independent* producers, while enlarging regulation of *majors* by extending controls into intrastate markets! They sprung the vote when Krueger and his forces were not expecting it. Balloting resulted in a tie, 196–196. Then, a few stragglers voted, and the announced vote was 204–202 for the amendment, capping the victory.

Yet, what the industry could not win in straight-up legislative battles to decontrol prices, they could often win in executive actions. In July 1976, the Federal Power Commission gave the industry much of what Eckhardt had taken from them in Congress. The Commission raised the price of new interstate natural gas from 52 cents per thousand cubic feet to $1.42—at a consumer price tag of nearly $2 billion.[15] The Federal Energy Administration had earlier won authority to modify price controls through administrative "energy actions," with potential legislative vetoes. Eckhardt proposed an amendment to stop FEA from presenting a lump "package" of energy actions, wrapping all its decontrol initiatives together. He won 200–175, forcing

FEA to come to Congress with individual actions on various oil products.[16] FEA exempted many energy products from the controls, essentially accomplishing decontrol bit by bit. Alarmed, Eckhardt pushed to block the phase-out of controls. He argued that FEA was planning to recommend decontrol of middle distillate petroleum, including home heating oil, diesel fuel, and jet fuel, but he lost miserably. Next, FEA went after Eckhardt's provision protecting small producers. Eckhardt again led the charge. He compared FEA to the mythical figure Cronus, who ate his offspring: "The FEA eats the charges that we have given to it to perform certain duties under the law." Again, he lost.[17]

Carter's Bitter Pills

The 1975 Energy Policy and Conservation Act had not saved Gerald Ford. Democrat Jimmy Carter rode the national disaffection with the economy, Watergate, and Ford's pardon of Nixon to a razor-thin victory in 1976. Georgian Stuart Eizenstat and Washingtonian James Schlesinger became his point men on energy. Eizenstat was Carter's domestic policy director; Schlesinger, who had been in the Ford administration, his energy adviser. Schlesinger was close to John Dingell and Scoop Jackson and was originally in favor of keeping price controls. Carter soon unveiled the administration's National Energy Plan, including gasoline taxes and increased crude oil prices. Its major thrust on natural gas was to push toward conversion to coal and on gas pricing to move toward a single national market (extending controls to intrastate markets), then ending controls.

Eckhardt was alarmed, convinced that Carter was intent on dismantling the 1975 act. He thought that Congress had stabilized oil prices in 1975, and that stabilization was a keystone of any good energy policy. Eckhardt had been so hopeful after the 1975 victory, then the Democratic victory in the 1976 election. But in his *Quarterly Report* he lamented, "What a Democratic Congress could do against the opposition of a Republican President, an oil-oriented Speaker and an initially adverse Senate, it cannot do in opposition to a Democratic President."[18]

The 1976–77 winter was a cold, hard one. Congress passed the Emergency Natural Gas Act of 1977, giving temporary presidential authority to order transfer of gas to the eastern United States. Commerce hurriedly approved its part of the bill, with one critical change: an Eckhardt amendment to keep price caps on emergency gas sales, with presidential authority to grant higher prices if essential. On the floor, Ohio Republican Bud Brown led the opposition, but Eckhardt won. Carter's chief lobbyist told House leaders that "we can live with it," but conferees stripped off Eckhardt's amendment.[19]

Ad Hoc-ing It on Energy

In late 1976, seeing the criticality of energy issues and the gridlock produced by multiple jurisdictions and powerful committee chairs, incoming Speaker Tip O'Neill tried to create a new standing committee on energy. But each committee with some energy jurisdiction protected its turf, so he failed. On April 20, 1977, the day that Jimmy Carter addressed a special joint session of Congress on the energy crisis, O'Neill urged the acceptance of a compromise Ad Hoc Select Committee on Energy. (It was remarkably like a concept that Eckhardt espoused in his published 1974–75 conversations with Charles Black.[20]) O'Neill promised, "The committee will not have authority to change the recommendations reported by the standing committees. It will have the authority to recommend amendments for consideration on the floor." The next day, the House approved the Ad Hoc Committee. Knowing that the real energy action would take place on that committee, Eckhardt immediately sought and got assignment from Speaker O'Neill to the committee.[21]

New Majority Leader Jim Wright sponsored Carter's package. It was carved up among five standing committees with jurisdiction, with short deadlines for markup. The Commerce Committee plowed into its part of the package. Krueger won a crucial deregulation amendment in the Energy and Power Subcommittee. Then, Eckhardt and others beat him back in full committee, 22–21. A grateful President Carter thanked Eckhardt.[22] Eckhardt also won votes to help power plants in Texas continue using natural gas.

After the standing committees acted, the bills were reported to the Ad Hoc Committee. One fear was that when the package emerged on the floor, Republicans and their deregulator Democratic supporters would coalesce to defeat it. Eckhardt and others knew that they must craft a compromise if they were to fish for enough floor votes to assure victory. Natural gas companies and their congressional allies were planning a vigorous lobbying campaign, so Eckhardt decided that the only way to stave off a natural gas deregulation victory on the floor was to accept higher prices than he would really like. But rather than just striking at the price issue, which would divide people over whether it was too high or too low, he went at the *base* on which price would be set.

"New" gas discoveries under the Carter plan would be eligible for a ceiling price of $1.75 per thousand cubic feet; "old" gas would be controlled at lower prices. Carter's proposal limited "new gas" to new reservoirs at least 2.5 miles away from or 1,000 feet deeper than existing wells. Eckhardt and Charlie Wilson fashioned a compromise to expand Carter's definition of "new" natural gas. Eckhardt's proposal allowed more potential gas reserves to receive that "new" gas designation, so producers of wells from those properties could make more money from gas production. Moreover, Eckhardt's amendment would place Texas natural gas prices under the federal price ceiling, finally doing away with the intrastate/interstate two-tier pricing system.

All thirteen Republicans on the Ad Hoc Committee voted against it, as did two southern Democrats. But the Democratic majority held, and Eckhardt's amendment passed 24–15. Consumer groups disagreed with the strategy, believing that the Carter plan could have won without the compromise. A senior White House energy adviser wrote that it was "acceptable" if it helped build a mandate in Congress behind the Carter program.

With his reputation as a staunch consumer advocate, Eckhardt and others knew that the deregulators would not follow his lead. So, on the House floor, Charlie Wilson led the effort to attract more votes from the right. Eckhardt felt that although Wilson did not know the details as well as he did, he was a very good politician, he supported independent producers, and he could help sell the deal.

Jim Wright had been a supporter of Krueger's 1975–1976 deregulation thrusts, but he was now the majority leader and, as such, supported the Wilson-Eckhardt amendment in an effort to save the president's bill. "Henry Clay once pleaded with his colleagues: 'Do not despise compromise. It is the cement which holds the Union together,'" Wright said. Wilson told the House that he had made concessions "that have been like taking castor oil" and that his oil friends were angry with him. Indeed, J. R. Parten scolded "about you joining Bob Eckhardt" in the compromise, criticizing Wilson for letting the federal government "impress permanently the natural resources of Texas."[23] On the other side, Toby Moffett's consumer friends were angry with him. Moffett "had to hold his nose" to support the compromise.[24] When it became obvious that Wilson-Eckhardt would win, it was approved on a voice vote, and the opponents went on to their straight up-or-down deregulation amendment.

A tense House debated Krueger's deregulation amendment for hours. Speaker O'Neill blasted "big oil" in a rare floor speech. "Never have I seen such an influx of lobbyists in this town. . . . Believe me, the future of this nation . . . is at stake," O'Neill ended, to great applause. Eckhardt, Wilson, and Wright won, 227–199. The entire bill was finally approved on August 5, 1977, 244–177.

O'Neill was thrilled, seeing the victory as a great portent of things to come.[25] But he was wrong, as it would be more than a year before the battle was over. In the Senate, a fierce gas deregulation battle raged. After a long stalemate and bruising filibuster, Majority Leader Robert Byrd and Vice President Walter Mondale agreed to accept Bentsen's modified deregulation amendment.[26] Now, the conference battle was on, and it would last for a year.

The 1978 Energy Conference Huddle

Everyone dug into the trenches. Eckhardt headed to the White House with Toby Moffett, Ed Markey, Andy Maguire, Ab Mikva, Al Gore, and Jim Guy Tucker to press the House's position against the Senate's. White House lobbyist Frank Moore advised Carter that "this group of liberal progressive Members wishes to impress upon the Pres. their great concern over the possibility of giving the oil companies too much leeway in the final version of the energy bill. The group will not support the bill if it is not balanced in favor of consumer interests." A few weeks later, Moore warned Carter that Eckhardt, Moffett, and Phil Sharp had briefed House members on the negotiations and that the briefing outcome was not favorable to Carter's positions. He told Carter that Schlesinger and O'Neill had agreed that it was necessary for Carter to meet with Eckhardt again "since this group represents a sufficient number in the House to jeopardize the bill." Reluctantly, Carter agreed.[27]

Eckhardt was appointed to serve on the House-Senate Conference Committee, with twenty-four other House conferees. House conferees offered a compromise, but the Senate divided 9–9, so it was defeated. Carter then called Eckhardt and a small group of the conferees to the White House. He and Schlesinger pressed the members to agree to a compromise. As a result, a "Christmas Compromise" was brokered, but on December 22, Senate conferees rejected it, 16–2. Natural gas pricing was the sticking point. It was time for a long Christmas break.

Eckhardt devoted his winter *Quarterly Report* to an analysis of the Christmas Compromise, and he also wrote up a version of it for *The Journal of Energy and Development*.[28] While he slogged through the negotiations, Eckhardt would fly home to lecture on energy policy at the University of Houston; the next semester, he took the train to Haverford College to lecture on Congress. He was truly in his element.

After the Christmas break, with both sides still dug in, a long impasse ensued. On March 9, 1978, Carter accepted the Senate's phaseout of gas price controls.[29] John Dingell's subcommittee staff drafted a compromise, and Eckhardt and Dingell discussed it numerous times. Eckhardt wrote Dingell an eight-page letter, complete with hand-sketched figures and graphs on the GNP deflator over time. "I am in accord with much of the proposal that you and your staff have so diligently worked up," he wrote. However, he expressed concern about gas price escalation and effects on producers and consumers, as well as reservations about whether the proposals would gain the Senate votes or not.[30] The proposal was never presented as a whole, but it significantly affected future conference negotiations.

Eckhardt in the Oval Office. During the 1977–1978 negotiations over President
Carter's national energy program, Bob Eckhardt was a key negotiator for House
members championing regulation and price controls to protect consumers.
He repeatedly met with President Carter and his energy advisers. Here, he meets
with the president in the Oval Office, along with Texas Congressman Charlie
Wilson and Energy Secretary James Schlesinger. White House Photo; courtesy
of the Robert C. Eckhardt Collection, Center for American History,
University of Texas at Austin, CN 12143.

On March 21, Eckhardt wrote his fellow conferees: "The counter-proposal
of the House Conferees offered here today does not represent a step lightly
taken. It represents a significant departure from the House-approved natural
gas pricing measure and contains concessions beyond even those agreed to
by many House Members in the so-called Christmas Compromise." Their
proposal, he wrote, contained a "floating cap" mechanism (a price cap that
would float with market conditions), whereas the Senate's proposal had a
ceiling price mechanism, during the period leading up to termination of controls. As Eckhardt noted:

> The floating cap mechanism and study provisions afford an essential op-
> portunity for the President and the Congress to assess market conditions
> prior to the expiration of controls and prior to the termination of the time

deadline for extending controls for a two-year period. The price mechanism in the Senate proposal cannot afford the same degree of market eval-
uation because price ceilings, by their very nature, often act as a magnet
drawing all new prices to the ceiling level.

The House offered an extension of controls for up to two years, rather than
the Senate's *reimposition* of controls, which was a sword that "could hang
over industry well into the 1990s. . . . However, at the same time, the [House]
proposal affords protection to consumers by ensuring that Congress and the
President will have an opportunity to evaluate market conditions under the
floating cap and act to continue controls for two years if instability exists in
the marketplace."[31] The day after his statement, House conferees voted 13–12
with Eckhardt to reject the Senate natural gas language and adopt their own.

The travails of the oil and gas battles served as fodder for Mr. Hyde. Eckhardt, amused at the floating cap concept, whipped out his pen and sketched
caricatures of a cap floating on water, with a man trying not to drown beneath
the surface. He also recognized the complexity and seeming incoherence of
the cumbersome plan that the conferees were producing. He sketched out his
image of the result—an ugly beast—in a cartoon he called "Creature of the
Conferees," which *Science* magazine printed along with its article on "Congressman Eckhardt, Legislative Craftsman."[32]

But Eckhardt also became seriously alarmed at the direction of the conference. Without a strong outside push for price regulations, he thought the
Senate would pull the final decision far over to the side of industry. He spoke
with Ed Ball, now a top national director with the United Steelworkers of
America. They convinced the Steelworkers president to issue a news release
blasting the proposals for deregulation.[33]

Carter finally intervened again, meeting with conferees at the White
House on April 11, 12, and 13. Schlesinger proposed a compromise, moving
the House closer to the Senate's decontrol. He shuttled back and forth between small groups of conferees, pushing them. Schlesinger had to forge a
coalition in the middle, and he decided that they had to bring Eckhardt in to
do it, since he was a leader on the liberal side of the debate. That meant giving
more on the price control issues than they would have liked.

Simultaneously, Schlesinger and Carter were discussing with Eckhardt an
executive appointment in energy, a development that affected conference deliberations. Over the years, Eckhardt had come to know and respect Lynn
Coleman, who had worked at the Texas capitol while Eckhardt was there.
Coleman then went to work in Houston as a Vinson & Elkins law partner and
introduced Eckhardt to his colleagues there. John Connally sent Coleman to
Washington to open a new office for the firm in 1973, and he got to know

Eckhardt again as he lobbied for Vinson & Elkins clients, including Houston Natural Gas. Coleman found an apartment on the Hill, close to Eckhardt, who was living as a bachelor. Eckhardt would come over for supper, bring his laundry, and they would sit there folding clothes as they argued energy policy. In turn, Coleman would drop by Eckhardt's place for discussions, finding him at work with his carpentry tools building a bed or grilling out in the backyard.

Thus, when Carter and Schlesinger were staffing the new U.S. Department of Energy (DOE), Eckhardt urged that they appoint Coleman DOE general counsel. When Carter nominated him, Eckhardt went to bat for Coleman, despite widespread suspicion among consumer advocates of anyone associated with Connally and his oil-and-gas lobbying firm. Eckhardt defended his friend in a lengthy piece in *The Nation*.[34]

In the midst of the conference committee negotiations, the Senate finally confirmed Coleman as general counsel. Coleman respected Eckhardt and quickly became a negotiator, working with him, industry, and the administration. Schlesinger hosted a reception on April 21 to celebrate and welcome Coleman. As Schlesinger, Coleman, Eckhardt, and Charlie Wilson talked, Schlesinger finally convinced Eckhardt and Wilson to agree to split their differences over the bill. They all abruptly left the party and, a bit tipsy, they headed to the Capitol, where they wrote up details of the new proposal.

Dingell's staff estimated the compromise would give the gas industry $23 billion more than the House version would have. In a raucous meeting on May 3, House conferees backed away from the compromise. There was an atmosphere of political hysteria. On May 24, the deadlock was broken again, with another proposal for partial deregulation. Eckhardt believed that he had gotten as much as he would get and decided to support it—over the opposition of the Consumer Federation of America, Americans for Democratic Action, and the Independent Petroleum Association. Toby Moffett led the House conferees opposed to deregulation, trying to derail the compromise with amendments, but Eckhardt's vote made the difference and the measure was approved by House conferees 13–12. The Senate conferees voted for it 10–7. Robert Sherrill later bitterly wrote that Eckhardt had proved to be a valued ally of the natural gas industry, serving as a "Judas goat to lure other liberals into supporting decontrol."[35]

O'Neill appointed a task force to shepherd the measure to final approval, led by Eckhardt's ally, Phil Sharp. With conservatives opposing controls and liberals supporting tighter regulation, there was an intense Rules Committee battle, with the committee finally approving a rule permitting only one vote on the package. On October 13, the House voted 207–206 to accept the rule, with Eckhardt voting yes, against Moffett and Maguire, who had organized the effort to defeat it. The House then awaited Senate action and another

Eckhardt with President Carter, signing 1978 Energy Act. After two years of
battles, Congress passed a revised version of President Carter's energy package in
1978. Bob Eckhardt was one of the key players in the drawn-out battle, and here,
he looks on as Carter signs the 1978 Natural Gas Policy Act. Official White House
photograph. Courtesy of the Robert C. Eckhardt Collection, Center for American
History, University of Texas at Austin, CN 12141.

filibuster, then approved the package, 231–168. Eckhardt stood over Carter's
shoulder at the public signing ceremony.

After sixty years, the natural gas industry was finally on the road to shucking the monkey of regulation. New gas would be deregulated over time, even
if old gas remained regulated. Projections were that deregulation would increase production by a measly amount while bringing whopping profits to
the industry. "Even most advocates of price decontrol argue that decontrol
will only slow the decline in production of oil and gas, not increase the domestic supply of the fuels over current production," wrote the Democratic
Study Group.[36]

Bubbles, Coupons, Tilts, and Strippers

During the next round of oil and gas battles in 1979 and 1980, Eckhardt hosted
scores of O&I hearings on gasoline prices and distribution, DOE's gasoline

"tilt" rule, the so-called natural gas "bubble," industry cheating on classification of small "stripper" wells, and every energy scenario imaginable.

The most visible public manifestation of an energy crisis was long lines of people waiting at filling stations. Even Stuart Eizenstat sometimes couldn't get gasoline to drive to his White House meetings on gasoline shortages! Eckhardt's and Dingell's subcommittees held a joint hearing in May 1979 on the gasoline shortage. Eckhardt supported Carter's gasoline rationing plan that he submitted as required by the 1975 act. "Rationing by coupon is certainly fairer than rationing by price—or by gas lines," he told labor union members in a 1980 speech.[37] But the House rejected it.

The Natural Gas Policy Act of 1978 was based on a long-term shortage of natural gas. Yet a few months later, in early 1979, Carter officials incredibly decided that there was a glut of natural gas—surely, they said, a temporary "bubble"—that could be used to replace middle distillates as a boiler fuel. Eckhardt held a hearing and concluded that DOE had no independent estimate of the size of the alleged bubble and had not considered the side effects of their diversion program.[38]

Eckhardt, Dingell, and Moffett (now chairing the Government Operations' Subcommittee on Environment, Energy and Natural Resources) held three-committee joint hearings on the diesel and home heating oil shortages. They brought in marketing and supply experts from oil companies and state energy representatives, all of whom objected to DOE rules. Then, they brought in DOE's deputy secretary, who assured everyone that there would be adequate supplies of heating oil. To deal with the mix of refining the various products, DOE decided to implement a "tilt" toward higher gasoline prices as compared to prices for other uses of oil: as of March 1, 1979, refiners were allowed to pass through an increased percentage of their crude oil and refining costs to gasoline purchasers.

When Congress crafted the policy earlier, this tilt toward higher gasoline prices was meant to lower prices for home heating oil (by making more crude oil available for refining into heating oil), and DOE contended the tilt was necessary to increase refining capacity. Eckhardt believed it was just a way for oil companies to get higher prices for their products. He obtained major oil company testimony contradicting DOE's conclusions about shifts in refining, and he criticized EPA for giving in to DOE on the issue. Eckhardt calculated that the tilt policy would cost consumers $5 billion a year, on top of the $10 billion for increased crude oil prices. The *Washington Post* further researched the policy, interviewed Eckhardt, and published a front-page story, describing the tilt policy as a "financial bonanza" to oil companies.[39] Eckhardt contended that, with the demise of controls on the other products, there was nothing to "tilt" from, so the policy should not have been triggered by the administration. "These were vastly important and interlocking questions of policy," he said. "But who decided it? It was largely under the aegis of [DOE]. It was not a decision of Congress."[40]

The tilt issue also provided a wonderful stage for Eckhardt's mindplay and wordplay. He bewildered the committee and witnesses by conjuring an example of the possible uses of barley in Scotland to explain that producing more whiskey meant less food.[41] He also recalled an Aztecan "pulque" house he once saw in Mexico. The Aztecs used the maguey plant for needles, fibers, thread, clothing, sails, rope, and pulque (which can be refined into tequila). Eckhardt surmised:

> If one should decide to use more of the plant for pulque and less for clothing, there might be a quite adequate supply of pulque for a good time even in a bad maguey crop year. Of course, this would all be at the expense of rope, canoe sails, and clothing. But the happy child of nature might go on drinking pulque until he went naked without ever running into a 20 percent shortfall of that noble drink. . . . It is appropriate both to the Indian's pulque-induced euphoria and our own intoxification [sic] with the indulgent use of gasoline. The name of the pulque house was, translated, "The glorious History of the Future of the Past."[42]

Next came the "stripper" battle. Stripper wells were those that produced less than about ten barrels of oil per day. In 1976, Eckhardt had won a vote to exempt them from the interstate price ceiling to provide an incentive for continued production. Early in 1980, Dr. Lower discovered that DOE was allowing producers to claim the high "stripper" prices for wells that did not qualify. He calculated that more stripper oil was reported *sold* to the refineries than was reported as *produced* and concluded that the resulting overcharges totaled $1 billion for 1979, and more than that for 1980.

Eckhardt could not help but have fun with the name. "I call this the Mystery of the Billion Dollar Stripper," and the "Gypsy Rose Lee Rule: Once a stripper, always a stripper." He gained media attention, as the *New York Times* and others covered the unfolding scandal.

In Eckhardt's stripper hearings, Al Gore raked DOE officials over the coals, charging that oil companies were "getting away with it because the DOE is not enforcing the law. Let's tell it like it is. There's a lot of lying, cheating, and stealing. The oil industry has looked on this as in season."[43] Eckhardt asked, "Now, has any individual served as much as one day in jail for any type of willful violation of DOE petroleum price and allocation regulations?"[44] The answer was no; DOE admitted their audits revealed that the overcharges had not triggered even one citation. Eckhardt declared that the overcharges represented "a wholesale rip-off of American consumers. The term 'miscer-tification' which the DOE has used for this scheme seems far too mild and overly technical for such activity. I remember I used to have a schoolmate who frequently 'misclassified' his examination after looking at my papers. We used to call that cheating." The oil companies—and DOE—realized that they had been caught. Now DOE began fining companies for the cheating and the investigations that Eckhardt started led to prosecutions. Two years later, a DOE investigator wrote him as a case was making its way through court, saying, "Your determination of a 'billion dollar stripper' obviously was much more on point than anyone really thought possible two years ago." [45]

To Decontrol

The 1975 Energy Policy and Conservation Act set up a trigger date in 1979 for possible early presidential decontrol of domestic crude oil prices. In prepa-ration for the decision on whether to decontrol, Eckhardt and sixty other House members wrote President Carter urging him not to speed decontrol. In March 1979, Eckhardt held a well-reported news conference in which he laid out data showing that oil drilling was at its highest level ever. He outlined the inflationary impact of decontrol and blasted DOE for its tilt rule, which he thought was equivalent to administrative decontrol.[46] On March 29, Eck-hardt and other members met with Carter in the Oval Office and urged him not to decontrol.

Eckhardt, Moffett, Dingell, Gore, and Markey met to craft a strategy. Eck-hardt gave an hour-long lecture to the House on oil production, pricing, and inflation issues. He described the huge increases in income for oil companies, saying, "This does not look like the profit picture of a business that is going out of business." And "energy costs are clearly fueling an inflationary spi-ral." [47] He was not alone in his analysis—Secretary of Labor Ray Marshall was arguing inside the Carter administration that their policies were misguided and that oil prices were the primary cause of the inflation.[48]

Yet, the effort to head Carter off was to no avail; in April, he announced that he would gradually decontrol the price of domestic oil beginning June 1 and recoup some of the revenue through a windfall profits tax. That decision, Eck-hardt believed, destined the economy to hyperinflation and doomed the Carter presidency. Largely because of the economic fiasco, Ted Kennedy decided to run against Carter in the 1980 primary.[49] The Congressional Budget Office estimated that the cost to consumers would be a whopping $75 billion by 1982 and that inflation would be 4.6 points higher because of the decontrol—all to save 3 percent of then-current U.S. petroleum consumption.[50]

Eckhardt was not willing to accede to Carter's decision. He and his allies decided on a strategy of a legislative extension of controls to block Carter's decision. Eckhardt and Moffett battled before the Commerce Committee for an amendment to extend controls, but lost on a tie vote, 21–21. Next, they pushed to get the Democratic Caucus on record in favor of a recision of presidential authority. Moffett made the motion, and Eckhardt was a leading debater for the resolution. The caucus voted overwhelmingly, 138–69, in favor of Moffett's resolution. Even Speaker O'Neill was fed up with Carter and said if he voted, he would have supported Moffett. By this time, Kennedy had given up on Carter and was running against him in the Democratic presidential primaries, further muddying the waters on oil and gas issues. Clearly, only Republicans could rescue Carter. And they did. Moffett let the charge on the House floor, but lost 257–135.

To Restore Controls

Eckhardt, Moffett, and the others did not give up after they lost the vote in the spring to maintain crude oil price controls. They started beating the drum for a *restoration* of controls. In the autumn of 1979, the House had to reauthorize DOE. It was a worthy vehicle for all kinds of attacks on the Carter energy policies. Eckhardt spoke out for Peter Kostmayer's (D-Penn.) amendment to restore controls on heating oil and diesel fuel, but they lost 124–243. Republican James Courter from New Jersey won an amendment to prohibit funds to control gasoline prices *and* allocation, but his victory was razor thin. Eckhardt then lost, by a very slim margin, an amendment allowing controls during an emergency. Two weeks later, Eckhardt led the House to reverse the vote on the Courter amendment, 189–225.[51] The DOE bill was the obvious vehicle that Eckhardt and Moffett needed to offer their crude oil re-control proposal, and Moffett made the motion. Eckhardt's old union, the Oil, Chemical, and Atomic Workers International, wrote representatives that the union "strongly urges you to support the Eckhardt-Moffett amendment."[52] Lynn Coleman pled with Eckhardt to back off, arguing that even most Democrats had come around to supporting deregulation and that the issue would not help Eckhardt win reelection, but Eckhardt waved him off. Carter urged congressional members "in the strongest terms to join me in opposition to this amendment."[53] In an open letter to Carter in the *New York Times*, Eckhardt argued that the nation would face high prices and high inflation, but would not get higher oil production: "We cannot achieve [energy independence] through the impoverishment of our people and the concomitant enrichment of a few giant oil companies."[54] Kostmayer distributed

Eckhardt's letter to all members. Eckhardt spoke forcefully for it, but they lost decisively, 135 to 257. Decontrol was here, with its cascading economic and political repercussions.

Oil Profits and Inflation

In February 1979, Eckhardt had met with Stuart Eizenstat and Carter's economic adviser Alfred Kahn to discuss his concerns over inflation.[55] Knowing that administrations often push their policies by labeling their opponents as solely negative, Eckhardt developed "The Eckhardt Plan" in response to Carter's decontrol effort. Based on all the analysis that he and his O&I committee and staff had produced, he presented his energy and inflation-control scheme to the House in the midst of the debate on reimposing controls.[56] The day before the vote on Moffett's amendment to restore controls, Eckhardt wrote a letter to his colleagues alerting them to the vote on Moffett's amendment and enclosing his plan as a brief of arguments for a new direction.

Eckhardt was constantly speaking at labor union and oil and gas industry conferences around the nation, as well as at committee hearings, preaching his gospel of price controls and energy conservation. In January 1980, Eckhardt delivered his mountaintop sermon to the Edison Electric Institute: "A Secular View of Regulation and Deregulation, or There Is No Economic Ayatollah." He told the industry:

> Englishmen and Americans in designing the government process have—
> when they are at their best—been pragmatists. When men want to dig a
> ditch, one man does not become ideologically committed to the shovel
> and another to the pick. When he wants to loosen the dirt he uses a pick
> and when he wants to scoop it out he uses the shovel. So should it be with
> government. . . . Fortunately there is no economic Ayatollah to tell us the
> course dictated by the "true religion." What is one person's "true religion" is
> another's heresy. Some true believers say that if we would just "deregulate"
> everything would fall into place by the wisdom of that great "omnipres-
> ence in the skies," the marketplace. But there are other true believers who
> say "there is but one God, and his name is Bureaucrat. He is omniscient
> and omnipresent." There is but one appellation for both, and its name is
> hogwash.[57]

In December 1979, he held a hearing on "The Direct and Indirect Impact of Energy Prices on Inflation," calling Carter's deputy director of the Council on Wage and Price Stability to testify. Eckhardt began the hearing stating, "If we proceed with broad, theoretical policies which perpetuate the energy inflation in order to solve the long-term energy crisis, the immediate crisis will overtake and cripple the economy."[58] Eckhardt relied on one of Dr. Lower's signature pieces, an ongoing examination of the profitability of oil and gas companies. Oil and gas industry net income grew 24 percent from 1972 to 1978, while non-oil and gas companies grew 10.1 percent. Then the disparity really kicked in: eighty-two oil and gas companies got 96 percent of all of the net income increase from 1978 to 1980, while 918 companies shared the other 4 percent increase.

Lower's work confirmed for Eckhardt that energy was the dominant factor in the hyperinflation.[59] What, then, was Carter thinking? When he announced decontrol, he said, apparently with a straight face, that it would have only a slight effect on inflation.[60] The persuasive power of the free market hucksters was clearly winning in the fun house mirror world of production, prices, and regulations. As soon as Carter decontrolled, his Council on Wage and Price Stability had to order the industry to produce explanations of the huge profits they were reporting, and the whole administration was scrambling to deal with the catastrophic inflation, just as Eckhardt had predicted. New Energy Secretary Charles Duncan was seething as he had to admit under Eckhardt's O&I grilling that the consumer cost of decontrol was $47.4 billion, not the $16 billion the administration had claimed. (Eckhardt had no inclination to go easy on Duncan, who had just supported the opposition in Eckhardt's primary election.)

To Deregulate

Carter's oil decontrol initiative was but one part of his economic agenda. Carter (even Kennedy) strengthened the gathering winds of deregulation with airline, trucking, and rail deregulation initiatives. Eckhardt was headed the other direction, following in the footsteps of his great uncle, Congressman Rudolph Kleberg, who introduced legislation in the 1890s to increase the Interstate Commerce Commission's (ICC) power over railroads. Believing that high coal transportation prices had the effect of keeping more natural gas in use in Texas, Eckhardt argued that one way to free up more natural gas for the East was to make coal more affordable by stopping the monopolistic pricing of railroads. But he was pursuing his goal against the increasing gale force of deregulation.

Carter's effort to further deregulation came in the Staggers Rail Act of 1980. Eckhardt opposed Staggers working with fellow West Virginian Nick Joe Rahall. They led a coalition of interest groups that kept growing. Eckhardt rounded up the other Texas Democratic congressmen and went to the White House to meet with Vice President Mondale. They told Mondale that if coal rates were not limited, Carter would lose Harris County, and thus Texas, in the November election.[61] Eckhardt's significant amendment to the Staggers Act was to permit the Interstate Commerce Commission to review a rate where a captive shipper (an enterprise on a rail line with no shipping alternative to that line) was involved with a monopoly rail line. Eckhardt provided in effect more regulatory control over rates, protecting captive shippers.

Just as Eckhardt and the Texas delegation were meeting with White House officials, Eizenstat was meeting with O'Neill and telling him to run over Eckhardt, who angrily accused the White House of "using every trick in the book."[62] Eckhardt won his amendment. Carter officials later admitted that their vote count "was far off" and that they had underestimated Eckhardt's strength. "Will the Carter Administration never learn?" asked *Texas Monthly* in September 1980. "With Texas looming as a crucial state this fall, the administration not only botched the chance to make its railroad deregulation bill palatable to Texas but also managed to alienate most of the state's congressional delegation in the process."[63] But Congress recessed, and after an intense lobbying blitz in August, the Eckhardt amendment was voted on again and defeated.[64] In conference, the final version gave Eckhardt some of what he had originally won. He rushed back home for a final, fatal month of campaigning.

Readying for the Energy Battles of the 1980s

Once decontrol and deregulation were in place, it was clear that the energy wars of the 1980s would turn to questions about profit management, alternative sources, conservation of energy, and societal shifts to accommodate a new energy reality. Neither Jimmy Carter nor Bob Eckhardt would be in office for those battles. But not knowing their futures, both acted, of course, as if they would be around. Eckhardt jumped into those issues as they were being molded. In late 1979, he held hearings on renewable energy and residential energy conservation. In the Senate, Kennedy introduced a comprehensive package of energy conservation proposals to promote energy efficiency in residential, commercial, and industrial sectors, and he asked Eckhardt to carry it in the House. Throughout 1980, Eckhardt worked with Kennedy and John Durkin, sponsoring the Kennedy-Durkin-Eckhardt Energy Productivity Act.

Coal was the stand-in player in the oil and gas battles of the 1970s, and it was often called in to play its role. Eckhardt extended his interest in coal transportation by becoming the lead congressional advocate of "coal slurry pipelines," an effort to bypass expensive rail rates. Eckhardt got Morris Udall to support his effort to recall his bill to the full committee in October 1977. Opponents objected that he was stampeding the issue before it had been fully heard—this after four years of hearings. "If the buffalo had stampeded like we have," Eckhardt responded wryly, "the glaciers would have caught up with them!" Then, early in 1978, Transportation and Commerce Subcommittee Chair Fred Rooney, who was against coal slurry, planned to bring it up in Commerce, hoping to kill it there. Eckhardt got Rooney's assurance that he would not bring it up the next day while Eckhardt was in a physical exam. But in the midst of his exam, Eckhardt got a call, leapt up from the exam, and rushed back, finding Rooney pressing a vote. Staggers ruled against Eckhardt's objection and continued with the vote, which defeated coal slurry. Eckhardt was irate. "This member was deceived," he yelled in a speech on the House floor, reminiscent of his personal privilege speeches at the Texas capitol. If members could not count on each other's word, he said, "we make of this committee a jungle, a sort of Jim Bowie duel [in which] you turn two people with knives loose in a darkened room and let 'em go at each other." [65] But he never got his coal slurry bill passed.

Tip O'Neill had failed to win creation of a new standing Energy Committee in 1976. In 1979 and 1980, wary of the gridlock of competing committees, the House revisited the idea of committee realignment so that future energy conflicts would be fought on new battlefields. It was a bitter, bloody battle. The proposal brought to the floor would create an Energy Committee, realigning committee jurisdictions. Jonathan Bingham (D-N.Y.) pushed a counterproposal to not create a new Energy Committee, but rather to give the Commerce Committee greater jurisdiction over energy issues and re-name it the Committee on Energy and Commerce.

Dingell threw in with Bingham, hoping that he would soon get the full committee chairmanship when Staggers retired. Eckhardt had left Dingell's Energy and Power Subcommittee to chair his own subcommittees, so he was not in the heat of the battle, though his energy leadership meant he had to be wary of the fight and pick his path carefully, especially because both he and Dingell wanted to move up in the committee.

Eckhardt feared that a stand-alone Energy Committee would be easier for oil and gas to dominate. With energy as part of a broader commerce, health, and consumer affairs committee, "no single group can control a majority," Eckhardt argued.[66] He wrote that the proposal "is merely a shift of power to a place where that power is more easily influenced by the most powerful lobby in the country." [67] For its part, the industry understood what was happening. Knowing that Staggers was retiring and that Dingell was likely to chair the full committee, Eckhardt was telling people that he was confident that he would be the new chair of the Energy and Power Subcommittee. "If Bob gets to be chairman, God save the country!" exclaimed one oilman.[68]

Eckhardt's position on the energy wars of the 1970s was complex. He knew that, as he told the industry in 1977, "prices must inevitably go up," and he broadened his perspective beyond the discrete issue of Texas oil and gas to the broader energy availability (and conservation) issues. He told his constituents that his energy plan was a fair system of rationing gasoline, encouraging production of energy from new sources, conserving energy, developing energy efficiency, and facilitating transportation of coal.[69] His statement to the industry after the House had passed its version of Carter's plan is the best description of his legacy in those battles:

> Had I, as well as the representatives from industry, labor, consumers and independent producers with whom I worked throughout the House deliberations, decided to abandon this gradual process of improving the bill and had instead gone to one extreme or the other, we might well have been left with a definition that would be both too restrictive and geologically unsound, a coal conversion tax that was entirely punitive and an oil conversion program which would have reached deep into the pockets of industrial and residential consumers. Those who wanted to remain ideologically pure, either from industry's point of view or that of the consumers, played a losing game. The only votes that were to prevail were those that took into account the diverse interests that make up our society.[70]

But the arrogant leaders of the oil and gas industry would have none of it. They were right, Eckhardt was in the way, and he had to go. The patchwork congressional policies of the 1970s were doomed to failure in a world that was quickly turning away from the regulatory face of Roosevelt and Johnson. And, in the world of polarizing politics, the 1980 voters responded much more to a Ronald Reagan on an ideological horse than to a Bob Eckhardt on his mount of legislative craftsmanship coupled with populist ideals.

SIXTEEN

The 1980 Election

There is no disgrace, per se, in losing an election, as Bob Eckhardt did in 1980. A candidate's victories or losses in elections are influenced by many variables—personal characteristics, party dynamics, finances and organization, the opponent, and the dynamics of the era. The New Right eyed the race against Eckhardt and concluded, "Frankly, it's just a function of money."[1] Years later, Jake Pickle commented that Eckhardt didn't go home enough, and "the money boys got together on him" and defeated him. Eckhardt was neither a good nor a disciplined campaigner, and his reputation for constituent service was mixed. Yet, he had won twenty-three elections in a row by November 1980, so clearly his personal ambivalence to campaigning was but one variable in his victories, and but one variable in his 1980 defeat. When he first won in 1958, his victory was partly because of the anti-Eisenhower/anti-Republican backlash that swept liberal Democrats to victory across the country. Likewise, in 1980, Eckhardt would not have lost but for the surging New Right movement that brought down Eckhardt, Carter, and scores of Democrats.

National Treasure, Local Enigma

After fourteen years in Washington, Bob Eckhardt was well known in political leadership circles. Already showered with awards and recognition, he continued receiving accolades in 1980. With all these hosannas, Eckhardt's campaign finance chair proudly kicked off the fund-raising, writing, "We have a wonderful product to sell—Bob Eckhardt is a national treasure."[2] Yet the time Eckhardt spent chairing his subcommittees, negotiating legislative compromises, speaking around the nation, and attending international conventions had taken its toll. He now had only a 28 percent name recognition in the district![3]

Eckhardt got complaints that he had neglected his constituent service. In 1976, *Texas Monthly* commented on "his slipshod treatment of the folks back home." Robert Sherrill became alienated from him over the oil and gas wars, and wrote a post-election letter to the *Texas Observer* that described Eckhardt's staff as horrible (though he wrote a later *Observer* piece that was favorable to the Lowers).[4] For years, Eckhardt maintained his local office in the federal building in downtown Houston, eight miles outside the district, and that rankled some; he finally opened a Baytown branch office in 1978. Yet, there is evidence that many thought he and his staff were worthy and influential fighters for his constituents. In naming Eckhardt the state's "Best Liberal," *Texas Business* wrote, "He has worked hard, developed strong constituent services and has used his position . . . to excellent advantage for space-minded Houston."[5] So, some found good constituent service from Eckhardt, while others did not—which was enough for an opponent to play on.

The Changing Eighth—Foreground to Defeat

The seeds of Eckhardt's 1980 loss go back to the 1976 campaign, if not earlier. By 1976, Republicans could run viable campaigns in much of Harris County. Eckhardt's city and labor precincts were dependable Democratic areas, but the outlying areas were suburbanizing, with more sympathy for Republicans. Areas that were rice fields when he was first elected were now vibrant white-collar suburbs. Housing developments now surrounded his wooded sanctuary on Cypress Creek. The black proportion of the district steadily decreased, dipping from 29 percent in the mid-1960s to below 20 percent by 1980, while the Latino proportion remained fairly steady at 10 percent. Even more ominously for the labor-oriented Eckhardt, the blue-collar proportion plummeted from 71 percent before the 1971 redistricting to below 50 percent by the end of the decade.[6] Eckhardt's vote totals stayed about the same in 1978 compared to 1974, but the opposition gained considerably from Republican crossovers and new voters. And Eckhardt *dropped* in votes from white boxes, while his opposition gained considerably.[7]

Eckhardt's 1978 compromises had caused his oil and gas industry opponents to pull back briefly. Indeed, a few decided that the best way to deal with Eckhardt was to give him money, as they did everyone else, then ask for policy changes. Houston oilman Jack Warren constantly urged Eckhardt to do things for him. Without naming Warren, but apparently referring to him, Eckhardt told journalist Robert Sherrill, "Lapped into his contributions were requests for help in solving problems. Oil problems." But Eckhardt's vote for Carter's windfall profits tax caused the industry to come roaring back after him. "This time," Eckhardt said, "they may be thinking of the expression from Macbeth—'We have scotched the snake, not killed it.' This time they are really trying to kill me."[8]

The New Right

Accompanying the scares of Eckhardt's 1976 and 1978 races was the rise of an angry sociopolitical movement, the New Right, with its backlash against the cultural changes of the 1960s, its attacks on New Deal and Great Society programs, and its quasi-religious, militaristic nationalism. Think tanks such as the Heritage Foundation whipped up a free enterprise, anti-government public relations campaign, aided by coalitions such as the American Conservative Union. Ex-generals fanned out across the nation, arguing that U.S. military might was weakening. Conservative religious leaders organized their members behind Republican politics.[9]

Eckhardt recognized the corrosive effects of the movement. In 1976, he wrote a piece in *The Nation* decrying Reagan's and Ford's attitudes toward government. Reagan had stated that government should get out of the way, saying, "Let us have at it." In response, Eckhardt wrote:

> If "us" is not the American people acting through government, "us" as Mr. Reagan conceives it must be individual persons acting in some manner of voluntary concert. Corporations, I suppose, would be the principal vehicle of "having at it," because they are the principal way that the movers and the shakers act in concert. But if *people* are to be represented, who is to represent them other than . . . Congressmen and the executive branch, members of the regulatory agencies, and other governmental officials? It is the very institution of government that Mr. Reagan is attacking.[10]

In the world of electoral politics, the New Right caught on fast. By 1980, their largest funding entities were Citizens for the Republic, National Conservative Political Action Committee (known as NCPAC or "nick-pack"), Committee for the Survival of a Free Congress, Gun Owners of America, and the Conservative Victory Fund (from the American Conservative Union).[11] These organizations developed a new generation of savvy electoral leaders such as Richard Viguerie, who cut his teeth in Houston Republican politics; Paul Weyrich; and Terry Dolan, who in turn joined forces with Religious Right leaders such as Jerry Falwell.

NCPAC Chairman Terry Dolan worked out of offices in Arlington, Virginia, clustered with other New Right groups, including one that he directed, Conservatives Against Liberal Legislation (CALL), which would come into play in Eckhardt's election. The *Washington Post* quoted Dolan as saying that NCPAC "could lie through its teeth and the candidate it helps could stay clean."[12]

Like labor and business, New Right groups learned how to choose congressional votes that they could use to paint favorable portraits of their supporters and to demonize their opponents. The National Taxpayers' Union gave Eckhardt eleven out of one hundred points. They were more generous than other groups on the right. Eckhardt got zero ratings from the American Security Council (which labeled him anti-defense), National Alliance of Senior Citizens (a business-backed group formed to counter the American Association of Retired Persons), National Association for Neighborhood Schools, Christian Voice, and U.S. Chamber of Commerce. All this was fodder for his electoral opponents. Eckhardt spent so much time on his projects and issues that he did not focus on the challenge that the New Right social agenda presented.

Nationalization of the Campaign

In 1979, the economy slumped, the Soviet Union invaded Afghanistan, Americans were taken hostage in Iran, and Jimmy Carter became an albatross around the necks of Democrats, just as the New Right was pushing its well-financed army. The congressional Democratic Study Group sampled polls and intelligence from its members and reported that Republican Ronald Reagan was beating Carter *in Democratic congressional districts* across the nation. That did not bode well for Democratic congressmen like Eckhardt who were running tight races for reelection.[13]

In 1976, Jimmy Carter had carried Texas. In 1980, Bill Clements was governor of Texas, the first Republican in the governor's mansion in a century, and George Bush was the Republican vice presidential candidate. So the Right had a giant boost for its Texas efforts. The U.S. Chamber of Commerce wrote its members urging a strong effort to defeat Eckhardt.[14] The New Right targeted several Texas congressmen, but Eckhardt was in their bull's-eye. Paul Weyrich's Committee for the Survival of a Free Congress targeted ninety races across the nation. Weyrich made it plain that his committee would use both Democratic and Republican shills for their efforts:

> Conservatives can make meaningful gains in the United States House of Representatives. For example, we want to beat Bob Eckhart [*sic*] before he beats America! In Congress Eckhardt votes for: Double Digit Inflation, Big Government, Expanding Bureaucracy, Big Labor Bosses. If you think that's bad, that's not all. Eckhardt has worked hard to change the image of America to one of weakness and meekness. Bob Eckhardt . . . isn't very well known, most people don't recognize his name, but he's had a tremendous influence on your life and my life and the life of every American. Bob

votes wrong 86 percent of the time. But Bob's got a reelection problem. He's out of step with the voters back home and we can defeat him in 1980. We have a good conservative running against Bob Eckhardt in the Democratic primary, and a good conservative Republican in the general election.[15]

Jack Fields

Twenty-eight-year-old Jack Fields Jr. won the Republican nomination to challenge Eckhardt. Fields grew up and lived in Humble, a small town of 7,000 near the northeastern boundary of Harris County, where Humble Oil (Exxon) was founded. Jack Fields Sr. served as president of the local Chamber of Commerce. The Fields family owned and ran Rosewood Memorial Park. Jack Fields Jr. worked for the family business, selling cemetery plots. He was handsome, clean-cut, athletic, and had an unusually deep speaking voice, and he had drawn on all those attributes to win election as high school student body president.

Fields wanted to play college basketball, but didn't get a scholarship. The Fields were Baptists, so Jack Jr. decided to go to Baylor University in Waco, where he began his studies in 1970. There, he quickly became active with the conservative student political machine. By this time, moderates had learned how to organize and were winning student elections at Baylor. In the beginnings of polarized politics, though, conservative students were convinced that these religious and political moderates were extreme liberals. Fields was such an attractive candidate that the conservative machine's leaders decided to run him for student body president, even though he was only a sophomore. He won and served as president in his junior year, then won again the next year. It was unheard of for anyone at Baylor to serve two terms.

In the early 1970s, almost everyone in Texas was still a Democrat—even conservatives. As the 1972 presidential campaign geared up, Fields allied himself with the Republicans, wearing a "Re-elect Nixon" button around campus. Organizers of "University Chapel," a required course for undergraduates, scheduled a session on the presidential campaign. The ground rules were set for a debate,[16] with Fields to debate for President Nixon and this book's author to debate for Democratic nominee George McGovern. At the appointed time, Fields said privately that he would not debate. He gave his opening speech for Nixon, then, rather than debate, told the audience that he had to study for an exam, and walked off the stage.[17] It would not be the last time that Fields shied from debating.

Among some faculty and students, Fields had a reputation of being an intellectual lightweight. But he was unquestionably popular among the students, and he was a favorite of President Abner McCall and Dean of Students

W. C. Perry. Perry's son Bob, who had graduated from Baylor, would soon bankroll Fields's campaign against Eckhardt and later became the biggest financier of Texas Republicans in the 1980s and 1990s (and even going national, funding the anti-John Kerry "swift boat" ads in 2004).[18]

Fields graduated in 1974, then went to Baylor Law School, graduating in 1977. He moved back home, married the daughter of an Exxon executive, reestablished connections in Humble, and began drawing on his Baylor connections. In 1979, new Republican Governor Bill Clements appointed him to the Small Business Advisory Council. Taking note of the fierce battles waged against Eckhardt in his 1978 race against Nick Gearhart, Fields started building a campaign to prepare for 1980.[19]

Fields traveled to Washington where he met Paul Weyrich, who was eagerly recruiting New Right candidates. Weyrich liked what he saw in Fields and invited him to Weyrich's campaign school. In 1979, a Republican Congressional Committee organizer came to Humble and met with Fields, who then attended their campaign school as well. Congressman Bill Archer's aide Lloyd Pierson had moved to Houston to run against Eckhardt in the next race. Pierson, too, went to the campaign school, but Weyrich liked Fields better and helped him muscle Pierson out of the race.[20]

In mid-1979, Fields started knocking on doors and recruiting precinct captains. With Weyrich's connections, Fields hooked up with top New Right consulting firms, pollsters, and managers. Fields brought in as campaign manager the executive director of the College Republican National Committee, and he hired other staff from among his former campaigning school students. Soon, the Republican National Committee and the U.S. Chamber of Commerce both sent campaign advisers to Humble.[21] Fields recruited as his finance chairman Robert Allen from Gulf Resources and Chemical Corp. The New Right had a candidate fueled by the oil and gas industry. Eckhardt, according to Fields's campaign slogan, "represents everything that's wrong with this country."[22] The die was now cast.

Early Money

Labor unions had always been good to Eckhardt, though their contribution amounts were not staggering. He had to branch out beyond that base. Knowing that he faced a one-two punch of primary and general campaigns, Eckhardt had to raise a lot of money fast. As usual, he had not been aggressive with his fund-raising and first had to pay off $26,000 in lingering debts, much of it in consolidation loans from Walter Hall.

Eckhardt planned a March 1979 fundraiser with President Carter's chief of staff, Hamilton Jordan, and his top lobbyist, Frank Moore, coming to

Houston to headline it.[23] At the fund-raiser, a friend set up a meeting between Eckhardt and the director of the Texas Trial Lawyers Association, and Eckhardt thanked them both for helping mend the "painful and uncomfortable breach with some of my closest supporters."[24] Other breaches did not heal. J. R. Parten had always funded Eckhardt, but he had become alienated during the energy crisis years and did not give the congressman money for the 1980 race.[25]

Ann Lower requested Rosalynn Carter to come to Houston. The White House staff mulled it over, noting that "Eckhardt is one of our more dependable supporters (with a support rating of 85.7 percent) and I'm sure that an appearance could pay off."[26] The First Lady did come, making appearances for several politicians and groups. Bernard Rapoport also helped with the early fund-raising, and the money rolled in. Labor was still crucial; Eckhardt had a Washington fund-raiser in November 1979, and the AFL-CIO's national director urged labor leaders to attend.[27]

Ann was still playing dual roles as chief of staff of the congressional office and as head of Eckhardt's political operation. In March 1980, she developed her campaign budget and decided that the primary should cost no more than $50,000 and the general election just over $100,000—a serious miscalculation that the campaign quickly had to scramble to change. Even that early, news stories were reporting that Fields planned to spend $400,000 (he spent twice that). And they expected Democrat Larry Washburn to spend a lot in the primary. "I look on this year as one continuous campaign and believe that my opposition has a common strategy, combining the two campaigns into a double header," Eckhardt wrote his backers.[28] Still, after the primary, the campaign fund was nearly dry, and fund-raising became a time-consuming part of the campaign.

The Democratic Primary

Complicating the political calculations was the matter of Senator Kennedy challenging President Carter for the presidential nomination. What was Eckhardt to do in that face-off? Ann Lower spoke with former Houston Mayor Fred Hofheinz, who was organizing for Kennedy. They advised that Eckhardt sign on as local cochair of the Houston reception for Rosalynn Carter in order to protect his legislation and not anger Carter supporters such as oilman Jack Warren, whose support Eckhardt would need in his election.[29]

Eckhardt and Lower learned that local judge John Ray Harrison was planning on running against Eckhardt in the primary, funded by money from George Brown, Walter Mischer, Houston oilmen, and Republicans.[30] Eckhardt's political and fund-raising activities, though, worked to deflate

Harrison's effort. When Jimmy Carter fired James Schlesinger as his energy secretary in 1979, he replaced him with Houston businessman Charles Duncan. At primary filing time in January 1980, it was Duncan's brother-in-law, Larry Washburn, who popped up as the candidate to run against Eckhardt. Secretary Duncan gave $1,000 to Washburn, an unheard-of slight from an administration that rhetorically supported the incumbent congressman.[31] Eckhardt was furious.

Washburn's big contributors were oilmen and doctors.[32] Indeed, he picked up people like Walter Mischer and developer Bob Perry, who had learned from Richard Viguerie the value of funding fights against Democratic incumbents in the primary in order to weaken them for the fall campaign.[33] Washburn's news releases read like they were straight out of the Republican and New Right machines.[34] After Washburn lost, Perry jumped right over to Fields's Republican campaign in the fall.

Jack Fields ran unopposed for the Republican nomination, but he joined in Washburn's rhetorical battle against Eckhardt. Fields had learned the New Right playbook and was practicing it. He preached the message: Eckhardt voted against tax cuts, against decontrol of energy, against voluntary prayer in schools, and for forced busing. Even his wife got into the game—the campaign sent out a regular "campaign update," supposedly written by Roni Sue Fields. These updates were peppered with such articles as "Eckhardt Backs Marxists," charging that "Eckhardt has voted recklessly to give our hard earned dollars to communist nations."[35] In one of the most bizarre exchanges of the campaign, Jack Fields even blasted Eckhardt for responding to a plea to help a critically injured constituent get an Air Force flight (no private flights were available) from Mexico to a hospital in the United States; he would use anything to get free press.

Washburn had no qualms about appealing to Republicans and encouraging Fields's supporters to cross over and vote for him. "Republicans fed up with Bob Eckhardt's free-spending, inflationary policies have an excellent chance to get rid of him by supporting me in the Democratic primary," he told voters. Ann Lower responded that his statement was evidence of "a strategy to dirty Eckhardt up in the primary and set him up for the general election."[36] Eckhardt spent a little more than $100,000 in the primary (twice what Lower had originally budgeted), and Washburn spent a little less than $100,000.

The one-two punch of Washburn's and Fields's broadsides was effective, but still not enough to defeat Eckhardt. Washburn won 43 percent of the vote. Clearly, there was a strong anti-Eckhardt sentiment in the district, with some of that vote coming from Republican crossovers. Districtwide, Eckhardt's margin was larger than his 1978 primary victory, but turnout was horrible.

He won the minority boxes overwhelmingly, but in the white boxes, with higher turnout, Eckhardt lost 46 percent to 54 percent. He had barely won Baytown in 1976, and now he lost it decisively, two to one. He had lost the white boxes to Joe Archer in 1978, too; it was the black boxes that pulled him to victory. In the 1980 primary, blacks just did not vote, their numbers dropping from 6,321 votes in those precincts in the 1978 primary down to 1,131 votes in 1980.[37]

At the victory party on primary night, lawyer and political financier Gaylen Nix tried to talk with Eckhardt about the fall campaign and was irritated that Eckhardt was too busy to talk with him. Nix soon called Washburn to try to persuade him to endorse Eckhardt. Then Nix wrote Eckhardt, warning "of the difficult contest which awaits you against Jack Fields. You must begin immediately."[38]

Eckhardt had started attending the state Democratic conventions in the 1940s. Now, in 1980, he returned and spoke to the delegates in San Antonio. "What's the bottom line on Eckhardt?" Maury Maverick Jr. wrote in his newspaper column during the convention. "In a nutshell here's Bob Eckhardt: 60 percent Sam Houston, 20 percent Judge Louis Brandeis, and 20 percent Adlai Stevenson. Then mix well with some Fredericksburg sausage, and when his Wurzbach cousins are not looking, throw in a jalapeño." Maverick reminded his readers, "In the days of Joe McCarthy I walked through a valley of fire with him. He did not turn tail."[39] Eckhardt clearly had an opportunity to pull in support from his many followers around the state. Yet, even at the convention, among the die-hard politicos ready for battle, Eckhardt could not shuck his role as legislative craftsman. His speech focused on the San Antonio and Texas railroad and coal issue that he was fighting in Congress during the spring and summer.

Meanwhile, Paul Weyrich reported that Washburn said more than half of his voters would support Fields. Weyrich wrote that Ann Lower had a strong organization and that her campaign "will be a real, gut Chicago ward operation if she feels she needs it."[40] Back in Houston, Fields issued a debate challenge. Eckhardt accepted the challenge on May 16, and the general election race was on.

Nuts and Bolts

Ann Lower had decided that an on-site campaign coordinator would not be needed during the summer; Fields, on the other hand, was going full blast. Rifts began appearing in Eckhardt's organization. Celia had never liked Ann, and she and others tried to convince Bob to bring in another campaign manager. But he had valued Ann's help for four years; he knew that she was well connected with Hofheinz, the women's caucus, and the state legislators she had helped elect; and he would not abandon her.

Celia pulled together a meeting to stoke a volunteer effort, believing that Ann had neglected it. She then wrote Bob and Ann that they needed to "reverse some very unpleasant feelings that have got entrenched about the Eckhardt campaign efforts." She sorted out personality battles and argued that Eckhardt needed professional consultation on his television appearances. Celia urged Bob to have neighborhood meetings, and suggested that her son David, fifteen-year-old Sarah Eckhardt, and even Rosalind and her four-year-old son Robert Stanley should be pulled in to campaign (and they were).[41] Ann was furious at Celia's intervention.

Ann did indeed set up an extensive volunteer recruitment effort, assigning block walking in September. She involved labor and political leaders as coordinators. The staff produced talking points for the block walkers on gun control, busing, and school prayer, and information about positive Eckhardt work.[42] Ann designed a mail program and contracted for polling, voter identification, direct mail, and a block captain program. The consultants projected turnout and, on that basis, predicted an Eckhardt victory of 58,860 (52 percent) to Fields's 53,455 (48 percent). The percentages ended up being in the ballpark, but predicted turnout was much lower than the actual turnout. The projections showed Fields winning big in Baytown and the northwest sections, Eckhardt winning big in the black communities, and the other areas splitting more evenly or producing very small vote totals.[43]

Thus, Eckhardt knew that he had to have a big turnout in the black community if he were to pull out a victory. As in his previous campaigns, he developed material for the black community showing pictures of himself with Mickey Leland, Andy Young, Ted Kennedy, and Jimmy Carter. Young, Leland, and California Congressman Ron Dellums came in and campaigned for him. Eckhardt's longtime supporter Reverend Floyd Williams coordinated activities in the black community. He lobbied his fellow black ministers to deliver the vote to the Democratic ticket, arguing that "any support of the Republican Party and its Candidates is a vote against the black people and other minorities."[44]

Eckhardt went to New York for the Democratic National Convention in August, then spent September in Washington, while Fields was blanketing the district with TV ads and working full time on his campaign. When he was in Houston, Eckhardt would do media interviews at the headquarters, decrying the "horrible mistake" the administration had made on decontrol: "What they did was the height of irresponsibility."[45] He complained about the "terrible burden" of legislating in Washington and having to campaign at home. Belatedly, the campaign started filming TV ads.

The Debate Debate

Bob Eckhardt had a reputation as an accomplished trial lawyer, with cross-examination skills honed in years of congressional committee work. Did the young, inexperienced Jack Fields really want to debate this highly knowledgeable congressional leader?

A debate can be a wild card in a campaign, sometimes working against a candidate. Voters like the idea of debates, though, and a refusal to participate can be used against a candidate. So, candidates often make it seem like they want to debate, then do everything they can to avoid it and blame the opposition for the lost opportunities. Fields played this game beautifully. Just as he had avoided debating on behalf of Nixon's presidential campaign at Baylor by simply walking off the stage, so now in 1980 he found a way to appear eager to debate while avoiding it for as long as he could.

Eckhardt accepted Fields's debate challenge seven days after he made it in May, but Fields told reporters that Eckhardt had never responded. Then when he was caught, he said that Eckhardt had not responded until five weeks later (even though reporters had Eckhardt's letter of May 16).[46] Fields's invitation was not so much a challenge to debate as it was an invitation for Eckhardt to tag along as a foil at Fields campaign stops; Eckhardt's acceptance wasn't so much an acceptance as an opening of negotiations over debate formats and rules. Fields wanted to control the audience and the questioners, so he suggested events in the white areas of the district, before groups that should be favorable to him, and with his community newspaper supporters as the questioners. Eckhardt lined up free TV time and suggested possible dates. But televised debates were not in Fields's campaign playbook. Why go on television in a risky debate, when you have hundreds of thousands of dollars to blanket the district in skillfully scripted TV ads?

Fields's justification for refusing to debate on television was weak, but it kept him in control: he argued that any debate should happen *inside* the district, and the television studios were *outside* the district. Yet, disingenuously, he taped his TV commercials outside the district, he traveled downtown to speak to the Young Republicans at the University of Houston campus, and he finally did join Eckhardt at a forum outside the district, downtown at the Houston Club, before the Houston Chamber of Commerce. Eckhardt confronted Fields there, telling him they should debate both ways—in the district *and* on TV. Fields said he might, "if it will fit my schedule."[47]

At the Chamber of Commerce gathering, Fields was electrifying, repeating his campaign slogan that Eckhardt "represents everything that is wrong with America," while he, Fields, stood for hope and opportunity. He used the New Right's opposition research to mold Eckhardt's votes to fit his message.

Fields supported the legislative veto to rein in the FTC and criticized Eck-hardt's leadership against it. In rebuttal, Eckhardt discussed his leadership in the 1975 energy legislation, using specific price figures and technical descrip-tions.[48] He could not, or did not, play the game that Fields was playing, and he came across as flat. Fields was clearly well coached, and perhaps should not have been so shy about debating.

The rest of the campaign was one of brinksmanship on the debate debate. A television station would schedule a meeting to discuss the particulars; the Fields campaign would call and postpone the meeting until later in the day, then call to cancel. Money continued to flow in, so the Fields campaign decided to stick with paid ads. Fields wouldn't firmly say no to a televised debate—that could be used against him—he just made it impossible to orga-nize the details. He would go to a candidate forum that was actually a cam-paign rally organized by his supporters, then blast Eckhardt for not showing up. The *Chronicle's* political editor wrote, though, that "Fields would appear to be the clear loser in the debate debate. He's allowed Eckhardt to shift at-tention away from his liberal voting record—his chief liability. And, Eckhardt has made Fields appear uncertain and less than adept."[49]

Yet, in another sense, Fields had won the chess game. Eckhardt was forced to go into forums that favored Fields, while Fields avoided forums in Eckhardt's territory. On October 7, they debated before the Baytown League of Women Voters, then later before Fields's media supporters, the Houston Community Newspapers, then at a forum at the Baytown Community Center, and then, on October 29, before the North Channel Area Chamber of Commerce. The audiences were stacked with people wearing green and white Fields buttons. Eckhardt "represents everything that is wrong with America," Fields would repeat, skillfully going through his panoply of characterizations. Before the League of Women Voters, Eckhardt spent all his opening time discussing one issue—busing. The questions from the audiences were hostile to Eckhardt. Fields did a great job of hammering away on his themes. Eckhardt spoke in policy details, and, after one debate, complained, "You can't talk about these issues in two minutes."[50]

Dirty Tricks

In October, the campaign battled the scam of a planted letter. Mark Florio of Vienna, Virginia, wrote a $5 check to Eckhardt with a letter praising him for supporting "school busing and gun control" and saying, "I'm proud that you have stood up and worked against all those new weapons systems in Congress . . . [and] fought to keep prayers out of the schools." Florio mailed it to the Fields headquarters, where staffers opened the letter, supposedly addressed to Eckhardt, and then dutifully sent out a news release "exposing" the contents. Only later did it come out that Florio was a staffer for Terry Dolan's Conservatives Against Liberal Legislation.

Fields then got publicity out of the affair by issuing a news release apologizing for his staff opening Eckhardt's mail about his "liberal voting record which I have publicized throughout my campaign."[51] Eckhardt held a news conference and requested a ruling from the attorney general on mail fraud. "Mr. Fields has either tampered with my mail illegally, or he has resorted to the crudest kind of gutter politics." He called it "a scurrilous and amateurish campaign trick . . . not even worthy of Nixon."[52] Mark Raabe put his investigatory skills to work and located Florio. The *Houston Post* got Florio on the phone. He lied and said he was a "moderate-liberal" just working for CALL as a job. But his roommate had not been alerted to what was going on and described Florio to the reporter as a conservative. The reporters also got Terry Dolan on the phone. Dolan admitted what he had been quoted as saying earlier, that the New Right "can lie through our teeth and get away with it."[53] But they got caught on this one. After the election, Raabe found Florio working for Newt Gingrich, with a Jack Fields bumper sticker on his car. Journalist Mark Shields wrote about the affair as an example of the dirty tricks that had helped the Right win the watershed elections.[54]

The Homestretch

Robert Sherrill wrote a cover story on Eckhardt's campaign, "A Texan vs. Big Oil," for the October 12, 1980, *New York Times Magazine,* and its publication brought letters and checks from around the nation. The election week issues of *Newsweek* and *Time* mentioned Eckhardt as being in great peril. Would he be able to turn it around?

Fields proved to be a great student of campaigning. He skillfully got community newspapers behind him, with front-page favorable coverage (after the election, one of the managing editors went to work for him). His campaign plied those papers with news releases—including those announcing that local mayors were endorsing Fields, even when they had not done so.[55] Fields charged that Eckhardt voted to spend tax money to promote Communism abroad and homosexuality at home! He also played his campaign to the Religious Right drumbeat, telling voters "that the Christian Voice rates [Eckhardt] a zero, the National Christian Action Coalition rates him an 11 out of a possible 100, and his votes on Christian issues are bad." Fields included as "Christian" issues busing, abortion, the New York City loan guarantee, school prayer, balancing the budget, and the B-1 bomber and MX missile. The campaign leafleted white evangelical church parking lots with the anti-Eckhardt pieces. Eckhardt responded that Fields's campaign "has a lot of the elements of the Know Nothing Party, offering demagogic, self-serving, how-am-I-served positions. The idea that just because one is in a majority the majority is moral, tramples everything underfoot. Our religious background in America points to compassion, love and concern." [56]

In May, the Fields campaign had written potential contributors that their budget was $509,000.[57] When Eckhardt and Ann Lower learned that, Eckhardt commented to the *New York Times* during the fall campaign that he expected Fields to spend $500,000. The Fields campaign knew that they faced a public relations problem if the campaign centered on how much money they were spending, or where it came from. Full of bluster, they demanded a retraction from the *New York Times,* saying it was not true that they would spend that amount. But the reporter had Fields's fundraising letter boasting of their budget, read it to them, and refused to retract the story, so they shut up.[58]

President Carter was clearly in trouble and campaigned hard across the nation. He came to Houston, where Eckhardt joined him in campaigning.[59] With the political winds blowing hot fires across the nation and the New Right close to big victories, money started flowing even faster to Fields. Houston oilman Jack Warren, a friend and supporter of Carter, had courted Eckhardt for years, and Eckhardt him. But Warren proved true to his earlier warning to Celia: "If you can't get Bob to vote with us, we're just going to have to beat him." He wrote a fund-raising letter with George Brown endorsing Fields "to beat Bob Eckhardt, the Texas ultra liberal." The letter enraged Eckhardt. Now Carter's Secretary of Energy *and* his chief Houston oil supporter were both campaigning against him. "Carter doesn't give a good [expletive] about anybody else in this election," he said. "In 1976, while Carter was losing Houston and surrounding Harris County, he won in my district. He should realize that if I lose, he's almost certain to lose the district and the rest of the county—the largest in the state." [60]

Late in the campaign, Sherrill wrote that Eckhardt's opposition had raised more money "than by any side in any previous Congressional election in Texas history." [61] In early October, Fields upped his budget to $700,000. Lower's polls confirmed that Fields's negative TV campaign was working, and Eckhardt was losing, 38 percent to 55 percent.

In the meantime, Eckhardt was still not on TV. When Congress finally adjourned, Eckhardt rushed home and went on the air with TV and radio ads pushing pocketbook issues and a campaign against Big Oil. Celia made calls around Washington, convincing Phil Burton, Mickey Leland, and others that Eckhardt was in trouble, and coaxing their support.[62] Several Eckhardt and subcommittee staff people took leaves of absence and spent October in Houston, joining an intense block-walking program. The tide started to turn, as evidenced in weekly polls throughout October.[63] But the damage of $1.5 million spent against Eckhardt over four years had taken its toll. As one reporter put it, Eckhardt's problem "may be that he has spent so much time and money fighting the brush fires ignited by Fields in the more conservative areas that he won't have enough of either to rally the black and Hispanic voters."[64]

Labor and Democrats also saw the disaster in the making and bore down intensely to save what they could, with intense late campaign fund-raising. Eckhardt's longtime core supporters were alarmed, and when Eckhardt finally got back to Houston full time in October, he too realized that he was losing. Eckhardt had resisted when Celia implored him to dismiss Ann Lower. He never did, but now he called Sam Dawson with the Steelworkers, told him that he knew he was losing, and asked him to come over and run the campaign. Ann Lower focused on fund-raising for the rest of the campaign, and Dawson ran the day-to-day operations. He rented a motel room next to the headquarters and spent three weeks doing nothing but the campaign. Dawson did not like what he saw—he did not believe that the campaign was well organized or that it was producing the necessary kind of material or outreach. And, though he and Eckhardt had been allies for years, they had a tense yelling match in which Dawson told him forcefully that his highbrow campaign mail-outs and his above-the-fray, professorial approach would not win the votes they needed. The next day, Eckhardt told him he thought it was right for him to stand up to him.

Dawson immediately called Jim Hightower to help, and together, they kicked the campaign into high gear. Eckhardt had come to know Hightower in Washington and had praised him on the floor of the House for his populist analysis of the agricultural industry. Hightower went home to Texas in 1976 when Ronnie Dugger hired him to be editor of the *Texas Observer*. Four years later, he quit and ran a dynamite campaign in the spring 1980 primary, nearly upsetting an incumbent Railroad Commissioner. Hightower set up shop at the Eckhardt headquarters, using his campaign organization, writing skills, and fund-raising network for Eckhardt. Dawson had the campaign mail-outs burned, and Hightower rewrote the materials in a more populist language. "The Big Money Boys are solidly behind Mr. Fields," he wrote.[65] They reoriented the campaign to one of Eckhardt standing up for consumers against greedy oil and gas giants. They drew in endorsements from city officials and industrial and agricultural shippers who had worked with Eckhardt on the rail rate battle.

The whole of the old Texas movement—the Democrats of Texas, the Texas Social and Legislative Conference, the *Observer*—and the national liberal community came out for Eckhardt. B. Rapoport helped bring in thousands of dollars. Maury Maverick wrote a column about Eckhardt's battle, pleading for people to come to La Villita for an Eckhardt fund-raiser that he and Dugger sponsored. Rapoport, Hightower, Maverick, Dugger, and Margaret Carter paid for a *Texas Observer* ad to whip up the old constituency, blasting the lobby and oil and gas for their high-dollar anti-Eckhardt campaign. Philanthropist Stewart Mott hosted a fund-raiser on Capitol Hill, aimed at congressional staffers and government officials "who've turned into fans" of Eckhardt.[66] Dominique de Menil hosted a fund-raiser for him at her Houston home, with Ron Dellums and others flying in for it. Bill Hobby also hosted a fund-raiser, and John Henry Faulk came in to emcee a fund-raiser. Just two days before the election, local official (and future mayor) Kathy Whitmire hosted a fund-raiser for him. Eckhardt raised $111,000 in the last two weeks alone—a phenomenal amount, though not enough to cover the burgeoning expenses, as he had to borrow about $50,000. Fields raised $150,000 in those last two weeks, upping his total spending to nearly $800,000. Eckhardt ended up spending a little more than $400,000.[67]

Fields brought in Gerald Ford, Ronald Reagan, George Bush, Jack Kemp, and John Connally to campaign for him. Connally, now thoroughly Republicanized, told voters "I don't know of any more worthwhile endeavor that anyone can undertake than to unseat Bob Eckhardt."[68] The Dallas office of the Chamber of Commerce wrote a letter, chortling about the turn of public opinion that they had helped orchestrate and fawning over Fields as "a friend of business who can win." The letter advised companies how to get around campaign finance limits and four ways to "legally" use corporate money and resources to help Fields, then cautioned, "Of course, you will want to consult with your attorneys before you undertake any of these political activities."[69] In a speech in Houston, C. William Verity, the chairman of Armco Steel and of the U.S. Chamber of Commerce, said that Eckhardt was at the top of their hit list.

Eckhardt had worked hard to solidify his support among sportsmen, knowing the power of the National Rifle Association. He got the fishermen lined up with him. He had cast votes on gun issues that he was sure would inoculate him with the NRA. But as militants took over the NRA in the late 1970s, Eckhardt's local support from sportsmen was effectively countered. The NRA Political Victory Fund paid $10,000 just ten days before the election for radio and newspaper ads for Fields (on top of $12,000 they had already spent). The NRA's Washington director flew to Houston to campaign for Fields.[70] The NRA wasn't the only one to independently spend against

Eckhardt. His old shell-dredging opposition came back to haunt him, as a shell dredger placed full-page newspaper ads against Eckhardt.

On the Democratic side, Willie Nelson came to Houston and performed a concert for Carter and the Democratic ticket. Eckhardt was there and sang a song for Willie, based on the sketch he had drawn earlier:

> O, Lord, it's hard to be humble
> when the profits continue to soar.
> So we changed our name to Exxon.
> And we'll never be Humble no more.

Ted Kennedy came in, too. He knew that his campaign against Carter had not only weakened Carter, but also the entire Democratic ticket. On a barnstorming tour in October, he whipped up the Democratic troops, asking labor gatherings and others to work for Carter and to vote a straight Democratic ticket. A Houston steelworkers meeting, billed as a Carter-Mondale rally, instead turned into an Eckhardt rally when Sam Dawson pulled Kennedy aside and told him how much trouble Eckhardt was in. Dawson took Eckhardt's oversized EK button and pinned it on Kennedy's coat. (Some reporters didn't get it and mocked Kennedy for wearing a heart-shaped button with his own initials on it.) Kennedy shared the stage with Eckhardt, with an Eckhardt poster on the podium and "Welcome Ted and Bob" behind the podium.[71] Eckhardt introduced Kennedy, who then praised Eckhardt. "I can think of no member of the Congress of the United States who is prepared to take on the big boys like Bob Eckhardt," Kennedy yelled, decrying that "he's been targeted by the major oil and gas companies."[72]

Ralph Nader campaigned for Eckhardt in the district, then went on *The Phil Donahue Show*, singing the praises of Eckhardt and his fight against big oil companies and warning that, as a result, he was in a great struggle for reelection. Sam Dawson conferred with Nader frequently, and several Nader's Raiders descended on Houston to help with the campaign.

Hightower's and Dawson's effort to tie Fields's campaign to the unpopular oil and gas giants began to work—the momentum (and polls) started shifting back. Fields claimed that he had received "less than $30,000 in oil company contributions and not the hundreds of thousands of dollars" claimed by Eckhardt. The Fields campaign said that "not more than 10 percent" of their funds were from the oil industry. Eckhardt charged that oil and gas was buying a congressman, prompting Fields to file a complaint with the Fair Campaign Practices Committee claiming that Eckhardt's charges were untrue! It was too much of a softball. Hightower, Dawson, and others quickly scrambled and put together visuals for the press. Eckhardt held a news conference with a giant blow-up board showing, name by name, the 68 Fields contributors from oil and gas company PACs, 143 oil and gas company executives, and 35 oil and gas-related business PACs and their executives. Combined, they contributed $276,000—58 percent of Fields's itemized totals reported by that date to the Federal Elections Commission.[73]

That was the last shot before the polls opened. Which campaign would the voters reward? Would Fields's 10–12 point lead in the last polls hold? Would Carter's floundering campaign drag Eckhardt, and others down, or would they survive even with Reagan winning? About midday on Election Day, Sam Dawson commented that the undecideds were breaking to the Republicans. And the electorate just wasn't interested. Turnout in the Eighth District went down slightly from 141,502 votes cast in 1976 to 140,777—but it was down in the blue collar areas and up in the more affluent northeastern sections.

Still, as they huddled at the campaign headquarters, the race was close as the boxes came in. Eckhardt had momentum, and it was clear that Fields's 10–12 point lead had evaporated. After midnight, Eckhardt lit a cigar. Could he close a gap of 4,000 votes? Seven boxes were still out. "When we get it down to six, it'll be like a revolver with a bullet in every chamber," he re-marked.[74] By 4:00 a.m., it was apparent that those boxes were not enough to pull him to shore. Fields won 72,856 votes (51.8 percent) to Eckhardt's 67,921 (48.2 percent). Eckhardt was the only Texas incumbent congressman to be defeated.

Eckhardt later told Studs Terkel, "I did everything wrong from the stand-point of present-day politics. I was opposing the most powerful interest in my district: oil. . . . As politics became more polarized and people began to take it for granted that you ought to represent the biggest power interest in your district, I got defeated."[75] He believed he could have won if he had not had the primary expense and battle.[76] In his post-election letter to his sup-porters, Eckhardt wrote:

> It has given me much comfort in the last weeks of the 1980 campaign and since to receive a flood of letters of support and contributions. . . . I have tried to represent my constituents truly and well but, in the last analysis, as Edmund Burke said, "Your representative owes you not his industry only, but his judgment." He thought, as I do, that a legislator betrays you if he sacrifices this to an existing electoral opinion. Perhaps, in the ebb and flow of political opinion, one who holds these principles inviolate may not ex-pect to survive in office more than 14 years. I enjoyed my 14-year stay in office, but do not intend to linger in the past and am looking forward to continuing the fight for those principles in another arena.[77]

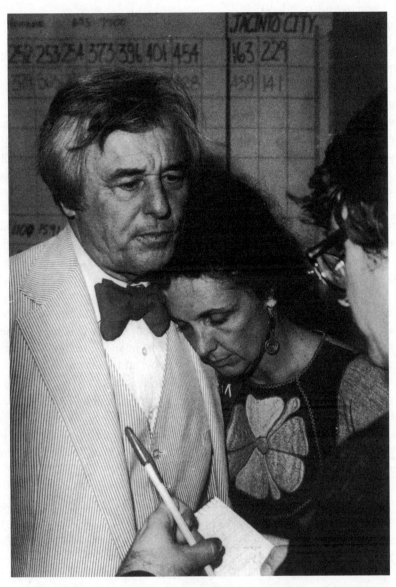

Bob and Celia Eckhardt, election night 1980. As the votes are tallied, the dispirited faces of Bob and Celia Eckhardt tell the story of his defeat. Courtesy of the Eckhardt family.

Cries of Anguish

The nation awoke the day after the 1980 election with many in a state of rapture and many others in a state of shock. Ronald Reagan had won the presidency (in Harris County, Carter garnered only 38 percent of the vote). The New Right had defeated so many of their Senate targets that Republicans won control of the Senate, and in the House, Eckhardt and thirty other longtime Democrats were gone. Celia wrote a bitter letter to the *Houston Post,* detailing the dirty tricks of Fields's campaign: "In the name of church and family, Mr. Fields ran the nastiest modern campaign I'd know of, with the possible exception of Richard Nixon's against Helen Gahagan Douglas." [78] The *Washington Post* printed an obituary on Eckhardt as Texas's political "snail darter" and included reproductions of six Eckhardt sketches. Dallas Congressman Jim Mattox told reporters that Eckhardt was the "social conscience" of the Texas delegation: "I think the worst part about it is the oil industry can basically say they beat a congressman." [79]

Congress came back to Washington for a lame duck session in December. It gave Eckhardt's colleagues a chance to say goodbye. But they did more than that. In a one-hour special order, arranged by Henry B. Gonzalez, they poured out their anguish and their admiration in speeches. Member after member praised Eckhardt as a man of principle and as one of the best and brightest members of Congress. Gonzalez said that Eckhardt was a seminal thinker in the legislative process, devoted to the greatest good for the greatest number. [80] Even Texas Republican Jim Collins said, "When he steps forward and goes to the well of the House to speak, you would think that Daniel Webster was again in the Halls of Congress." Pickle paid his old sparring partner the high compliment of naming him "the most qualified legislator in this Chamber. . . . His mind is as precise as his suits are rumpled. . . . To many people outside his district and even outside the State, Bob is regarded as their second Congressman. He has held a partnership with the interests of people and a love affair with the Constitution." Mickey Leland expressed his grief over "that gloomy night of November 4, 1980." He said, "Bob Eckhardt, for many years of my political life, was my mentor. . . . He leaves a legacy as a consummate constitutional authority and a supreme liberal strategist. Few can measure up to the heights of this man, this wonderful human being. . . . Thank you Bob Eckhardt . . . for being my standard, my friend, my brother." John Seiberling (D-Ohio) said that "it is the tall trees that draw the lightning," and that he would be replaced by a man "of lesser stature." An Eckhardt staffer penned an anonymous tribute: "Notwithstanding Jack Fields' complaint that you 'represented everything that's wrong with this country,' there are a large number of us who know you represented the best of this country." Claude

Pepper made an eloquent statement, saying that Eckhardt "would have been an equal with any of our past great, as a constitutional scholar, as a Member learned in the law, as a philosopher, as a political scientist, as a mellow man with distinctive dress, an especially gracious manner and charm. . . . It will be long before the glow of Bob Eckhardt's brilliant mind shall fade from this House."[81]

SEVENTEEN

Congressman Emeritus

From January 1981 until his death in November 2001, Robert Christian Eckhardt was no longer a voting member in the councils of government. But he still had his voice, and he spoke; he still had his pen, and he wrote; he still had his imagination, and he drew. He served for many years as a congressman-without-portfolio. After lawyering and lobbying for a while in Washington, he returned to Austin, back to Scholz's, Barton Springs, and his family and friends. He explored his German-Texas family history, helped defend his Open Beaches Act, and wrote presciently about constitutionalism and current events. He reengaged with his family on an emotional level that was deeper than when he was so focused on lawyering and legislating.

As Congressman Pepper had predicted, Eckhardt was, indeed, missed in the halls of the Capitol. Three years after his defeat, a congressional staffer wrote, "I watched every speech you made on the floor and took special pains to be in the gallery when I knew you were going to speak. Your grace under fire, your knowledge of the Constitution and your attention to the issues inspired many young staffers in the late seventies and continue to influence our work every day. The Congress is not the same without you."[1]

In those years after Congress, he continued to win acknowledgement for his years of public service. In 1981, the American Ethical Union awarded Eckhardt its annual John Lovejoy Elliott-Algernon Black Award "for his civic courage as defender of the United States Constitution and protector of the well being of the common people and his resistance to the pressures of powerful special interest groups."[2] In 1984, the Houston Sierra Club hosted Eckhardt as their honoree. In 1997, Texas Land Commissioner Garry Mauro established the Bob Eckhardt Lifetime Coastal Achievement Award. The Texas Chapter of the Surfrider Foundation established a Robert Christian Eckhardt Memorial Scholarship in honor of his open beaches advocacy. In 2002, shortly after his death, the *Texas Observer* placed Eckhardt's name permanently on its masthead and established the Bob Eckhardt Investigative Journalism Fund.

Those last two decades of his life started, though, with coming to terms with the nation's political turn to the Right.

Aftermath of a Defeat

Back in Texas, political leaders and citizens alike adjusted to the new realities. The 1981 session of the Texas legislature got underway with a commendatory resolution for Eckhardt. A few weeks later, Eckhardt and Yarborough got standing ovations at a Bernard Rapoport/Jim Hightower affair. As for the Eighth District of Texas, it got a complete turnaround in representation. Whereas Eckhardt earned 100 percent ratings from Americans for Democratic Action, Fields got 5 percent. And it stayed that way for a long time. In the 1980 campaign, Fields blasted Eckhardt for being in Congress for fourteen years and promised that he would only serve two terms.[3] He served sixteen years.

Immediately after the shock of his defeat, Eckhardt realized that he had about eight weeks to finish projects that were near and dear to him. His subcommittee staff quickly pushed out a host of reports. Eckhardt produced his final *Quarterly Report.* Entitled "The Tragic Error," it was a broadside at the Federal Reserve Board and Carter for ruining the economy. It was an encapsulation of his congressional era of the late 1970s. "In short," he wrote:

> President Carter's accelerated decontrol of oil was very inflationary, and the inflationary impact hit the poor and the median-to-lower income brackets much more heavily than it did those above the median.... To these Americans the situation of the 1980s looked grim indeed. Their real incomes were cut. Since high interest rates especially impact particular sectors such as housing, their prospects for planning a secure family establishment were blasted. Is it any wonder that the American public was at the time of the 1980 election disillusioned and cynical? Where was the "Great Society" Lyndon Johnson promised? The great expectations of the early '70s sank into the slough of the Vietnam War, and people concluded that government could not deliver. The Nixon fiasco convinced them that government had no intention of delivering for them but only for itself. Government existed only to maintain and expand its own power—that was the message of Watergate. The Carter Administration was amateurish and inept.[4]

Ronald Reagan immediately ended price and allocation controls on crude oil, gasoline, and propane, foreshortening by eight months Carter's decontrol. Dr. Lower analyzed the Carter and Reagan decontrols, decrying "the structural distortions and massive redistribution of income engendered by the sudden run-up of crude oil prices.... The redistribution of corporate profits from the rest of manufacturing industry to energy companies poses serious problems for the allocation of investment, economic growth, productivity, and further inflation."[5] But Eckhardt's and Lower's critical analyses of the nation's economic direction were now shelved. The nation sunk into its deepest recession since the Great Depression, before rebounding in time for the 1984 presidential election.

Eckhardt's campaign debt of nearly $50,000 would hang over his head for years. His loyal staff and volunteers plugged away at retiring it. In spring 1981, Ted Kennedy and Morris Udall hosted a fund-raising "roast" for Bob in Washington, attracting more than five hundred to Stewart Mott's house.[6] Ralph Yarborough couldn't come, but wrote a passionate letter:

> Texas has never had a better Congressman in the history of this State, and your service in Washington ranked you as among the top in the Nation. . . . It was bought away from you just as my seat in the Senate was bought from me in 1970. We each had become Chairman of powerful committees and in doing our duty there, we failed to have enough time to protect our flanks in Texas. I am grateful and proud for your great services. Sit down and write about it; enumerate it before you forget it, while you still have it fresh on your mind. Tell the world, tell us about it. Let Texas and the Nation know that there was once a Congressman from Texas.[7]

By 1983, Eckhardt still had $20,000 in campaign debts. J. Edwin Smith would file the official reports and implore Eckhardt to work with him on it, but Eckhardt was lackadaisical. "Do you realize that since your defeat I've had no word from you whatsoever," Smith wrote two years after the election. "What gives?"[8] Smith, exasperated, finally resigned as treasurer and Chris Dixie took over. Eckhardt would periodically sit down and write letters appealing for contributions. He finally wrote J. R. Parten, asking futilely for help. Eckhardt wrote that he had not wanted to ask Parten for money in 1980 because they had come to disagree on oil and gas. But now, "I know we have been very much together in issues that I believe we both think are much more important than oil or balanced budgets or regulation and deregulation—issues such as Viet Nam, slowing the arms race, and preventing the permanent poisoning of the country with nuclear waste."[9]

Congressman Without Portfolio

After wrapping up his congressional office, Eckhardt had to decide what to do. He had been away from Houston labor law practice for fourteen years. His contacts now were in Washington. So, like many ex-congressmen, he stayed on there. Charles Black tried to help him get on with Washington law firms. Within months, he became Of Counsel to the McCarthy, Spencer, Sweeney, & Harkaway Law Firm. There, he provided legal services to clients, but his chief value was in legislative advice and lobbying. He had been so close to the Consumer Federation of America that they hired Ann Lower as their associate director and Eckhardt as a consultant on energy. Milton Lower stayed on with the O&I Subcommittee, now chaired by John Dingell.

Bob Eckhardt was still in demand as a speaker. He would ride the train to New Haven and teach at Yale Law School; he and Celia lectured at Hampshire College in Massachusetts; he continued to lecture at the Brookings Institution's seminars; and he spoke around the nation on toxic substances, consumer protection, energy policy, and congressional politics. A year after his defeat he served, with the new powers in Washington, on an energy symposium panel. Texas Congressman Phil Gramm relished the chance to match wits with Eckhardt, "clearly the most articulate spokesman for evil on [natural gas deregulation]." New Energy Secretary James Edwards asked Eckhardt to sign the doodle he had sketched of him.[10]

Eckhardt often found himself in the Capitol testifying, by invitation of his former colleagues, who were interested in his constitutional analysis and in buttressing their cases against Republican colleagues. Max Baucus (D-Mont.) served as the ranking minority member of the Republican-controlled Senate Judiciary Committee's Subcommittee on Separation of Powers. In 1981, they were considering a bill to overturn the effect of *Roe v. Wade,* and Baucus wrote Eckhardt: "I am writing to you in your capacity as a leading expert on American constitutional law," asking for his assessment of the constitutional authority for Congress to so act.[11] Later that same year, he was back before the Subcommittee testifying on an amendment to restrict judicial jurisdiction in school busing. He followed and countered arch-conservative UT Law Professor Lino Graglia on points of constitutional interpretation, then engaged in a debate with North Carolina Republican Senator John East on the role of courts in the governmental system.[12]

In 1982, he testified on natural gas issues to his former colleagues on the renamed Energy and Commerce Committee. He pooh-poohed the testimony of an industry representative with his supposed concern for the poor by describing to the committee Mark Twain's "Hyde v. Morgan" case, where the court agreed that one side made sense—and the observer then knows that the court was going to decide for the other side.[13] Eckhardt also continued to write legislation. He worked with Congressman Seiberling, writing a bill on railroad regulation. Though it did not pass, it helped build the pressure that forced the opening of some rail lines, and he wrote a detailed article on the battle.

After the debacle of 1980, Democrats pressed electoral reforms. Republicans, now in charge in the Senate, were understandably hostile to the proposals. Eckhardt worked with the Committee for the Study of the American Electorate on a "Truth in Political Ads" project to require a candidate's voice and image to be in an ad. He testified before the House Task Force on Elections, recounting his electoral history and blasting the new world of campaign consulting. "Incumbent congressmen *are* warped by the demagogy used against them. They *are* corrupted by the need for money to conduct expensive counter campaigns. During their tenure they *are* diverted from legislative duties by the fear of the next election. . . . Thus money has dehumanized politics."[14] He was determined to raise a cry against the electoral system that had done him in. Politics, he told the *Houston Chronicle,* "have institutionalized and made respectable a series of sellouts to single-interest groups. Computer devices send information to every single interest group about how you supported them last week. Finally, your opponents pick up a composite of special interest and minority groups who make up a majority. That unfortunately is what our representative system is descending into."[15]

By 1986, Eckhardt was restless. "I'm beginning to get a little tired of lobbying," he wrote, "and would like to do a little more writing and teaching. . . . The more one moves into the business of selling a bill, always with some tacit promise of reward, the less congenial the process is to my preferences."[16] His relationship with Celia had completely broken down, too, and friends suggested that perhaps it was time to go back to Austin.

Heading Home to Austin

Just as Bob had fallen passionately in love with Nadine in the early 1960s, so in 1976 and 1977, he had fallen passionately in love with Celia. Celia was writing a biography of the nineteenth-century feminist and abolitionist Fannie Wright, and Bob was proud of her work.[17] He wrote to Elmo and Jenny Hegman, the Austin friends whose parties had inspired young Lawyer Eckhardt to verse ("Oh, what Elysium, Hegman's Kitchen!"), describing Fannie Wright and telling them that he wanted them to meet Celia.[18] But theirs was a stormy relationship. Celia was disgusted with him for the divorce arrangement he had negotiated with Nadine. Then, once they moved in together, she quickly learned that Bob kept his domestic affairs, both physical and financial, in a shambles. "If he was not a class five hurricane," she wrote, "he was at least a three." His procrastination also antagonized her, as when he did not put the time or money into remodeling their kitchen.[19]

Celia demanded that he clean up his living environment and straighten up his financial affairs—including selling the land in Houston. When Bob did not, she moved out and they maintained two residences, occasionally spending the night at each other's place. In the early years after Congress, they spent two years in therapy, got back together, then separated; they would reinvigorate their love, then lose it again.

Eckhardt's health since his 1978 heart surgery was shaky. His doctor told him he had to cut back his drinking to no more than one drink a day. So, he would fill the tallest glass he had with his scotch or his wine and drink that one drink! On the night of April 2, 1987, after he drank too much, he could sense that something was wrong. He had a stroke and was rushed to the hospital. His left side was paralyzed, and he lost his speech. Friends, family, and former aides hurried to Washington to his side. Ronnie Dugger came in. Celia, Orissa, and Rosalind were there. His brother Norman came, playing his flute at the bedside. Bob experienced the frustration of not being able to communicate. He tried to talk, and no one could understand him. The left-handed Eckhardt would hold a pen with his right hand and try to draw what he wanted to communicate, in a charades-like game. He was amazed to find that he could so quickly learn to draw right-handed. He wanted to get word to Don Kennard, in Harpers Ferry, West Virginia, but he couldn't come up with Kennard's name. In his frustration, he sketched out a drawing of John Brown and Harpers Ferry and a train track and wrote "A long way" on it. Celia and the others finally guessed what he was trying to tell them, and they got hold of Kennard. Nadine wrote from Austin, "I'm thinking of you a lot and visualizing your full recovery. I guess one never really stops loving someone who has been in one's life so long. You are a wonderful person, Bob, and the love from your daughters and all the women in your life will help your recovery." [20]

In the months of his recovery, Celia was very kind to him, helping to care for him. She and Gloria Cochran went through his mess at home, trying to sort out his finances. Soon, though, Bob and Celia's differences returned, and she returned to her apartment. Former staff aides would come by his house to help. His doctor told him that it would be good therapy for him to revisit his drawings and writings in an effort to get back his memory and his speech. So, they spread out a supply of his sketches. Milton Lower picked one up and recognized it as a caricature of a UT math professor from the 1930s to 1950s. "Is that Co-Sine Red!?" he asked. Eckhardt stared at it and a look of recognition came across his face. "Why, yes!" he replied. [21] He was on the way back. His speech returned, though never to full capacity. He could not regain his oratorical splendor.

His friends decided to make one last push to help him get on his feet financially. Long-time campaign aide Jocelyn Gray organized a fund-raiser at Scholz's Beer Garden and Saengerrunde Hall in Austin on September 11, 1987. Molly Ivins emceed, with help from John Henry Faulk, Maury Maverick, Don Kennard, and others. The effort worked: Eckhardt was finally able to settle his debt.

Back in Washington, Bob finally decided that he did not want to stay in his nonrelationship with Celia, so he initiated divorce proceedings. Celia was furious, but the divorce was finalized in May 1988, with Celia getting the house. He still liked Celia very much, though he also knew that she vented her rage in letters to their friends. The two of them never spoke to each other again.

Eckhardt, ever his cheap self, wandered Washington and found a basement apartment. He took Don Kennard to see it, and Don was alarmed at the rundown and potentially dangerous neighborhood and at the shabby abode. He persuaded Eckhardt instead to rent a house jointly (with occasional roommates), so that Eckhardt would have a nicer place to live and Kennard would have a city place to stay when he came in from Harpers Ferry for his lobbying work. So, Bob resumed his disheveled bachelor lifestyle, meticulously labeling and filing papers and odds and ends, yet making a mess of their new place with his food and clothes habits. Sometimes, Bob would take the train out to Harpers Ferry, where he would search for field corn—he had a way of judging whether it was just to the right point of ripeness or not—and push it through his corn scraper, getting silk and flecks of corn all over his sweater and overalls.[22] Bob invited Julya to Washington, seeing her for the first time since the early 1960s, and they went out to the Kennards. She marveled that Bob, "a hapless male creature, who looks like he does not belong in a kitchen at all, can produce fresh orange juice with noteworthy ease and dispatch."[23]

As the 1980s ended, Eckhardt was persuaded by friends that, especially with his stroke, his lawyering and lobbying days were over. So, he returned to Austin. There, he bought a house that Tommy Sutherland's family had lived in near downtown, complete with a giant live oak in which he built a tree house. He would sit in the tree house, sipping his whiskey, reading, writing, and conversing. It was there that we had conversations about his life and this book.

Humor

Historians have already discovered Bob Eckhardt's cartooning. George Norris Green included three of Eckhardt's 1940s and 1950s cartoons in *The Establishment in Texas Politics;* Maury Forman and Robert A. Calvert published *Cartooning Texas,* with three selections from Eckhardt's work.[24] In retirement, Mr. Hyde still made his appearances, often coaxed out by the outrages of the Reagan era. In 1981, Eckhardt penned a classic cartoon on Reagan's tax cut plan for the *Washington Star.* Similar to his 1940s *Texas Spectator* cartoons, this drawing showed Big Oil as an auctioneer selling the shackled Texas congressional delegation, with Reagan and Ways and Means Chairman Dan Rostenkowski as the bidders.[25] With the severe recession in the Reagan years and the resulting rise in homelessness, Congress and the nation debated what

Eckhardt family at his cartoon exhibit, 1996. Retired in Austin, Bob Eckhardt turned over his papers to the Center for American History at the University of Texas at Austin. In 1996, the Center sponsored a six-month exhibit of Eckhardt's cartoons and sketches. His family joined him at the opening of the exhibit in November 1996. Pictured with him are Rosalind and her daughter Summer, Sarah, Orissa, Nadine, and Sidney. Courtesy of the Eckhardt family.

to do about this issue. Eckhardt drew a sketch of a homeless person sleeping on a grate across from the White House, and wrote an accompanying poem ("Home, Home on the Grate").

Eckhardt loved playing with words as well as pictures. In 1984, he supported his friend Walter Mondale in his race against Gary Hart for the Democratic presidential nomination. "I have read the polls this morning," he wrote to Mondale, "and, to be sure, they show us the magnitude of our task. But they also tell us something about how we may master it. So don't be discouraged, Fritz; take Hart!"[26] In 1989, he couldn't help but spoof the goings-on for a constitutional amendment to ban flag burning, writing a great satirical piece, "A Report of the President on Flag Burning, Office of Flag Licensing and Incineration Prevention."[27] By the 1990 Texas gubernatorial campaign, Eckhardt was supporting Ann Richards against Republican oilman Clayton Williams. He wrote an op-ed piece for the *Houston Post* to counter their endorsement of Williams, then he skewered Williams's gaffes in a cartoon published in both the *Texas Observer* and the *Houston Post*. Finally, in 1996–1997, the University of Texas hosted an exhibit of Eckhardt's cartoons and sketches.[28]

Of Constitutions, Wars, and Presidents

Eckhardt did not write his congressional life story that Yarborough urged him to write. Instead, he wrote manuscripts, articles, and book chapters on energy policy, on presidential authority, on congressional government, and on Reaganism. In 1989, he wrote two articles defending Jim Wright, who was by then Speaker and under attack. Eckhardt wrote that the press engaged in character assassination, similar to a matador delivering the coup de grace to the crippled bull.[29]

As Eckhardt watched Reagan's foreign policy bellicosity, he would write about it, criticizing Reagan on the Lebanon fiasco and other misadventures. After the *Chadha* decision upheld his view of the unconstitutionality of a one-house legislative veto, he was concerned about the possibility of it being used to further marginalize the War Powers Act. He wrote an article defending the congressional resolution in the War Powers Act as being different from the one-House veto that *Chadha* had rightly thrown out; he also wrote that the only real power Congress has to back up its war powers is the impeachment process.[30]

Eventually, Eckhardt developed his thinking on the broader issue of constitutional restraints on abuse of power. In his last years in Washington, he wrote a book-length manuscript titled *Why Not Try the Constitution?* He wrote a friend saying, "Originally, I had almost finished it; but, of course, there's a long space between the cup and the lip, and I think the book is too much of a diatribe against Reagan and becomes dated."[31] Thus, he revised it extensively. He and Ronnie Dugger tried to push the revised manuscript to publication, but did not succeed.

It did not matter to Bob Eckhardt whether presidential war making was by a Republican or a Democrat—he believed fervently in a strong congressional role. He was convinced in the Clinton years that Clinton "is in violation of the War Powers Act."[32] Later, he was relieved to find that Clinton recognized the need to go to Congress to introduce troops into Bosnia, but he thought it wrong that Clinton had tried to avoid that question, wanting to wait until after he had gone in, then go to Congress. He argued that Clinton could have carried the decision in Congress and then been able to send in troops, to protect the safe havens.[33]

Out of all this came a new large manuscript on presidential war making powers, reviewing the whole of twentieth-century wars and the presidential-congressional determinations on war, though he never completely finished it. In 1999, he wrote then-Texas Governor George W. Bush, perhaps hoping that he was planting a seed for a future president, describing some of the history of presidents and Congress on war: "we have ignored this fundamental constitutional requirement and the War Powers Act. In the coming century our presidents will recognize these constitutional and legal concepts, if you shall be elected." [34]

The Lion in Winter

In Eckhardt's retirement years, he continued to travel and made new, loyal friends around the nation and beyond. He would occasionally get back to his log cabin in Houston or go to San Antonio to visit his centenarian cousin Emily Wurzbach (Mickler). He would ride his bicycle to Barton Springs, where he had swum eighty years earlier as a boy. On his birthday in 1998, when he turned 85, the Austin City Council approved an ordinance authorizing a free lifetime pass for Barton Springs to Eckhardt. Austinites, including his stepson Willie, would frequently see him there and stop to talk. Sarah, Nadine, Sidney, and Shelby returned to Austin and saw him frequently. He would visit Orissa in New Orleans and bicycle around the city, outriding his daughter and her friends. Or he would visit Rosalind in Colorado, riding her horses and spending hours mending fences.

He rejoined Morris Akin and many of his old labor allies in a convention of retired CIO leaders in 1992.[35] When he read the news and felt the urge to implore congressional action, he would go to the *Observer* offices a few blocks away and use their fax machine to send his analysis to his former congressional colleagues or administration officials. He kept up with Ronnie Dugger and other old *Observer* colleagues and was lauded at *Observer* affairs, including sharing the head table with Kennedy and Yarborough. There were funerals and memorial services to attend, of course, including John Henry Faulk's in 1990 and Ralph Yarborough's and Fred Schmidt's in 1996. Eckhardt would talk with visitors in his tree house. Journalist Jan Reid interviewed him there, writing a *Texas Monthly* article about "The Last of a Breed," with a photo of Eckhardt peering down from his tree house, cigar in hand.[36] Bob and Julya rode out into the Texas Hill Country in 2001, where they picnicked and sipped wine while taking in the panoramic views.

Bob Eckhardt died of a stroke on November 13, 2001, with Sarah and Julya by his side in the hospital, not far from 2300 Rio Grande, not far from the University of Texas, not far from the Texas capitol, where he once roamed the halls as a giant. He was buried in Austin alongside his father, Joseph Eckhardt, and his mother, Norma Wurzbach Eckhardt. At his memorial service in Washington three months later, his staffers eulogized him. Al Gore spoke passionately about the humor and intellectual leadership that Eckhardt had brought to Congress.

Afterword

Bob Eckhardt lived another twenty years after his 1980 defeat. If he could have escaped his narrow defeat in 1980, what would have happened a few months later when the Texas legislature met to redistrict? Texas gained three congressional seats, the legislature was still Democratic, and Bill Hobby was still in charge of the Senate. Conceivably, Eckhardt could have fashioned a district that would have kept him in office through much of the 1980s. But he would likely have been miserable in the new atmosphere. In his interview with Studs Terkel, he said that he had been beaten by an overwhelming abundance of twenty-second television spots. "A record of twenty-two years in an elective office in essentially the same district can be overwhelmed in three months." He reflected on the new era and political style: "Political advisers have learned that if they use generalities and get them fixed in people's minds, they'll win. People remember Big Government and forget big crooks."[1] In a 1984 interview with Chandler Davidson, Eckhardt said, "I think that so much that happens is more or less accidental, and a lot of it is just a question of a kind of predilection by people in a certain direction, which may lead them to rather clever tricks, or it may lead them to absolute disaster . . . what I call stragedy. . . . All progress moves on great strides of stupidity."[2]

Eckhardt fully understood the frailties of even his beloved legislative institutions. As he told Charles Black, "It always makes me shiver a little bit when I see a court say 'Congress in its wisdom has done so-and-so,' and I remember walking from the Longworth Building to the House Floor to vote, asking someone on the way, 'What is this amendment?'"[3] But Eckhardt's was primarily a world of faith in government and politics. "I have never believed . . . that we can promote the general welfare and extend human rights by a *less active,* as opposed to a *more effective* government," he said shortly after his defeat. We need "a *more* active promotion of the general welfare, not less."[4]

Did he accomplish as much as he could have? No. Eckhardt had monumental achievements with very real impacts—the Open Beaches Act, the Toxic Substances Control Act, his contribution to the War Powers Act, auto safety requirements, the preservation of the Big Thicket. But Bob Eckhardt could have been more. Had he been aggressive enough, had the era of liberalism gelled again, as it did in 1932 and in 1958, he could have been a senator, governor, and yes, even president, and with those more powerful positions, he could have changed the system as a Hogg, a Roosevelt, and an Allred did.

Why did he not? Partly himself, and partly the system. Here political science and biography come together. He could have contributed more even staying in the House, but the system was listing rightward and cast him off. Though he was a tremendous resource for the American political system, he needed, as he observed, a wide margin of safety, because he was aligned against the society's power centers. And by the late 1970s, that margin of safety was gone. He could be a good politician, leading the ticket, appealing to people and their better nature. He was a superior person, and his peers knew it. Voters knew it. But sometimes we turn to those who shout to our baser nature, and the nation did that in 1980 and beyond.

Eckhardt's world of progressive politics slipped away in the waning years of the twentieth century. In the never-ending battles between competing power centers, the populist and labor power center from which Eckhardt emerged (all the way back to Jim Hogg and William Jennings Bryan) lost out to the Establishment power center. Jim Hightower and others carried the battle forward for awhile in the 1980s, but the new Republican Establishment power center wiped them out quickly. Populism, progressivism, and liberalism would have to await a new day in the twenty-first century. There are always signs of movement one way or the other; 1994 sent the nation surging farther right for a decade, yet by 2006, George W. Bush's popularity vanished and the nation became appalled and disgusted with the new order. And in that year, Sarah Eckhardt won an election in Austin. Perhaps . . . perhaps.

In *Lateral Thinking,* Edward De Bono wrote that we too often miss the alleyways and detours of life.[5] Bob Eckhardt explored those alleyways. He was always more than just politics. He was a keen observer of his world, detouring off into antique shops, into cathedrals, into books, into new relationships. He reveled in his world through his imagination and storytelling, his cartoons, his writing, and his traveling. Early in his electoral career, he wrote that we should celebrate "a reverse Lent," when people would "embrace all that is most happy-making, a time of shucking off, if but for a short while, artificial busy-work like politics and law and business, a time for pilgrimages."[6] He knew that, to be a public character, he had to guard his inner self. In politics, he wrote after his very first victory, he had to "block that unguarded door of the imagination. I've blocked it in the campaign. I pass out these little cards and brochures and say 'good morning,' 'how are you today,' 'may I give you one of my folders,' 'thanks.' But the door leaks a little."[7] In his retirement, he wrote to a friend, remembering his European trips during his congressional years:

> I want to go to Rothenburg and Tauber and once more gaze at noon day (as has been done for some four hundred years) at the opening of the wooden doors high over the Rathhaus. I'd like again to see the Burgermeister and the victorious Catholic general who held the town forfeit on the wager that the Burgermeister could drink down the giant flagon. Then I would watch that wooden figure raise his clock-work arm to drain the great flagon to win the bet and save the Protestant town of Rothenburg. Away with all this modern, partisan foppery![8]

Still, Lyndon Johnson and Albert Thomas were right: Bob Eckhardt was born to be a congressman. Despite partisan foppery, and perhaps because his imagination did leak through the door between private life and public life, Eckhardt was the best congressman that Texas had produced since Maury Maverick's brief Washington sojourn in the 1930s. More than that, he was, for many years, America's Second Congressman. As Ralph Yarborough wrote with passion, there once was, indeed, a true Congressman from Texas.

Robert Christian Eckhardt:
A Chronology

1913.   Born July 16 to Joseph Carl Augustus Eckhardt, M.D. and Norma Wurzbach Eckhardt (sister of San Antonio Congressman Harry Wurzbach and State Representative William Wurzbach).

1931.   Graduated Austin High School, where he was humor editor of the *Comet*.

1931–1935.   Undergraduate pre-med major, University of Texas.

1935–1939.   Law student, University of Texas (LLB, 1939). Lost student body president election to (future congressman) J. J. "Jake" Pickle, whose campaign manager was (future governor) John Connally. Served as editor of the *Texas Ranger,* 1937–1938. Muralist, including mural at Hillbilly Café on the Drag.

1939.   Established law practice in Austin with Creekmore Fath and Clay Cochran.

1940.   Ran losing campaign for state legislature from Austin.

1942.   Married Orissa Stevenson. Enlisted in Air Corps (1942–1944).

1944–1945.   Published cartoons in *State Observer.*

1944–1946.   Worked for Nelson Rockefeller's Office of Inter-American Affairs (OIAA).

1945–1948.   Produced cover art for *Texas Spectator* under pseudonym "Jack o' Diamonds."

1946.   Daughter Orissa born. Named Travis County Coordinator for Homer Rainey for Governor campaign and was a founding member of People's Legislative Committee.

1946–1947.   Consulted for Texas Good Neighbor Commission.

1946–1951.   One of the founders, executive committee member, and chair, Texas Social and Legislative Conference (TS&LC).

1947.   Daughter Rosalind born.

1947–1958.   Lobbied for the CIO.

1948.   Moved to Dallas and served as attorney for Oil Workers International Union in Fort Worth, then for Communication Workers of America in Dallas.

1950.   Moved to Houston. Practiced law with Chris Dixie, Thomas Ryan, Meyer Jacobson, Al Schulman, Ed Ball. Formed partnership: Ryan, Eckhardt, and Adams.

1952.   Led bolting delegation from the Harris County Democratic Convention, chaired credentials committee of bolting delegation at the San Antonio state Democratic convention, and campaigned for Ralph Yarborough for governor.

1953.   Joined Lake Buchanan gathering that led to formation of Democratic Organizing Committee, which Sam Rayburn reformed to Democratic Advisory Council.

1954.   Helped found the *Texas Observer* and contributed cartoons and artwork. Campaigned for Yarborough for governor.

1956.   Keynoted the Harris County Democratic Convention. Helped organize Democrats of Texas. Campaigned for Yarborough for governor.

1957.   Campaigned for Yarborough for U.S. Senate.

1958.   Chaired Harris County Democrats. Elected to Texas House of Representatives.

1959.   Passed the Texas Open Beaches Act.

1961.   Divorced from Orissa Eckhardt. Appointed chair of Criminal Jurisprudence Committee.

1962.   Married Nadine Ellen Cannon Brammer (children: Sidney, Shelby, and Willie).

1964.   Daughter Sarah born.

1966.   Elected to Congress.

1968.   Joined Members of Congress for Peace Through Law.

1970.   Ralph Yarborough defeated for Senate reelection.

1972.   Passed the Automobile Bumper Safety Act.

1974.   Won passage of the Big Thicket National Preserve. Awarded the National Recreation and Parks Associations' National Congressional Award.

1975.   Elected chair of the Democratic Study Group.

1976.   Passed the Toxic Substances Control Act. Published *The Tides of Power: Conversations on the American Constitution,* with Professor Charles Black, a lifelong friend and former Austinite. Divorced from Nadine Eckhardt.

1977.   Elected chair, subcommittee on Consumer Protection and Finance (House Interstate and Foreign Commerce Committee). Married Celia Morris (son: David Morris).

1978.   Underwent heart bypass surgery. Won Consumer Federation of America's Philip Hart Public Service Award. Served on conference committee that produced Natural Gas Policy Act.

1979.   Elected chair of Subcommittee on Oversight and Investigation (House Interstate and Foreign Commerce Committee).

1980.   Listed by columnist Jack Anderson as one of the fifteen most effective members of Congress. Defeated for reelection to Congress.

1981.   Taught, on fellowship, at Yale University. Joined firm of McCarthy, Spencer, Sweeney, & Harkaway.

1987.   Suffered stroke.

1989.   Moved back to Austin.

2001.   Died November 13, in Austin.

Notes

Introduction

1. Letters from Maury Maverick Jr. to Nadine Eckhardt, August 5, 1966, March 15, 1967, in Nadine Eckhardt Personal Papers, Folders: 1966 and 1967.

2. Willie Morris, "Legislating in Texas," *Commentary* 38, no. 4 (November 1964): 44.

3. Letter from Ralph Yarborough to Bob Eckhardt, April 29, 1981, in Bob Eckhardt Personal Papers, Box 1 (Persons), Folder: Yarborough.

4. Jack Anderson and Tony Capaccio, "Jack Anderson Rates the Congress," *The Washingtonian,* October 1980; Robert Sherrill, "A Texan vs. Big Oil," *New York Times Magazine,* October 12, 1980.

5. "Political Profile: Harris' Eckhardt," *Texas Observer,* June 15, 1962.

6. "Political Profile: Harris' Eckhardt."

1. The German Texas Pioneers

1. Glen E. Lich, *The German Texans* (San Antonio: University of Texas Institute of Texan Cultures, 1981), 22, 44; Annelies Schlickenrieder, "German Texan Ethnicity: Through History and Present" (MA thesis, University of Texas at Austin, 1986), 46.

2. Cat Spring Agricultural Society, *The Cat Spring Story* (San Antonio: Lone Star Printing Co., 1956), 1; "Rosalie von Roeder Kleberg," *Handbook of Texas Online,* www.tsha .utexas.edu/handbook/online/articles/KK/fkl12.html (accessed October 22, 2002); John H. Brown, *Indian Wars and Pioneers of Texas* (Austin: L. E. Daniell, 189?), 338–342, quote on 289; Lich, *The German Texans,* 43, 194.

3. "Dick Kleberg," notes by Bob Eckhardt, undated in Bob Eckhardt Personal Papers, Box 4, Folder: Miscellaneous; R. L. Biesele, *The History of the German Settlements in Texas 1831–1861* (Austin: Von Boeckmann-Jones, 1930), 49; "The First Piano Comes to Texas," in Rudolph Kleberg Family Papers, Center for American History, University of Texas at Austin, Box 2J52, Folder: Family history and genealogy, 1961 and undated.

4. Bob Eckhardt interview, March 11, 1994.

5. Brown, *Indian Wars and Pioneers of Texas,* 289–295; "Robert Justus Kleberg," www .sanjacinto-museum.org/Herzstein_Library/veteran_Biographies/Browse_Biographies/ biographies/default.asp?action=bio&id=3300 (accessed May 30, 2003, and October 31, 2006); Lich, *The German Texans,* 40.

6. Translation of letter from Ernst Kleberg to General Houston, February 15, 1837, with letter from Robert Stayton to Rudolph Kleberg, November 15, 1921, in Rudolph Kleberg Family Papers, Center for American History, University of Texas at Austin, Box 2J51, Folder: Miscellaneous letters, K-Z, 1871–1963.

7. "Robert Justus Kleberg," www.sanjacinto-museum.org/; Biesele, *The History of the German Settlements*, 68, 193.

8. "Dick Kleberg," notes by Bob Eckhardt; Lich, *The German Texans*, 110; Cat Spring Agricultural Society, *The Cat Spring Story*, 2, 33, 154.

9. Review of *A Political History of the Texas Republic, 1836–1841*, by Stanley Siegel, *Texas Observer*, December 12, 1956.

10. "Rosalie von Roeder Kleberg," *Handbook of Texas Online*, www.tsha.utexas.edu/handbook/online/articles/print/KK/fkl12.html (accessed October 22, 2002); Brown, *Indian Wars and Pioneers of Texas*, 338–342; Lich, *The German Texans*, 47; Biesele, *The History of the German Settlements*, 130–131n.

11. See Eckhardt, Kleberg, von Roeder, and Fisher lineage described in letter from Mrs. W. R. Eckhardt to Tillie V. Kleberg, January 23, 1959, in Rudolph Kleberg Family Papers, Center for American History, University of Texas at Austin, Box 2J51, Folder: Eckhardt family members, 1864–1959.

12. Biesele, *The History of the German Settlements*, 57; Brownson Malsch, *Indianola: The Mother of Western Texas* (Austin: Shoal Creek Publishers, 1977), 36.

13. *Texas and Texans* (Chicago: American Historical Society, 1914), 1210; "Robert Justus Kleberg," www.sanjacinto-museum.org/; Brown, *Indian Wars and Pioneers of Texas*, 289–295.

14. "Early Pioneers of West Texas—Notes," in Ann and Milton Lower Personal Papers, Box 55: Miscellaneous Political Material; "Robert Justus Kleberg," www.sanjacinto-museum.org/; Brown, *Indian Wars and Pioneers of Texas*, 289–295.

15. Lich, *The German Texans*, 123, 145.

16. Charles Ramsdell, "100 Years of Yorktown," *San Antonio Express Magazine*, 1948(?).

17. Lich, *The German Texans*, 66.

18. "Harry Wurzbach and Family," www.lsjunction.com/ (accessed June 5, 2003).

19. Bob Eckhardt, "Hame Cam' His Gude Horse," in Bob Eckhardt Personal Papers, Box: "Writings."

20. Eckhardt, "Hame Cam' His Gude Horse."

21. Eckhardt, "Hame Cam' His Gude Horse"; *Texas and Texans*, 1210.

22. Brown, *Indian Wars and Pioneers of Texas*, 338–342; *Texas and Texans*, 1210.

23. *Personnel of the Texas State Government for 1885*, pp. 85–86; "A Guide to the Rudolph Kleberg Family Papers," in Center for American History, University of Texas at Austin, www.lib.utexas.edu/taro/utcah/00012/cah-00012.html (accessed July 18, 2003).

24. Caesar Kleberg letters, in Rudolph Kleberg Family Papers, Center for American History, University of Texas at Austin, Box 2J50, Folder: Letters by writer, Caesar Kleberg, 1884–1904.

25. "Harry Wurzbach and Family," www.lsjunction.com/ (accessed June 5, 2003); Emily Wurzbach Mickler interview, June 6, 2003.

26. "Otto Eckhardt," notes by Bob Eckhardt, undated, in Bob Eckhardt Personal Papers, Box 4, Folder: Miscellaneous; "Why Not Try the Constitution," notes, in Bob Eckhardt Personal Papers, Box 10: "Politics," Folder: "Notes."

27. *Texas and Texans*, 1212; "Otto Eckhardt" notes by Bob Eckhardt; memo from Keith Ozmore to Bob Eckhardt, February 27, 1980, in Bob Eckhardt Personal Papers, Box: Publications, Writings, Notes, Folder: Eckhardt Brand.

28. See J. Frank Dobie, "The Mexican Vaquero of the Texas Border," *Southwestern Political and Social Science Quarterly* 8, no. 1 (June 1927); Nadine Eckhardt, personal communication, June 7, 2006.

29. Bob Eckhardt interview, 1984, with Chandler Davidson, Rice University Fondren Library, Woodson Research Center, Tape 1, Side 1; Norman Eckhardt interview, July 19, 2003.

30. *Southwestern Historical Quarterly,* April 1962, 65, 465.

31. Carol Hoff, *Johnny Texas* (Chicago: Wilcox & Follett Co., 1950), winner of the first Charles W. Follett Award for Worthy Contributions to Children's Literature; *Johnny Texas on the San Antonio Road* (Chicago: Wilcox & Follett Co., 1953).

32. "Robert Justus Kleberg," www.sanjacinto-museum.org/kemp/v463.html (accessed May 30, 2003).

2. Bobby Eckhardt in Austin

1. Emily Wurzbach Mickler interview, June 6, 2003; letterhead, "Drs. Schwab & Eckhardt, Yoakum, Texas" (Dr. E. H. Schwab and Dr. Jos. C. A. Eckhardt), undated, in Rudolph Kleberg Family Papers, Center for American History, University of Texas at Austin, Box 2J50, Letters by writer: Mathilde (Til) Violet Kleberg, 1896, 1913–1916, and undated.

2. *Texas and Texans,* 1211.

3. Anthony M. Orum, *Power, Money and the People: The Making of Modern Austin* (Austin: Texas Monthly Press, 1987), 20–28; Lich, *The German Texans,* 152.

4. Orum, *Power, Money and the People,* 29–30, 46; Diana Dworin, "Man Awarded Lifetime Pass to Barton Springs," *Austin American-Statesman,* October 10, 1996.

5. Orum, *Power, Money and the People,* 90–128.

6. Ann Lower, "The Capitol Well: A Texas Tradition," incomplete draft with remembrances from Bob Eckhardt, in Bob Eckhardt Personal Papers, Box 21.

7. Letter from Mrs. Fred Fischer (Bessie Olle), August 15, 1977, in Bob Eckhardt Personal Papers, Box: Publications, Writings, Notes, Folder: Norma Eckhardt Fund.

8. Robert L. Zangrando, *The NAACP Crusade Against Lynching, 1909–1950* (Philadelphia: Temple University Press, 1980), 52; Orum, *Power, Money and the People,* quotation on 25–26 and 203, 362; Patricia Bernstein, *The First Waco Horror* (College Station: Texas A&M University Press, 2005), 140; Melvin J. Banks, "The Pursuit of Equality: The Movement for First Class Citizenship Among Negroes in Texas, 1920–1950" (DSS diss., Syracuse University, 1962), 181.

9. Bob Eckhardt interview, July 16, 1996.

10. Letter from Joe Eckhardt to Bob Eckhardt, March 20, 1985, in Bob Eckhardt Personal Papers, Box 13, Folder: Service in Congress.

11. Quotation from Bob Eckhardt interview, 1984, with Chandler Davidson; Norman Eckhardt interview, July 19, 2003; Orissa Arend interview, March 27, 1997.

12. Bob Eckhardt interview, 1984, with Chandler Davidson.

13. "Why Not Try the Constitution," notes, in Bob Eckhardt Personal Papers, Box 10: "Politics," Folder: "Notes."

14. Bob Eckhardt interview, 1984, with Chandler Davidson; Julya Kirkpatrick interview, July 13, 2002.

15. Bob Eckhardt interview, 1984, with Chandler Davidson.

16. Norman Eckhardt interview, July 19, 2003.

17. Bob Eckhardt interview, September 5, 1996.

18. Emily Wurzbach Mickler interview, June 6, 2003; undated sympathy card from Carolyn Barnes upon Norma's death, in Bob Eckhardt Personal Papers, Box: Publications and Writings.

19. Lawsuit against the Eckhardts, 1915–1916, in Rudolph Kleberg Family Papers, Center for American History, University of Texas at Austin, Box 2J49, Folder: Financial and legal records, 1874–1924.

20. *Austin American,* April 23 and 24, 1951; *Austin American,* February 2, 1960; *Austin American-Statesman,* April 20, 1983.

21. Norman Eckhardt interview, July 16, 1995.

22. Bob Eckhardt interview, 1984, with Chandler Davidson.

23. Bob Eckhardt, "The Miscellanist," *Yale Law Journal* 95, no. 8 (July 1986): 1555.

24. Emily Wurzbach Mickler interview, June 6, 2003.

25. Eckhardt, "The Miscellanist."

26. In the 1970s, she would have a school named after her in Austin. Letter from Katherine Cook to Bob Eckhardt, July 8, 1976, in Robert C. Eckhardt Collection, Center for American History, University of Texas at Austin, Box 3M-26, Folder: Black/Eckhardt Book.

27. Letter (handwritten) from Bob Eckhardt to Gloria Cochran, November 25, 1984, in Bob Eckhardt Personal Papers, Folder: Cochran, Gloria.

28. Bob Eckhardt, "Remembering Johnny and Things Gone By," unsigned manuscript, in Bob Eckhardt Personal Papers, Box 21, Folder: John Henry Faulk.

29. For the story of Faulk's life, see Michael C. Burton, *John Henry Faulk: The Making of a Liberated Mind* (Austin: Eakin Press), 1993.

30. Eckhardt, "Remembering Johnny and Things Gone By."

31. Eckhardt, "Remembering Johnny and Things Gone By"; quote from Bob Eckhardt interview, 1984, with Chandler Davidson; Burton, *John Henry Faulk,* 4–5, 7.

32. Robert C. Eckhardt Collection, Center for American History, University of Texas at Austin, Box 3J308, Folder: Personal Items.

33. Henry Holman personal communication, January 16, 1996; *The Comet* (Austin High School yearbook), 1931.

34. Eckhardt, "Remembering Johnny and Things Gone By." Quote is from *Oliver Twist.*

35. Creekmore Fath interview, July 6, 1994.

36. Bob Eckhardt Personal Papers, Box 5: Caricatures and Cartoons; Bob Eckhardt memorabilia, in Nadine Eckhardt Personal Papers.

37. *Austin Statesman,* September 25, 1931.

38. *Meatloaf Gazette,* no. 6 (November 30, 1930).

39. Eckhardt, "The Miscellanist."

40. Emily Wurzbach Mickler interview, June 6, 2003.

41. Bob Eckhardt interview, March 11, 1994.

42. Roger M. Olien, *From Token to Triumph: The Texas Republicans Since 1920* (Dallas: SMU Press, 1982), 40–52.

43. Emily Wurzbach Mickler interview, June 6, 2003.

44. Judith Kaaz Doyle, "Out of Step: Maury Maverick and the Politics of the Depression and the New Deal" (PhD diss., University of Texas at Austin, 1989), 92–93, 724.

45. Richard B. Henderson, *Maury Maverick: A Political Biography* (Austin: University of Texas Press, 1970), 51.

46. Bob Eckhardt interview, December 14, 1994.

3. Student Eckhardt on the Forty Acres

1. Homer P. Rainey, *The Tower and The Dome: A Free University Versus Political Control* (Boulder, CO: Pruett Publishing Company, 1971), 20; *State Observer,* December 11, 1939.

2. Jane Gracy Bedichek, *The Roy Bedichek Family Letters* (Denton: University of North Texas Press, 1998); Creekmore Fath interview, June 10, 1994.

3. Fred Schmidt interview, October 21, 1994.

4. Mark Adams, *Glimpses of an American Century: By a Mouse in the Halls of the Mighty* (Oak Harbor, Wash.: Packrat Press, 1997), 80.

5. Joe B. Frantz, *The Forty-Acre Follies* (Austin: Texas Monthly Press, 1983), 3, 47; Richard B. Henderson, *Maury Maverick: A Political Biography* (Austin: University of Texas Press, 1970), 38; Don E. Carleton, *A Breed So Rare: The Life of J. R. Parten, Liberal Texas Oil Man, 1896–1992* (Austin: Texas State Historical Society, 1998), 17.

6. See Jake Pickle and Peggy Pickle, *Jake* (Austin: University of Texas Press), 1997.

7. See Willie Morris, "The Search for Billy Goat Hill," in *Always Stand in Against the Curve and Other Sports Stories* (Oxford, Miss.: Yoknapatawpha Press, 1983).

8. See Margaret Berry, *Brick by Golden Brick: A History of Campus Buildings at the University of Texas at Austin, 1881–1993* (Austin: LBCo., 1993).

9. Bob Eckhardt Collection, Center for American History, University of Texas at Austin, Box 3J308, Folder: Personal Items.

10. Julya Kirkpatrick interview, July 13, 2002.

11. Letter from Mary Bartelt Leader to Bob Eckhardt, October 27, 1980, in Bob Eckhardt Personal Papers, Box: Publications, Writings, Notes; William Sterling, *Trails and Trials of a Texas Ranger* (Norman: University of Oklahoma Press, 1959), 178, 187, 191, 214; Norman Eckhardt interview, July 19, 2003.

12. From *Richard II*.

13. "Political Profile: Harris' Eckhardt," *Texas Observer*, June 15, 1962.

14. Eckhardt, "The Miscellanist."

15. Bob Eckhardt, "Some of My Compatriots in Politics," in Bob Eckhardt Personal Papers, Box 4, Folder: Jottings.

16. Kay Sutherland, "Gone With Gypsy Time," in Bob Eckhardt Personal Papers, Box 21; Liz Carpenter, Remarks (Women's National Democratic Club, May 15, 1975), in Ann and Milton Lower Personal Papers, Box 37: Eckhardt Biographical.

17. D. B. Hardeman, "Shivers of Texas: A Tragedy in Three Acts," *Harper's*, November 1956, 50–56.

18. Jake Pickle interview, May 24, 1999; Pickle and Pickle, *Jake*, 17–21.

19. Bernard Rapoport interview, January 16, 1995. See also Carleton, *Being Rapoport* (Austin: University of Texas Press, 2002).

20. Fred Schmidt, "Shoving that Pushcart," *Texas Observer* Benefit Banquet program, October 15, 1994; Bernard Rapoport, "Fred Schmidt: Optimistic About the World, 1918–1999," *Texas Observer*, March 19, 1999, 23; Biography, Fred H. Schmidt Collection, in Special Collections, University of Texas at Arlington Libraries.

21. Fred Schmidt interview, October 21, 1994; Clay Cochran Memorial Tribute Program.

22. Julya Kirkpatrick interview, July 13, 2002.

23. May 9, 1942, wedding invitation, and clipping from *Houston Post*, May 17, 1942, from scrapbook at Orissa Arend's house.

24. Henderson, *Maury Maverick*, 61.

25. Bob Eckhardt interview, September 8, 1994; "Dick Kleberg," notes by Bob Eckhardt, in Bob Eckhardt Personal Papers, Box 4, Folder: Miscellaneous; *Congressional Record*, December 4, 1944, H8912.

26. John Connally, with Mickey Herskowitz, *In History's Shadow: An American Odyssey* (New York: Hyperion, 1993), 42.

27. Larry Hufford, *D. B.: Reminiscences of D. B. Hardeman* (Austin: AAR/Tantalus, 1984), 16, 21.

28. "Political Profile: Harris' Eckhardt," *Texas Observer,* June 15, 1962.

29. Henderson, *Maury Maverick,* 82.

30. Orum, *Power, Money and the People,* 148.

31. See, for example, Cochran's thesis done under Montgomery, "Corporate Control of the Tobacco Industry" (MA thesis, University of Texas, 1938), and his dissertation, "Hired Farm Labor and the Federal Government" (PhD diss., University of North Carolina, 1950); Orum, *Power, Money and the People; Congressional Record,* July 20, 1970, no. 122, E6803.

32. Orum, *Power, Money and the People,* 149–151; "Red Hearing Will Resume Tonight," *Austin Statesman,* October 14, 1936, clipping from Otto Mullinax scrapbook.

33. Bob Eckhardt interview, 1984, with Chandler Davidson.

34. Creekmore Fath interview, September 18, 2003; Carleton, *A Breed So Rare,* 139–140; e-mail message from Sarah Eckhardt to author, November 5, 2006.

35. See http://ideas.repec.org/p/vic/vicddp/0104.html and www.tsha.utexas.edu/handbook/online/articles/view/HH/fha38.html.

36. Texas House of Representatives, *House Journal,* Third Called Session, October 1936, 27.

37. Otto Mullinax interview, July 12, 1996. See *House Journal,* October 1, 1936, 27; October 6, 1936, 78; and October 14, 1936, 227.

38. "Students Storm House Communism Investigation," *Austin American,* October 15, 1936, 1.

39. "Probe Will be Again Closed to Spectators," *Austin Dispatch,* n.d., clipping from Otto Mullinax scrapbook.

40. "Red Hearing Will Resume Tonight," *Austin Statesman,* October 14, 1936, clipping from Otto Mullinax scrapbook.

41. "Red Inquiry Blamed on Utilities," *Austin Statesman,* October 27, 1936, 1.

42. Adams, *Glimpses of an American Century,* 87.

43. Bob Eckhardt letter, undated, in Otto Mullinax scrapbook.

44. Richard Doyle card, in Bob Eckhardt Personal Papers, Box 1 (Persons), Folder: Houston, Bill.

45. Bob Eckhardt interview, July 8, 1996; Bob Eckhardt journal, September 29, 1959, in Bob Eckhardt Personal Papers; Bob Eckhardt interview, 1984, with Chandler Davidson.

46. Untitled paper, in Bob Eckhardt Personal Papers, Box 13, Folder: Texas Ranger.

47. "Mirrors of Austin," *State Observer,* July 15, 1940, 6.

48. Campaign card in Nadine Eckhardt Personal Papers.

49. See *Texas Ranger,* March 1935, for the first appearance of the Hobbs Boys; letter to Eckhardt, c/o the *Ranger,* from William Lieberson, directors of the College Magazine Editorial Group, New York City, May 8, 1940, in scrapbook at Orissa Arend's house.

50. Henderson, *Maury Maverick,* 126.

51. Bob Eckhardt interview, October 7, 1994.

52. *Texas Ranger,* May 1937.

53. Bob Eckhardt interview, March 11, 1994.

54. *Texas Ranger,* November 1936.

55. "Mirrors of Austin," *State Observer,* July 15, 1940, 6; comments of Congressman Chick Kazen, *Congressional Record,* December 4, 1980, H12049.

56. *Texas Ranger,* January 1948, 14–15; Bob Eckhardt Personal Papers, Box 1, Folder: Olcutt Sanders, April 16, 1979, letter on Fellowship of Reconciliation letterhead, Nyack, NY.

57. Bob Eckhardt interview, March 18, 1994.

58. Connally, *In History's Shadow,* 44.

59. Ann Fears Crawford and Jack Keever, *John Connally: Portrait in Power* (Austin: Jenkins Publishing Company, 1973), 32–33; *Daily Texan,* March 16, 1937, 1.

60. Bob Eckhardt interview, July 17, 1999.

61. *Daily Texan,* April 6, 1937.

62. Pickle and Pickle, *Jake,* 27–29.

63. *Texas Ranger,* April 1937, 7.

64. Crawford and Keever, *John Connally,* 30–31.

65. *Texas Ranger,* March 1937, 5.

66. Eckhardt, "The Miscellanist."

67. Bob Eckhardt, "Bob Booty and Lewis and Luther McQuirter," in Bob Eckhardt Personal Papers, Box 16, Folder: Personal Experiences.

4. Eckhardt's Shingle and Pen

1. Liz Carpenter Remarks (Women's National Democratic Club, May 15, 1975), in Ann and Milton Lower Personal Papers, Box 37: Eckhardt Biographical.

2. Patrick Cox, *Ralph W. Yarborough: The People's Senator* (Austin: University of Texas Press, 2001); Mark Adams and Creekmore Fath, *Yarborough: Portrait of a People's Senator* (Austin: Chaparral Press, 1957).

3. Bob Eckhardt interview, 1984, with Chandler Davidson.

4. Bob Eckhardt journal, November 1, 1939, in Bob Eckhardt Personal Papers.

5. *State Observer,* July 15, 1940, 6.

6. "Young Lawyers Begin Careers with Victory in Loan Case," and "Loan Victim Wins Usury Litigation," *Austin Times,* August 4, 1939, 1.

7. Bob Eckhardt, "Lawyer Eckhardt," ms., January 25, 1978, in Bob Eckhardt Personal Papers, Box 13.

8. "Mirrors of Austin," *State Observer,* September 9, 1940, 3.

9. Eckhardt, "Lawyer Eckhardt."

10. Bob Eckhardt interview, 1984, with Chandler Davidson; "Political Profile: Harris' Eckhardt," *Texas Observer,* June 15, 1962.

11. One version of this story is in Bob Eckhardt's speech to National Council of Urban Education Associations, June 28, 1968, Robert C. Eckhardt Collection, Center for American History, University of Texas at Austin, Box 3M-16, Folder: Speeches.

12. Bob Eckhardt, "Souls of Poets Dead and Gone," 1984, from the original 1940, in Bob Eckhardt Personal Papers, Box 21: E. J. Hegman.

13. Letters from Otto Mullinax to Cecil Burney and James L. Lattimore, September 18, 1939, in Otto Mullinax Personal Papers, Folder: Young Democrats.

14. *State Observer,* June 17, 1940, July 15, 1940; "Mirrors of Austin," *State Observer,* July 8, 1940, 3.

15. Bob Eckhardt interview, July 10, 1994.

16. "Mirrors of Austin," *State Observer,* October 28, 1940, 1. Another version of the poem is in Bob Eckhardt Personal Papers, Folder: UT.

17. Edwin M. Yoder Jr., "Washington Notes: Eckhardt of Texas," *Harper's,* June 1970, 34.

18. Creekmore Fath interview, July 6, 1994. See also the *Texas Observer* series on Fath, March 21, 1958, 1; March 28, 1958, 1; April 14, 1958, 1.

19. Bob Eckhardt interview, March 18, 1994.

20. Joe Dibrell interview, August 12, 2003.

21. Fourteenth Annual Architects' Wind-up, Stephen F. Austin Hotel, May 9, 1942, in Orissa Eckhardt Arend Personal Papers; *Houston Post,* May 17, 1942; *Houston Chronicle,* April 26, 1942.

22. *Houston Post,* June 7, 1942; *Houston Chronicle,* June 7, 1942; *Austin American-Statesman,* June 7, 1942.

23. Joe Dibrell interview, August 12, 2003.

24. Julya Kirkpatrick interview, July 13, 2002.

25. Undated newsletter, in Orissa Arend family scrapbook.

26. "Eckhardt Man of Many Arts," *Houston Post,* February 5, 1950, 24.

27. Letter from Brigadier General Robert S. Young to Congressman Bob Eckhardt, February 11, 1977; questionnaire about military service, in Bob Eckhardt Personal Papers, Box: Publications, Writing, Notes, Folder: Military Service.

28. Bob Eckhardt interview, March 18, 1994.

29. Quotation from Shakespeare's "Bird of Dawning." Christmas card from Bob Eckhardt Personal Papers.

30. *Austin American-Statesman,* undated clipping, in Orissa Arend family scrapbook.

31. Adams, *Glimpses of an American Century,* 164–165.

32. Richard Ray Cole, "A Journal of Free Voices: The History of *The Texas Observer,*" (MA thesis, University of Texas, 1966), 7–15, 20, 46, 49.

33. *State Observer,* October 16, 1944 and February 12, 1945.

34. J. Edwin Smith, manuscript on Hubert Mewhinney, in Bob Eckhardt Personal Papers, Box 21: Ed Smith, April 20, 1995.

35. *Texas Spectator* collection, Center for American History, University of Texas at Austin.

36. "Breathe Again, O Lover," *Texas Observer,* December 20, 1954, 6.

37. Bob Eckhardt interview, 1984, with Chandler Davidson.

38. *Dallas News,* September 21, 1969.

39. *Texas Spectator,* November 1, 1946, 8.

40. Unidentified newspaper, clipping from June 30, 1946, article by J. Frank Dobie, in Orissa Arend family scrapbook.

41. See, for instance, *Texas Week,* December 7, 1946, identifying Eckhardt as Jack o' Diamonds.

42. *Texas Ranger,* January 1948, 14–15.

43. "Breathe Again, O Lover."

5. Civil Rights and Labor

1. Bob Eckhardt, "Lawyer Eckhardt," ms., January 25, 1978, in Bob Eckhardt Personal Papers, Box 13.

2. Eckhardt, "Lawyer Eckhardt."

3. Carl Allsup, *The American G.I. Forum: Origins and Evolution,* Monograph No. 6 (Center for Mexican American Studies, University of Texas at Austin, 1982), 25; Nellie Ward Kingrea, *History of the First Ten Years of the Texas Good Neighbor Commission* (Fort Worth, Tex: TCU Press, 1954), 18–19; 42–47.

4. Pauline R. Kibbe, *Latin Americans in Texas* (Albuquerque: University of New Mexico Press, 1946), 23.

5. Kingrea, *History of the First Ten Years of the Texas Good Neighbor Commission,* 30–31; Kay Sutherland, "Gone With Gypsy Time," in Bob Eckhardt Personal Papers, Box 21, Folder: Tom Sutherland.

6. Letter from Paul Vickers, Manager, McAllen Chamber of Commerce, to State Department Latin-American Division, August 3, 1943, in Robert C. Eckhardt Collection, Center for American History, University of Texas at Austin, Box 3J305, Folder: Chambers of Commerce Correspondence.

7. Kibbe, *Latin Americans in Texas,* 209; *State Observer,* August 7, 1944; letter from Tom Sutherland to William McGill, Governor's Office, August 6, 1943, in Robert C. Eckhardt Collection, Center for American History, University of Texas at Austin, Box 3J305, Folder: Governor's Office Correspondence.

8. Letter from Oscar Dancy to Pauline Kibbe, January 5, 1944, in Robert C. Eckhardt Collection, Center for American History, University of Texas at Austin, Box 3J305, Folder: Oscar Dancy Correspondence; *Brownsville Herald,* April 3, 1944, editorial page; Morris Akin, *Tales of a Texas Union Pioneer* (Austin: self published, circa 1992), 59.

9. Undated typed notes, in Robert C. Eckhardt Collection, Center for American History, University of Texas at Austin, Box 3J306, Folder: Rocky Mountain Council of Inter-American Affairs.

10. Letter from Bob Eckhardt to Mr. Hisle, Budget & Finance director, October 23, 1944, in Robert C. Eckhardt Collection, Center for American History, University of Texas at Austin, Box 3J306, Folder: OI-AA Administrative Records: Budget and Finance Division.

11. Correspondence between Sally Guinn and Robert C. Eckhardt, undated and November 25, 1944, in Robert C. Eckhardt Collection, Center for American History, University of Texas at Austin, Box 3J306, Folder: Administrative Records: Materials Division; correspondence between Bob Eckhardt and Adelfa Guerrero, Box 3J305, Folder: Adelfa Guerrero Correspondence; letter from Bob Eckhardt to Fred Much, November 25, 1944, and Eckhardt correspondence with Joe Gonzales and Jacob Ancira, July 23, 1945, and August 17, 1945, Box 3J306, Folder: Administrative Records: Requests for Information.

12. See correspondence between Adelfa Guerrero and Bob Eckhardt, in Robert C. Eckhardt Collection, Center for American History, University of Texas at Austin, Box 3J305, Folder: Adelfa Guerrero Correspondence, and Folder: Texas State Department of Education Correspondence; Guadalupe San Miguel, *"Let All of Them Take Heed": Mexican Americans and the Campaign for Educational Equality in Texas, 1910–1981* (Austin: University of Texas Press, 1987), 101.

13. See Department of Education Correspondence, in Robert C. Eckhardt Collection, Center for American History, University of Texas at Austin, Box 3J375, Folder: 1940s Administrative Records.

14. Kibbe, *Latin Americans in Texas,* 250–252.

15. See Box 56, Folder 11, in George I. Sanchez Collection, Benson Latin American Collection, University of Texas at Austin.

16. Fred H. Schmidt Collection, in Special Collections, University of Texas at Arlington Libraries, Box 296-1-4.

17. The meeting and Eckhardt's speech quotations are found in a news clipping in Bob Eckhardt Personal Papers, but the identifying information had been cut off.

18. Robert C. Eckhardt Collection, Center for American History, University of Texas at Austin, Box 3J306, Folder: U.S. Dept. of Labor.

19. Kibbe, *Latin Americans in Texas,* 253; Bob Eckhardt interview, April 28, 1994; "Good Neighbor Com. Holds First Meeting," *State Observer,* October 8, 1945; Kingrea, *History of the First Ten Years of the Texas Good Neighbor Commission,* 63–64, 134.

20. Bob Eckhardt, "Incidents of the Past," in Bob Eckhardt Personal Papers, Box 17.

21. *Houston Press,* November 26, 1946, clipping, in Orissa Arend family scrapbook.

22. *Fort Worth Star-Telegram,* September 4, 1947, reported in Kingrea, *History of the First Ten Years of the Texas Good Neighbor Commission,* 80.

23. "Mission to El Paso," *Texas Spectator,* December 27, 1947, 9; Kingrea, *History of the First Ten Years of the Texas Good Neighbor Commission,* 79; letter from Bob Smith to Allan Shivers, September 22, 1947, and reply October 1, 1947, in Allan Shivers Papers, 4–15/206, Texas State Archives, reported in George N. Green, "The Good Neighbor Commission," in *Ethnic Minorities in Gulf Coast Society,* ed. Jerrell Shofner and Linda Ellsworth (Pensacola, Fla.: Gulf Coast History and Humanities Conference, 1979), 115.

24. *Fort Worth Star-Telegram,* September 5, 1947, reported in Kingrea, *History of the First Ten Years of the Texas Good Neighbor Commission,* 80.

25. "Consultant Quits Good Neighbor Job," September 5, 1947, 1, news clipping from unidentified Houston newspaper, in Orissa Arend family scrapbook.

26. Kingrea, *History of the First Ten Years of the Texas Good Neighbor Commission,* 81; *Texas Spectator,* September 22, 1947.

27. Austin bureau of the *Monitor,* undated news release, in Orissa Arend family scrapbook.

28. Mary L. Dudziak, *Cold War Civil Rights: Race and the Image of American Democracy* (Princeton, N.J.: Princeton University Press, 2000), 23–24.

29. *Mendez v. Westminster School District,* 64 F.Supp. 544, 559 (N.D. Cal., 1946); 161 F.2d 774 (9th Cir., 1947); Attorney General Opinion V-128, April 8, 1947.

30. Ricardo Romo, "George I. Sanchez and the Civil Rights Movement: 1940–1960," *La Raza Law Journal* 1, no. 3 (fall 1986): 342–362; "Gustavo C. Garcia," *Handbook of Texas Online,* www.tsha.utexas.edu/handbook/online/articles/view/GG/fga51.html (accessed October 22, 2002).

31. Letter from George Sanchez to Gus C. Garcia, June 26, 1947; letter from Gus Garcia to A. L. Wirin, August 22, 1947, in George I. Sanchez Collection, Benson Latin American Collection, University of Texas at Austin, Box 16, Folder 17.

32. Allsup, *The American G.I. Forum,* 33.

33. See Julie Leininger-Pycior, *LBJ and Mexican-Americans: The Paradox of Power* (Austin: University of Texas Press, 1997), 56.

34. Quote from Bob Eckhardt interview, 1984, with Chandler Davidson; letter from George Sanchez to Bob Eckhardt, June 22, 1948, in George I. Sanchez Collection, Benson Latin American Collection, University of Texas at Austin, Box 12, Folder 18.

35. *Delgado v. Bastrop Independent School District,* Civil No. 388 (W.D. Tex., June 15, 1948).

36. Bob Eckhardt interview, 1984, with Chandler Davidson.

37. Charles Black helped Thurgood Marshall write the legal brief for Linda Brown.

38. Myrtle Tanner, "History of the Good Neighbor Commission," 1952 MS, 60–61, reported in Kingrea, *History of the First Ten Years of the Texas Good Neighbor Commission,* 85. Later, Dr. Sanchez became interested in the jury qualification issue, and he and Eckhardt testified in a case in Beeville, where the sheriff had killed several Mexicans at one time. Eckhardt testified that the issue was a social one, rather than a genetic one, because, in reality, in Texas communities, classification for jury purposes was based on some combination of one's wealth, English-speaking ability, and darkness of skin.

39. Letter from Al Wirin to Gus Garcia, copy to Bob Eckhardt, January 6, 1948, in George I. Sanchez Collection, Benson Latin American Collection, University of Texas at Austin, Box 16, Folder 18.

40. Wirin then followed up with a victory in a similar case in Arizona: *Gonzales v. Sheehy,* 96 F.Supp. 1004 (D. Ariz., 1951).

41. Kingrea, *History of the First Ten Years of the Texas Good Neighbor Commission,* 119–129. See also Jorge C. Rangel and Carlos M. Alcala, "De Jure Segregation of Chicanos in Texas Schools," Project Report, *Harvard Civil Rights–Civil Liberties Law Review* 7, no. 2 (March 1972): 307–392.

42. Letter from Thurgood Marshall to George Sanchez, July 1, 1948, in George I. Sanchez Collection, Benson Latin American Collection, University of Texas at Austin, Box 24, Folder 8; letter from Al Wirin to George Sanchez, July 1, 1948, Box 62, Folder 15.

43. Murray Polakoff, "The Development of the Texas State C.I.O. Council" (PhD diss., Columbia University, 1955), 353–360.

44. Polakoff, "The Development of the Texas State C.I.O. Council," iv–v, 110–111; George Norris Green, "Organizing: Past, Present, and Future" (24th Annual Southwest Labor Studies Association Conference, St. Edward's University, Austin, April 24–26, 1998).

45. Bob Eckhardt interview, 1984, with Chandler Davidson.

46. *House Journal,* 47th Legislature, 1231.

47. Polakoff, "The Development of the Texas State C.I.O. Council," 35–46.

48. The original case was *Thomas v. Collins,* 323 U.S. 516 (1945). Others were *AFL et al. v. Mann et al.,* 188 S.W. (2d) 276 (1945); *Ludine v. McKinney,* 183 S.W. (2d) (1944); *CIO v. City of Dallas,* 198 S.W. (2d) 143 (1946); Polakoff, "The Development of the Texas State C.I.O. Council," 280–296.

49. Bob Eckhardt interview, 1984, with Chandler Davidson.

50. Polakoff, "The Development of the Texas State C.I.O. Council," 7, 12.

51. Morris Akin, "A Texas CIO Pioneer," ms., in Bob Eckhardt Personal Papers, Box 1: Persons, Folder: Morris Akin; Polakoff, "The Development of the Texas State C.I.O. Council," vi, viii; Bob Eckhardt interview, 1984, with Chandler Davidson; Akin, *Tales of a Texas Union Pioneer,* 38.

52. Polakoff, "The Development of the Texas State C.I.O. Council," 142–158, 362, 364–365, 400–407.

53. Polakoff, "The Development of the Texas State C.I.O. Council," ix–x, 392–393.

54. Adams, *Glimpses of an American Century,* 172–174; *Austin American-Statesman,* January 26, 1947, 1; Bob Eckhardt, "Jim Wright, The Speaker and the Institution," unpublished ms. in Bob Eckhardt Personal Papers, Box 1: Persons, Folder: Jim Wright.

55. Ronnie Dugger, "A Fair Tax on the Oil Industry," *Texas Observer,* August 29, 1986, 9.

56. Akin, *Tales of a Texas Union Pioneer,* 45; Polakoff, "The Development of the Texas State C.I.O. Council," 200–204.

57. Bob Eckhardt interview, 1984, with Chandler Davidson.

58. Bob Eckhardt interview, March 11, 1994.

59. Bob Eckhardt Personal Papers, Box 1: Persons, Folder: Friends, Carl & Laura Brannin.

60. Mullinax, Wells Labor Case Records, in Special Collections, University of Texas at Arlington Libraries.

61. "Eckhardt Man of Many Arts," *Houston Post,* February 5, 1950, 24.

6. Eckhardt in 1940s Texas Politics

1. See Charles W. Stephenson, "The Democrats of Texas and Texas Liberalism, 1944–1960: A Study in Political Frustration" (MA thesis, Southwest Texas State College, 1967).

2. Letter from Lyndon B. Johnson to Caesar Kleberg, March 15, 1934, in Rudolph Kleberg Family Papers, Center for American History, University of Texas at Austin, Box 2J50, Folder: Letters by writer: Caesar Kleberg, 1927–1944.

3. Creekmore Fath interview, September 18, 2003; Judith N. McArthur and Harold L. Smith, *Minnie Fisher Cunningham: A Suffragist's Life in Politics* (Oxford: Oxford University Press, 2003), 163.

4. Mrs. Albert (Lera) Thomas Oral History, interview with David G. McComb, October 11, 1968, transcript, in Lyndon Baines Johnson Library, AC 74-47.

5. David Welsh, "Building Lyndon Johnson," *Ramparts,* December 1967, 53–65; Hart Stilwell, "Will He Boss Texas?" *The Nation,* November 10, 1951, 398.

6. Hufford, *D. B.: Reminiscences of D. B. Hardeman,* 29; Welsh, "Building Lyndon Johnson," 55.

7. See Fagan Dickson, "The Texas Poll Tax," *Texas Bar Journal* 11, no. 11 (December 1948): 619ff.

8. Banks, "The Pursuit of Equality," 317–331.

9. William J. Tolleson, "The Rift in the Texas Democratic Party—1944" (MA thesis, University of Texas, 1953), 8–17.

10. *Austin American,* May 27, 1944, quoted in Tolleson, "The Rift in the Texas Democratic Party—1944," 47.

11. Tolleson, "The Rift in the Texas Democratic Party—1944," 50–65.

12. *Austin American,* August 18 and 19, 1944, quoted in Tolleson, "The Rift in the Texas Democratic Party—1944," 79–80.

13. Tolleson, "The Rift in the Texas Democratic Party—1944," 71–75, 89–93.

14. *Dallas News,* October 7, 1944, quoted in Tolleson, "The Rift in the Texas Democratic Party—1944," 103.

15. Tolleson, "The Rift in the Texas Democratic Party—1944," 97–117.

16. *Texas Spectator,* October 11, 1946, and November 22, 1946.

17. McArthur and Smith, *Minnie Fisher Cunningham;* Mark Sonntag, "Hyphenated Texans: World War I and the German-Americans of Texas" (MA thesis, University of Texas at Austin, 1990), 55–56; Patricia Ellen Cunningham, "The Fight for Woman Suffrage in Texas: The Final Years, 1915–1919" (paper presented at Joe C. Thompson Conference Center, University of Texas, April 3, 1986), in Bob Eckhardt Personal Papers, Folder: Cunningham, Minnie Fisher.

18. Photo and caption, unidentified magazine, in Orissa Arend family scrapbook.

19. Bob Eckhardt interview, 1984, with Chandler Davidson.

20. Rainey, *The Tower and The Dome,* 97–98.

21. Rainey, *The Tower and The Dome*, 42; Carleton, *A Breed So Rare*, 237.

22. Rainey, *The Tower and The Dome*, 6–7, 29, 87; Ronnie Dugger, *Our Invaded Universities: Form, Reform and New Starts* (New York: W. W. Norton & Co., 1974), 43.

23. Rainey, *The Tower and The Dome*, 85.

24. Carleton, *A Breed So Rare*, 307.

25. Rainey, *The Tower and The Dome*, 98.

26. Rainey, *The Tower and The Dome*, 118–122; Carleton, *A Breed So Rare*, 315; *Washington Post*, November 27, 1944; *Harper's*, November 1945.

27. Bob Eckhardt interview, October 7, 1994; *Texas Spectator*, August 9, 1946.

28. Seth S. McKay, *Texas and the Fair Deal 1945–1952* (San Antonio: The Naylor Co., 1954), 98; Carleton, *A Breed So Rare*, 364.

29. Letter from Lillian Bedichek to Jane Bedichek, August 3, 1946, in Bedichek, *The Roy Bedichek Family Letters*, 264; McKay, *Texas and the Fair Deal 1945–1952*, 127.

30. Bob Eckhardt interview, March 18, 1994.

31. Stephenson, "The Democrats of Texas and Texas Liberalism, 1944–1960," 7.

32. Letter from Chris Dixie to Walton Hamilton, April 3, 1946; letter from Hamilton to Dixie, April 12, 1946; letter from Dixie to Hamilton, August 28, 1946, in Walton H. Hamilton Papers, Tarlton Law Library, University of Texas Law School.

33. Bernard Rapoport interview, January 16, 1995.

34. *Texas Week*, December 7, 1946; Orum, *Power, Money and the People*, 164.

35. *The Nation*, May 3, 1947, 512.

36. Polakoff, "The Development of the Texas State C.I.O. Council," 405, 421.

37. Texas Social and Legislative Conference brochure and Margaret Reading, "A Report 1951," in Margaret B. Carter Papers, Special Collections, University of Texas at Arlington Libraries, AR-239, Box 239-20-1; Polakoff, "The Development of the Texas State C.I.O. Council," 425.

38. Bob Eckhardt interview, 1984, with Chandler Davidson.

39. Letter from Jeff Hickman to local unions, November 27, 1949, quoted in Polakoff, "The Development of the Texas State C.I.O. Council," 425.

40. Letter from Bob Eckhardt, chairman, Division 20 Legislative Committee, Communication Workers of America, to William Dunn, legislative director, Communication Workers of America, December 21, 1949, quoted in Polakoff, "The Development of the Texas State C.I.O. Council," 429–431.

41. Minutes, December 11, 1949, Executive Committee, meeting in Waco Texas Social and Legislative Conference Records, in Special Collections, University of Texas at Arlington Libraries, AR-120, Box: 120-1-4.

42. Orum, *Power, Money and the People*, 164–167.

43. Brochures in Walter G. Hall Papers, Rice University Fondren Library, Woodson Research Center.

44. Bernard Rapoport interview, January 16, 1995.

45. O. Douglas Weeks, *Texas Presidential Politics in 1952*, Public Affairs Series no. 16, Institute of Public Affairs, University of Texas, 1953, 8.

46. Stephenson, "The Democrats of Texas and Texas Liberalism, 1944–1960," 15; Burton, *John Henry Faulk*, 90.

47. "Progressive Leader Asks Pertinent Question," *State Observer*, March 8, 1948, 1; *Wichita Daily Times*, February 28, 1948; Weldon Hart column, *Austin American-Statesman*, February 28, 1948.

48. *Dallas News*, May 25, 1948.

49. Stephenson, "The Democrats of Texas and Texas Liberalism, 1944–1960," 11.

50. Creekmore Fath interview, cited in Stephenson, "The Democrats of Texas and Texas Liberalism, 1944–1960," 13.

51. Stephenson, "The Democrats of Texas and Texas Liberalism, 1944–1960," 9–10.

52. Fath interview, cited in Stephenson, "The Democrats of Texas and Texas Liberalism, 1944–1960," 13.

53. Bob Eckhardt interview, July 16, 1996.

54. Letter from Jack and Margaret Carter to Walter G. Hall, June 11, 1949, RE: Appointment of J. Edwin Smith as federal judge, in Walter Gardner Hall Papers, Rice University Fondren Library, Woodson Research Center, MS 280-3.

55. D. B. Hardeman and Donald C. Bacon, *Rayburn: A Biography* (Austin: Texas Monthly Press, 1987), 339.

56. *State Observer,* September 20, 1948.

57. Hardeman and Bacon, *Rayburn,* 339–341; J. W. Jackson, "Texas Politics in 1948," *Southwestern Social Science Quarterly* 30, no. 1 (June 1949): 45–48; Weeks, *Texas Presidential Politics in 1952,* 9.

7. Brother Eckhardt Goes to Houston

1. "Eckhardt Man of Many Arts," *Houston Post,* February 5, 1950, 24.

2. "Top Political Figures," *Houston Chronicle,* December 12, 1999.

3. Bob Eckhardt journal entry, undated, in Bob Eckhardt Personal Papers.

4. Hubert Mewhinney, *A Manual for Neanderthals* (Austin: University of Texas Press, 1957), with Eckhardt sketches on the cover and p. 10.

5. Rosalind Eckhardt letter, 1968, in Bob Eckhardt Personal Papers, Box 13; Orissa Arend interview, November 25, 2003.

6. Leah Brooke Tucker, "The Houston Business Community, 1945–1965" (PhD diss., University of Texas, 1979), 19–20, 53–61.

7. Tucker, "The Houston Business Community, 1945–1965," 220.

8. See Tucker, "The Houston Business Community, 1945–1965"; also see Kenneth Lipartito and Joseph Pratt, *Baker & Botts in the Development of Modern Houston* (Austin: University of Texas Press, 1991).

9. Tucker, "The Houston Business Community, 1945–1965," 26, quote on 74.

10. Welsh, "Building Lyndon Johnson," 59.

11. Lipartito and Pratt, *Baker & Botts in the Development of Modern Houston,* 184–185.

12. Chandler Davidson, *Biracial Politics: Conflict and Coalition in the Metropolitan South* (Baton Rouge: Louisiana State University Press, 1972), 14–16.

13. Minutes, September 13, 1950, Houston Area Industrial Union Council Papers, in Special Collections, University of Texas at Arlington Libraries, AR 104, Box 1, Folder 1, 104-1-2.

14. Davidson, *Biracial Politics,* 19.

15. Southern Regional Council Voter Education Project data, reported in Davidson, *Biracial Politics,* 6.

16. Davidson, *Biracial Politics,* 94, 195.

17. See Arnoldo DeLeon, *Ethnicity in the Sunbelt: Mexican Americans in Houston* (College Station: Texas A&M University Press), 2001.

18. Data from Industrial Development Department, Bank of the Southwest, reported in Davidson, *Biracial Politics,* 242; Polakoff, "The Development of the Texas State C.I.O.

Council," 133; Marvin Ray Felder, "The Politics of the Texas Gulf Coast, 1945 to 1960" (MA thesis, University of Texas, 1960), 71.

19. Letter from Walton Hamilton to Robert Eckhardt, January 25, 1950, in Bob Eckhardt Personal Papers, Box 1, (Persons) Folder: Hammy.

20. Robert C. Eckhardt, "Labor Law Section Report," *Texas Bar Journal*, June 1954, 342; "Labor Law," August 1952, 387; June 1953, 386; August 1953, 522.

21. "Eckhardt Man of Many Arts," *Houston Post*, February 5, 1950, 24; Bob Eckhardt interview, 1984, with Chandler Davidson.

22. Al Shulman interview, June 4, 1998.

23. Bob Eckhardt interview, July 8, 1996.

24. Fred Schmidt interview, October 21, 1994.

25. Houston Area Industrial Union Council Papers, August 8, 1951, in Special Collections, University of Texas at Arlington Libraries, AR 104, Box 1, Folder 1, 104-1-2.

26. Story told by Eckhardt to Fred Schmidt, Fred Schmidt interview, October 21, 1994.

27. CWA Local 6215, in Special Collections, University of Texas at Arlington Libraries, AR 353-1-1.

28. Letter from Bonnie Clark, Seymour, Texas, to the CWA, May 20, 1981, in Bob Eckhardt Personal Papers, Box 13, Folder: Letters Answered.

29. Bob Eckhardt interviews, March 11, 1994, and July 8, 1996; Bob Eckhardt journal entry, undated, in Bob Eckhardt Personal Papers.

30. Stilwell, "Will He Boss Texas?" 398.

31. Bob Eckhardt interview, July 8, 1996.

32. Bob Eckhardt interview, 1984, with Chandler Davidson; Ed Ball interview, May 8, 2004.

33. Don E. Carleton, *Red Scare!: Right-wing Hysteria, Fifties Fanaticism, and Their Legacy in Texas* (Austin: Texas Monthly Press, 1985), 231.

34. See Carleton, *Red Scare!;* "Seeking Martin Luther King Jr.'s Mountain," *Huntsville Item,* January 22, 1993, in Bob Eckhardt Personal Papers, Box 21: Keith Ozmore.

35. Minutes, September 13, 1950, and April 11, 1951, Houston Area Industrial Union Council Papers, in Special Collections, University of Texas at Arlington Libraries, AR-104, Box 1, Folder 2.

36. Minutes of the Executive Committee, 1950–1951, Texas Social and Legislative Conference Records, in Special Collections, University of Texas at Arlington Libraries, AR-120-1-7.

37. *Fort Worth Star Telegram,* July 3, 1950; Texas Social and Legislative Conference Records, in Special Collections, University of Texas at Arlington Libraries, AR-120-1-2, 120-1-4, 120-1-7; Walter Gardner Hall Papers, Rice University Fondren Library, Woodson Research Center, MS 280.

38. Letter from Walter Gardner Hall to J. Edwin Smith re: Mineral Wells convention, August 19, 1950, and letter from Walter Gardner Hall to Baker Hotel in Mineral Wells, August 23, 1950, in Walter Gardner Hall Papers, Rice University Fondren Library, Woodson Research Center, MS 280, 280-4, MS 280, 280-4; McArthur and Smith, *Minnie Fisher Cunningham,* 193.

39. Maury Maverick, "Thumbs Up for Henry B." *Texas Observer,* August 28, 1998, 30–31.

40. Hufford, *D. B.: Reminiscences of D. B. Hardeman.*

41. Edgar Berlin, personal communication, June 17, 1995.

42. Ann Fears Crawford and Crystal Sasse Ragsdale, *Women in Texas: Their Lives, Their Experiences, Their Accomplishments* (Austin: Eakin Press, 1982), 250; e-mail message from Bill Hobby to author, February 24, 2006.

43. Letter from Bob Eckhardt letter to Jeff Hickman, January 3, 1951, and letter from George Parkhouse to Bob Eckhardt, February 17, 1951, quoted in Polakoff, "The Development of the Texas State C.I.O. Council," 433.

44. Minutes of the Executive Committee, January 7, March 11, 1951, Texas Social and Legislative Conference Records, in Special Collections, University of Texas at Arlington Libraries, AR-120-1-7; Walter Gardner Hall Papers, Rice University Fondren Library, Woodson Research Center, MS 280.

45. Margaret Carter letter to Bob Eckhardt, February 16, 1951, in Walter Gardner Hall Papers, Rice University Fondren Library, Woodson Research Center, MS 280.

46. Letter from Maury Maverick Jr. to the editor, *Texas Observer,* March 5, 1999.

47. Bob Eckhardt Personal Papers, Box 21, Folder: Johnny Barnhart; *Daily Texan,* March 16, 1951; letter from Maury Maverick Jr. to Bob Eckhardt, March 5, 1994, Box 21, Folder: Maury Maverick.

48. Maury Maverick Jr. interview, March 6, 2002.

49. Denny O. Ingram Jr., "Reminiscences About an Old House, Some Poor Boys, and a Tax Fight," *Texas Observer,* March 21, 1955.

50. September 22, 1991, column, in Bob Eckhardt Personal Papers, Box 21, Folder: Maury Maverick.

51. Hufford, *D. B.: Reminiscences of D. B. Hardeman,* 34.

52. *State Observer,* June 11, 1951, and January 14, 1952; Walter Gardner Hall Papers, Rice University Fondren Library, Woodson Research Center, MS 280.

53. Letter from Margaret Reading to Walter and Helen Hall, August 27, 1951, in Walter Gardner Hall Papers, Rice University Fondren Library, Woodson Research Center, MS 280.

54. Letter from Walter G. Hall to Loyal Democrats, October 17, 1951, in Walter Gardner Hall Papers, Rice University Fondren Library, Woodson Research Center, MS 280.

55. Texas Social and Legislative Conference Records in Special Collections, University of Texas at Arlington Libraries, AR-120-1-14.

56. Letter from Fagan Dickson to Walter G. Hall, October 11, 1951; letter from Creekmore Fath to Hall, November 5, 1951; letter from Hall to John Cofer, November 8, 1951; letter from Hall to Fath, November 8, 1951, in Walter Gardner Hall Papers, Rice University Fondren Library, Woodson Research Center, MS 280.

57. Proceedings of the Sixteenth Annual Convention of the Texas State CIO Council, 27–28, quoted in Polakoff, "The Development of the Texas State C.I.O. Council," 71.

58. Minutes of the Executive Committee, monthly meetings, 1951, quotations from December 9, 1951 minutes, Texas Social and Legislative Conference Records, in Special Collections, University of Texas at Arlington Libraries, AR-120-1-7.

59. Eddie Ball interview, May 28, 2004.

60. Ann Fears Crawford, *Frankie: Mrs. R. D. Randolph and Texas Liberal Politics* (Austin: Eakin Press, 2000), 26; draft of Ronnie Dugger article, in Bob Eckhardt Personal Papers, Box 21: Frankie Randolph, and edited and published version in Handbook of Texas Online, www.tsha.utexas.edu/handbook/online/articles/view/RR/fra34.html.

61. "HCD—The Early Years," www.harriscountydemocrats.org/history.php (accessed July 1, 2003).

62. Davidson, *Biracial Politics*, 44–46.

63. Stephenson, "The Democrats of Texas," 21–22.

64. Loyal Democrats of Texas, "YOUR Democratic Party—And How to Keep It That Way," brochure in Walter Gardner Hall Papers, Rice University Fondren Library, Woodson Research Center, MS 280; Polakoff, "The Development of the Texas State C.I.O. Council," 71.

65. Weeks, *Texas Presidential Politics in 1952*, 3, 41.

66. Minutes of the Democratic State Convention of the State of Texas held May 27, 1952, at La Villita. Walter Gardner Hall Papers, Rice University Fondren Library, Woodson Research Center, MS 280; Henderson, *Maury Maverick*, 275.

67. Weeks, *Texas Presidential Politics in 1952*, 46.

68. Letter from Walter G. Hall to Fagan Dickson, June 13, 1952, on plans for Chicago convention: "Bob Eckhart [*sic*] is today writing Stuart about a meeting of the Organization Committee."

69. Weeks, *Texas Presidential Politics in 1952*, 75; Stephenson, "The Democrats of Texas," 26; Paul B. Holcomb, "How Texas Became 'A No-Party State,' " *State Observer*, October 19, 1953, 7; Weeks, *Texas Presidential Politics in 1952*, 80; J. Wendell Knox, "Democratic Schism in Texas, 1952–1957: Emergence of National Liberalism in the South" (MA thesis, North Texas State College, 1959), 13.

70. Minutes of the Executive Committee, August 17, 1952, minutes, Texas Social and Legislative Conference Records, in Special Collections, University of Texas at Arlington Libraries, AR-120-1-7.

71. Letter from Minnie Fisher Cunningham to Jack Carter, October 7, 1952, Texas Social and Legislative Conference Records, in Special Collections, University of Texas at Arlington Libraries, 265-3-11.

72. Polakoff, "The Development of the Texas State C.I.O. Council," 100–102.

73. O. Douglas Weeks, *Texas One-Party Politics in 1956*, Public Affairs Series no. 32, Institute of Public Affairs, University of Texas, 1957, 5.

74. Bob Eckhardt, "Texas and Taxes—It's Up to You," n.d. Texas Social and Legislative Conference Records, in Special Collections, University of Texas at Arlington Libraries, AR-120 120-1-6.

75. Polakoff, "The Development of the Texas State C.I.O. Council," 31, 76–77; "Specifically, Bob Eckhardt, representing the Conference at the regular session of the 53rd Legislature, worked for defeat of the Ford Bill Amendment to the unemployment compensation law and HB 261 which, under cover of increasing compensation, would have taken away the right of jury trial in workmen's compensation cases." Quote from "What is the Texas Social and Legislative Conference?" brochure, Texas Social and Legislative Conference Records, in Special Collections, University of Texas at Arlington Libraries, AR-120-1-6.

76. Maury Maverick Jr., interview, March 6, 2002; *House Journal*, May 27, 1953.

77. Stephenson, "The Democrats of Texas," 32–33.

78. Sam and Cele Keeper personal communication, June 4, 1998; Ronnie Dugger interview, December 6, 1997.

79. Letterhead, May 4, 1953 and 1954, Texas Social and Legislative Conference Records, in Special Collections, University of Texas at Arlington Libraries, 265-3-11; *Texas Observer*, April 25, 1956.

80. Orissa Arend interview, November 25, 2003.

8. Eckhardt, the *Texas Observer,* and Yarborough Come of Age

1. Quoted by Hardeman, "Shivers of Texas: A Tragedy in Three Acts," 54.

2. *Austin American,* July 6, 1954, in Polakoff, "The Development of the Texas State C.I.O. Council," 85.

3. Two of these unions had been expelled from the CIO in 1949 and 1950 in the internal battles over Communist influence. The Distributive, Processing and Office Workers Union had since been reconstituted and, in late 1953, went on strike against twenty-two retail businesses in Port Arthur. DPOW withdrew after the Industrial Commission's allegations of Communism, and the national CIO took over the strike and bargaining. CIO revoked DPOW's charter and issued a local charter to the Sabine Area Local Industrial Union No. 1814. Polakoff, "The Development of the Texas State C.I.O. Council," 88.

4. Quoted in Carleton, *Red Scare!,* 262.

5. Knox, "Democratic Schism in Texas, 1952–1957," 33, 35.

6. Pickle and Pickle, *Jake,* 72.

7. *Dallas Morning News* series on Port Arthur, May 2–7, 1954; quotation from May 5, 1954, editorial.

8. Polakoff, "The Development of the Texas State C.I.O. Council," 89–90.

9. Robert Eckhardt, "First Things First—The Convention," *State Observer,* September 6, 1954, 2.

10. Stephenson, "The Democrats of Texas," 34.

11. Jake Pickle interview, May 24, 1999.

12. Polakoff, "The Development of the Texas State C.I.O. Council," 94f; Cole, "A Journal of Free Voices," 109; *State Observer,* October 12, 1953.

13. *State Observer,* September 10, 1954.

14. Cole, "A Journal of Free Voices," 53.

15. Patricia Ellen Cunningham, "Too Gallant a Walk: Minnie Fisher Cunningham and Her Race for Governor of Texas in 1944" (MA thesis, University of Texas, 1985), 127.

16. Crawford, *Frankie,* 34–35; "Tentative Plan of Organizing an Independent Newspaper in Texas," undated, Margaret B. Carter Papers, in Special Collections, University of Texas at Arlington Libraries, AR-239, 239-19-10.

17. McArthur and Smith, *Minnie Fisher Cunningham,* 197.

18. Letter from Ronnie Dugger to Mrs. R. D. Randolph, October 22, 1954, Margaret B. Carter Papers, in Special Collections, University of Texas at Arlington Libraries, AR-239, 239-19-10.

19. McArthur and Smith, *Minnie Fisher Cunningham,* 197.

20. Ronnie Dugger interview, December 6, 1997; Ronnie Dugger remarks, *Texas Observer* banquet, October 15, 1994.

21. Letter from Robert C. Eckhardt, Attorney at Law, to Minnie Fisher Cunningham, November 2, 1954, Margaret B. Carter Papers, in Special Collections, University of Texas at Arlington Libraries, AR-235, 235-19-10. There were those who would chafe at Dugger's independence over the years. "Brother Payne," reported a 1956 union report, "voiced disapproval of the *Texas Observer,* Texas's only liberal newspaper, giving first page spread to [Price] Daniel." (Minutes, July 25, 1956, Houston Area Industrial Union Council Papers, AR 104, Box 1, Folder 1, in Special Collections, University of Texas at Arlington Libraries, 104-1-3).

22. Ronnie Dugger, draft of "Frankie Carter Randolph," in Bob Eckhardt Personal Papers, Box 21, Folder: Frankie Randolph; Handbook of Texas Online, www.tsha.utexas.edu/handbook/online/articles/RR/fra34.html.

23. Bob Eckhardt journal, undated, in Bob Eckhardt Personal Papers.

24. "Breathe Again, O Lover," *Texas Observer,* December 20, 1954, 6.

25. Bob Eckhardt letter to Ronnie Dugger, September 19, 1955, in Bob Eckhardt Personal Papers, Box 1 (Persons).

26. Bob Eckhardt journal, August 13 and September 29, 1959, in Bob Eckhardt Personal Papers.

27. Bob Eckhardt journal, November 1, 1959, in Bob Eckhardt Personal Papers.

28. Ronnie Dugger letter to John Fischer, June 6, 1956, in Bob Eckhardt Personal Papers, Box 1 (Persons).

29. Malcolm McGregor interview, February 19, 1996; "Observations," *Texas Observer,* November 11, 1966, 11; Ronnie Dugger, "To a Novelist Dying Young," *Washington Post,* June 18, 1978, F1.

30. *Texas Observer,* February 28, 1955, January 10, 1955, January 17, 1955.

31. Knox, "Democratic Schism in Texas, 1952–1957," 46–47.

32. Robert C. Eckhardt, "Senate-Passed Parkhouse Strike Bill Would be Worst of Anti-Labor Laws," *Texas Observer,* April 25, 1955, 3–4.

33. Bob Eckhardt Personal Papers, Box 1 (Persons), Folder: Jamison, Liz: This Old House lyrics to sine die song.

34. *Texas Observer,* June 6, 1955.

35. *Texas Observer,* November 2 and 9, 1955; Stephenson, "The Democrats of Texas, 1952–1957," 35; *Dallas Morning News,* November 5, 1955, in Knox, "Democratic Schism in Texas, 1952–1957," 54; Democratic Advisory Council, in Special Collections at University of Texas at Arlington Library, AR 360; Weeks, *Texas One-Party Politics in 1956,* 13.

36. Hardeman, "Shivers of Texas: A Tragedy in Three Acts," 54–55.

37. *Austin American,* May 3, 1956, 1, 5, quoted in Stephenson, "The Democrats of Texas," 37.

38. Stephenson, "The Democrats of Texas," 40.

39. Ronnie Dugger, "Harris Convention Liberals Hit Hard," *Texas Observer,* May 9, 1956, 8.

40. Bob Eckhardt, "The Issue: Who Shall Control," *Texas Observer,* May 9, 1956, 3.

41. Bob Eckhardt note, November 27, 1957, in Bob Eckhardt Personal Papers.

42. Felder, "The Politics of the Texas Gulf Coast, 1945 to 1960," 52.

43. *Texas Observer,* September 12, 1956.

44. David Richards, *Once Upon a Time in Texas: A Liberal in the Lone Star State* (Austin: University of Texas Press, 2002), 11.

45. Fred Schmidt interview, October 21, 1994.

46. Stephenson, "The Democrats of Texas," 42; *Texas Observer,* May 23, 1956, June 4 and 6, 1956, 2; Weeks, *Texas One-Party Politics in 1956,* 25.

47. Crawford, *Frankie,* 48.

48. Stephenson, "The Democrats of Texas," 41; Knox, "Democratic Schism in Texas, 1952–1957," 69–71.

49. Stephenson, "The Democrats of Texas," 43–44.

50. Bob Eckhardt interview, 1984, with Chandler Davidson.

51. Davidson, *Biracial Politics,* 253.

52. Stephenson, "The Democrats of Texas," 46–48; *Texas Observer,* September 19, 1956; McArthur and Smith, *Minnie Fisher Cunningham,* 199.

53. Carleton, *A Breed So Rare,* 472; McArthur and Smith, *Minnie Fisher Cunningham,* 200.

54. May 15, 1958 column, quoted in *Archer Fullingim: A Country Editor's View of Life,* ed. Roy Hamric (Austin: Heidelberg Publishers, 1975), 89–90.

55. Bob Eckhardt, "Some of My Compatriots in Politics," in Eckhardt Personal Papers, Box 4, Folder: Jottings.

56. Bob Eckhardt interview, 1984, with Chandler Davidson.

57. Bob Eckhardt journal, June 15, 1960, in Bob Eckhardt Personal Papers.

58. *Texas Observer,* March 5 and 19, 1957.

59. Felder, "The Politics of the Texas Gulf Coast, 1945 to 1960," 61.

60. "So in this case a single stone was enough to elevate two birds," commented Hamilton to Montgomery. Letter from Walton Hamilton to Robert Montgomery, February 17, 1958, in Walton H. Hamilton Papers, University of Texas School of Law, Tarlton Law Library.

61. *Texas Observer,* December 19, 1956, and January 2, 1957.

62. Crawford, *Frankie,* 58.

63. Bob Eckhardt journal, May 31, 1960, in Bob Eckhardt Personal Papers.

64. Stephenson, "The Democrats of Texas," 59.

65. Afterward, Mark Adams printed a twenty-four-page slick brochure for the DOT, detailing the meeting and listing all the officials, in "Statewide Meeting Democrats of Texas" (Austin: Chaparral Press), copy in Ralph Yarborough Collection, Center for American History, University of Texas at Austin; Stephenson, "The Democrats of Texas," 60–61.

66. *Texas Observer,* February 7 and June 13, 1958.

67. Crawford, *Frankie,* 58.

68. "Political Ethics Code Urged by Liberal Dems," *Houston Chronicle,* September 29, 1957.

69. *Texas Observer,* March 26, 1957, 6.

70. Stephenson, "The Democrats of Texas," 87, 96, 98.

71. "Group Official Cool to Birch Endorsement," May 24, 1961, news clipping, source unidentified, in Harris County Democratic Party Records, Center for American History, University of Texas at Austin, Box 4C521, Folder: Freedom in Action.

72. Letter from Robert C. Eckhardt, Harris County Democrats, to Loyal Democratic Precinct Judges and Leaders, March 6, 1958, in Harris County Democratic Party Records, Center for American History, University of Texas at Austin, Box 4C505, Folder: Liberals/ DOT 1957–58.

73. Stephenson, "The Democrats of Texas," 84–88, 99.

74. Minutes, December 17, 1957; letter from Don Ellinger to James McDevitt, National Director, his Texas Report, January 15 and January 28, 1958 follow-up letter, W. Don Ellinger Papers, in Special Collections, University of Texas at Arlington Libraries, 110 Series 9, Box 1.

75. Bob Eckhardt journal, undated, in Bob Eckhardt Personal Papers.

76. Letter from Don Ellinger to James McDevitt, May 17, 1958, W. Don Ellinger Papers, in Special Collections, University of Texas at Arlington Libraries, 110 Series 9, Box 1; Stephenson, "The Democrats of Texas," 77–78.

77. Crawford, *Frankie,* 70.

78. Stephenson, "The Democrats of Texas," 83, 85; *Texas Observer,* June 6, 1958.

79. Stephenson, "The Democrats of Texas," 82–83.

80. See Pickle and Pickle, *Jake,* 74–75.

81. Letter from Bob Eckhardt to Sherman Miles, February 24, 1958, Texas AFL-CIO Collection, in Special Collections, University of Texas at Arlington Libraries, AR 110, Series 11, Box 8, 8–5.

82. Bob Eckhardt, "Another Surrender to Special Interests," *Texas Observer,* March 21, 1958, 1.

83. *Houston Post,* July, 12, 1958; Texas AFL-CIO Collection, in Special Collections, University of Texas at Arlington Libraries, AR 110, Series 11, 8–5.

84. Bob Eckhardt, journal, July 25, 1958, and April 26, 1960, in Bob Eckhardt Personal Papers.

85. *Texas Observer,* August 15, 1958.

86. *Texas Observer,* August 29, 1958, 1, 8; Bob Eckhardt, journal, August 8, 1958, in Bob Eckhardt Personal Papers.

87. Al Hieken, "Liberals Sweep Houston Runoffs," *Texas Observer,* August 29, 1958, 1, 8; Bob Eckhardt journal, July 25, 1958, in Bob Eckhardt Personal Papers.

88. Crawford, *Frankie,* 72.

89. Minutes, September 2, 1958, Harris County AFL-CIO Council Papers, in Special Collections, University of Texas at Arlington Libraries, AR-20, Box 6, Folder 1.

90. Letter from Don Ellinger to James McDevitt, August 27, 1958, W. Don Ellinger Papers, in Special Collections, University of Texas at Arlington Libraries, 110 Series 9, Box 1.

91. Stephenson, "The Democrats of Texas," 95.

9. Freshman Legislator of the Year, 1959

1. Morris, "Legislating in Texas," 46.
2. "Political Profile: Harris' Eckhardt," *Texas Observer,* June 15, 1962.
3. See *Texas Observer,* May 9, 1959, 1.
4. Willie Morris, "Legislating in Texas," 42.
5. Bob Eckhardt 1962 campaign brochure, in Nadine Eckhardt Personal Papers.
6. "Why Not Try the Constitution," notes, in Bob Eckhardt Personal Papers, Box 10: Politics, Folder: Notes.
7. Quoted in letter from Franklin Jones to J. Edwin Smith, in Ann Adams, ed., *The Public and Private Letters of Franklin Jones Sr., Vol. II: Mellow Manana, 1975–1980* (Oak Harbor, Wash.: Packrat Press, 1983), 44.
8. Letter from Bob Eckhardt to Joel Fleishman, September 8, 1986, in Bob Eckhardt Personal Papers, Box 1, Folder: Joel Fleishman.
9. "Political Profile: Harris' Eckhardt," *Texas Observer,* June 15, 1962.
10. "Speaker Race Claim Bumps," *Austin Times,* August 28, 1958, 7; Bob Eckhardt, journal, July 13, 1959, in Bob Eckhardt Personal Papers.
11. *J. W. Luttes et al. v. State of Texas,* 159 Tex. 500, 324 S.W.2d 167 (1958).
12. Handwritten draft of letter from Bob Eckhardt to Assistant Attorney General Ken Cross, n.d. (circa 1987), in Bob Eckhardt Personal Papers, Box 16, Folder: Letter to Ken Cross.
13. Bob Eckhardt, journal, January 1959, in Bob Eckhardt Personal Papers.
14. Jean Dugger Sherrill conversation with Gary Keith, February 27, 1999.
15. Malcolm McGregor interview, February 19, 1996.
16. See letters from Franklin Jones to J. Edwin Smith, July 14, 1978, and Ann Adams, October 10, 1984, in Adams, *The Public and Private Letters of Franklin Jones Sr., Vol. II,* 110.

17. Bob Eckhardt, journal, August 11, 1959, in Bob Eckhardt Personal Papers.

18. Cartoon in *Texas Observer,* November 6, 1959, 1; "Dr. Jekyll and Mr. Hyde," *Texas Observer,* December 4, 1959, 1.

19. Letter from Franklin Jones to Bob Eckhardt, June 15, 1983, in Bob Eckhardt Personal Papers, Box 1, Folder: Franklin Jones.

20. Haverford Lectures, February 14, 1977, in Bob Eckhardt Personal Papers, Box 11 (Eckhardt's edit of the transcripts in some places, others unedited).

21. *Texas Observer,* January 16, 1959, 1–8.

22. Texas Legislative Service, *Roster* (Blue Book), 1959, 1961.

23. Undated lecture on the Texas legislature and January 24, 1977, lecture, Haverford Lectures, in Bob Eckhardt Personal Papers, Box 11 (Eckhardt's edit of the transcripts in some places, others unedited).

24. Don Gladden interview, August 24, 1978.

25. See *Texas State AFL-CIO News,* March 1959, Fred H. Schmidt Collection, AR 296, Box 1, Folder 5; *Houston Post,* May 1, 1960, AR 110 Series 11, 8-5, in Special Collections, University of Texas at Arlington Libraries.

26. "Take a Look at the 56th Legislature," Texas State AFL-CIO, Don Kennard Collection, in Special Collections, University of Texas at Arlington Libraries, AR-128, 128-2-6.

27. *House Journal,* May 6, 1959, 2625; "Eckhardt Labor Bill Move Fails," *Houston Post,* May 7, 1959, 15.

28. Fred Schmidt interview, October 21, 1994.

29. *House Journal,* May 19, 1959, First Called Session, 75–76; Bob Eckhardt, journal, May 31, 1959, in Bob Eckhardt Personal Papers.

30. Letter from Bob Eckhardt to Fred Schmidt, August 25, 1960, and attached material, Fred H. Schmidt Collection, in Special Collections, University of Texas at Arlington Libraries.

31. *Texas Observer,* August 28, 1959.

32. *Texas Observer,* April 11, 1959, 3.

33. Letter from Walter G. Hall to Bob Eckhardt, February 16, 1959, in Walter Gardner Hall Papers, Rice University Fondren Library, Woodson Research Center, MS 280-6.

34. *House Journal,* May 4, 1959.

35. Haverford Lectures, January 24, 1977, in Bob Eckhardt Personal Papers, Box 11, (Eckhardt's edit of the transcripts in some places, others unedited.)

36. Letter from Hall to Eckhardt, February 16, 1959.

37. Bob Eckhardt, journal, April 4, 1959, in Bob Eckhardt Personal Papers.

38. Letter from Robert C. Eckhardt to Russell Riggins, Texas Gas Corporation, September 12, 1960, in Robert C. Eckhardt Collection, Center for American History, University of Texas at Austin, Box 3J308, Folder: Personal Items.

39. *House Journal,* March 2, 1959, 547–548.

40. Malcolm McGregor interview, February 19, 1996.

41. Dugger, "A Fair Tax," quoting 1959 *Observer* interviews; Ronnie Dugger, "Three Clichés and the Natural Gas Tax," *Texas Observer,* March 21, 1959, and April 25, 1959.

42. *Texas Observer,* April 4, 1959, 1.

43. Bob Eckhardt, journal, July 6, 1959, in Bob Eckhardt Personal Papers.

44. Letter from Bob Eckhardt to Russell Riggins, September 12, 1960, in Robert C. Eckhardt Collection, Center for American History, University of Texas at Austin, Box 3J308, Folder: Personal Items.

45. *House Journal,* June 16, 1959, 833; June 30, 1959, 321.

46. *Transcontinental Pipeline Corp and Tennessee Gas Transmission Co.* Lee Jones, Associated Press story, December 15, 1960, Don Kennard Collection, in Special Collections, University of Texas at Arlington Libraries, 128-9-6.

47. *Luttes v. Texas.*

48. This account of Eckhardt's passage of the Open Beaches Act draws heavily from his accounts in an untitled handwritten manuscript (Eckhardt Personal Papers, Box 16); in Robert C. Eckhardt, "A Rational National Policy on the Public Use of Beaches," *Syracuse Law Review* 24, no. 3 (summer 1973); "The Galveston Storm of 1983—How Hurricane Alicia spawned a Legal Tornado," Box 3M42, in Robert C. Eckhardt Collection, Center for American History, University of Texas at Austin; Haverford Lecture, January 24, 1977, in Bob Eckhardt Personal Papers, Box 11, (Eckhardt's edit of the transcripts in some places, others unedited); and Bob Eckhardt journal, in Bob Eckhardt Personal Papers.

49. Malcolm McGregor interview, February 19, 1996; Rosalind Eckhardt interview, August 23, 1994.

50. Eckhardt, "A Rational National Policy on Public Use of the Beaches," 967–988, quotation on 968.

51. Eckhardt, "A Rational National Policy on Public Use of the Beaches," 967–988, and Hargrave's Law Tract, quoted in *Bagott v. Orr* (1801), 972.

52. Bob Eckhardt, handwritten manuscript, in Bob Eckhardt Personal Papers, Box 16.

53. *San Luis Gazette,* April 13, 1841, quoted in Eckhardt untitled manuscript, in Bob Eckhardt Personal Papers, Box 16.

54. Bob Eckhardt, handwritten manuscript, in Bob Eckhardt Personal Papers, Box 16.

55. Handwritten draft of letter from Bob Eckhardt to Assistant Attorney General Ken Cross, n.d. (circa 1987), in Bob Eckhardt Personal Papers, Box 16, Folder: Letter to Ken Cross.

56. Keith Ozmore, "Can't Take Texas' Open Beaches for Granted," *Houston Chronicle,* August 6, 1989, H1; Ed Overholser, "Beach Bill Would Penalize Public," *Austin American,* July 5, 1959, A8.

57. "Beach Bill Eludes Knife," *Texas Observer,* July 11, 1959, 2.

58. "Beach Bill Advanced by House," *Austin American,* July 10, 1959, A3.

59. *House Journal,* July 9, 1959, 469–486; July 10, 1959, 504–505.

60. Bob Eckhardt interview, March 1, 1994.

61. Bo Byers, "Afterthoughts on Legislature," *Houston Chronicle,* August 9, 1959.

62. *Seaway Co. v. Attorney General,* 375 S.W.2d 923 (Tex. Civ. App. 1964); see Steve McKeon, "Public Access to Beaches," *Stanford Law Review* (February 1970), 564–586; Daniel A. Degnan, "Public Rights in Ocean Beaches: A Theory of Prescription," *Syracuse Law Review,* 24 (1973): 935; Luise Welby, "Public Access to Private Beaches," *UCLA Journal of Environmental Law and Policy,* 69 (1986): 71.

63. In *Hirtz v. State of Texas,* the court said that the Open Beaches Act "did not create an easement that the public did not already own at common law." *Seaway v. Attorney General, Matcha and Matcha v. Mattox,* and *Feinman* beat back arguments that there was an unconstitutional taking of property through the state's regulatory activity. In 1983, Hurricane Alicia roared aground, moving the line of vegetation inward up to 100 and 200 feet in places, even destroying structures. Texas Attorney General Jim Mattox moved to stop reconstruction and, with Eckhardt's help with briefs and testimony, won a ruling that the easement does move with the natural movement of the vegetation line. See also Ozmore, "Can't Take Texas' Open Beaches for Granted."

10. The Veteran Legislator

1. *Texas Observer,* January 15, 1960, 1; Bob Eckhardt, journal, January 11, 1960, in Bob Eckhardt Personal Papers.

2. "Political Profile: Harris' Eckhardt," *Texas Observer,* June 15, 1962.

3. Bob Eckhardt and Charles L. Black Jr., *The Tides of Power: Conversations on the American Constitution* (New Haven: Yale University Press, 1976), 154.

4. Bob Eckhardt, journal, August 16, September 9, and July 15, 1960, in Bob Eckhardt Personal Papers.

5. Bob Eckhardt interview, February 27, 1999; letter from Rosalind Eckhardt to Bob Eckhardt, 1968, in Bob Eckhardt Personal Papers, Box 13.

6. Bob Eckhardt, journal, November 26 and December 20, 1960–January 2, 1961, in Bob Eckhardt Personal Papers.

7. Bob Eckhardt, journal, February 19, 1961, in Bob Eckhardt Personal Papers; Ed Ball interview, May 28, 2004.

8. Nadine Brammer letters, February 2, March 6, and July 28, 1961, in Nadine Eckhardt Personal Papers, Folder: 1961; Bill Brammer letters, Billy Lee Brammer Papers, Collection 007, Box 2 (Nadine Eckhardt Papers), Special Collections, Texas State University.

9. Handwritten letter from Bob Eckhardt to Nadine Eckhardt, December 6, 1975, in Bob Eckhardt Personal Papers, Box 1 (Persons).

10. Letter from Bill Brammer to Nadine Brammer, undated, in Nadine Eckhardt Personal Papers, Folder: 1961.

11. Letters from Bob Eckhardt to Nadine Brammer, August 20, 21, September 27, October 8, 10, 16, November 1, 1961, and undated letter on St. Louis Hilton letterhead, in Nadine Eckhardt Personal Papers, Folder: 1961.

12. Nadine Eckhardt letters, March 13, May 10, and August 23, 1963, and undated, in Nadine Eckhardt Personal Papers, Folder: 1963.

13. Rosalind Eckhardt interview, August 23, 1994.

14. Letters from Orissa Eckhardt, in Nadine Eckhardt Personal Papers, File: Bob Eckhardt Memorabilia.

15. Nadine Eckhardt letters, November 19, and July 28, 1962, in Nadine Eckhardt Personal Papers, Folder: 1962.

16. Willie Morris, *North Toward Home* (Boston: Houghton Mifflin, 1967).

17. Morris, "Legislating in Texas," 40, 42, 44.

18. "Celia Eckhardt the Distaff Side of Scholarly Pair," *Houston Post,* December 18, 1977, 1D.

19. Bernard Rapoport interview, January 16, 1995.

20. *Texas State AFL-CIO News,* January 1961; Ronnie Dugger, "A Quirky Integrity," *Texas Observer,* April 2, 1999, 23; Polakoff, "The Development of the Texas State C.I.O. Council," 408–409; letter from Fred Schmidt to O. A. Knight, June 14, 1955, Fred H. Schmidt Collection, in Special Collections, University of Texas at Arlington Libraries, 296-1-3; *The Texas Federationist* (Texas State Federation of Labor newspaper), n.d., Fred H. Schmidt Collection, in Special Collections, University of Texas at Arlington Libraries.

21. *Dallas Morning News,* January 31, 1960, Texas AFL-CIO Collection, in Special Collections, University of Texas at Arlington Libraries, AR 110 Series 11, 8–5.

22. Bob Eckhardt, journal, February and April 27, 1960, in Bob Eckhardt Personal Papers.

23. Bob Eckhardt, journal, April 2 and 21, 1960, in Bob Eckhardt Personal Papers.

24. Crawford, *Frankie,* 95.

25. Bob Eckhardt handwritten note, April 1960, in Bob Eckhardt Personal Papers.

26. Orissa Eckhardt Arend interview, March 27, 1997.

27. Rosalind Eckhardt interview; Bob Eckhardt interview, 1984, with Chandler Davidson.

28. Democrats of Texas Clubs Democratic Reporter, March 1960, Harris County Democratic Party Records, in Center for American History, University of Texas at Austin, Box 4C507, Folder: State Convention, Austin, Texas, June 14, 1960.

29. Felder, "The Politics of the Texas Gulf Coast, 1945 to 1960," 82, 85.

30. Davidson, *Biracial Politics,* 100, Table 7.3, 196, 199, 200–202.

31. Walter Mansell, "Top Liberal Dems Lose Places at Convention," *Houston Chronicle,* May 10, 1960, 1.

32. *Texas Observer,* September 23, 1960.

33. Crawford, *Frankie,* 84–85, 95.

34. Crawford, *Frankie,* 87; Nadine Eckhardt notes, in Nadine Eckhardt Personal Papers.

35. Frankie Carter Randolph Papers, Rice University Fondren Library, Woodson Research Center, Box 5, Folder 5.9.

36. Harris County AFL-CIO Council Papers, AR-20, Box 6, Folder 1, in Special Collections, University of Texas at Arlington Libraries; *Texas State AFL-CIO News,* March 1961.

37. Bo Byers, "Liberal Dems Map Plans in Austin Meet," *Houston Chronicle,* September 14, 1961.

38. Letter from Franklin Jones to Bob Eckhardt, June 16, 1981, in Adams, *The Public and Private Letters of Franklin Jones Sr., Vol. III,* 51.

39. *Austin Statesman,* October 24, 1961; *Baytown Sun,* October 24, 1961.

40. Sherrill, "A Texan vs. Big Oil," 42; Ed Ball interview, May 28, 2004.

41. Welsh, "Building Lyndon Johnson," 59.

42. Letter from Teresa Green to Nadine Eckhardt, April 11, 1962; Bob Eckhardt letter to Nadine, April 16, 1962, in Nadine Eckhardt Personal Papers, Folder: 1962.

43. 1962 Eckhardt campaign brochure, in Nadine Eckhardt Personal Papers, Folder: 1962.

44. Davidson, *Biracial Politics,* 38–42; Mary Beth Rogers, *Barbara Jordan: American Hero* (New York: Bantam Books, 1998), 84.

45. Bob Eckhardt, "In Memory of Barbara Jordan," January 18, 1996, in Bob Eckhardt Personal Papers, Box 1, Folder: Barbara Jordan; Rogers, *Barbara Jordan,* 99.

46. "Money Isn't Everything in Political Campaign," *Houston Chronicle,* May 20, 1962, 2.

47. Davidson, *Biracial Politics,* 101, 199; Rogers, *Barbara Jordan,* 90.

48. Bob Eckhardt, journal, May 6, 1960, in Bob Eckhardt Personal Papers.

49. Nadine Eckhardt letters, November 19, 1962, in Nadine Eckhardt Personal Papers, Folder: 1962.

50. Pryor campaign leaflet and 1962 Eckhardt campaign brochure and statement, in Nadine Eckhardt Personal Papers, Folder: 1962.

51. Haverford Lectures, March 21, 1977, in Bob Eckhardt Personal Papers.

52. List of Turman Pledges (75), including Eckhardt, in Kennard Collection 128-11-1; Neil Caldwell interview, August 27, 1978.

53. Bob Eckhardt, journal, April 11, 1961, in Bob Eckhardt Personal Papers.

54. Stuart Long, "Austin Report," April 9, 1961, Don Kennard Collection, in Special Collections, University of Texas at Arlington Libraries, 128-3-11.

55. *House Journal,* April 12, 1961, 1134.

56. The following material is from Bob Eckhardt, "How We Got the Dirtiest Stream in America: Regulation of Local Hazards—The Houston Ship Channel," *Texas International Law Journal,* 7:1 (1971): 5–28.

57. Stuart Long, "Austin Report" May 14, 1961, 3, in Don Kennard Collection, Special Collections, University of Texas at Arlington Libraries, 128-3-1.

58. Eckhardt, "How We Got the Dirtiest Stream in America," 17.

59. Stuart Long, "Austin Report" May 14, 1961, in Don Kennard Collection, Special Collections, University of Texas at Arlington Libraries, 128-3-1.

60. "Price's Choice: Payroll Levy, Deficit Plan," and "Early Proposals on State Taxes," *Texas Observer,* January 21, 1961, 1, 8.

61. Morris, "Legislating in Texas."

62. "Political Profile: Harris' Eckhardt," *Texas Observer,* June 15, 1962.

63. HB 481, *House Journal,* May 16, 1961, 2091–2093; May 22, 1961, 2385–2393.

64. Untitled ms., signed by Bob Eckhardt, March 3, 1987, in Bob Eckhardt Personal Papers, Box 16, Folder: State of Texas—Taxes; *House Journal,* April 20, 1961, 1293–1294.

65. *Texas Observer,* July 8, 1961, 4.

66. Harris County AFL-CIO Council Papers, June 14, 1961, in Special Collections, University of Texas at Arlington, AR-20, Box 6, Folder 1.

67. *Austin American,* July 11, 1961, 1.

68. "Political Profile: Harris' Eckhardt"; *House Journal,* July 19, 1961, 235–236.

69. Bob Eckhardt, journal, July 30, 1961, in Bob Eckhardt Personal Papers.

70. Morris, "Legislating in Texas."

71. *House Journal,* August 4, 1961, 784–786.

72. *House Journal,* August 12, 1961, 70–72.

73. "Lobbyists Jubilant Over Tax Vote; Some Solons Cheer, Others Sulk," *Houston Chronicle,* August 9, 1961.

74. Bob Eckhardt, "The Worst Tax in Texas History and Why I Voted Against It," in Special Collections, University of Texas at Arlington Librarien.

75. *House Journal,* January 16, 1962, 131–135.

76. HSR 77, Third Called Session, 57th Legislature, Texas State Archives; *House Journal,* January 17, 1962, 152; Haverford Lecture, January 24, 1977, in Bob Eckhardt Personal Papers, Box 11; "Congress Urged to Reciprocate," *Texas Observer,* January 19, 1962, 7.

77. Connally, *In History's Shadow,* 224.

78. Connally, *In History's Shadow,* 242.

79. *Corpus Christi Caller,* January 8, 1963; "The 1963 Legislature," *Texas Observer,* January 10, 1963, 3. Shakespeare wrote in "Measure for Measure," Act II, Sc. 2, 1.108: "Oh, it is excellent to have a giant's strength, But it is tyrannous to use it like a giant."

80. Neil Addington, "Eckhardt Protests House Rules Change," *Houston Post,* May 28, 1963.

81. Bob Eckhardt interview, March 2, 1995.

82. Morris, "Legislating in Texas," 45.

83. Crawford and Keever, *John Connally,* 149.

84. *Texas Observer,* May 30, 1963.

11. Readying for Congress

1. Letter from Orissa Eckhardt to Bob and Nadine Eckhardt, September 27, 1964, in Nadine Eckhardt Personal Papers, Folder: Bob Eckhardt Memorabilia, Letters from Orissa.

2. Ronnie Dugger, ed., *Three Men in Texas: Bedichek, Webb, and Dobie* (Austin: University of Texas Press, 1967), vii.

3. McArthur and Smith, *Minnie Fisher Cunningham,* 203.

4. Creekmore Fath interview, July 6, 1994.

5. Crawford, *Frankie,* 95.

6. Quotations from Marge Crumbaker article, *Houston Post,* reprinted in *Texas Observer,* November 25, 1966.

7. Bob Eckhardt untitled ms., March 3, 1987, in Bob Eckhardt Personal Papers, Box 16, Folder: State of Texas—Taxes.

8. James Hyatt, "Forbes Top Spender in Primary—$26,875," *Houston Chronicle,* May 17, 1964, 16.

9. Letter from Mrs. Bob Eckhardt to Lyman Jones and Sherman Miles at AFL-CIO, April 13, 1964, in Nadine Eckhardt Personal Papers, Folder: Bob Eckhardt Memorabilia.

10. Bob Eckhardt untitled ms., March 3, 1987, in Bob Eckhardt Personal Papers, Box 16. Folder: State of Texas—Taxes.

11. Photo, *Corpus Christi Caller,* May 27, 1965, 12.

12. AFL-CIO Committee on Political Education, "How Your Senators and Representatives Voted 1947–1956," in Ann and Milton Lower Personal Papers, Box 55, Folder: Labor Record.

13. Letter from Charles Black to Bob Eckhardt, July 20, 1963, in Nadine Eckhardt Personal Papers, Folder: 1963.

14. Letter from Nadine Eckhardt to mother, June 10, 1963, in Nadine Eckhardt Personal Papers, Folder: 1963.

15. Letter from Charles Black to Bob Eckhardt, July 20, 1963, in Nadine Eckhardt Personal Papers, Folder: 1963.

16. Crawford and Keever, *John Connally,* 160–161, 183; Connally, *In History's Shadow,* 226.

17. Crawford and Keever, *John Connally,* 186–187.

18. Chandler Davidson, *Race and Class in Texas Politics* (Princeton, N.J.: Princeton University Press, 1990), 54.

19. Crawford and Keever, *John Connally,* 160–161.

20. Redistricting information from Wesley S. Chumlea, "The Politics of Legislative Apportionment in Texas 1921–1957," (PhD diss., University of Texas, 1959).

21. Davidson, *Biracial Politics,* 60.

22. *Bush v. Martin,* 224 F. Supp. 499; *Bush v. Martin,* 84 S. Ct. 709 (1964).

23. *Kilgarlin v. Martin,* 252 F. Supp. 404 (S.D. Tex. 1966); see Bob Tutt, "State Reapportionment to be Pushed in Texas," *Houston Chronicle,* June 16, 1964, 15.

24. *House Journal,* January 27, 1965, 84.

25. Bob Eckhardt interview, December 14, 1994.

26. "Harris County Election Analysis," in Harris County Democratic Party Records, Center for American History, The University of Texas at Austin, Box 4C516.

27. "Harris Legislators Show Mixed Reaction to Districting Proposal," *Houston Chronicle,* January 12, 1965, 21.

28. "Harris County Plan for Legislative Districts, Using Plan-A Congressional Districts," in Harris County Democratic Party Records, Center for American History, University of Texas at Austin, Box 4C516.

29. Curtis Graves interview, December 22, 2005.

30. Mickey Herskowitz, *Sharpstown Revisited: Frank Sharp and a Tale of Dirty Politics in Texas* (Austin: Eakin Press, 1994), 145.

31. "Houston is Accommodated; San Antonio on the Rack," *Texas Observer,* June 11, 1965, 8; Davidson, *Biracial Politics,* 69, 71; Dennis M. Simon, "Texans in the United States House of Representatives: A History of Electoral, Partisan, and Ideological Change, 1936–2000" (paper presented at Jim Wright Symposium on Texas Congressional Leaders, Texas Christian University, Fort Worth, Texas, April 19, 2002).

32. Jake Johnson, personal communication, June 4, 1998.

33. *House Journal,* May 31, 1965.

34. *Harper v. Virginia Board of Elections,* 383 U.S. 663 (1966).

35. University of Texas Institute of Public Affairs, "The Fifty-Ninth Texas Legislature: A Review of Its Work," 1966; *House Journal,* February 21, 1966, 39–40.

36. Herskowitz, *Sharpstown Revisited,* 133–136.

37. Curtis M. Graves, "Negro Proclamation," certificate, May 14, 1966, in Nadine Eckhardt Personal Papers.

38. Letter from Curtis Graves to Bob Eckhardt, February 14, 1967, in Robert C. Eckhardt Collection, Center for American History, University of Texas at Austin, Box 15 House of Representatives 90–93, Folder: Texas, State of . . . Legislation.

39. Rogers, *Barbara Jordan,* 104.

40. Edward Stumpf interview, Benjamin N. Woodson Papers, in Fran Dressman, *Gus Wortham: Portrait of a Leader* (College Station: Texas A&M University Press, 1994), 178.

41. February 18 and 23, 1966, minutes; Minutes of Harris County COPE, March 23, 1966; Harris County AFL-CIO Council Papers, AR-20, Box 6, Folder 1 and 7, in Special Collections, University of Texas at Arlington Libraries.

42. Letter from Bob Eckhardt to Rudd Ross Jr., June 2, 1966, in Walter Gardner Hall Papers, Woodson Research Center, Rice University Fondren Library.

43. Curtis Graves interview, December 22, 2005.

44. Bob Eckhardt 1966 campaign brochure, in Nadine Eckhardt Personal Papers, Folder: Bob Eckhardt memorabilia.

45. Bob Tutt, "Labor Studies Low Turnout in Primary," *Houston Chronicle,* June 23, 1966.

46. Welsh, "Building Lyndon Johnson," 59.

47. Bob Eckhardt interview, October 7, 1994.

48. Nadine Eckhardt, journal, May 10, 1966, in Nadine Eckhardt Personal Papers, Folder: 1962.

49. Richard Scammon, *America Votes* 7 (1966), Congressional Quarterly Press, 1968, 392; *Congressional Quarterly Weekly,* May 13, 1966, 973.

50. Harold Scarlett, "Eckhardt Seems to be Victor," *Houston Post,* May 8, 1966, 1; "McKaskle Decides to Drop Election Contest Plans," unidentified news clipping, in Harris County Democratic Party Records, Center for American History, University of Texas at Austin, Box 4C513, Folder: Candidates—1966.

51. Letter from Victor Emmanuel to Robert Eckhardt, November 21, 1966, in Nadine Eckhardt Personal Papers, Folder: 1966.

52. Bob Eckhardt handwritten note, October 3, 1966, in Nadine Eckhardt Personal Papers.

53. Letters from Orissa Eckhardt, September 20 and 21, October 19, 1966, in Nadine Eckhardt Personal Papers, Folder: Bob Eckhardt Memorabilia.

54. Letter from Dr. Harold G. Scheie to Bob Eckhardt, in Nadine Eckhardt Personal Papers, Folder: Bob Eckhardt Memorabilia; Orissa Arend interview, March 27, 1997.

55. Great Issues Committee Political Forum, Texas A&M University, November 29, 1966.

12. Inside Congress, Inside Washington

1. Bob Eckhardt interview, 1980, with Studs Terkel, *The Great Divide: Second Thoughts on the American Dream* (New York: Pantheon Books, 1988), 364–367.

2. Tip O'Neill and William Novak, *Man of the House: the Life and Political Memoirs of Speaker Tip O'Neill* (New York: Random House, 1987).

3. Eckhardt news release, February 2, 1968, in Nadine Eckhardt Personal Papers, Folder: Bob Eckhardt Memorabilia.

4. Jake Pickle interview, May 24, 1999.

5. Yoder, "Washington Notes: Eckhardt of Texas," 34–36.

6. Bob Eckhardt quotation, in Robert C. Eckhardt Collection, Center for American History, University of Texas at Austin, Box 3M-56, Folder: Eckhardt Words of Wisdom.

7. Letter from Bob Eckhardt to constituent, February 1967, in Robert C. Eckhardt Collection, Center for American History, University of Texas at Austin, Box 17, Folder: Form Letters.

8. Letter from Bill White to *Texas Monthly,* July 7, 1994, in Jan Reid Collection, Special Collections, Texas State University, Box 769, Folder 8.

9. *Congressional Record* 78 (May 25, 1971): H4303. Quote is from *Measure for Measure.*

10. Bob Eckhardt quotation, in Robert C. Eckhardt Collection, Center for American History, University of Texas at Austin, Box 3M-56, Folder: Eckhardt Words of Wisdom.

11. Bob Eckhardt quotation, Gloria Cochran Memorandum, August 1, 1980, in Robert C. Eckhardt Collection, Center for American History, University of Texas at Austin, Box 3M-56, Folder: Jack Anderson.

12. "Texan Offers Plan to Replace Tax Surcharge," UPI article, undated, in Nadine Eckhardt Personal Papers, Folder: 1969.

13. Quoted in Daniel Rapoport, *Inside the House* (Chicago: Follett Publishing Company, 1975), 92.

14. Bernard Rapoport interview, February 20, 2002.

15. Tom Whatley interview, June 30, 1994.

16. Bob Eckhardt interview, February 26, 1995.

17. "The Ear," *Washington Star,* December 16, 1976; Tom Whatley personal communication, March 11, 2004.

18. *Washington Post Magazine,* September 14, 1986, 72–73.

19. Bob Eckhardt interview, March 18, 1994.

20. "'Bow Tie Gang' Eckhardt among 10 Worst-Dressed in 'Schlump City' Report," *Houston Post,* December 6, 1977, B4; letter from Tom Turner to Bob Eckhardt, October 20, 1975, in Robert C. Eckhardt Collection, Center for American History, University of Texas at Austin, Box 3M-56.

21. Curtis Graves interview, December 22, 2005.

22. Shel Holtz, Atlantic Richfield Co., *ARCOspark* 5, no. 46 (November 18, 1977), in Ann and Milton Lower Personal Papers, Box 37, Folder: Eckhardt Biographical.

23. Sherrill, "A Texan vs. Big Oil," 38*ff.*, quote on 38.

24. Carl Bernstein, "Commuter Cycling Picks Up 'Speed,'" *Washington Post*, June 14, 1970, E1.

25. Evie Dubrow comments, Bob Eckhardt memorial service, Washington, D.C., February 26, 2002; Joan Sanger, personal communication, July 16, 2000.

26. Letter in Robert C. Eckhardt Collection, Center for American History, University of Texas at Austin, Box 3M56, Folder: Bicycle Stories.

27. Letter from *Family Weekly* to Representative Eckhardt, May 4, 1979, in Robert C. Eckhardt Collection, Center for American History, University of Texas at Austin, Box 3M56; Nina Dougherty Rowe, "This Congressman Commutes," *Bicycling*, March 1980.

28. Memo from Jake Jacobsen to President Johnson, January 9, 1967, in LBJ Library, University of Texas at Austin, Names file: Eckhardt.

29. See, for example, John Jacobs, *A Rage for Justice: The Passion and Politics of Phillip Burton* (Berkeley: University of California Press, 1995), 240, on Pickle's opposition to Phil Burton and Democratic Study Group reformers.

30. Bob Eckhardt interview, March 18, 1994.

31. Bob Eckhardt, "Some of My Compatriots in Politics," in Bob Eckhardt Personal Papers, Box 4, Folder: Jottings.

32. Versions of this poem appear in handwritten card, in Bob Eckhardt Personal Papers, Box 4; in Box: Writings, Folder: Poem; in Yoder, "Washington Notes: Eckhardt of Texas," 35; and in Terkel, *The Great Divide*, 365–366.

33. Bob Eckhardt note, in Bob Eckhardt Personal Papers, Box 18 (Legislative Issues), Folder: Persons—Dingell.

34. Bob Eckhardt, "In Memory of Barbara Jordan," January 18, 1996, in Bob Eckhardt Personal Papers, Folder: Barbara Jordan.

35. Curtis Graves interview, December 22, 2005.

36. Bob Eckhardt, "Some of My Compatriots in Politics," in Bob Eckhardt Personal Papers, Box 4, Folder: Jottings.

37. Lecture Notes, Washington School, in Robert C. Eckhardt Collection, Center for American History, University of Texas at Austin, Box 3M-22, Folder: Washington School 2nd Lecture, February 2, 1982.

38. Jake Pickle interview, May 24, 1999.

39. See A. Lee Fritschler, *Smoking and Politics: Policymaking and the Federal Bureaucracy*, 3rd ed., Englewood Cliffs, N.J.: Prentice-Hall, 1983.

40. *Congressional Quarterly Almanac* 25 (1969), 886.

41. "Congress and Government," *Congressional Quarterly Almanac* 30 (1974), 641.

42. Griffen Smith, Jr. and Paul Burka, "The Best, the Worst, and the Fair-to-Middlin'," *Texas Monthly*, May 1976, 106.

43. Memo from Frances Gray to Ann Lower, July 16, 1980, in Ann and Milton Lower Personal Papers, Box 35.

44. Robert Cochran, "It was Just a Function of Money," unpublished ms.; John L. Pery, *Rome News-Tribune*, November 25, 1984, and letter from Robert Cochran to Bob Eckhardt, March 1, 1983, in Bob Eckhardt Personal Papers, Box: 1 (Persons), Folder: Cochran, Bob.

45. Gloria Cochran and Frances Gray interviews, August 13, 2004.

46. Gloria Cochran interview, August 14, 2004, and correspondence, May 29, 2004.

47. Vera Glaser, "Clayton Powell Bad Boy of Congress and Likes It," *Houston Chronicle*, June 27, 1965, 28; Morris K. Udall, *Too Funny to be President* (New York: Henry Holt and Co., 1988), 109–116, Young quote on 116; Bob Eckhardt, "My Most Difficult Vote," Robert C. Eckhardt Collection, Center for American History, University of Texas at Austin, Box 3M-26, Folder: My Most Difficult Vote.

48. The Constitution has no provision for "exclusion," though the House had excluded seven members in its history up to this time. See Rapoport, *Inside the House*, 172–176.

49. Robert C. Eckhardt, "The Adam Clayton Powell Case: Observation," *Texas Law Review* 45 (July 1967): 1205–1211.

50. See *Powell v. McCormack*, 395 U.S. 486 (1969), Eckhardt material on 510–511.

51. Bob Eckhardt interview, April 28, 1994.

52. "The U.S. Should De-escalate Unilaterally, Eckhardt Says," *Texas Observer*, April 28, 1967; copy of speech in Robert C. Eckhardt Collection, Center for American History, University of Texas at Austin, Box 95-147/33, Folder: Speech—Young Democratic Clubs of Texas, April 1967.

53. Card from Bob Eckhardt to Nadine Eckhardt, June 2, 1967, in Nadine Eckhardt Personal Papers, Folder: 1967.

54. Nadine Eckhardt letter, August 2, 1967, in Nadine Eckhardt Personal Papers, Folder: 1967.

55. Postcard from John Faulk to Bob and Nadine Eckhardt, November 8, 1967, in Nadine Eckhardt Personal Papers, Folder: Bob Eckhardt Memorabilia.

56. Letter from Bob Eckhardt to George Chandler, Baytown City Attorney, September 14, 1967, in Nadine Eckhardt Personal Papers.

57. Udall, *Too Funny to be President*, 120.

58. Yoder, "Washington Notes: Eckhardt of Texas," 34.

59. *New York Post*, November 17, 1967; Prepared Comments, in Robert C. Eckhardt Collection, Center for American History, University of Texas at Austin, Box 95-147/33, Folder: Vietnam Symposium New York, November 16, 1967.

60. Bob Eckhardt interview, March 1, 1994. See also Yoder, "Washington Notes: Eckhardt of Texas," 28–36; Jacobs, *A Rage for Justice*, 155–156; Erwin Knoll, ed., *American Militarism 1970: A Dialogue on the Distortion of our National Priorities and the Need to Reassert Control over the Defense Establishment* (New York: Viking Press, 1969); Erwin Knoll, ed., *War Crimes and the American Conscience* (New York: Holt, Rinehart, and Winston, 1970); Pat Kraus, ed., *Anatomy of an Undeclared War: Congressional Conference on the Pentagon Papers* (New York: International Universities Press, 1972).

61. Bob Eckhardt interview, December 14, 1994.

62. Sam Dawson interview, September 14, 2004.

63. Bob Eckhardt, statement on LBJ's March 31, 1968, announcement, April 1, 1968, in Nadine Eckhardt Personal Papers, and similar statement in *Congressional Record* 60 (April 9, 1968): E2865.

64. Letter from Bob Eckhardt to J. Sears McGee, October 1, 1968, in Robert C. Eckhardt Collection, Center for American History, University of Texas at Austin, Box 4, Folder 2.

65. Letter from Rosalind Eckhardt to Bob Eckhardt, April 3, 1968, in Nadine Eckhardt Personal Papers, Folder: Bob Eckhardt Memorabilia.

66. Bob Eckhardt, statement, April 5, 1968, in Nadine Eckhardt Personal Papers, and similar statement in *Congressional Record* 59 (April 8, 1968): H2656.

67. "Yazoo . . . Notes on Survival," *Harper's,* June 1970; Celia Morris, *Finding Celia's Place* (College Station: Texas A&M University Press, 2000), 165–166.

68. Michael Barone, Grant Ujifusa, and Douglas Matthews, *The Almanac of American Politics* (Boston: Gambit, 1972).

69. Bob Eckhardt interview, April 28, 1994.

70. *Congressional Record* 190 (November 30, 1970): H10907.

71. *Congressional Record* 84 (May 25, 1970).

72. Representative Bob Eckhardt, *Face the Nation* transcript, April 4, 1971, 13–14, in Robert C. Eckhardt Papers, Center for American History, University of Texas at Austin, Box 95-147/33, Folder: Transcript—*Face the Nation,* April 4, 1971.

73. "Eckhardt Joins Tour to Protest War," *Houston Chronicle,* May 7, 1971.

74. "Presidential Candidate Nomination," *Bob Eckhardt's Quarterly Report* 4 (Fall 1968): 3.

75. Bob Eckhardt, "Dear Colleague" letter, September 15, 1969, in Nadine Eckhardt Personal Papers. Folder: Bob Eckhardt Memorabilia.

76. Yoder, "Washington Notes: Eckhardt of Texas"; *Congressional Record* 116 (May 18, 1970).

77. Cumulative voting records, 1967–1979, compiled by Congressman Eckhardt's staff, in Ann and Milton Lower Personal Papers, Box 55, Folder: Voting Record '67–'79.

78. *Congressional Quarterly Almanac* 23 (1967), and vol. 24 (1968), 25 (1969), 26 (1970); 1974 campaign brochure, in Nadine Eckhardt Personal Papers.

79. Eckhardt and Black, *The Tides of Power,* 34.

80. "District 8 Candidates Discuss Issues," *Houston Post,* April 26, 1970, 15; "8th District Congressional Candidates," *Houston Chronicle Voter's Guide,* April 26, 1970, 6–7.

81. Eckhardt interview, April 28, 1994; Walter Mansell, "Independent Liberal Democrats Plan Permanent Organization," *Houston Chronicle,* July 16, 1967.

82. Statement from Bill and Teresa Green to Bob Hall, chairman of Harris County Democrats, November 17, 1969, in Nadine Eckhardt Personal Papers, Folder: Bob Eckhardt Memorabilia; Bob Eckhardt quotation in Fred Bonavita, "Liberal Demos Ask New Blood, Reorganization," *Houston Post,* December 9, 1968, 20.

83. Bob Eckhardt interview, April 28, 1994.

84. Letter from Bob Eckhardt to Hank Brown, December 21, 1970; telegram from Bob Eckhardt to Hank Brown, January 5, 1971; letter from Bob Eckhardt to Hank Brown, January 28, 1971, in Bob Eckhardt Personal Papers, Box 1 Persons, Folder: Hank Brown.

13. The Veteran Congressman

1. E-mail message from Lynn Coleman to author, November 26, 2006.

2. Leon Hale, "Roasted Oysters in Eckhardt's Woods," *Houston Post,* May 1, 1977, B3.

3. "Eckhardt Telephone Conversation with Ken Klutsam of the Northeast News RE: Desegregation Plan for Houston," May 22, 1980, transcript of Tape III, in Robert C. Eckhardt Collection, Center for American History, University of Texas at Austin, Box 3M-26, Folder: Transcribed Tapes (Radio).

4. Letter from Bob Eckhardt to students, March 18, 1969, and letter to Dr. Donald Ford, March 29, 1972, in Robert C. Eckhardt Collection, Center for American History, University of Texas at Austin, Box: HISD Busing and Integration.

5. Rogers, *Barbara Jordan;* Ben Barnes interview, December 6, 2004.

6. Transcript, *60 Minutes,* November 28, 1971, in Robert C. Eckhardt Collection, Center for American History, University of Texas at Austin, Box 95–147/33, Folder: Transcript: 60 Minutes (CBS).

7. "McGovern Supporters Stage Rally," *Houston Post,* July 4, 1972, A14.

8. *New York Times,* July 5, 1972. McGovern also considered Senators Thomas Eagleton, Reubin Askew, Edmund Muskie, Hubert Humphrey, Abraham Ribicoff, and Gaylord Nelson; Boston Mayor Kevin White; and Wisconsin Governor Patrick Lucey. McGovern eventually named Sargent Shriver as his running mate.

9. Typed statement for Congressman Eckhardt's Meeting with the Press, July 6, 1972, in Nadine Eckhardt Personal Papers, Folder: Bob Eckhardt Memorabilia.

10. Bob Eckhardt interview, April 28, 1994.

11. *Houston Chronicle,* May 5, 1974.

12. Many are collected at the Center for American History, University of Texas at Austin.

13. Letter from Bob Eckhardt to *New Yorker,* October 3, 1975, in Robert C. Eckhardt Collection, Center for American History, University of Texas at Austin, Box 3M-56, Folder: Eckhardt cartoons.

14. Bob Eckhardt, "The 'Art' of Politics: A Short History of Political Cartooning," *Lithopinion* 5, no. 2, issue 18 (summer 1970).

15. See, for example, "A Representative from Texas Doodles House Tedium Away," *New York Times,* May 9, 1975; also, *Washington Evening Star,* April 6, 1971.

16. Bernard Rapoport letters, July 3, 1969, in Bernard Rapoport Papers, Center for American History, University of Texas at Austin, Box 4C595, Folder: Robert Eckhardt.

17. "Eckhardt's Newsletter a Winner: Houston Lawmaker Cashes in on Former Experience," *Dallas Morning News,* September 21, 1969.

18. "Eckhardt's Newsletter a Winner."

19. See, for instance, Congressman Peter Kyros's comments and Eckhardt's "Oil Prices and Inflation," *Congressional Record* 55 (April 23, 1974): E2427.

20. See articles by Bob Eckhardt: "The Adam Clayton Powell Case," 1205; "Consumer Class Actions," *Notre Dame Law Review* 45 (1970): 663; "How We got the Dirtiest Stream in America," 5; "A Rational National Policy on the Public Use of Beaches," 967; "The Presumption of Openness Under House Rules," *Harvard Journal on Legislation* 2 (1974): 279; "Citizens' Groups and Standing," *North Dakota Law Review* 51 (winter 1974): 360.

21. Letter from Charles Black to Nadine Eckhardt, February 1, 1969, in Nadine Eckhardt Personal Papers, Folder: 1968; Nadine Eckhardt, personal communication, March 26, 2003.

22. Bob Eckhardt untitled ms. for Taylor Branch, in Robert C. Eckhardt Collection, Center for American History, University of Texas at Austin, Box 3M-26, Folder: Articles for Publication; O'Neill and Novak, *Man of the House,* 299.

23. Bob Eckhardt, "Impeachment Explained," review of *Impeachment: A Handbook,* by Charles L. Black Jr., *Washington Post,* July 10, 1974, B10.

24. Bob Eckhardt and Charles L. Black Jr., *The Tides of Power: Conversations on the American Constitution* (New Haven: Yale University Press), 1976.

25. Frank Wozencraft, "Fabric of Government," *Houston Post,* April 18, 1976; Max Beloff, "The Bounds of the Constitution," *Times Literary Supplement,* October 1, 1976, with handwritten note from Charles Black, in Robert C. Eckhardt Collection, Center for American History, University of Texas at Austin, Box 3M-26, Folder: *Tides of Power* Book Reviews.

26. Dear Colleague letter from Bob Eckhardt, December 1, 1969, and attached statement, in Robert C. Eckhardt Collection, Center for American History, University of Texas at Austin, Box 3M-16, Folder: Vietnam.

27. See House Committee on Foreign Affairs, *The War Powers Resolution: A Special Study of the Committee on Foreign Affairs,* 1982, 130–131.

28. Eckhardt and Black, *The Tides of Power.*

29. House Committee on Foreign Affairs, *The War Powers Resolution,* 162–164.

30. *Congressional Record* 170 (November 7, 1973): H9648.

31. Nadine Eckhardt Divorce Petition, in Robert C. Eckhardt Collection, Center for American History, University of Texas at Austin, Box 3M56, Folder: Eckhardt—Personal Notes.

32. Bob Eckhardt interview, March 2, 1995.

33. See "Historic Cabin Transplanted," *News-Messenger,* October 23, 1980, 8A.

34. Letter from Neil Caldwell to Gary Keith, October 1, 1996.

35. Martha Patterson interview, 1994.

36. Barone, Ujifusa, and Matthews, *The Almanac of American Politics,* 1972 and 1974.

37. "Eckhardt Big Winner," *Houston Chronicle,* May 5, 1974.

38. See handwritten speech notes, in Robert C. Eckhardt Collection, Center for American History, University of Texas at Austin, Box 95–147/38, Folder: Speech: Texas State Convention, Austin, TX, September 17, 1976; quoted in Nicholas Von Hoffman, "The Texas Liberal," *Los Angeles Times-Washington Post* News Service, 1971, news clipping in John Henry Faulk Papers, Center for American History, University of Texas at Austin, Box 3E204, Folder: Texas Politics.

39. Ronnie Dugger interview, December 6, 1997.

40. Eckhardt and Black, *The Tides of Power,* 184.

41. Bob Eckhardt typed notes for speech on the "buying of elections," Speaker Foley, and congressional reform, in Bob Eckhardt Personal Papers, Folder: Tom Foley.

42. Bob Eckhardt, "The Process of Election," in Bob Eckhardt Personal Papers, Box 6, Folder: The Process of Election.

43. Democratic Study Group Campaign Fund, "8th Congressional District Texas, A Survey of Voter Attitudes and Opinions," July 1976, in Ann and Milton Lower Personal Papers, Box 33, Folder: Memos/Eckhardt.

44. "Vote Tally on Natural Gas," *Petroleum Independent,* May–June 1976, 64–65.

45. Letter from Gloria Cochran to Professor Larry Dodd, December 15, 1976, in Robert C. Eckhardt Collection, Center for American History, University of Texas at Austin, Box 3M26, Folder: *Tides of Power.*

46. Bob Eckhardt letters, September 1, 1976, in Ann and Milton Lower Personal Papers, Box 36, Folder: Black Community.

47. Letter from Charles Frandolig, Gearhart Campaign Director, to Union Carbide, August 23, 1976, in Ann and Milton Lower Personal Papers, Box 36, Folder: Nick Gearhart Material.

48. Bob Eckhardt handwritten note, in Robert C. Eckhardt Collection, Center for American History, University of Texas at Austin, Box 3M56, Folder: Grimes, Fablemacher, & Smoot.

49. *Congressional Quarterly Almanac* 32, 1976; 33, 1977, 36A, 37A, 43A; Barone, Ujifusa, and Matthews, *The Almanac of American Politics,* 1978.

50. Ann Lower speech to Harris County Democrats, in Ann and Milton Lower Personal Papers, Box 36, Folder: Archer News Clippings; Walter De Vries and Lance Tarrance

Jr., *The Ticket-splitter: A New Force in American Politics* (Grand Rapids, Mich.: Eerdmans, 1972).

51. "Eckhardt For Increasing Public Debt," *Baytown Sun,* March 10, 1978; National Republican Campaign Committee, "Other Side" news release, in Ann and Milton Lower Personal Papers, Box 36, Folder: Archer news clippings.

52. "Eckhardt Sits Atop NRA Hit List," *Dallas Morning News,* July 21, 1980.

53. *Houston Post,* April 11, 1978.

54. Federal Election Commission General Counsel's Report MUR 909, August 24, 1979, in Ann and Milton Lower Personal Papers, Box 36, Folder: Archer/Finance Reports; Bob Eckhardt interview, April 28, 1994; memo from Ann Lower to Bob Eckhardt with 1978 Primary budget comparisons, March 5, 1980, in Robert C. Eckhardt Collection, Center for American History, University of Texas at Austin, Box 3M21, Folder: Campaign 80-Primary; Barone, Ujifusa, and Matthews, *The Almanac of American Politics,* 1980.

55. David Broder, *Washington Post,* February 27, 1978, A6.

56. *Congressional Record,* no. 151 (October 12, 1971), H9364.

57. Jane Ely, "Eckhardt Convinces Few on ERA Vote," *Houston Post,* August 24, 1978, A3.

58. Letter from Willie Morris to Bob Eckhardt, August 2, 1977, in Bob Eckhardt Personal Papers, Box 21, Folder: Willie Morris.

59. Morris, *Finding Celia's Place,* 193, 196.

60. Letter from Norman Eckhardt to Bob Eckhardt, February 16, 1976; letter from Bob Eckhardt to Norman Eckhardt, February 24, 1976, in Nadine Eckhardt Personal Papers, Folder: Letters Regarding Mother Eckhardt.

61. Morris, *Finding Celia's Place,* 197.

62. Bob Eckhardt quotation, in Robert C. Eckhardt Collection, Center for American History, University of Texas at Austin, Box 3M-56, Folder: Eckhardt Words of Wisdom.

63. Jacobs, *A Rage for Justice,* 231.

64. Bob Eckhardt interview, June 4, 1998.

65. *Houston Chronicle,* January 28, 1977.

66. *Houston Post,* January 7, 1979.

67. Barbara Canetti, "Survival of GOP Worries Young—a Little," *Houston Post,* November 2, 1978, A12.

68. "Wrong Man for a Key Job," *New York Post,* January 6, 1979, editorial.

69. "Fox in the Chicken Coop," *Wall Street Journal,* January 29, 1979, 16.

70. "Not Qualified," *New York Times,* January 29, 1979, editorial.

71. *Houston Chronicle,* January 30, 1979; Eckhardt memorial service, February 26, 2002.

72. Al Gore, comments, Bob Eckhardt memorial service, February 26, 2002.

73. See, for instance, Luther Carter, "Congressman Eckhardt, Legislative Craftsman," *Science,* March 9, 1979, 983–984.

74. Mark Raabe resume, in Bob Eckhardt Personal Papers, Box 1 (Persons), Folder: Mark Raabe.

75. "To Keep the Big Boys Honest," and "To Keep the Government Frugal and Responsive," *Bob Eckhardt's Quarterly Report* 22 (spring 1980) and 23 (summer 1980).

76. Jim Wright interview, July 12, 1996; Jim Wright, *Balance of Power: Presidents and Congress from the Era of McCarthy to the Age of Gingrich* (Atlanta: Turner Publishing, 1996), 260; see also John M. Barry, *The Ambition and the Power* (New York: Penguin Books, 1989), chap. 1.

77. Ronnie Dugger, "A Fair Tax on the Oil Industry," *Texas Observer,* August 29, 1986, 10, in Bob Eckhardt Personal Papers, Box: 1 (Persons).

78. Dennis M. Simon, "Texans in the United States House of Representatives: A History of Electoral, Partisan, and Ideological Change, 1936–2000" (paper presented at Jim Wright Symposium on Texas Congressional Leaders, Texas Christian University, Fort Worth, Texas, April 19, 2002), 3.

79. Jacobs, *A Rage for Justice,* 312–313.

80. Dennis M. Simon, "Texans in the United States House of Representatives."

14. Public v. Special Interest

1. Sam Dawson interview, September 14, 2004.

2. See Robert N. Mayer, *The Consumer Movement: Guardians of the Marketplace,* Boston: Twayne Publishers, 1989, chap. 2.

3. Ralph Nader, *Unsafe at Any Speed: The Designed-in Dangers of the American Automobile* (New York: Grossman Publishers), 1965.

4. *Washington Post,* October 21, 1980, B1.

5. Sources for this section include Bob Eckhardt's review of *The Big Thicket* by Pete A. Y. Gunter, *Texas Books in Review* XIV, no. 4 (winter 1991): 17–18; Big Thicket notebook, in Bob Eckhardt Personal Papers, Box 9; Big Thicket Files in Bob Eckhardt Personal Papers, Box 16; Howard Peacock, *The Big Thicket of Texas: America's Ecological Wonder* (Boston: Little, Brown, 1984); Roy Hamric, ed., *Archer Fullingim: A Country Editor's View of Life* (Austin: Heidelberg Publishers, 1975); Bob Eckhardt campaign ad, 1976, in Ann and Milton Lower Personal Papers, Box 36, Folder: Joe Archer; Bob Eckhardt Legislative Report on H.R. 5941, Big Thicket National Biological Reserve, in Bob Eckhardt Personal Papers, Box 16; "Big Thicket," Handbook of Texas Online, www.tsha.utexas.edu/handbook/online/articles/view/BB/gkb3.html (accessed October 22, 2002); Debra Jacobson, "Big Thicket National Preserve," September 23, 1976, MS, in Ann and Milton Lower Personal Papers, Box 36, Folder: Big Thicket; Alexander Kress, *Ralph Yarborough: The Big Thicket's Advocate in Congress—An Annotated Congressional Record Bibliography 1962–1970* (Austin: Kress, 1970).

6. William A. Owens, "On Top of Tallman Mountain," in *Three Men in Texas: Bedichek, Webb, and Dobie: Essays by their Friends in the Texas Observer,* ed. Ronnie Dugger (Austin: University of Texas Press, 1967), 36.

7. Bob Eckhardt ms., with handwritten notes for review of Gunter, *The Big Thicket,* in Bob Eckhardt Personal Papers, Box 16.

8. Bob Eckhardt interview, April 28, 1994.

9. Charlie Wilson interview, September 17, 2004.

10. *Congressional Record* (March 21, 1973): 8928.

11. United States Code, *Congressional and Administrative News,* 93d Cong., 2d sess., 1974, vol. 3, Legislative History, 5558.

12. United States Code, *Congressional and Administrative News,* 93d Cong., 2d sess., 1974, vol. 3, Legislative History, 5554.

13. Bob Eckhardt campaign ad, 1976, in Ann and Milton Lower Personal Papers, Box 36, Folder: Joe Archer.

14. Bob Eckhardt news release, January 31, 1975, in Ann and Milton Lower Personal Papers, Box 36, Folder: Big Thicket; "The Plot Thickets," *Houston Post,* January 28, 1977, editorial, E2.

15. See "Senators' Backing Gives Big Thicket Expansion a Boost," *Austin American-Statesman,* June 11, 1991.

16. *Congressional Quarterly Almanac* 33 (1977): 638.

17. David Zwick and Marcia Benstock, *Water Wasteland: Ralph Nader's Study Group Report on Water Pollution* (New York: Grossman Publishers, 1971), 19–20.

18. *Houston Post,* July 1, 1967, in Tucker, "The Houston Business Community, 1945–1965," 352.

19. Zwick and Benstock, *Water Wasteland,* 21, 189–190.

20. Don Kennard interview, www.texaslegacy.org.

21. "Proceedings of the EPA Conference in the Matter of Pollution of Navigable Waters of Galveston Bay and Its Tributaries—Texas, November 2–3, 1971," vol. 1, 319; see also Rep. Bob Eckhardt Statement, Pollution Enforcement Conference on Galveston Bay, June 7–9, 1971, in Robert C. Eckhardt Collection, Center for American History, University of Texas at Austin, Box 95-147/33, Folder: Statement: Pollution Enforcement Conference.

22. "Proceedings of the EPA Conference in the Matter of Pollution of Navigable Waters of Galveston Bay and Its Tributaries—Texas, June 7–12, 1971," vol. 1, follow-up meeting of the Conference in the Matter of Pollution of the Navigable Waters of Galveston Bay and Its Tributaries, Houston, Texas, December 5, 1972, transcript of proceedings; see also Rep. Bob Eckhardt Statement, Pollution Enforcement Conference, November 3, 1971, in Robert C. Eckhardt Collection, Center for American History, University of Texas at Austin, Box 95-147/33, Folder: Statement: Pollution Enforcement Conference.

23. Zwick and Benstock, *Water Wasteland,* 177.

24. Bob Eckhardt, "Death of Galveston Bay," in Robert C. Eckhardt Collection, Center for American History, University of Texas at Austin, Box 3M16, Folder: Water Pollution; Zwick and Benstock, *Water Wasteland,* 19–20.

25. Subcommittee on Fisheries and Wildlife Conservation, transcript, March 9, 1967, in Robert C. Eckhardt Collection, Center for American History, University of Texas at Austin, Box 3, Folder: Conservation Legislation; Jack Walker statement, *Humble News-Messenger,* April 27, 1978, B-6, B-7; "The Shell Reefs," *Bob Eckhardt's Quarterly Report* 1 (fall 1968).

26. Bob Eckhardt, "Welcome" (Southwestern Symposium on Conservation Education, October 13–15, 1968, Lee College, Baytown, Texas), symposium booklet.

27. "Our 10 Best Friends in Congress," *Outdoor Life,* October 1980.

28. HR 11016 in 1970, HR 4932 in 1973, in Bob Eckhardt Personal Papers, Box 9, Folder: Big Thicket. See *Bob Eckhardt's Quarterly Report* (summer 1969); Eckhardt news release, January 20, 1975, in Ann and Milton Lower Personal Papers, Box 36, Folder: Flood and Coastal Management.

29. Eckhardt, "A Rational National Policy on Public Use of the Beaches," 967–988; Charles Black, "Constitutionality of the Eckhardt Open Beaches Bill," *Columbia Law Review* 74:3 (1974): 439–447.

30. "The Nation's Beaches: A View from Texas and from Washington" (ABA Environmental Law Course, February 9, 1974, San Francisco).

31. Bob Eckhardt, "Assault on Environmental Protection," chap. 5, unpublished ms. on the Constitution, in Bob Eckhardt Personal Papers, Box 6, Folder: Constitution, 64.

32. Eckhardt, unpublished ms. on the Constitution, 64.

33. "Remarks of Congressman Bob Eckhardt, Atlantic Richfield Annual Chemical Division Meeting."

34. See Irvin Schwartz and Larry Marion, "Anatomy of a Bill," *Chemical Week,* April 27, 1977, 52–61.

35. Bob Eckhardt, news release, January 12, 1977, in Ann and Milton Lower Personal Papers, Box 35.

36. Schwartz and Marion, "Anatomy of a Bill," 55.

37. Eckhardt, news releases, May 26 and June 9, 1976, in Ann and Milton Lower Personal Papers, Box 35.

38. Schwartz and Marion, "Anatomy of a Bill," 59.

39. Elizabeth Wiley, "New Toxic Bill Should Aid Environment—Eckhardt," *Bay Area Life Style,* League City, August 26, 1975.

40. Subcommittee on Oversight and Investigations, "Oversight Activities—1979," in Ann and Milton Lower Personal Papers, Box 57.

41. Janet Raloff, "Abandoned Dumps: A Chemical Legacy," *Science News* 115, no. 21 (May 26, 1979), 348*ff.*

42. "Eckhardt Proposes Superfund Alternative," *Hazardous Waste Report* 1, no. 17, 3 (Aspen Systems Corp., Germantown, MD), in Ann and Milton Lower Personal Papers, Box 37, Folder: Eckhardt Biographical File.

43. See U.S. EPA Mid-Atlantic Regional Center for Environmental Information, "What is the Eckhardt Report?" www.epa.gov/region3/rcei/faq/eckhardt.htm (accessed May 30, 2003).

44. Mark Raabe and Peter Kinzler interview, February 27, 2002; *Congressional Quarterly Almanac* 36 (1980).

45. Al Gore comments, Bob Eckhardt memorial service, February 26, 2002.

46. "A Program on Consumer Matters," *Bob Eckhardt's Quarterly Report* (summer 1969), 6:2.

47. See Jerry Mashaw and David Harfit, *The Struggle for Auto Safety* (Cambridge, Mass.: Harvard University Press, 1990).

48. *Congressional Quarterly Almanac,* 28 (1972): 320.

49. Bob Eckhardt, "John Dingell's Comments on Joan Claybrook," in Bob Eckhardt Personal Papers, Box 16, Folder: "Personal Experiences."

50. Bob Eckhardt quotation, January 28, 1974, Subcommittee on Commerce and Finance oversight hearing on the Motor Vehicle Information and Cost Savings Act, in Robert C. Eckhardt Collection, Center for American History, University of Texas at Austin, Box 3M-56, Folder: Eckhardt Words of Wisdom.

51. Bob Eckhardt news release, March 7, 1975, in Ann and Milton Lower Personal Papers, Box 35, Folder: Miscellaneous.

52. Subcommittee on Consumer Protection and Finance, press releases, May 5 and 25, 1977, in Ann and Milton Lower Personal Papers, Box 56, Folder: Press Releases.

53. Subcommittee on Consumer Protection and Finance, September 9, 1977 hearing; letter from Susan Baker, associate professor, Johns Hopkins University to Bob Eckhardt, December 28, 1982, in Bob Eckhardt Personal Papers, Box 1 (Persons), Folder: Baker, Susan; *Congressional Quarterly Almanac* 33 (1977): 531–532; letter from Jimmy Carter to Bob Eckhardt, October 26, 1977, in Jimmy Carter Library, Names File: Eckhardt.

54. Bob Eckhardt, "No-Fault Legislation Lacks Humane and Equitable Answers," *Trial* 7, no. 3 (May/June 1971): 43; "No-Fault Without Fraud," *Trial Lawyer Forum* (July-December 1971): 17.

55. *Congressional Quarterly Almanac* 28 (1971).

56. Bob Eckhardt, quotation in *Consumer Federation News,* July 1978, in Ann and Milton Lower Personal Papers, Box 57.

57. Bob Eckhardt, press releases, March 18, 1977; Subcommittee on Consumer Protection and Finance press release, April 7, 1977, in Ann and Milton Lower Personal Papers, Box 56, Folder: Press Releases.

58. Bob Eckhardt, typed, unsigned remarks, in Ann and Milton Lower Personal Papers, Box 35, Folder: No-fault.

59. Letter from W. James Kronzer to Bob Eckhardt, and Subcommittee on Consumer Protection and Finance testimony, June 17, 1977, in Ann and Milton Lower Personal Papers, Box 35, Folder: No-fault; see September 22, 1977, memorandum from Peter Kinzler to Bob Eckhardt, in Ann and Milton Lower Personal Papers, Box 35.

60. "No Fault Auto Insurance Bill Rejected," *Congressional Quarterly Almanac* 34 (1978).

61. Letter from John G. Patterson to Bob Eckhardt, January 24, 1978, in Ann and Milton Lower Personal Papers, Box 35, Folder: Trial Lawyers; *Texas Observer,* January 1978.

62. Letter from Bob Eckhardt and Harley Staggers to Jimmy Carter, May 24, 1978, in Jimmy Carter Library, Names File: Eckhardt.

63. "Consumer Policy," *Congressional Quarterly Almanac* 30 (1974): 330.

64. "The Consumer Class Action Bill," *Bob Eckhardt's Quarterly Report* 6 (summer 1969), 2, quotation from Shakespeare, *Measure for Measure.*

65. Stephen Brobeck, ed., *Encyclopedia of the Consumer Movement* (Santa Barbara, Calif.: ABC-CLIO, 1997), 611. See also "Consumer Class Actions," *Bob Eckhardt's Quarterly Report* (winter 1970–1971), 3.

66. Bob Eckhardt, news release, February 2, 1970, in Texas AFL-CIO Collection, Special Collections, University of Texas at Arlington Libraries, AR 100, Series 11.

67. Bob Eckhardt, "Statement on the Consumer Class Action Bill," (lecture, Seminar for Business Executives, Brookings Institution, April 15, 1970), in Robert C. Eckhardt Collection, Center for American History, University of Texas at Austin, Box 3M-16, Folder: Consumer Protection.

68. Bob Eckhardt, comments on administration's consumer proposals, February 26, 1971, in Robert C. Eckhardt Collection, Center for American History, University of Texas at Austin, Box 95-147/33, Folder: Comments on Nixon Consumer Proposals.

69. Confidential letter from Bob Eckhardt to Harley Staggers, September 21, 1970, in Robert C. Eckhardt Collection, Center for American History, University of Texas at Austin, Box: Commerce Committee, Folder: Committee Materials.

70. See Brobeck, *Encyclopedia of the Consumer Movement,* 592–593, 601–604.

71. "Office of Consumer Representation," *Congressional Quarterly Almanac* 34 (1978): 473.

72. "Congressional 'Veto' over Federal Regulations Proposed," *Congressional Quarterly Almanac* 31 (1975), 571.

73. See *Congressional Quarterly Almanac* 33 (1977): 701.

74. White House memorandum from Si Lazarus to Frank Moore re: Koch-Eckhardt Class Action Bill, March 14, 1977; letter from Jimmy Carter to Bob Eckhardt, June 30, 1977, in Jimmy Carter Library, Names File: Eckhardt.

75. *Congressional Quarterly Almanac* 35 (1979): 342.

76. *Congressional Quarterly Almanac* 33 (1977): 554–554.

77. Michael Pertschuk, *Revolt Against Regulation: The Rise and Pause of the Consumer Movement* (Berkeley: University of California Press, 1982) 91.

78. Pertschuk, *Revolt Against Regulation*, 16, 56–57; quote from Thomas B. Edsall, "Business Learns to Play New Politics," *Baltimore Sun,* February 25, 1980, A7.

15. The Oil and Gas Wars

1. This material draws on an unpublished manuscript by Bob Eckhardt on oil and gas, in Bob Eckhardt Personal Papers, Box 9, Notebook: Oil/Gas: Prices in the World Market In Six Years, n.d.; Democratic Study Group, "Special Report: The Congressional Energy Record," no. 96-31, September 10, 1980, in Ann and Milton Lower Personal Papers; and memorandum, in Bob Eckhardt Personal Papers, Box: Oil & Gas Policy 1970s-1980s, Folder: Natural Gas Policy Act 1978.

2. Morris, *Finding Celia's Place,* 226.

3. Robert Sherrill, "The Case Against the Oil Companies," *New York Times Magazine,* October 14, 1979.

4. Table 2, "Natural Gas Production," from *American Gas Association AGA Gas Facts,* in "The Economics of the Natural Gas Controversy, A Staff Study for the Subcommittee on Energy," Joint Economic Committee, September 19, 1977, 14.

5. "Energy and Environment," *Congressional Quarterly Almanac* 30 (1974): 734, 780–781; "Why the President's Decontrol of Oil Should be Reversed by Congress," *Bob Eckhardt's Quarterly Report* 18 (spring 1979).

6. Sherrill, "A Texan vs. Big Oil," 101.

7. Robert Sherrill, *The Oil Follies of 1970–1980: How the Petroleum Industry Stole the Show (and Much More Besides)* (Garden City, N.Y.: Anchor Press/Doubleday, 1983), 293.

8. Eckhardt and Black, *The Tides of Power,* 198.

9. Daniel Rapoport, "Oh Congress!" *Washingtonian,* November 1978, 177–181.

10. Paul Burka, "So Close, So Far," *Texas Monthly,* April 1976, 27, 38.

11. "Energy and Environment," *Congressional Quarterly Almanac* 31 (1975): 236.

12. *Congressional Record* (July 30, 1975), votes 347, 348, 106-H; "Energy and Environment," *Congressional Quarterly Almanac* 31 (1975): 243–244.

13. Charlie Wilson interview, September 17, 2004.

14. Burka, "So Close, So Far," 37.

15. "Energy and Environment," *Congressional Quarterly Almanac* 32 (1976): 172.

16. *Congressional Quarterly Almanac* 31 (1975): 70-H, vote 231.

17. "Energy and Environment," *Congressional Quarterly Almanac* 32 (1976): 180, 181.

18. *Bob Eckhardt's Quarterly Report* (spring 1977).

19. *Congressional Quarterly Almanac* 33 (1977): 649–650.

20. Eckhardt and Black, *The Tides of Power,* 157.

21. This section draws from Debra Jacobson, "Legislative History of the Natural Gas Policy Act of 1978," April 8, 1980, in Bob Eckhardt Personal Papers, Box: Oil & Gas Policy 1970s-1980s, Folder: Natural Gas Policy Act 1978.

22. Letter from Jimmy Carter to Bob Eckhardt, July 19, 1977, in Jimmy Carter Library, Names File: Eckhardt.

23. Letter from J. R. Parten to Charles Wilson, August 5, 1977, in Bernard Rapoport Papers, Center for American History, University of Texas at Austin, Box 4C514b, AR 92-414, Folder: J. R. Parten.

24. *Congressional Quarterly Almanac* 33 (1977): 723; Toby Moffett interview, April 27, 2004.

25. Letter from Speaker Tip O'Neill to Bob Eckhardt, August 5, 1977, in Ann and Milton Lower Personal Papers, Box 55, Folder: Eckhardt Correspondence.

26. "Carter Energy Bill Fails to Clear," *Congressional Quarterly Almanac* 33 (1977): 708–746.

27. Frank Moore, White House memorandum, October 25, 1977; memorandum from Frank Moore to the president, November 30, 1977, with Carter's handwritten notes, in Jimmy Carter Library, Names File: Eckhardt.

28. Bob Eckhardt, "On the Gas Price Issue," *Journal of Energy and Development* 3, no. 2 (spring 1978): 270–276; "The Gas Price Issue," *Bob Eckhardt's Quarterly Report* 14 (winter 1977).

29. See "Energy Bill: The End of an Odyssey," *Congressional Quarterly Almanac* 34 (1978): 639–667.

30. Letter from Bob Eckhardt to John Dingell, February 2, 1978, quoted in Jacobson, "Legislative History."

31. Quoted in Jacobson, "Legislative History."

32. Carter, "Congressman Eckhardt, Legislative Craftsman," 983–984.

33. United Steelworkers of America news release, March 28, 1978, and memo from Ed Ball to Ann Lower indicating that the news release was "made in accordance with our request," in Ann and Milton Lower Personal Papers, Box 35, Folder: Steel Industry.

34. Bob Eckhardt, "A Good Word for the Revolving Door: The Lynn Coleman Appointment," *The Nation,* February 18, 1978, 173–176.

35. Sherrill, *The Oil Follies of 1970–1980,* 370–371fn.

36. Democratic Study Group, "The Congressional Energy Record," 15–16, in Ann and Milton Lower Personal Papers.

37. Congressman Bob Eckhardt (remarks, Energy and Jobs Conference of the Industrial Union Department, AFL-CIO, Washington, D.C., May 5, 1980), in Ann and Milton Lower Personal Papers, Box 56, Reference File: Energy Speeches.

38. Subcommittee on Oversight and Investigations, "Oversight Activities—1979," 12, in Ann and Milton Lower Personal Papers, Box 57.

39. Subcommittee on Oversight and Investigations, "Oversight Activities—1979," 11, in Ann and Milton Lower Personal Papers, Box 57; *Washington Post,* August 6, 1979, 1, and August 7, 1979.

40. "Oversight Panel off to Fast Start Under Eckhardt," *ESC Weekly Bulletin,* April 2, 1979, C5, in Ann and Milton Lower Personal Papers, Box 55, Folder: Miscellaneous Political Material.

41. Al Gore, comments, Bob Eckhardt memorial service, February 26, 2002.

42. "The Energy Department's High Price Game: A Non-Inflationary Alternative," *Bob Eckhardt's Quarterly Report* 19 (summer 1979), 4.

43. *Houston Post,* April 19, 1980.

44. Sherrill, *The Oil Follies of 1970–1980,* 477.

45. "The Case of the Billion Dollar Stripper: The Evasion of Price Controls on Domestic Crude Oil by Resellers," Subcommittee on Oversight and Investigations, 96th Cong., 2d sess., 1980, 96-IFC 58; Subcommittee news releases, April 25 and October 19, 1980, in Ann and Milton Lower Personal Papers, Box 37, Folder: Press Releases; letter from Sherry Tucker, Of Counsel to DOE to Bob Eckhardt, November 12, 1982, in Bob Eckhardt Personal Papers, Box: Large Miscellany and Duplicates, "U.S. District Court vs. Sutton."

46. Roberta Hornig, "Even with Price Control, Oil Drilling Booms in U.S.," *Washington Star,* March 24, 1979.

47. Bob Eckhardt, comments, *Congressional Record* (May 17, 1979).

48. Interview with Ray Marshall, Miller Center Interviews, Carter Presidency Project, vol. 25, May 4, 1988, Jimmy Carter Library, 42.

49. Interview with Ray Marshall, 42.

50. Democratic Study Group, "The Congressional Energy Record," 9.

51. HR 3000, October 12, 1979, Courter amendment, 191–188; Eckhardt amendment 182–191; October 24, 1979, reconsider and reverse Courter amendment, 225–189; October 11 vote.

52. Letter from Robert F. Goss, President, Oil, Chemical and Atomic Workers International Union to Members of Congress, August 31, 1979, in Ann and Milton Lower Personal Papers, Box 56, Folder: The Eckhardt Plan.

53. Letter from Jimmy Carter to Members of Congress, July 26, 1979, in Ann and Milton Lower Personal Papers, Box 56, Folder: Letter to Carter.

54. Bob Eckhardt, "To Reverse the President on Oil Decontrol," letter to the editor, *New York Times,* September 12, 1979.

55. Letter from Stuart Eizenstat to Bob Eckhardt, February 6, 1979, in Jimmy Carter Library, Names File: Eckhardt.

56. See *Congressional Record,* October 9, 1979.

57. Bob Eckhardt, "A Secular View of Regulation and Deregulation, or There Is No Economic Ayatollah" (speech, 1980 Legislative Conference of the Edison Electric Institute, Palm Springs, CA, January 3, 1980), in Ann and Milton Lower Personal Papers, Box 35.

58. Bob Eckhardt, Chairman's Opening Statement, Subcommittee on Oversight and Investigations, December 20, 1979, hearing on "The Direct and Indirect Impact of Energy Prices on Inflation," in Ann and Milton Lower Files, Box 55, Folder: Oil and Gas.

59. Memorandum from Milton Lower to Congressman Eckhardt, "Growth, Profitability, and Employment of Oil Companies in the 'Fortune 1000 Largest Industrial Corporations' 1972–1976," December 7, 1977, in Ann and Milton Lower Personal Papers, Box 57; "The Changing Distribution of Industrial Profits: The Oil and Gas Industry Within the Fortune 500, 1978–1980," staff report, Subcommittee on Oversight and Investigations, Committee on Energy and Commerce, 97th Cong., 1st sess., November 1981, Committee Print 97-W.

60. Walter S. Mossberg, "President will Gradually Phase Out Price Controls on Crude Oil to Spur Production, Curb Consumption," *Wall Street Journal,* April 6, 1979.

61. Rush Loving Jr., "The Railroads' Bad Trip to Deregulation," *Fortune,* August 25, 1980, 47.

62. William E. Clayton Jr., "Eckhardt Tacks Amendment on Rail Bill," *Houston Chronicle,* July 25, 1980.

63. "Coal Shoulder," *Texas Monthly,* September 1980; "House Vote Jams Rail Deregulation," *National Journal,* August 2, 1980.

64. See Robert C. Eckhardt, "The Western Coal Traffic League Case: Condoning ICC Eschewal of Rail Monopoly Ratemaking," *Transportation Law Journal* 13, no. 2 (1984): 307–328.

65. "Energy and Environment," *Congressional Quarterly Almanac* 33 (1977) and 34 (1978), 649–650.

66. Richard E. Cohen, "Energy Turf Fight," *National Journal,* October 6, 1979, 1652; "House May Get an Energy Committee, and Dingell May be Left Out in the Cold," *Na-*

tional Journal, February 2, 1980, 188–191; and "Not Quite the Status Quo," *National Journal,* April 5, 1980, 568.

67. Manuscript for *New Republic,* in Robert C. Eckhardt Collection, Center for American History, University of Texas at Austin, Box 3M-26, Folder: *New Republic* magazine.

68. *The Echo,* October 29, 1980, in Ann and Milton Lower Personal Papers, Box 35; Sherrill, "A Texan vs. Big Oil," 38*ff.,* quote on 38.

69. "What We Should do about Energy/Inflation," *Bob Eckhardt's Quarterly Report* 21 (winter 1980), 4.

70. Bob Eckhardt (remarks, Atlantic Richfield Annual Chemical Division meeting, White Sulphur Springs, WV, September 13, 1977), in Ann and Milton Lower Personal Papers, Box 55, Position Papers, 4, 14.

16. The 1980 Election

1. Robert Cochran, "It was Just a Function of Money," unpublished ms.

2. Daniel Rapoport, "Oh Congress!" 181; Larry L. King, "The Ten Brightest Congressmen," *New Times,* April 4, 1975; Smith and Burka, "*The Best, The Worst,*" 106–107; memorandum from James Calaway to Finance Committee members, February 12, 1979, in Robert C. Eckhardt Collection, Center for American History, University of Texas at Austin, Box 3M21, Folder: Campaign—Spring 1979 Fundraiser.

3. Martin Tolchin, "Rep. Eckhardt Fights Conservative for Houston Seat," *New York Times,* November 3, 1980, D15.

4. Letter from Robert Sherrill to *Texas Observer,* January 16, 1981, 21.

5. Scott Bennett, "First Annual Congressional Awards," *Texas Business,* February 1980, 21–22.

6. See Steven K. Smith, "Southern Congressional Politics Since the Great Society" (PhD diss., University of South Carolina, 1983); Barone, Ujifusa, and Matthews, *The Almanac of American Politics,* 1972–1980 eds.

7. Vote summary tables, in Ann and Milton Lower Personal Papers, Box 56, Folder: Surveys.

8. Sherrill, "A Texan vs. Big Oil," quotes on 38*ff.* and 42.

9. See Richard Viguerie, *The New Right: We're Ready to Lead* (Falls Church, Va.: The Viguerie Co., 1981); Jonathan Kolkey, *The New Right, 1960–1968: With Epilogue, 1969–1980* (Washington, D.C.: University Press of America, 1983).

10. Bob Eckhardt, "Reverse English of Watergate: Running Against Washington," *The Nation,* June 26, 1976, 773–774.

11. Democratic Congressional Campaign Committee Report, vol. 3, no. 1, January 31, 1980, in Bob Eckhardt Personal Papers, Box 10: Politics, Folder: Conservative Victory Fund.

12. *Washington Post,* August 10, 1980.

13. "The Presidential Election in Democratic Congressional Districts," Democratic Study Group Special Report No. 96-27, August 7, 1980, in Ann and Milton Lower Personal Papers, Box 55, Folder: Miscellaneous Political Materials.

14. U.S. Chamber of Commerce National Chamber Alliance for Politics, "Opportunity Races in the House and Senate for the 1980 Elections," in Ann and Milton Lower Personal Papers, Box 35.

15. Letter from Paul M. Weyrich to Louis Gerber, February 26, 1980, in Bob Eckhardt Personal Papers, Box 10: Politics, Folder: Committee for the Survival of a Free Congress.

16. See Ann Thompson, "Politics Emphasized in Week before Election," *Baylor Lariat,* October 31, 1972, 1.

17. See Cindy Musick, "No Communication: Political Program Sparks Verbal Attacks," *Baylor Lariat,* November 7, 1972, 2.

18. "Texan a Reluctant Player in Swift Boat Flap," *Austin American-Statesman,* August 28, 2004, 1.

19. *Humble News-Messenger,* April 20, 1978, A1.

20. *Humble Echo,* December 13, 1979, in Ann and Milton Lower Personal Papers, Box 35.

21. Nicholas Lemann, "Jack Fields: How Money, Expertise Aid Unknown Candidate," *Washington Post,* September 29, 1980, A14.

22. *Houston Chronicle,* October 10, 1980.

23. Letter from Bob Eckhardt to Frank Moore, March 2, 1979, in Jimmy Carter Library, Names File: Eckhardt.

24. Letters from Bob Eckhardt to Jim Calaway, Gary Webb, and Phil Gauss, April 6, 1979, in Robert C. Eckhardt Collection, Center for American History, University of Texas at Austin, Box 3M21, Folder: Campaign 79 Fundraiser.

25. Letter from Bob Eckhardt to J. R. Parten, June 22, 1983, in Bob Eckhardt Personal Papers, Box 1 (Persons), Folder: J. R. Parten.

26. White House Memorandum from Cathy Hotka to Jane Fenderson, October 3, 1979, in Jimmy Carter Library, Names File: Eckhardt.

27. Letter from Bernard Rapoport to James C. Calaway, March 15, 1979, in Bernard Rapoport Papers, Center for American History, University of Texas at Austin, Box 4C595, Folder: Robert Eckhardt; memo from Al Barkan to COPE Operating Committee, October 31, 1979, in Robert C. Eckhardt Collection, Center for American History, University of Texas at Austin, Box 3M21, Folder: Campaign 80—Political.

28. Bob Eckhardt form letter, March 17, 1980, in Ann and Milton Lower Personal Papers, Box 56, Folder: Finances/Fundraising.

29. Letter from Ann Lower to Congressman Eckhardt, October 10, 1979, in Robert C. Eckhardt Collection, Center for American History, University of Texas at Austin, Box 3M21, Folder: Campaign—Spring 1979 Fundraiser.

30. John Ray Harrison financial filing, December 1979, in Ann and Milton Lower Personal Papers, Box 35; *Houston Echo,* December 13, 1979.

31. *Houston Post,* May 28, 1980.

32. "Rep. Eckhardt Outspends Foe in 8th District," *Houston Post,* April 26, 1980, A28.

33. Viguerie, *The New Right,* 88.

34. Larry Washburn campaign memos, in Ann and Milton Lower Personal Papers, Box 35.

35. "Campaign Update by Roni Sue Fields," April 1980, in Ann and Milton Lower Personal Papers, Box 35.

36. Joe Nolan, "Washburn asks Republicans to help Unseat Rep. Eckhardt," *Houston Chronicle,* April 30, 1980.

37. Vote summary tables, in Ann and Milton Lower Personal Papers, Box 56, Folder: Surveys.

38. Letter from Gaylen L. Nix to Bob Eckhardt, May 5, 1980, in Bob Eckhardt Personal Papers, Box 10, Folder: Politics.

39. Maury Maverick, "S.A.'s Friend by Conviction and by Blood," *San Antonio Express-News,* October 5, 1980, H3.

40. Paul Weyrich, *Political Report,* September 26, 1980, in Ann and Milton Lower Personal Papers, Box 35.

41. Letter from Celia Morris to Ann Lower and Bob Eckhardt, June 16, 1980, in Robert C. Eckhardt Collection, Center for American History, University of Texas at Austin, Box 3M21, Folder: Campaign 80—Assistance.

42. Material in Ann and Milton Lower Personal Papers, Box 57, Folder: Campaign Literature.

43. Vote projection table, in Ann and Milton Lower Personal Papers, Box 33, Folder: Election Statistics; memo from Ann Lower, May 20, 1983, in Ann and Milton Lower Personal Papers, Box 57, Folder: 1980 General Election.

44. Letter from Rev. F. N. Williams, area coordinator, Democratic Headquarters, to ministers, October 8, 1980, in Ann and Milton Lower Personal Papers, Box 56, Folder: Finances/Fundraising.

45. Judith Bender, "Oilmen Aided, Consumers Hurt," *Newsday,* October 14, 1980, 6.

46. Juan Ramon Palomo, *Houston Post,* October 19, 1980, A7.

47. Juan Ramon Palomo, "It's Debatable: Eckhardt, Fields Clash Again over Format," *Houston Post,* September 30, 1980.

48. Chamber of Commerce debate transcript, September 29, 1980, in Ann and Milton Lower Personal Papers, Box 38, Folder: Chamber of Commerce Debate.

49. Joe Nolan, "Rep. Bob Eckhardt, Jack Fields Debating," *Houston Chronicle,* October 5, 1980, 22.

50. League of Women Voters debate transcript, in Ann and Milton Lower Personal Papers, Box 38, Folder: Debate Eckhardt-Fields.

51. Jim Giles, "Letter Leads to Controversy," *Sentinel,* October 30, 1980.

52. "Eckhardt Asks Civiletti to Probe Letter Incident," *Houston Post,* October 29, 1980, A8.

53. Monica Reeves and Juan Ramon Palomo, *Houston Post,* October 22, 1980, 1, 17.

54. Mark Shields column, undated, in Ann and Milton Lower Personal Papers, Box 55, Folder: Big Oil Fields.

55. Letter from Jerry Lindsley, Fields campaign manager, RE lack of permission for announcing La Porte Mayor J. J. Meza's endorsement, *Deer Park Progress,* n.d., in Robert C. Eckhardt Collection, Center for American History, University of Texas at Austin, Box 3M-20.

56. Quoted in Martin Tolchin, "Rep. Eckhardt Fights Conservative for Houston Seat," *New York Times,* November 3, 1980, D15.

57. Letter from Jerry Lindsley and Rick Hawks (Jack Fields Campaign) to National Committee for an Effective Congress, May 5, 1980, in Ann and Milton Lower Personal Papers, Box 38, Folder: Debate.

58. Memo from Christine Moore to Ann Lower, September 25, 1980, in Ann and Milton Lower Personal Papers, Box 38, Folder: Debate.

59. Letter from Jimmy Carter to Bob Eckhardt, September 15, 1980, in Ann and Milton Lower Personal Papers, Box 38, Folder: Debate: Eckhardt/Fields.

60. Morris, *Finding Celia's Place,* 226; Saul Friedman, "Party Unity: A Forgotten Battle Cry," *Fort Worth Star-Telegram,* October 10, 1980, 1–2.

61. Sherrill, "A Texan vs. Big Oil," 38*ff.,* quote on 38.

62. Morris, *Finding Celia's Place,* 224.

63. Ann and Milton Lower Personal Papers, Box 33.

64. Palomo, *Houston Post,* October 19, 1980, A7.

65. Sam Dawson interview, September 14, 2004; Statement of Congressman Bob Eckhardt on Campaign Contributions to Jack Fields, October 31, 1980, in Ann and Milton Lower Personal Papers, Box 55, Folder: Big Oil Fields.

66. *Texas Observer,* August 22, 1980, 13; *Washington Post,* October 21, 1980, B1.

67. Friends for Fields filing and Bob Eckhardt Campaign Fund filing, Federal Election Commission, December 4, 1980, in Ann and Milton Lower Personal Papers, Box 33, Folder: Budget—Campaign; FEC filing, August 21, 1984, in Robert C. Eckhardt Collection, Center for American History, University of Texas at Austin, Box: "Campaign 1980," Folder: Campaign FEC 1983.

68. John Connally, quoted in *Humble News Messenger,* April 10, 1980, in Ann and Milton Lower Personal Papers, Box 33, notebook; also in Sherrill, "A Texan vs. Big Oil," 38*ff.,* quote on 38.

69. Letter from John C. Bailey, Chamber of Commerce of the United States, Southwest Region, to "Mr. Erwin," August 4, 1980, in Ann and Milton Lower Personal Papers, Box 57, Folder: 1980 General Election.

70. Letter from James Featherstone, Treasurer, NRA Political Victory Fund to Federal Election Commission, October 24, 1980, in Ann and Milton Lower Personal Papers, Box 57, Folder: Campaign Expenditures.

71. "Wearing a heart-shaped badge bearing his initials on the lapel, Kennedy . . . ." See Bill Coulter, "Kennedy Urges Party Unity," *Houston Post,* October 22, 1980; Sam Dawson interview, September 14, 2004.

72. Jim Barlow, "Kennedy Solicits Carter Support Here, Praises Eckhardt," *Houston Chronicle,* October 22, 1980, 10.

73. Joe Chapman, "Fields Camp Fails to Deny Higher Donation Figures," *Pasadena Citizen,* November 1, 1980, 1; Joe Nolan, "Eckhardt Names Names in Claim that Oil Industry Bankrolls Fields," *Houston Chronicle,* November 1, 1980; William Barrett, "Eckhardt Fights for Political Life in Oil Country," *Dallas Times Herald,* October 24, 1980.

74. "Last Day of the Lion," *Texas Observer,* November 28, 1980, 6–7.

75. Terkel, *The Great Divide,* 365–368.

76. Bob Eckhardt interview, February 26, 1995.

77. Form letter from Bob Eckhardt to supporters, December 18, 1980, in Bob Eckhardt Personal Papers, Box 1 , Folder: Hally Wood.

78. Letter from Celia Eckhardt to *Houston Post,* December 11, 1980.

79. "Last Day of the Lion," *Texas Observer,* November 28, 1980, 7.

80. Ward Sinclair, "Texas Rep. Eckhardt: The Fall of a Sort of Political Snail Darter," *Washington Post,* December 13, 1980, A2.

81. "A Tribute to the Honorable Bob Eckhardt," *Congressional Record* (December 4, 1980): H12046-12053; Special Order, attached to letter from Claude Pepper to Bob Eckhardt, December 18, 1980, in Bob Eckhardt Personal Papers, Box 13, Folder: Commendatory Letters.

17. Congressman Emeritus

1. Letter from Carolyn Blaydes to Bob Eckhardt, September 28, 1983, in Bob Eckhardt Personal Papers, Folder: Blaydes, Carolyn.

2. American Ethical Union, "Elliott-Black Award," www.ethicalculture.org/neac/elliott-black/ebalist.html (accessed May 30, 2003).

3. Kathy Lewis, "Texans on the Potomac: Jack and Roni Sue Fields," *Houston Post,* February 9, 1981, B1.

4. "Triggering Recession: The Tragic Error," *Bob Eckhardt's Quarterly Report* 24 (fall 1980).

5. Milton D. Lower, "Decontrol Déjà Vu," *Journal of Post Keynesian Economics* 3, no. 4 (summer 1981): 597–601, quote on 601.

6. *Houston Post,* May 1, 1981.

7. Letter from Ralph Yarborough to Bob Eckhardt, April 29, 1981, in Bob Eckhardt Personal Papers, Box 1 (Persons), Folder: Yarborough.

8. J. Edwin Smith letter to Bob Eckhardt, October 18, 1982, in Bob Eckhardt Collection, Center for American History, University of Texas at Austin, Box Campaign 1980, Folder campaign refunds.

9. Letter from Bob Eckhardt to J. R. Parten, June 22, 1983, in Bob Eckhardt Personal Papers, Box 1 (Persons), Folder: J. R. Parten.

10. *Houston Post,* November 22, 1981.

11. Letter from Max Baucus to "Bob & Celia," April 14, 1981, in Bob Eckhardt Personal Papers, Box 1 (Persons), Folder: Baucus, Max.

12. Statement of Robert C. Eckhardt and Transcript, Senate Judiciary Committee, October 1, 1981, in Bob Eckhardt Personal Papers, Box 6.

13. Bob Eckhardt, testimony transcript, House Committee on Energy and Commerce, July 26, 1982, in Bob Eckhardt Personal Papers, Box: Gas, Folder: Statement of Robert Eckhardt.

14. Bob Eckhardt, testimony transcript, House Task Force on Elections, June 10, 1982, in Bob Eckhardt Personal Papers, Box 6.

15. *Houston Chronicle,* November 30, 1981.

16. Letter from Bob Eckhardt to Joel Fleishman, September 8, 1986, in Bob Eckhardt Personal Papers, Box: 1 (Persons), Folder: Fleishman, Joel.

17. Celia Morris, *Fannie Wright: Rebel in America* (Cambridge, MA: Harvard University Press, 1984).

18. Letter from Bob Eckhardt to Elmo and Jenny Hegman, November 26, 1982, in Bob Eckhardt Personal Papers, Box: 1 (Persons) Folder: Hegman, Elmo.

19. Morris, *Finding Celia's Place,* 220–222; Celia Morris interview, December 3, 2004.

20. Card from Nadine Eckhardt to Bob Eckhardt, April 4, 1987, in Bob Eckhardt Personal Papers, Box: 1 (Persons) Folder: Nadine Eckhardt.

21. Milton and Ann Lower, personal communication, July 23, 1996.

22. Don Kennard interview; Don Kennard, speech, Bob Eckhardt memorial service, February 26, 2002.

23. Letter from Julya Kirkpatrick to Bob Eckhardt, March 14, 1988, in Bob Eckhardt Personal Papers.

24. George Norris Green, *The Establishment in Texas Politics* (Westport, Conn.: Greenwood Press, 1979); Maury Forman and Robert A. Calvert, *Cartooning Texas: One Hundred Years of Cartoon Art in the Lone Star State* (College Station: Texas A&M University Press, 1993), 103, 106, 123.

25. *Washington Star,* July 31, 1981, A10.

26. Letter from Bob Eckhardt to Fritz Mondale, July 3, 1984, in Robert Eckhardt Personal Papers, Box 10: Politics, Folder: Political-Mondale.

27. "A Report of the President on Flag Burning, Office of Flag Licensing and Incineration Prevention," in Bob Eckhardt Personal Papers, Box 6, Folder: Flag Burning.

28. Bob Eckhardt, "Williams' Stand is just Vacuous, with no Real Answers Advanced," *Houston Post,* October 31, 1990; Crusade in Caricature, Center for American History, University of Texas at Austin; Gary Keith, "A Fine Line," *Texas Observer,* 1996, 30–31.

29. Bob Eckhardt, "Wright was the Best Speaker Since Sam Rayburn," *Houston Chronicle,* June 11, 1989, H5.

30. Letter from Bob Eckhardt to Cora Weiss, November 15, 1983, in Bob Eckhardt Personal Papers, Box 1 (Persons), Folder: Weiss, Cora.

31. Letter from Bob Eckhardt to Kristine Jutrczenka, March 18, 1989, in Bob Eckhardt Personal Papers, Folder: von Jutrczenka, Kristine.

32. "Why It's Illegal," *Texas Observer,* September 11, 1998, 5.

33. Bob Eckhardt interview, April 28, 1994.

34. Letter from Bob Eckhardt to Governor George W. Bush, December 15, 1999, in Bob Eckhardt Personal Papers.

35. Akin, *Tales of a Texas Union Pioneer,* 151–152.

36. Jan Reid, "Last of a Breed," *Texas Monthly,* May 1994, 46*ff.*

Afterword

1. Studs Terkel, *The Great Divide,* 365–368.

2. Bob Eckhardt interview, 1984, with Chandler Davidson.

3. Eckhardt and Black, *The Tides of Power,* 122.

4. Bob Eckhardt, speech, Rothko Chapel, Houston, December 14, 1980, in Ann and Milton Lower Personal Papers, Box 56, Folder: CFA-Eckhardt Speeches.

5. Edward De Bono, *Lateral Thinking: Creativity Step by Step* (New York: Harper, 1970).

6. Bob Eckhardt, journal, April 13, 1960, in Bob Eckhardt Personal Papers.

7. Bob Eckhardt, journal, August 14, 1958, in Bob Eckhardt Personal Papers.

8. Letter from Bob Eckhardt to Kristine Jutrczenka, March 19, 1989, in Bob Eckhardt Personal Papers, Folder: von Jutrczenka, Kristine.

Sources

Books

Adams, Ann, ed. *The Public and Private Letters of Franklin Jones Sr., vol. 2: Mellow Manana 1975–1980,* Oak Harbor, WA: Packrat Press, 1983.

———. *The Public and Private Letters of Franklin Jones Sr., vol. 3: Firestarter Files 1981–1984,* Oak Harbor, WA: Packrat Press, 1983.

Adams, Mark. *Glimpses of an American Century: By a Mouse in the Halls of the Mighty,* Oak Harbor, WA: Packrat Press, 1997.

Adams, Mark, and Creekmore Fath. *Yarborough: Portrait of a People's Senator,* Austin: Chaparral Press, 1957.

Akin, Morris. *Tales of a Texas Union Pioneer,* Austin: self published, n.d., ca. 1992.

Allsup, Carl. *The American G.I. Forum: Origins and Evolution,* Monograph No. 6, Austin: Center for Mexican American Studies, University of Texas at Austin, 1982.

Barnes, Ben, and Lisa Dickey. *Barn Burning, Barn Building: Tales of a Political Life, from LBJ to George W. Bush and Beyond,* Albany, TX: Bright Sky Press, 2006.

Barone, Michael, Grant Ujifusa, and Douglas Matthews. *The Almanac of American Politics,* 1972, 1974, 1976, 1978, 1980 editions, Boston: Gambit.

Barry, John M. *The Ambition and the Power,* New York: Penguin Books, 1989.

Bedichek, Jane Gracy. *The Roy Bedichek Family Letters,* Denton: University of North Texas Press, 1998.

Bernstein, Patricia. *The First Waco Horror,* College Station: Texas A&M University Press, 2005.

Berry, Margaret. *Brick by Golden Brick: A History of Campus Buildings at the University of Texas at Austin, 1881–1993,* Austin: LBCo. Publishing, 1993.

Biesele, R. L. *The History of the German Settlements in Texas 1831–1861,* Austin: Von Boeckmann-Jones, 1930.

Brobeck, Stephen. *Encyclopedia of the Consumer Movement,* Santa Barbara, CA: ABC-CLIO, 1997.

Brown, John H. *Indian Wars and Pioneers of Texas,* Austin: L. E. Daniell, 189?.

Burton, Michael C. *John Henry Faulk: The Making of a Liberated Mind,* Austin: Eakin Press, 1993.

Carleton, Don E. *A Breed So Rare: The Life of J. R. Parten, Liberal Texas Oil Man, 1896–1992,* Austin: Texas State Historical Society, 1998.

Carleton, Don E. *Being Rapoport,* Austin: University of Texas Press, 2002.

Carleton, Don E. *Red Scare!: Right-wing Hysteria, Fifties Fanaticism, and Their Legacy in Texas,* Austin: Texas Monthly Press, 1985.

Cat Spring Agricultural Society. *The Cat Spring Story,* San Antonio: Lone Star Printing Co., 1956.

Congressional Quarterly, *Congressional Almanac,* Washington, DC: Congressional Quarterly Press (annually, 1967–1981).

Connally, John, with Mickey Herskowitz. *In History's Shadow—An American Odyssey,* New York: Hyperion, 1993.

Cox, Patrick. *Ralph W. Yarborough: The People's Senator,* Austin: University of Texas Press, 2001.

Crawford, Ann Fears. *Frankie: Mrs. R. D. Randolph and Texas Liberal Politics,* Austin: Eakin Press, 2000.

Crawford, Ann Fears, and Jack Keever. *John Connally: Portrait in Power,* Austin: Jenkins Pub. Co., 1973.

Crawford, Ann Fears and Crystal Sasse Ragsdale. *Women in Texas: Their Lives, Their Experiences, Their Accomplishments,* Austin: Eakin Press, 1982.

Davidson, Chandler. *Biracial Politics: Conflict and Coalition in the Metropolitan South,* Baton Rouge: Louisiana State University Press, 1972.

———. *Race and Class in Texas Politics,* Princeton, NJ: Princeton University Press, 1990.

de Bono, Edward. *Lateral Thinking: Creativity Step by Step,* New York: Harper, 1970.

De Leon, Arnoldo. *Ethnicity in the Sunbelt: Mexican Americans in Houston,* College Station: Texas A&M University Press, 2001.

DeVries, Walter, and Lance Tarrance Jr., *The Ticket-Splitter: A New Force in American Politics,* Grand Rapids, MI: Eerdmans, 1972.

Dressman, Fran. *Gus Wortham: Portrait of a Leader,* College Station: Texas A&M University Press, 1994.

Dudziak, Mary L. *Cold War Civil Rights: Race and the Image of American Democracy,* Princeton, NJ: Princeton University Press, 2000.

Dugger, Ronnie. *Our Invaded Universities: Form, Reform and New Starts,* New York: W. W. Norton & Co., 1974.

Dugger, Ronnie, ed. *Three Men in Texas: Bedichek, Webb, and Dobie,* Austin: University of Texas Press, 1967.

Eckhardt, Bob, and Charles L. Black Jr. *The Tides of Power: Conversations on the American Constitution,* New Haven: Yale University Press, 1976.

Feagin, Joe R. *Free Enterprise City: Houston in Political and Economic Perspective,* New Brunswick: Rutgers University Press, 1988.

Forman, Maury, and Robert A. Calvert. *Cartooning Texas: One Hundred Years of Cartoon Art in the Lone Star State,* College Station: Texas A&M University Press, 1993.

Frantz, Joe B. *The Forty-Acre Follies,* Austin: Texas Monthly Press, 1983.

Green, George Norris. *The Establishment in Texas Politics,* Westport, CT: Greenwood Press, 1979.

Hamric, Roy, ed. *Archer Fullingim: A Country Editor's View of Life,* Austin: Heidelberg Publishers, 1975.

Hardeman, D. B., and Donald C. Bacon. *Rayburn: A Biography,* Austin: Texas Monthly Press, 1987.

Henderson, Richard B. *Maury Maverick: A Political Biography,* Austin: University of Texas Press, 1970.

Herskowitz, Mickey. *Sharpstown Revisited: Frank Sharp and a Tale of Dirty Politics in Texas,* Austin: Eakin Press, 1994.

Hoff, Carol. *Johnny Texas,* Chicago: Wilcox & Follett Co., 1950.

———. *Johnny Texas on the San Antonio Road,* Chicago: Wilcox & Follett Co., 1953.

Hufford, Larry, *D. B.: Reminiscences of D. B. Hardeman,* Austin: AAR/Tantalus, 1984.

Sources

Jacobs, John. *A Rage for Justice: The Passion and Politics of Phillip Burton*, Berkeley: University of California Press, 1995.

Kemerer, Frank R. *William Wayne Justice: A Judicial Biography*, Austin: University of Texas Press, 1991.

Kibbe, Pauline R. *Latin Americans in Texas*, Albuquerque: University of New Mexico Press, 1946.

King, Larry L. *In Search of Willie Morris: The Mercurial Life of a Legendary Writer and Editor*, New York: Public Affairs, 2006.

Kingrea, Nellie Ward. *History of the First Ten Years of the Texas Good Neighbor Commission*, Fort Worth, TX: TCU Press, 1954.

Knoll, Erwin, ed. *American Militarism 1970: A Dialogue on the Distortion of our National Priorities and the Need to Reassert Control over the Defense Establishment*, New York: Viking Press, 1969.

———, ed. *War Crimes and the American Conscience*, New York: Holt, Rinehart, and Winston, 1970.

Kolkey, Jonathan. *The New Right 1960–1968: with epilogue, 1969–1980*, Washington, DC: University Press of America, 1983.

Kraus, Pat, ed. *Anatomy of an Undeclared War: Congressional Conference on the Pentagon Papers*, New York: International Universities Press, 1972.

Kress, Alexander. *Ralph Yarborough: The Big Thicket's Advocate in Congress—An Annotated Congressional Record Bibliography 1962–1970*, Austin: Kress, 1970.

Leininger-Pycior, Julie. *LBJ and Mexican-Americans: The Paradox of Power*, Austin: University of Texas Press, 1997.

Lich, Glen E. *The German Texans*, San Antonio: University of Texas Institute of Texan Cultures, 1981.

Lipartito, Kenneth, and Joseph Pratt, *Baker & Botts in the Development of Modern Houston*, Austin: University of Texas Press, 1991.

McArthur, Judith N., and Harold L. Smith. *Minnie Fisher Cunningham: A Suffragist's Life in Politics*, Oxford: Oxford University Press, 2003.

McKay, Seth S. *Texas and the Fair Deal 1945–1952*, San Antonio: The Naylor Co., 1954.

Malsch, Brownson. *Indianola: The Mother of Western Texas*, Austin: Shoal Creek Publishers, 1977.

Mashaw, Jerry, and David Harfit. *The Struggle for Auto Safety*, Cambidge, MA: Harvard University Press, 1990.

Mayer, Robert N. *The Consumer Movement: Guardians of the Marketplace*, Boston: Twayne Publishers, 1989.

Mewhinney, Hubert. *A Manual for Neanderthals*, Austin: University of Texas Press, 1957.

Morris, Celia. *Fannie Wright: Rebel in America*, Cambridge, MA: Harvard University Press, 1984.

———. *Finding Celia's Place*, College Station: Texas A&M University Press, 2000.

Morris, Willie. *North Toward Home*, Boston: Houghton Mifflin, 1967.

———. "The Search for Billy Goat Hill," in *Always Stand in Against the Curve and Other Sports Stories*, Oxford, MS: Yoknapatawpha Press, 1983.

Murphree, Nellie. *A History of DeWitt County*, Victoria, TX, 1962.

Nader, Ralph. *Unsafe at Any Speed: The Designed-in Dangers of the American Automobile*, New York: Grossman Publishers, 1965.

Olien, Roger M. *From Token to Triumph: The Texas Republicans Since 1920*, Dallas: SMU Press, 1982.

Sources

O'Neill, Tip, and William Novak. *Man of the House: the Life and Political Memoirs of Speaker Tip O'Neill,* New York: Random House, 1987.

Orum, Anthony M. *Power, Money and the People: The Making of Modern Austin,* Austin: Texas Monthly Press, 1987.

Peacock, Howard. *The Big Thicket of Texas: America's Ecological Wonder,* Boston: Little Brown, 1984.

Personnel of the Texas State Government for 1885.

Pertschuk, Michael. *Revolt Against Regulation: The Rise and Pause of the Consumer Movement,* Berkeley: University of California Press, 1991.

Pickle, Jake, and Peggy Pickle. *Jake,* Austin: University of Texas Press, 1997.

Rainey, Homer P. *The Tower and The Dome: A Free University Versus Political Control,* Boulder, CO: Pruett Publishing Company, 1971.

Rapoport, Daniel. *Inside the House,* Chicago: Follett Publishing Company, 1975.

Richards, David. *Once Upon a Time in Texas: A Liberal in the Lone Star State,* Austin: University of Texas Press, 2002.

Rogers, Mary Beth. *Barbara Jordan: American Hero,* New York: Bantam Books, 1998.

San Miguel, Guadalupe. *"Let All of Them Take Heed": Mexican Americans and the Campaign for Educational Equality in Texas, 1910–1981,* Austin: University of Texas Press, 1987.

Scammon, Richard. *America Votes,* Washington, DC: Congressional Quarterly Press (annual).

Sherrill, Robert. *The Oil Follies of 1970–1980: How the Petroleum Industry Stole the Show (and Much More Besides),* Garden City, NY: Anchor Press/Doubleday, 1983.

Shofner, Jerrell, and Linda Ellsworth, eds. *Ethnic Minorities in Gulf Coast Society,* Pensacola, FL: Gulf Coast History and Humanities Conference, 1979.

Sterling, William. *Trails and Trials of a Texas Ranger,* Norman: University of Oklahoma Press, 1959.

Terkel, Studs. *The Great Divide: Second Thoughts on the American Dream,* New York: Pantheon Books, 1988.

Texas and Texans, Chicago: American Historical Society, 1914.

Udall, Morris K. *Too Funny to be President,* New York: Henry Holt and Co., 1988.

University of Texas Institute of Public Affairs. *The Fifty-Seventh Texas Legislature: A Review of Its Work,* 1962.

———. *The Fifty-Ninth Texas Legislature: A Review of Its Work,* 1966.

Viguerie, Richard. *The New Right: We're Ready to Lead,* Falls Church, VA: Viguerie Co., 1981.

Weeks, O. Douglas. *Texas One-Party Politics in 1956,* Public Affairs Series no. 32, Institute of Public Affairs, University of Texas, 1957.

———. *Texas Presidential Politics in 1952,* Public Affairs Series no. 16, Institute of Public Affairs, University of Texas, 1953.

Wright, Jim. *Balance of Power: Presidents and Congress from the Era of McCarthy to the Age of Gingrich,* Atlanta: Turner Publishing, 1996.

Zangrando, Robert L. *The NAACP Crusade Against Lynching, 1909–1950,* Philadelphia: Temple University Press, 1980.

Zwick, David, and Marcia Benstock, *Water Wasteland: Ralph Nader's Study Group Report on Water Pollution,* New York: Grossman Publishers, 1971.

Sources

Theses, Dissertations, and Unpublished Works

Banks, Melvin J. "The Pursuit of Equality: The Movement for First Class Citizenship Among Negroes in Texas, 1920–1950," DSS diss., Syracuse University, 1962.

Barker, Carol. "A Case Study of Why Bob Eckhardt Lost His House Seat," unpublished manuscript, Rice University, 1982.

Chumlea, Wesley S. "The Politics of Legislative Apportionment in Texas 1921–1957," PhD diss., University of Texas, 1959.

Cochran, Clay. "Corporate Control of the Tobacco Industry," MA thesis, University of Texas, 1938.

——. "Hired Farm Labor and the Federal Government," PhD diss., University of North Carolina, 1950.

Cole, Richard Ray. "A Journal of Free Voices: The History of *The Texas Observer*," MA thesis, University of Texas, 1966.

Cunningham, Patricia Ellen. "Too Gallant a Walk: Minnie Fisher Cunningham and Her Race for Governor of Texas in 1944," MA thesis, University of Texas at Austin, 1985.

Doyle, Judith Kaaz. "Out of Step: Maury Maverick and the Politics of the Depression and the New Deal," PhD diss., University of Texas at Austin, 1989.

Felder, Marvin Ray. "The Politics of the Texas Gulf Coast, 1945 to 1960," MA thesis, University of Texas, 1960.

Knox, J. Wendell. "Democratic Schism in Texas, 1952–1957: Emergence of National Liberalism in the South," MA thesis, North Texas State College, 1959.

Polakoff, Murray. "The Development of the Texas State C.I.O. Council," PhD diss., Columbia University, 1955.

Schlickenrieder, Annelies. "German Texan Ethnicity: Through History and Present," MA thesis, University of Texas at Austin, 1986.

Simon, Dennis M. "Texans in the United States House of Representatives: A History of Electoral, Partisan, and Ideological Change, 1936–2000," unpublished paper presented at Jim Wright Symposium on Texas Congressional Leaders, Texas Christian University, Fort Worth, Texas, April 19, 2002.

Smith, Steven K. "Southern Congressional Politics Since the Great Society," PhD diss., University of South Carolina, 1983.

Sonntag, Mark. "Hyphenated Texans: World War I and the German-Americans of Texas," MA thesis, University of Texas at Austin, 1990.

Stephenson, Charles W. "The Democrats of Texas and Texas Liberalism, 1944–1960: A Study in Political Frustration," MA thesis, Southwest Texas State College, 1967.

Tolleson, William J. "The Rift in the Texas Democratic Party—1944," MA thesis, University of Texas, 1953.

Tucker, Leah Brooke. "The Houston Business Community, 1945–1965," PhD diss., University of Texas, 1979.

Web Sites

"American Ethical Union Elliott-Black Award," www.ethicalculture.org/neac/elliott-black/ebalist.html (accessed May 30, 2003).

"Big Thicket," *Handbook of Texas Online*, www.tsha.utexas.edu/handbook/online/articles/view/BB/gkb3.html (accessed October 22, 2002).

Sources

"Gustavo C. Garcia," *Handbook of Texas Online*, www.tsha.utexas.edu/handbook/online/ articles/view/GG/fga51.html (accessed October 22, 2002).

"Harris County Democrats—The Early Years," www.harriscountydemocrats.org/history .php (accessed July 1, 2003).

"Harry Wurzbach and Family," www.lsjunction.com/ (accessed June 5, 2003).

"Robert Justus Kleberg," www.sanjacinto-museum.org/Herzstein_Library/veteran_ Biographies/Browse_Biographies/biographies/default.asp?action=bio&id=3300 (accessed May 30, 2003, and November 1, 2006).

Ronnie Dugger, "Frankie Carter Randolph," *Handbook of Texas Online*, www.tsha.utexas .edu/handbook/online/articles/view/RR/fra34.html.

"Rosalie von Roeder Kleberg," *Handbook of Texas Online*, www.tsha.utexas.edu/handbook/ online/articles/KK/fkl12.html (accessed October 22, 2002).

"Top Political Figures," *Houston Chronicle*, www.chron.com/CDA/archives/archive .mpl?id=1999_3183703 (accessed July 3, 2003, and November 24, 2006).

Walton Hale Hamilton, see http://ideas.repec.org/p/vic/vicddp/0104.html and www.tsha .utexas.edu/handbook/online/articles/view/HH/fha38.html.

"What is the Eckhardt Report?" U.S. EPA Mid-Atlantic Regional Center for Environmental Information, www.epa.gov/region3/rcei/faq/eckhardt.htm (accessed May 30, 2003).

Archival Collections

BOB ECKHARDT PERSONAL PAPERS

Bob Eckhardt kept files in his personal possession, well organized by subject and by persons. (Unfortunately, many papers from his early career were lost in a flood.) Most of these files are post-congressional letters, manuscripts, articles, and clippings. Upon his death, the family retained some of these files and others were consolidated with the Robert C. Eckhardt Collection, Center for American History, University of Texas at Austin.

UNIVERSITY OF TEXAS AT AUSTIN
Center for American History

Robert C. Eckhardt Collection

The Robert C. Eckhardt Collection is the most comprehensive collection of Eckhardt papers, as several collections have been consolidated here. The original collection consisted of a scattering of boxes, including some from his early years. Congressman Eckhardt gave his congressional papers to the Houston Metropolitan Research Center at the Houston Public Library. In 1995, those papers were transferred to the Center for American History and consolidated with the earlier papers. Additionally, Mr. Eckhardt donated cartoons and sketches to the Center in 1996. (Upon his death, the family donated some of his personal papers to this collection, but in this work, they are cited as Bob Eckhardt Personal Papers rather than here with this collection.)

John Henry Faulk Papers
Box 3E204, Folder: Texas Politics.

Bernard Rapoport Papers
Box 4C595, Folder, Robert Eckhardt; Box 4C514b, AR 92-414, Folder: J. R. Parten; Box 4C595, Folder: Robert Eckhardt.

Rudolph Kleberg Family Papers

Box 2J52, Folder: Family history and genealogy, 1961 and undated.
Box 2J51, Folder: Miscellaneous letters, K-Z, 1871–1963; Folder: Eckhardt family members, 1864–1959.
Box 2J49, Folder: Financial and legal records, 1874–1924.
Box 2J50, Folder: Letters by writer.

Harris County Democratic Party Records
Box 4C513, Folder: Liberals 1965/66; Folder: Candidates—1966.
Box 4C521, Folder: Freedom in Action.
Box 4C505, Folder: Liberals/DOT 1957–1958.
Box 4C507, Folder: State Convention Austin Texas June 14, 1960.
Box 4C516. Harris County Election Analysis.

Ralph Yarborough Collection

Mark Adams, "Statewide Meeting Democrats of Texas," Austin: Chaparral Press.

Benson Latin American Collection

George I. Sanchez Collection
Box 24, Folder 8; Box 62, Folder 15; Box 16, Folder 18; Box 12, Folder 18; Box 16, Folder 17; Box 56, Folder 11.

University of Texas School of Law, Tarlton Law Library

Walton H. Hamilton Papers
Letter from Chris Dixie to Walton Hamilton, April 3, 1946; letter from Hamilton to Dixie, April 12, 1946; letter from Dixie to Hamilton, August 28, 1946; letter from Walton Hamilton to Robert Montgomery, February 17, 1958.

J. Edwin Smith Collection

Lyndon Baines Johnson Library

Mrs. Albert (Lera) Thomas Oral History, interviewer: David G. McComb, transcript, October 11, 1968, AC 74-47.

OTHER COLLECTIONS

Nadine Eckhardt Personal Papers

Special Collections, Texas State University

Billy Lee Brammer Papers
Bill Brammer letters, Collection 007, Box 2 (Nadine Eckhardt Papers).

Jan Reid Collection
Letter from Bill White to *Texas Monthly*, July 7, 1994, Box 769, Folder 8.

Ann and Milton Lower Personal Papers

Both Ann and Milton Lower worked for Congressman Eckhardt from about 1976 through the end of his congressional career in 1981, and Ann Lower ran all his political campaigns, starting in 1976. Their personal papers include official correspondence, memos, and papers, plus political files. The files have since been donated to the Center for American History, University of Texas at Austin.

Sources

Orissa Eckhardt Arend Personal Papers

Orissa Arend Family Scrapbook

Otto Mullinax Personal Papers

Otto Mullinax and Bob Eckhardt went to the University of Texas together, then both served as labor lawyers. Mr. Mullinax kept scrapbooks containing correspondence and news clippings from their political activities at the University of Texas, then gave those files to this author when I interviewed him.

Special Collections, University of Texas at Arlington Libraries

Democratic Advisory Council

Fred H. Schmidt Collection

Don Kennard Collection (permission to author to quote from collection)

Houston Area Industrial Union Council Papers

Harris County AFL-CIO Council Papers

Mullinax, Wells Labor Case Records

Texas Social and Legislative Conference Records

Margaret B. Carter Papers

Texas AFL-CIO Collection

W. Don Ellinger Papers

Rice University Fondren Library, Woodson Research Center

Walter Gardner Hall Papers

Frankie Carter Randolph Papers

Jimmy Carter Library

Names File: Eckhardt

Interview with Ray Marshall, Miller Center Interviews, Carter Presidency Project, vol. 25, May 4, 1988.

Texas State Archives

Bill Files, 1959–1965

Periodicals

FULL CITATIONS

Addington, Neil. "Eckhardt Protests House Rules Change," *Houston Post,* May 28, 1963.

Anderson, Jack, and Tony Capaccio, "Jack Anderson Rates the Congress," *Washingtonian,* October 1980.

Barlow, Jim. "Kennedy Solicits Carter Support Here, Praises Eckhardt," *Houston Chronicle,* October 22, 1980, 10.

Barrett, William. "Eckhardt Fights for Political Life in Oil Country," *Dallas Times Herald,* October 24, 1980.

Bender, Judith. "Oilmen Aided, Consumers Hurt," *Newsday,* October 14, 1980, 6.

Bennett, Scott. "First Annual Congressional Awards," *Texas Business,* February 1980, 21–22.

Bernstein, Carl. "Commuter Cycling Picks Up 'Speed," *Washington Post,* June 14, 1970, E1.

Black, Charles. "Constitutionality of the Eckhardt Open Beaches Bill," *Columbia Law Review,* 74:3, 439–447, 1974.

Bonavita, Fred. "Liberal Demos Ask New Blood, Reorganization," *Houston Post,* December 9, 1968, 20.

Broder, David. *Washington Post,* February 27, 1978, A6.

Burka, Paul. "So Close, So Far," *Texas Monthly,* April 1976, 27, 38.

Byers, Bo. "Afterthoughts on Legislature," *Houston Chronicle,* August 9, 1959.

Canetti, Barbara. "Survival of GOP Worries Young—a Little," *Houston Post,* November 2, 1978, A12.

Carter, Luther. "Congressman Eckhardt, Legislative Craftsman," *Science,* March 9, 1979, 983–984.

Chapman, Joe. "Fields Camp Fails to Deny Higher Donation Figures," *Pasadena Citizen,* November 1, 1980, 1.

Clayton, William E., Jr. "Eckhardt Tacks Amendment on Rail Bill," *Houston Chronicle,* July 25, 1980.

Cohen, Richard E. "Energy Turf Fight," *National Journal,* October 6, 1979, 1652.

———. "House May Get an Energy Committee, and Dingell May be Left Out in the Cold," *National Journal,* February 2, 1980, 188–191.

———. "Not Quite the Status Quo," *National Journal,* April 5, 1980, 568.

Coulter, Bill. "Kennedy Urges Party Unity," *Houston Post,* October 22, 1980.

Degnan, Daniel A. "Public Rights in Ocean Beaches: A Theory of Prescription," *Syracuse Law Review* 24 (1973): 935.

Dickson, Fagan. "The Texas Poll Tax," *Texas Bar Journal* 11, no. 11 (December 1948): 619*ff.*

Dobie, J. Frank. "The Mexican Vaquero of the Texas Border," *Southwestern Political and Social Science Quarterly* 8, no. 1 (June 1927).

Dugger, Ronnie. "A Fair Tax on the Oil Industry," *Texas Observer,* August 29, 1986, 9.

———. "Harris Convention Liberals Hit Hard," *Texas Observer,* May 9, 1956, 8.

———. "A Quirky Integrity," *Texas Observer,* April 2, 1999, 23.

———. "To a Novelist Dying Young," *Washington Post,* June 18, 1978, F1.

———. "Three Clichés and the Natural Gas Tax," *Texas Observer,* March 21, 1959, and April 25, 1959.

Dworin, Diana. "Man Awarded Lifetime Pass to Barton Springs," *Austin American-Statesman,* October 10, 1996.

Eckhardt, Bob. "The 'Art' of Politics: A Short History of Political Cartooning," *Lithopinion* 5, no. 2, issue 18 (summer 1970).

———. "Citizens' Groups and Standing," *North Dakota Law Review* 51 (winter 1974): 360.

———. "Consumer Class Actions," *Notre Dame Law Review* 45 (1970): 663.

———. "A Good Word for the Revolving Door: The Lynn Coleman Appointment," *The Nation,* February 18, 1978, 173–176.

———. "How We Got the Dirtiest Stream in America: Regulation of Local Hazards—The Houston Ship Channel," *Texas International Law Journal* 7:1 (1971): 5–28.

———. "The Issue: Who Shall Control," *Texas Observer,* May 9, 1956, 3.

———. "The Miscellanist," *Yale Law Journal* 95, no. 8 (July 1986): 1555.

———. "No-Fault Legislation Lacks Humane and Equitable Answers," *Trial* 7, no. 3 (May/June 1971): 43.

——. "No-Fault Without Fraud," *Trial Lawyer Forum* (July-December 1971): 17.

——. "On the Gas Price Issue," *Journal of Energy and Development* 3, no. 2 (spring 1978): 270–276.

——. "The Presumption of Openness Under House Rules," *Harvard Journal on Legislation* 2 (1974): 279.

——. "Reverse English of Watergate: Running Against Washington," *The Nation*, June 26, 1976, 773–774.

——. Review of *Impeachment: A Handbook*, by Charles L. Black Jr., *Washington Post*, July 10, 1974.

——. "To Reverse the President on Oil Decontrol," Letter to the Editor, *New York Times*, September 12, 1979.

——. "Williams' Stand is just Vacuous, with no Real Answers Advanced," *Houston Post*, October 31, 1990.

——. "Wright was the Best Speaker Since Sam Rayburn," *Houston Chronicle*, June 11, 1989, H5.

Eckhardt, Robert C. "The Adam Clayton Powell Case: Observation," *Texas Law Review* 45 (July 1967): 1205–1211.

——. "First Things First—The Convention," *State Observer*, September 6, 1954, 2.

——. "Labor Law Section Report," *Texas Bar Journal*, June 1954, 342.

——. "A Rational National Policy on the Public Use of Beaches," *Syracuse Law Review* 24, no. 3 (summer 1973).

——. "Senate-Passed Parkhouse Strike Bill Would be Worst of Anti-Labor Laws," *Texas Observer*, April 25, 1955, 3–4.

——. "The Western Coal Traffic League Case: Condoning ICC Eschewal of Rail Monopoly Ratemaking," *Transportation Law Journal* XZIII, no. 2, (1984): 307–328.

Ely, Jane. "Eckhardt Convinces Few on ERA Vote," *Houston Post*, August 24, 1978, A3.

Friedman, Saul. "Party Unity: A Forgotten Battle Cry," *Fort Worth Star-Telegram*, October 10, 1980, 1–2.

Giles, Jim. "Letter Leads to Controversy," *Sentinel*, October 30, 1980.

Glaser, Vera. "Clayton Powell Bad Boy of Congress and Likes It," *Houston Chronicle*, June 27, 1965.

Hale, Leon. "Roasted Oysters in Eckhardt's Woods," *Houston Post*, May 1, 1977, B3.

Hardeman, D. B. "Shivers of Texas: A Tragedy in Three Acts," *Harper's*, November 1956, 50–56.

Hieken, Al. "Liberals Sweep Houston Runoffs," *Texas Observer*, August 29, 1958, 1, 8.

Holcomb, Paul B. "How Texas Became 'A No-Party State,'" *State Observer*, October 19, 1953.

Hornig, Rebecca. "Even with Price Control, Oil Drilling Booms in U.S.," *Washington Star*, March 24, 1979.

Hyatt, James. "Forbes Top Spender in Primary—$26,875," *Houston Chronicle*, May 17, 1964, 16.

Ingram, Denny O., Jr. "Reminiscences About an Old House, Some Poor Boys, and a Tax Fight," *Texas Observer*, March 21, 1955.

Jackson, J. W. "Texas Politics in 1948," *Southwestern Social Science Quarterly* 30, no. 1 (June 1949): 45–48.

Keith, Gary. "A Fine Line," *Texas Observer*, 1996, 30–31.

King, Larry L. "The Ten Brightest Congressmen," *New Times*, April 4, 1975.

Lemann, Nicholas. "Jack Fields: How Money, Expertise Aid Unknown Candidate," *Washington Post*, September 29, 1980, A14.

Lewis, Kathy. "Texans on the Potomac: Jack and Roni Sue Fields," *Houston Post*, February 9, 1981, B1.

Loving, Rush, Jr. "The Railroads' Bad Trip to Deregulation," *Fortune*, August 25, 1980, 47.

Lower, Milton D. "Decontrol Déjà Vu," *Journal of Post Keynesian Economics* 3, no. 4 (summer 1981): 597–601.

Mansell, Walter. "Independent Liberal Democrats Plan Permanent Organization," *Houston Chronicle*, July 16, 1967.

———. "Top Liberal Dems Lose Places at Convention," *Houston Chronicle*, May 10, 1960, 1.

Maverick, Maury. "S.A.'s Friend by Conviction and by Blood," *San Antonio Express-News*, October 5, 1980, H3.

Nolan, Joe. "Washburn asks Republicans to help Unseat Rep. Eckhardt," *Houston Chronicle*, April 30, 1980.

McKeon, Steve. "Public Access to Beaches," *Stanford Law Review* (February 1970), 564–586.

Morris, Willie. "Legislating in Texas," *Commentary* 38, no. 4 (November 1964): 44.

———. "Yazoo . . . Notes on Survival," *Harper's*, June 1970.

Mossberg, Walter S. "President will Gradually Phase Out Price Controls on Crude Oil to Spur Production, Curb Consumption," *Wall Street Journal*, April 6, 1979.

Nolan, Joe. "Eckhardt Names Names in Claim that Oil Industry Bankrolls Fields," *Houston Chronicle*, November 1, 1980.

———. "Rep. Bob Eckhardt, Jack Fields Debating," *Houston Chronicle*, October 5, 1980, 22.

Overholser, Ed. "Beach Bill Would Penalize Public," *Austin American*, July 5, 1959, A8.

Ozmore, Keith. "Can't Take Texas' Open Beaches for Granted," *Houston Chronicle*, August 6, 1989, H1.

Palomo, Juan Ramon. *Houston Post*, October 19, 1980, A7.

———. "It's Debatable: Eckhardt, Fields Clash Again over Format," *Houston Post*, September 30, 1980.

Pery, John L. *Rome News-Tribune*, November 25, 1984.

Raloff, Janet. "Abandoned Dumps: A Chemical Legacy," *Science News* 115, no. 21 (May 26, 1979), 348*ff.*

Ramsdell, Charles. "100 Years of Yorktown," *San Antonio Express Magazine*, 1948.

Rangel, Jorge C., and Carlos M. Alcala. "De Jure Segregation of Chicanos in Texas Schools," Project Report, *Harvard Civil Rights-Civil Liberties Law Review* 7, no. 2 (March 1972): 307–392.

Rapoport, Bernard. "Fred Schmidt: Optimistic About the World, 1918–1999," *Texas Observer*, March 19, 1999, 23.

Rapoport, Daniel. "Oh Congress!" *Washingtonian*, November 1978, 181.

Reeves, Monica, and Juan Ramon Palomo. *Houston Post*, October 22, 1980, 1, 17.

Reid, Jan. "Last of a Breed," *Texas Monthly*, May 1994, 46*ff.*

Romo, Ricardo. "George I. Sanchez and the Civil Rights Movement: 1940–1960," *La Raza Law Journal* 1, no. 3 (fall 1986): 342–362.

Rowe, Nina Dougherty. "This Congressman Commutes," *Bicycling*, March 1980.

Scarlett, Harold. "Eckhardt Seems to be Victor," *Houston Post*, May 8, 1966, 1.

Schwartz, Irvin, and Larry Marion. "Anatomy of a Bill," *Chemical Week,* April 27, 1977, 52–61.

Sherrill, Robert, "The Case Against the Oil Companies," *New York Times Magazine,* October 14, 1979.

———. "A Texan vs. Big Oil," *New York Times Magazine,* October 12, 1980.

Sinclair, Ward. "Texas Rep. Eckhardt: The Fall of a Sort of Political Snail Darter," *Washington Post,* December 13, 1980, A2.

Smith, Griffen, Jr., and Paul Burka, "The Best, the Worst, and the Fair-to-Middlin'," *Texas Monthly,* May 1976, 106–107.

Stilwell, Hart. "Will He Boss Texas?" *The Nation,* November 10, 1951, 398.

Thompson, Ann. "Politics Emphasized in Week before Election," *Baylor Lariat,* October 31, 1972, 1.

Tolchin, Martin. "Rep. Eckhardt Fights Conservative for Houston Seat," *New York Times,* November 3, 1980, D15.

Tutt, Bob, "Labor Studies Low Turnout in Primary," *Houston Chronicle,* June 23, 1966.

———. "State Reapportionment to be Pushed in Texas," *Houston Chronicle,* June 16, 1964, 15.

Welby, Luise. "Public Access to Private Beaches," *UCLA Journal of Environmental Law and Policy* 69 (1986): 71.

Welsh, David. "Building Lyndon Johnson," *Ramparts,* December 1967, 53–65.

Wiley, Elizabeth. "New Toxic Bill Should Aid Environment—Eckhardt," *Bay Area Life Style,* League City, August 26, 1975.

Wozencraft, Frank. "Fabric of Government," *Houston Post,* April 18, 1976.

Yoder, Edwin M., Jr., "Washington Notes: Eckhardt of Texas," *Harper's,* June 1970, 34.

OTHER PERIODICALS

Arcospark
Austin American
Austin American-Statesman
Austin Dispatch
Austin Statesman
Austin Times
Baltimore Sun
Bay Area Life Style (League City, Texas)
Baylor Lariat
Baytown Sun
Bicycling
Brownsville Herald
Chemical Week
Columbia Law Review
Comet (Austin High School yearbook)
Commentary
Congressional Quarterly
Corpus Christi Caller
Daily Texan
Dallas Morning News
Dallas News

Sources

Dallas Times Herald
Fortune
Fort Worth Star-Telegram
Harper's
Harvard Civil Rights-Civil Liberties Law Review
Harvard Journal on Legislation
Houston Chronicle
Houston Echo
Houston Post
Humble Echo
Humble News-Messenger
Huntsville Item
Journal of Energy and Development
Journal of Post Keynesian Economics
La Raza Law Journal
Lithopinion
Meatloaf Gazette (Austin High School)
Nation
National Journal
New Times
New York Post
New York Times
New York Times Magazine
Newsday
North Dakota Law Review
Notre Dame Law Review
Outdoor Life
Pasadena Citizen
Petroleum Independent
Ramparts
San Antonio Express Magazine
San Antonio Express-News
Science
Science News
Sentinel
Southwestern Historical Quarterly
Southwestern Social Science Quarterly
Stanford Law Review
State Observer
Syracuse Law Review
Texas State AFL-CIO News
Texas Bar Journal
Texas Books in Review
Texas International Law Journal
Texas Law Review
Texas Monthly
Texas Ranger

Sources

Texas Spectator
Texas Observer
Texas Week
Transportation Law Journal
Trial
Trial Lawyer Forum
UCLA Journal of Environmental Law and Policy
Wall Street Journal
Washington Post
Washington Post Magazine
Washington Evening Star
Washington Star
Washingtonian
Wichita Daily Times
Yale Law Journal

Interviews

INTERVIEWS BY OTHERS

Bob Eckhardt interview, 1984, with Chandler Davidson, Rice University Fondren Library, Woodson Research Center.
Bob Eckhardt interview, 1980, with Bob Sherrill (transcript).
Bob Eckhardt interview, 1980, with Studs Terkel, in *The Great Divide: Second Thoughts on the American Dream.*
Don Kennard interview by www.TexasLegacy.org.

INTERVIEWS BY GARY KEITH

Arend, Orissa	New Orleans, March 27, 1997
	Austin, November 25, 2003
Ball, Ed	May 28, 2004
Barnes, Ben	December 6, 2004
Caldwell, Neil	August 27, 1978
Cochran, Gloria	August 13, 2004
Coleman, Lynn	August 11, 2004
Dawson, Sam	September 14, 2004
Dibrell, Joe	August 12, 2003
Dugger, Ronnie	December 6, 1997
Eckhardt, Bob	March 1, 1994
	March 11, 1994
	March 18, 1994
	April 28, 1994
	July 10, 1994
	September 8, 1994
	October 7, 1994
	December 14, 1994
	February 2, 1995

	February 26, 1995
	March 2, 1995
	June 17, 1995
	January 16, 1996
	July 8, 1996
	July 16, 1996
	September 5, 1996
	June 4, 1998
	February 27, 1999
	July 17, 1999
Eckhardt, Nadine	June 17, 1995
	March 26, 2003
	June 7, 2006
Eckhardt, Norman	July 19, 2003
	July 16, 1995
Eckhardt, Rosalind	August 23, 1994
Fath, Creekmore	July 6, 1994
	June 10, 1994
	September 18, 2003
Giesen, Clare	August 12, 2004
Gladden, Don	August 24, 1978
Graves, Curtis	December 22, 2005
Gray, Frances	August 13, 2004
Jacobson, Debra	August 13, 2004
Kennard, Don	October 2002
Kinney, Janie	August 13, 2004
Kirkpatrick, Julya	July 13, 2002
Kinzler, Peter	February 27, 2002
McGregor, Malcolm	February 19, 1996
Maverick, Maury Jr.	March 6, 2002
Mickler, Emily Wurzbach	June 6, 2003
Moffett, Toby	April 27, 2004
Morris, Celia	December 3, 2004
Mullinax, Otto	July 12, 1996
Patterson, Martha	August 26, 1996
	August 13, 2004
Pickle, Jake	May 24, 1999
Raabe, Mark	February 27, 2002
Rapoport, Bernard	January 16, 1995
Sanford, Rosalind	June 29, 2005
Schmidt, Fred	October 21, 1994
Seddon, Kathy	August 13, 2004
Shulman, Al	June 4, 1998
Schwartz, A. R. "Babe"	2003
Whatley, Tom	June 30, 1994
Wilson, Charlie	September 17, 2004
Wright, Jim	July 12, 1996

Sources

Government Records

Roster (Blue Book), 1959, 1961, Texas Legislative Service.

HOUSE JOURNAL, TEXAS HOUSE OF REPRESENTATIVES

HSR 77, Third Called Session, 57th Legislature.
Attorney General Opinion V-128, April 8, 1947.

CONGRESSIONAL RECORD

House Committee on Foreign Affairs, *The War Powers Resolution: A Special Study of the Committee on Foreign Affairs*, 1982, 130–131.
United States Code, Congressional and Administrative News.
"The Economics of the Natural Gas Controversy, A Staff Study for the Subcommittee on Energy, Joint Economic Committee, September 19, 1977, 14.

COURT DECISIONS

Delgado v. Bastrop Independent School District, Civil No. 388 (W.D. Tex, June 15, 1948).
Mendez v. Westminister School District, 64 F.Supp. 544, 559 (N.D. Cal. 1946); 161 F.2d 774 (9th Cir. 1947).
J. W. Luttes et al. v. State of Texas, 159 Tex. 500, 324 S.W.2d 167 (1958).
Seaway Co. v. Attorney General, 375 S.W.2d 923 (Tex. Civ. App. 1964).
Bush v. Martin, 224 F. Supp. 499; *Bush v. Martin,* 84 S. Ct. 709 (1964).
Powell v. McCormack, 395 U.S. 486 (1969).

Miscellaneous

Clay Cochran Memorial Tribute program, Otto Mullinax Collection.
Ronnie Dugger remarks, *Texas Observer* banquet, October 15, 1994.
Bob Eckhardt, "Welcome," Southwestern Symposium on Conservation Education, October 13–15, 1968, Lee College, Baytown, Texas, symposium booklet, Bob Eckhardt Personal Papers.
Al Gore and Don Kennard, comments, Bob Eckhardt memorial service, Washington, DC, February 26, 2002.
Great Issues Committee Political Forum, Texas A&M University, November 29, 1966.
Loyal Democrats of Texas, "YOUR Democratic Party—And How to Keep It That Way," Walter Gardner Hall Papers, Rice University, Fondren Library, Woodson Research Center, MS 280.
"The Nation's Beaches: A View from Texas and from Washington," ABA Environmental Law Course, February 9, 1974.
George Norris Green remarks, "Organizing: Past, Present, and Future," 24th Annual Southwest Labor Studies Association Conference, April 24–26, 1998, St. Edward's University, Austin.
Kathleen Russell, "Knowing Bob," videotape.
Fred Schmidt, "Shoving that Pushcart," *Texas Observer* Benefit Banquet program, October 15, 1994.
Dennis M. Simon, "Texans in the United States House of Representatives: A History of Electoral, Partisan, and Ideological Change, 1936–2000," paper presented at Jim Wright Symposium on Texas Congressional Leaders, Texas Christian University, Ft. Worth, Texas, April 19, 2002.

Index